TATTOOS

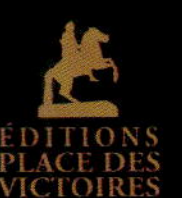

ÉDITIONS
PLACE DES
VICTOIRES

KÖNEMANN

TATTOOS

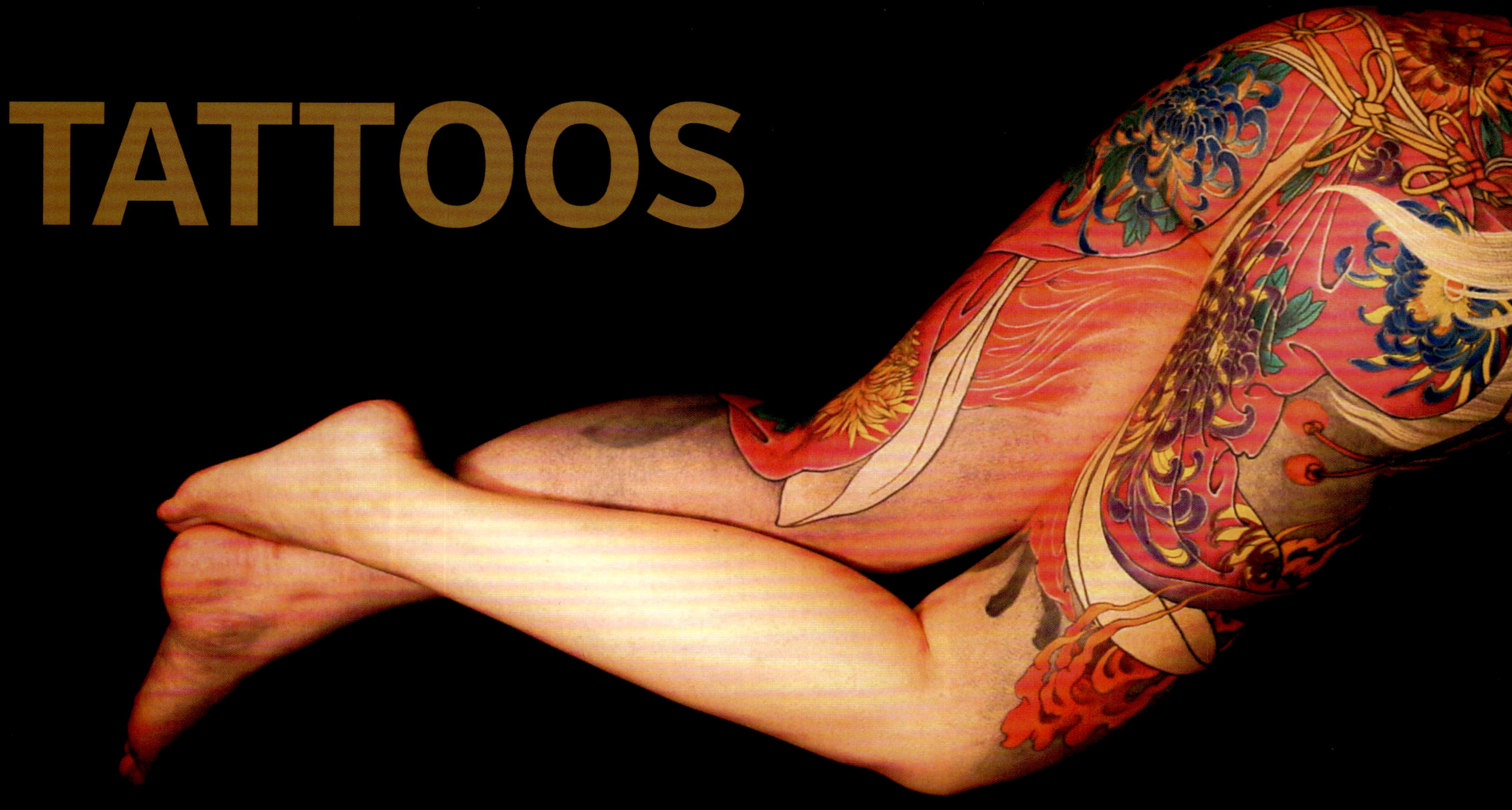

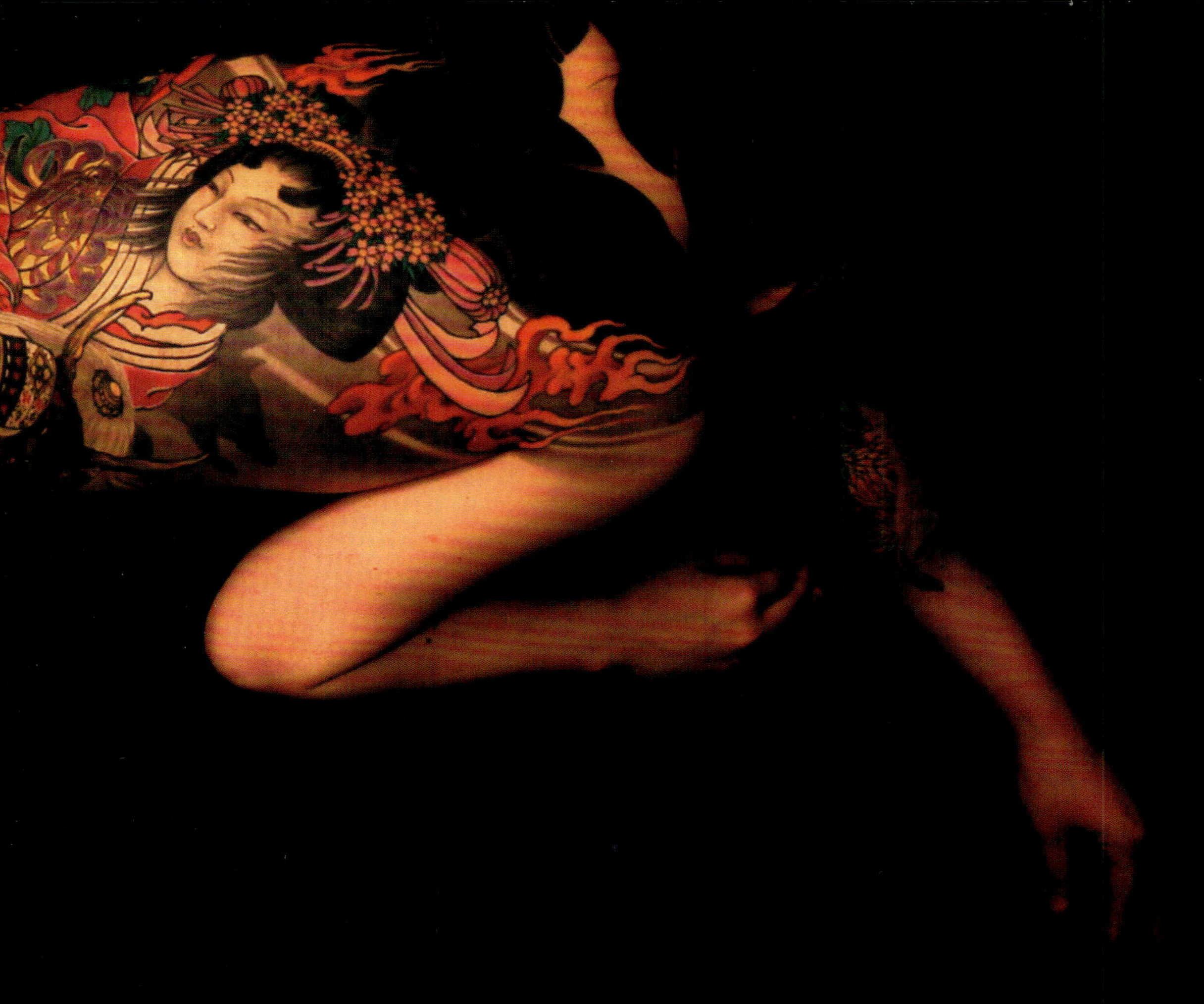

UNTIL THE COWS COME HOME

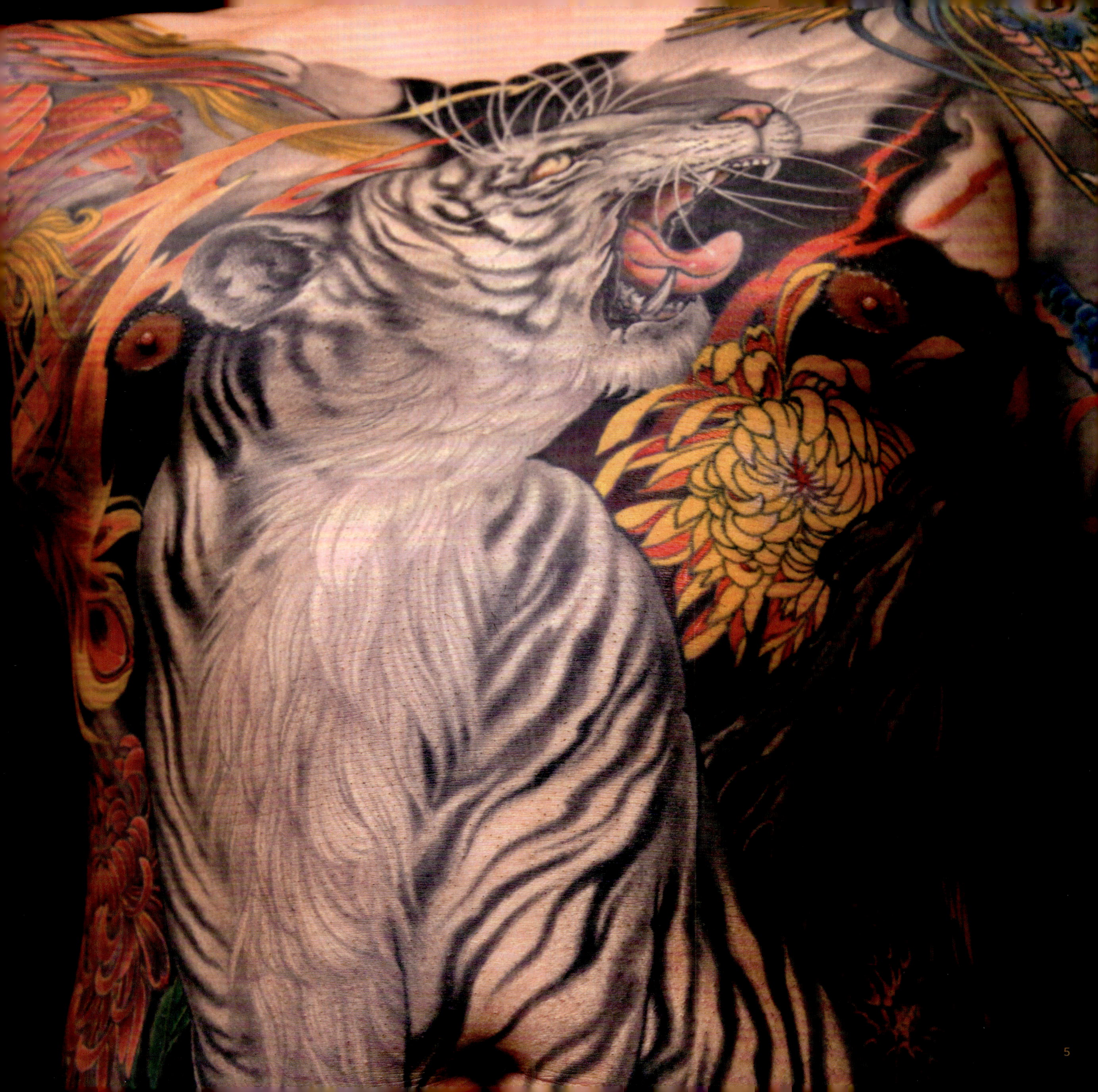

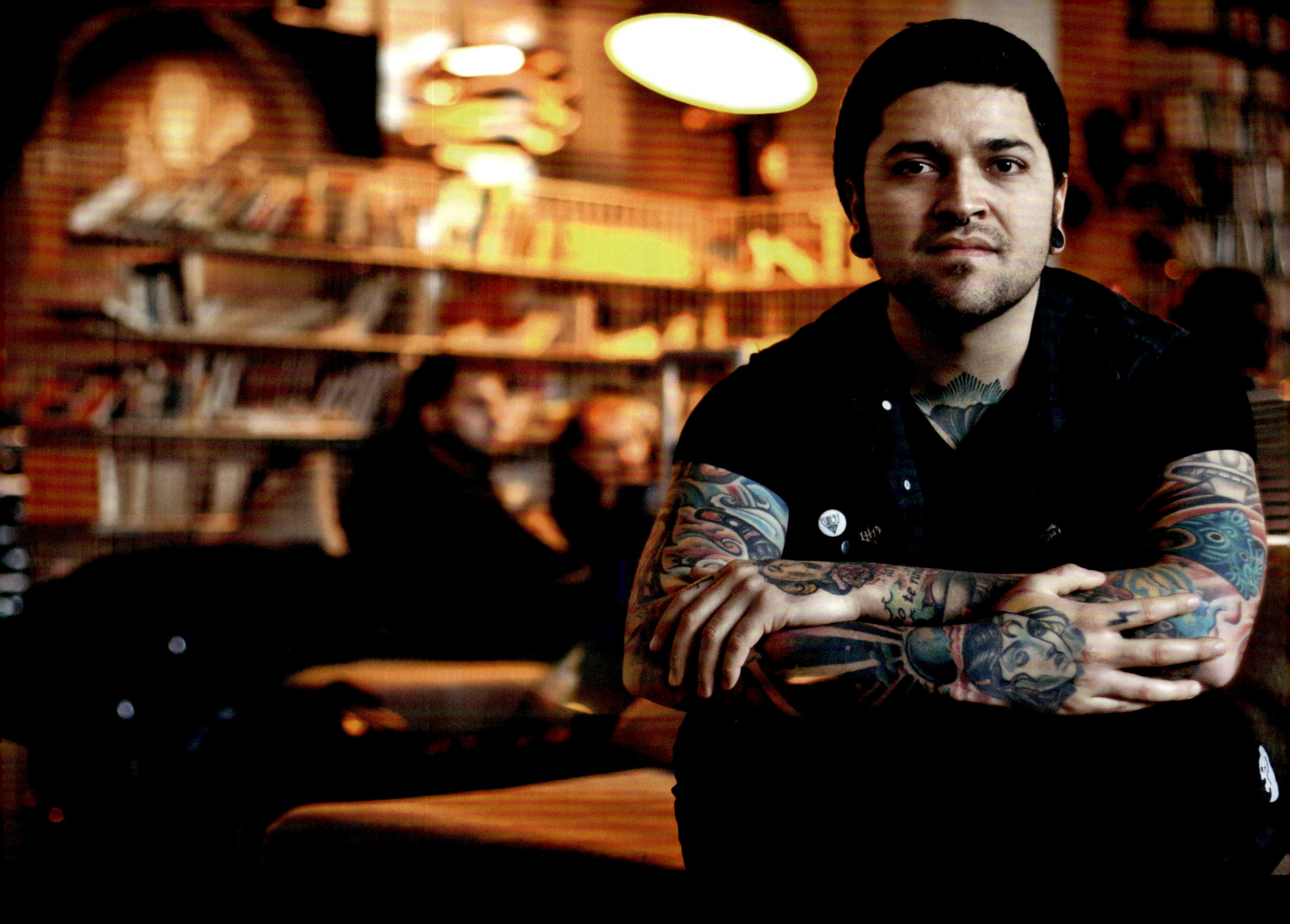

ADRIAAN MACHETE

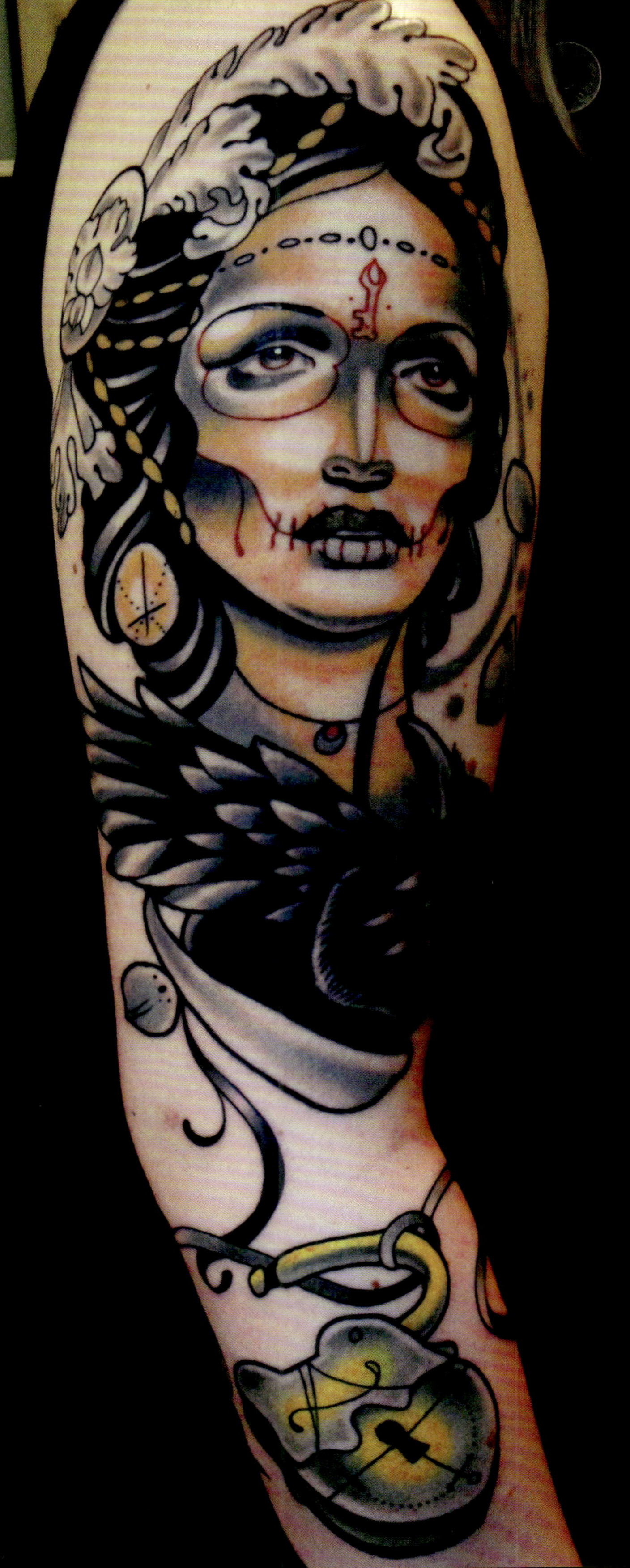

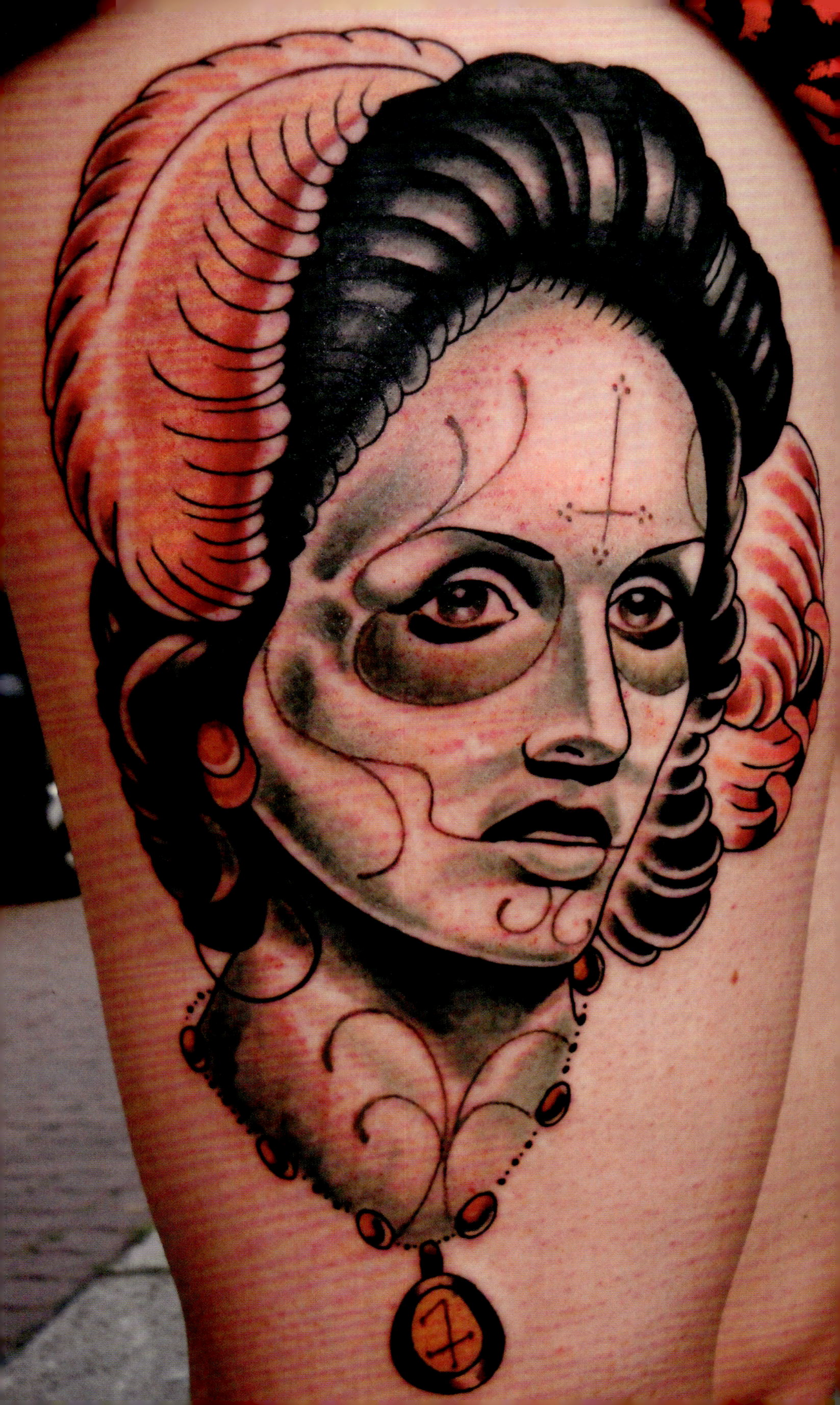

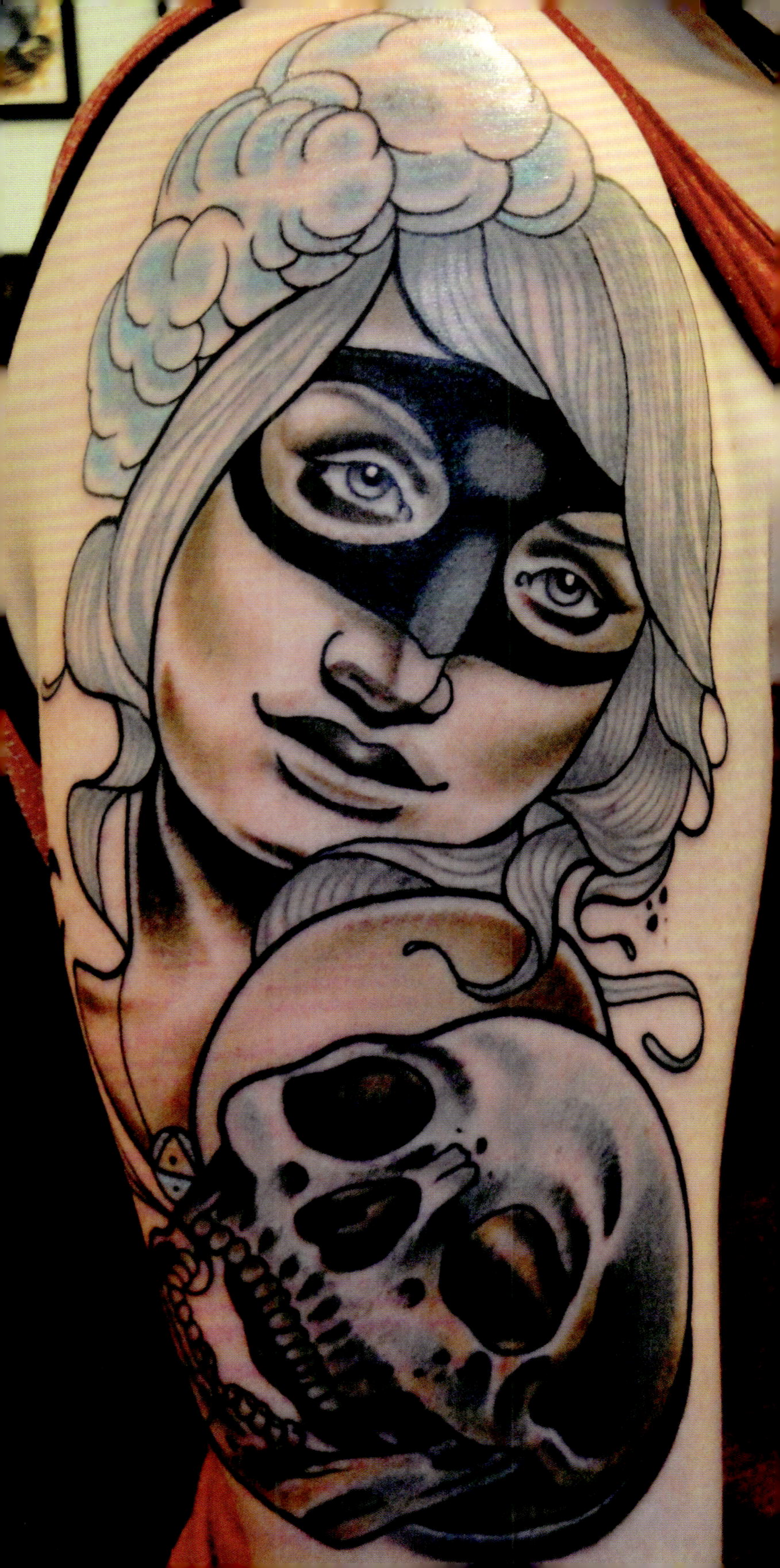

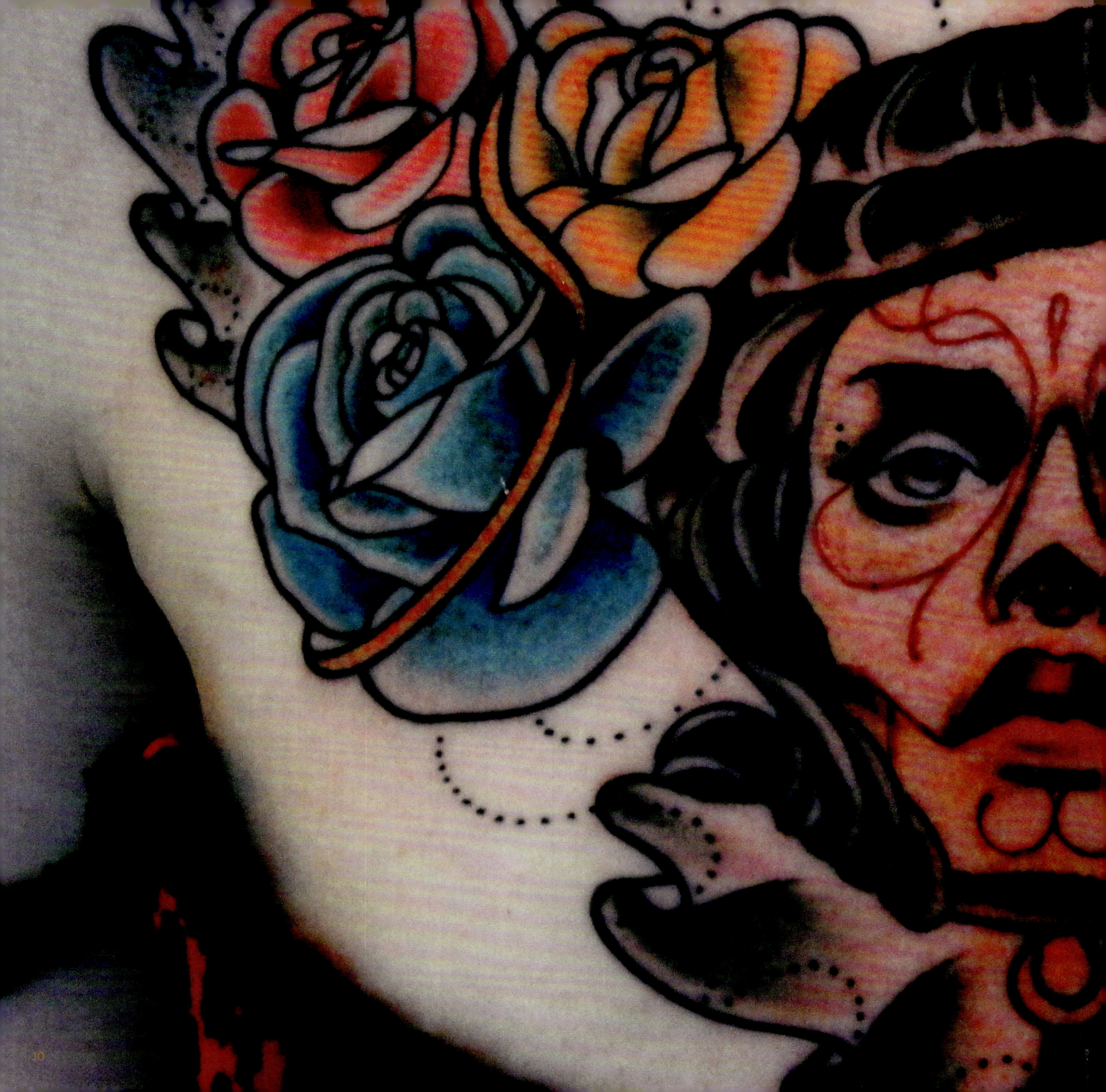

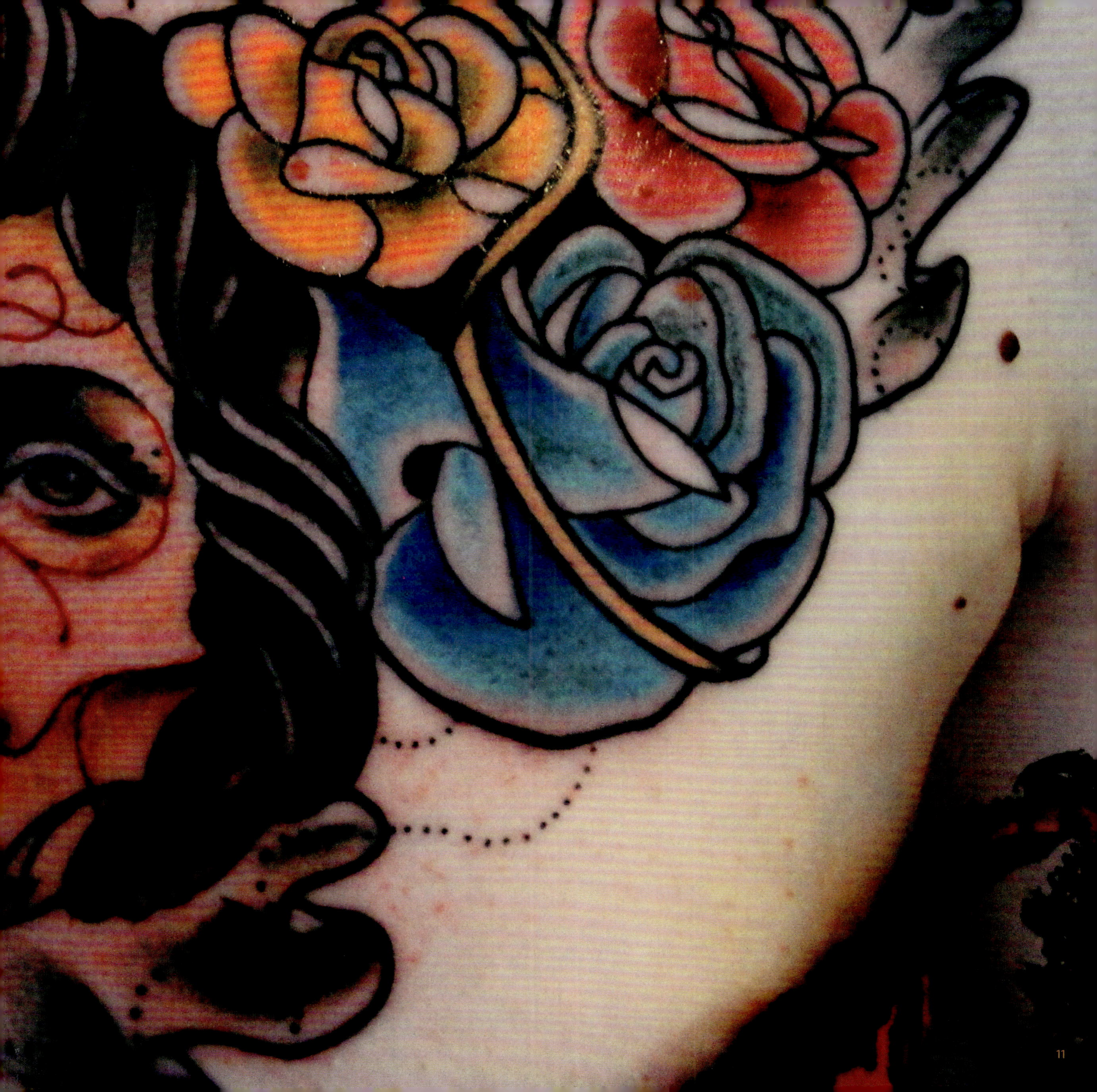

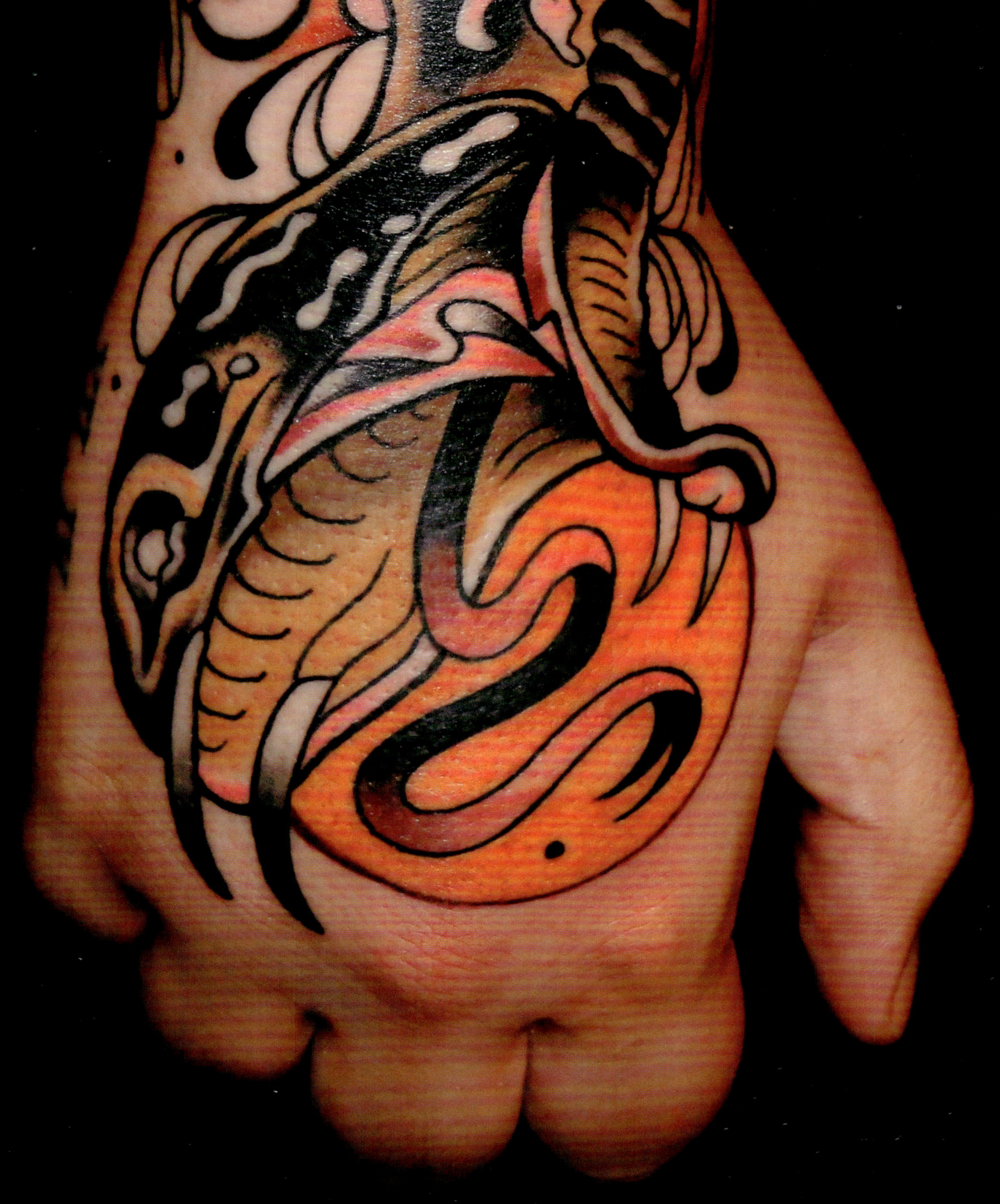

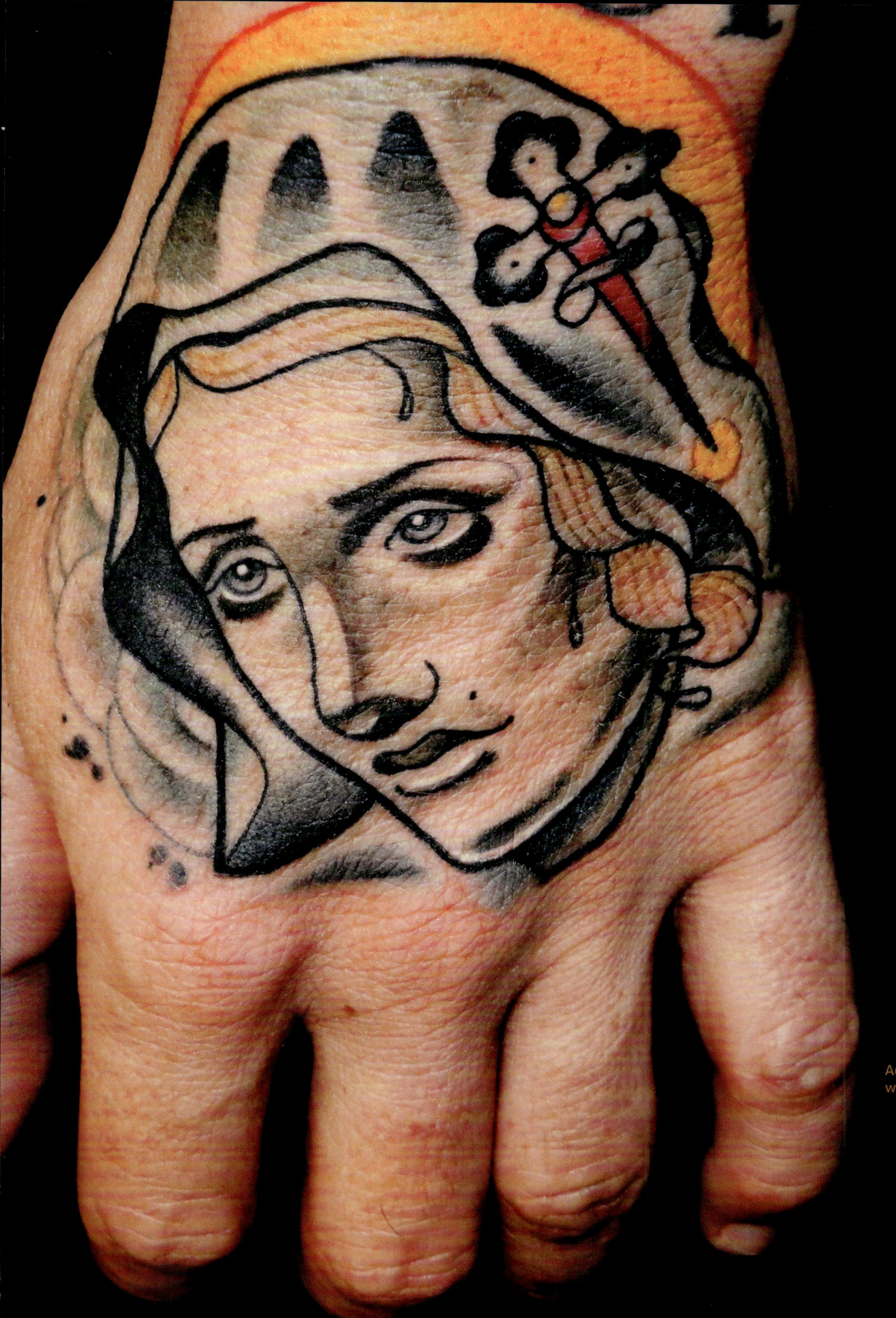

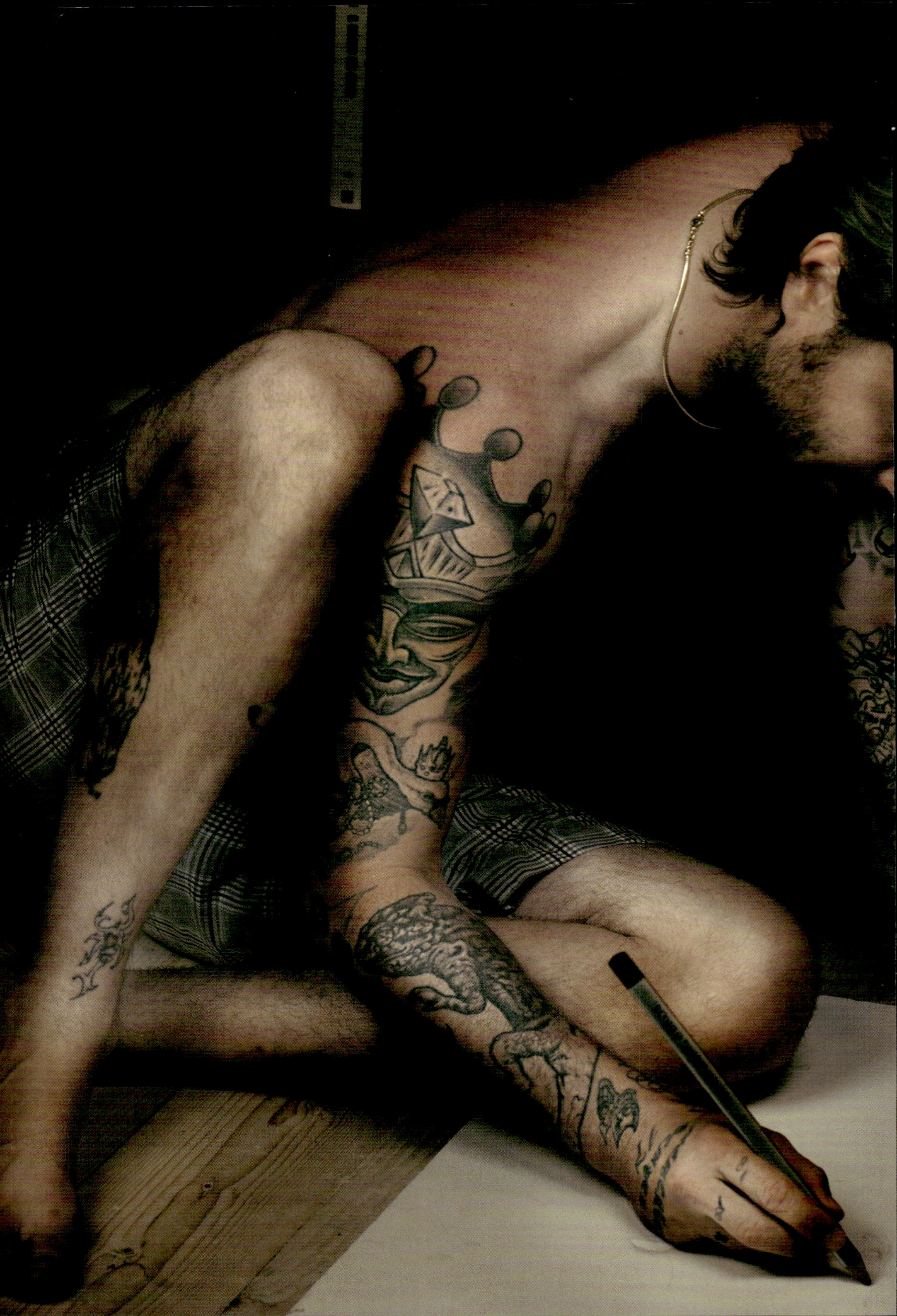

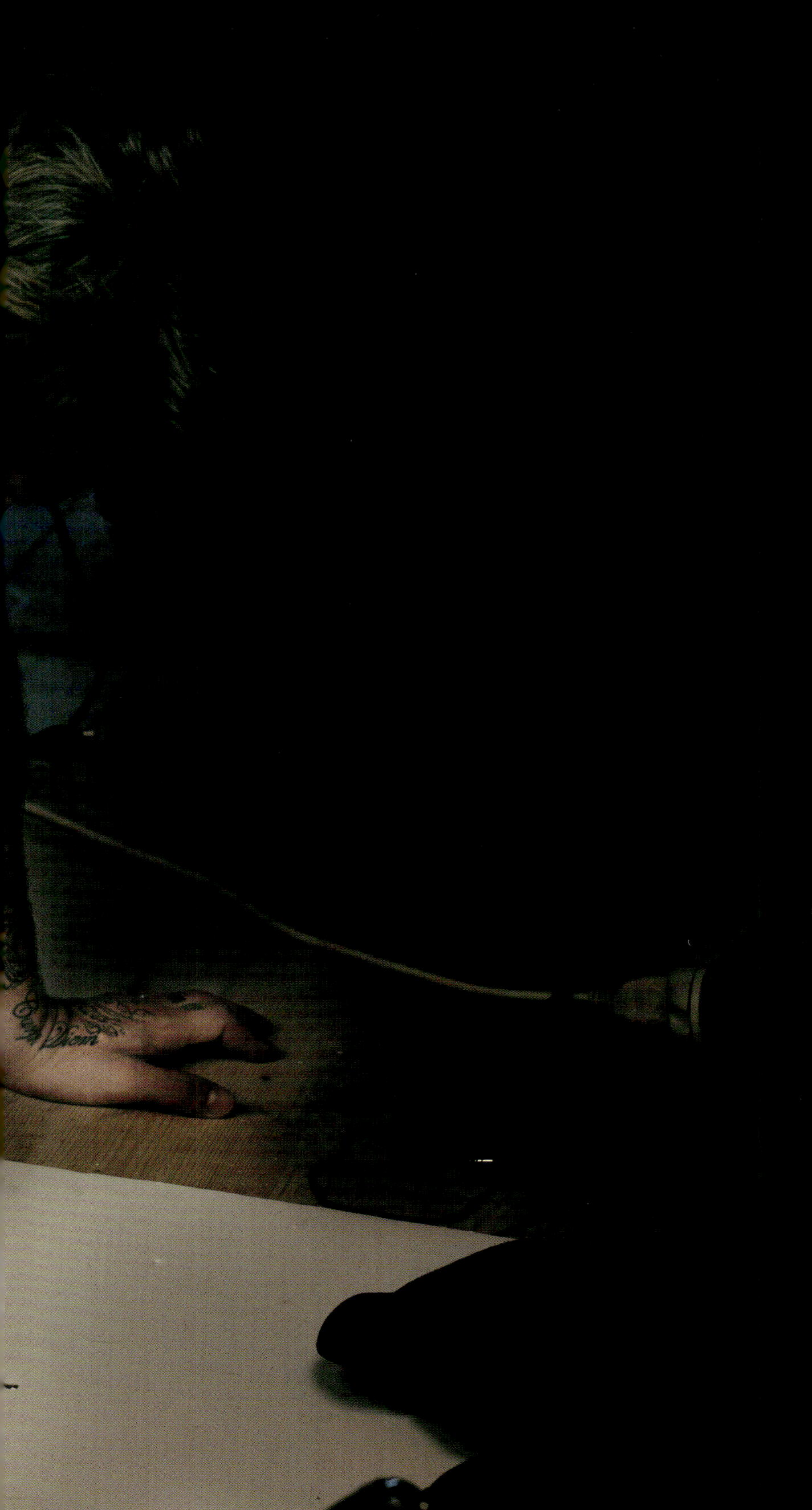

ALEX DE PASE

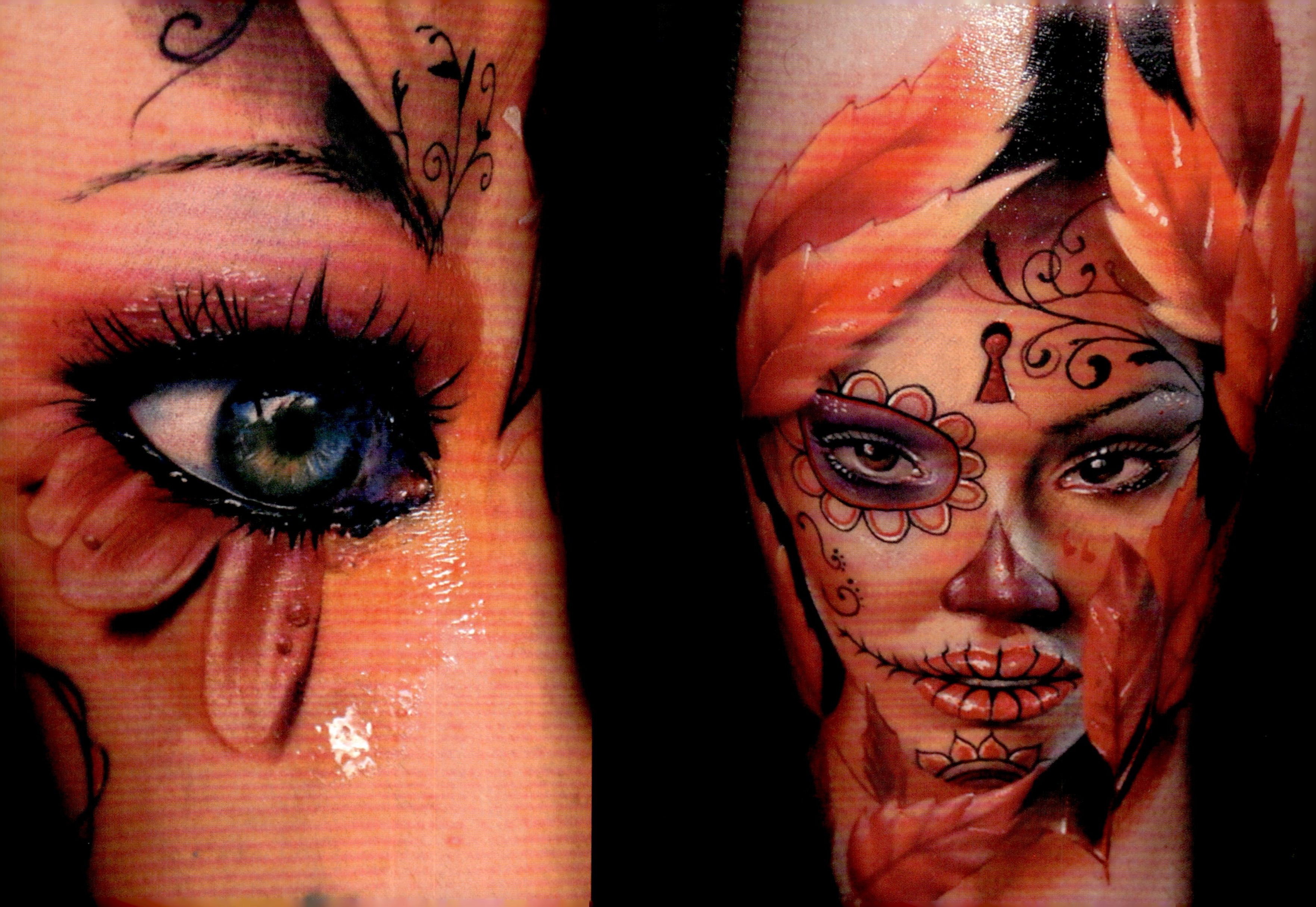

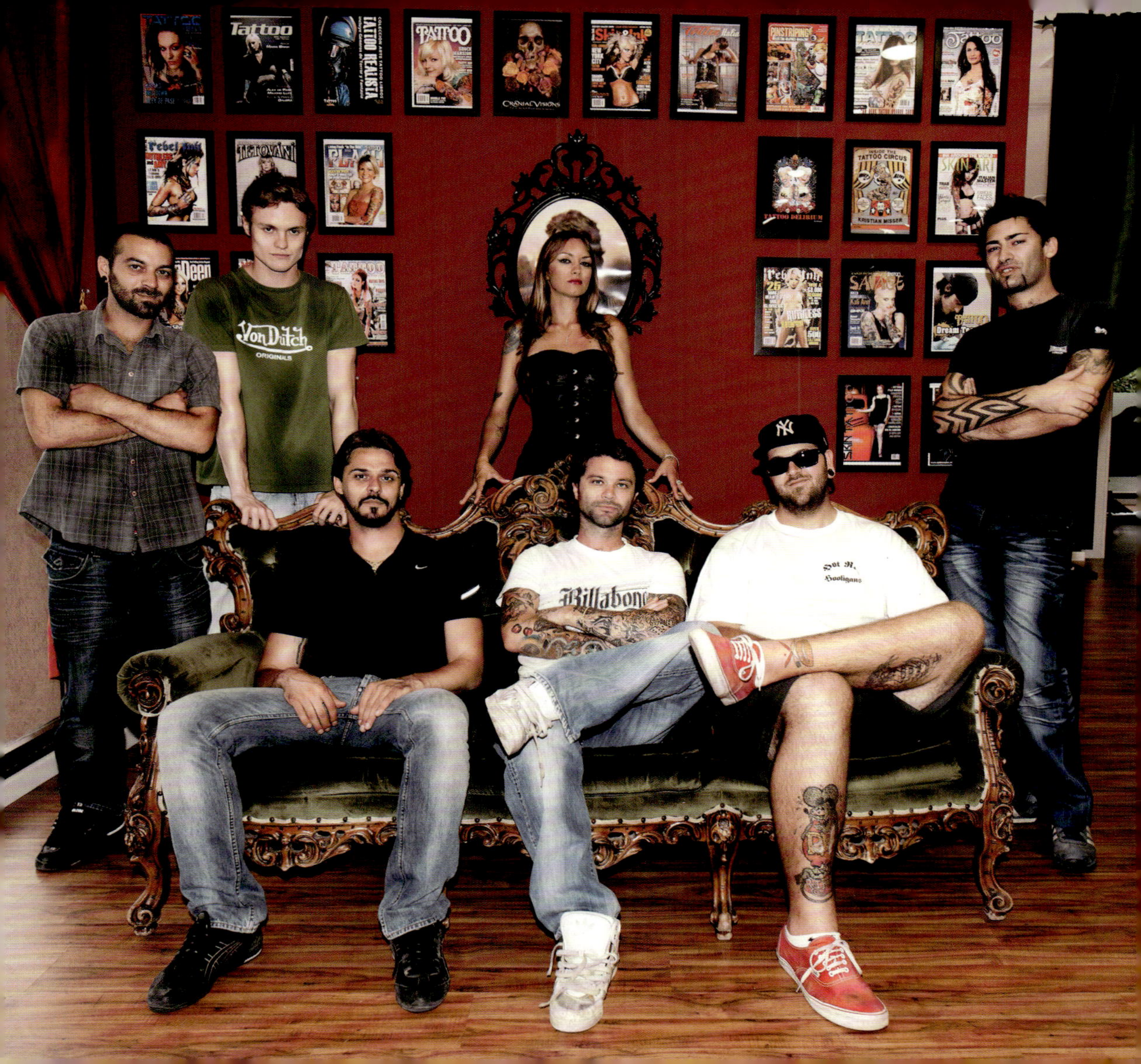

AMANDA RUBY

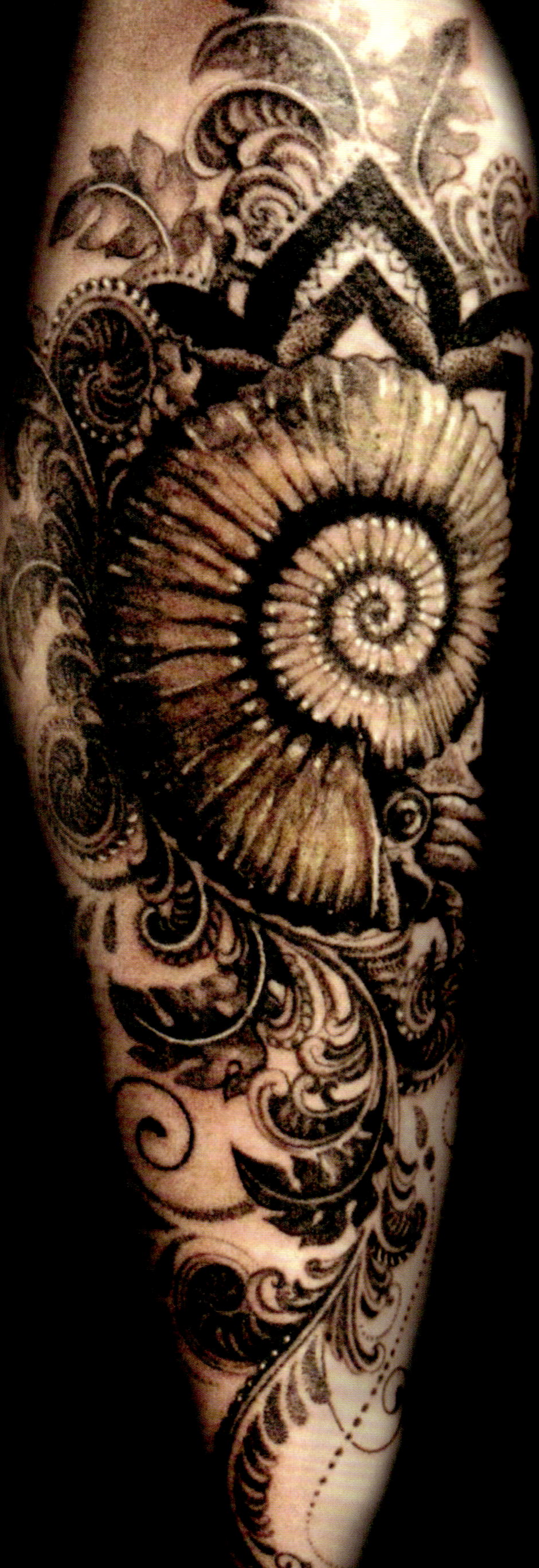

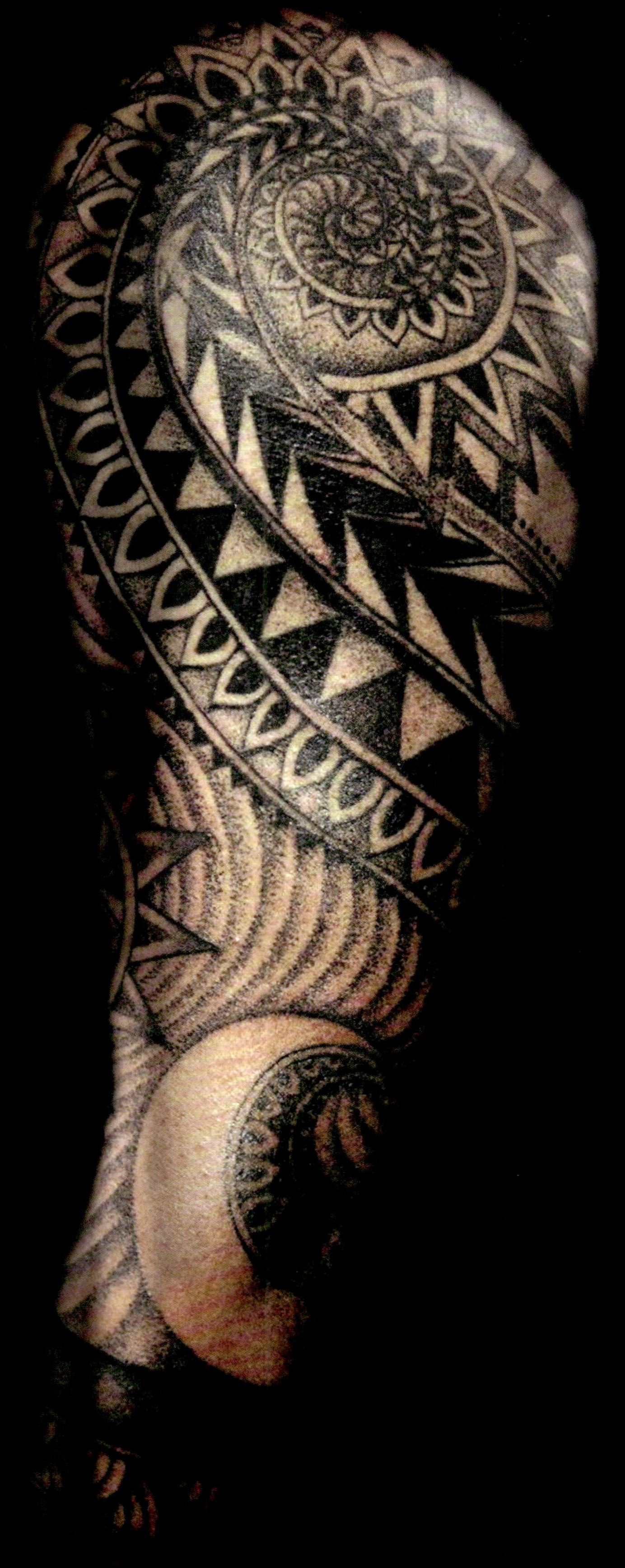

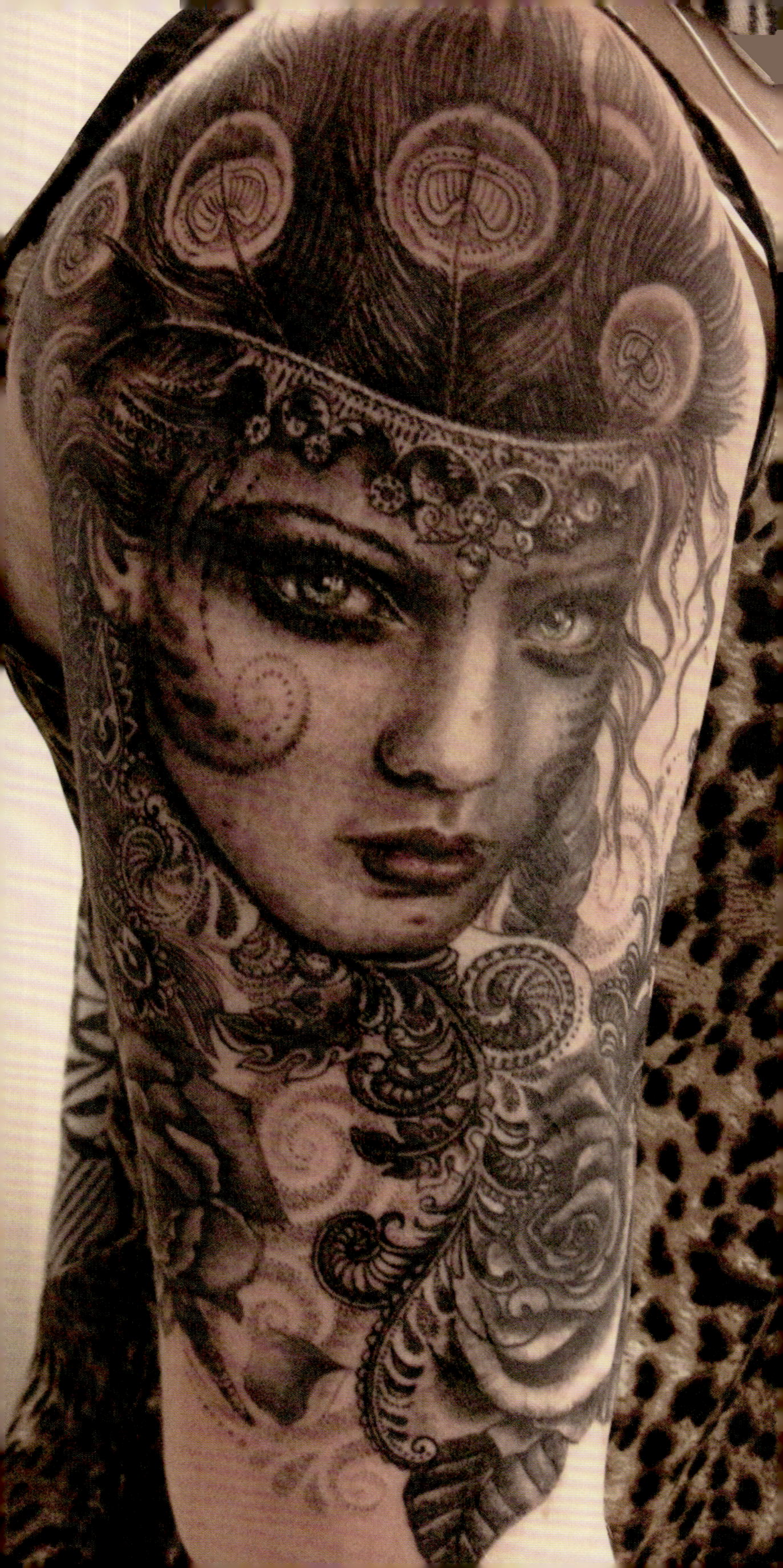

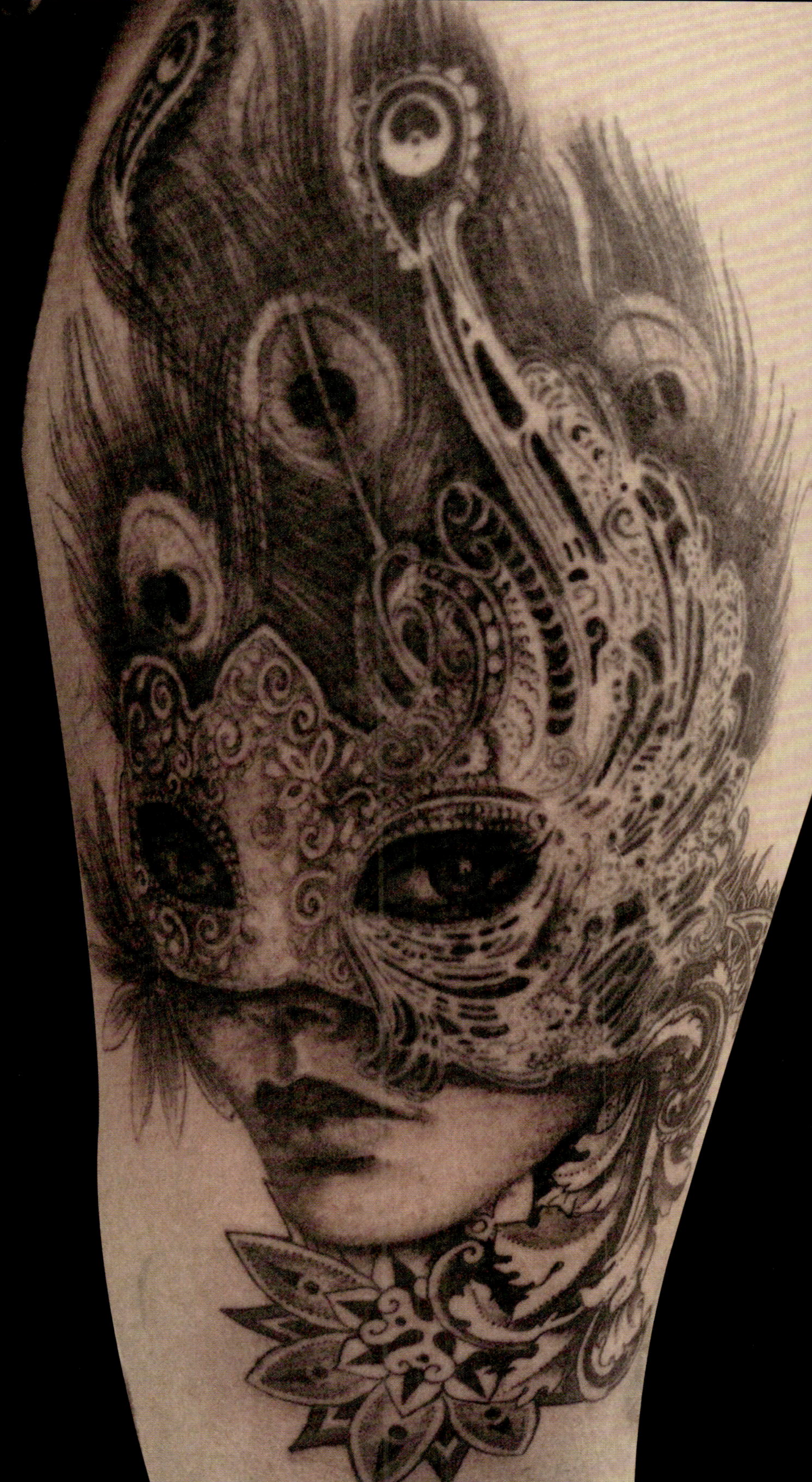

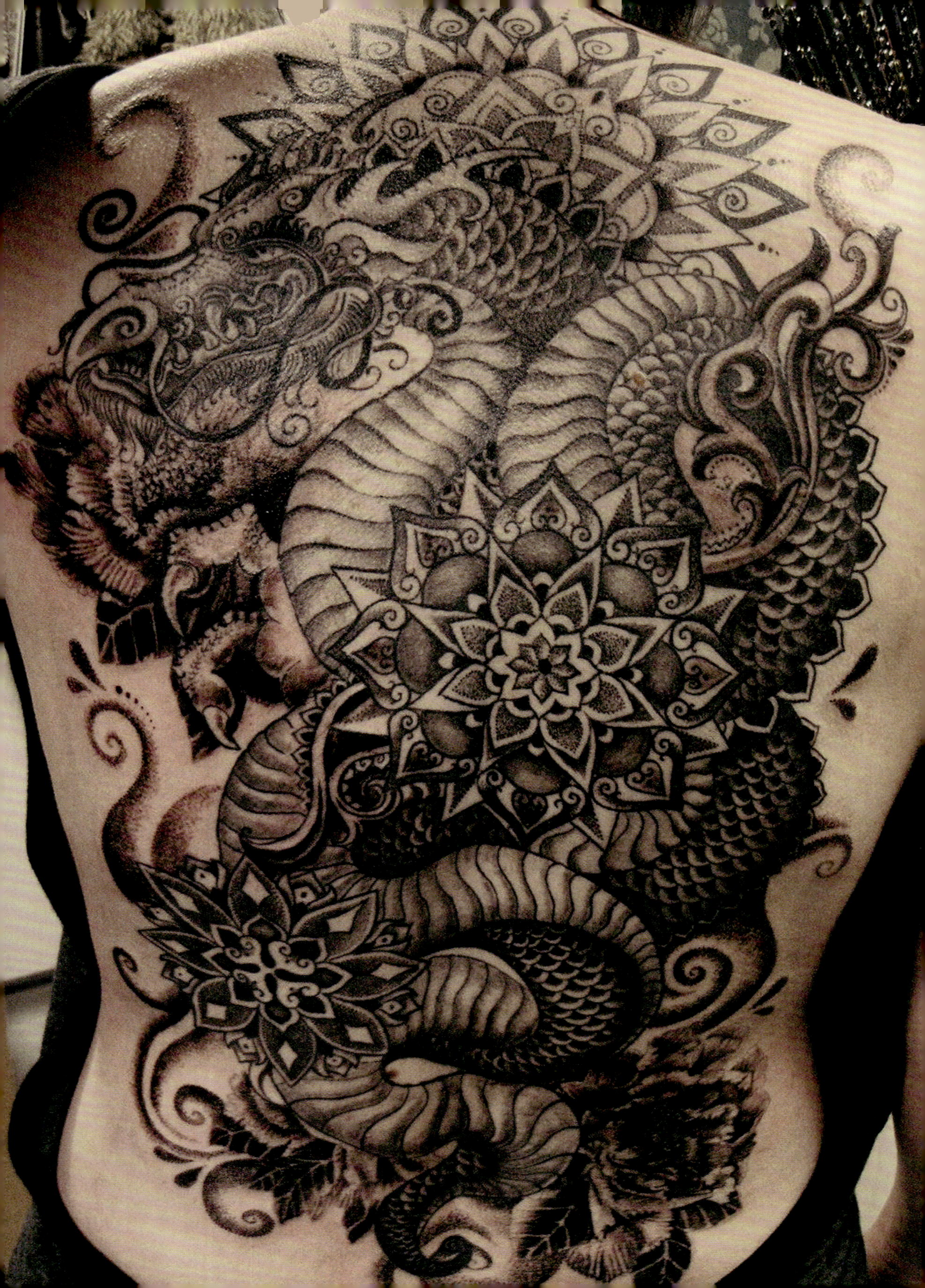

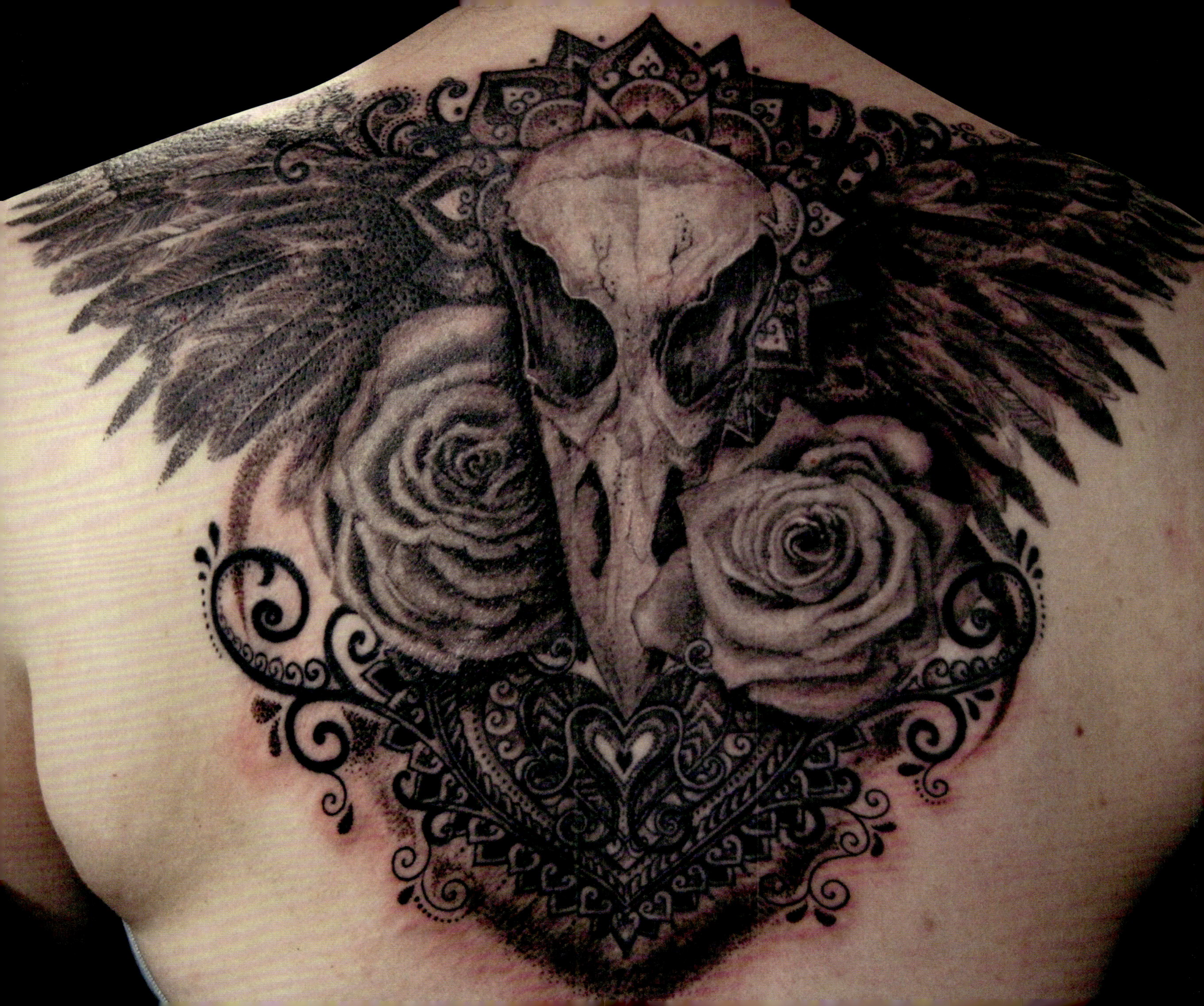

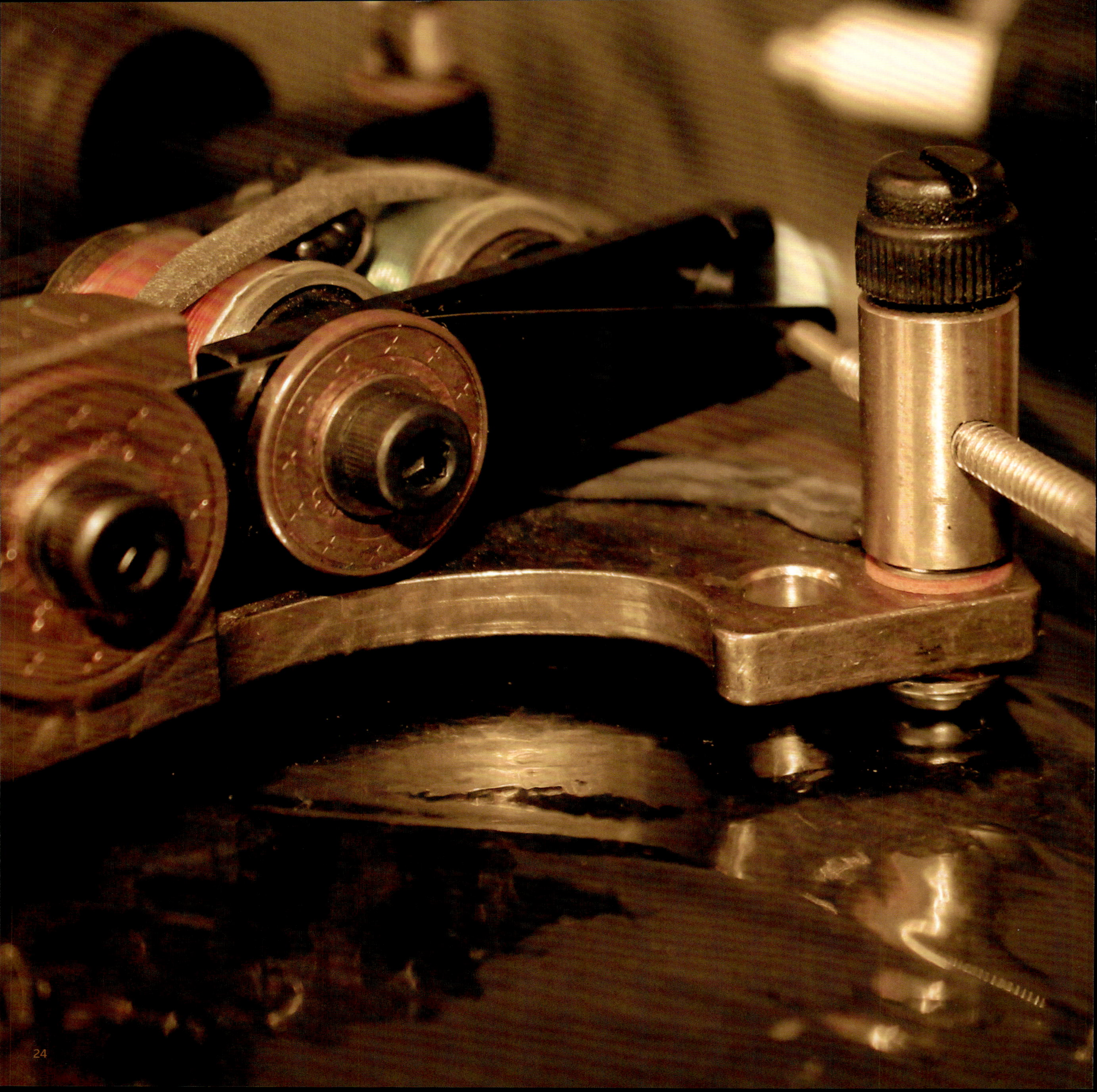

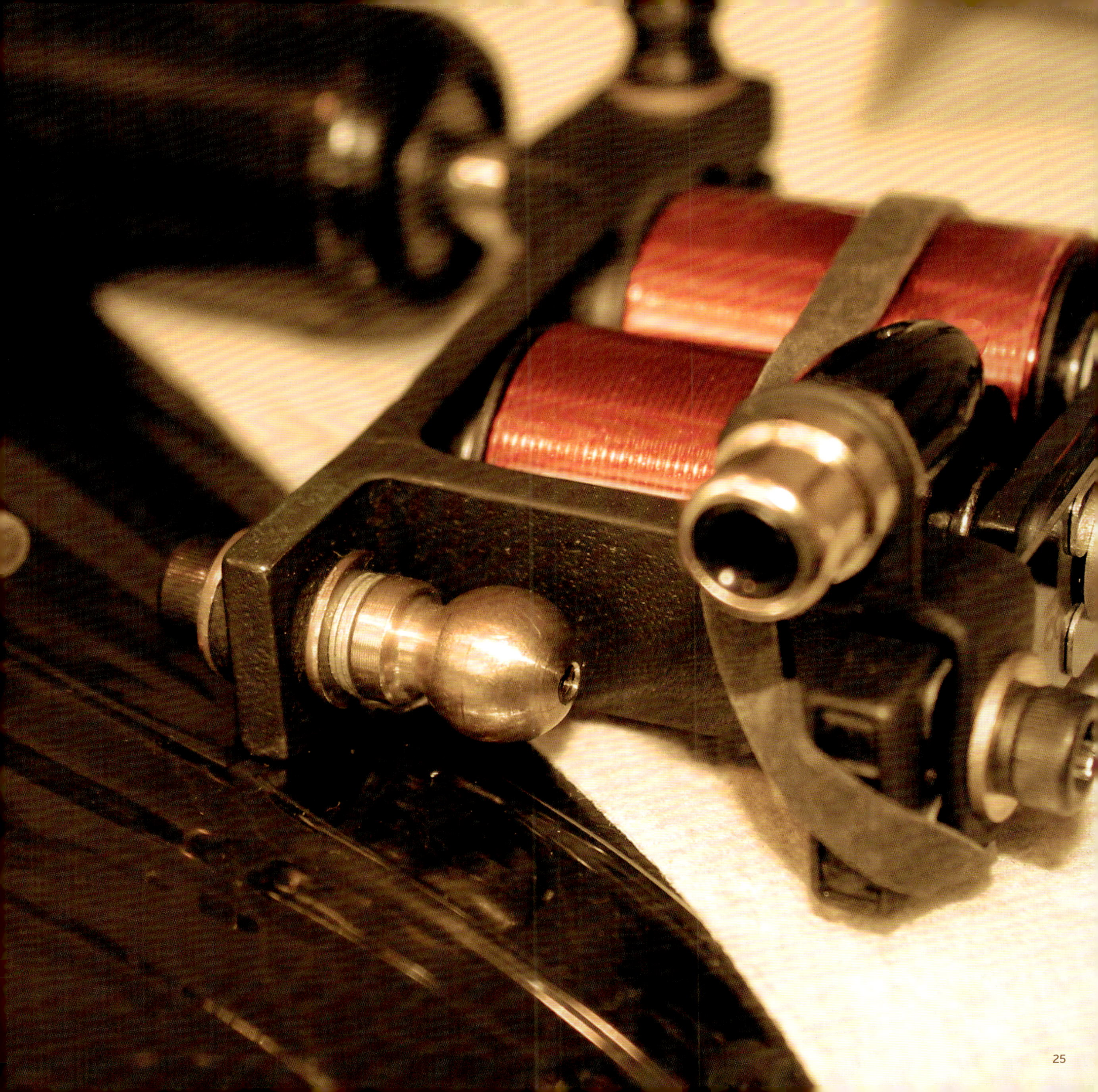

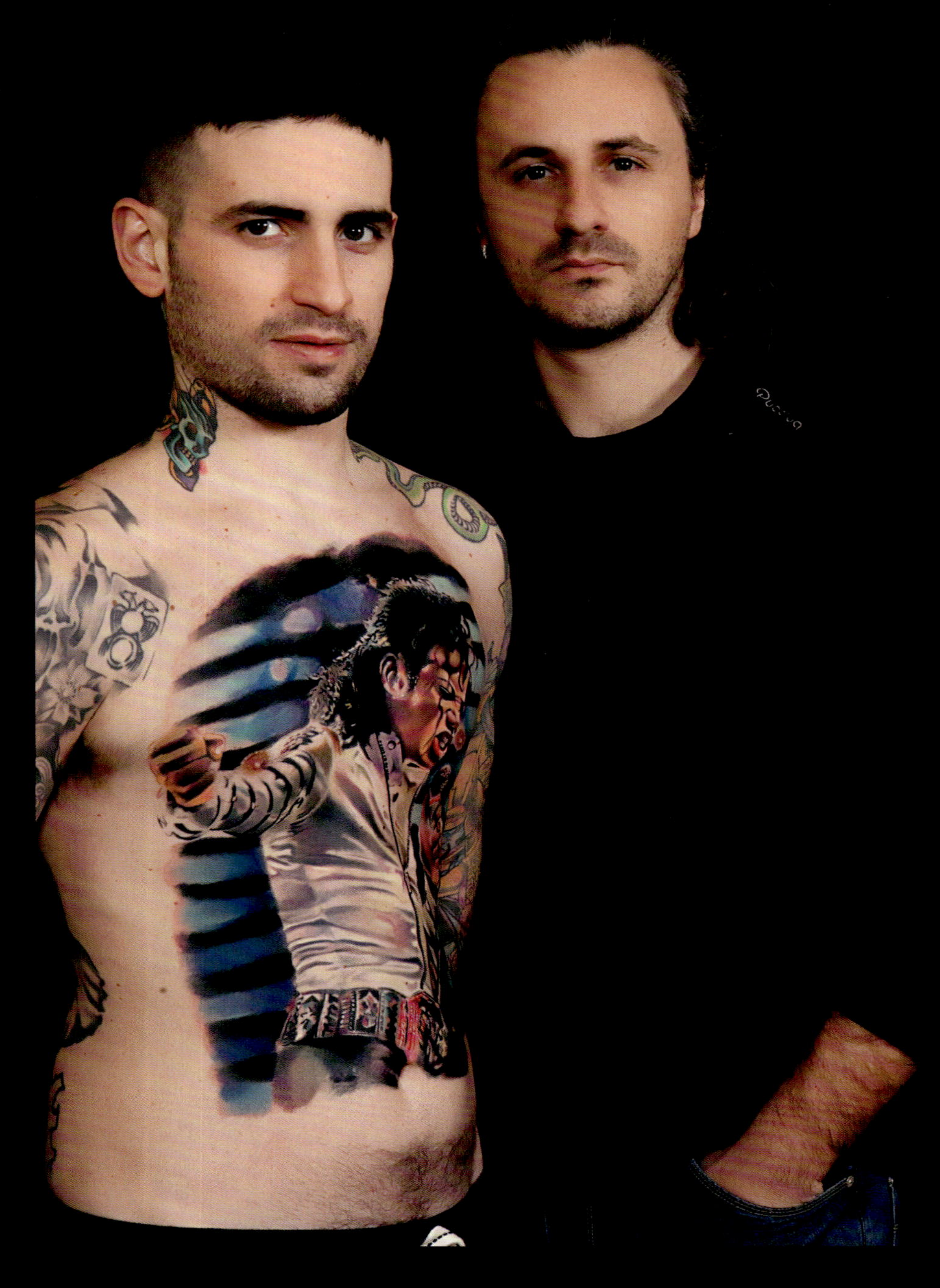

ANDREA AFFERNI

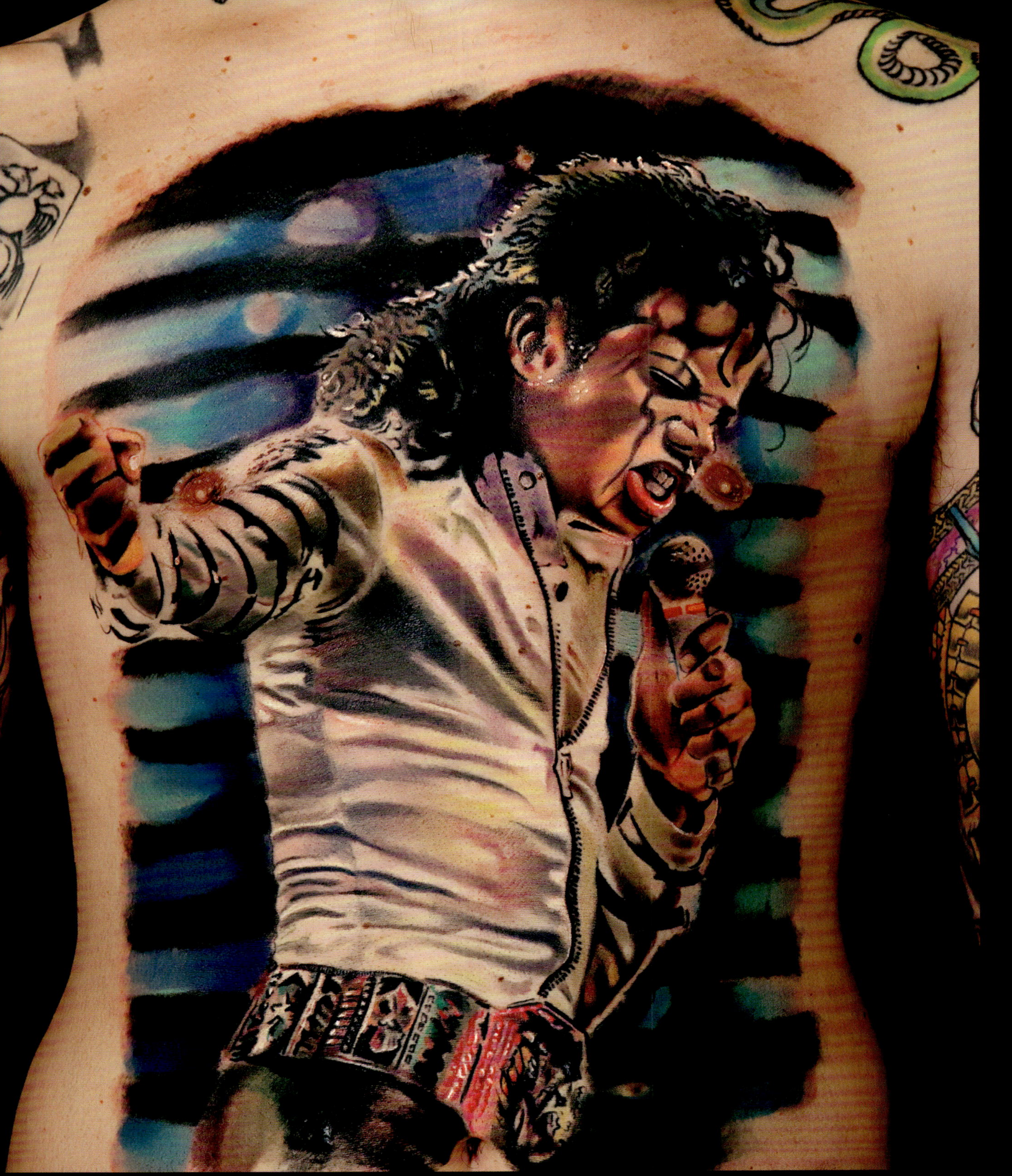

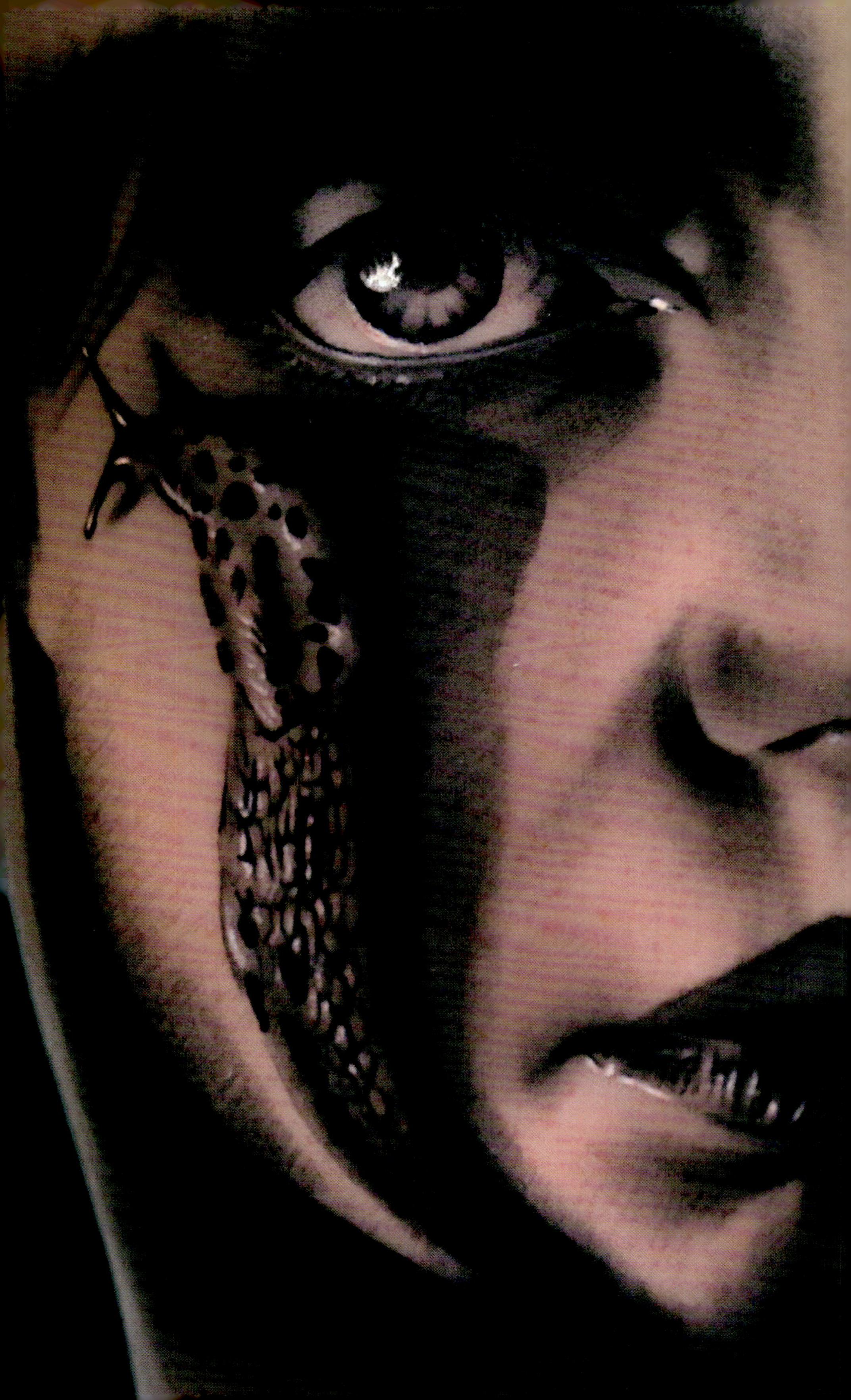

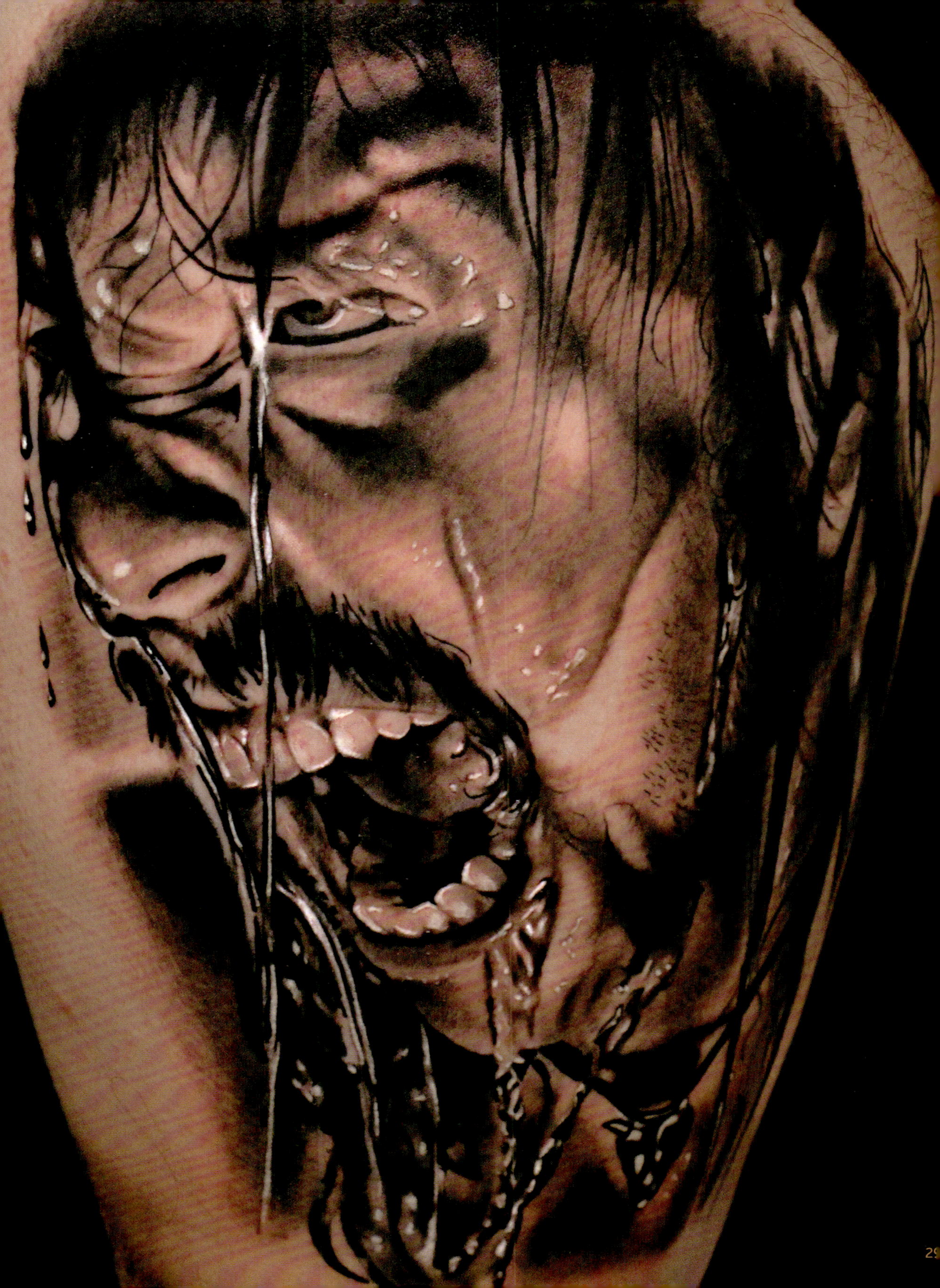

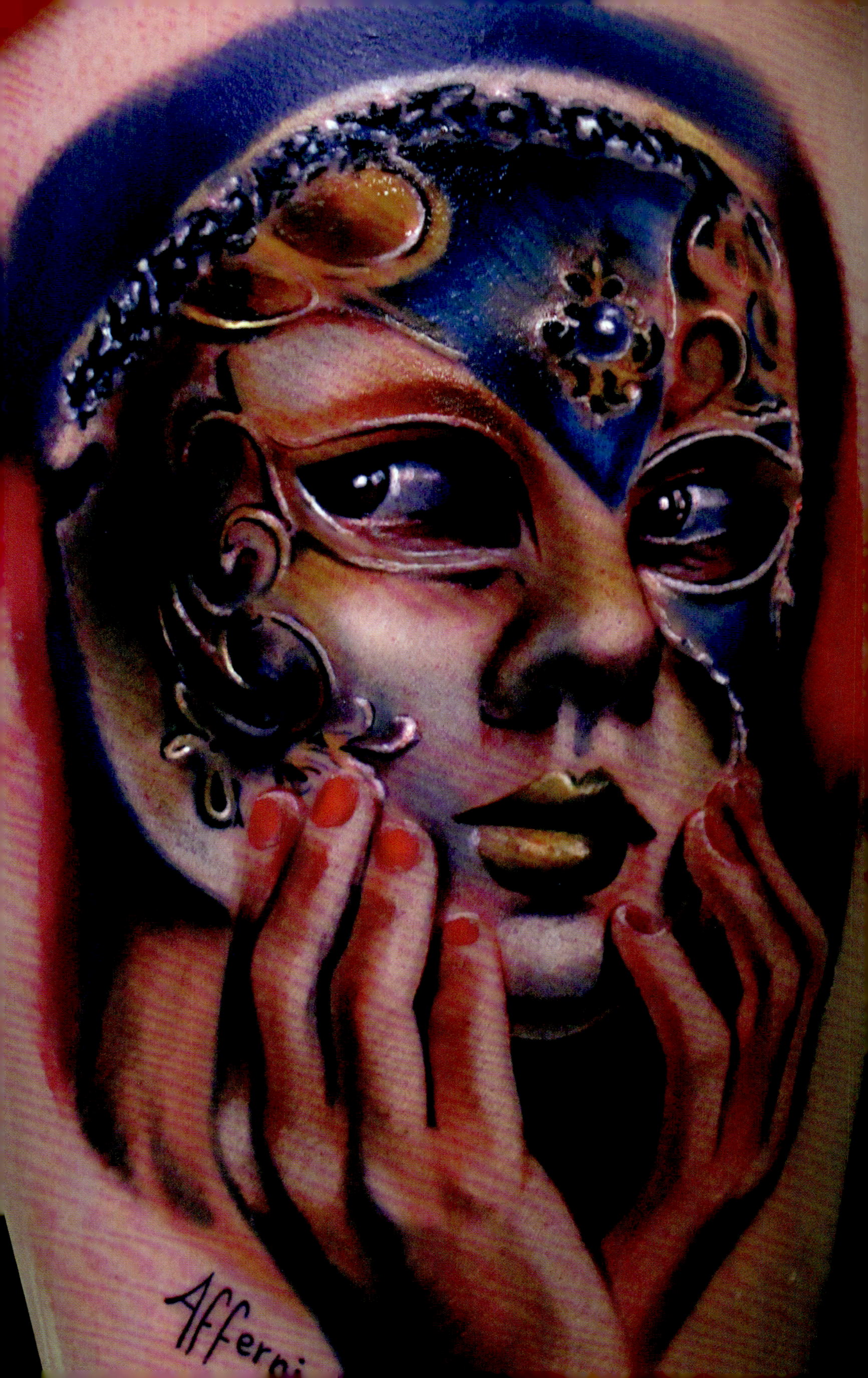
Afferni

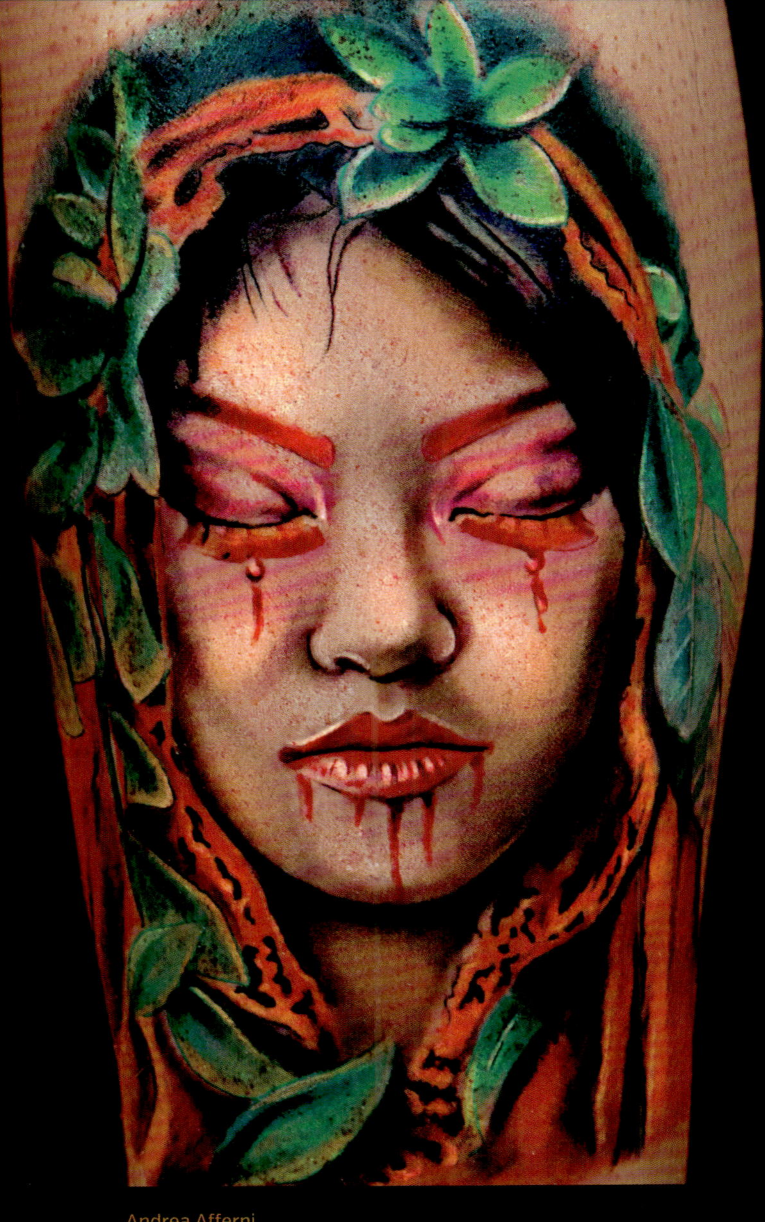

Andrea Afferni
www.afferniandrea.com

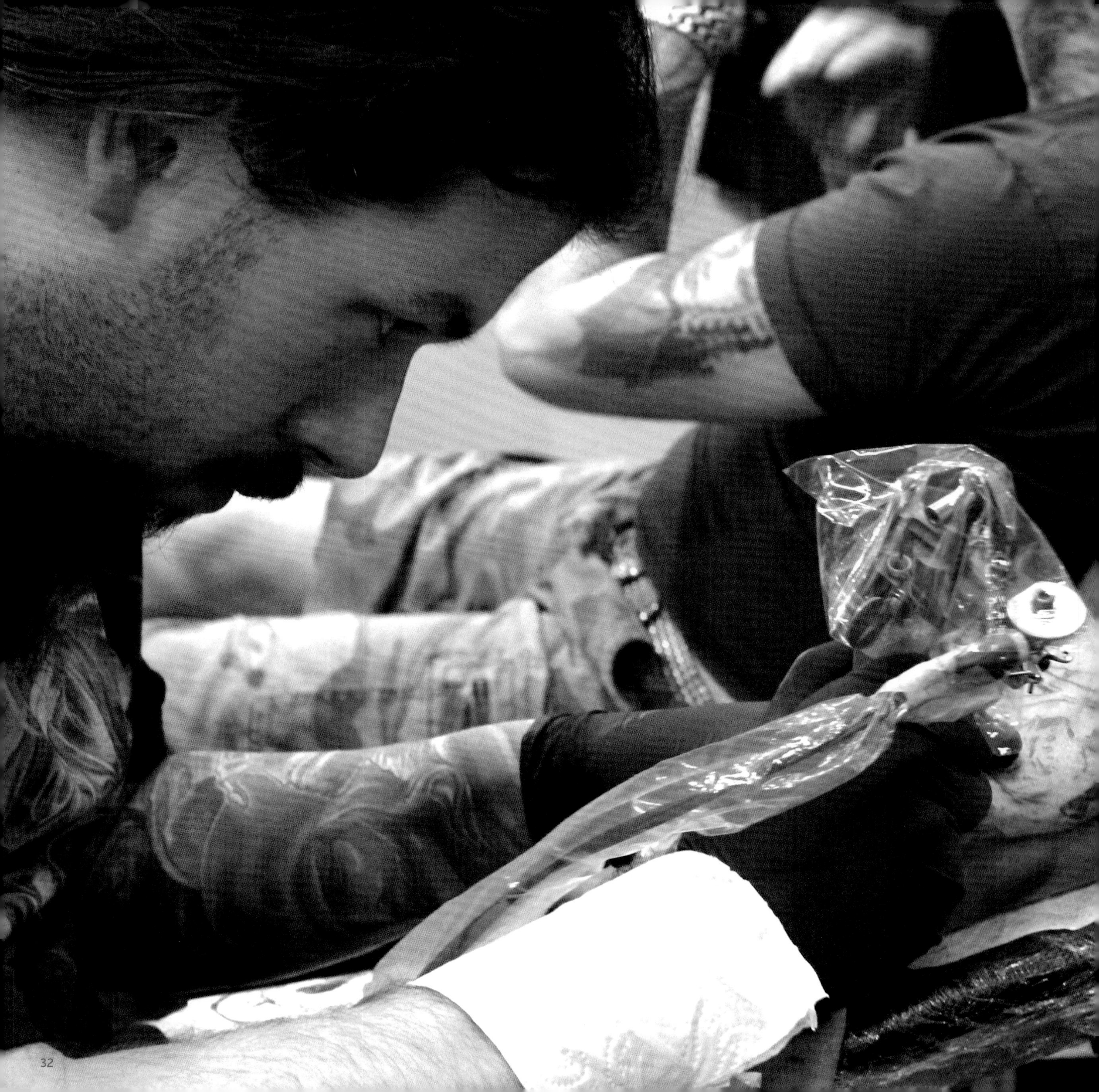

ARON SZABO
IMMORTAL INK

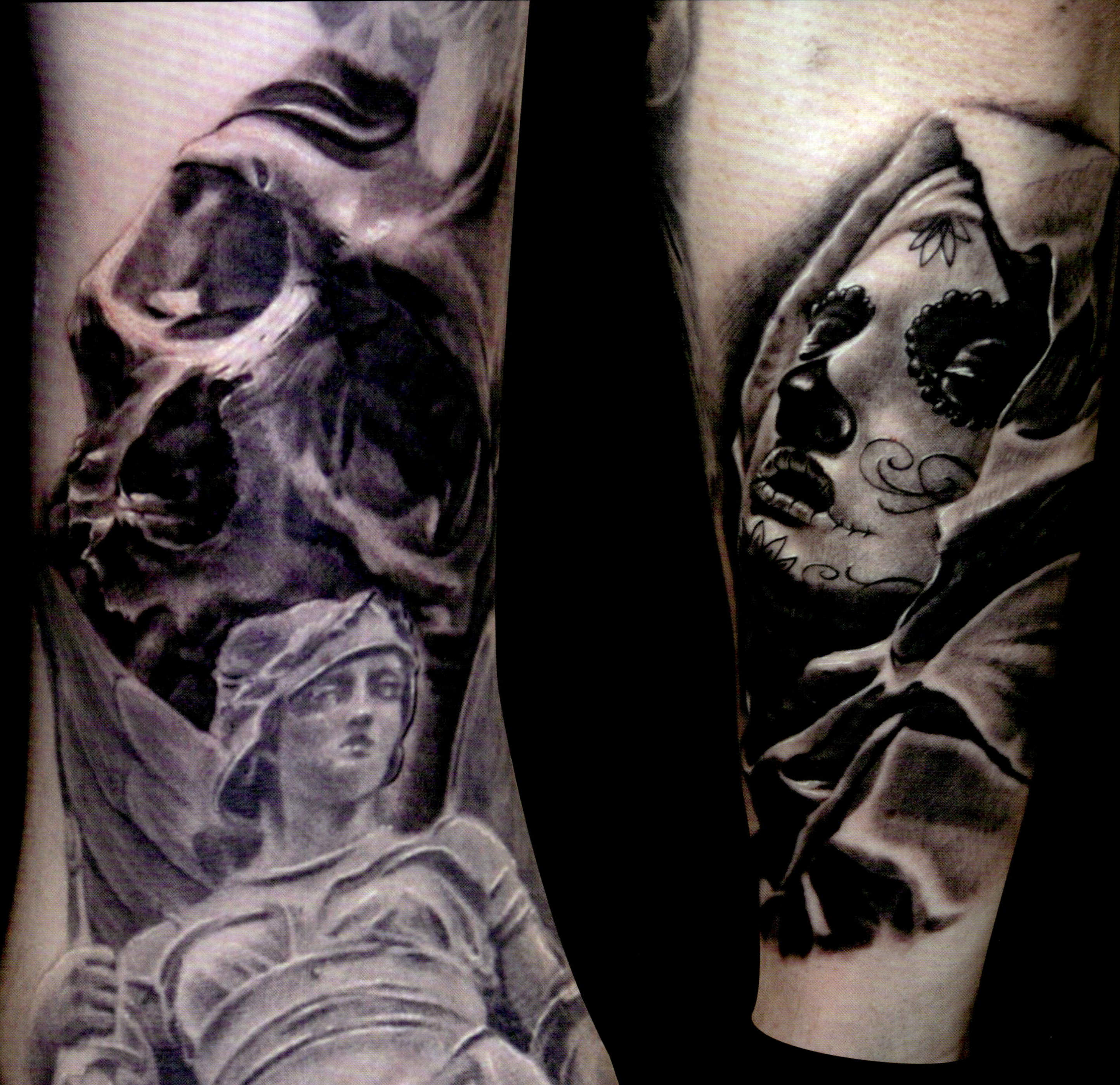

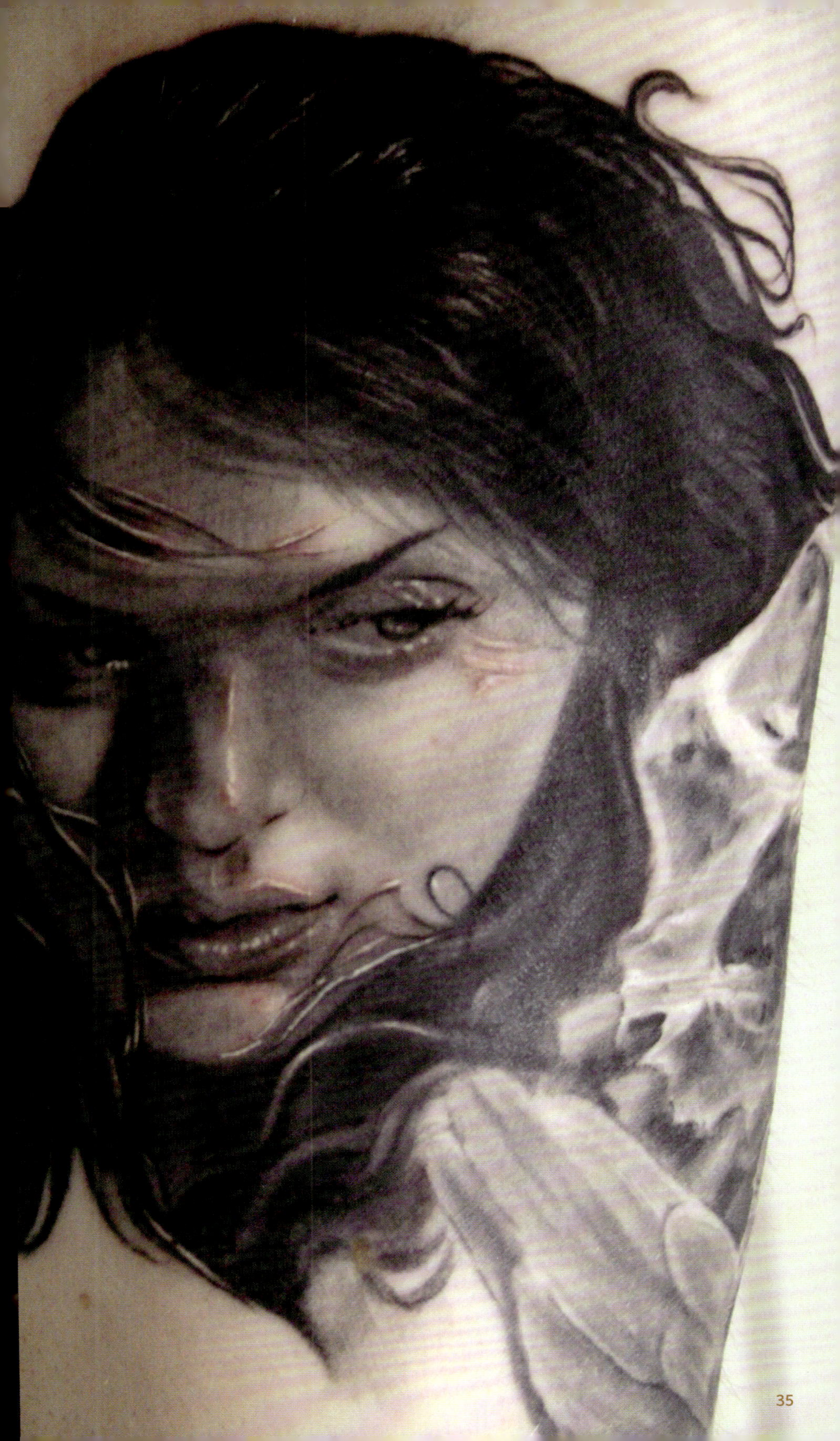

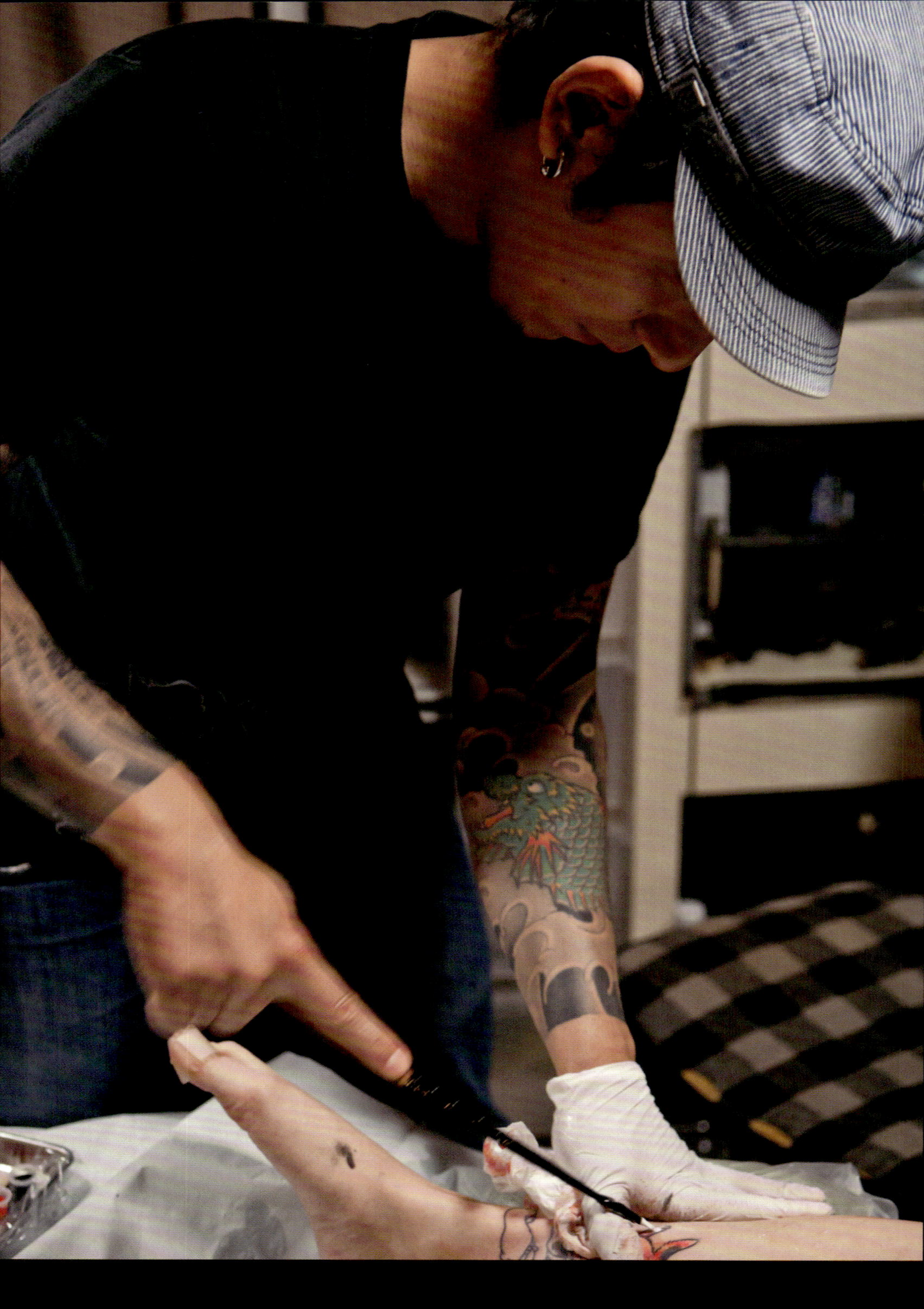

BUNSHIN HORITOSHI

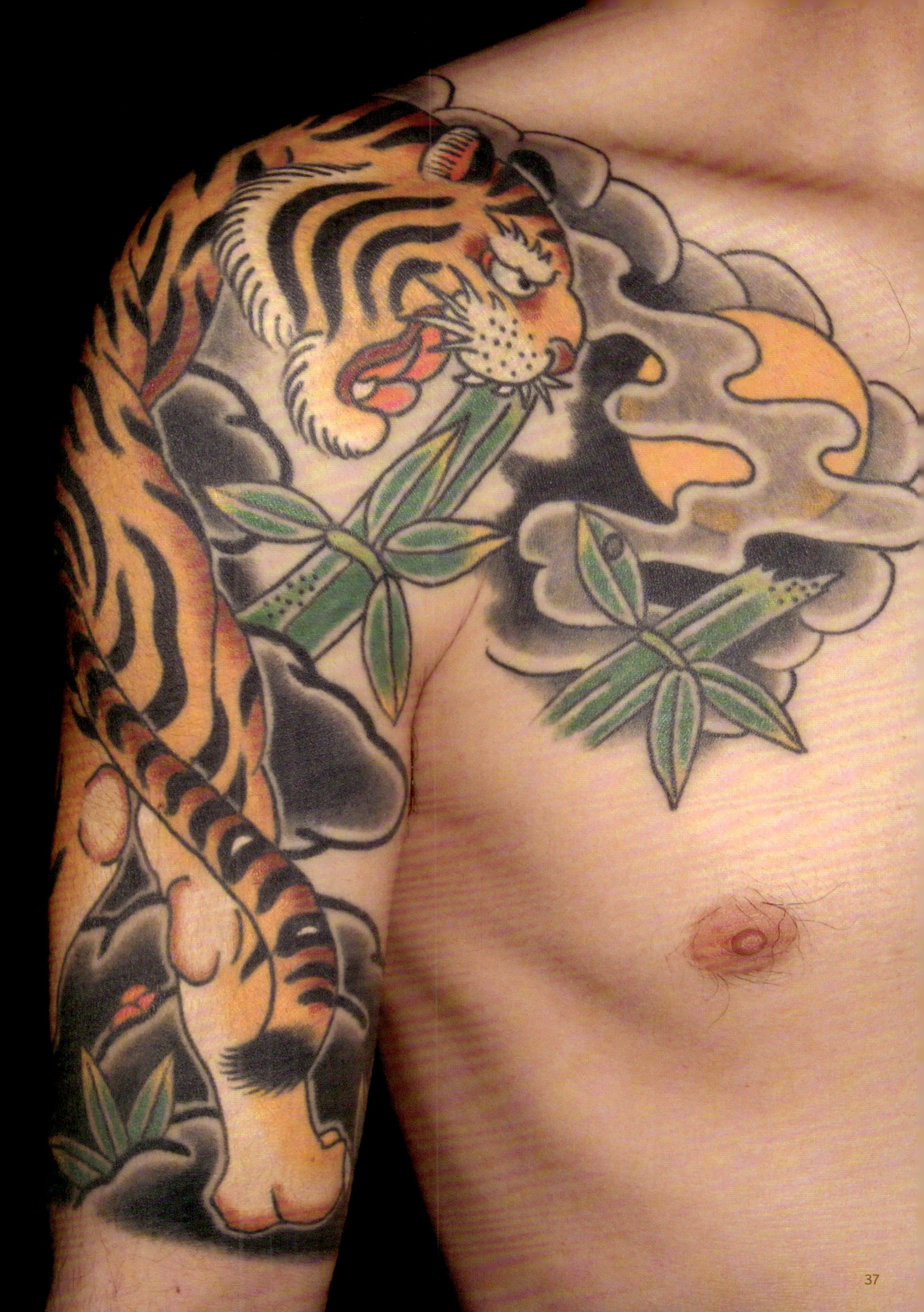

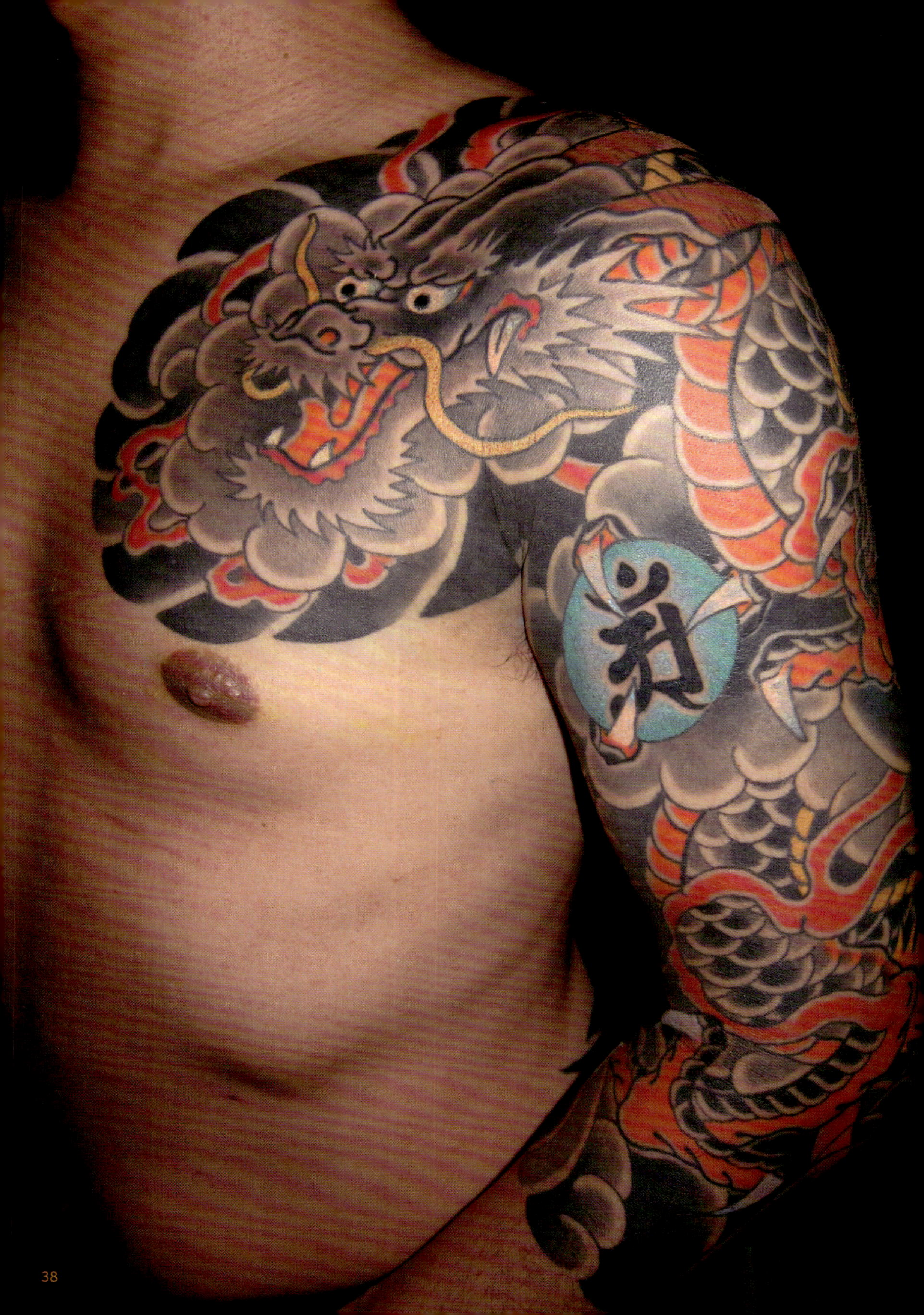

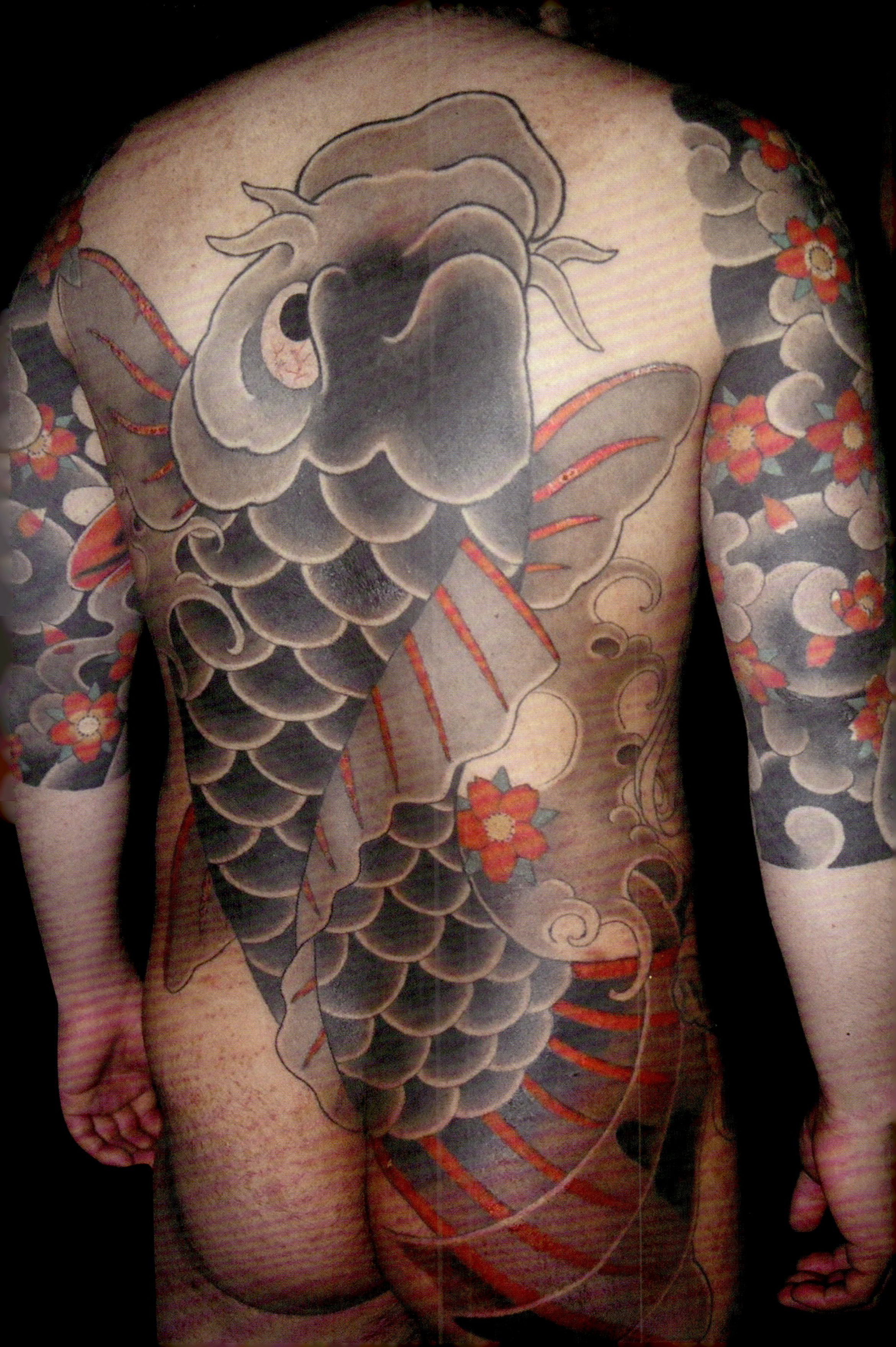

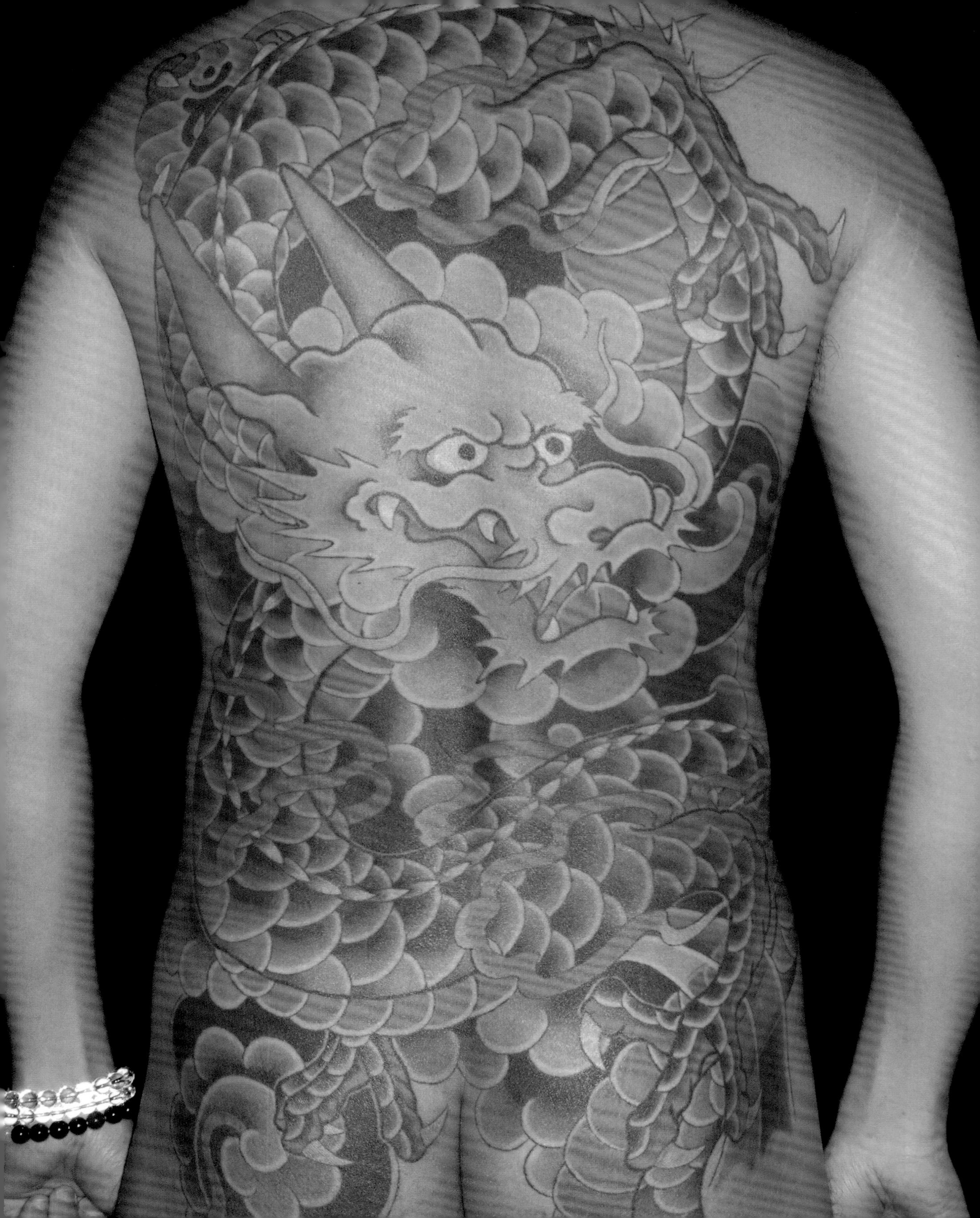

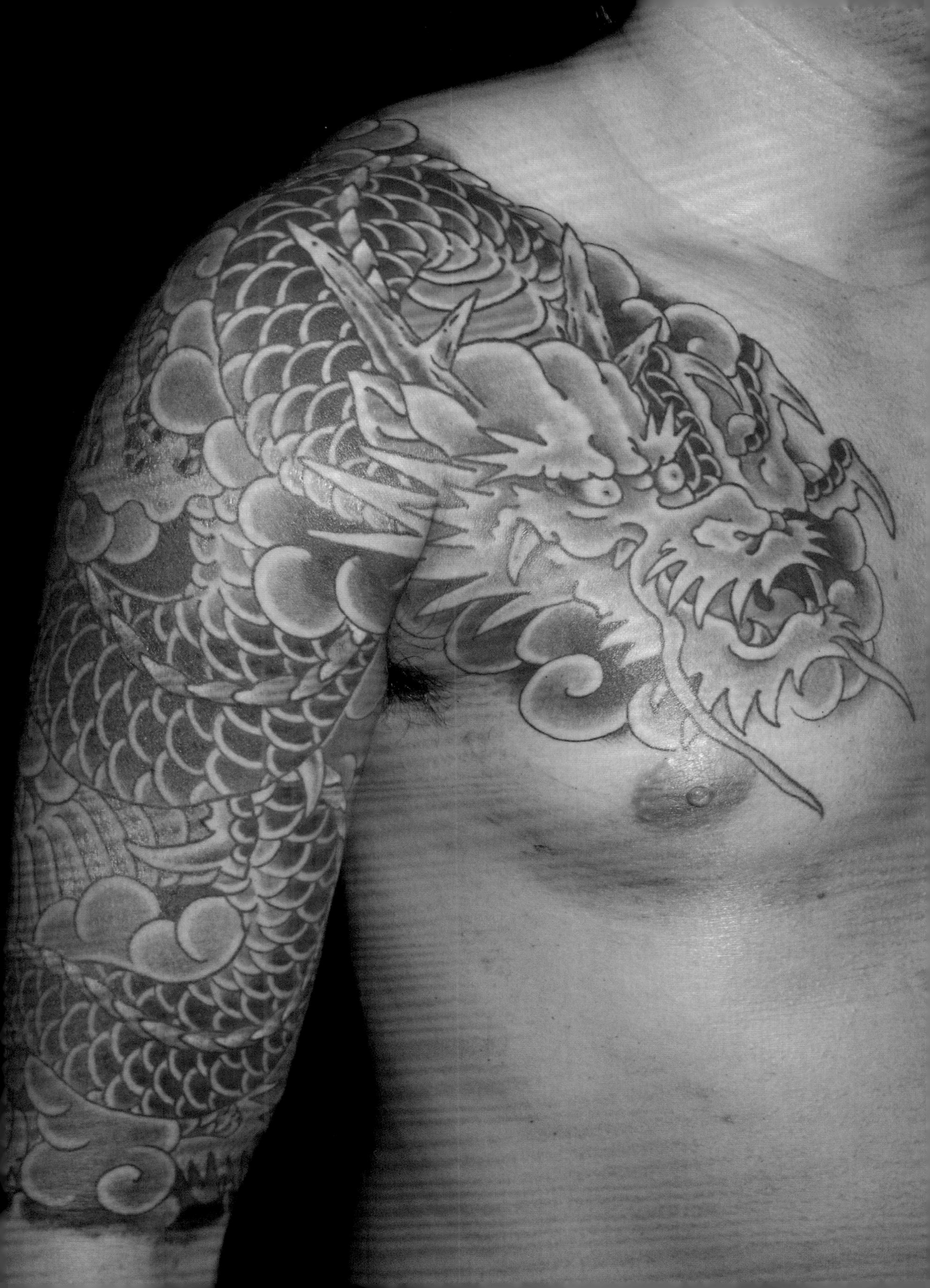

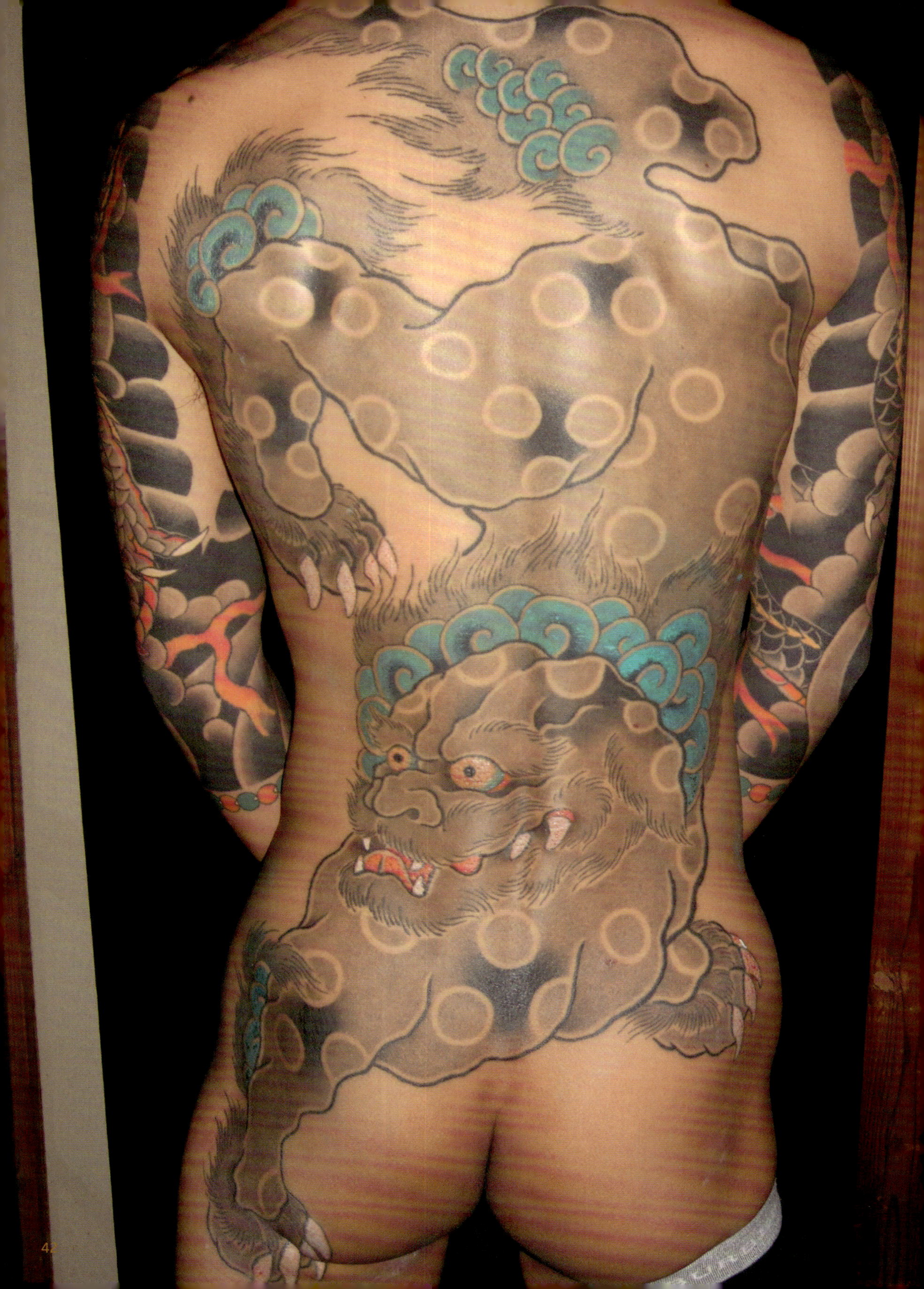

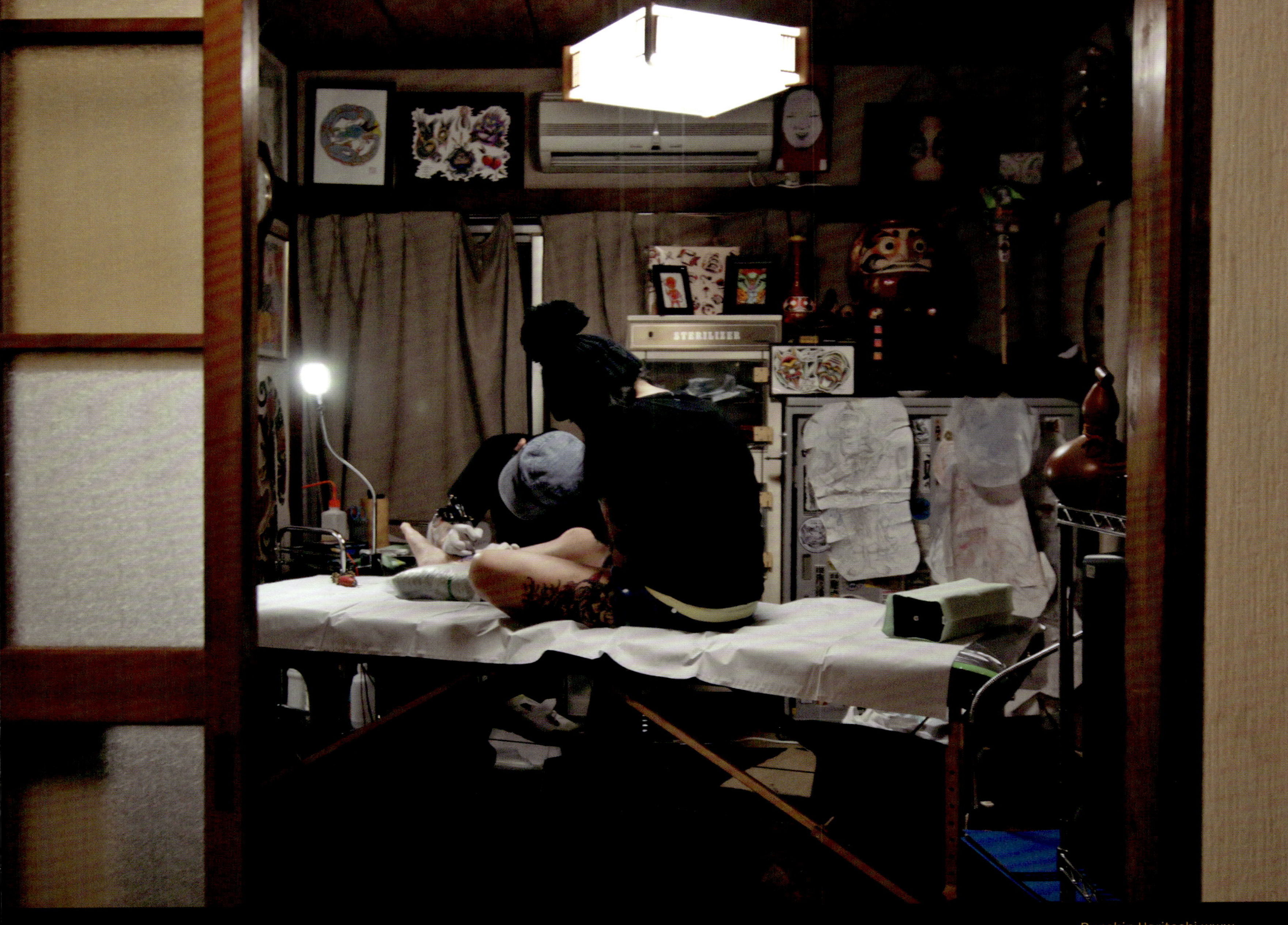
Bunshin Horitoshi www.
bunshin-horitoshi.jp

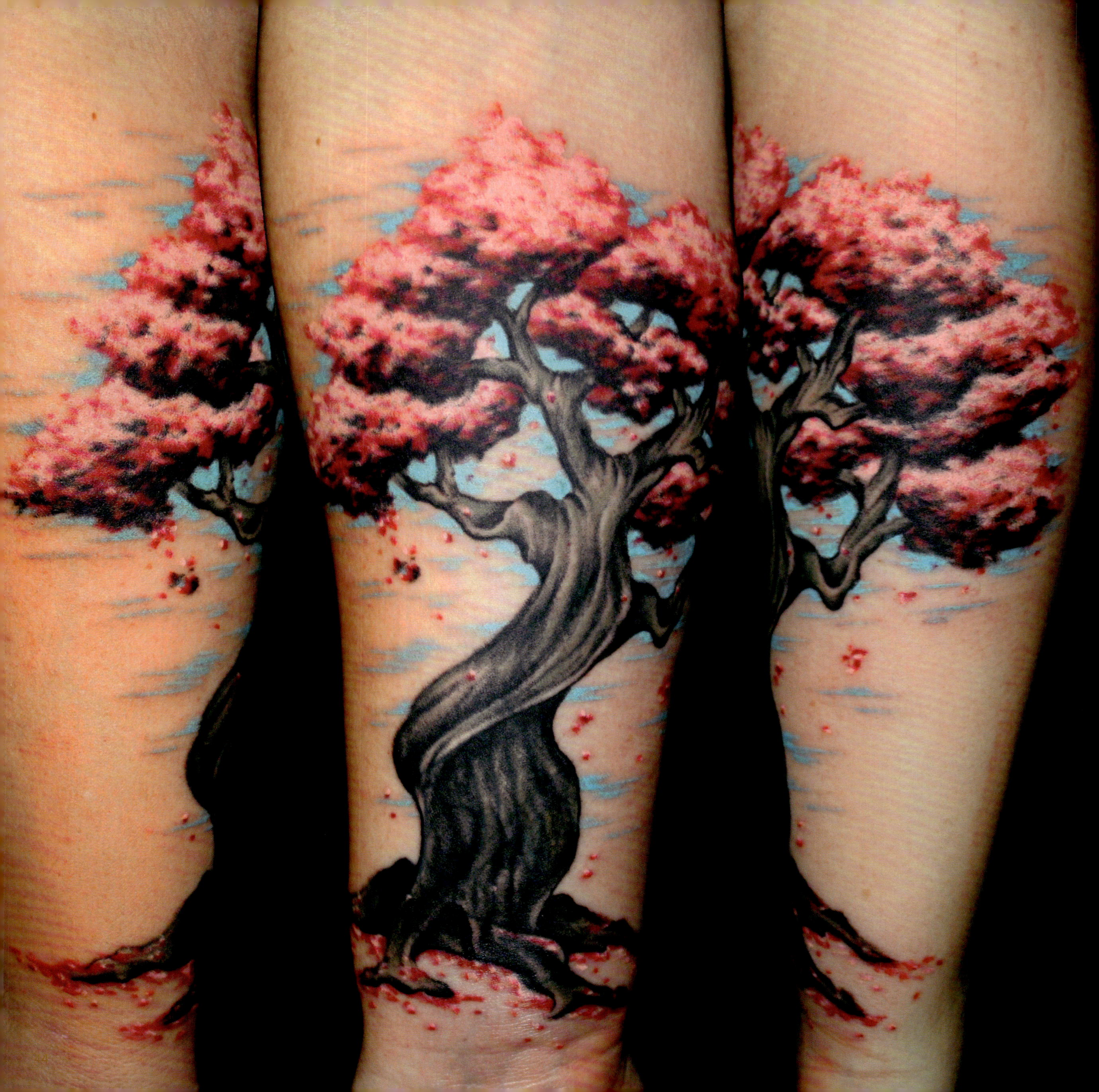

CHRIS 51

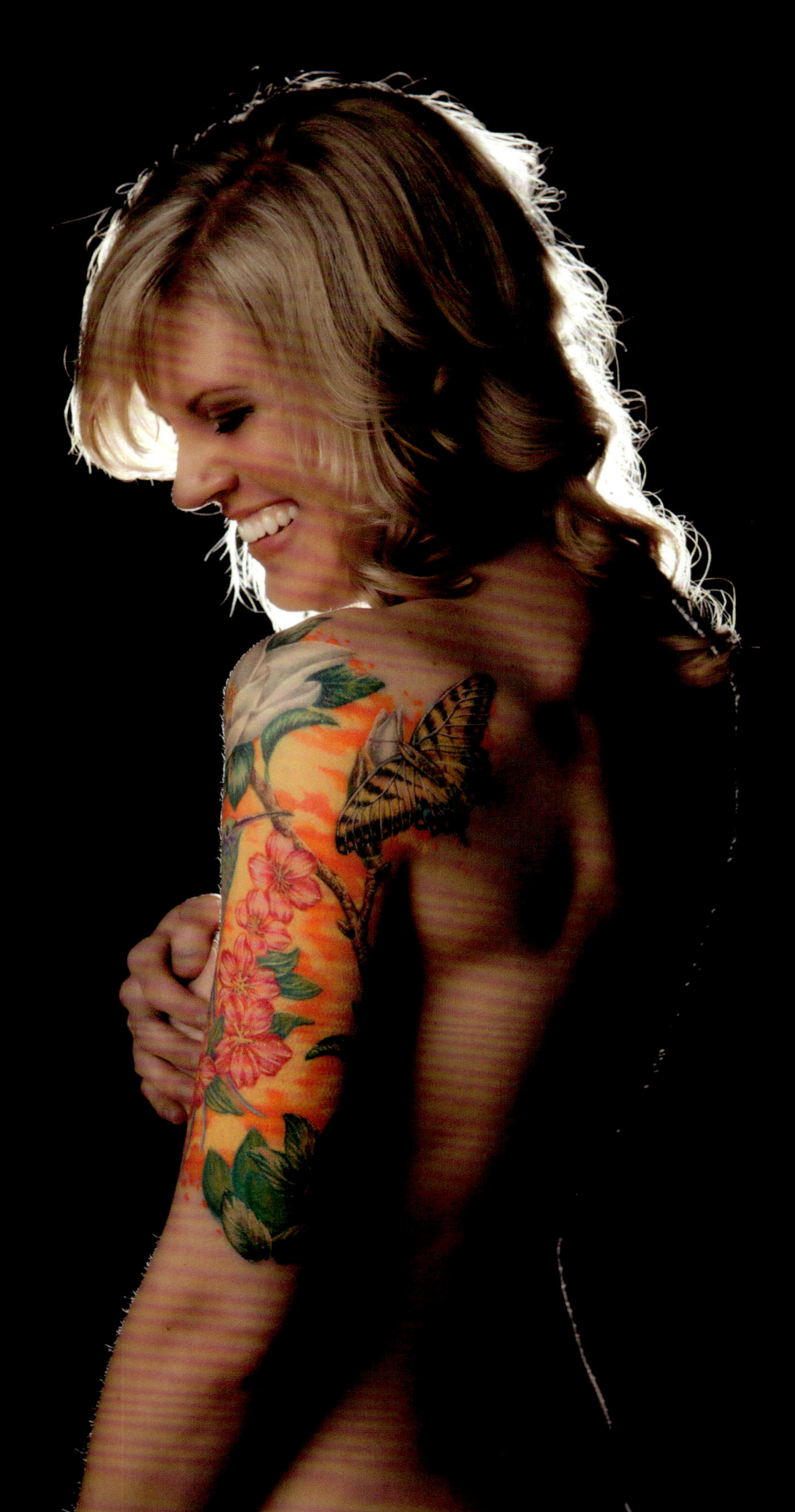

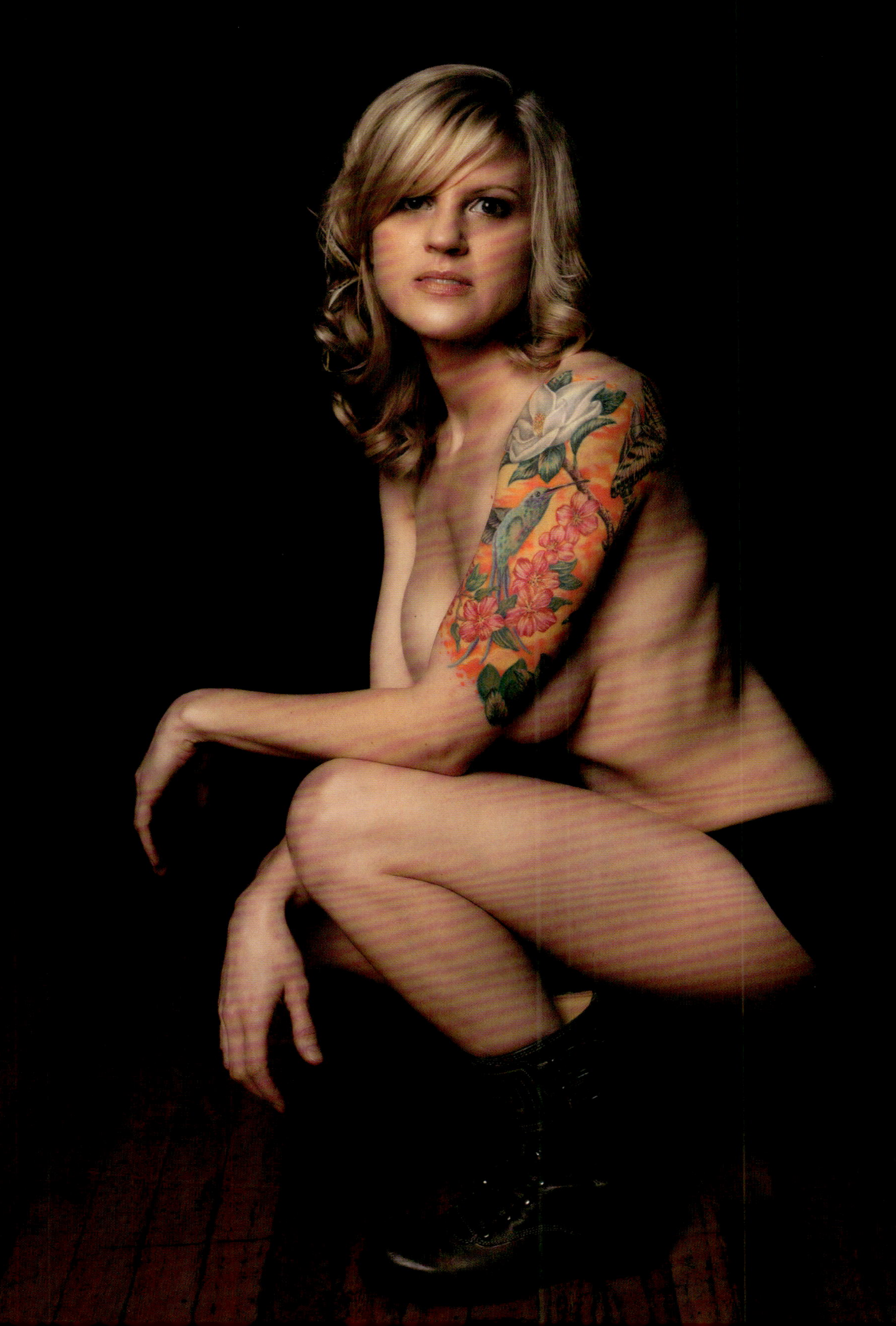

Chris 51
www.chris51.com

CORU FAMILY

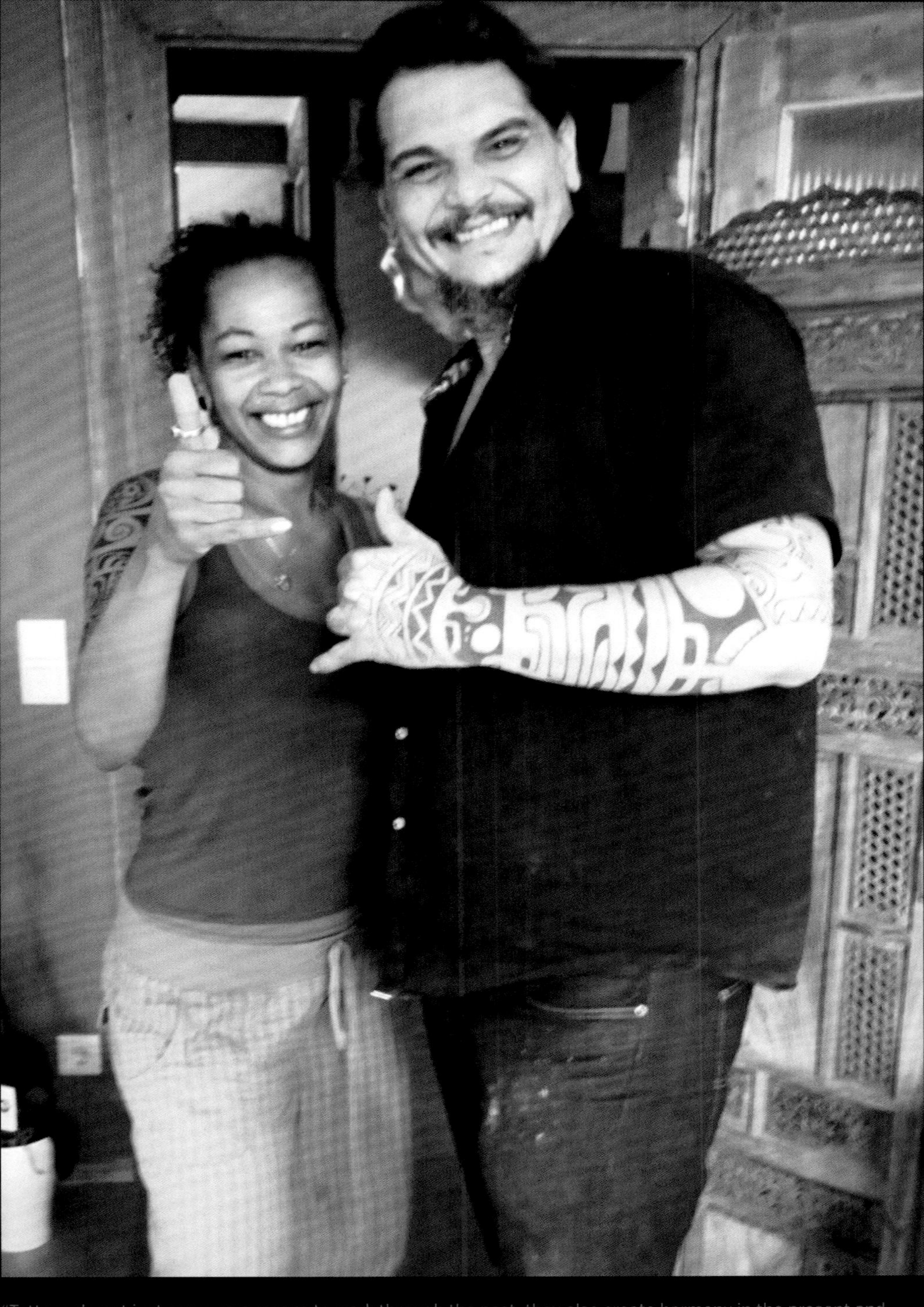

"Tattoos do not just serve as a means to work through the past; they also create harmony in the present and have an influence on future goals."

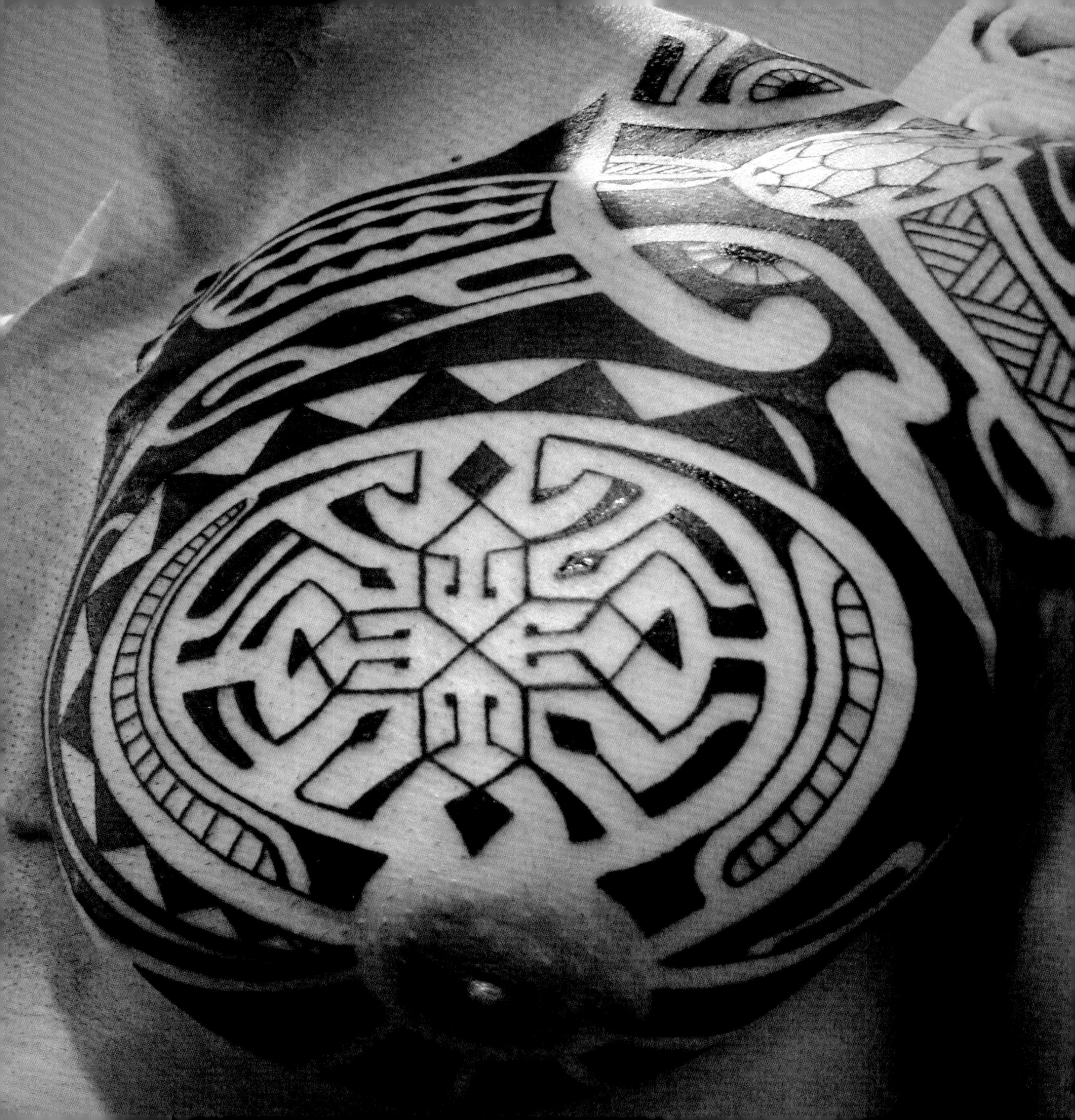

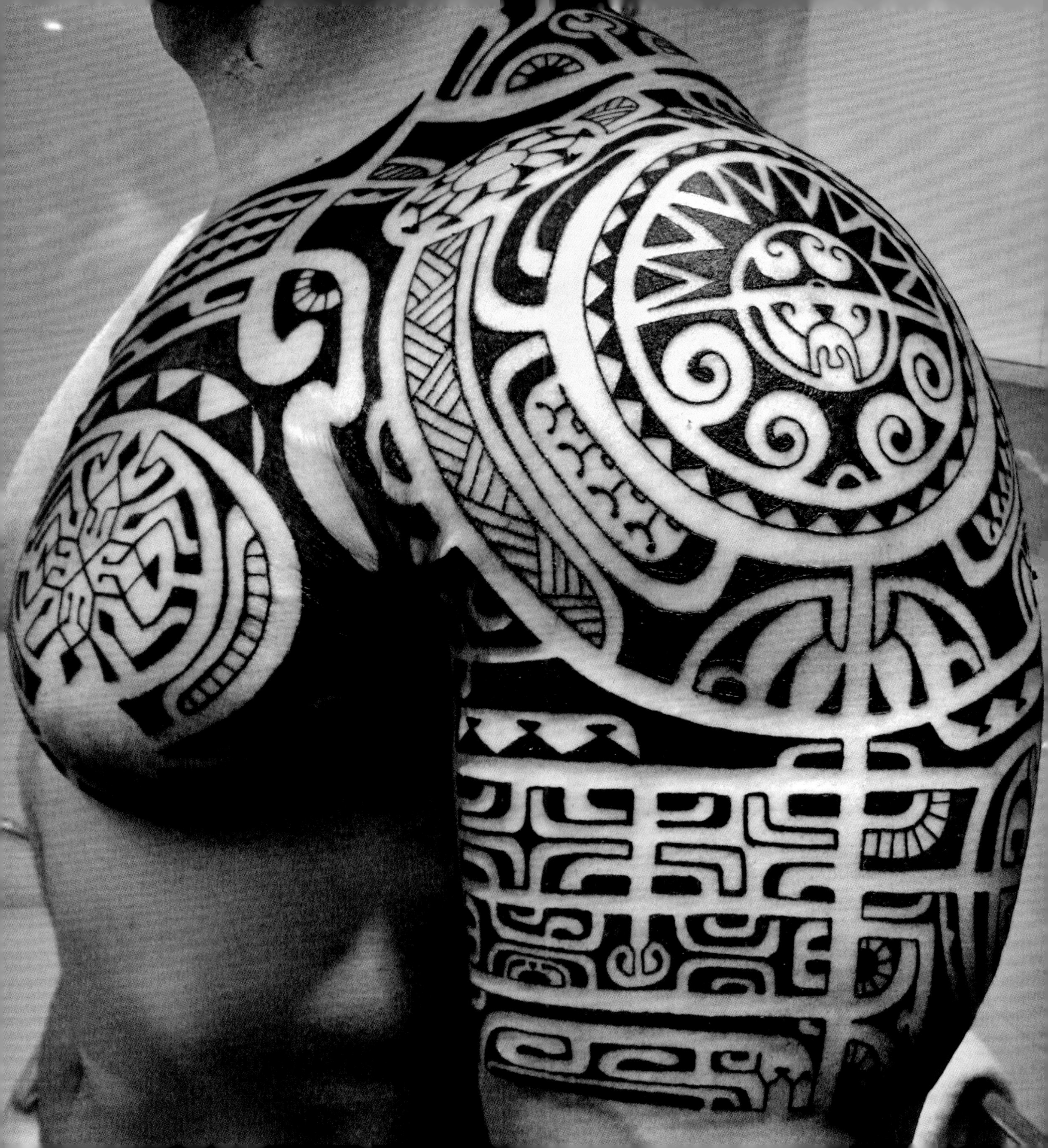

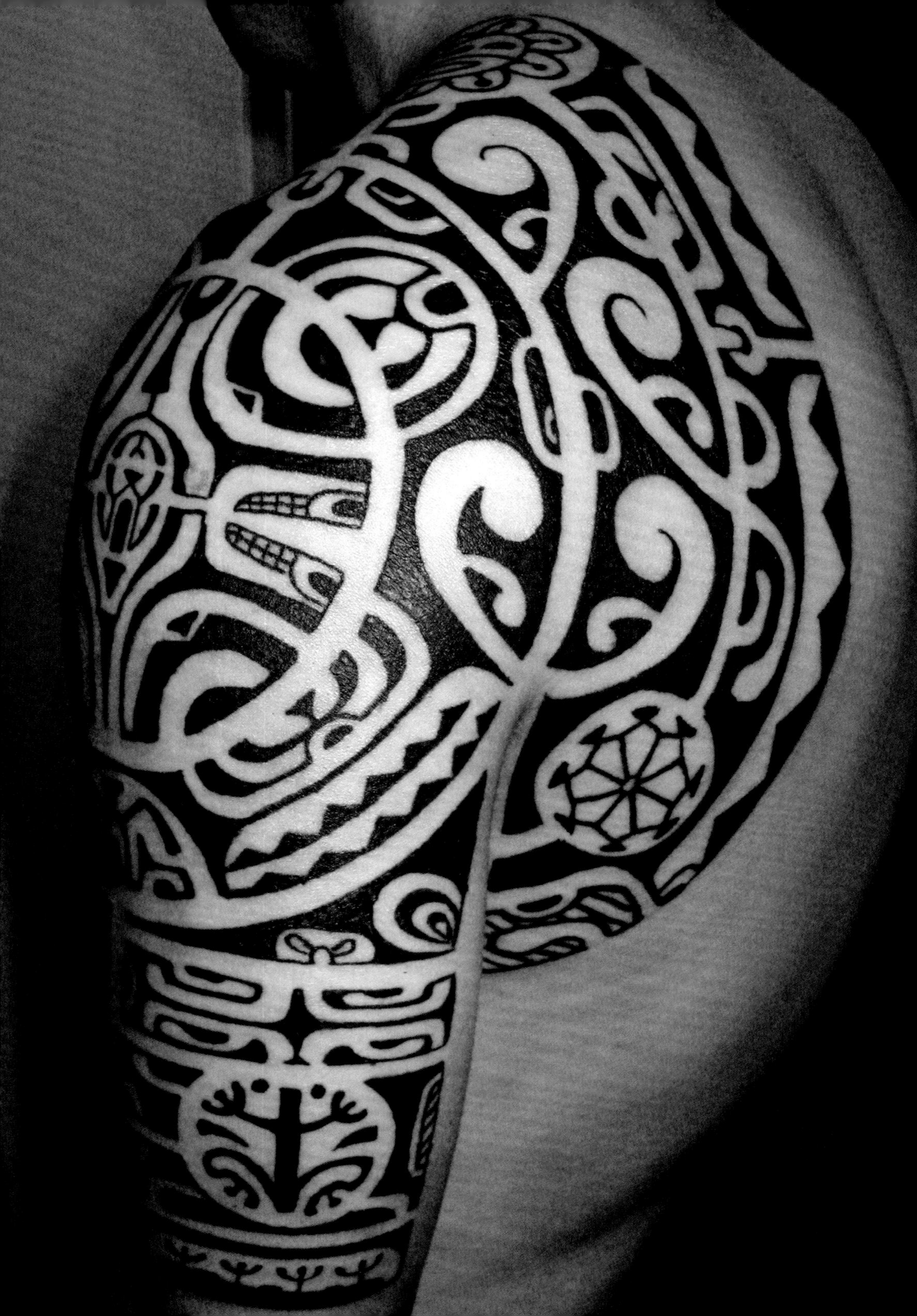

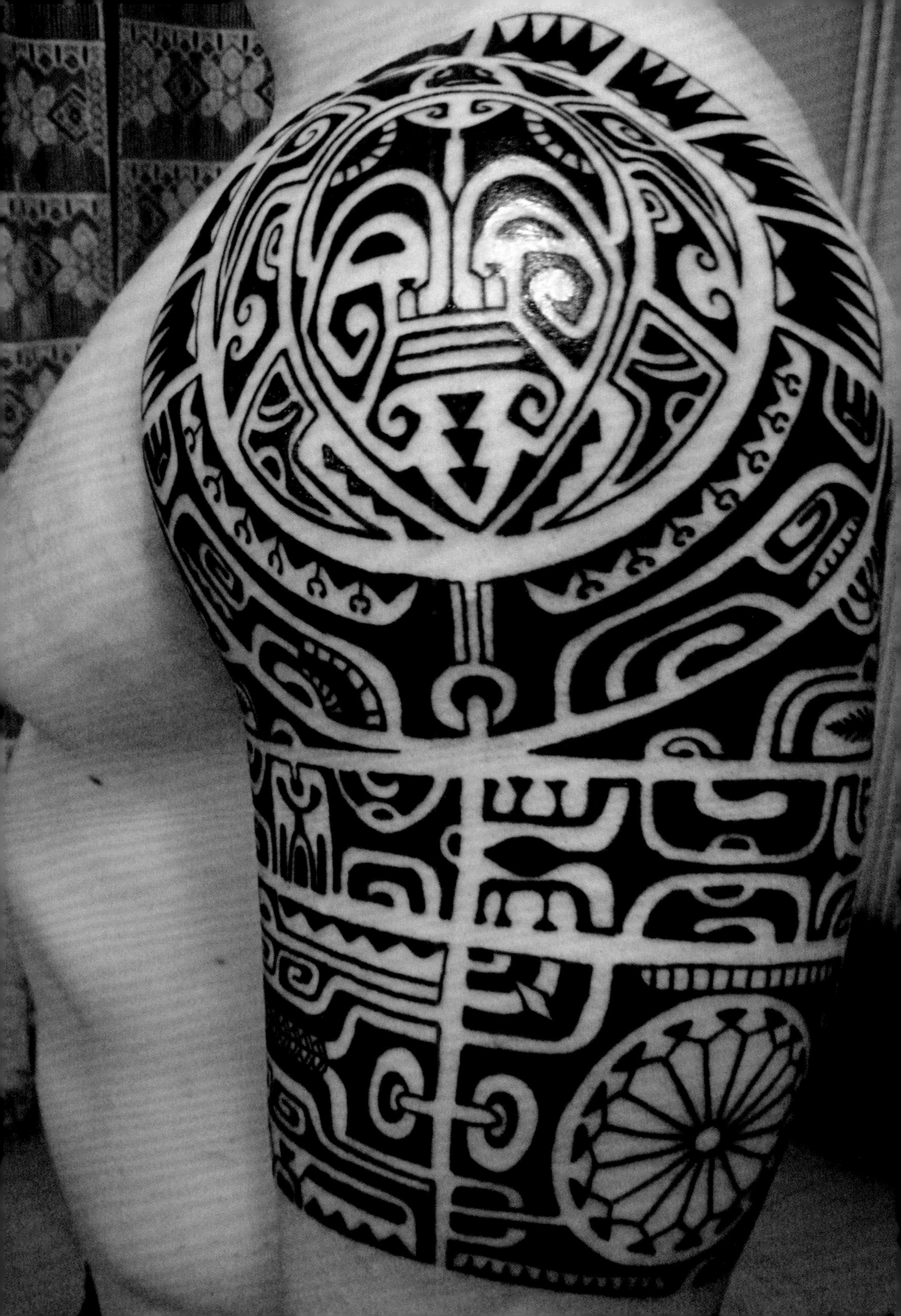

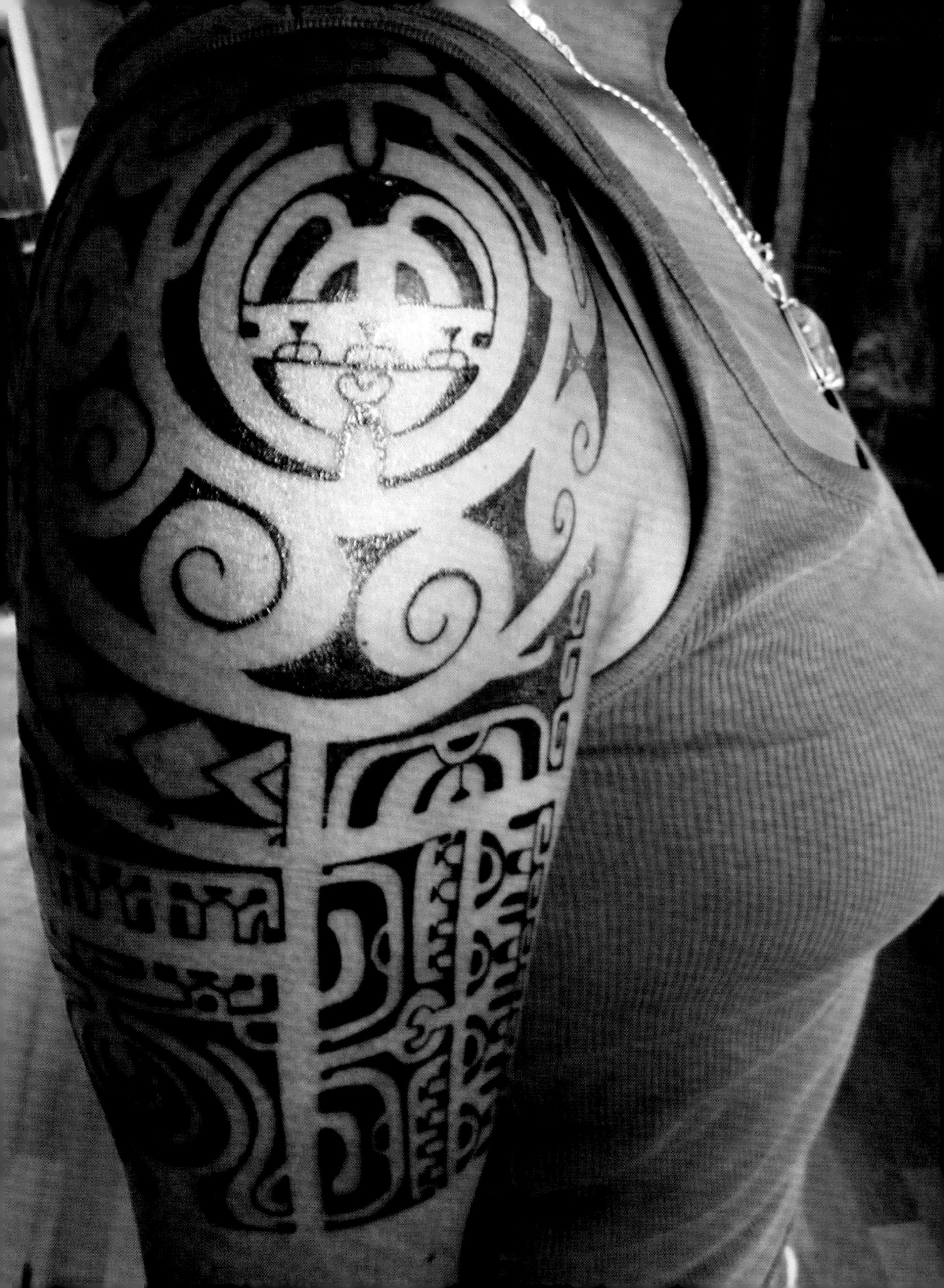

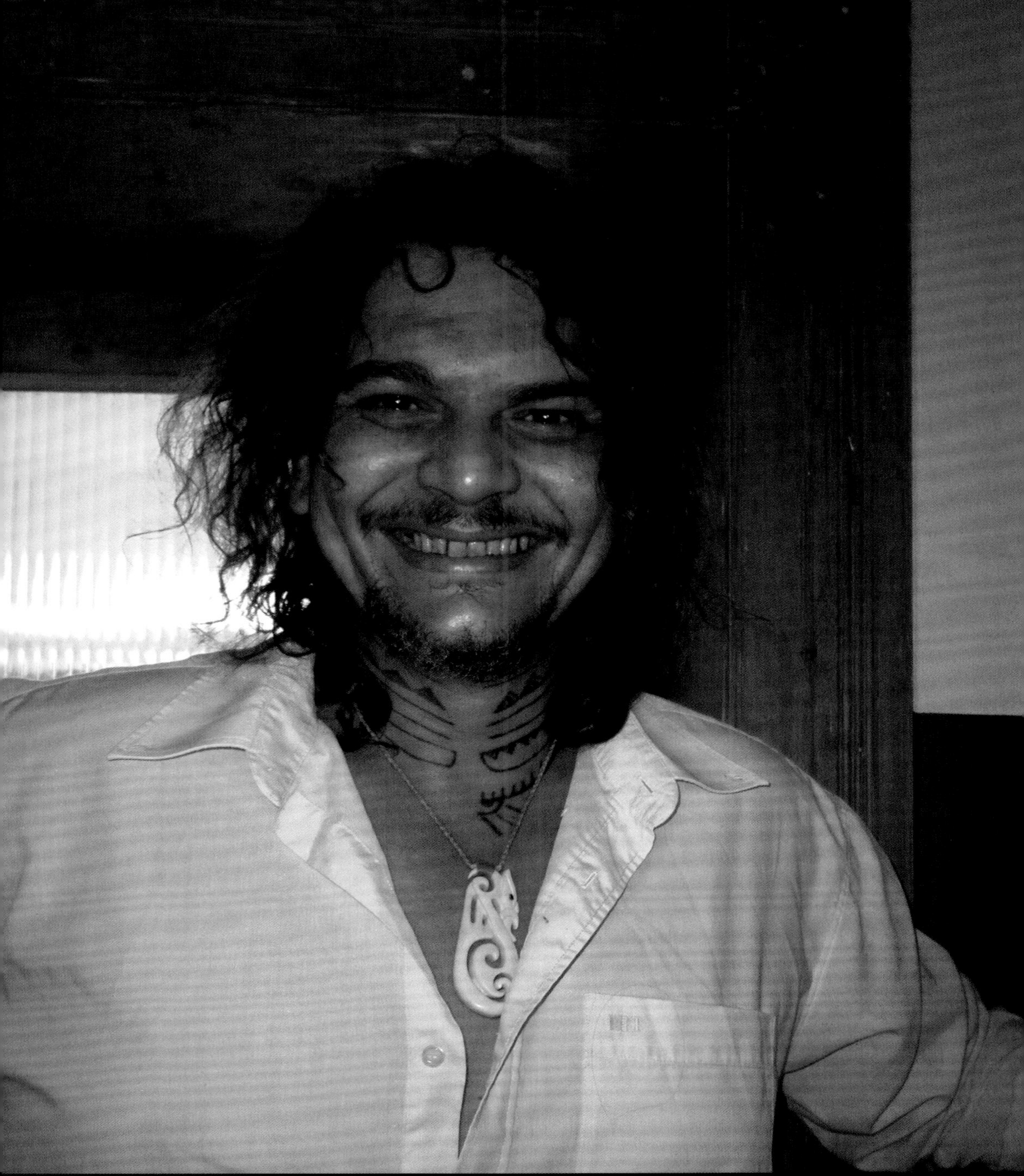

Po'oino Yrondi's tattoos represent traditional symbols of protection from his home country of French Polynesia.

Tattoos have the power to positively influence the life of those who wear them.

Coru Family
www.TatauStudio.de

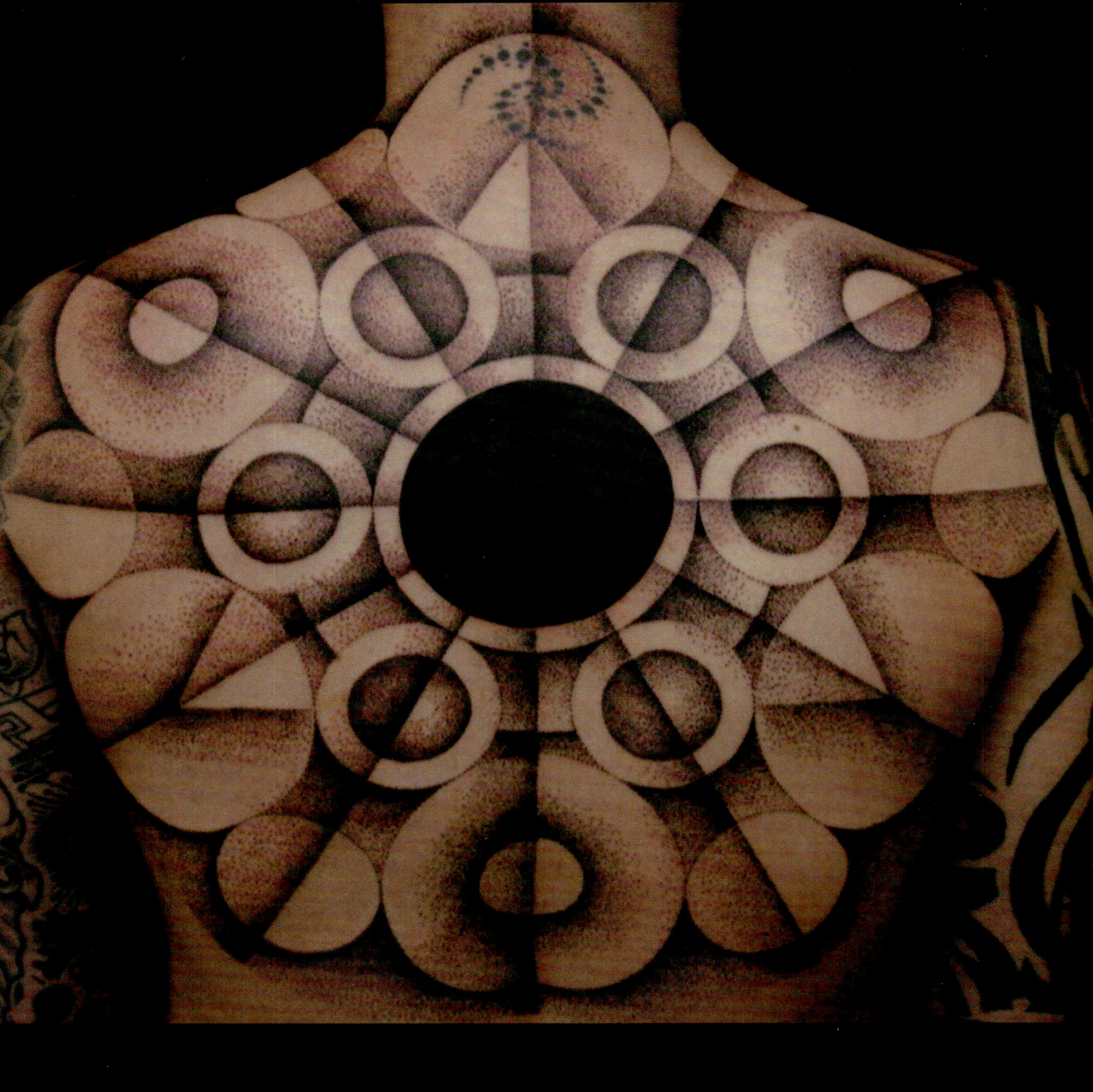

CORY FERGUSON
GOOD POINT TATTOOS

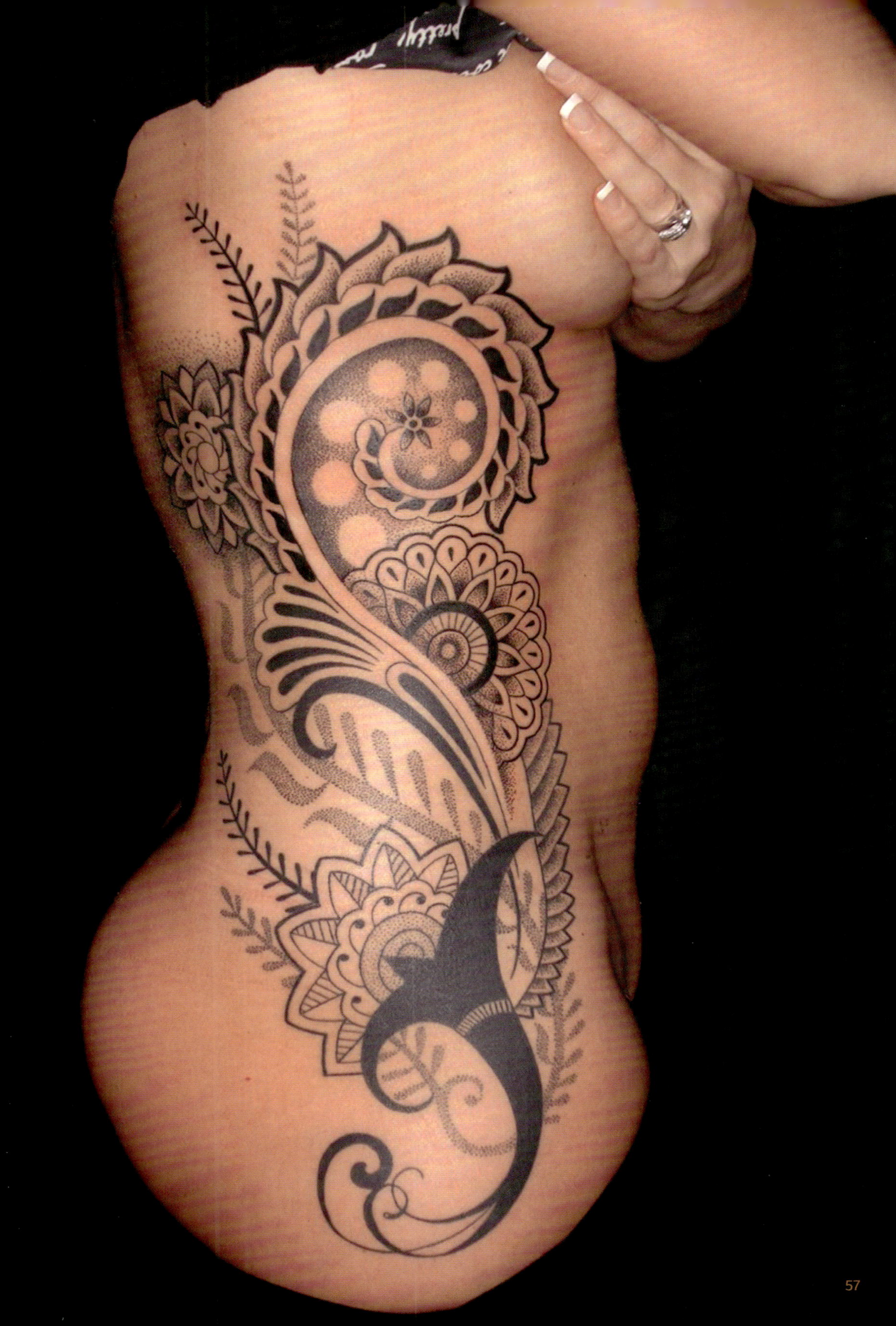

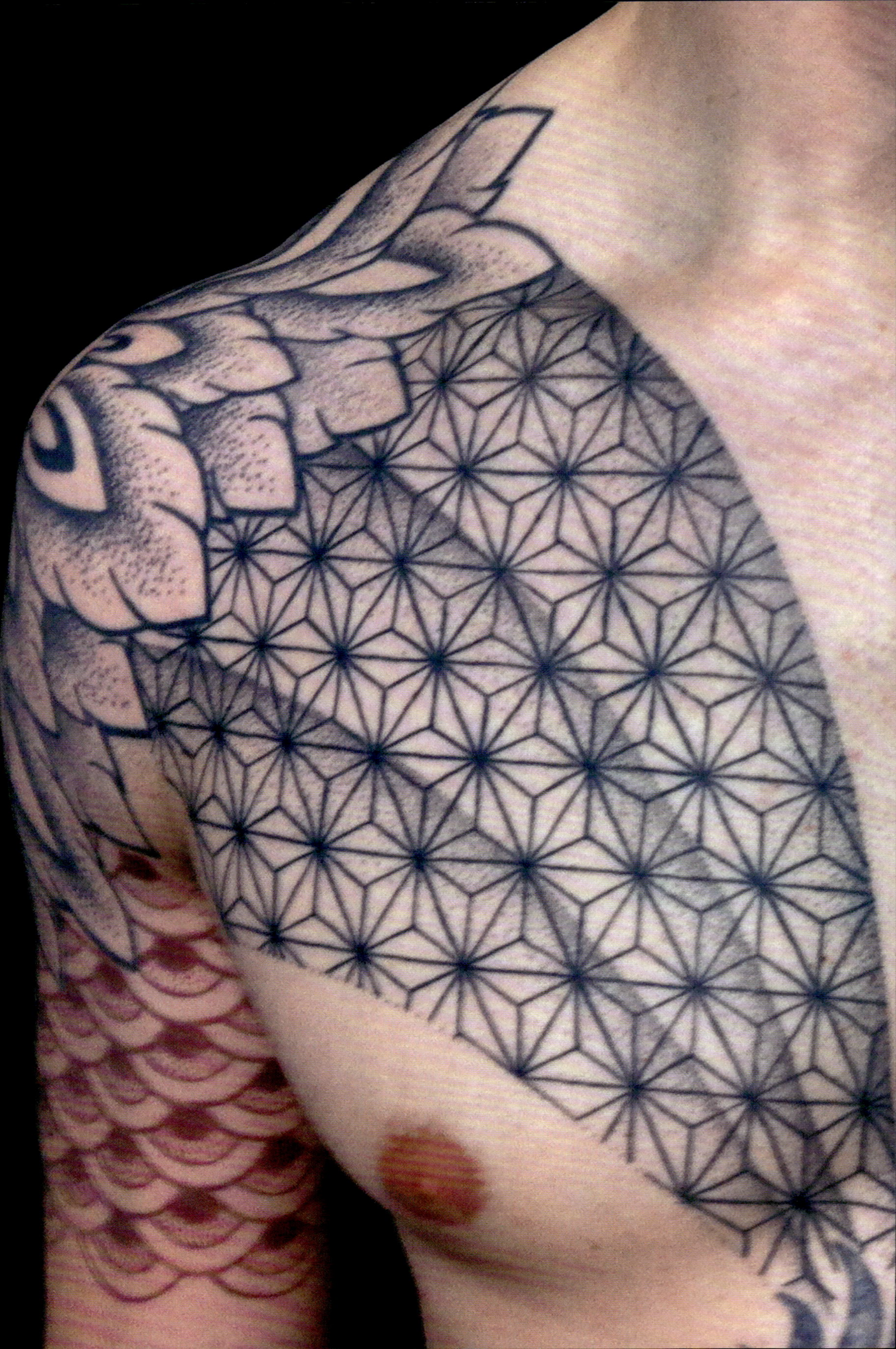

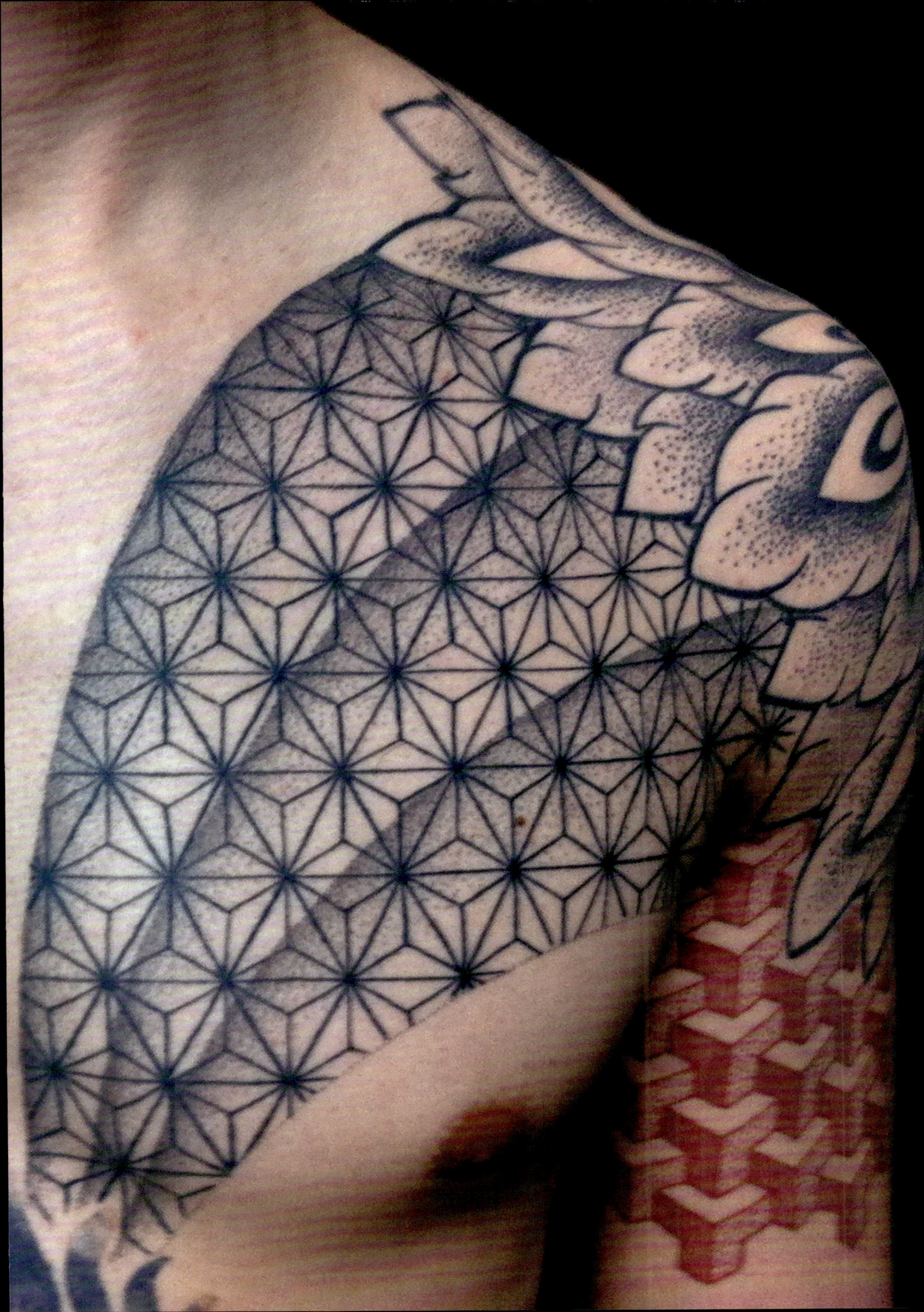

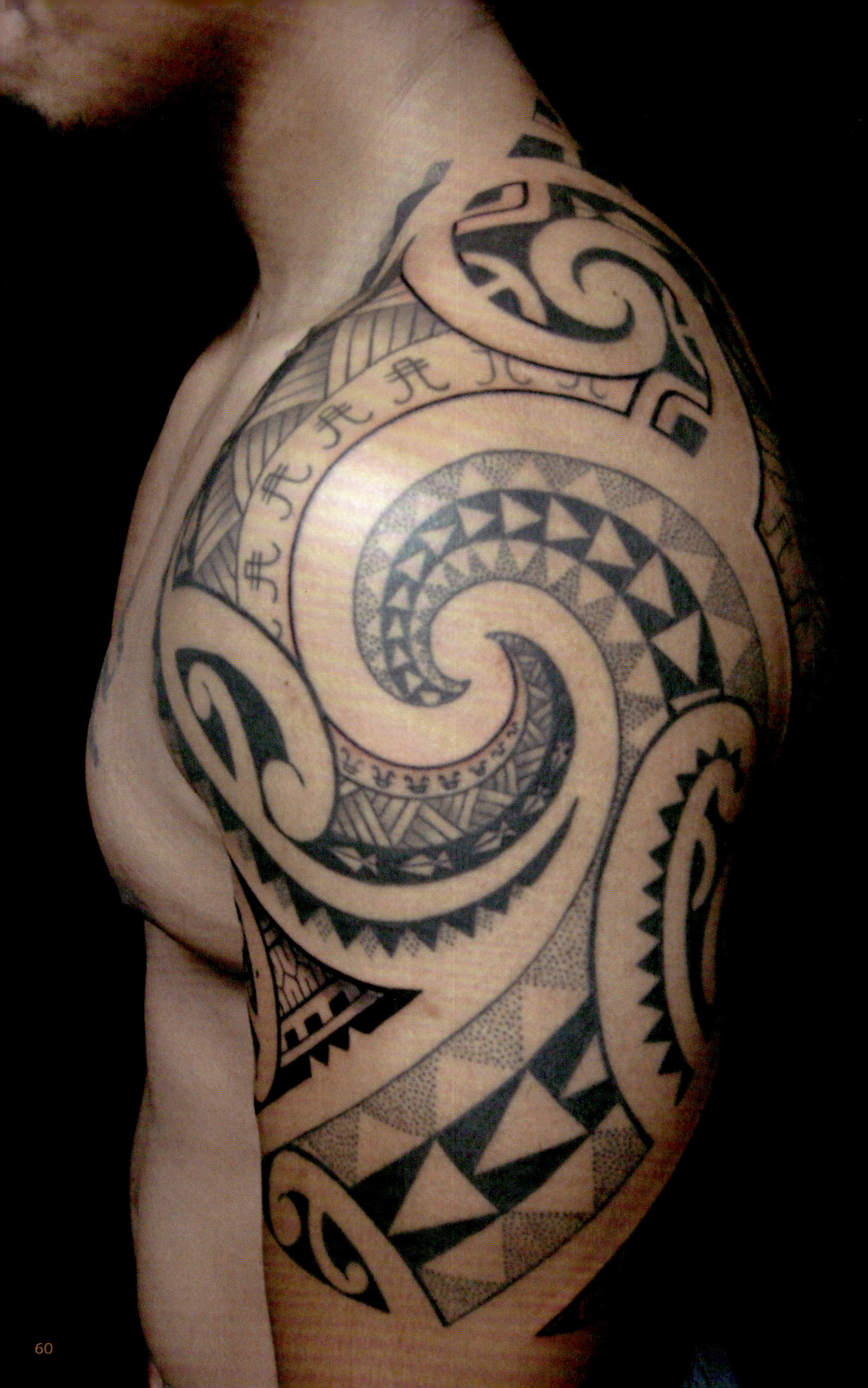

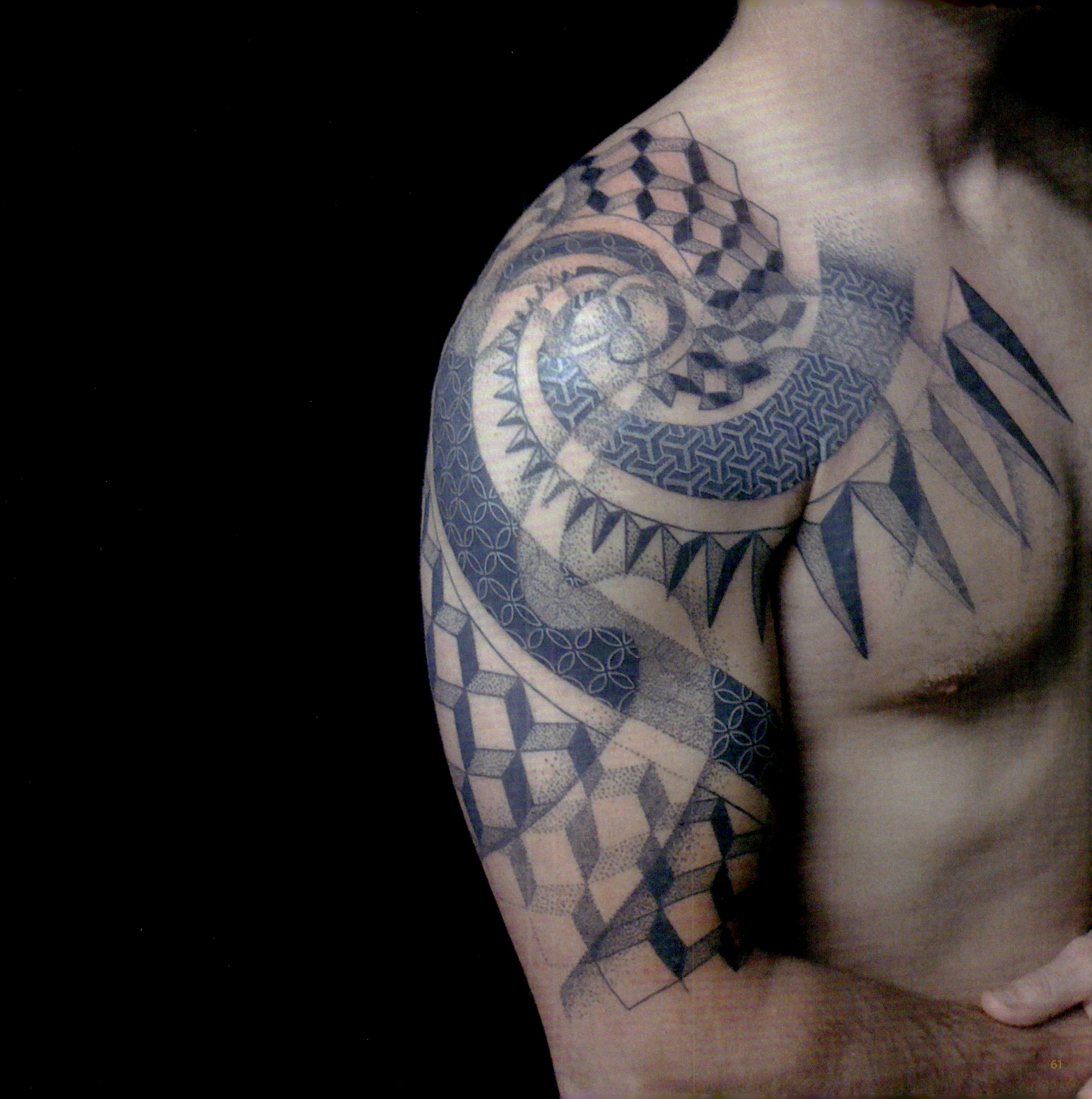

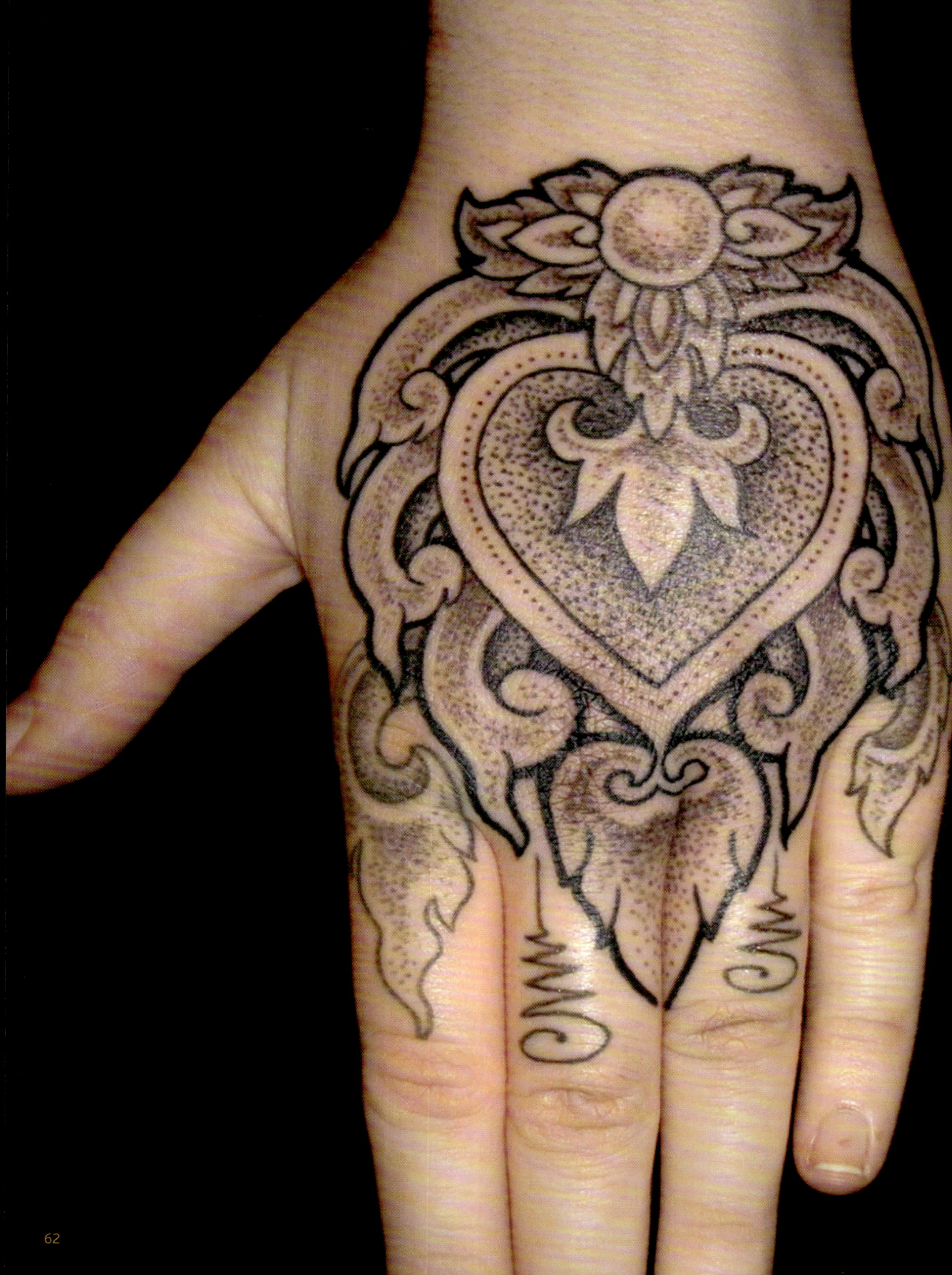

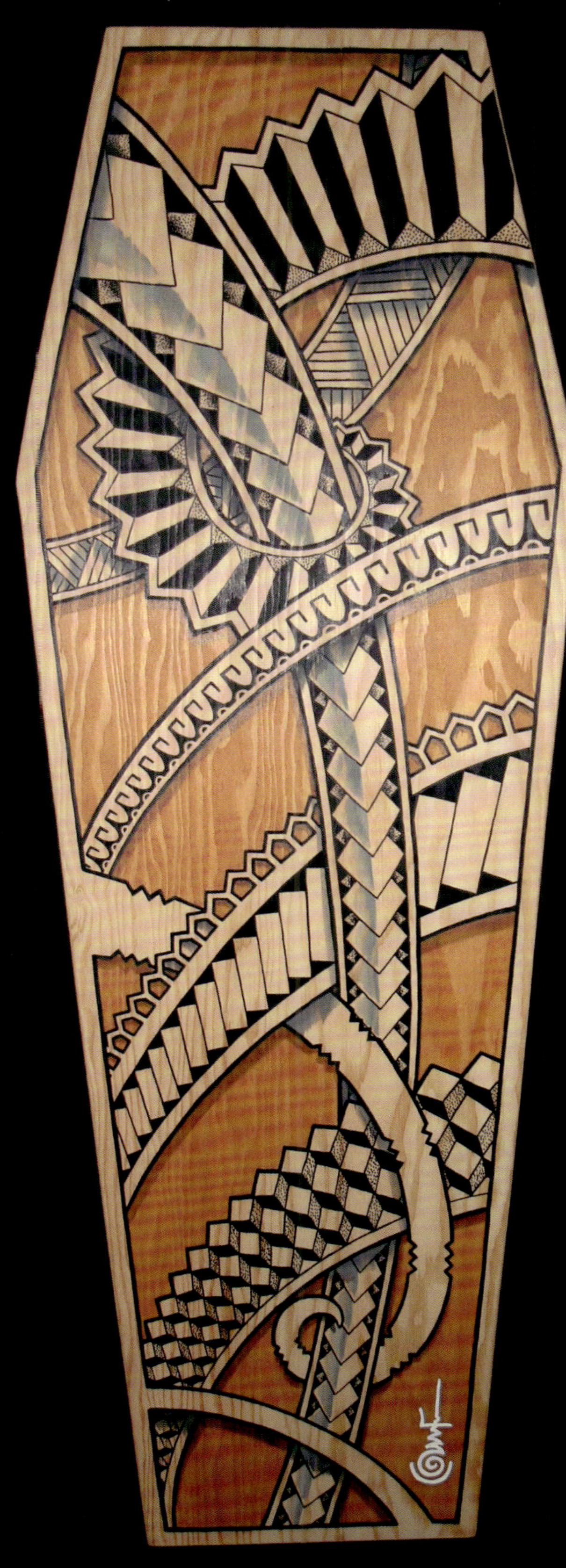

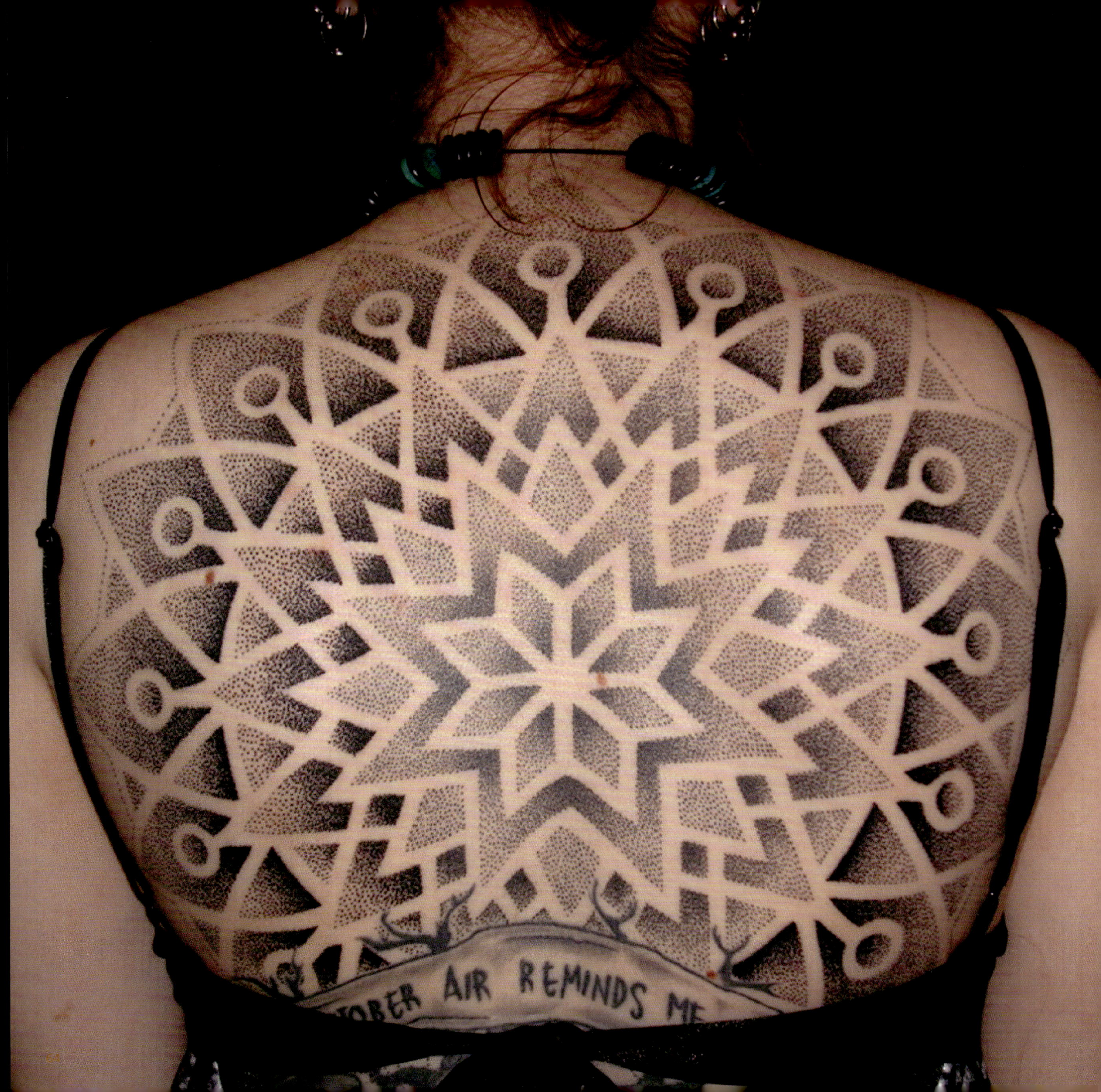
TOBER AIR REMINDS ME

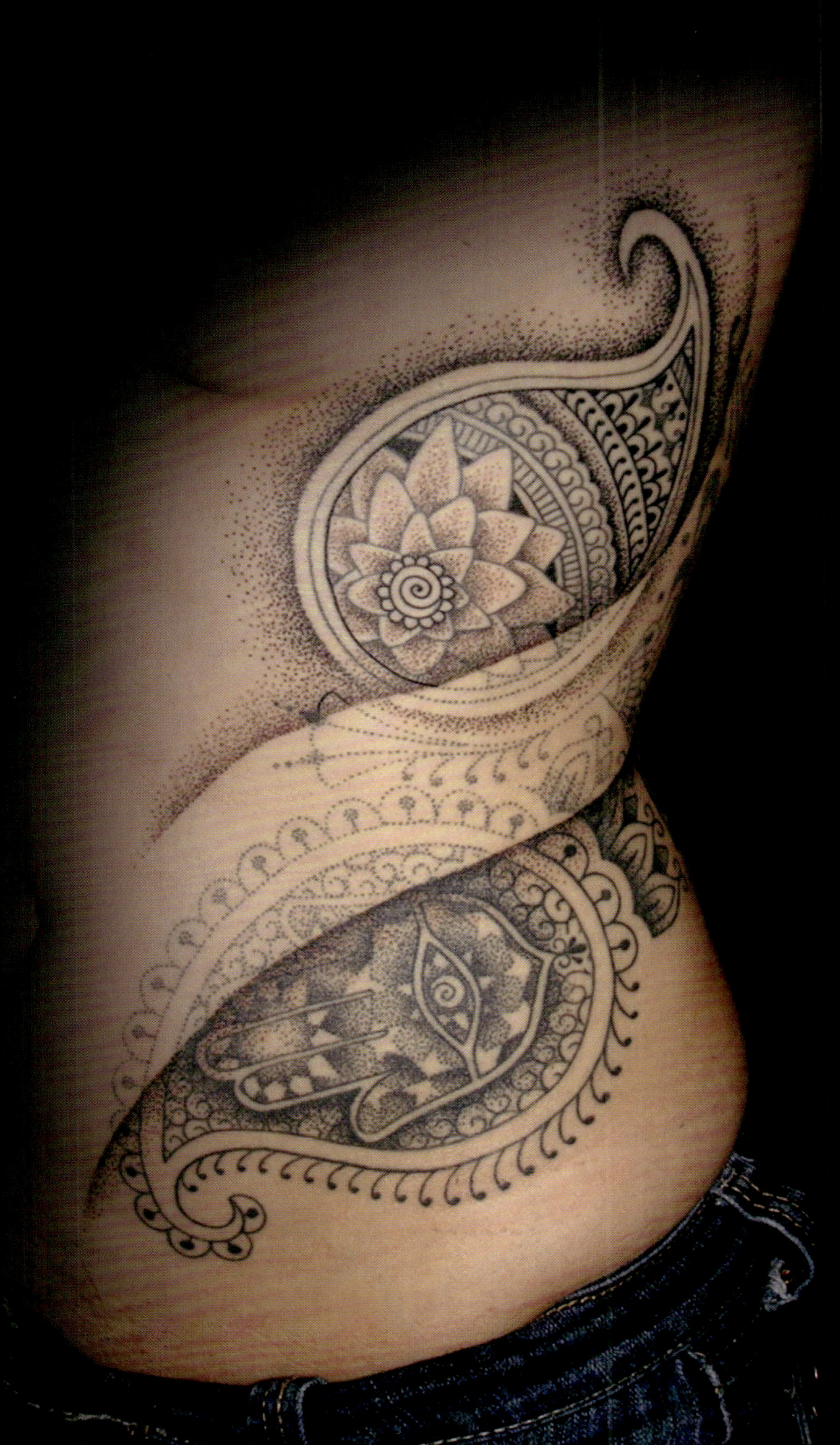

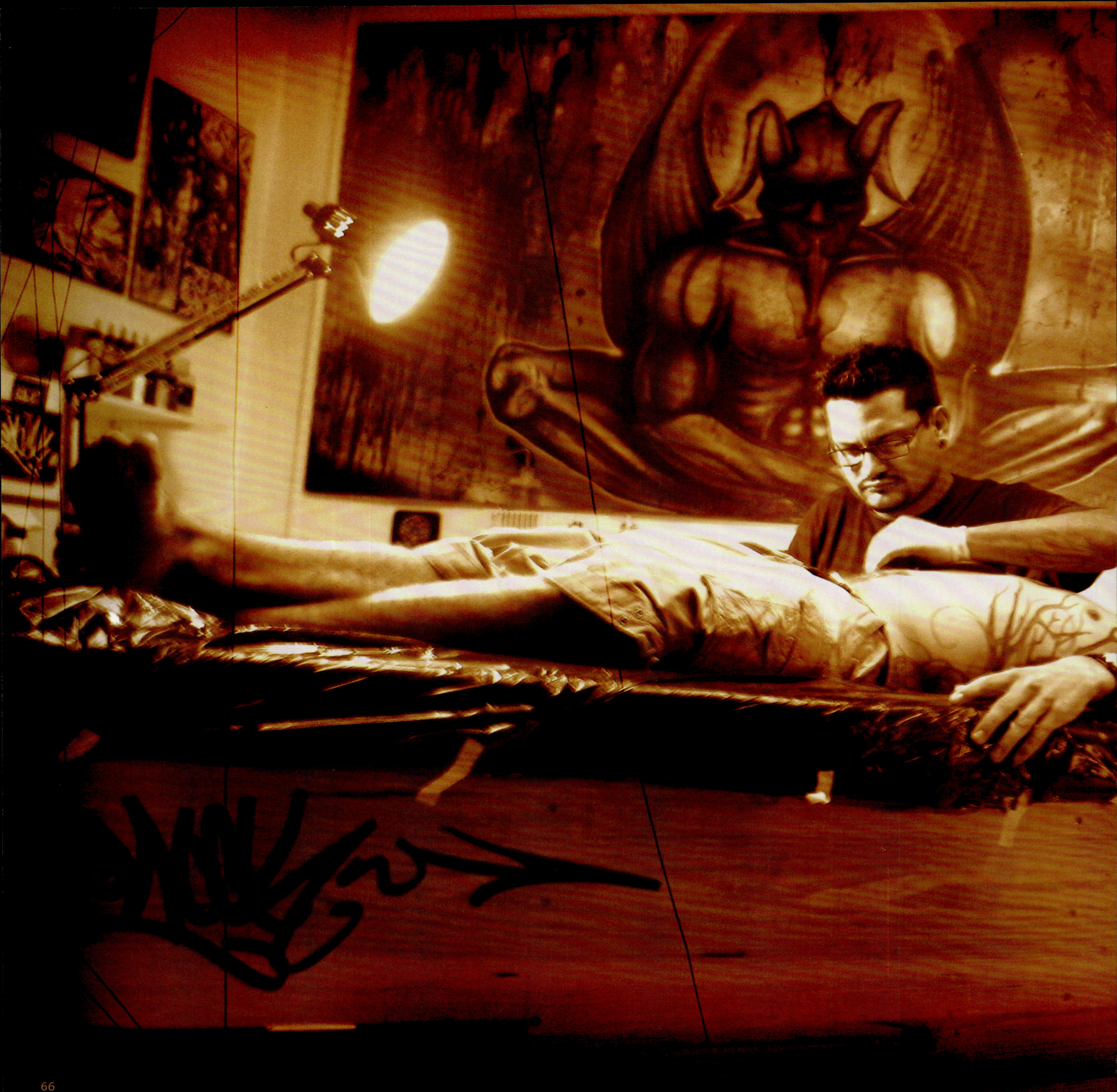

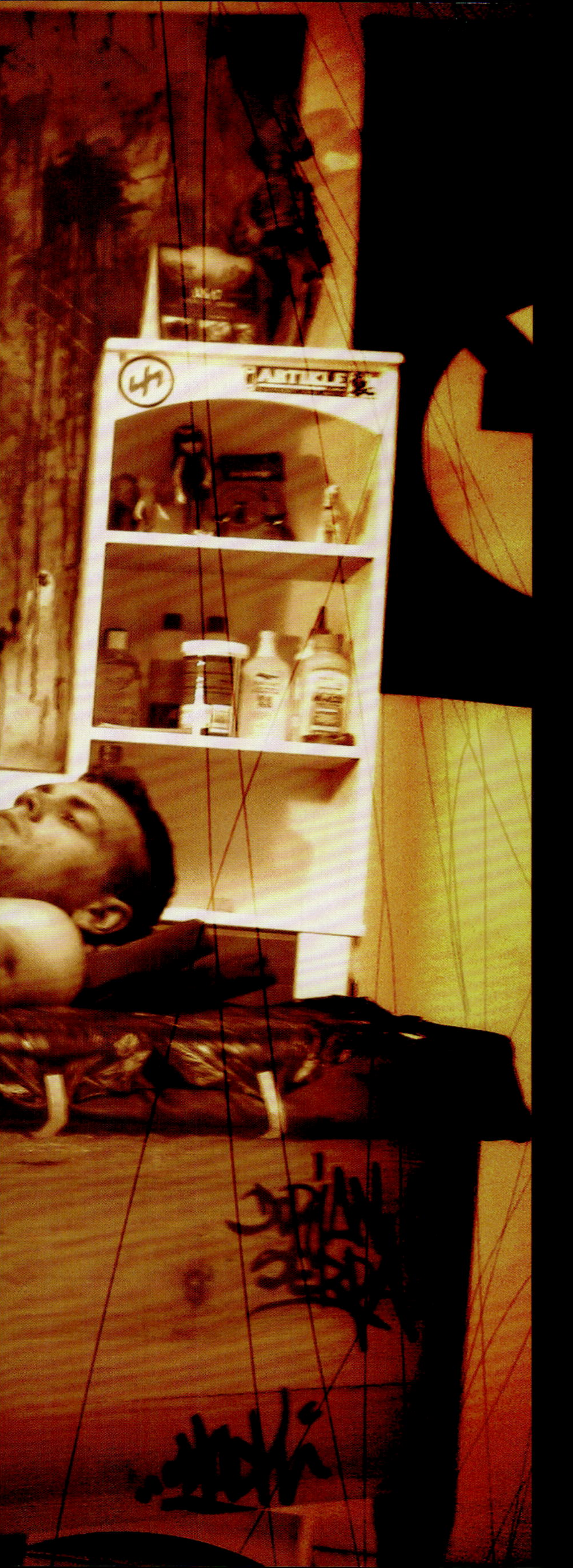
DORI
AK47

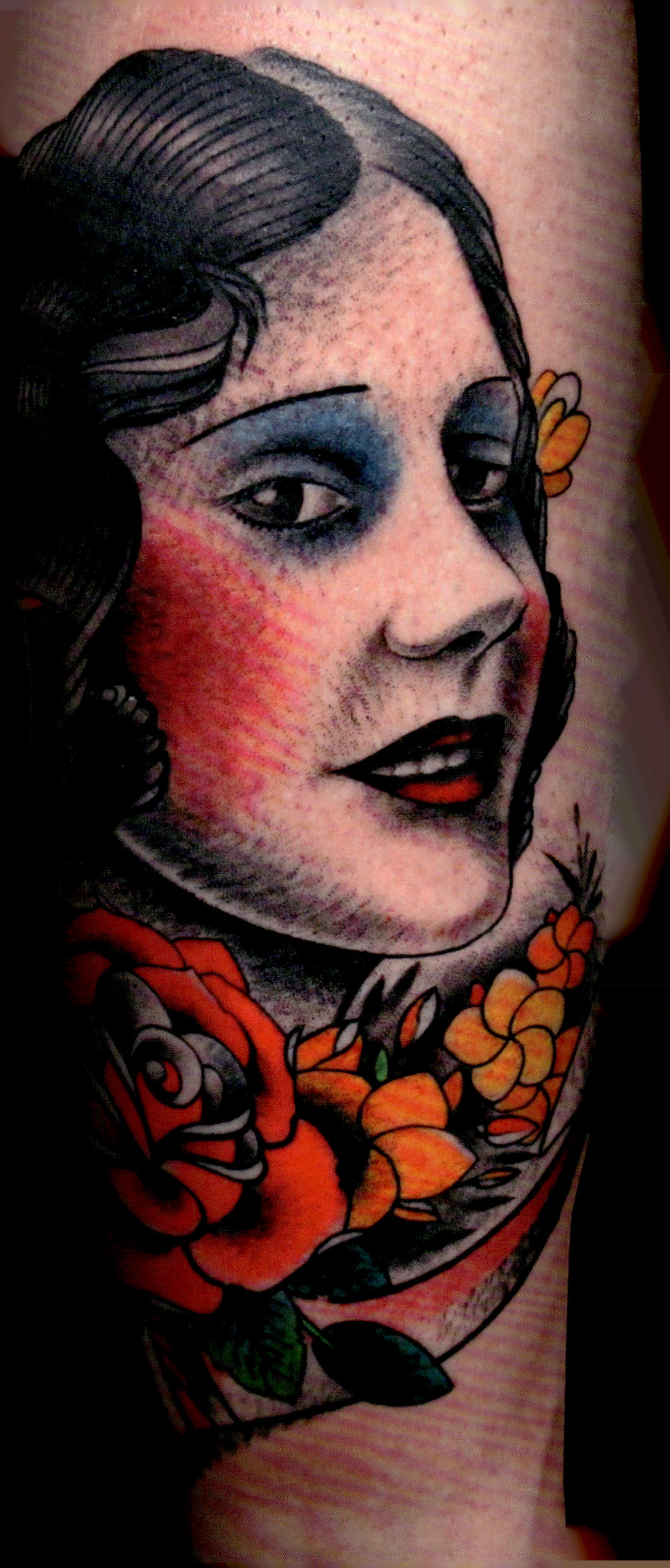

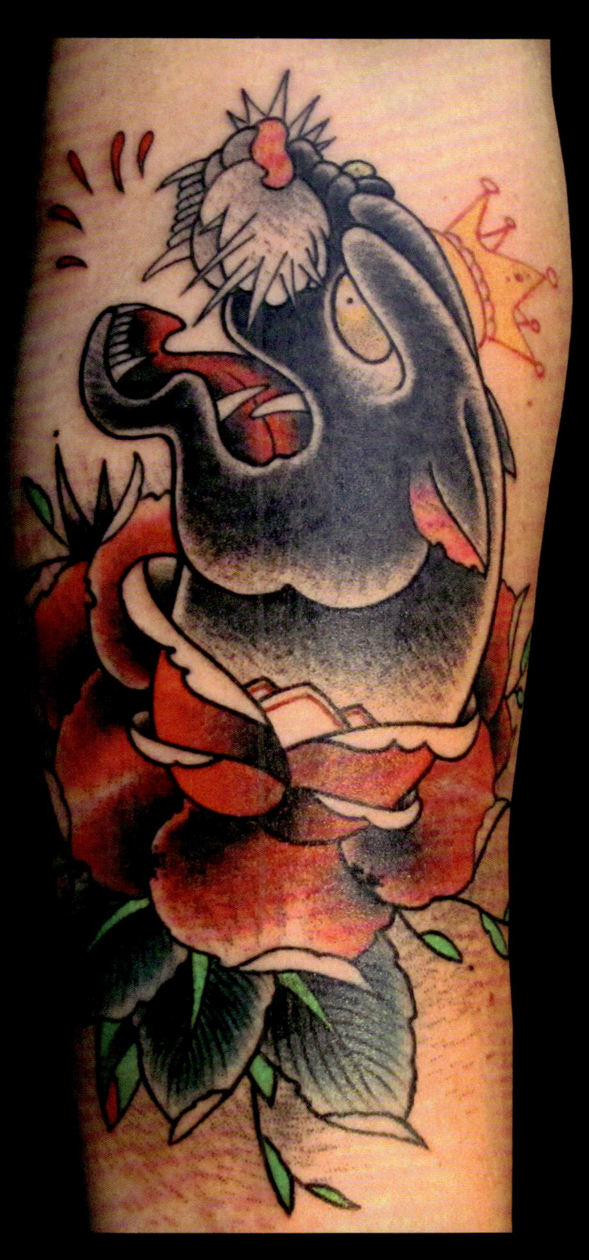

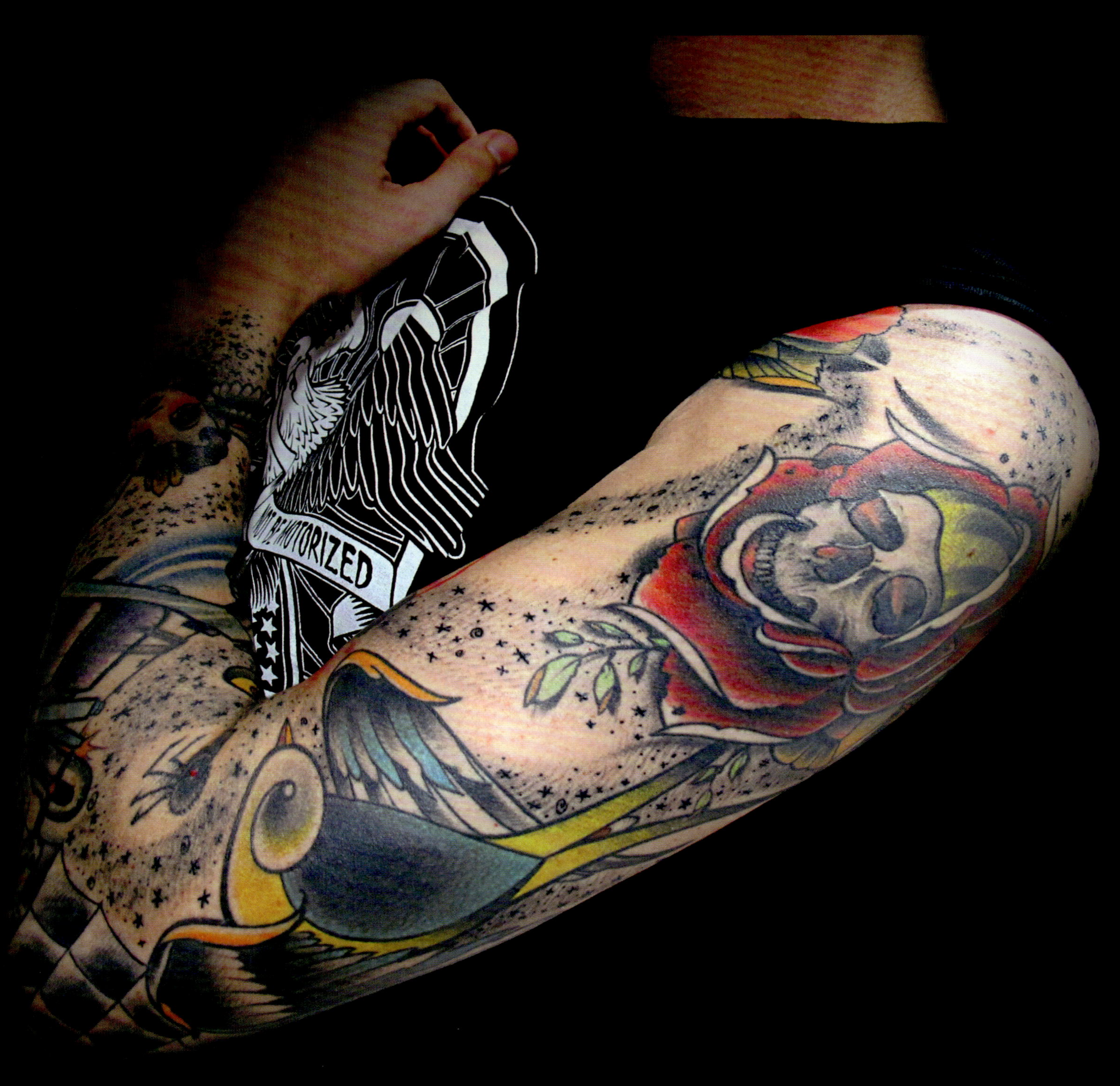

MOTORIZED

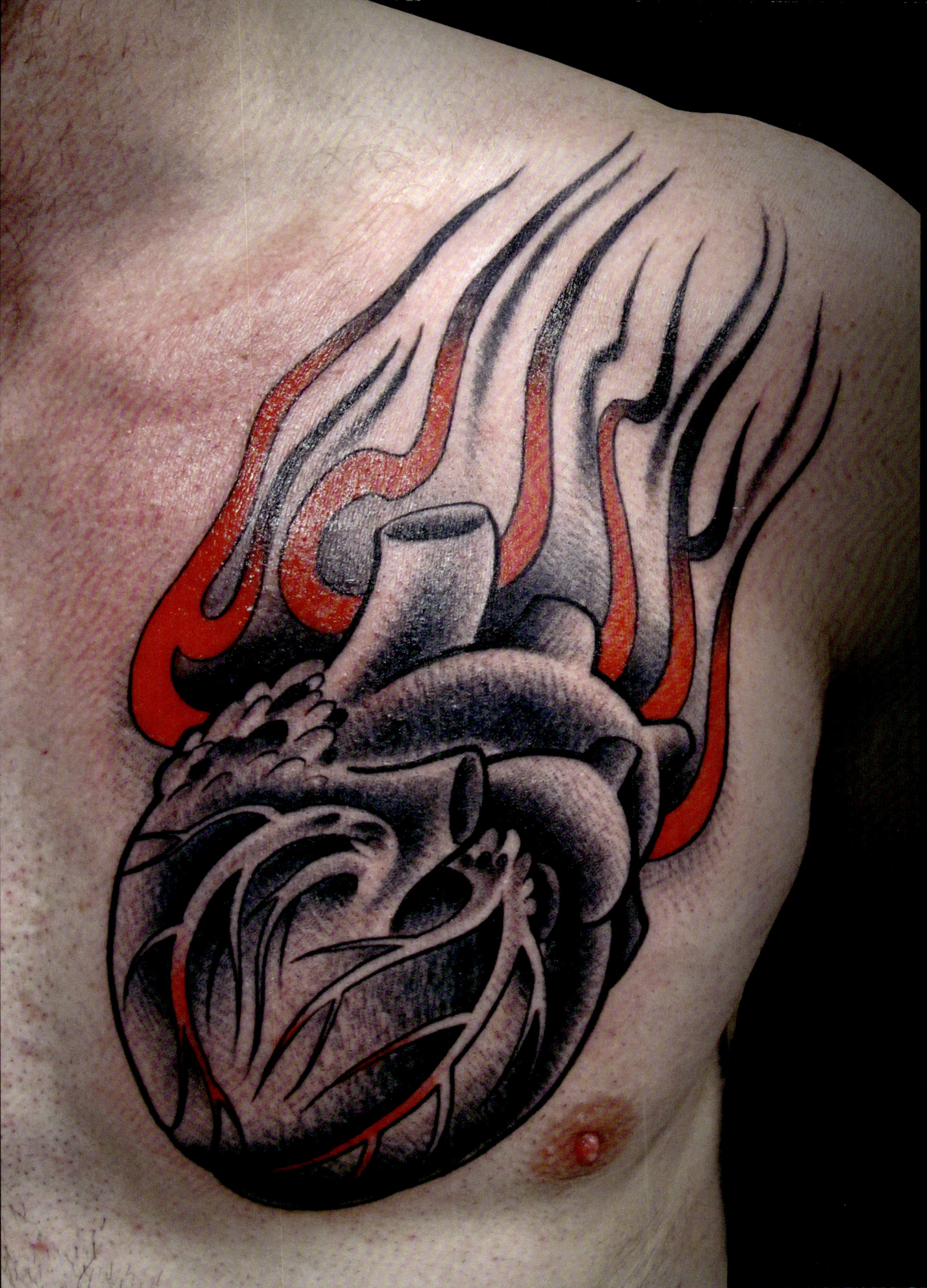

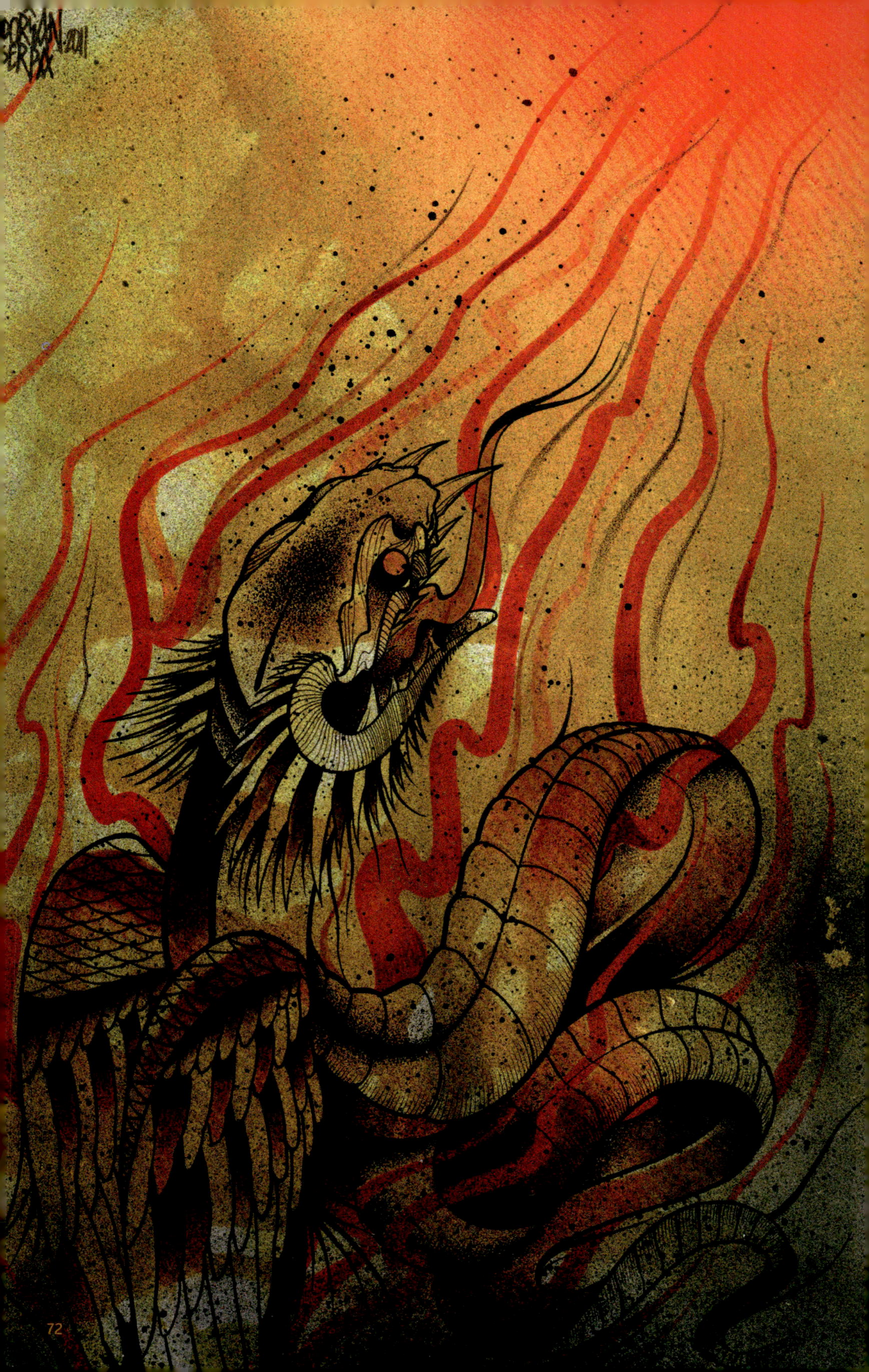
72

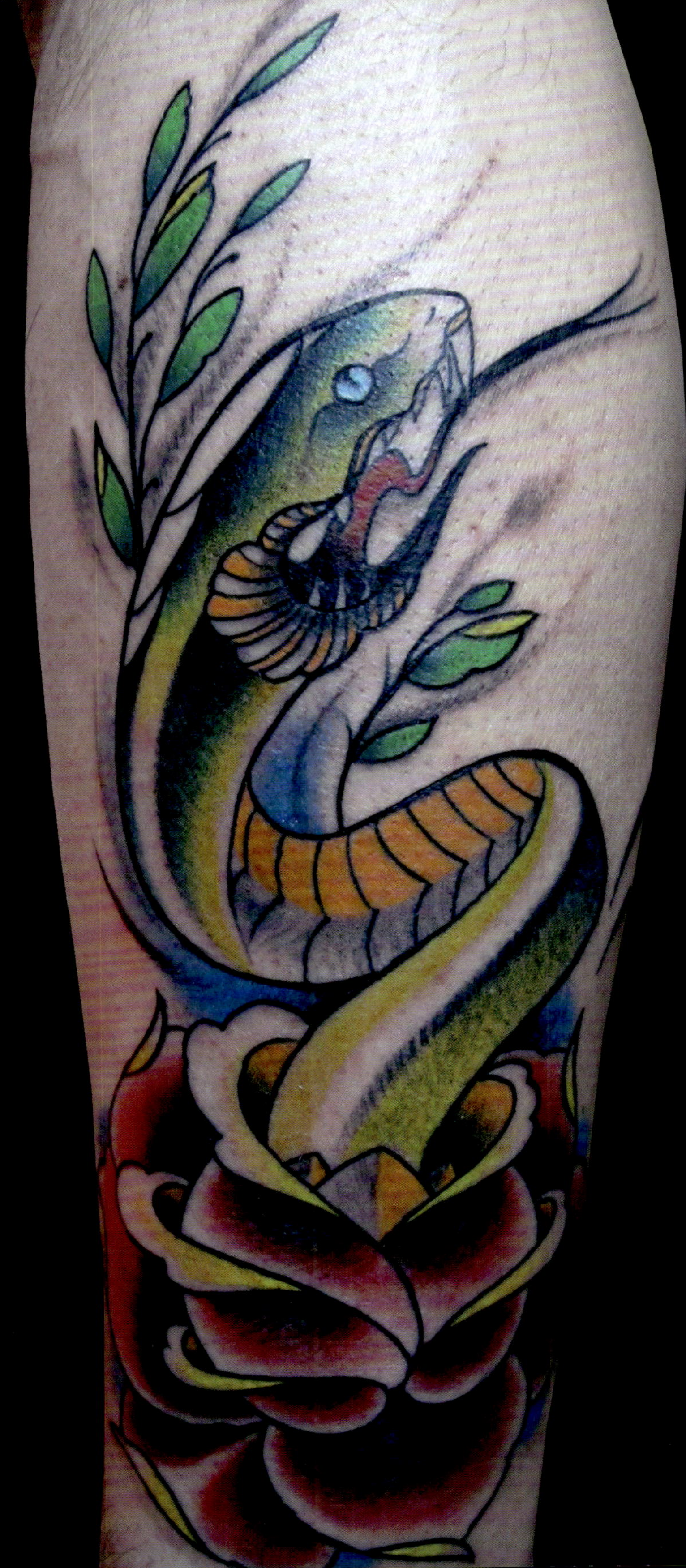

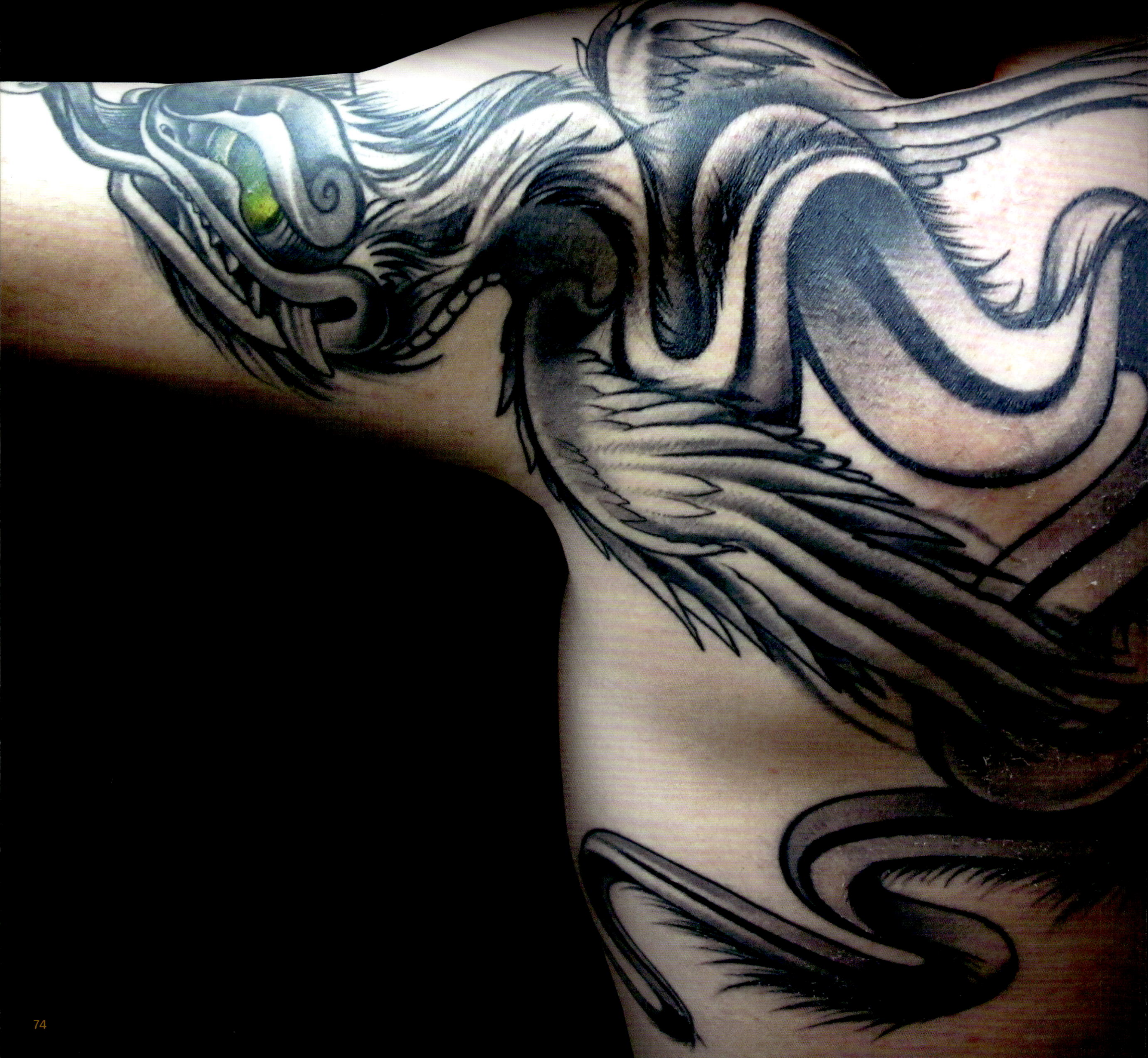

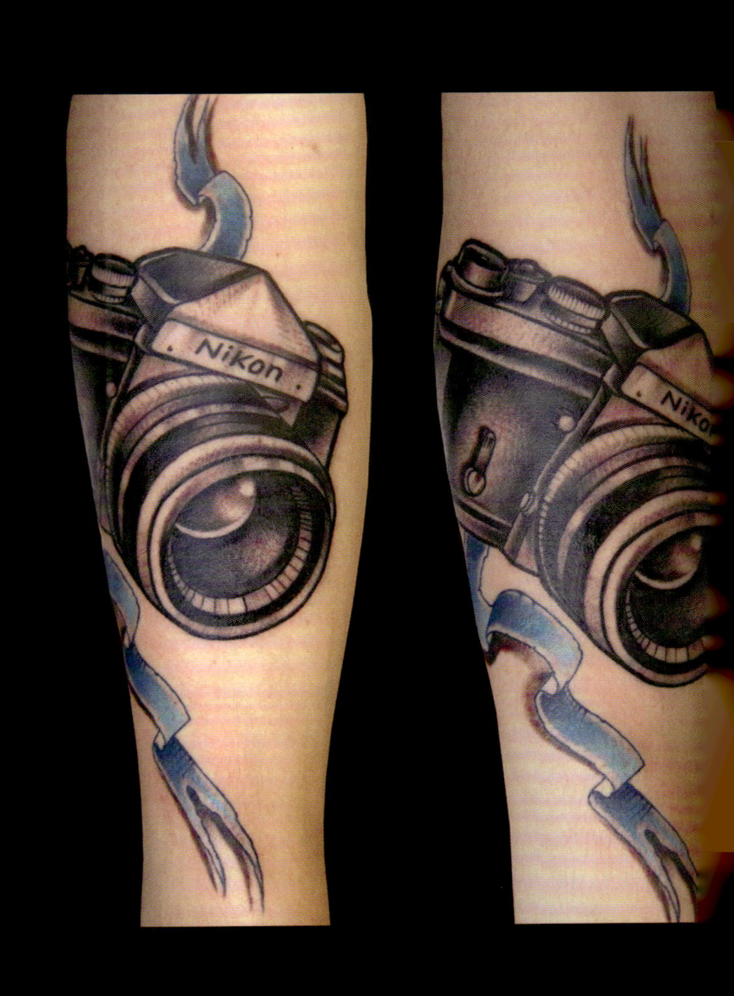

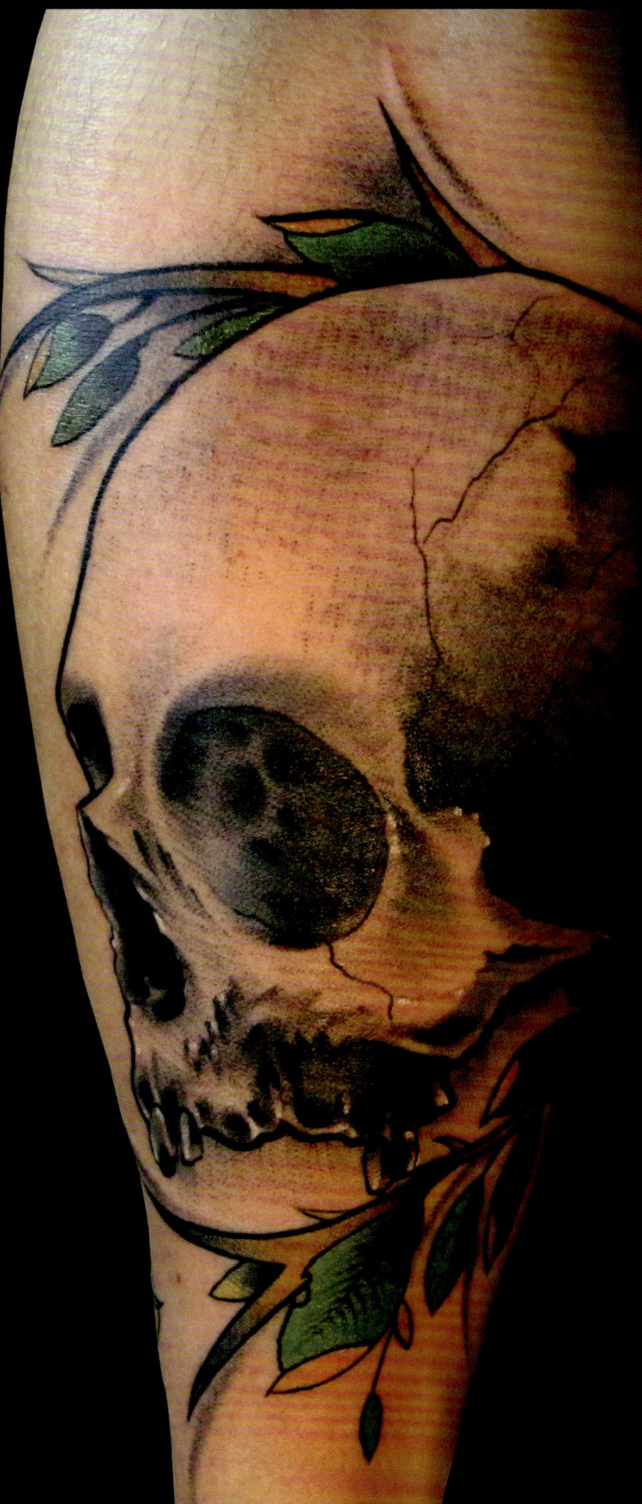

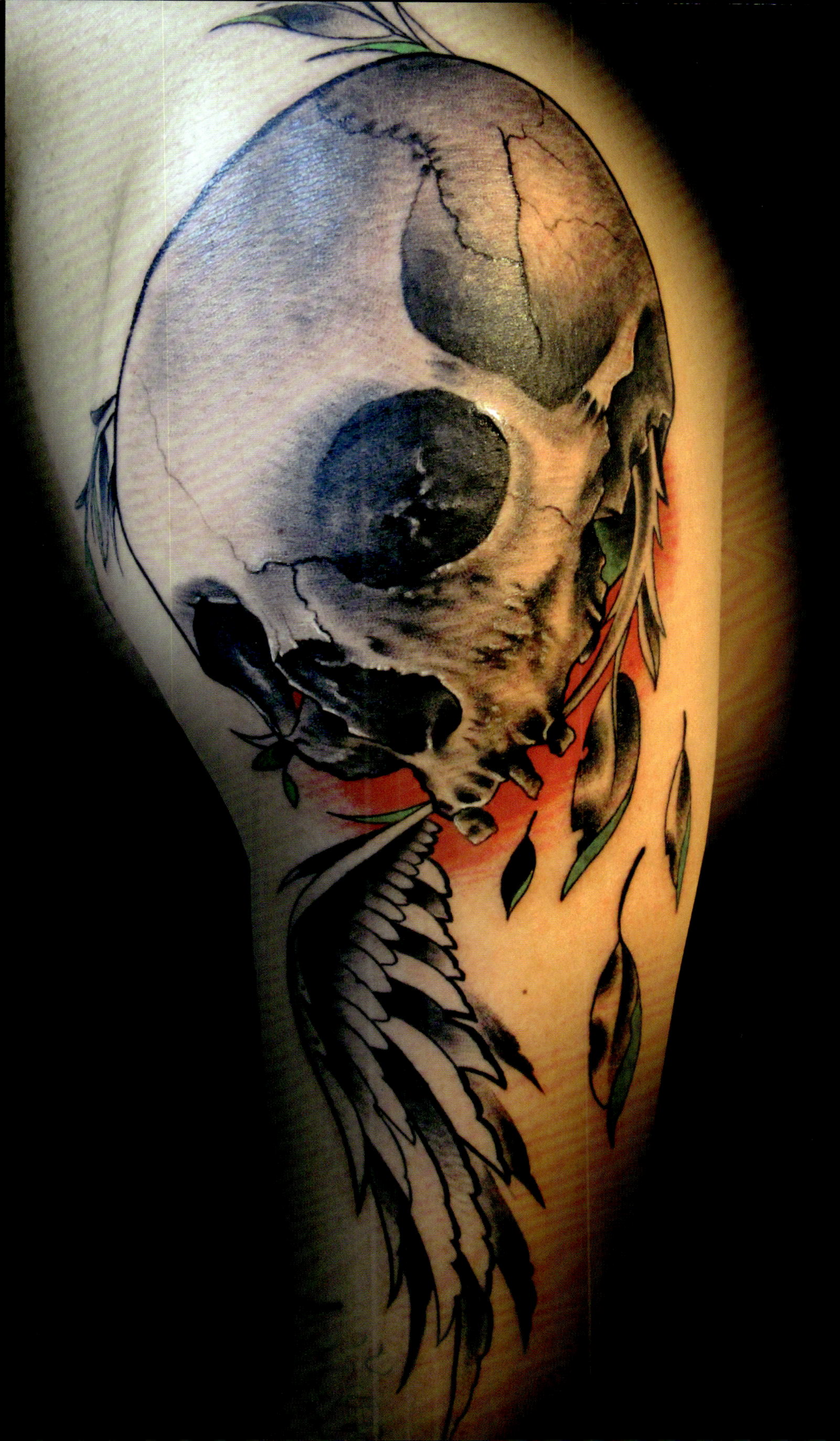

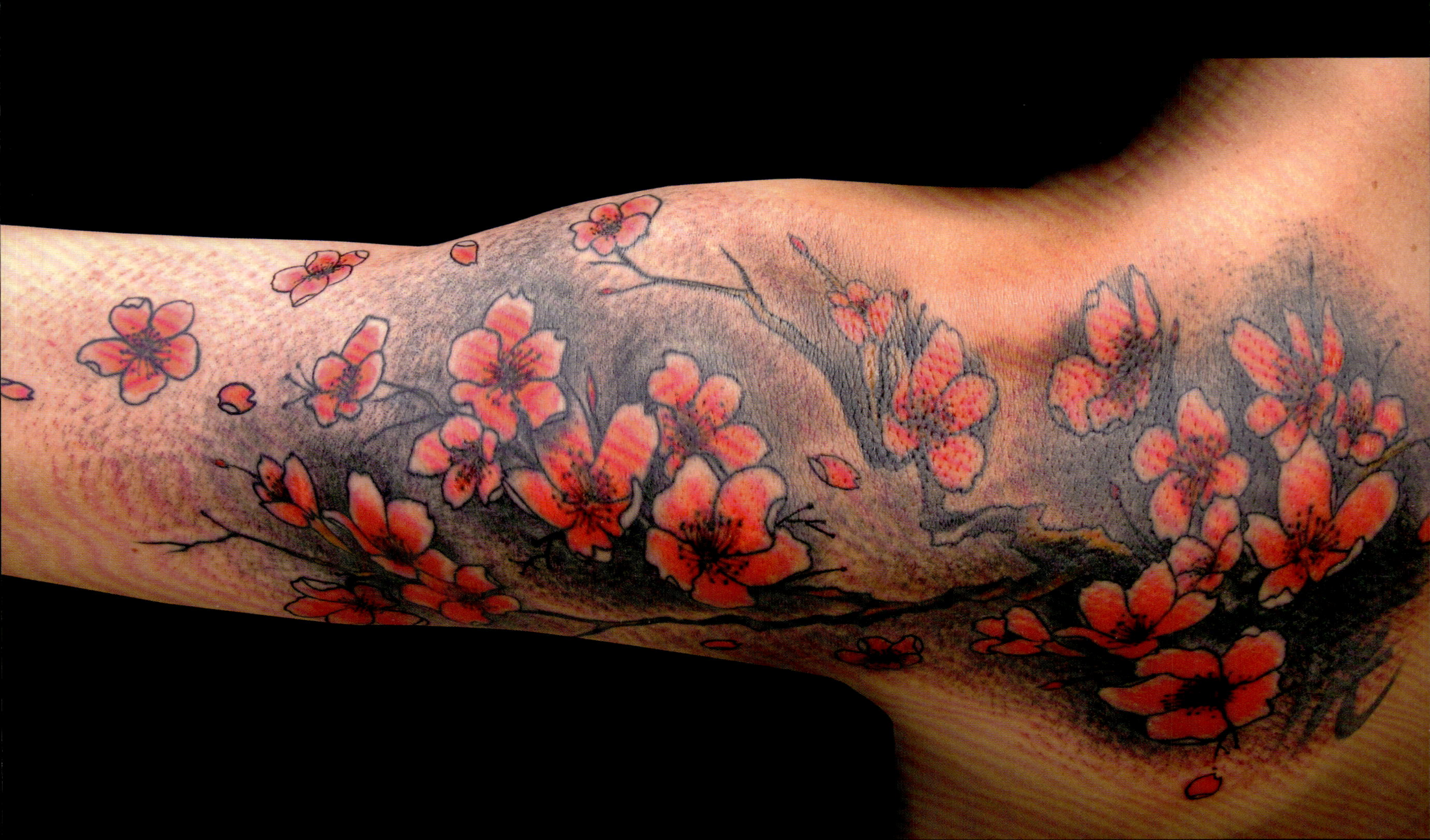

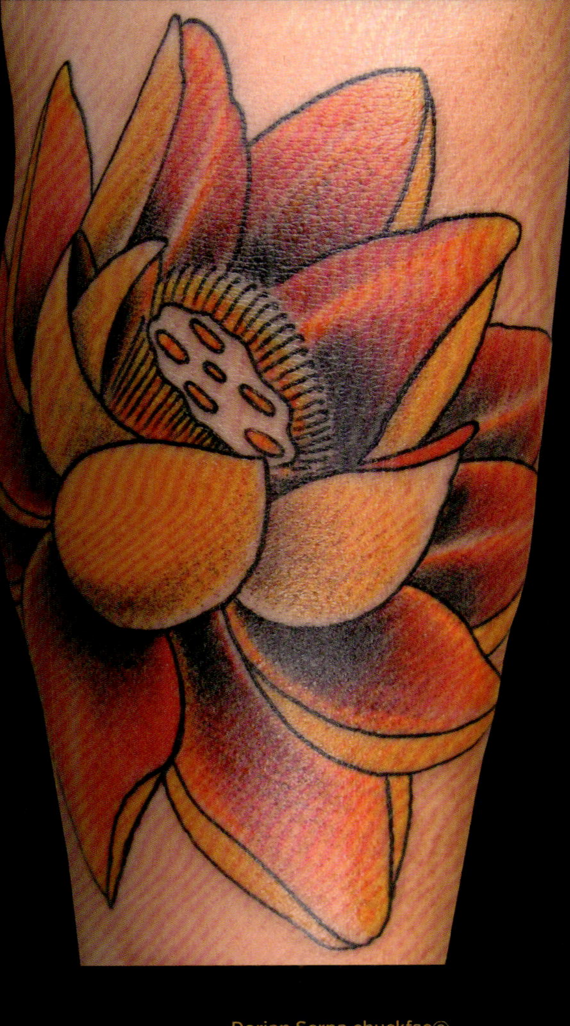
Dorian Serpa chuckfsc@
hotmail.com

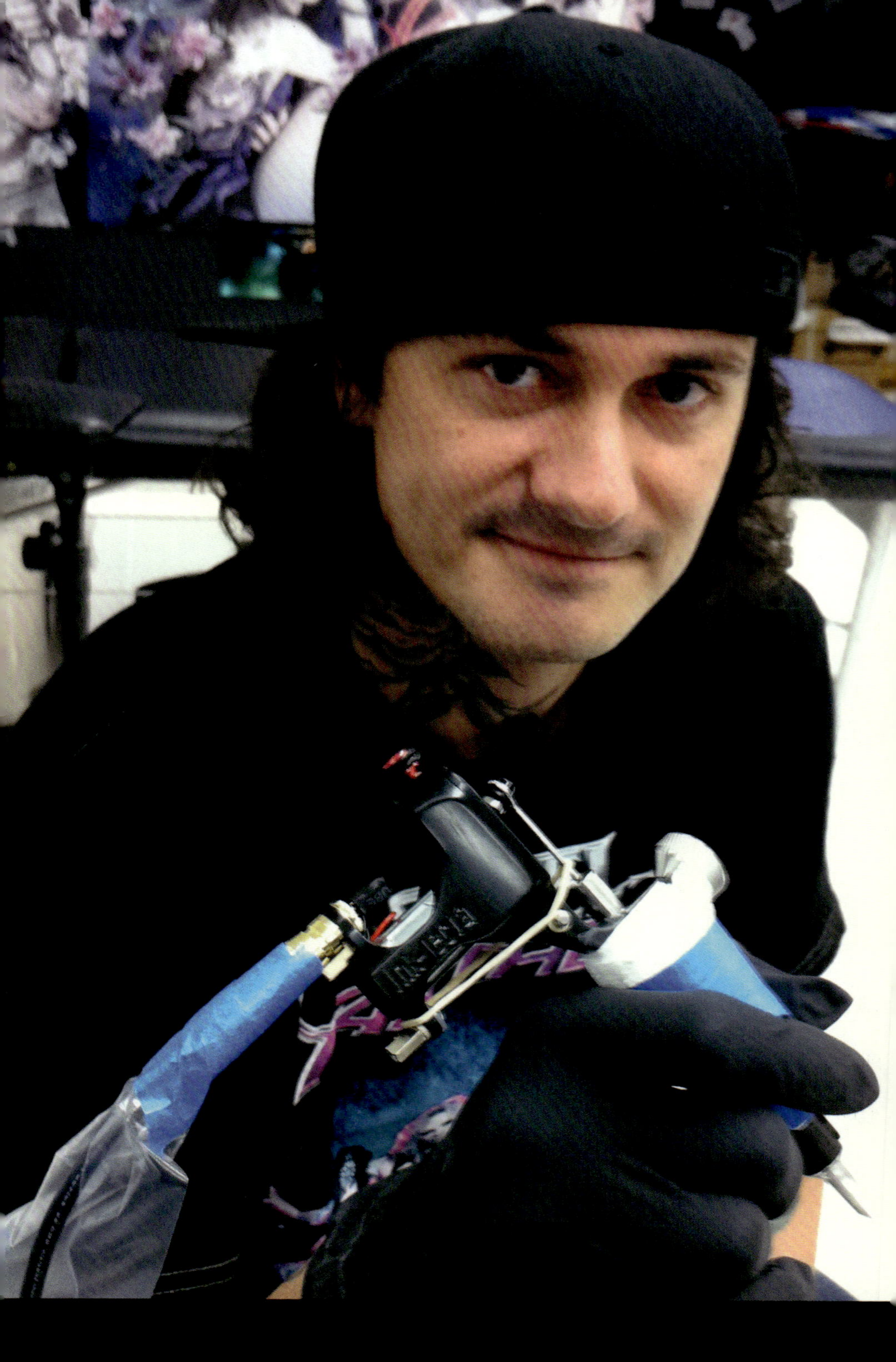

FABIAN DE GAILLANDE

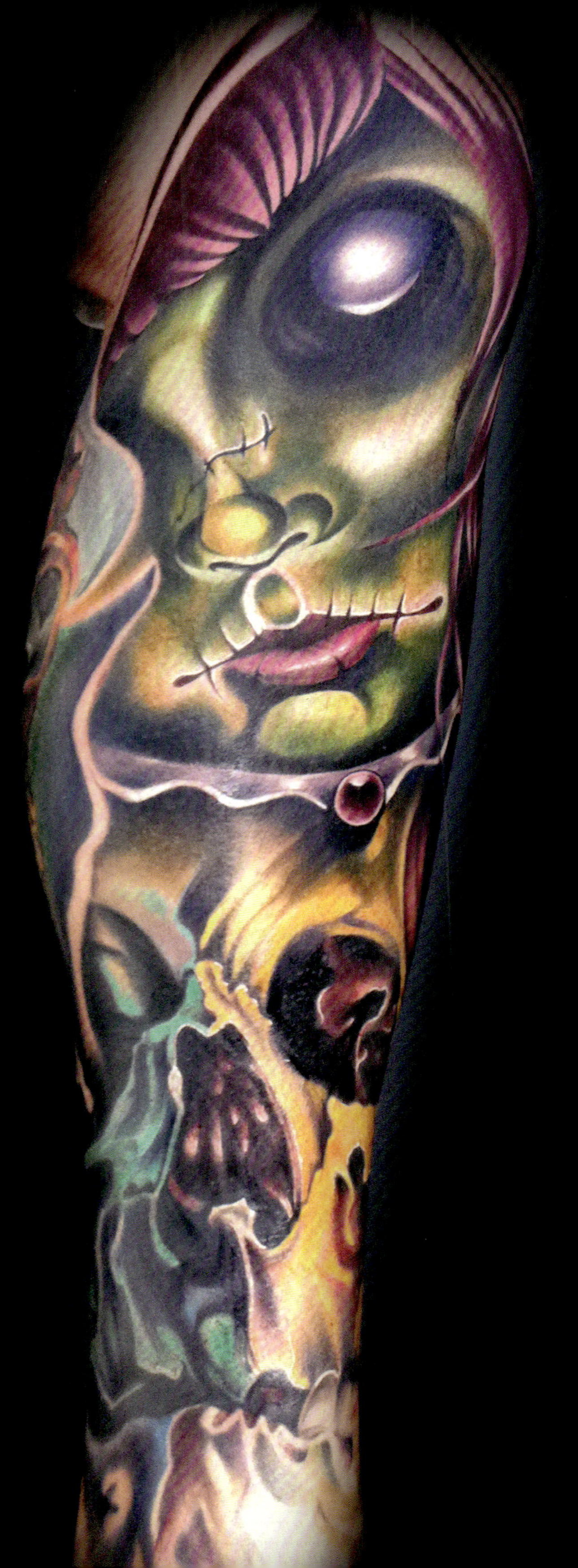

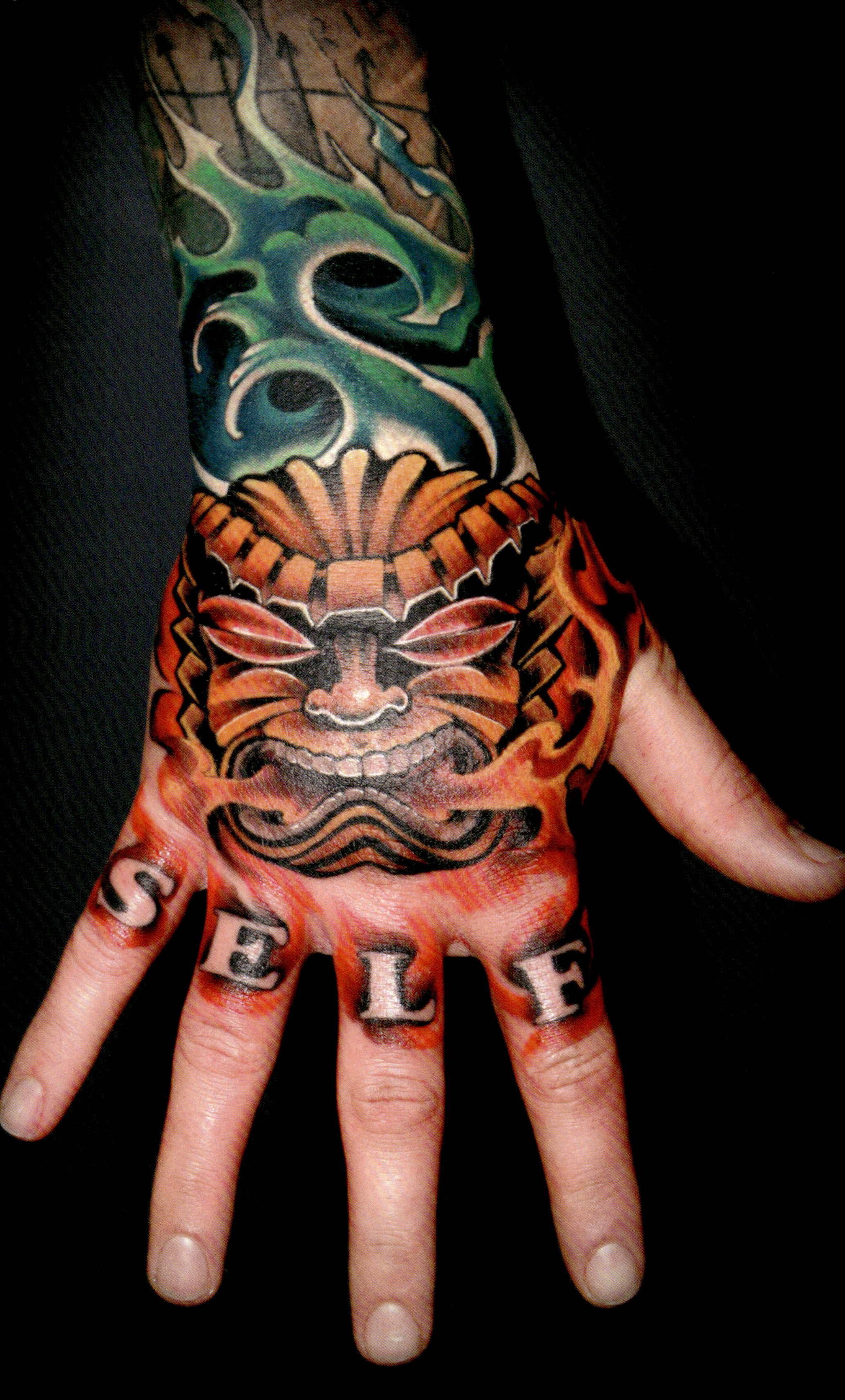
SELF

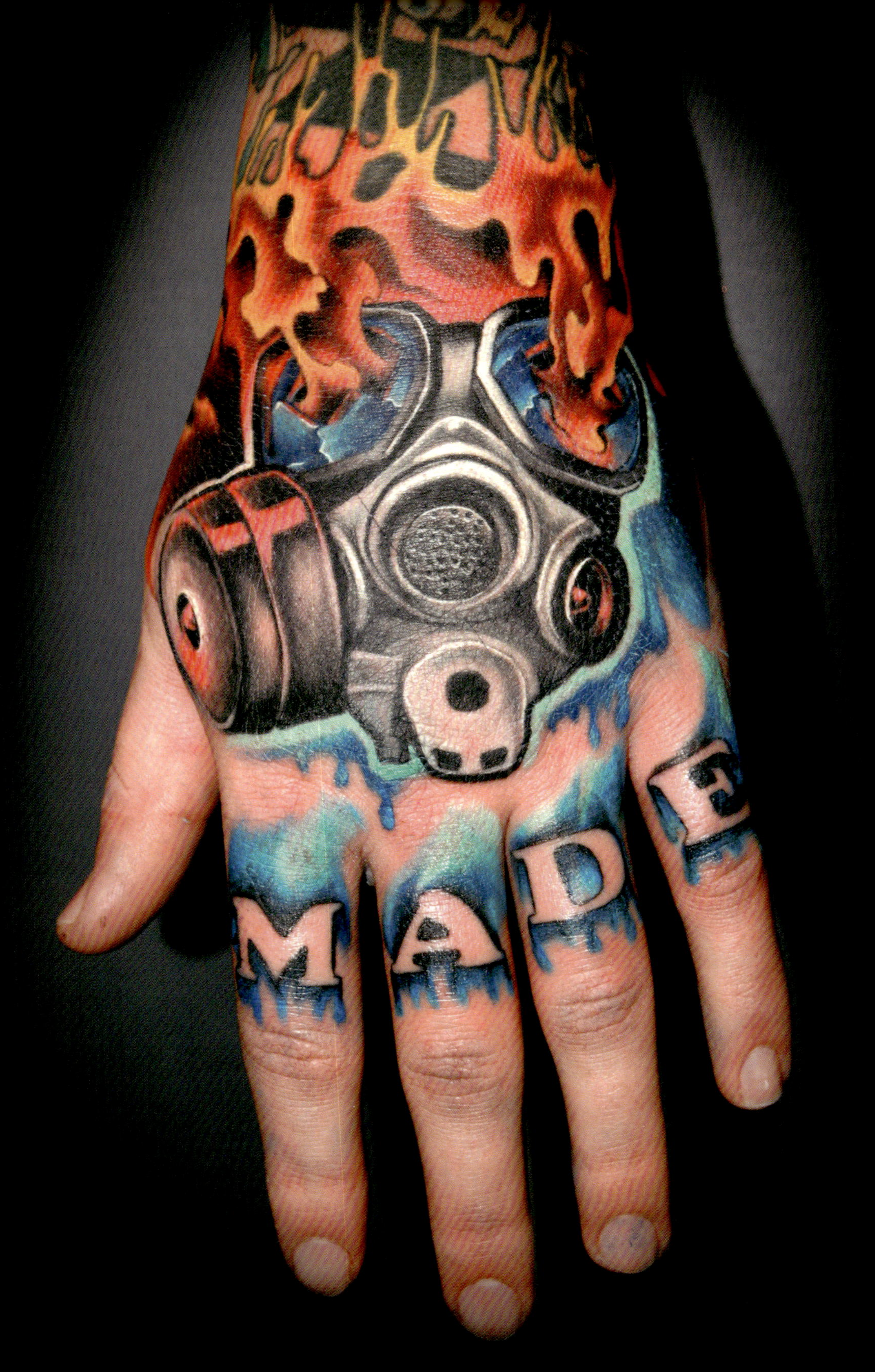

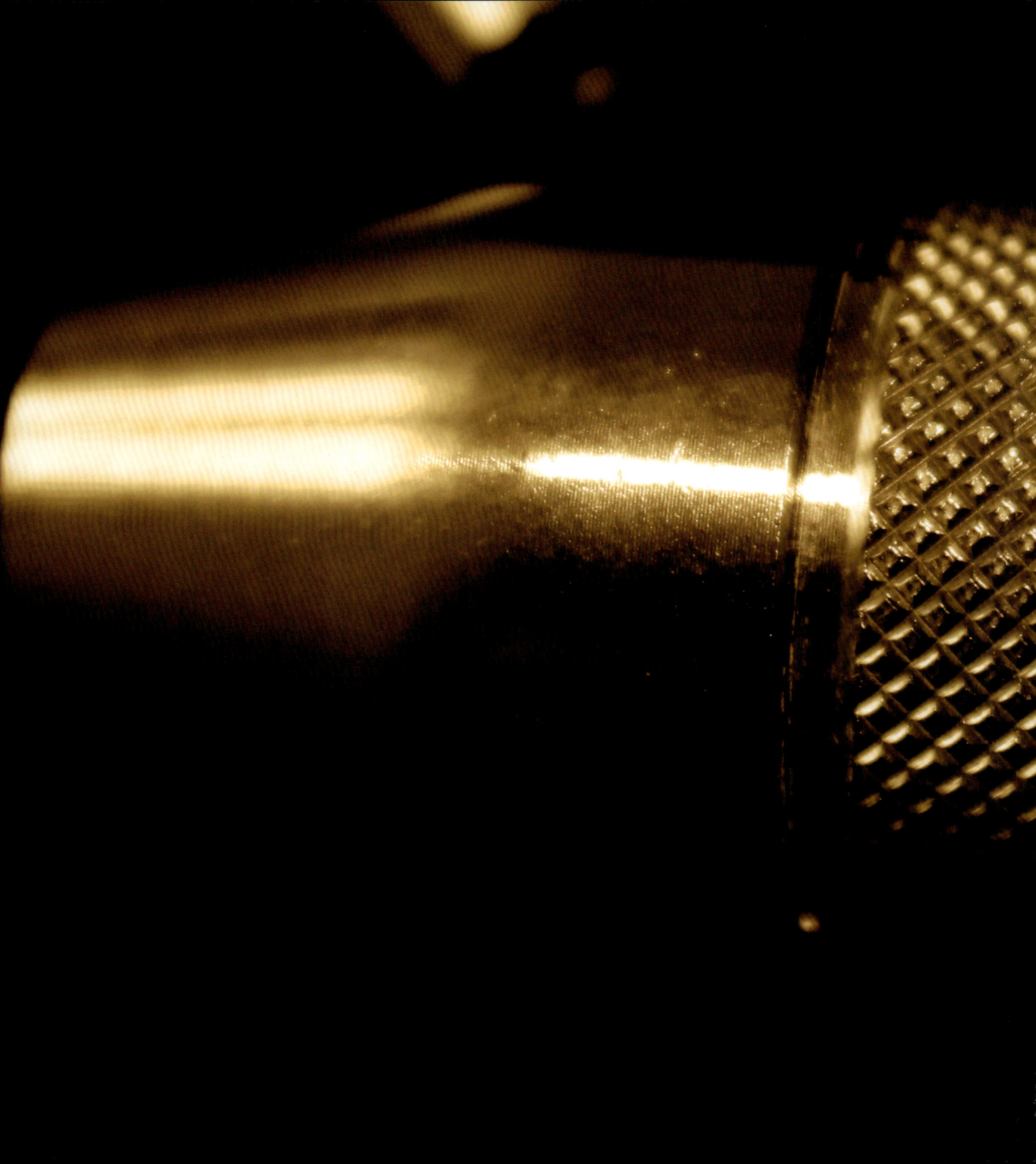

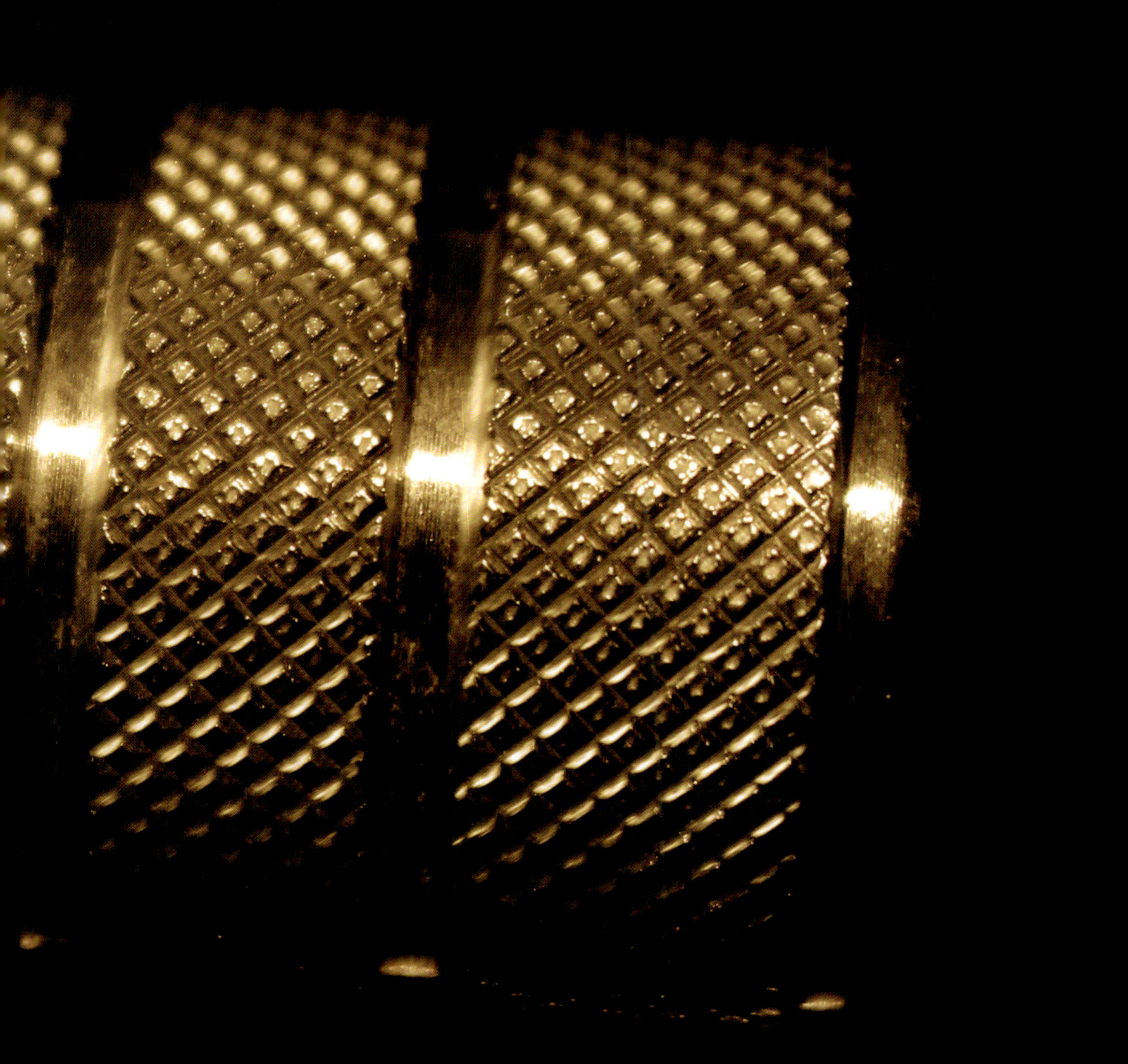

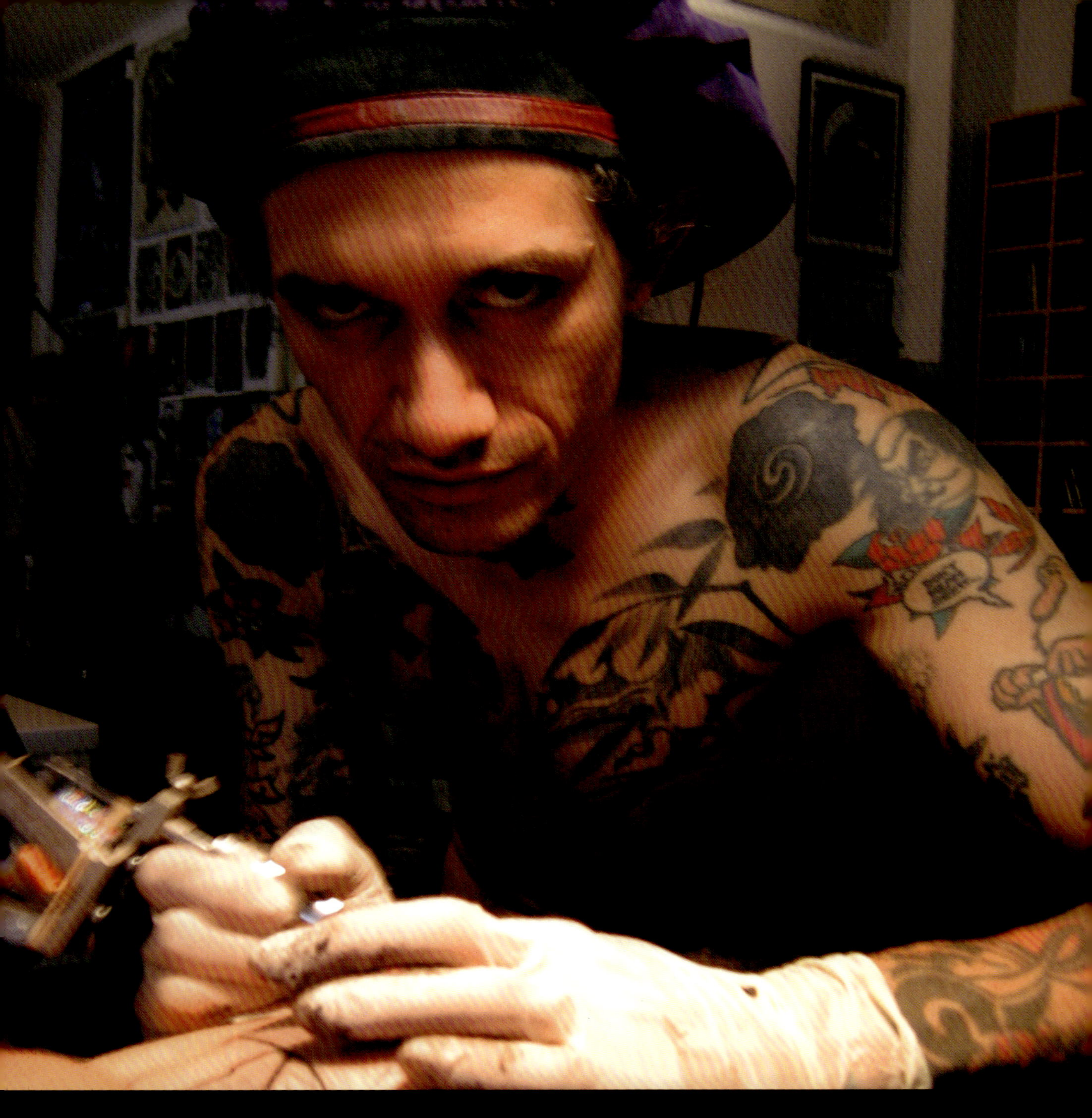

FILIP LEU
THE LEU FAMILY'S FAMILY IRON

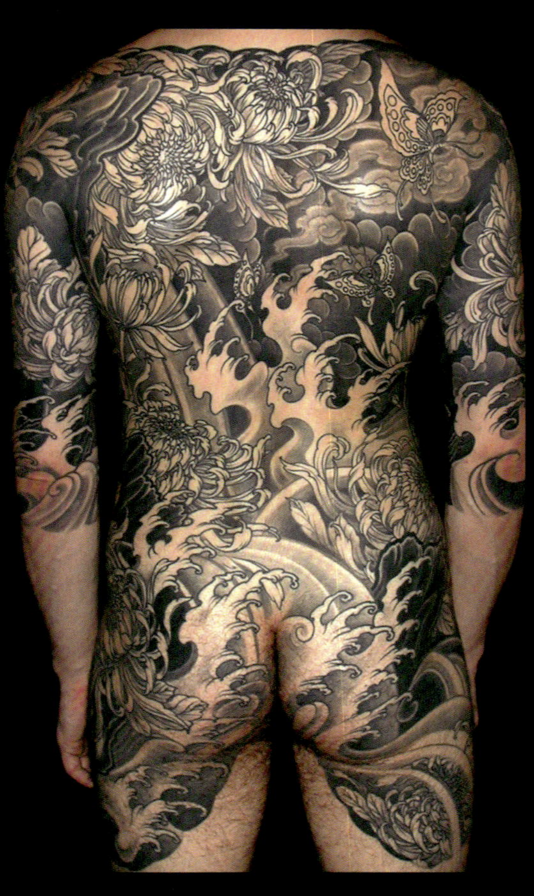
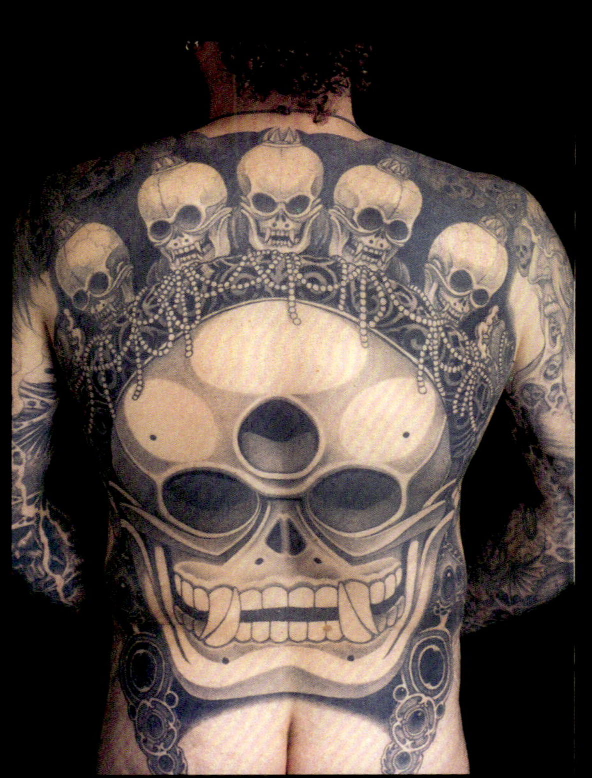

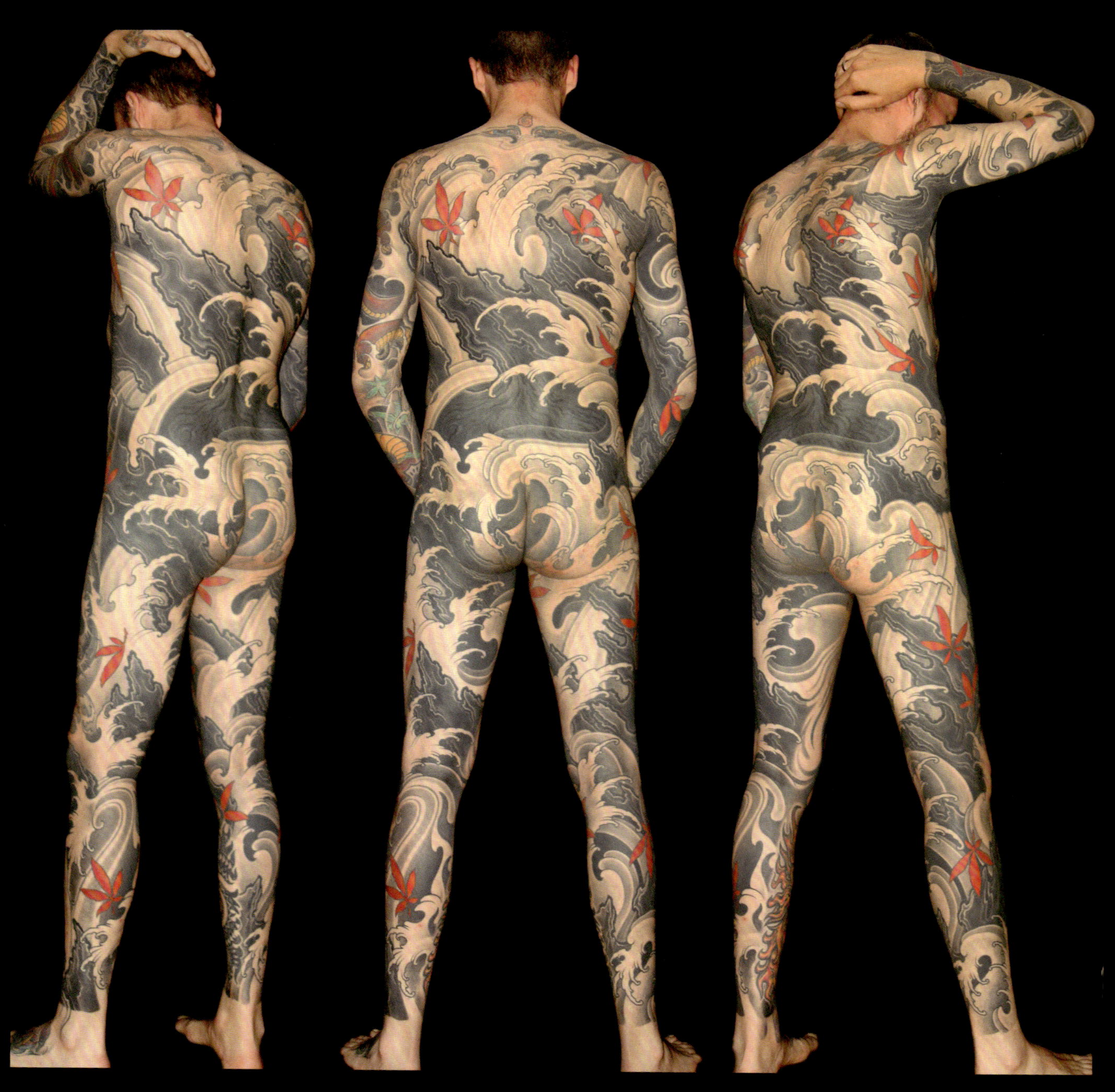

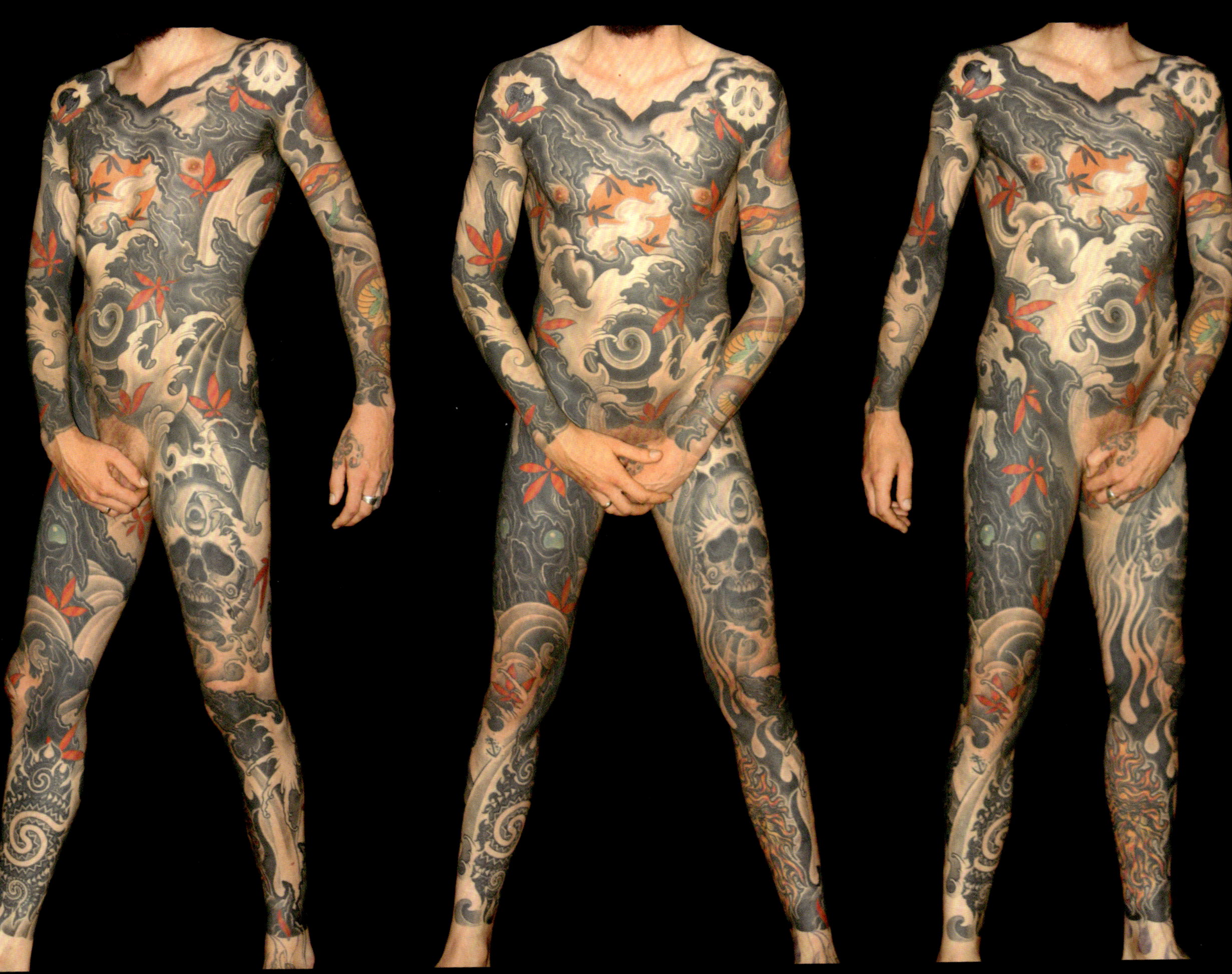

Filip Leu www.
leufamilyiron.com

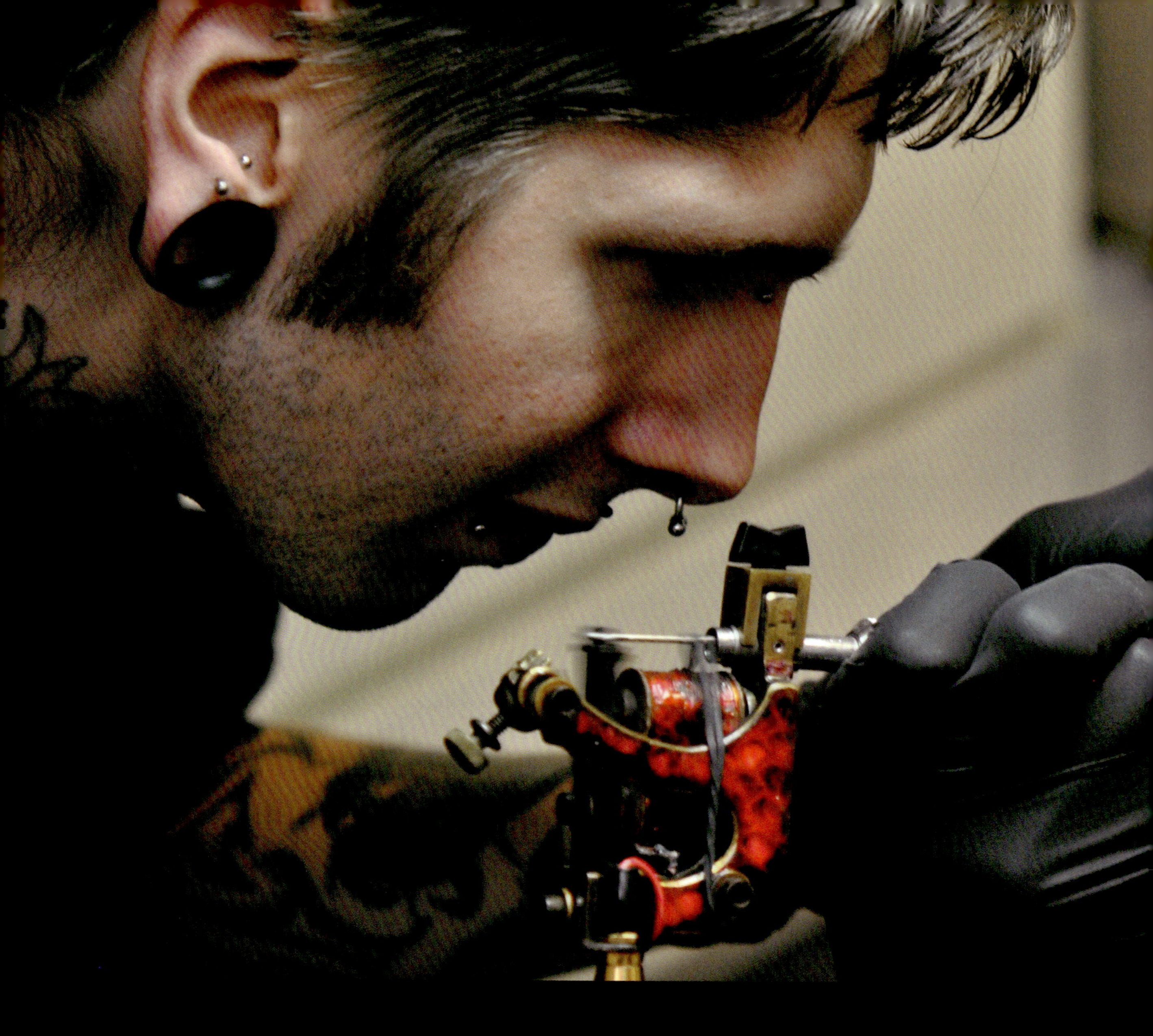

FLORIAN KARG
VICIOUS CIRCLE TATTOO

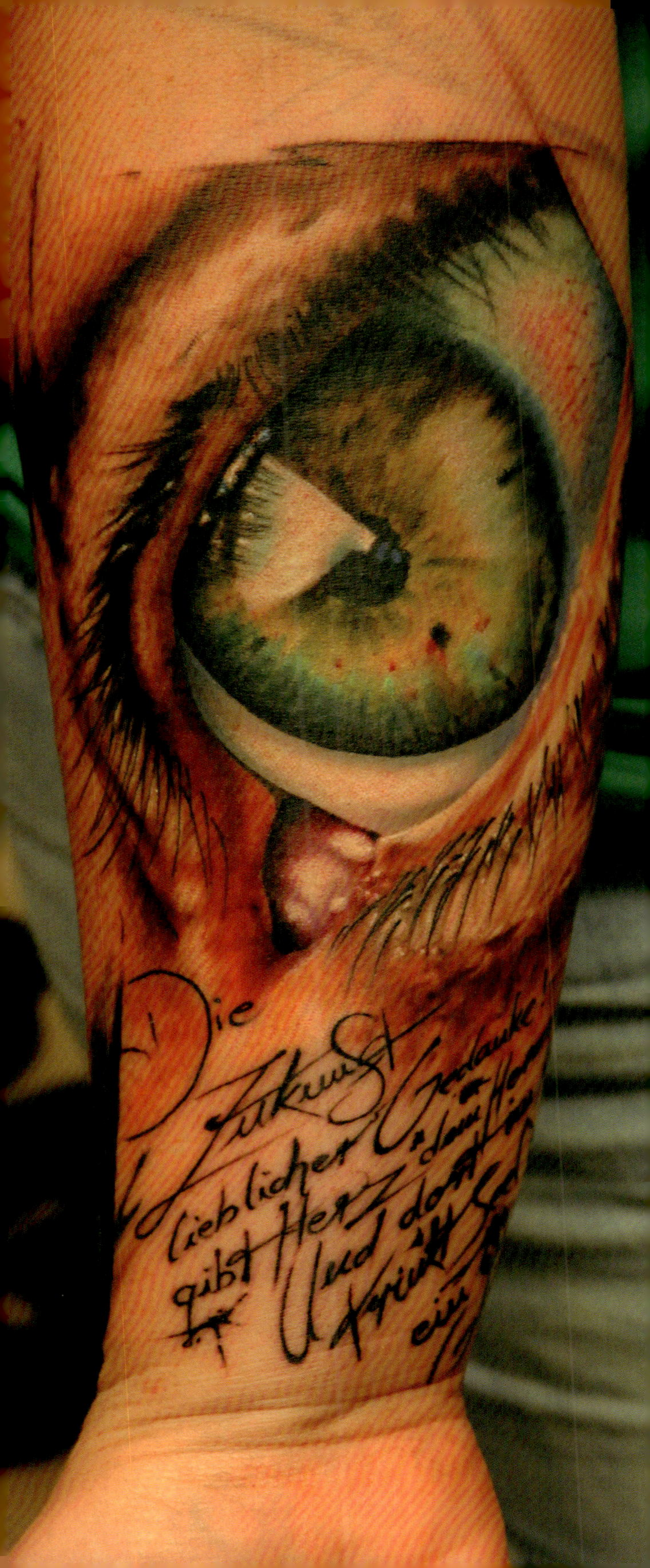
Die
Zukunft
lieblicher Gedanke!
gibt Herz und Hand
Und dort
ein

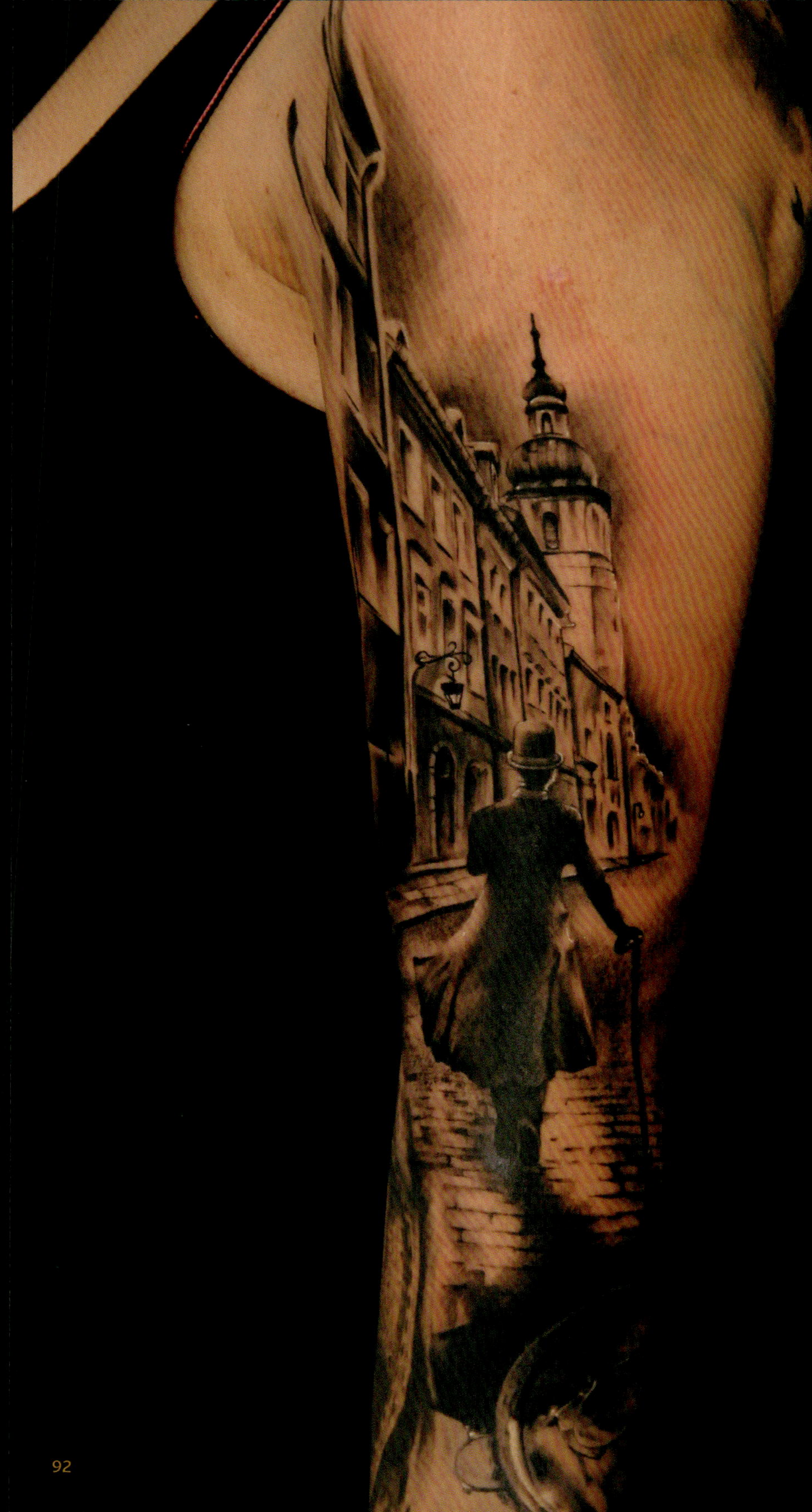

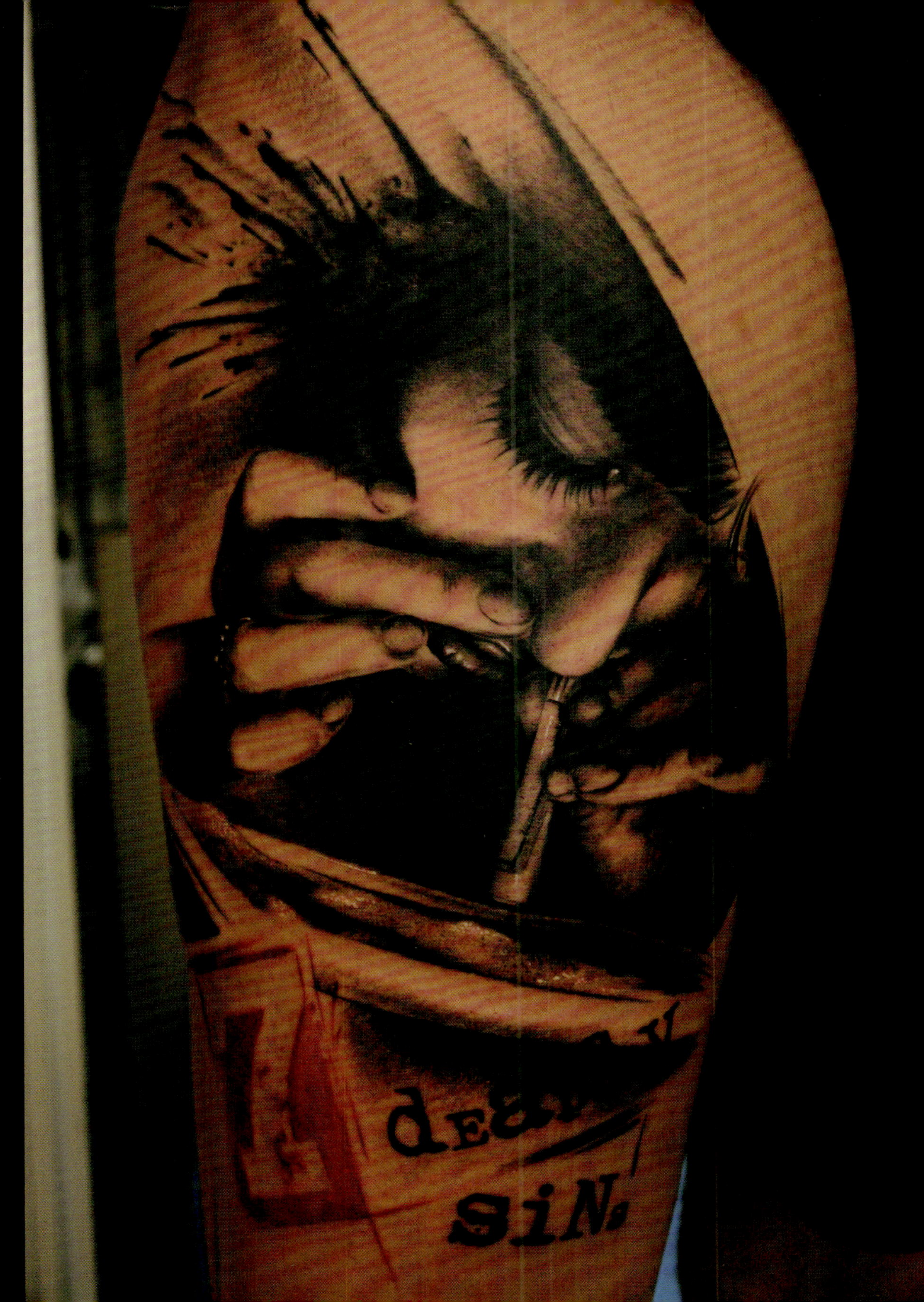
deadly
siN.

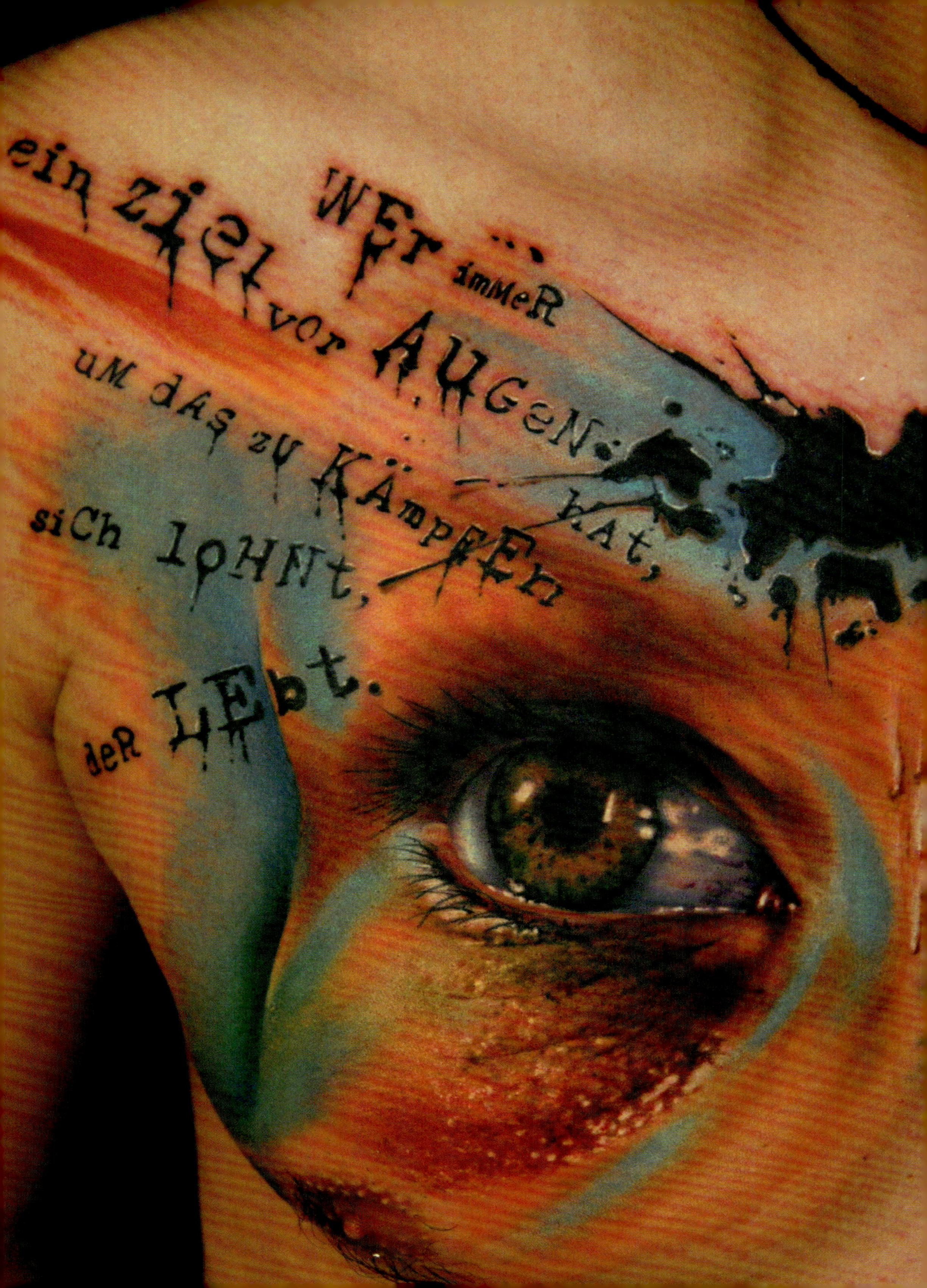

WEr ... immeR
ein ziel vor AUGeN ...
uM das zu KämpFEn ... hat,
sich loHNt,
deR LEbt.

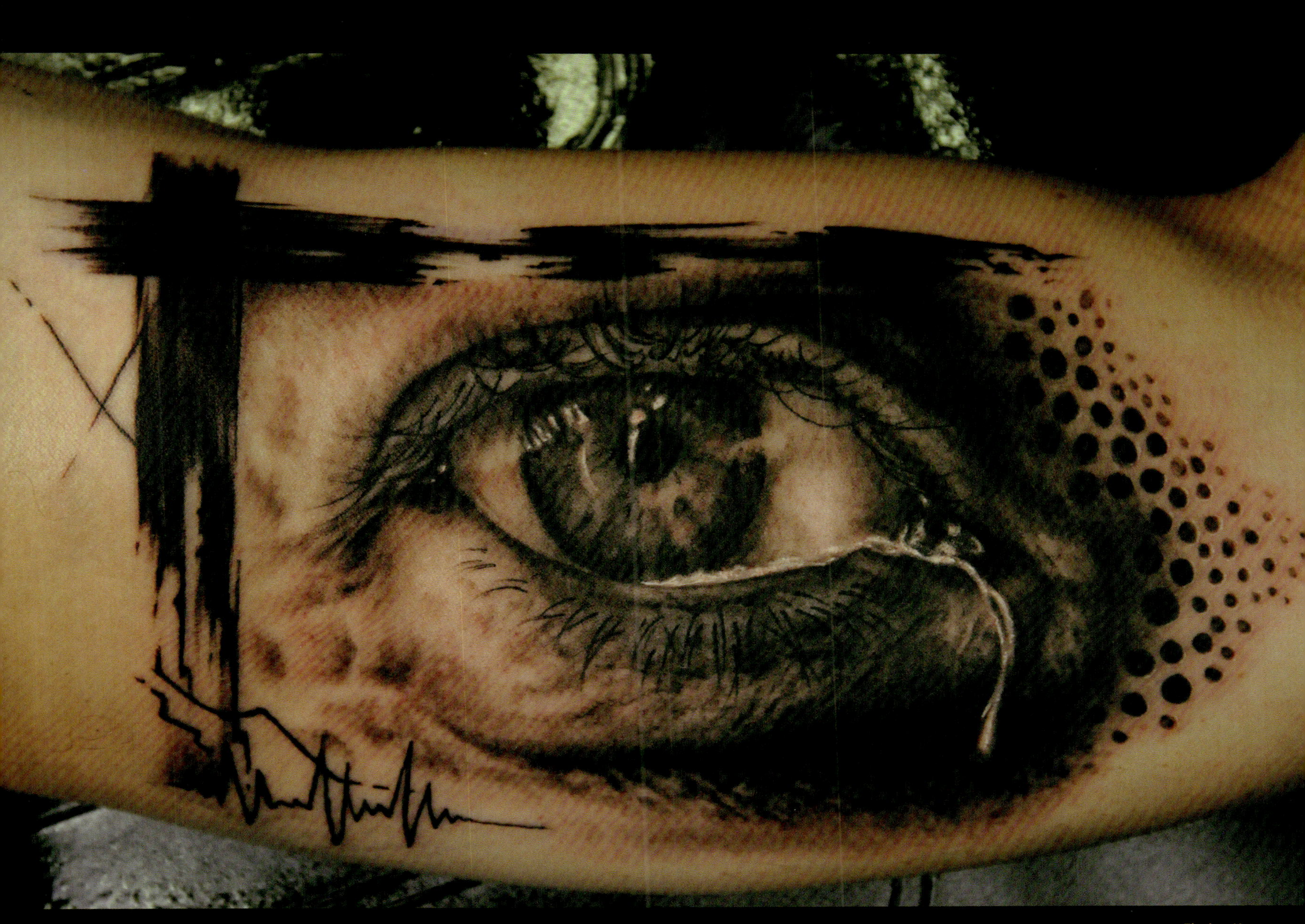

GENKO

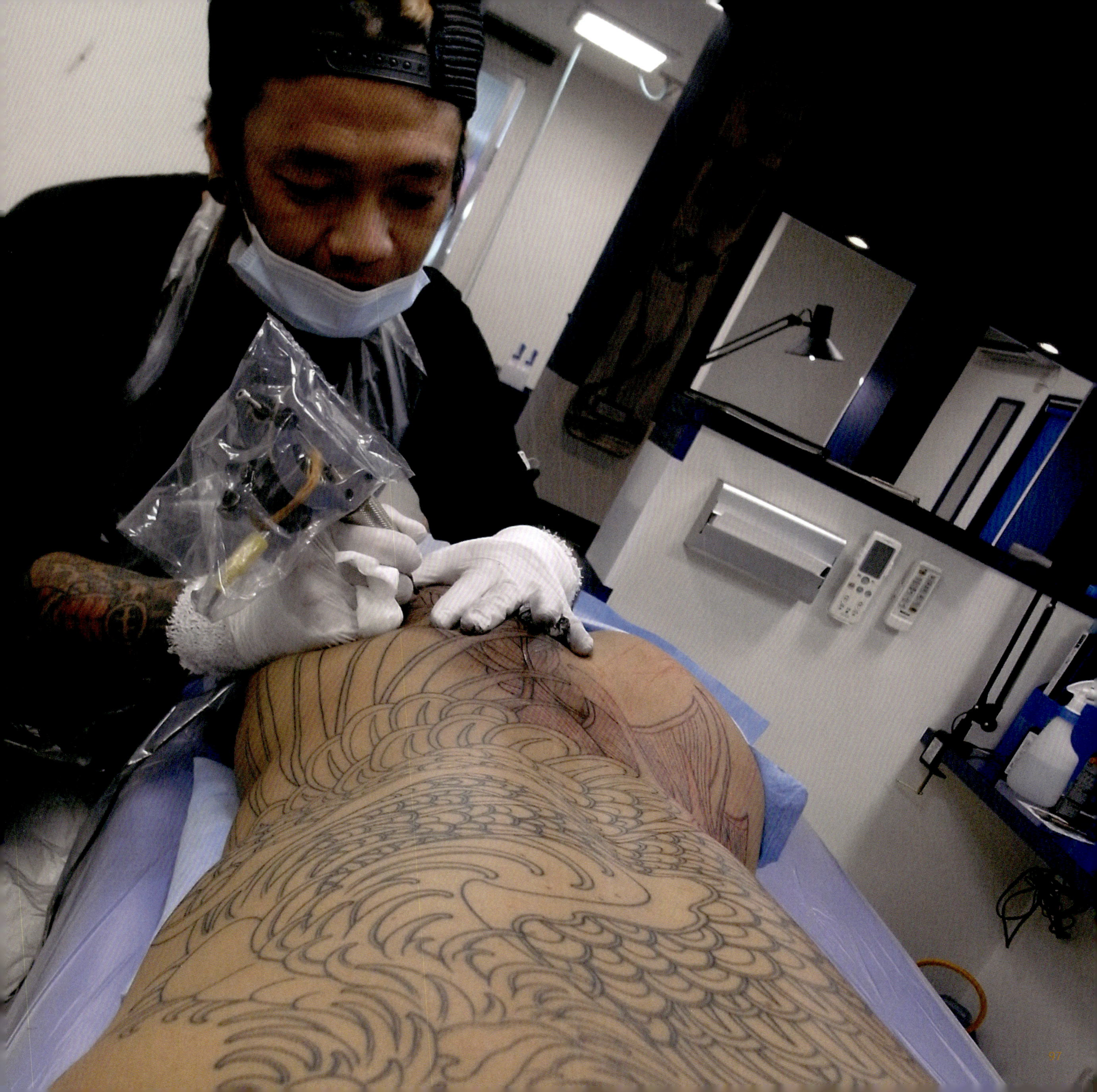

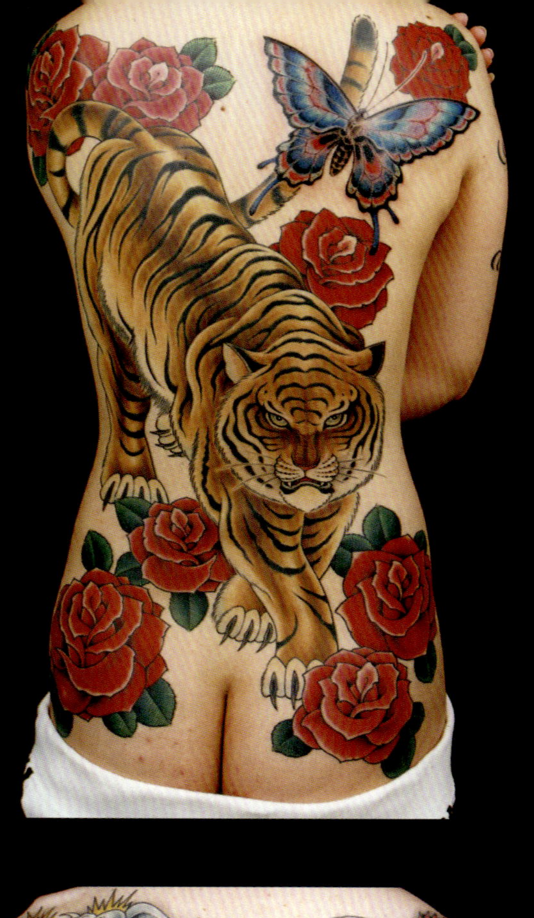
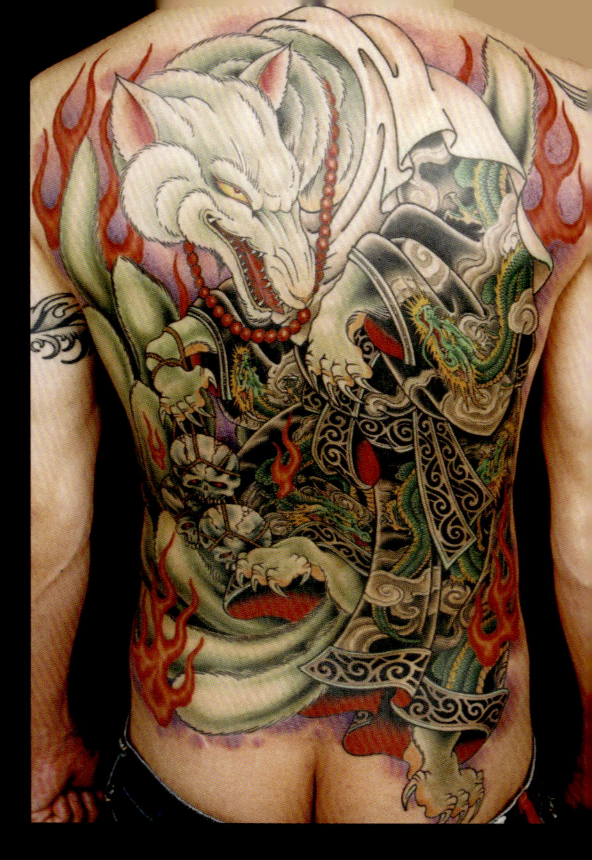
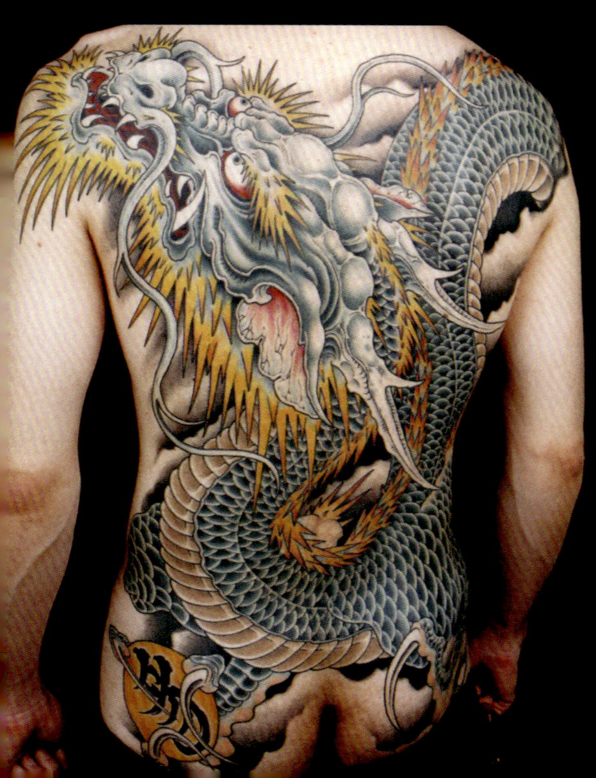
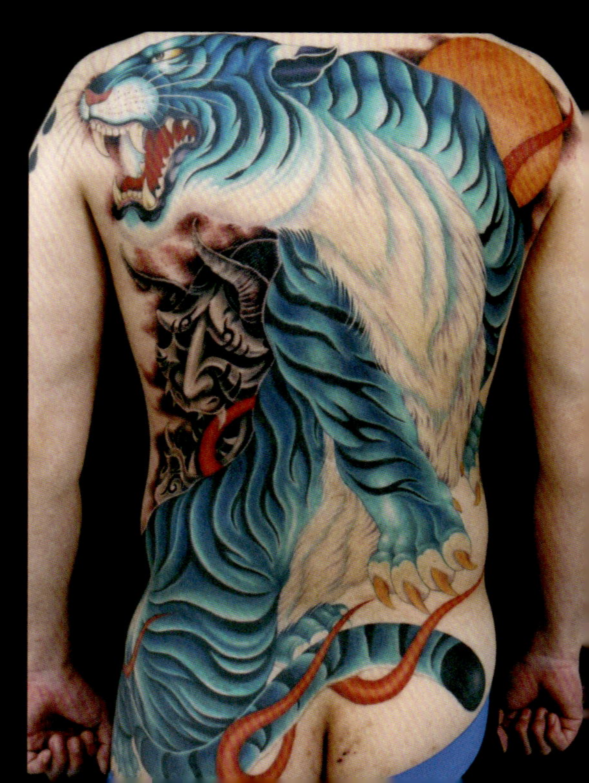

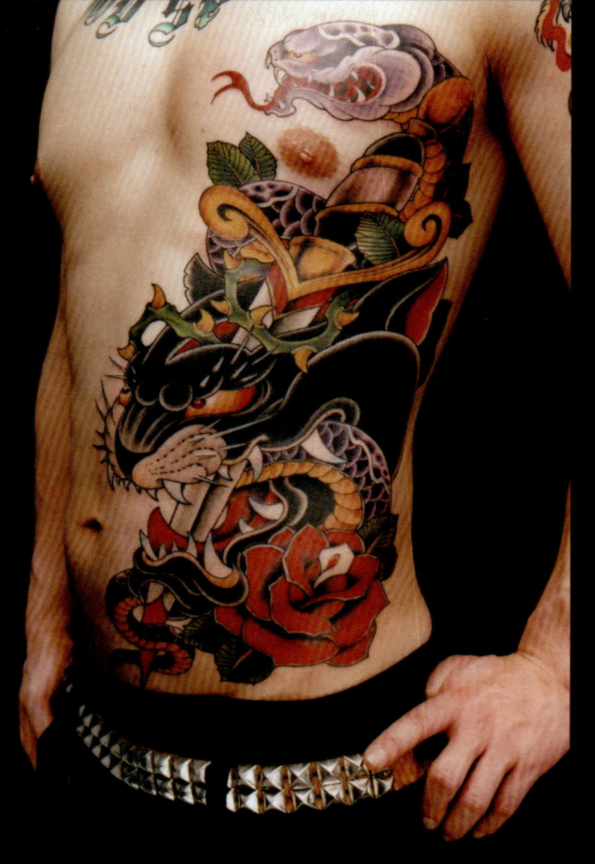
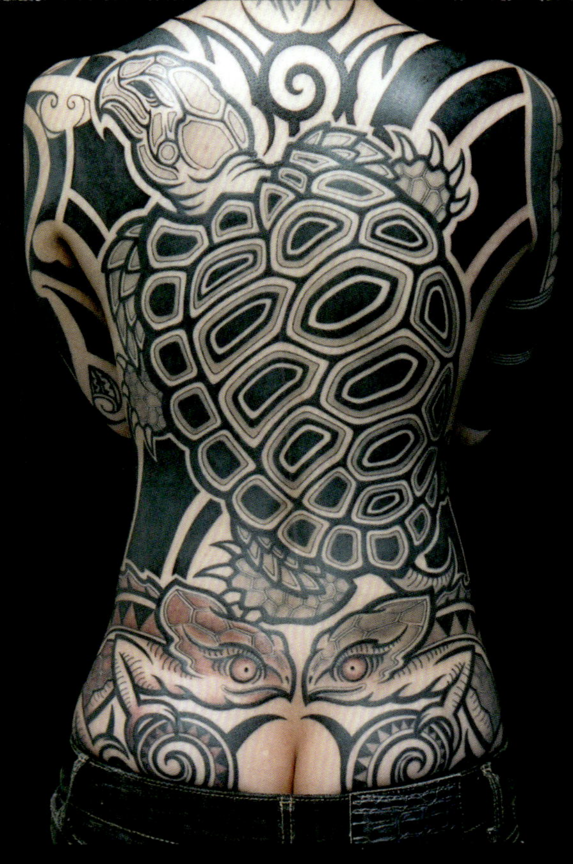
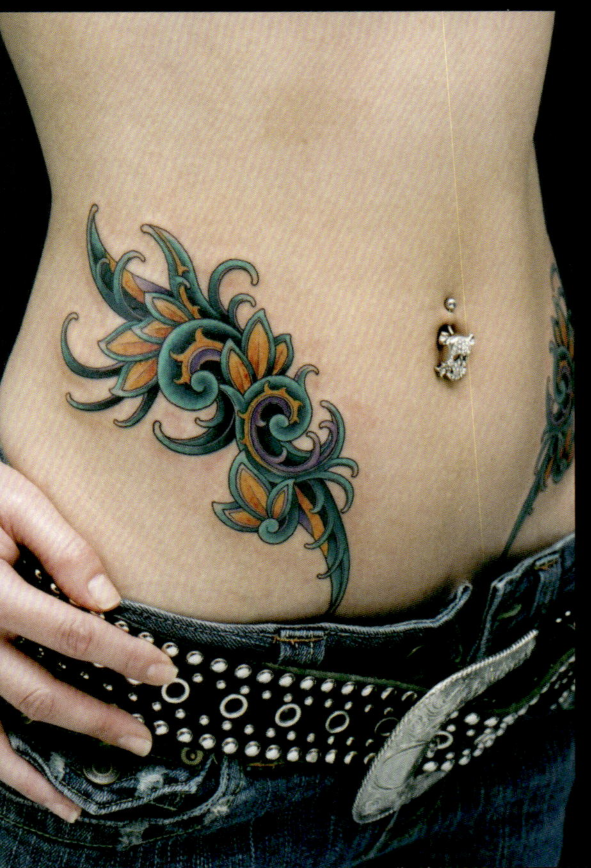
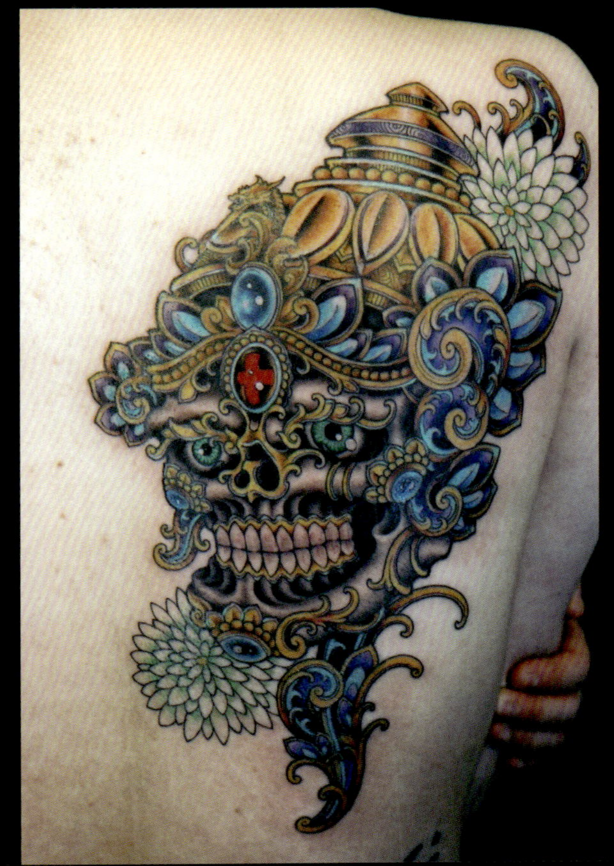
Ge
ww

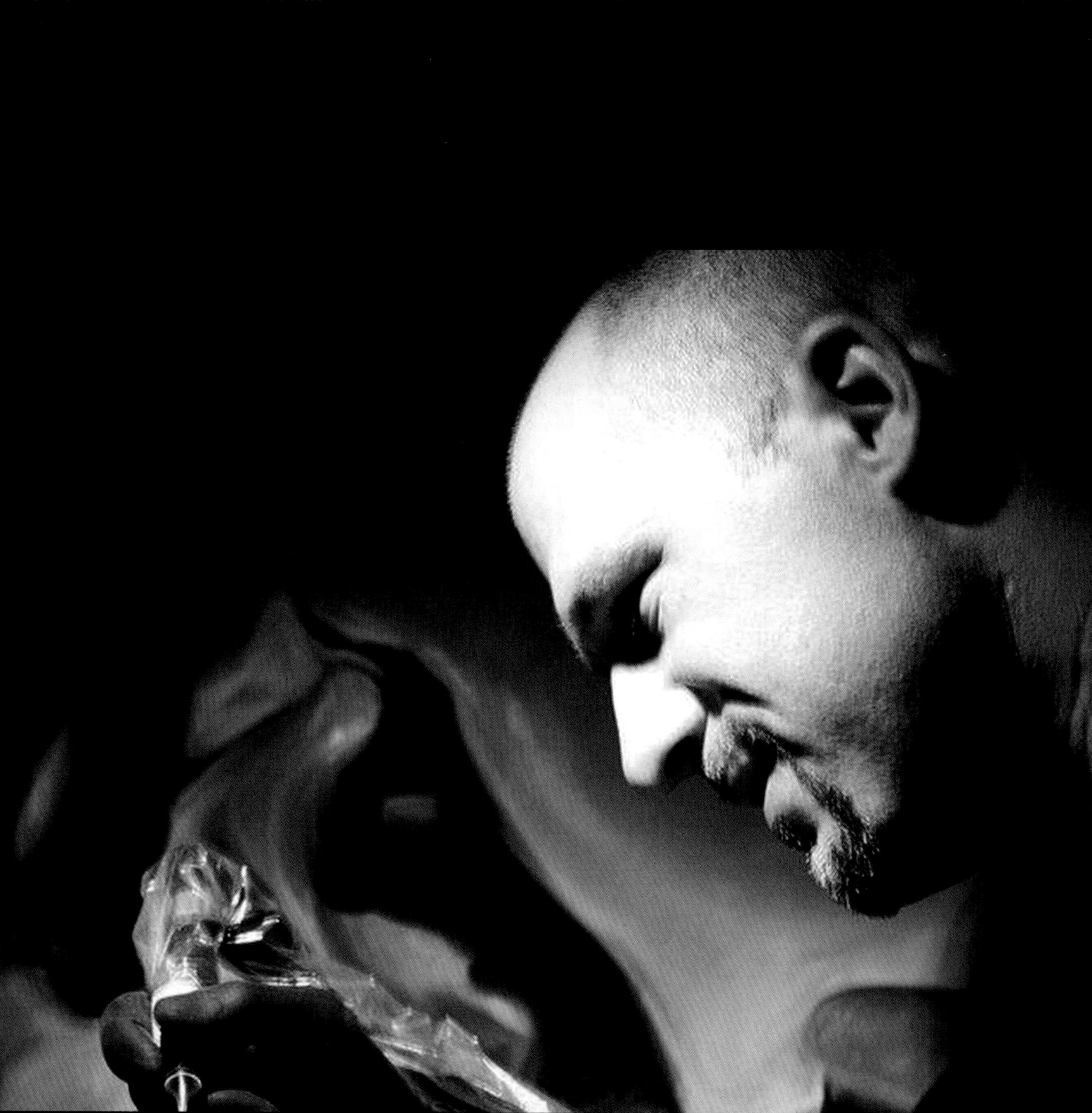

GEZA OTTLECZ
IMMORTAL INK

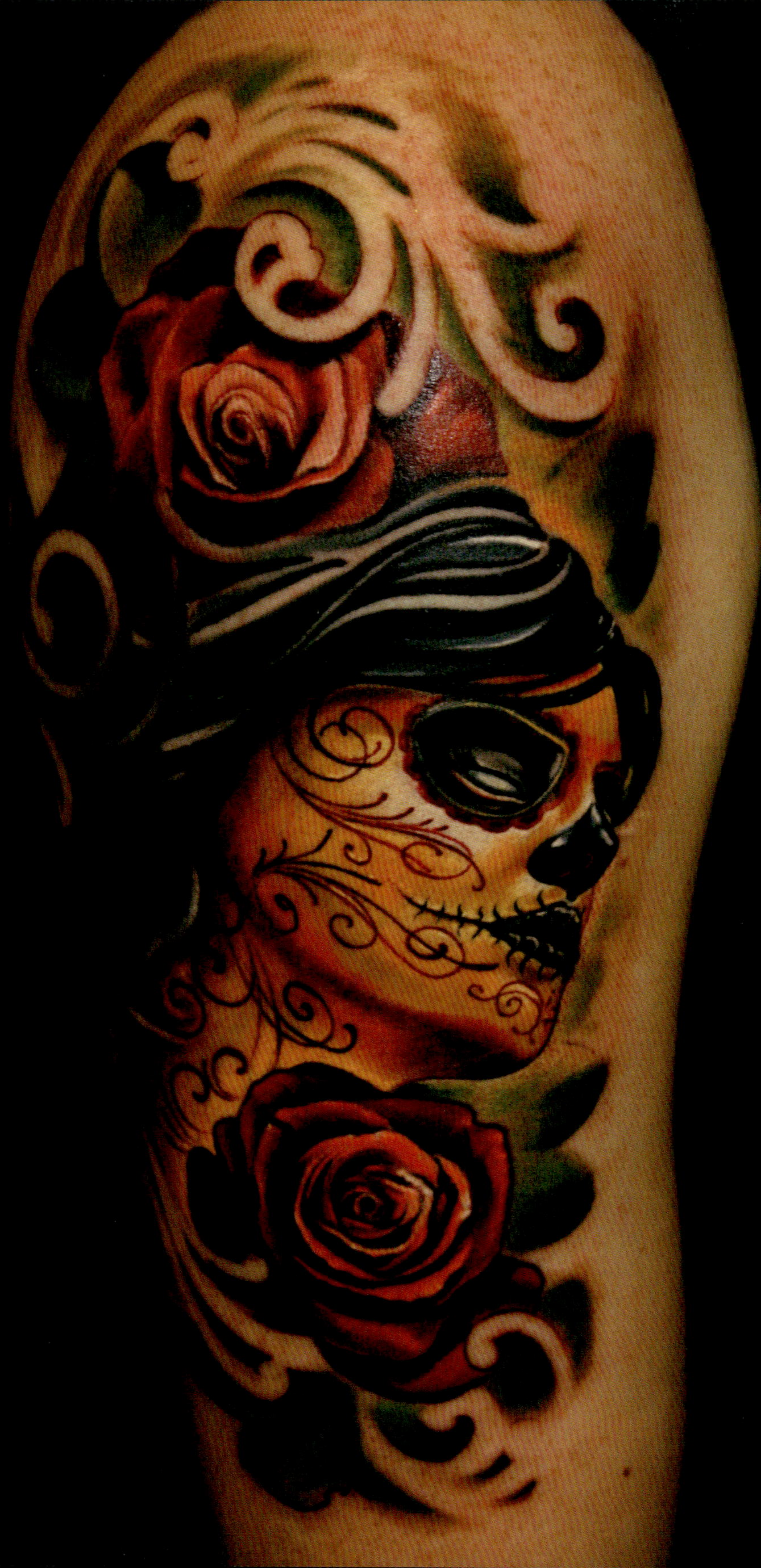

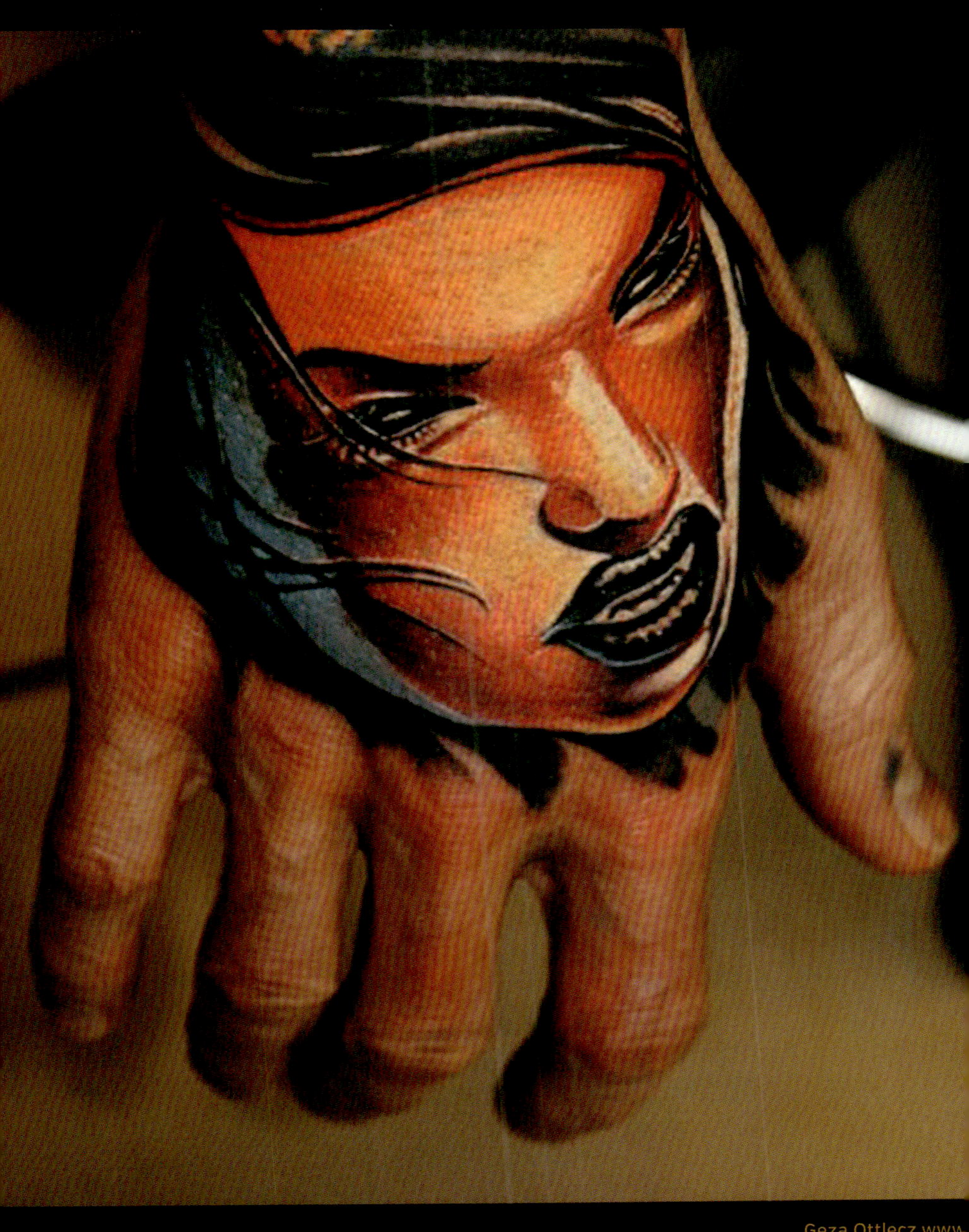

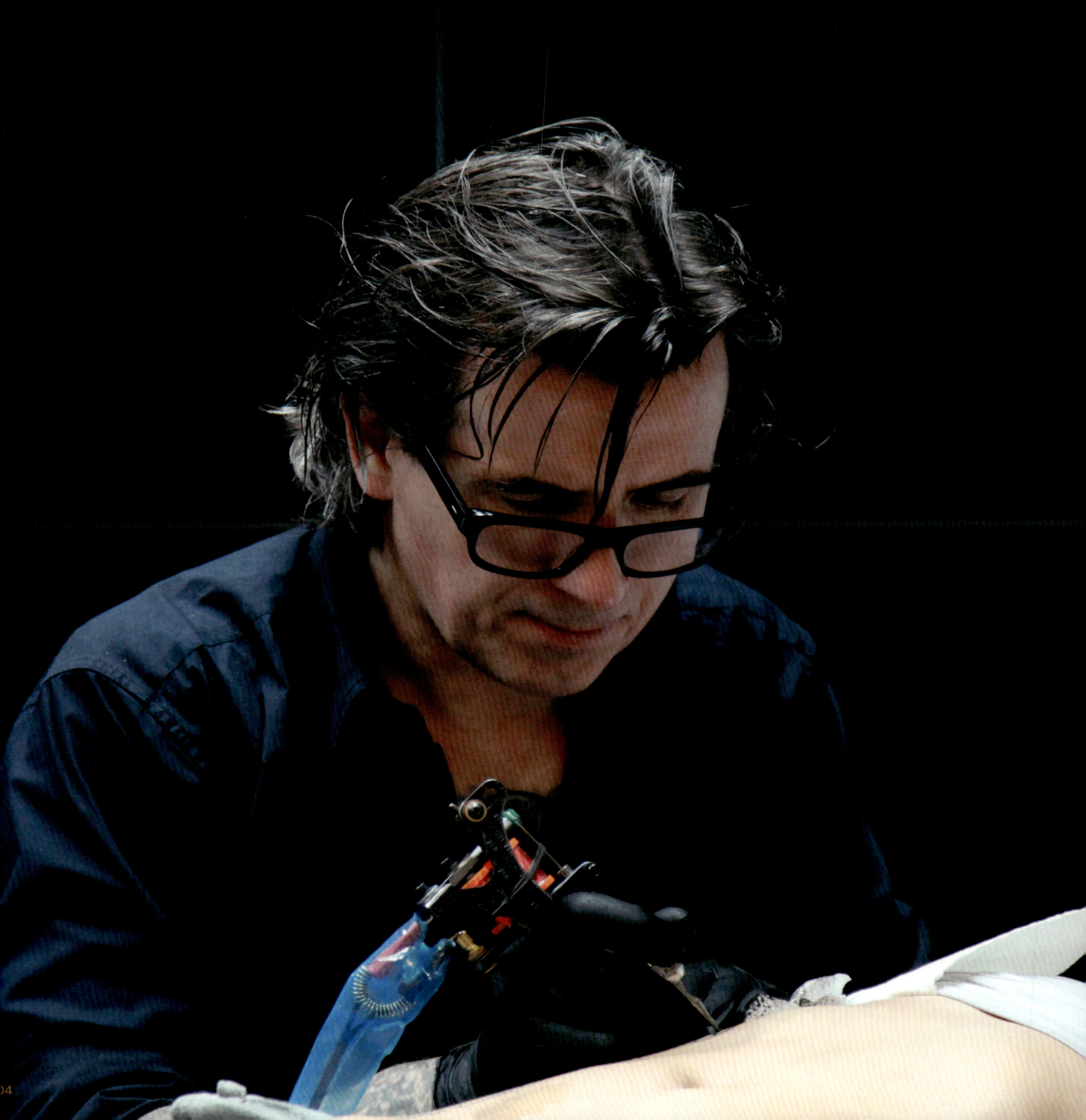

HENNING JØRGENSEN
ROYAL TATTOO

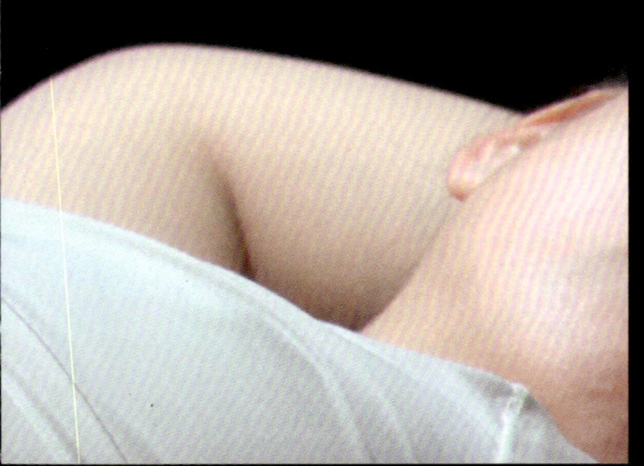

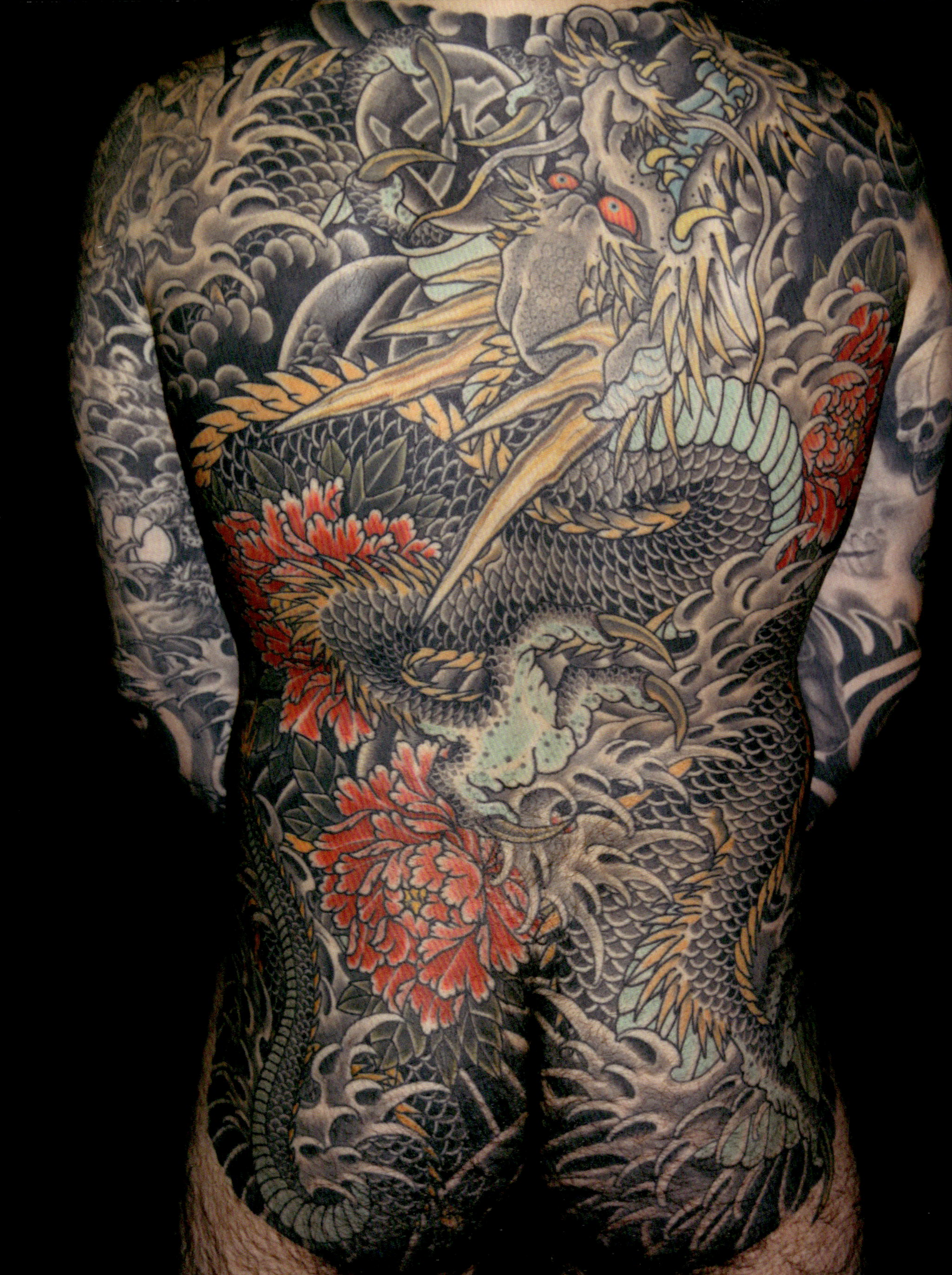

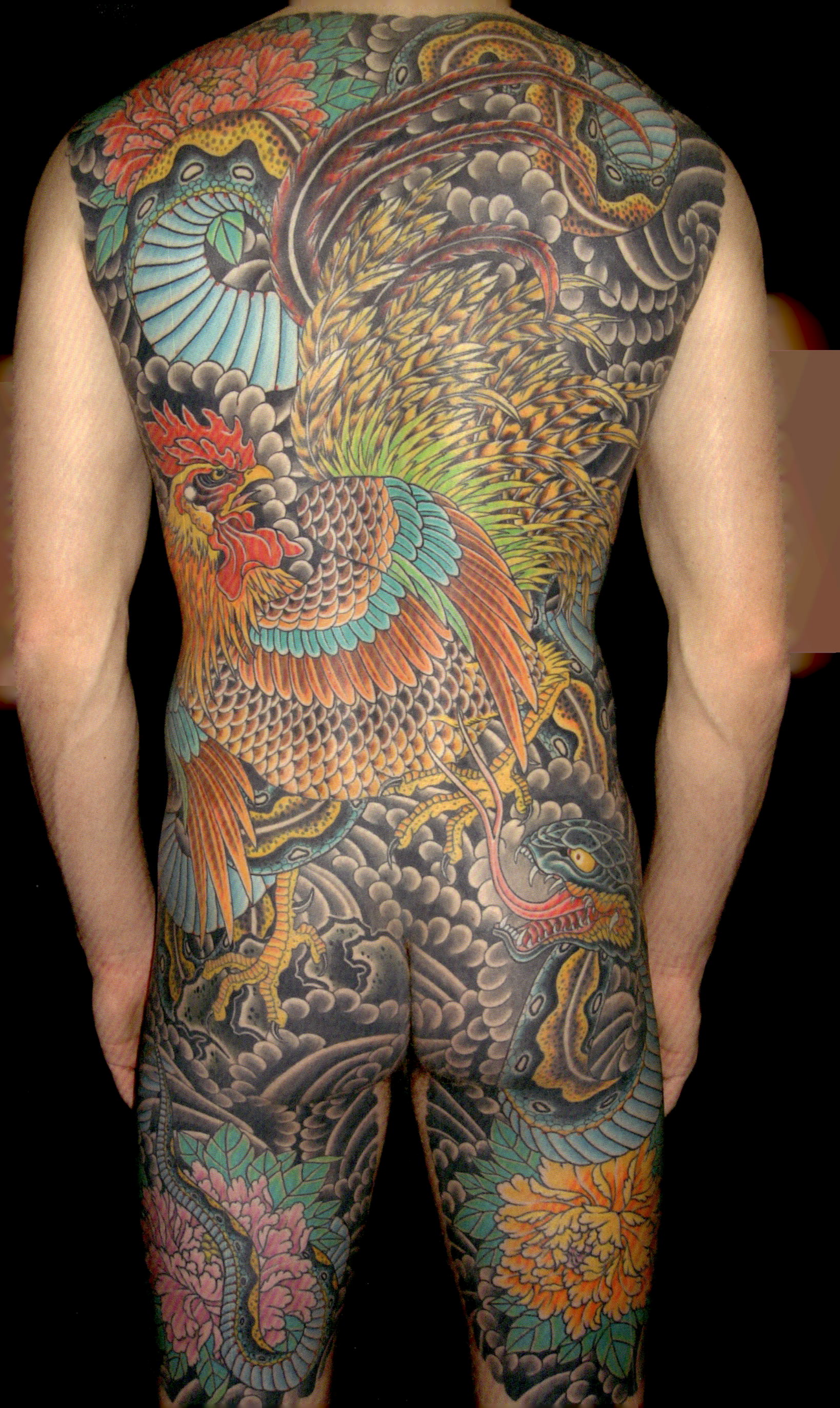

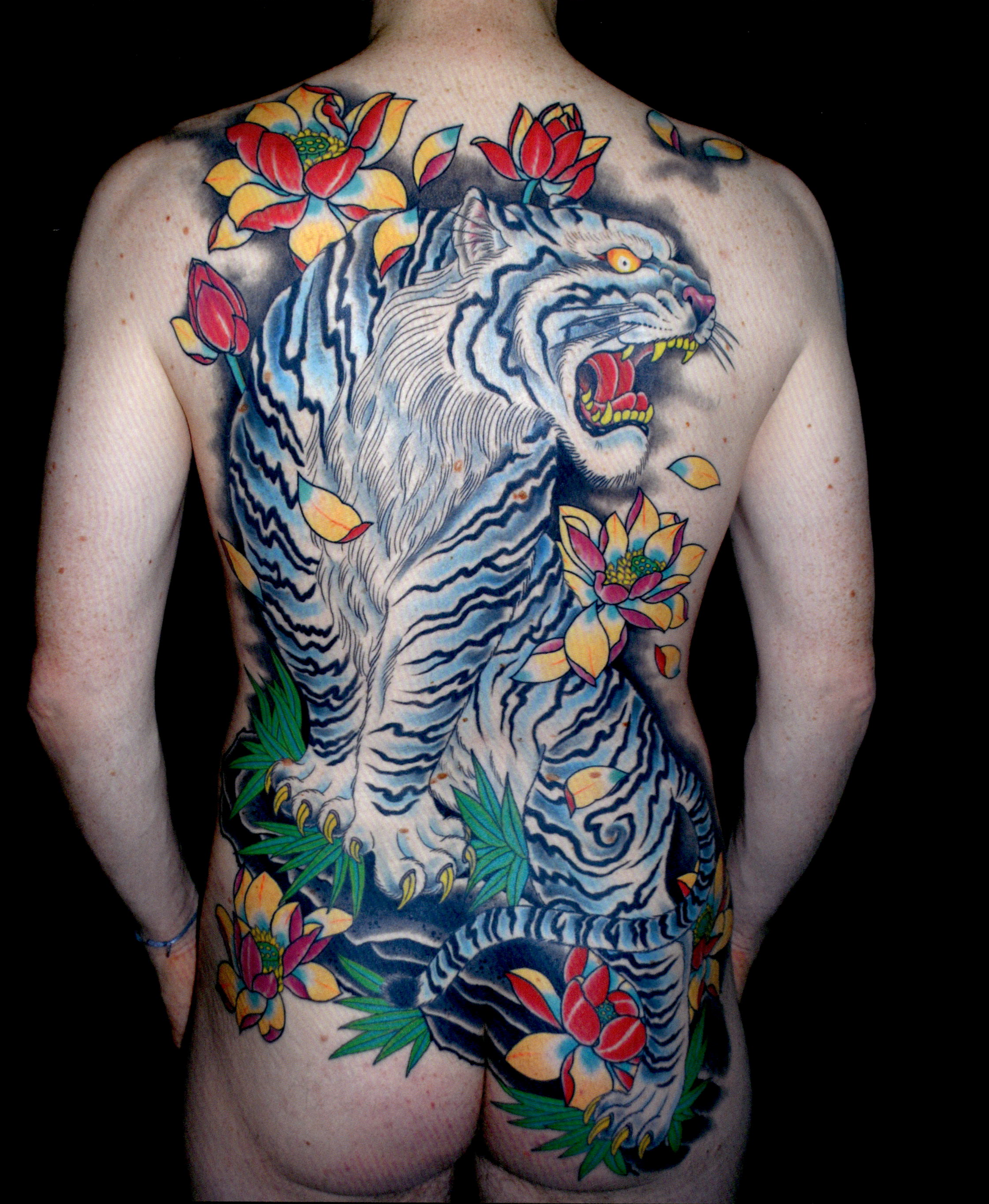

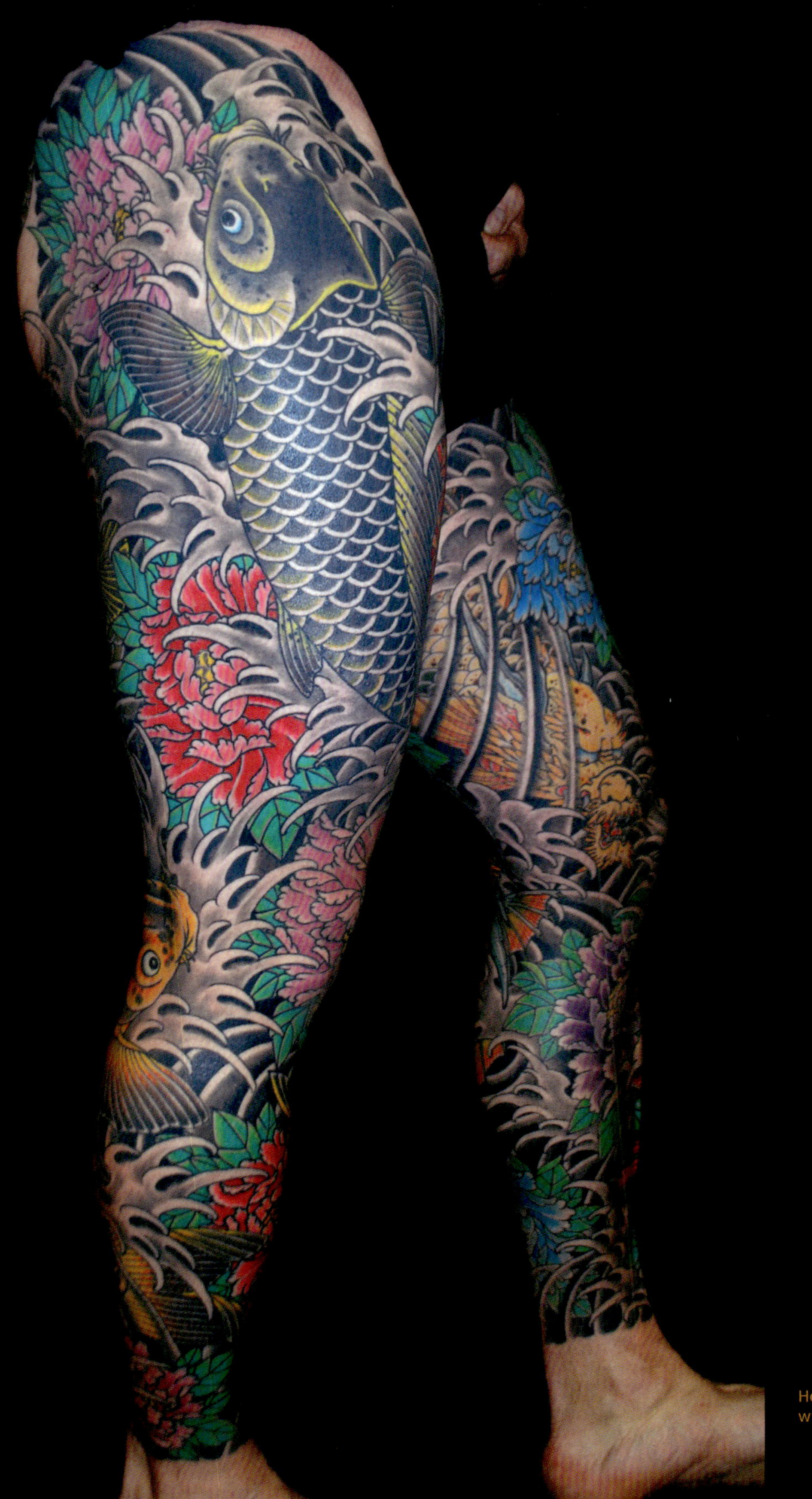

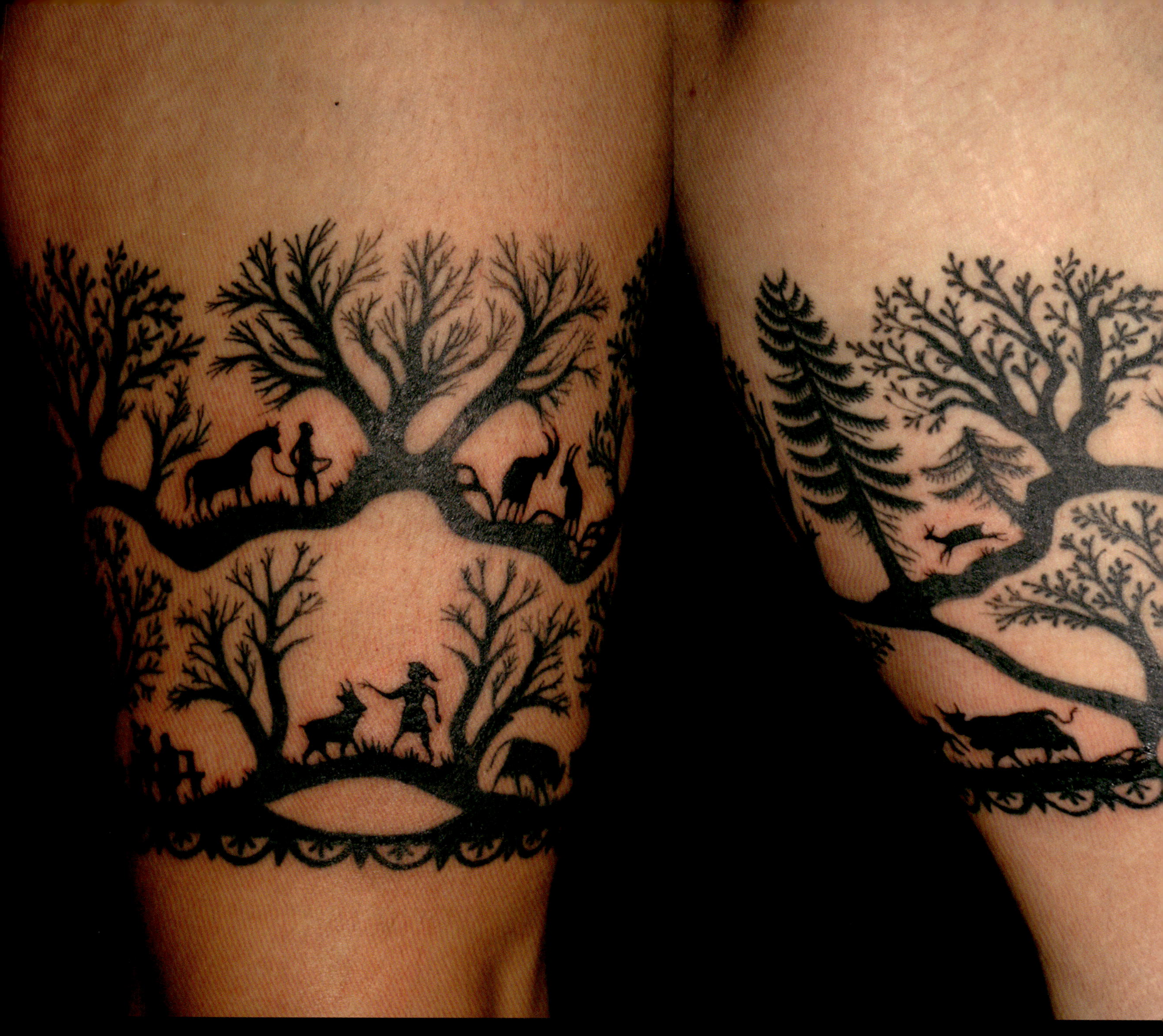

JACQUELINE SPOERLÉ
CORAZON TATTOO

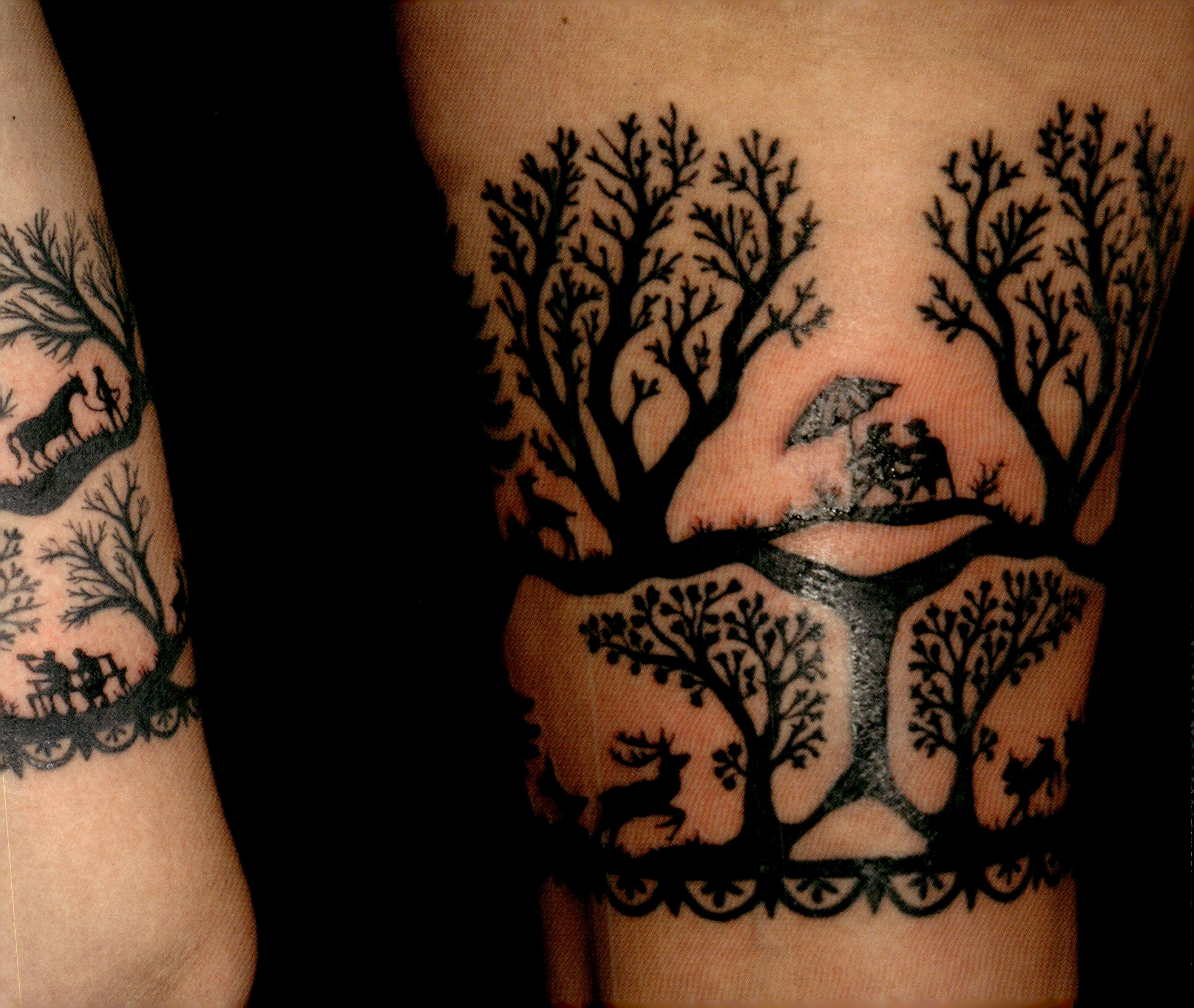

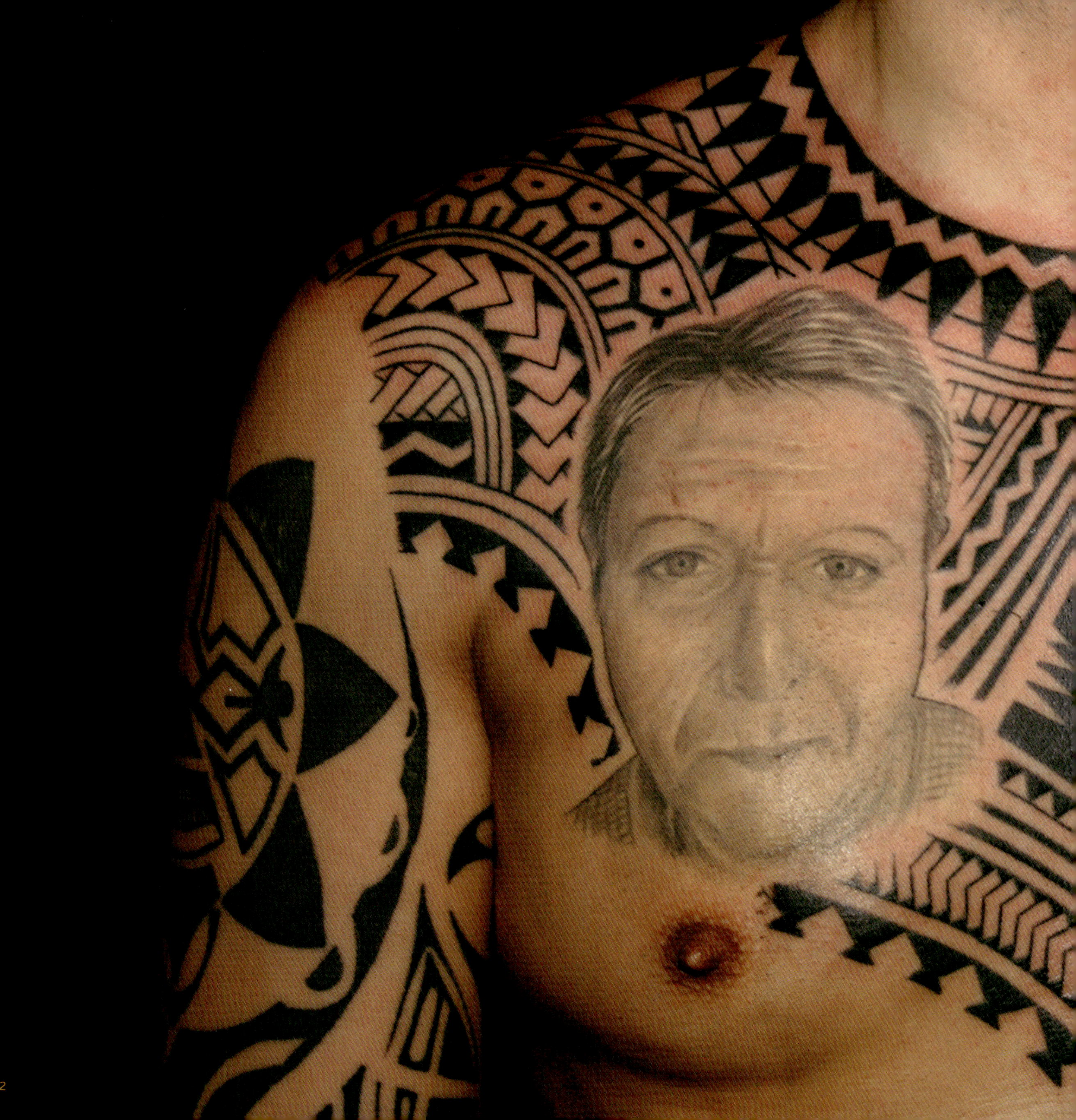

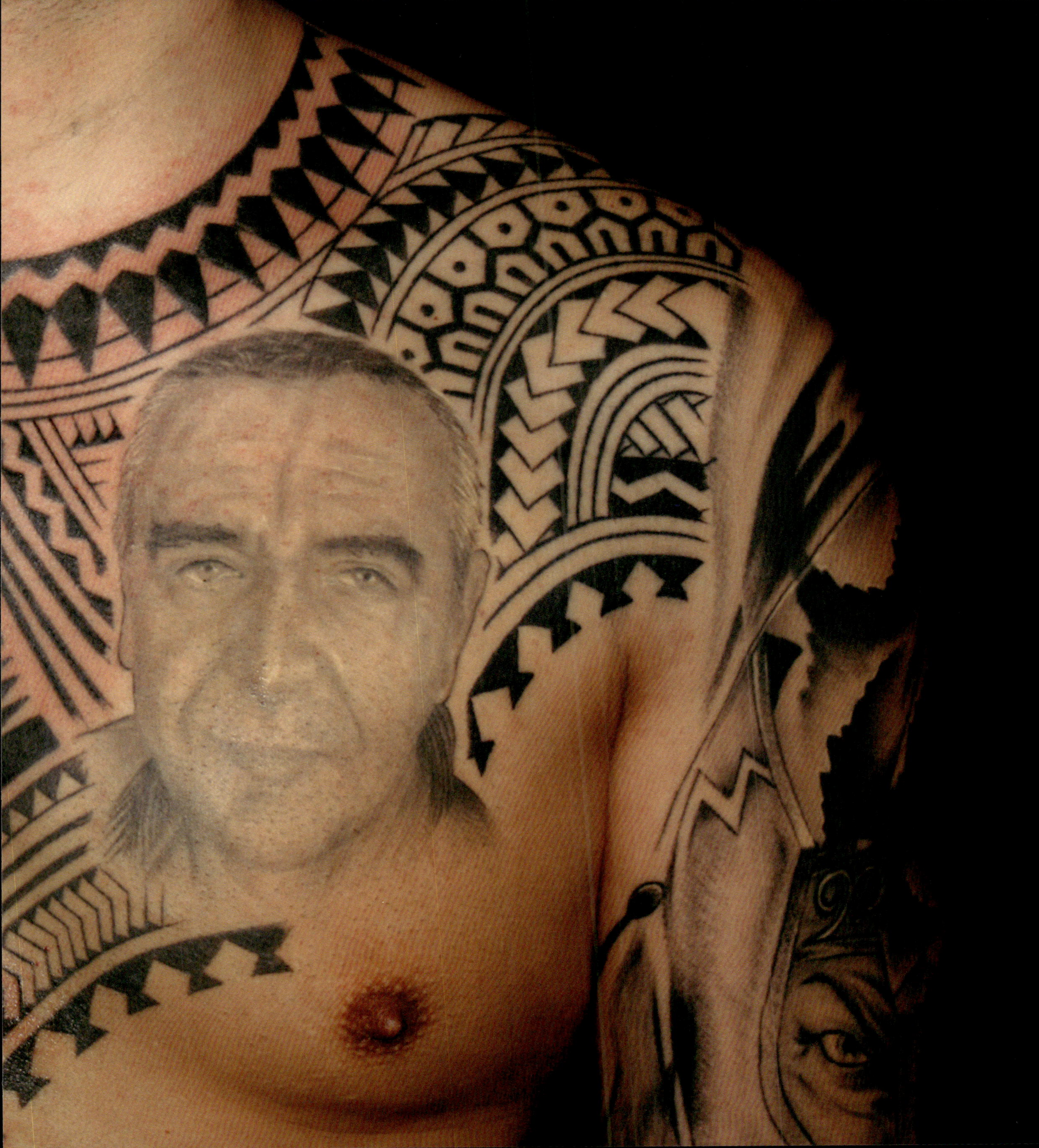

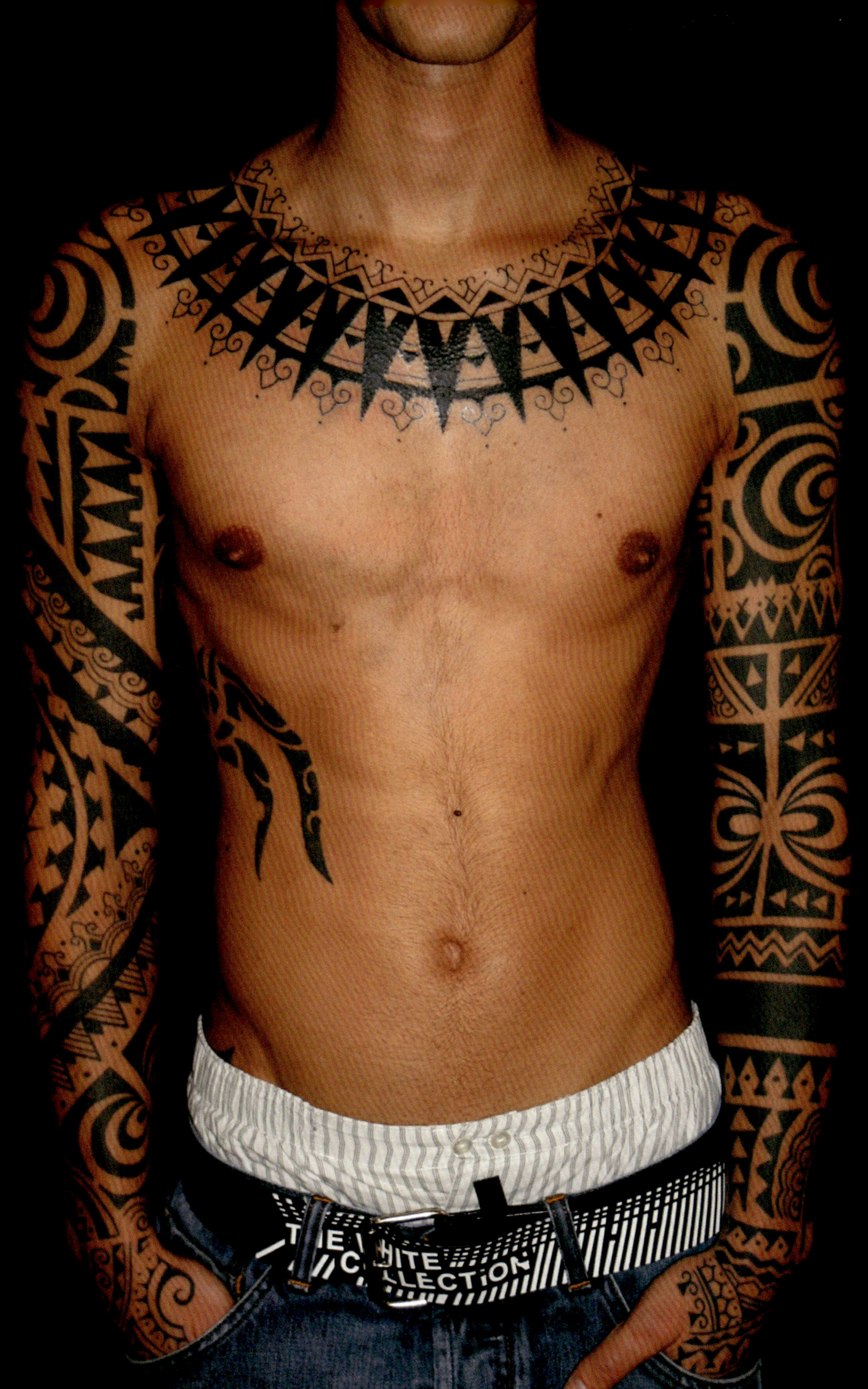

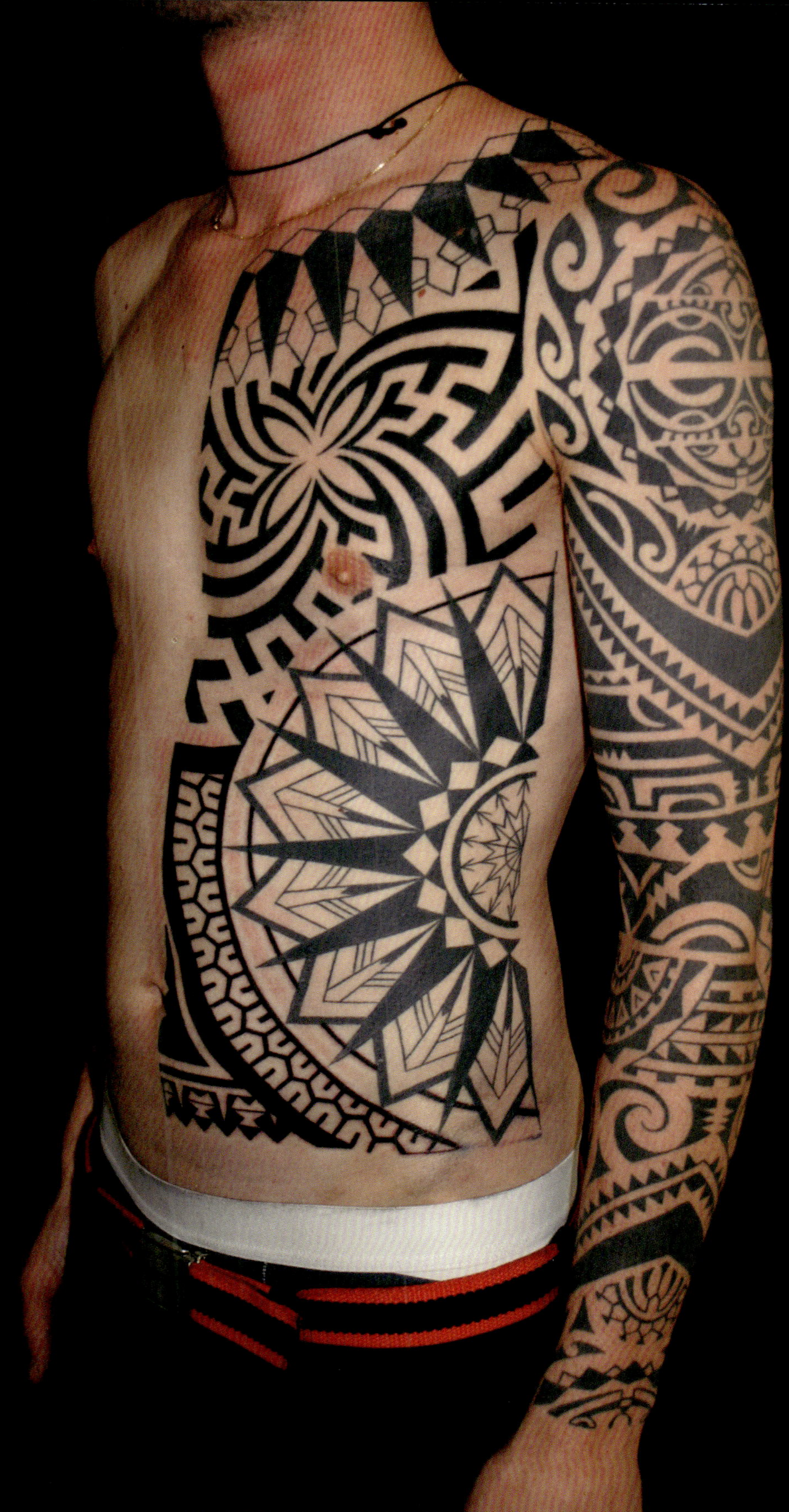

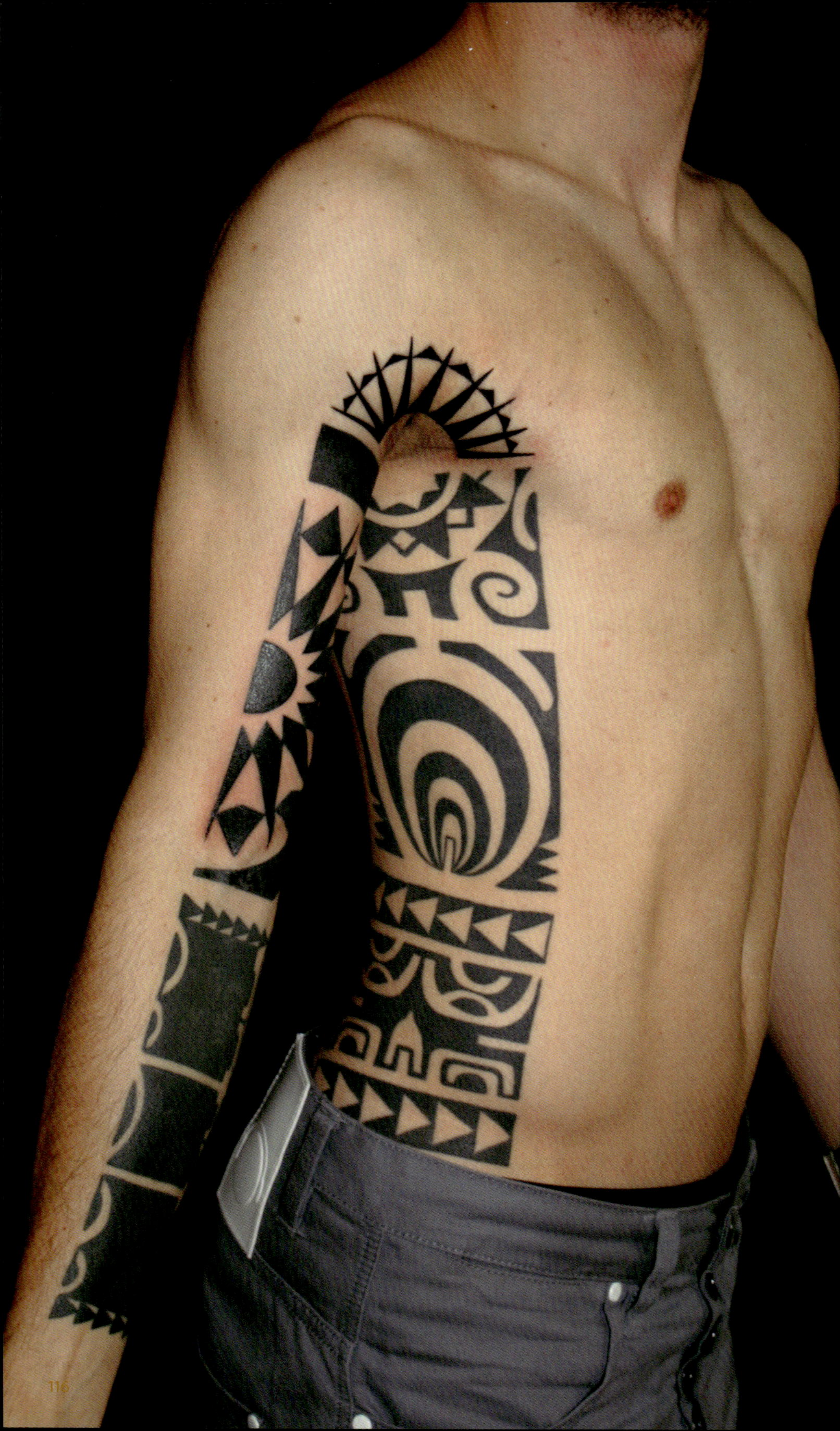

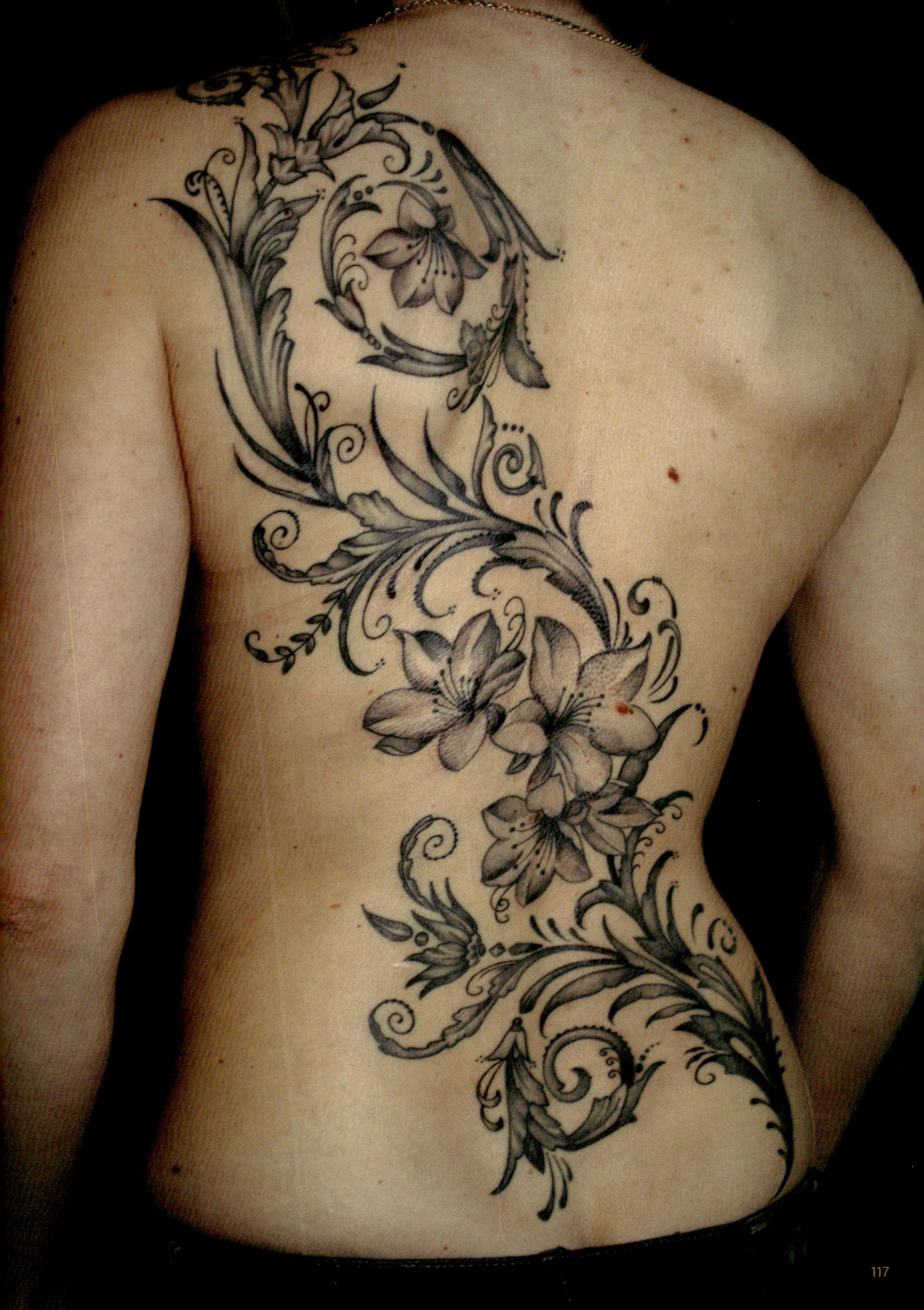

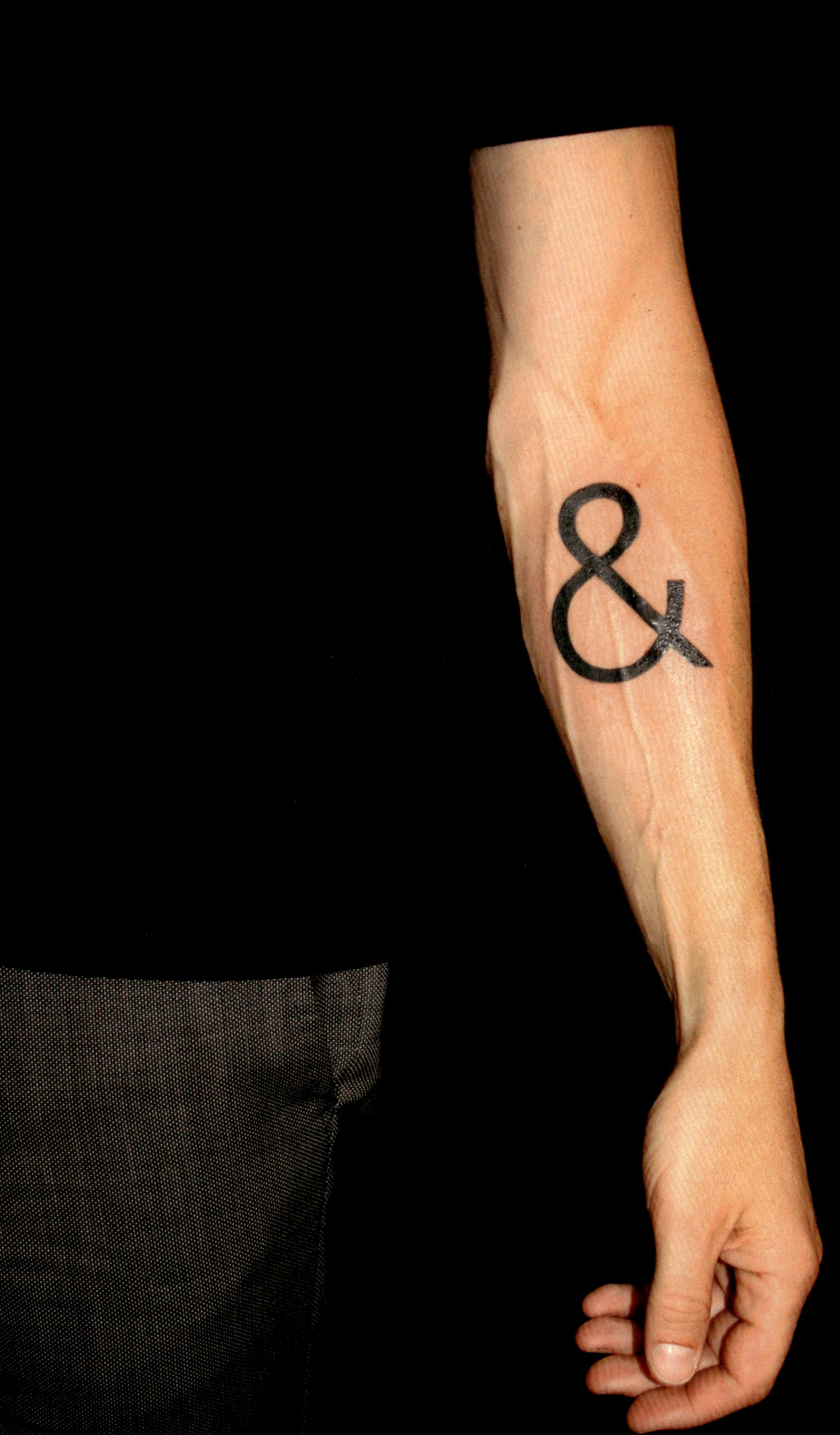

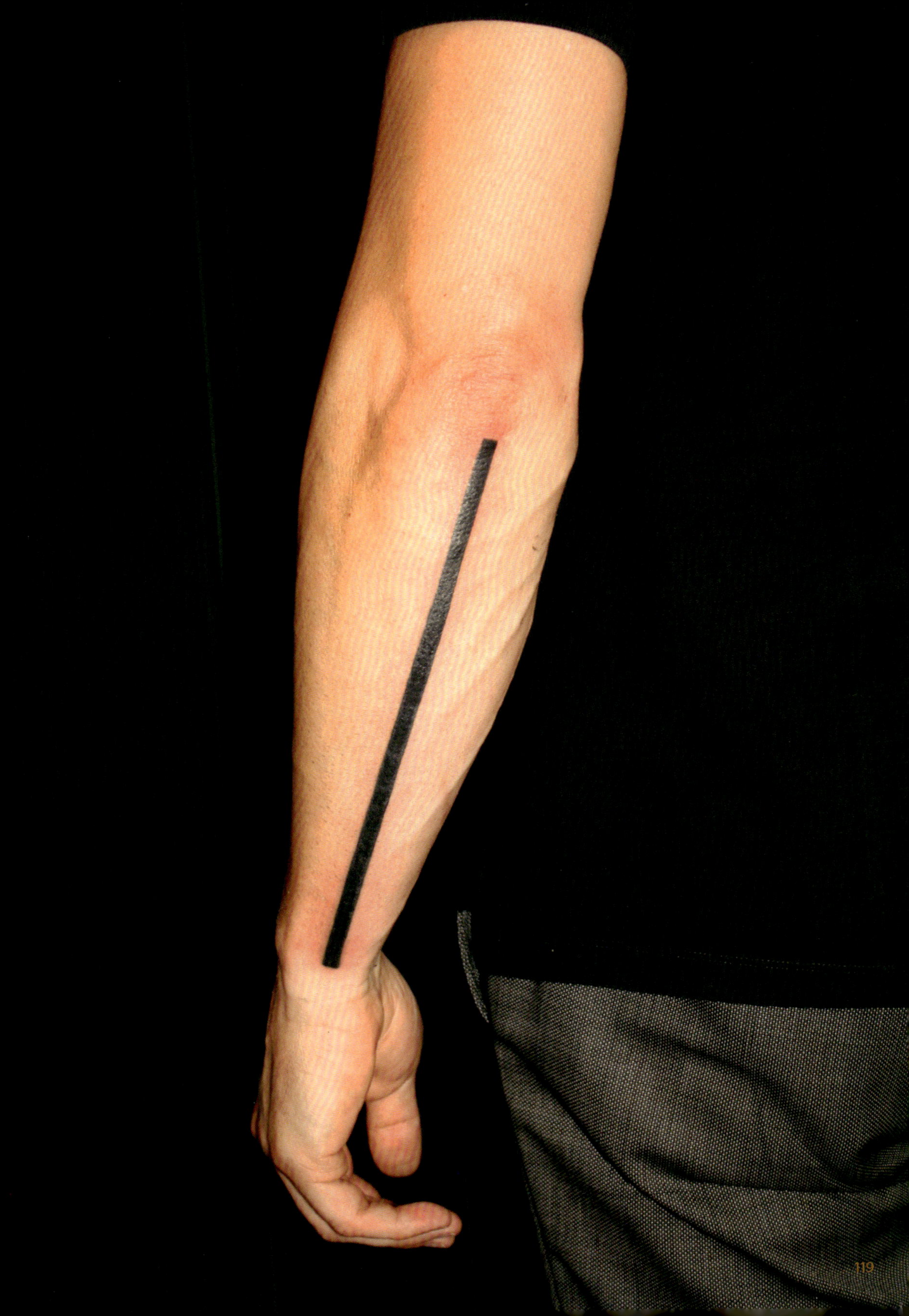

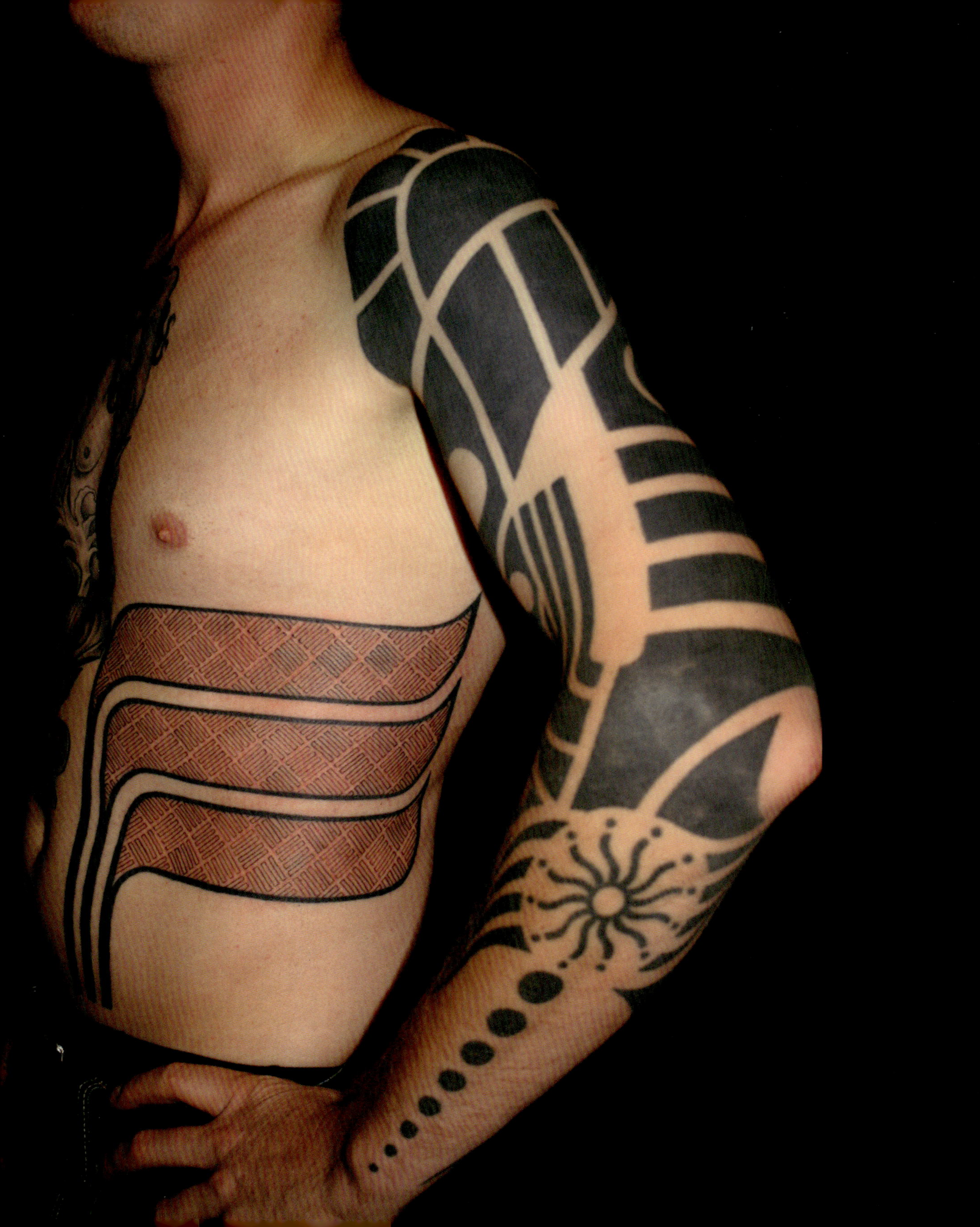

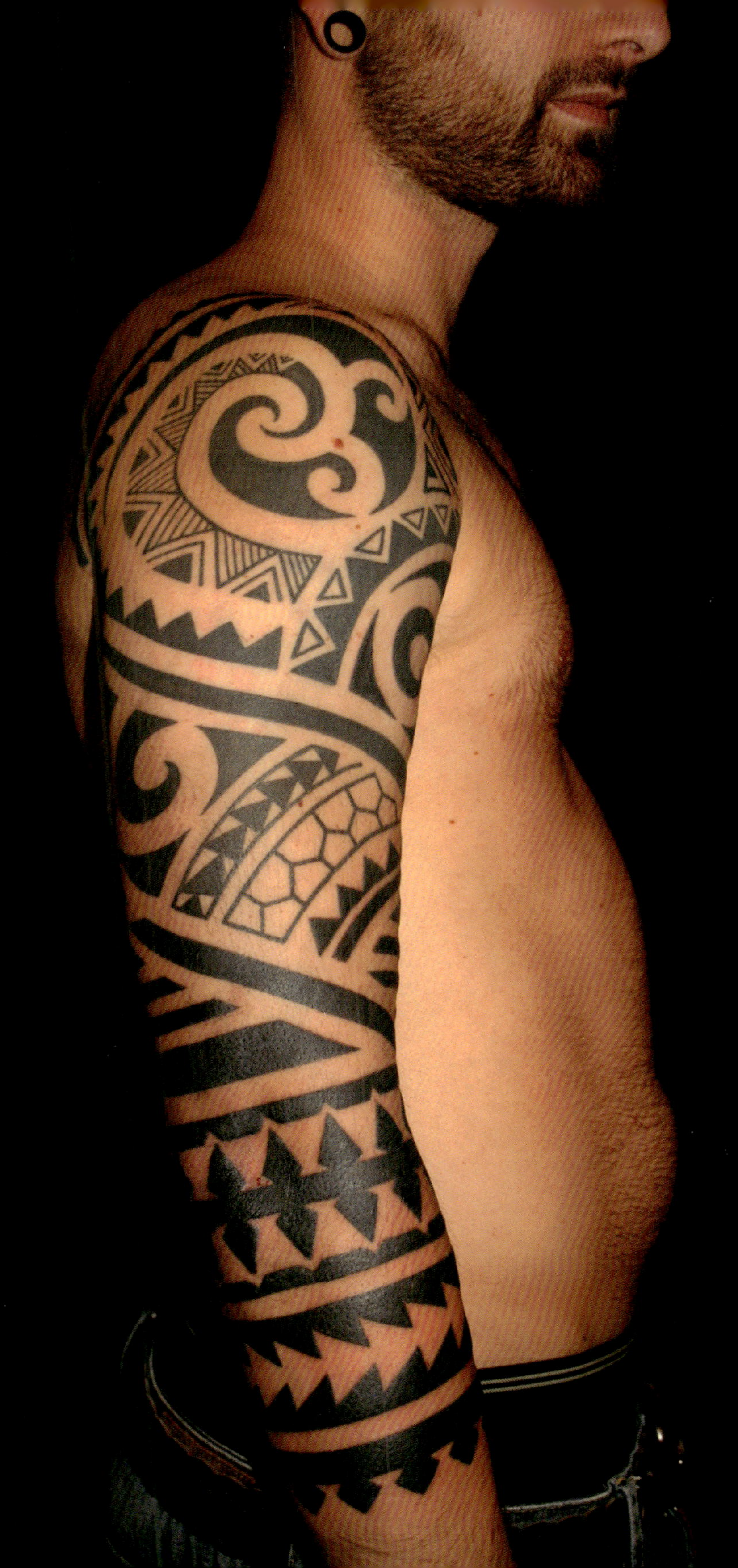

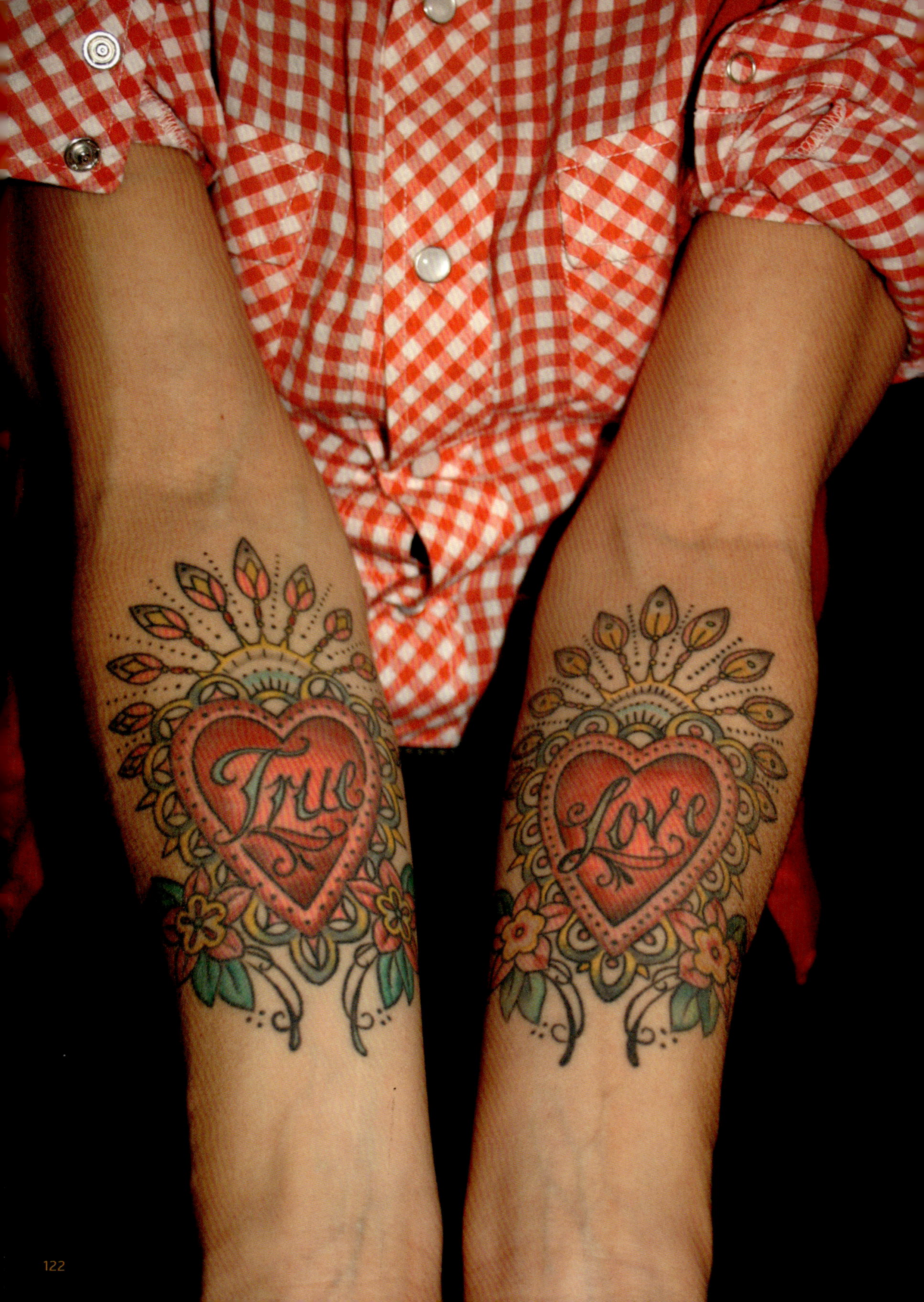
True
Love

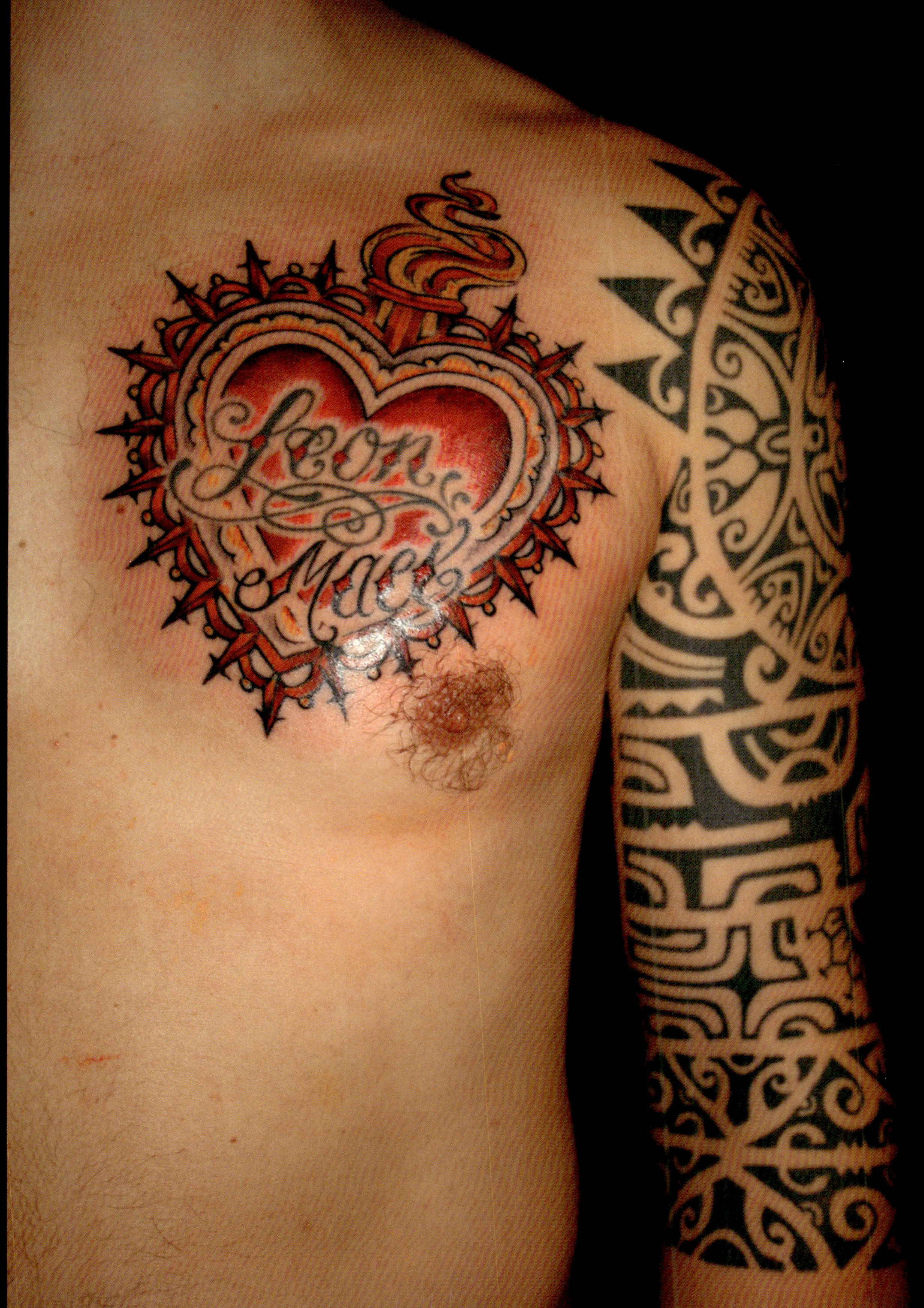

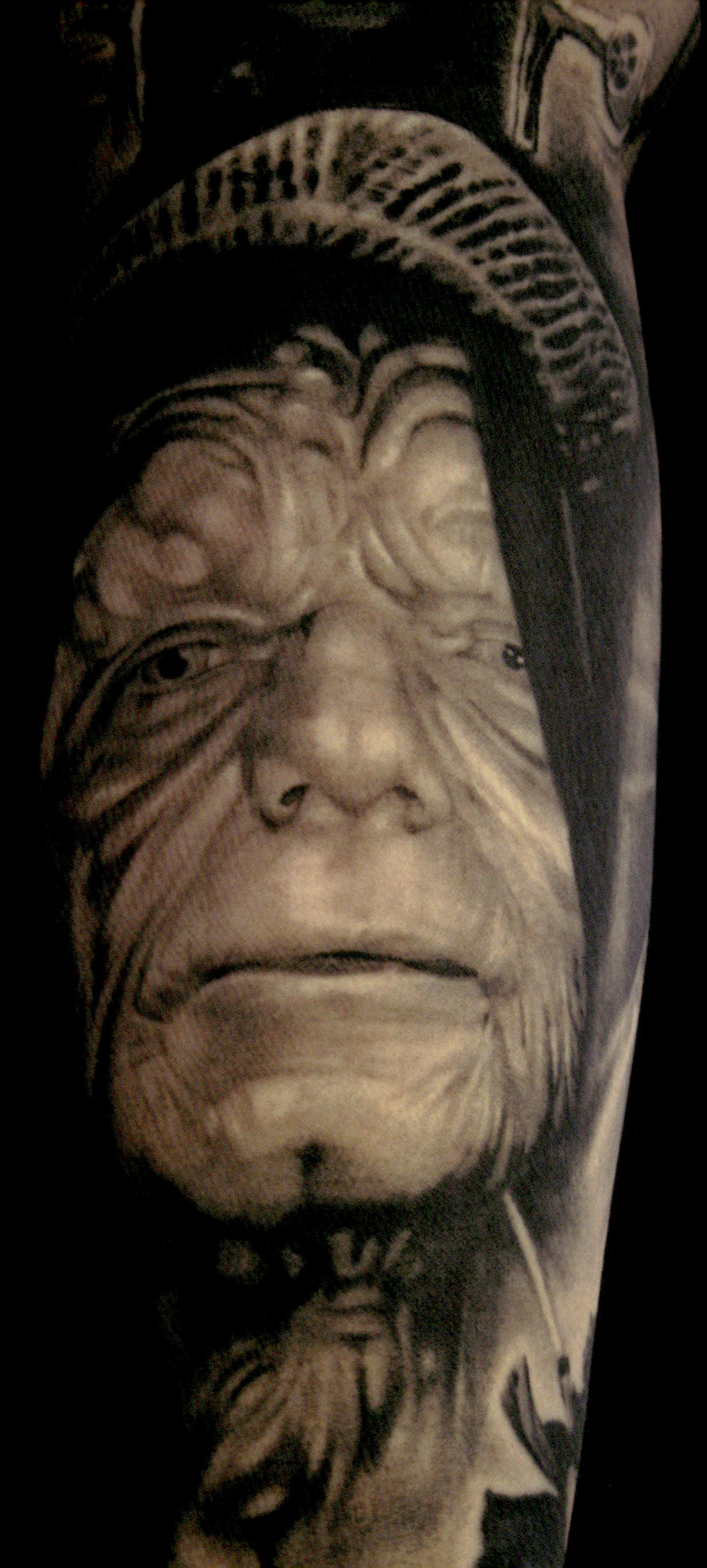

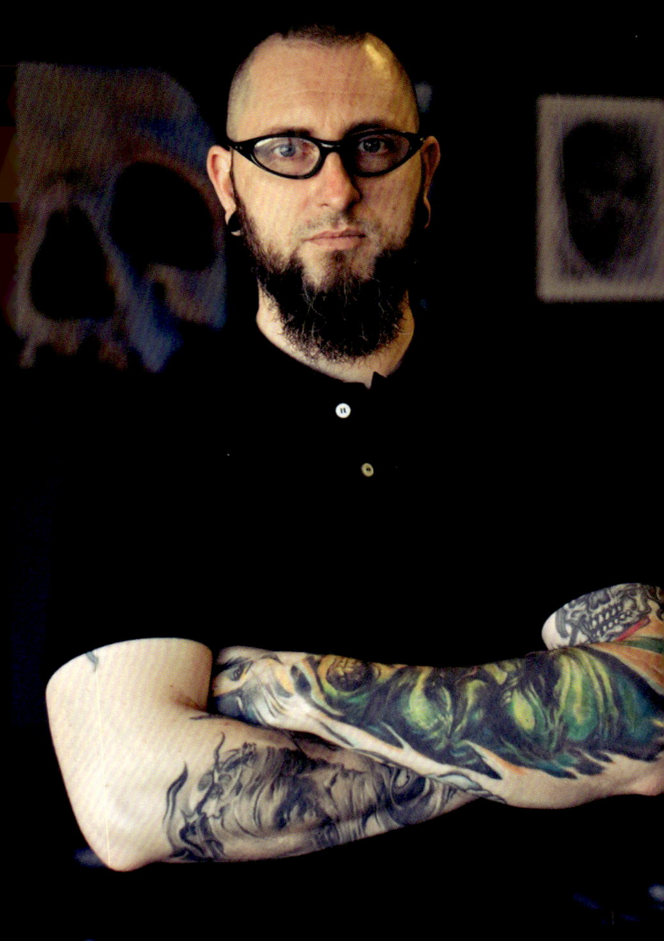

JASON BUTCHER
IMMORTAL INK

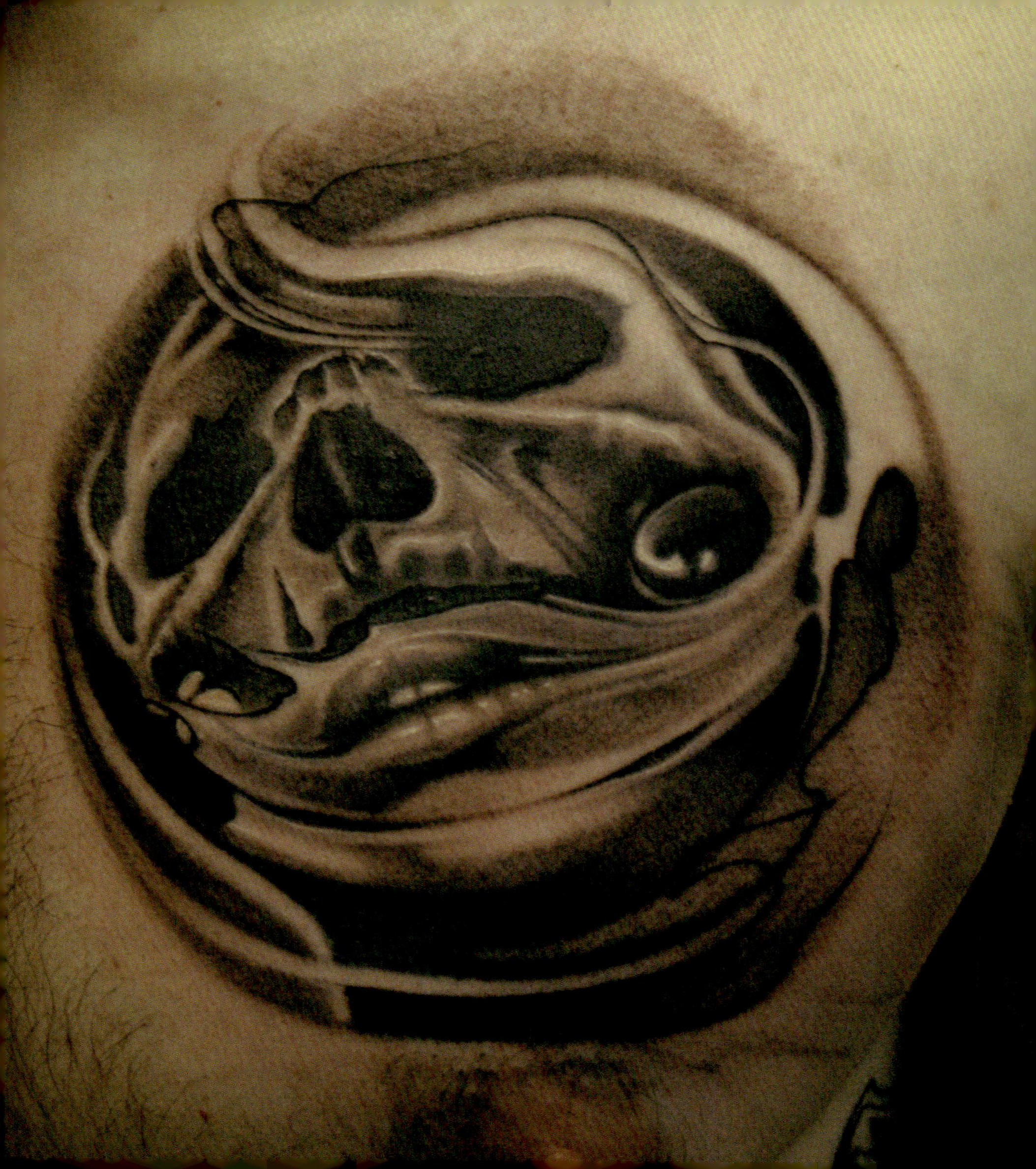

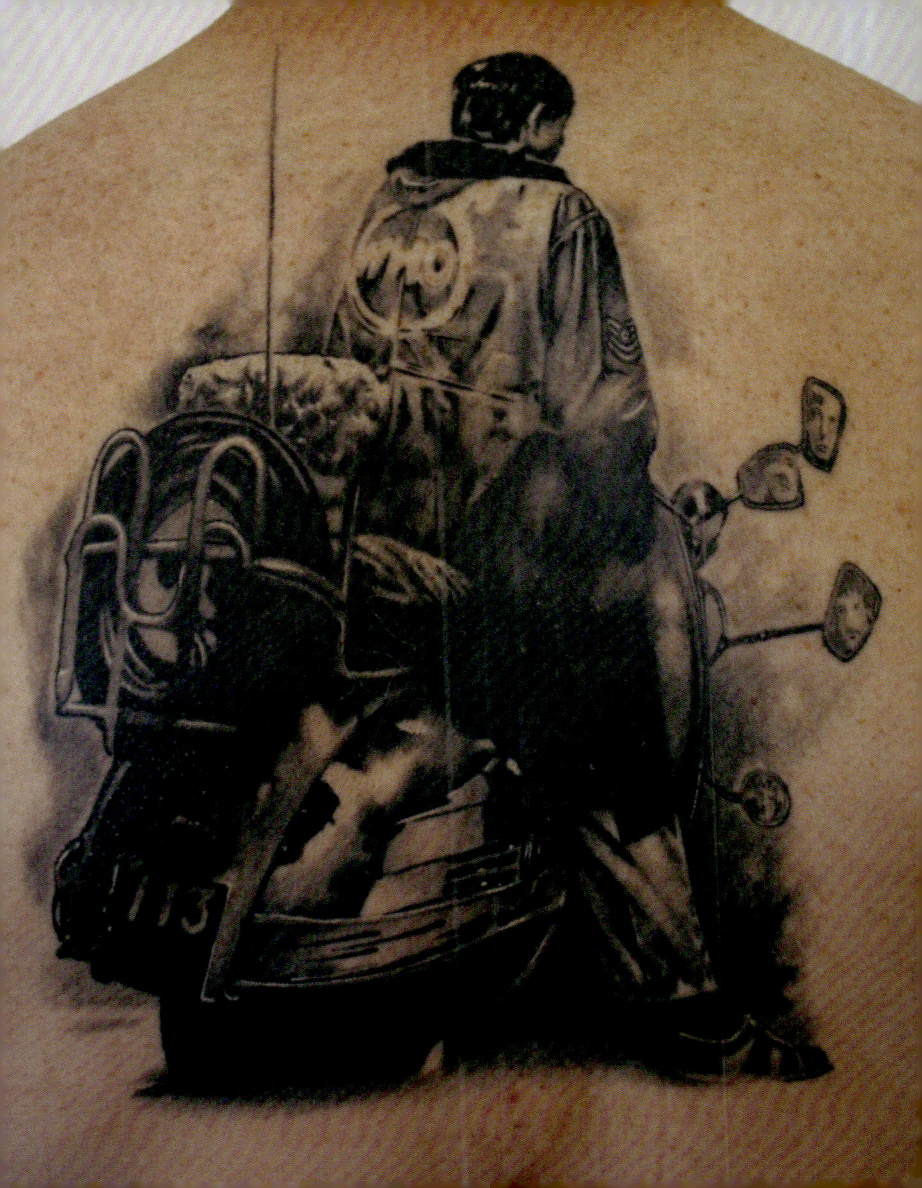

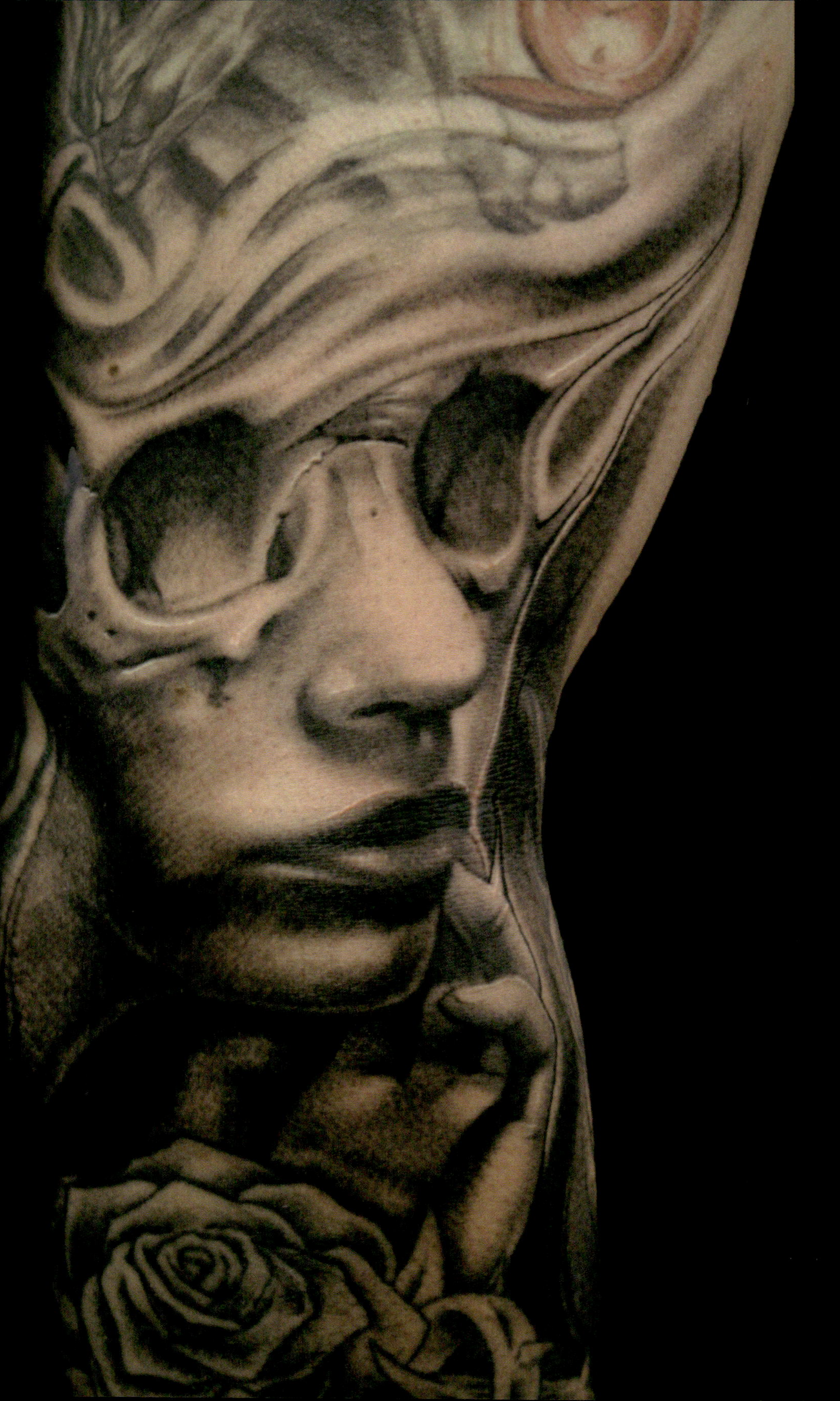

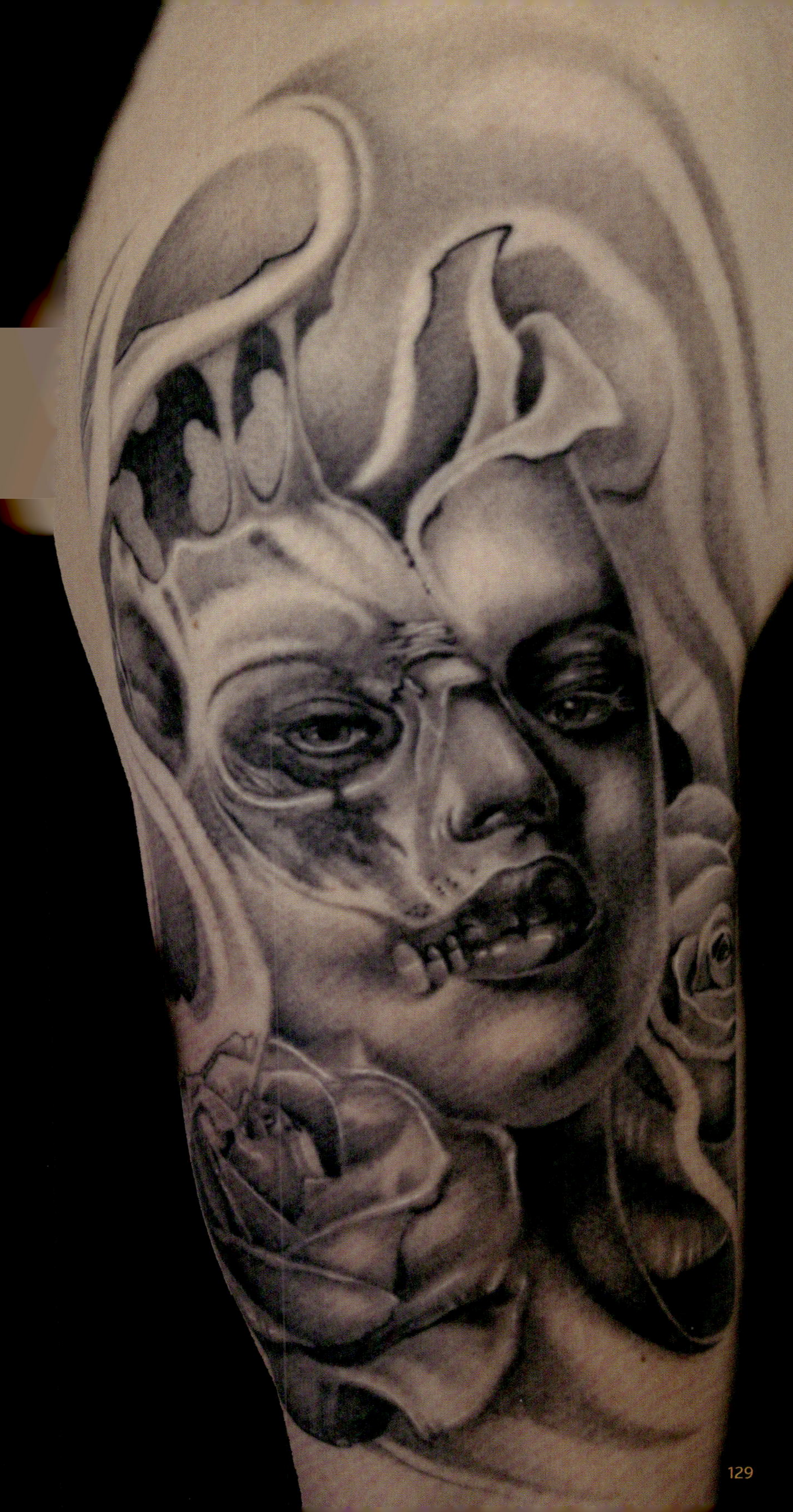

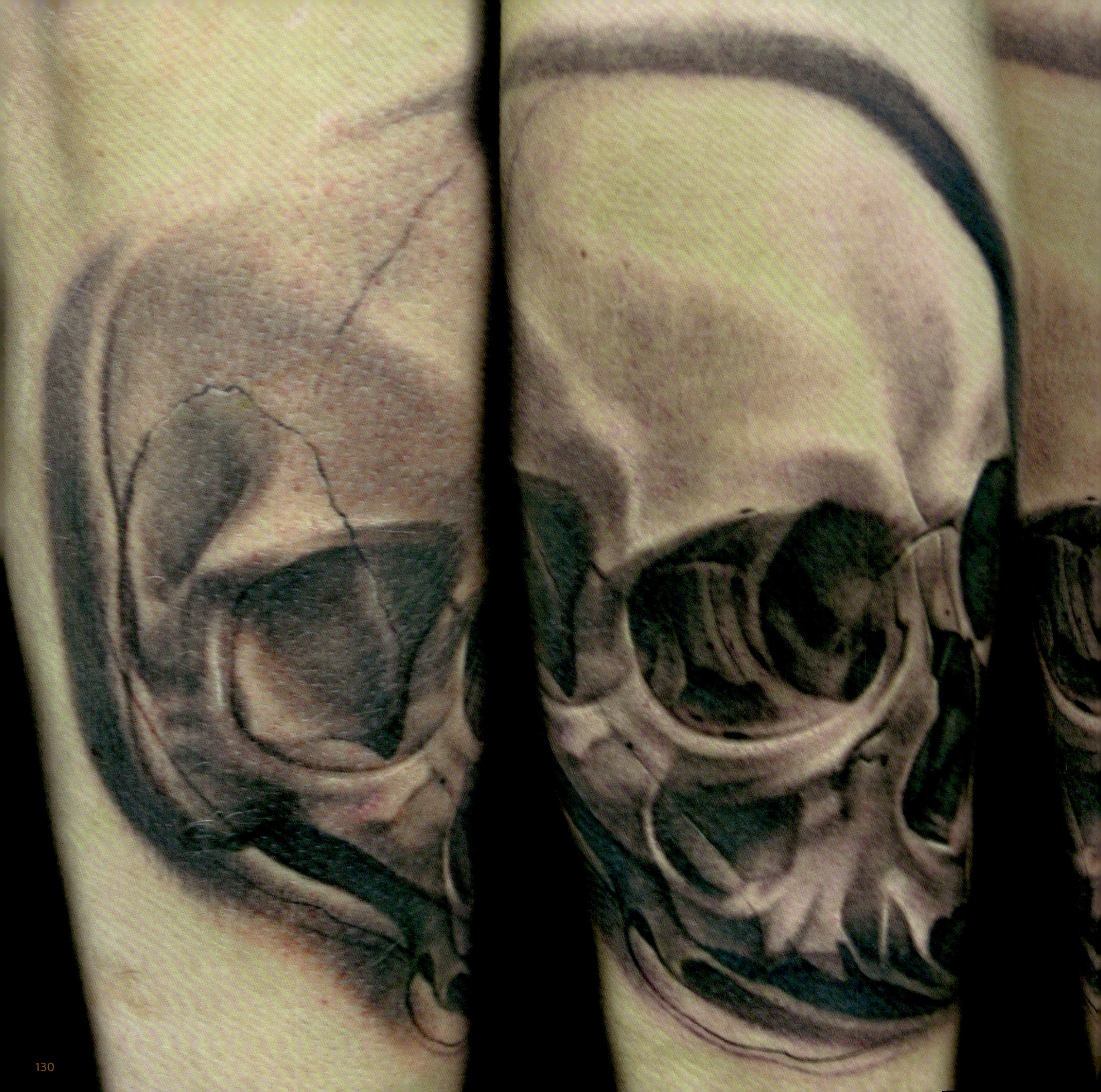

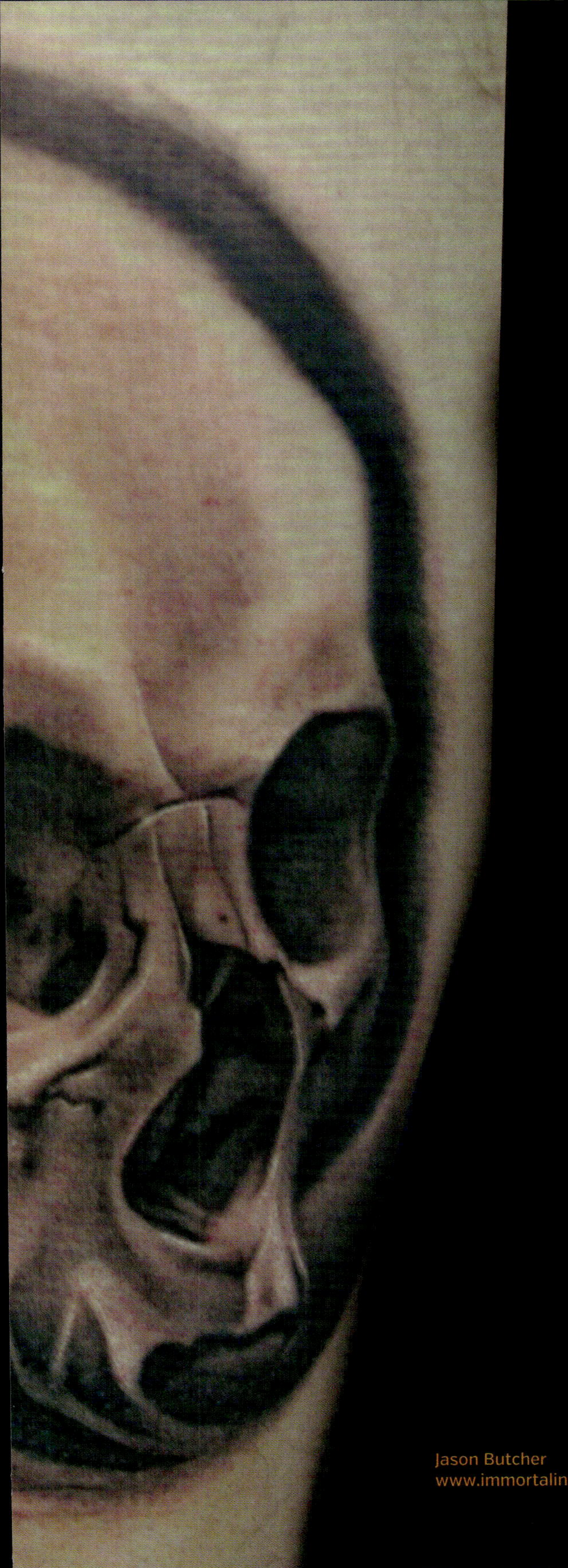
Jason Butcher
www.immortalin

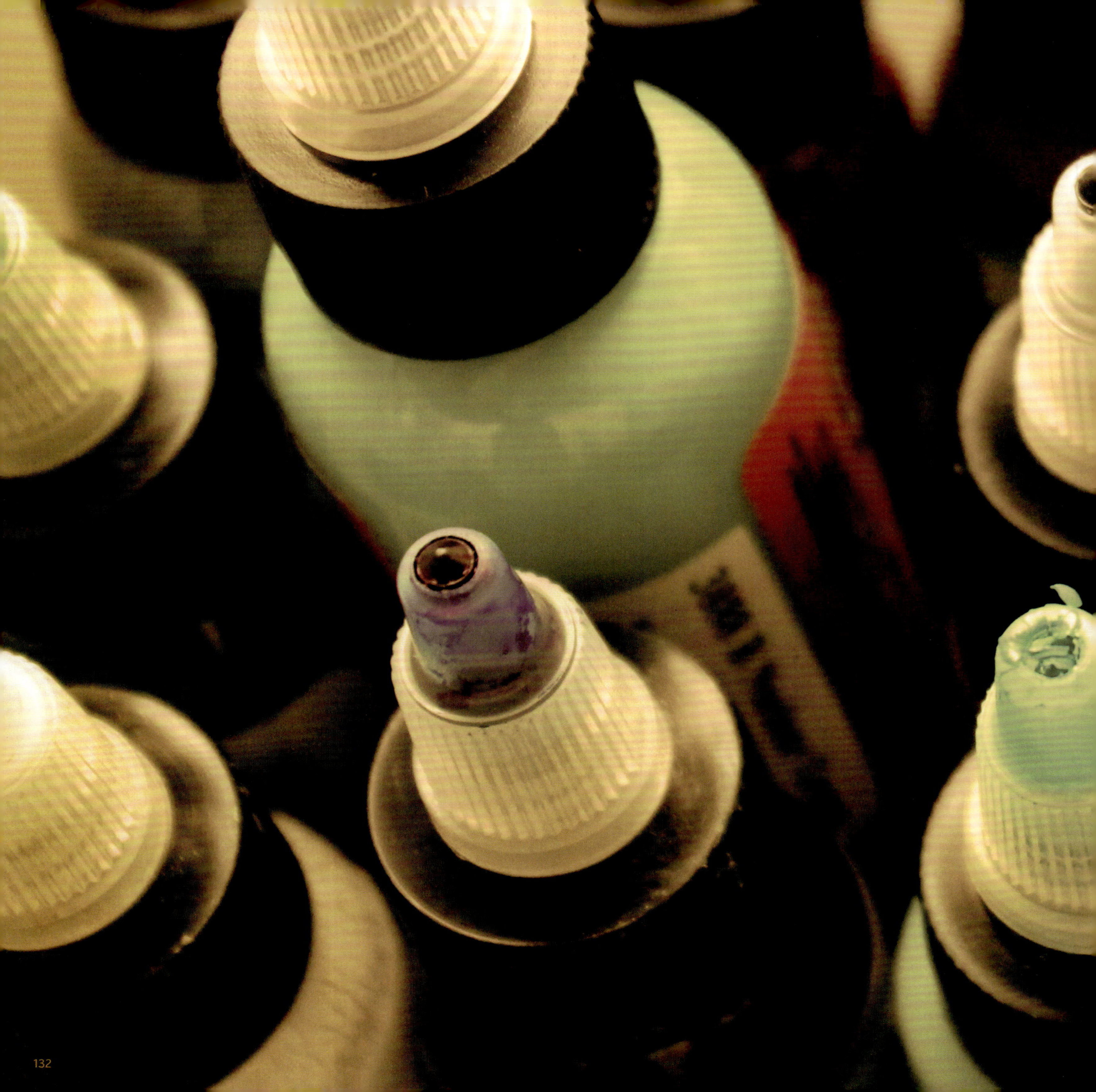

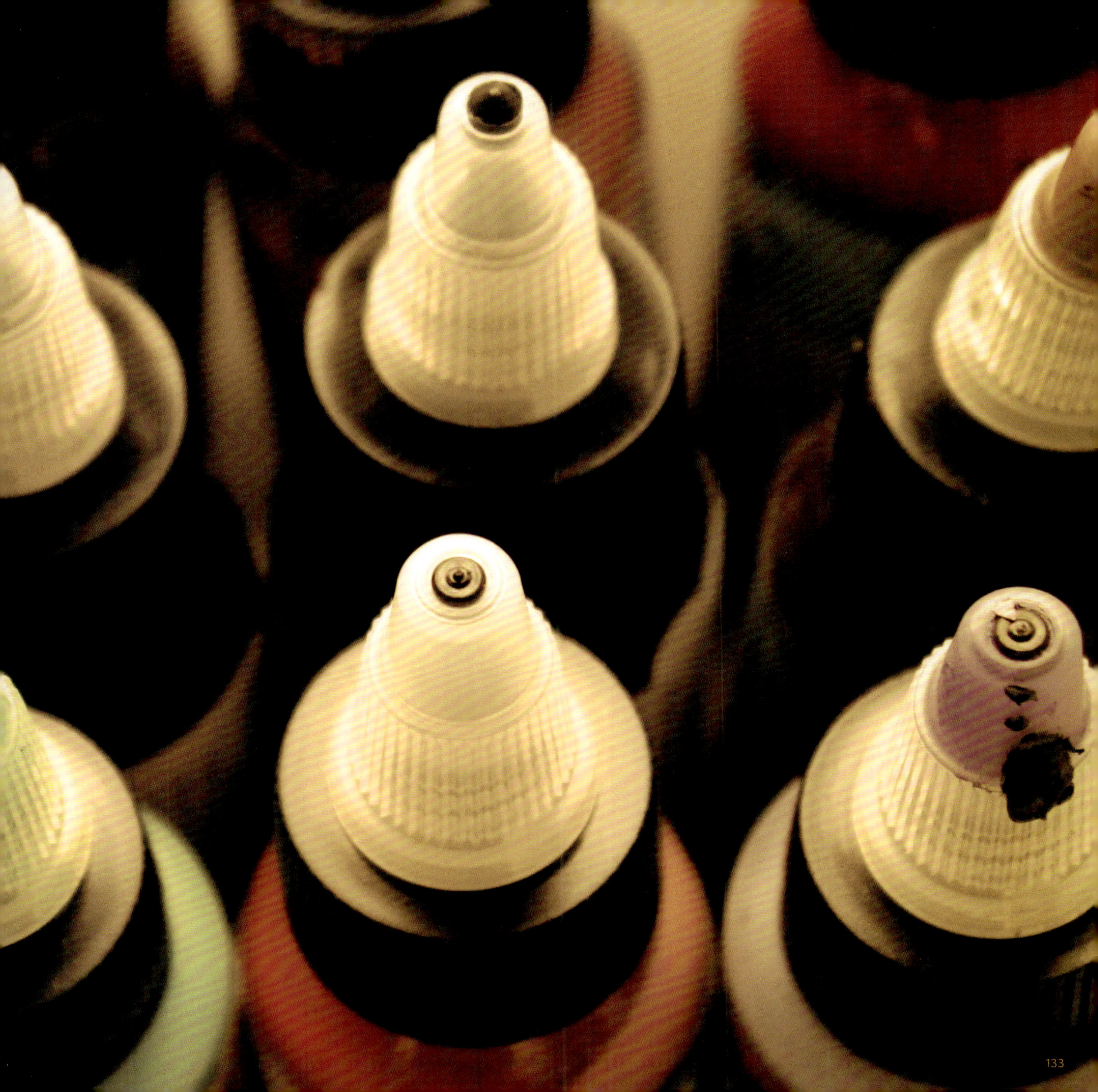

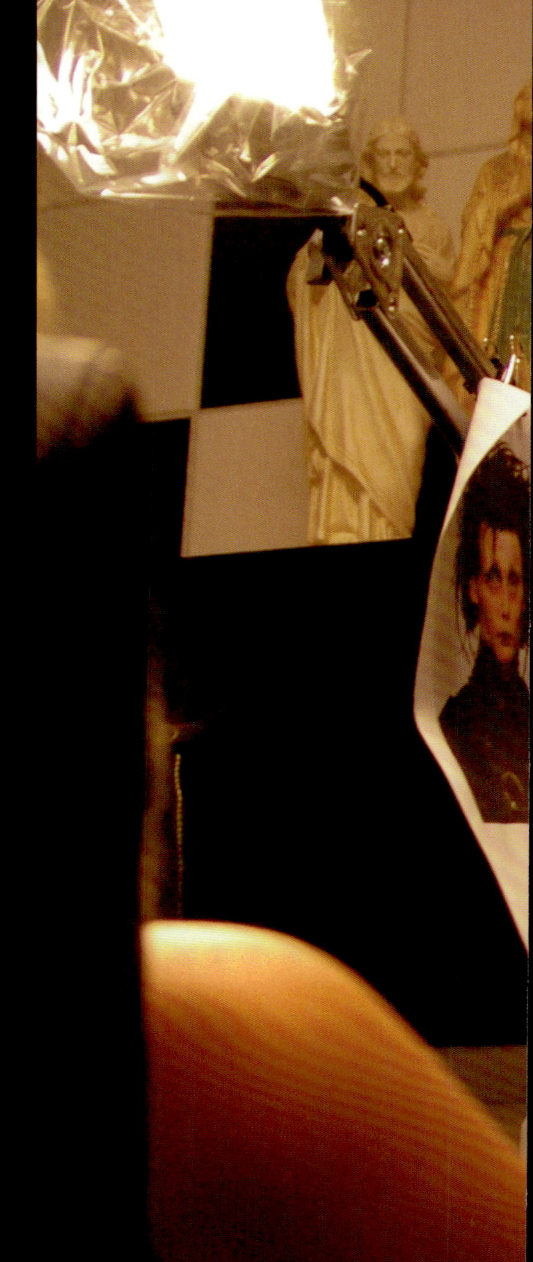

ENS BERGSTRÖM

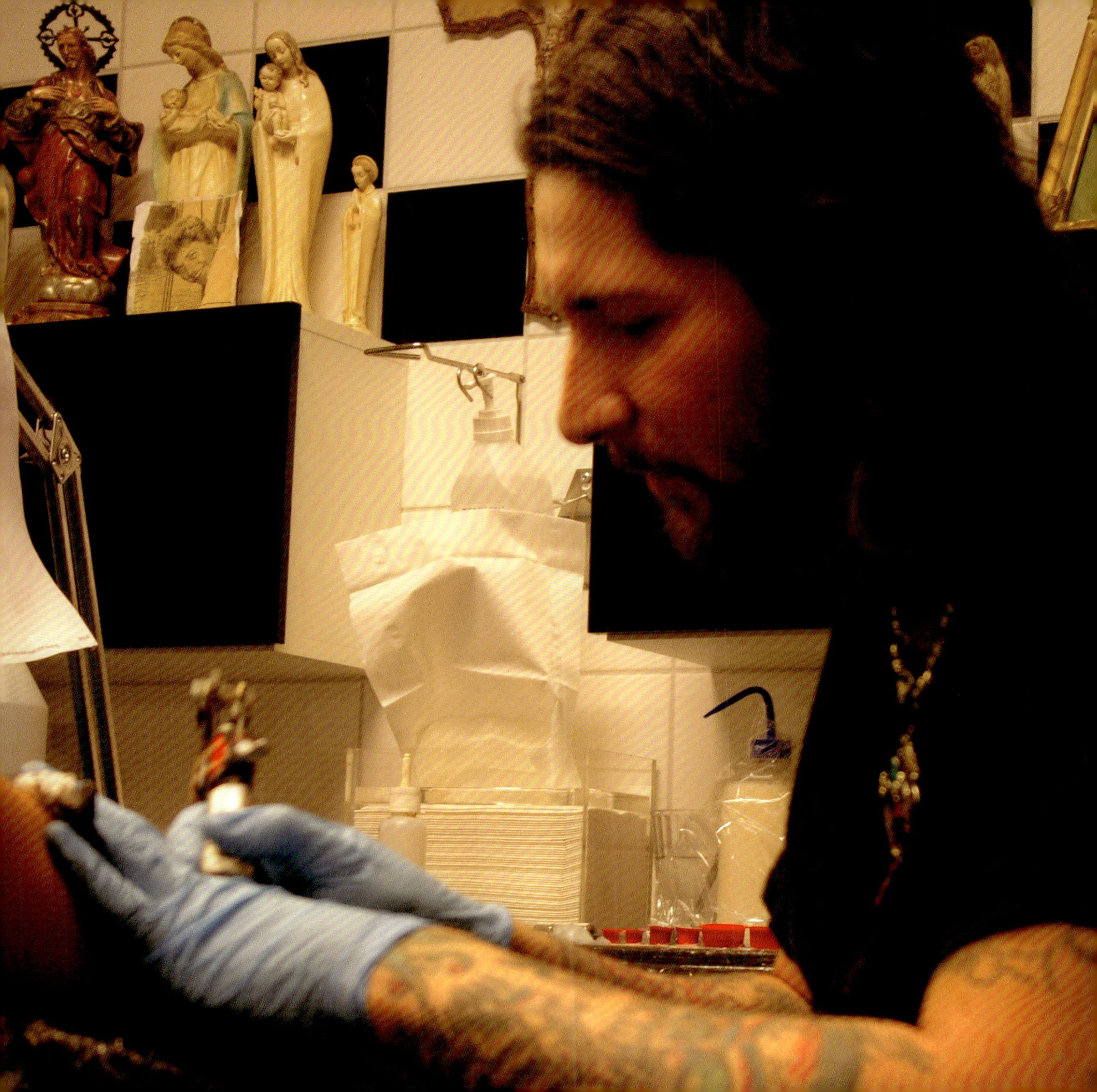

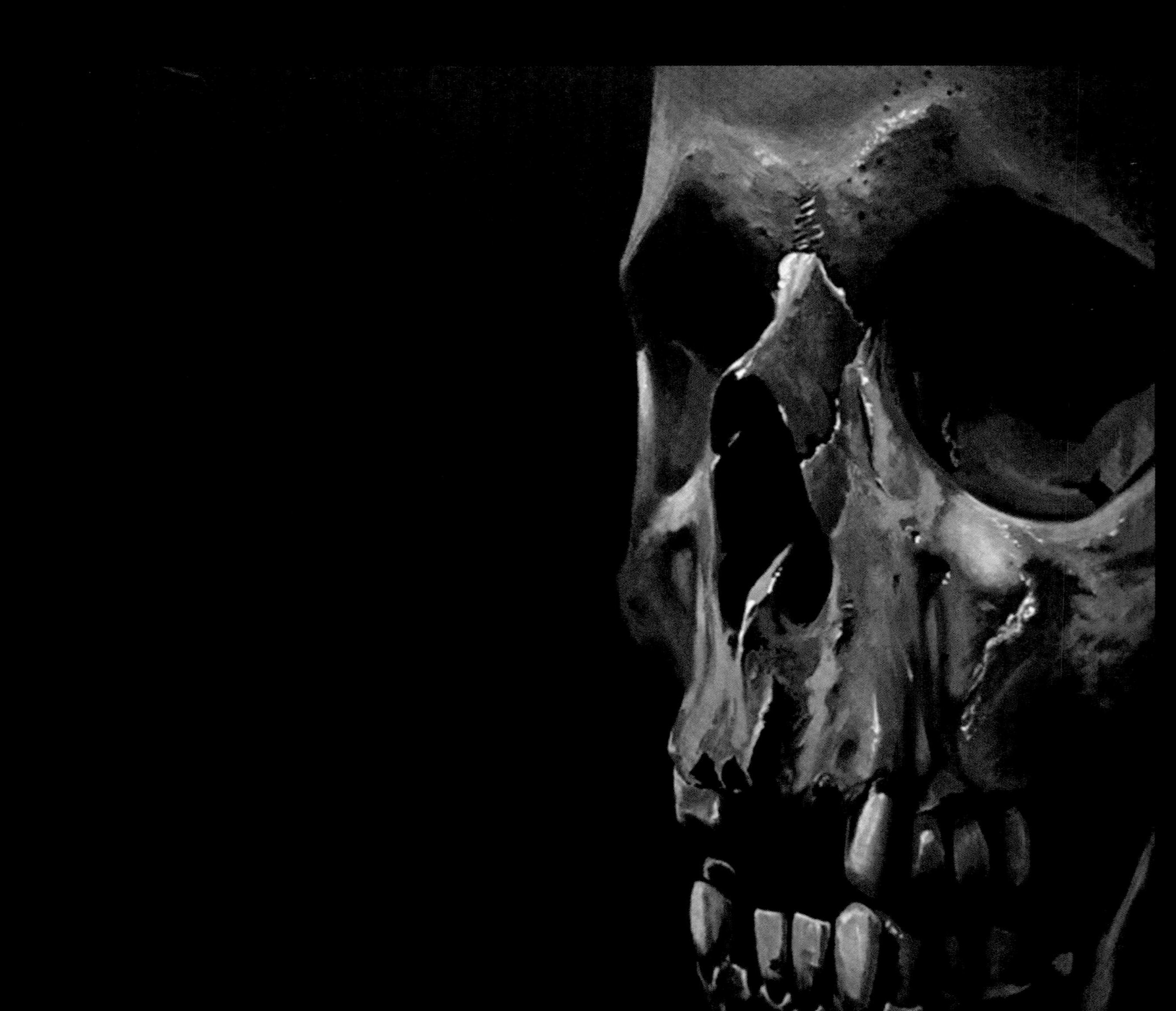

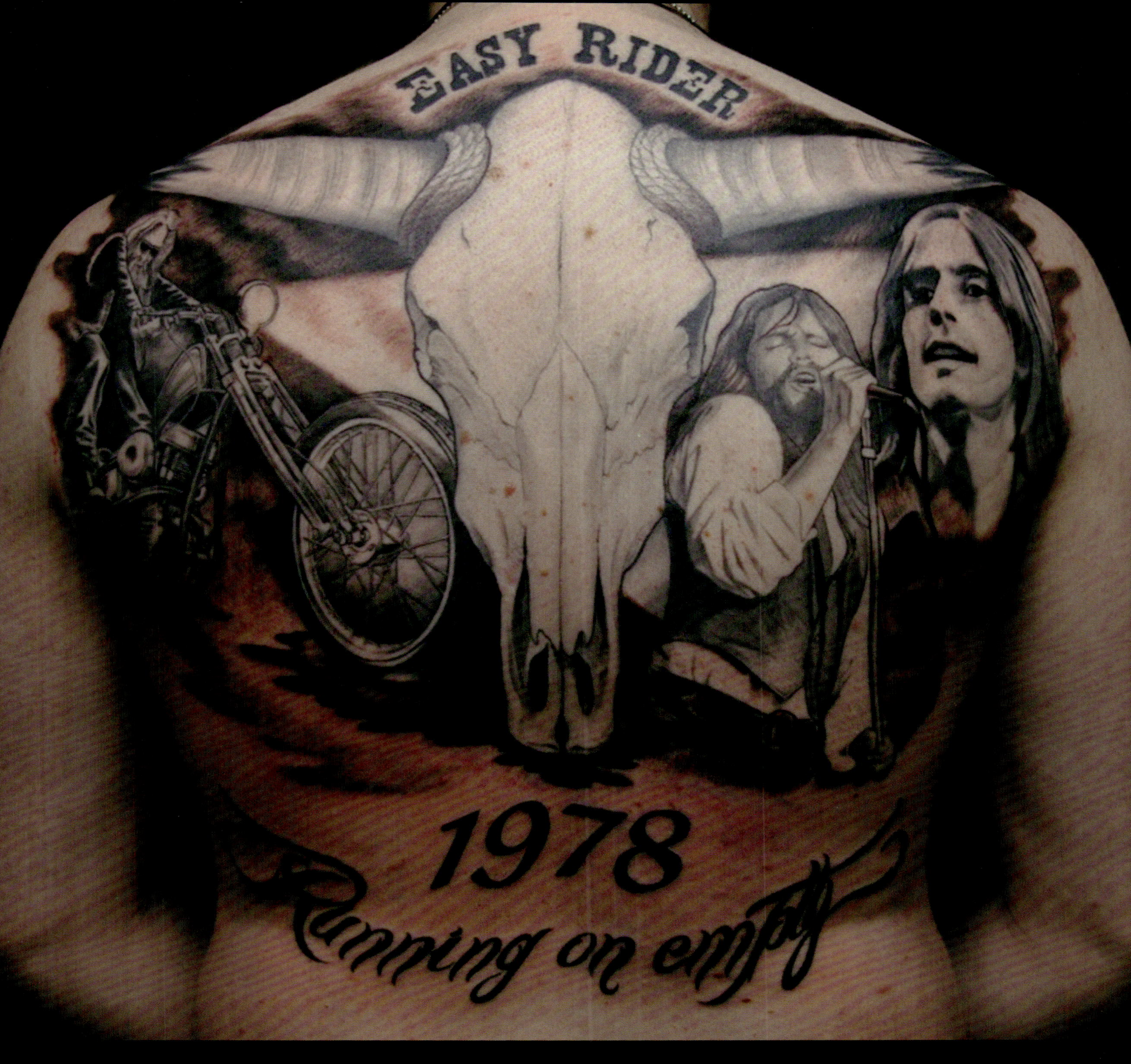
EASY RIDER
1978
Running on empty

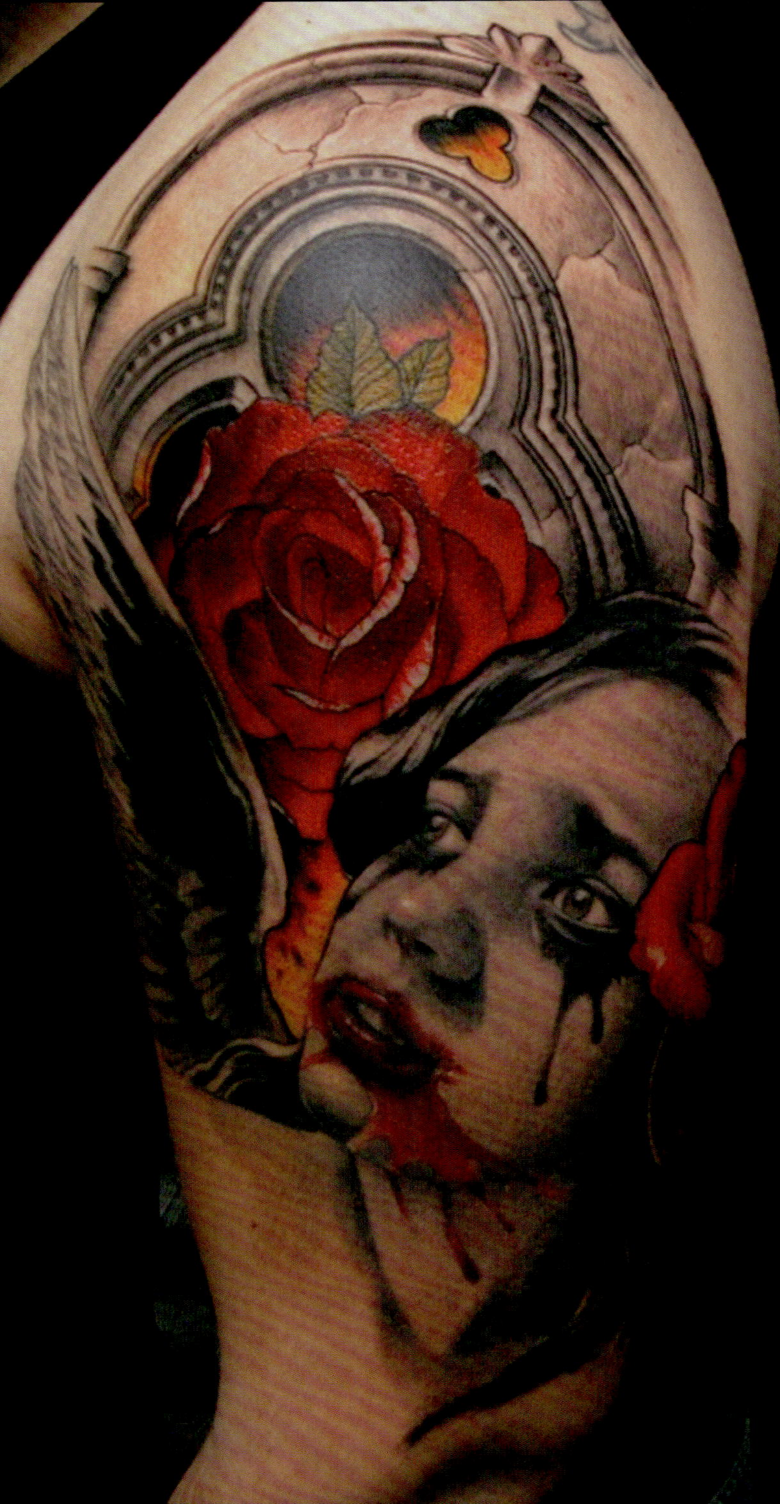

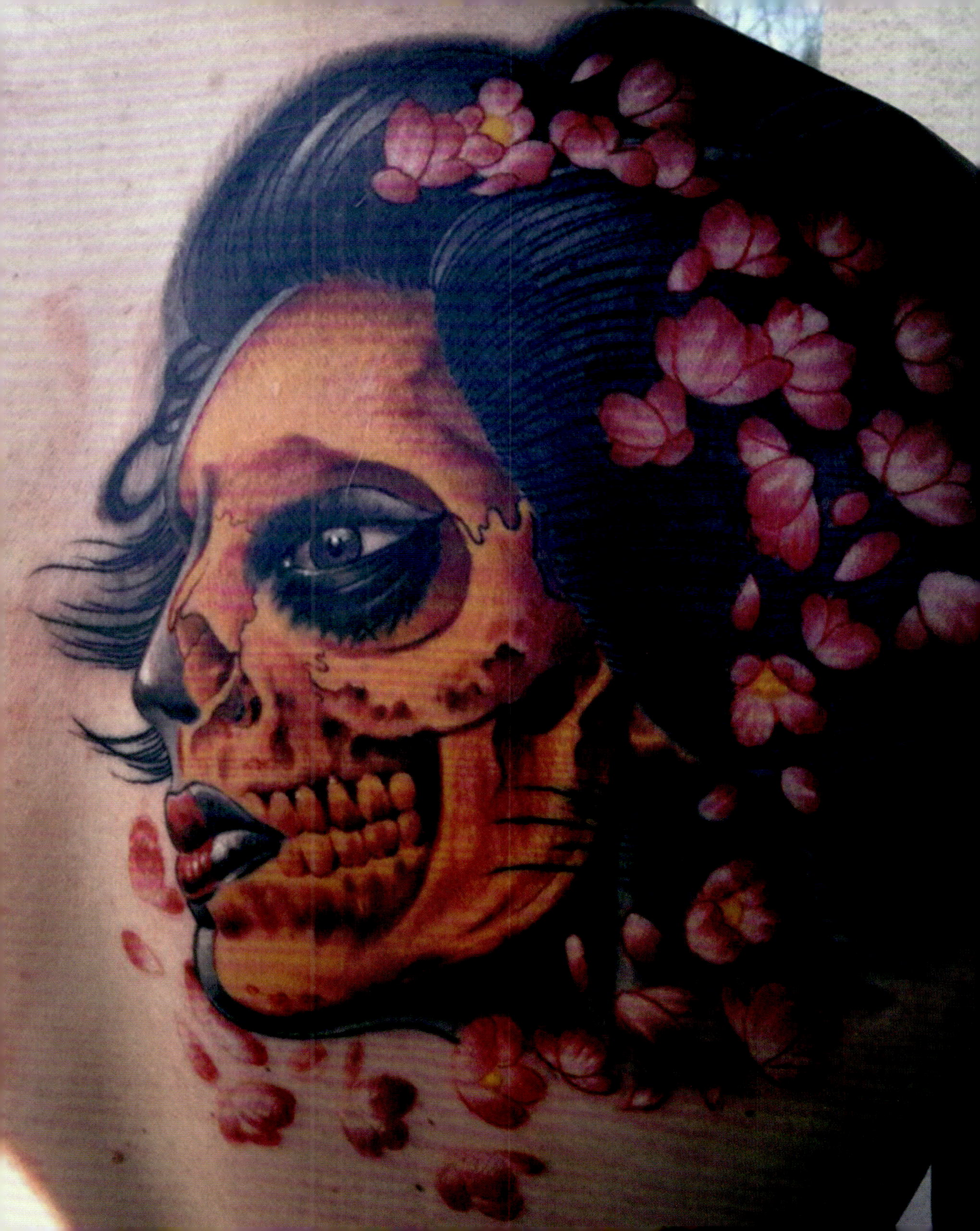

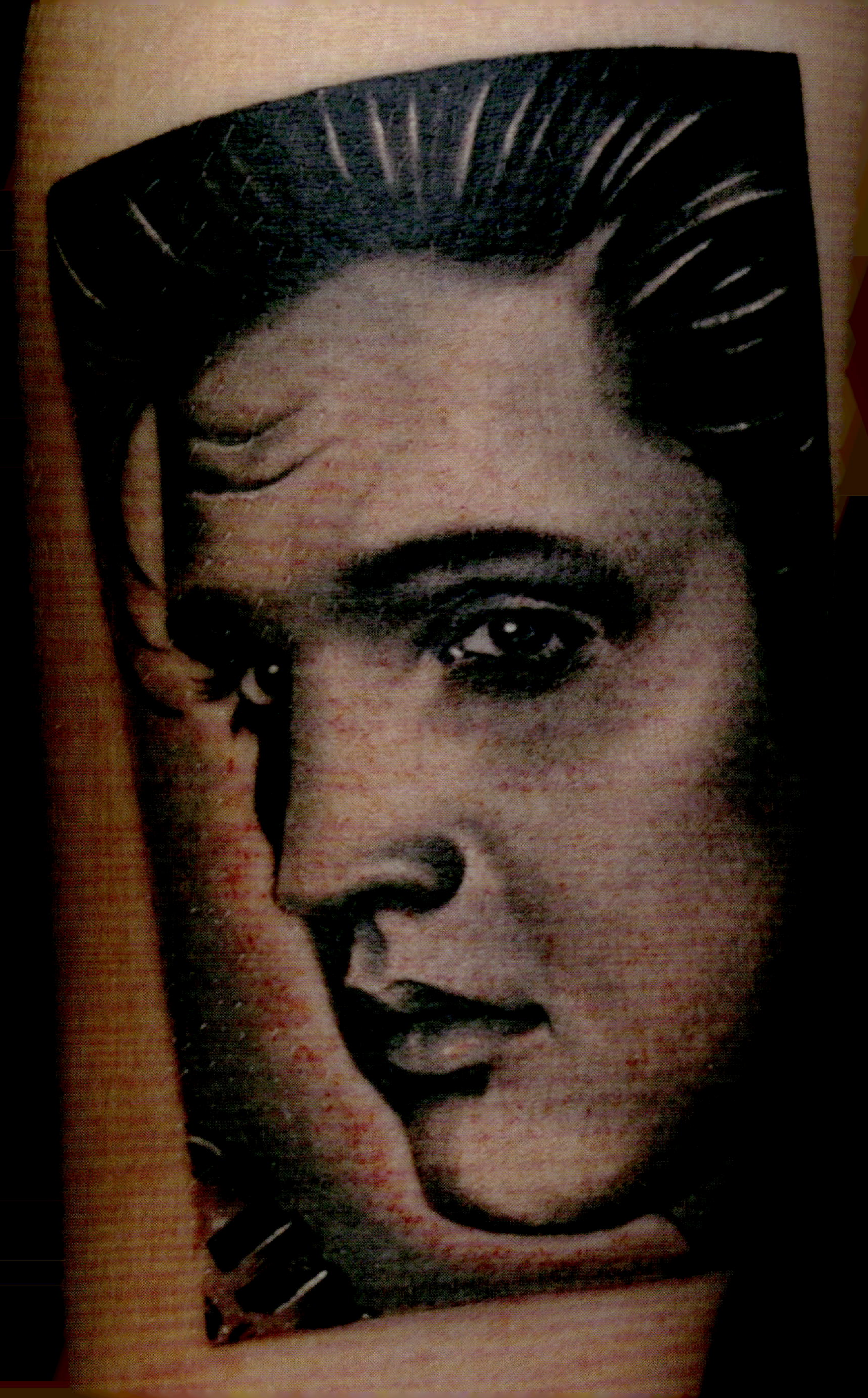

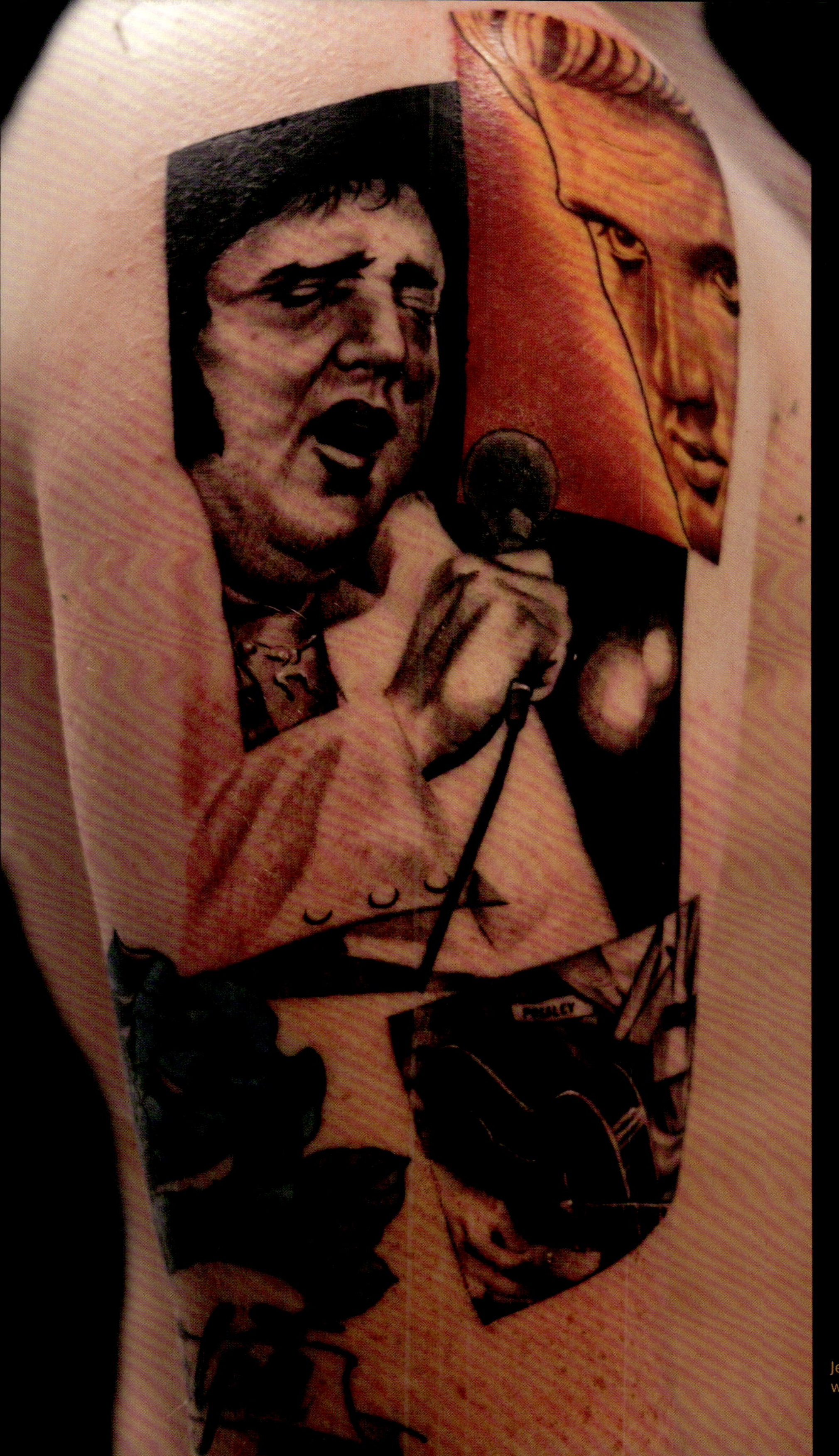

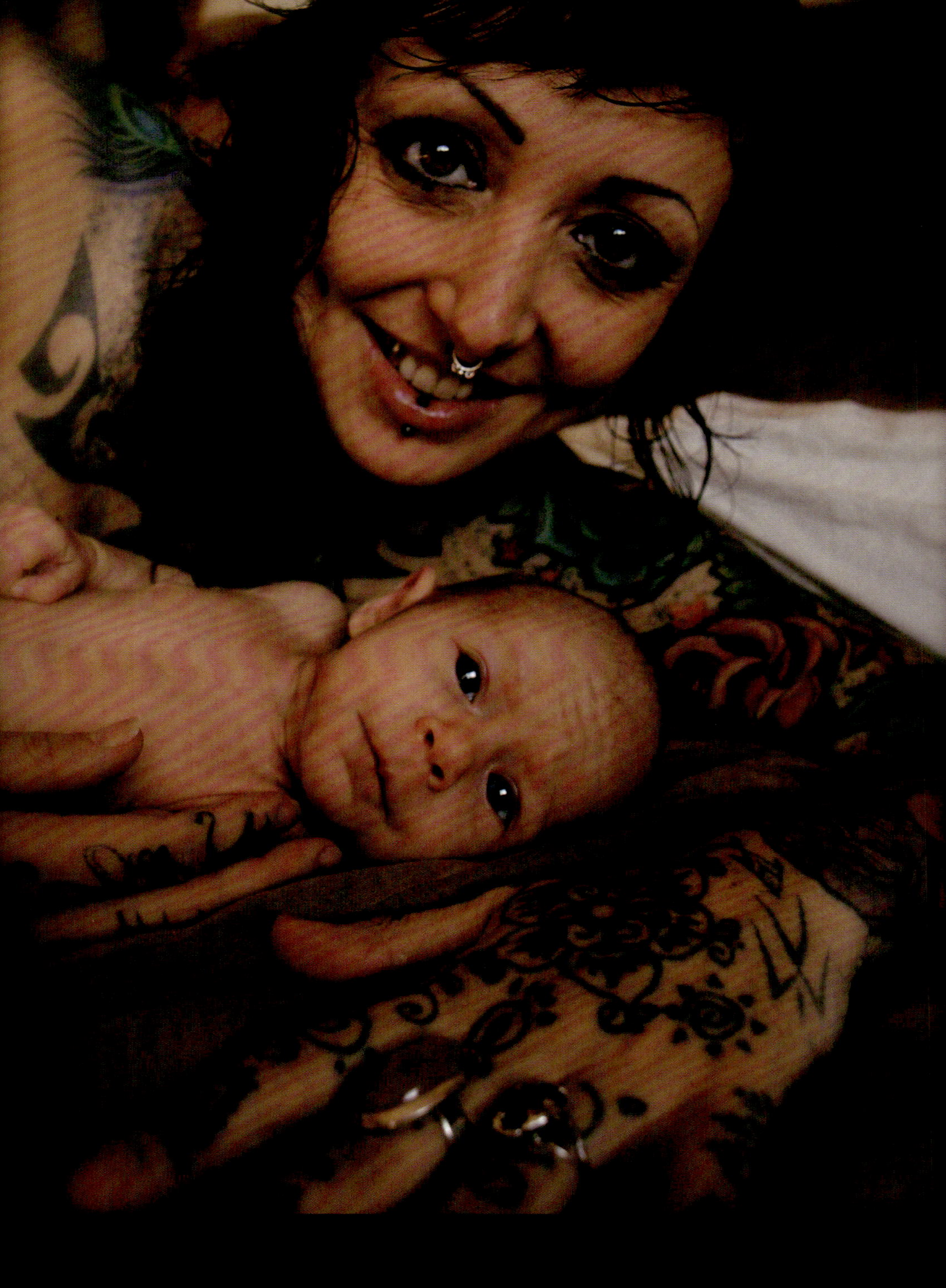

JO HARRISON

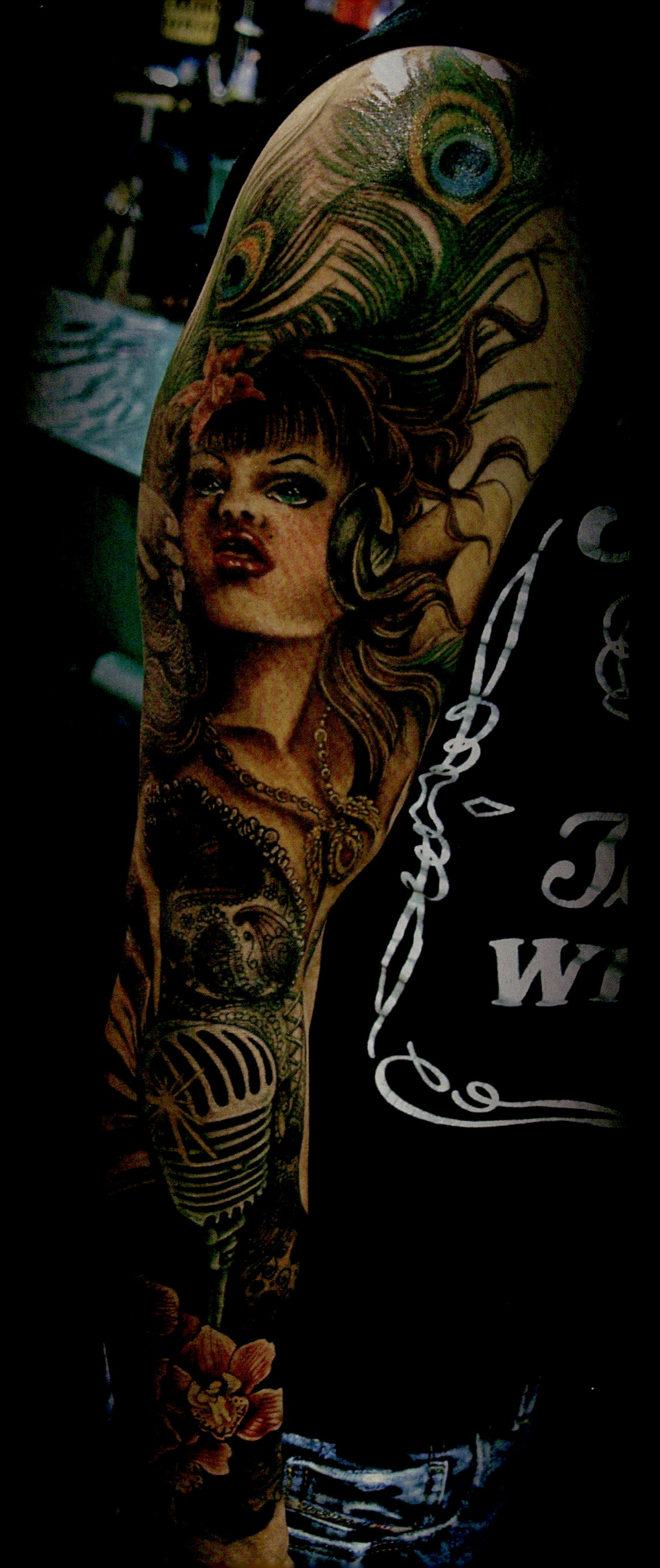

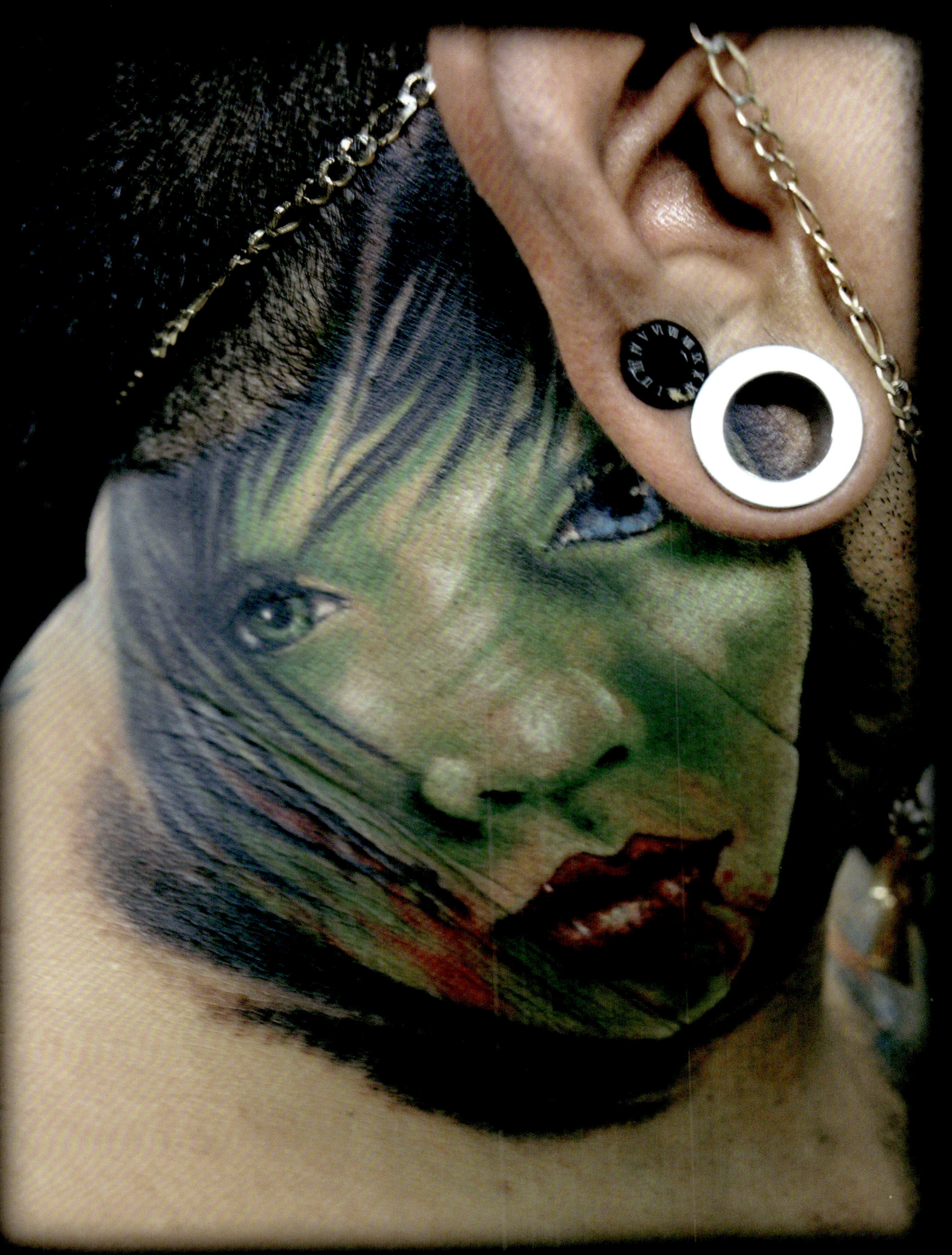

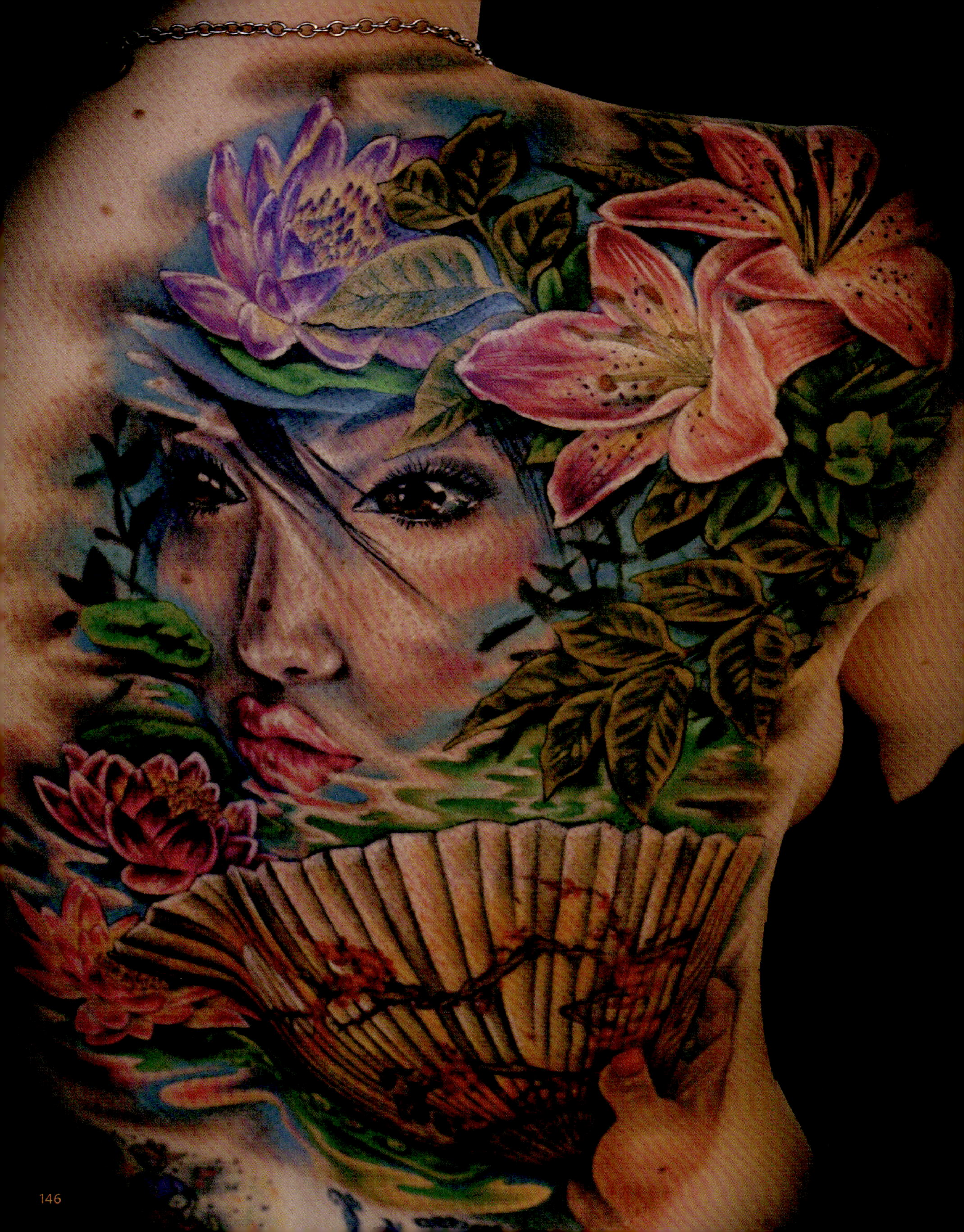

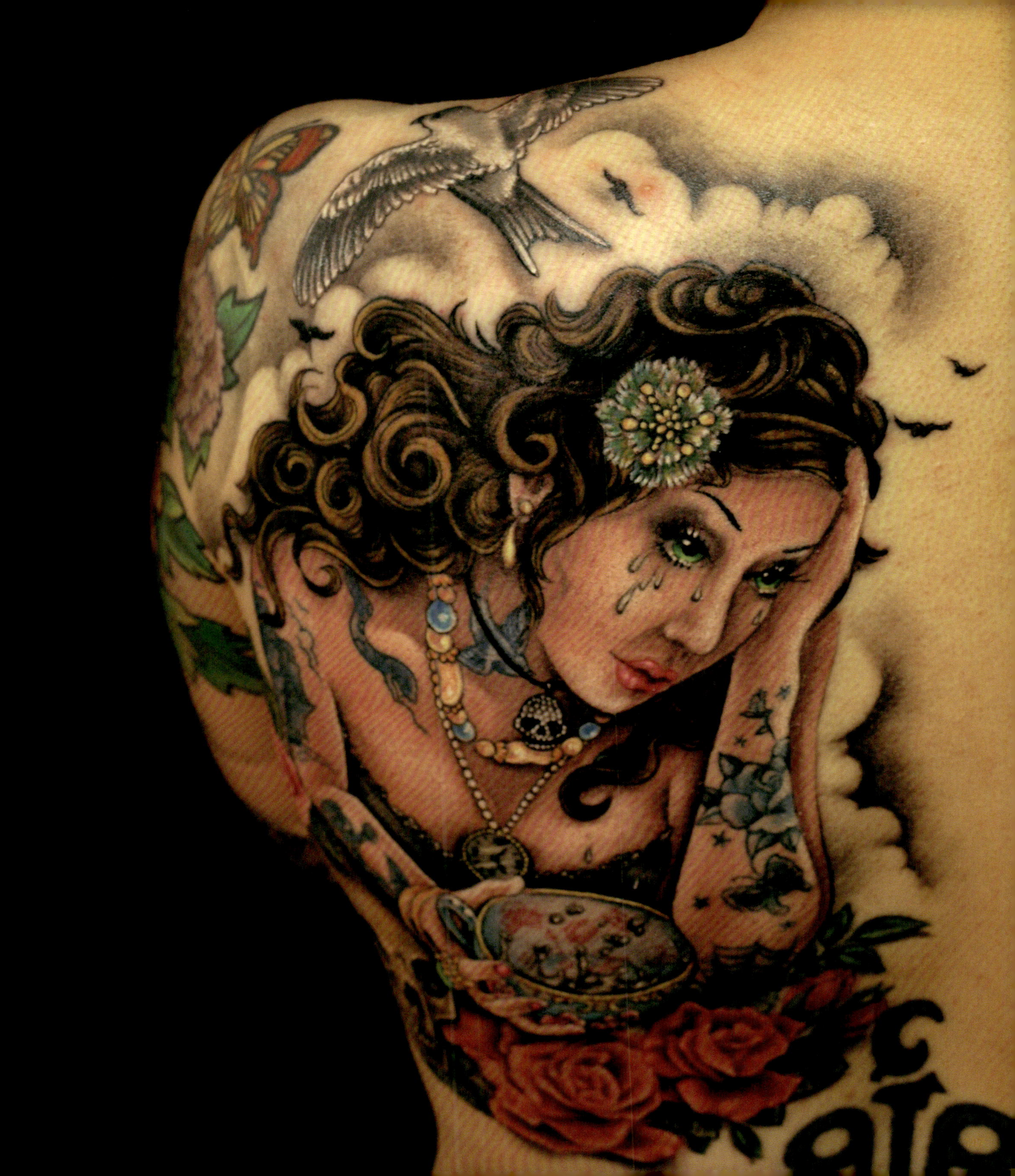

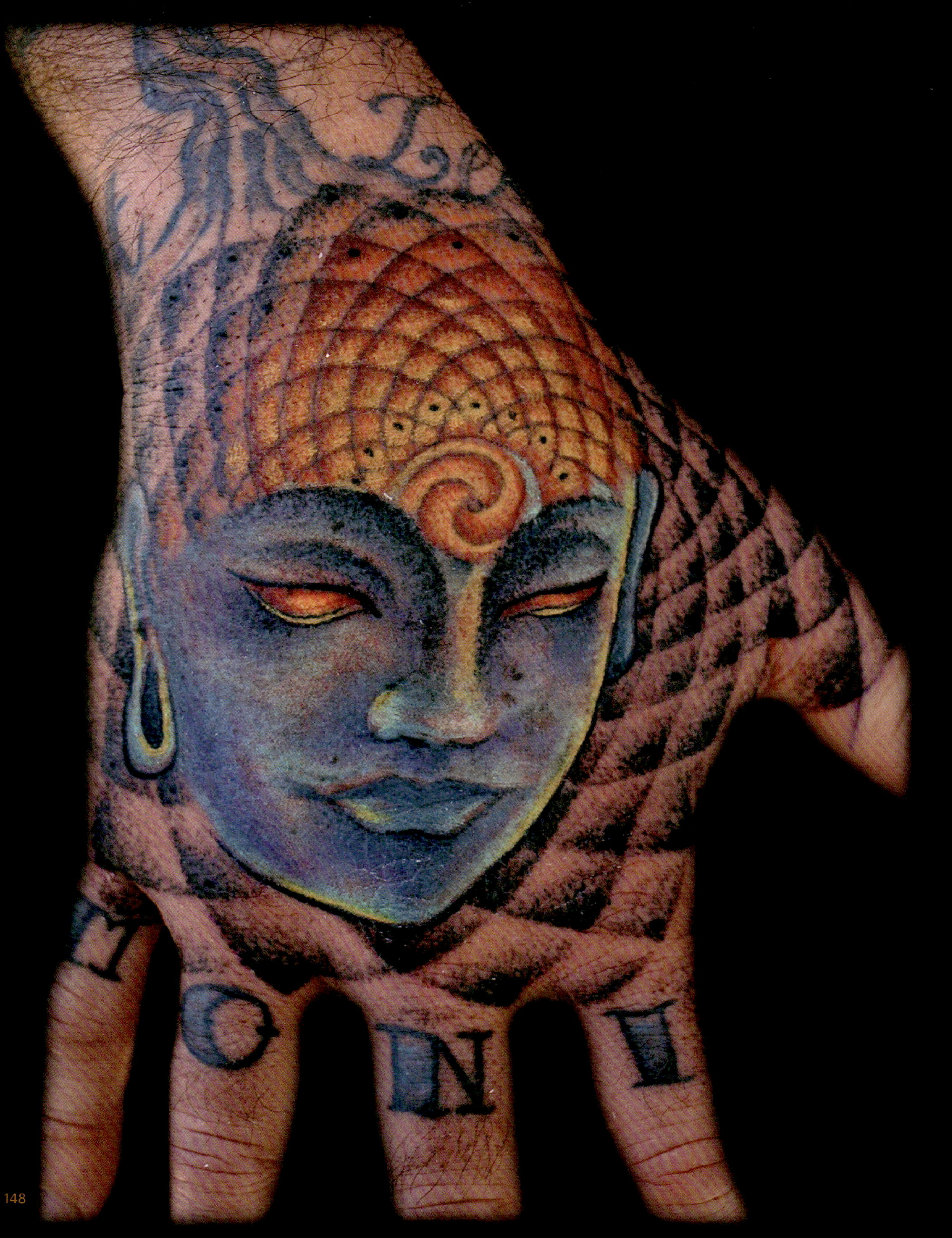

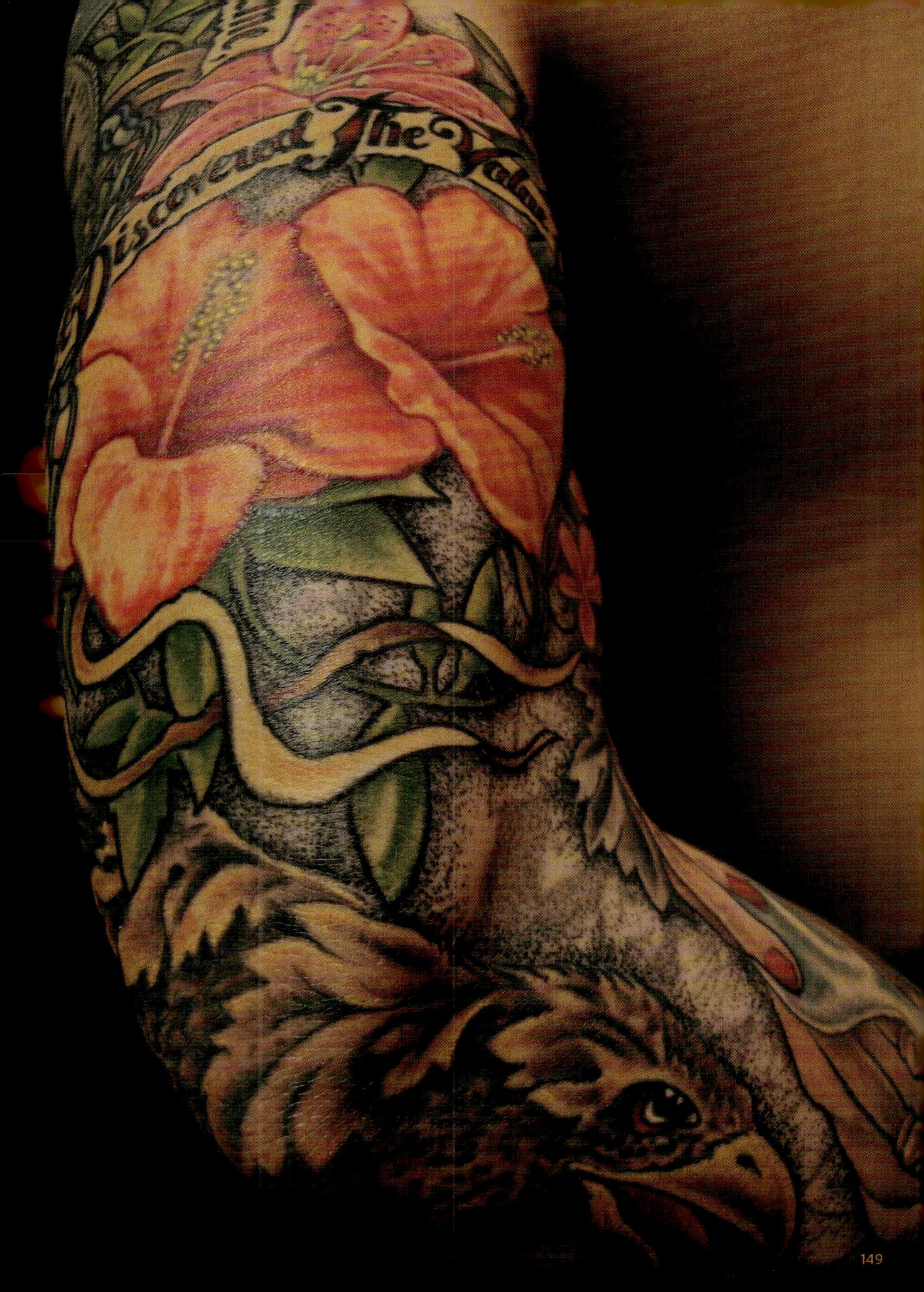

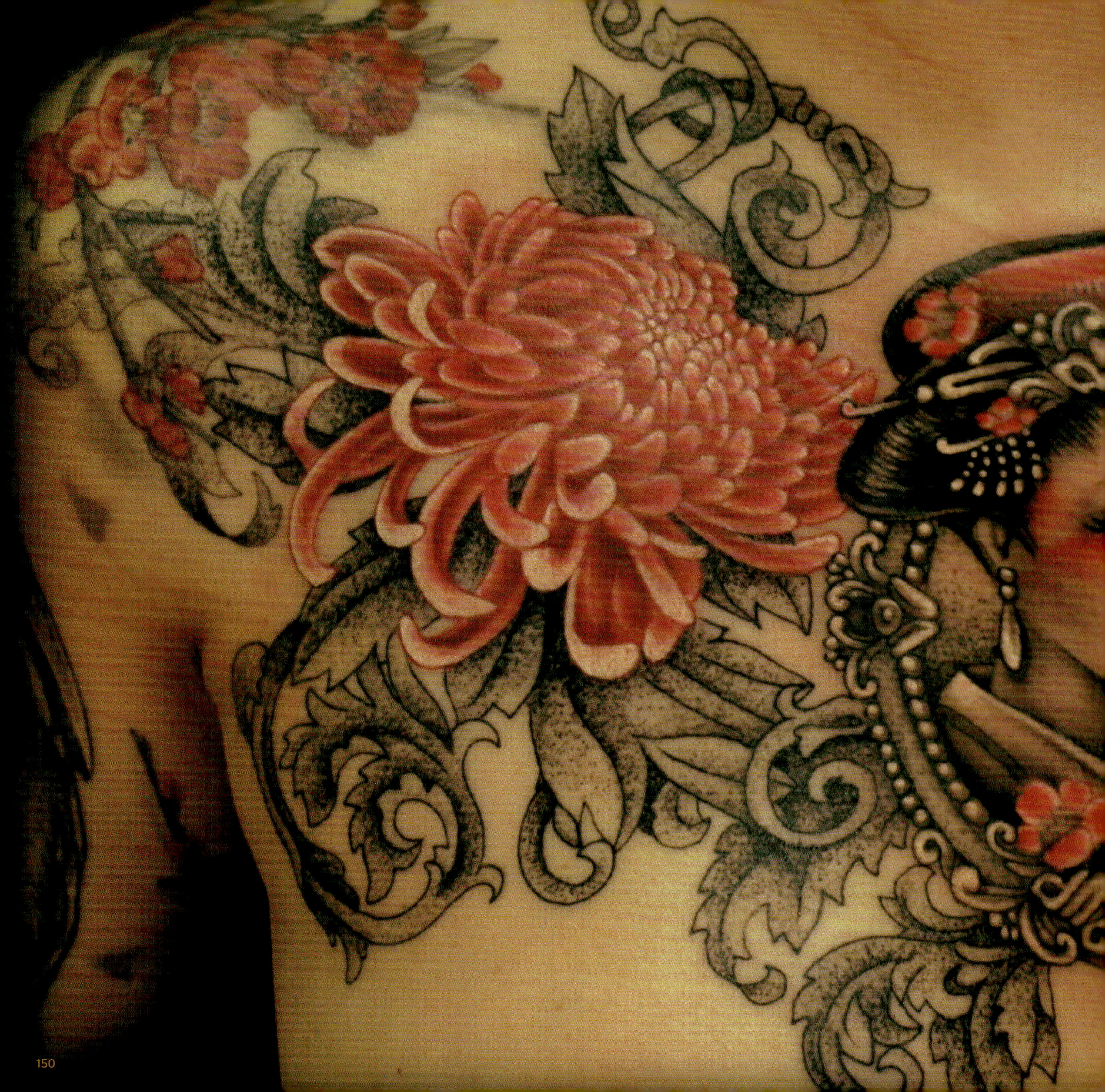

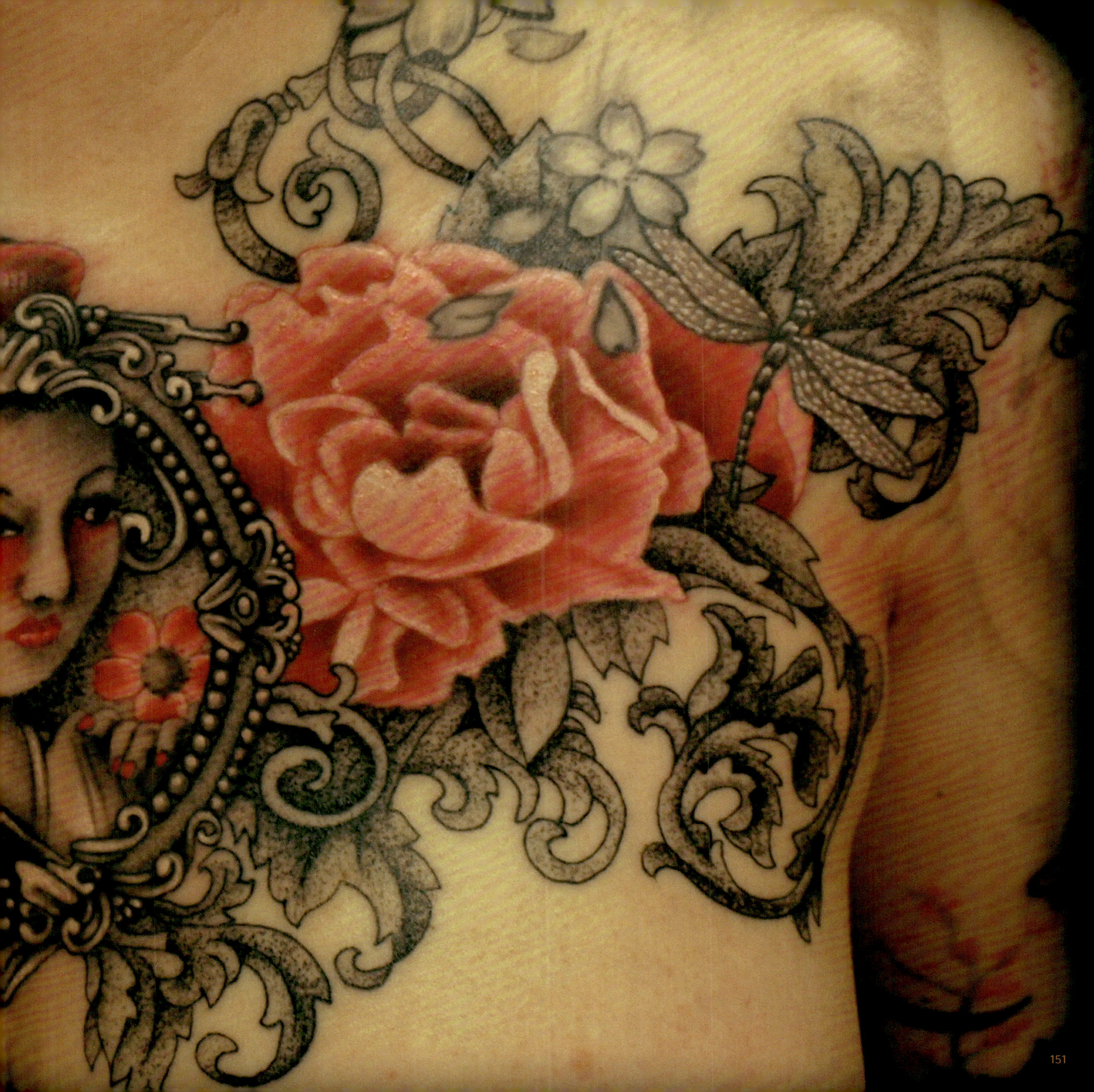

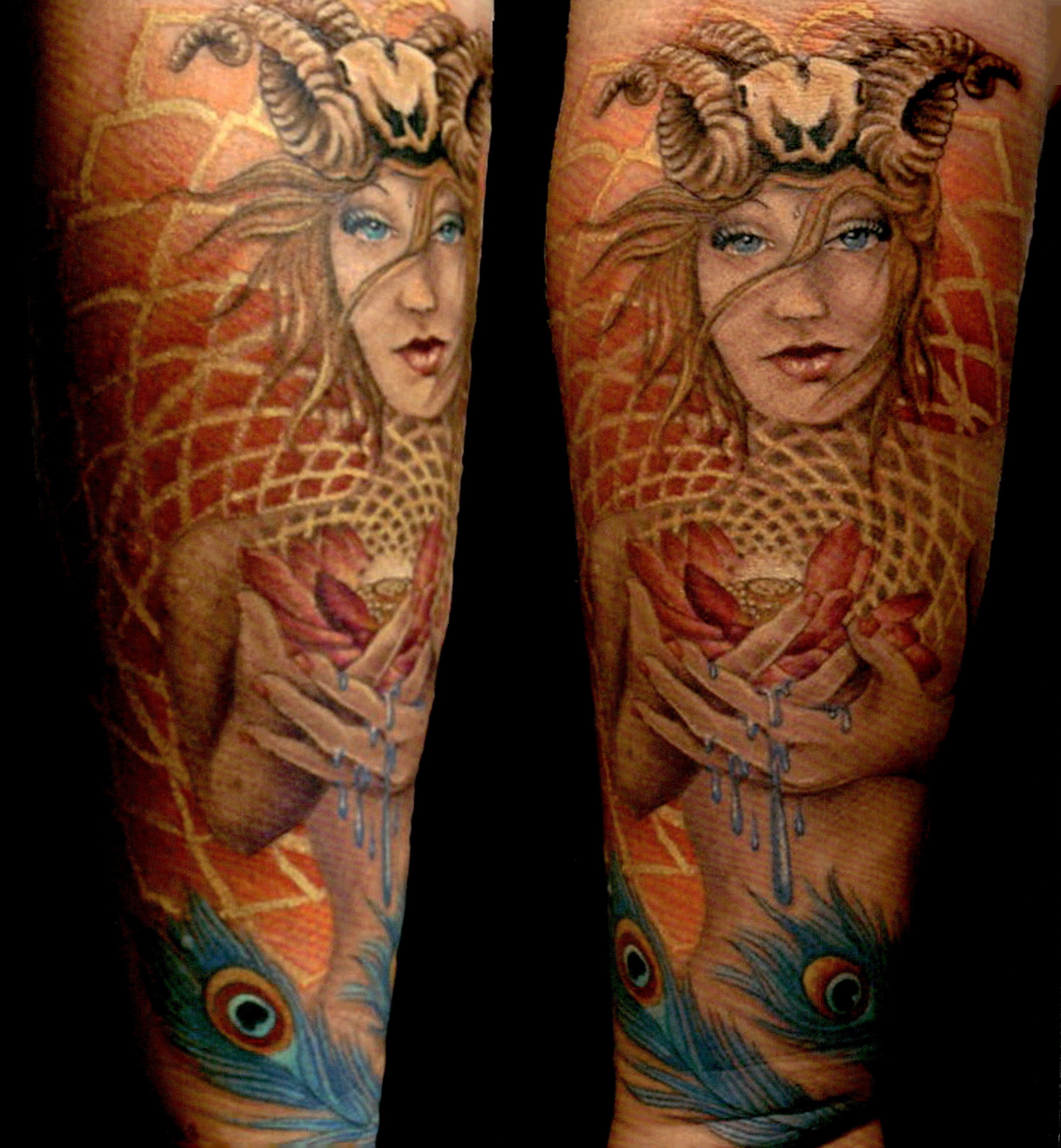

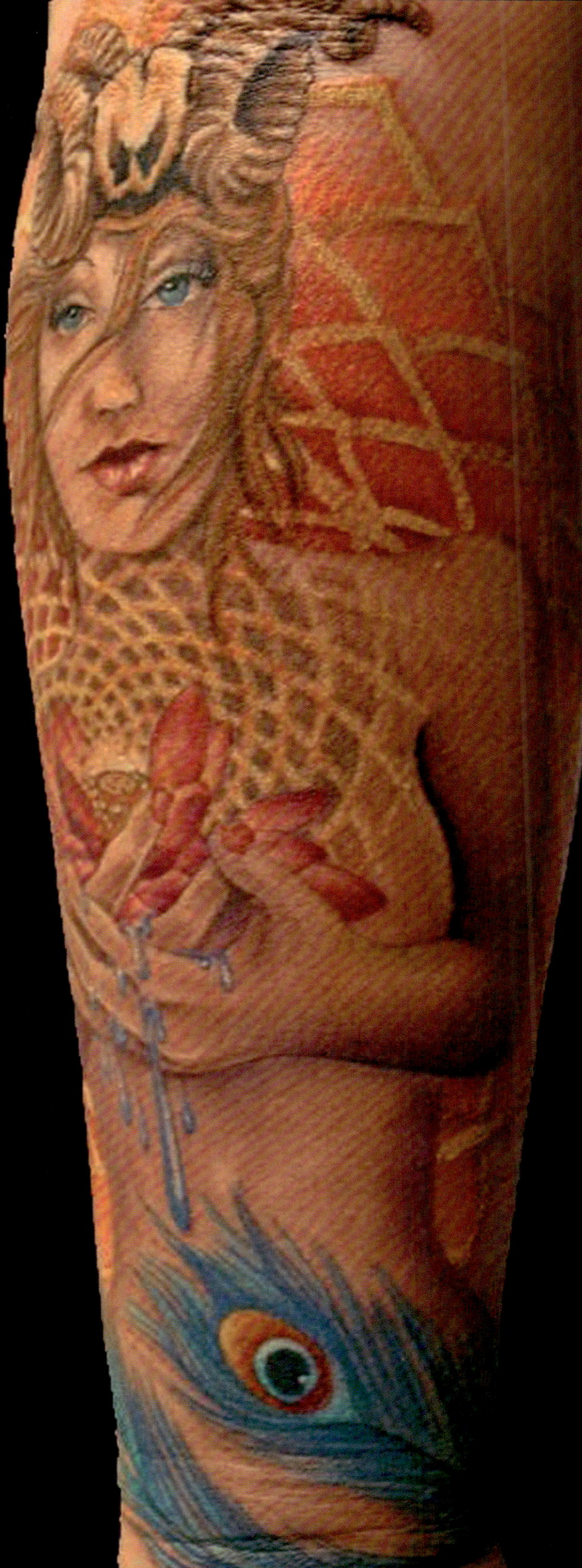

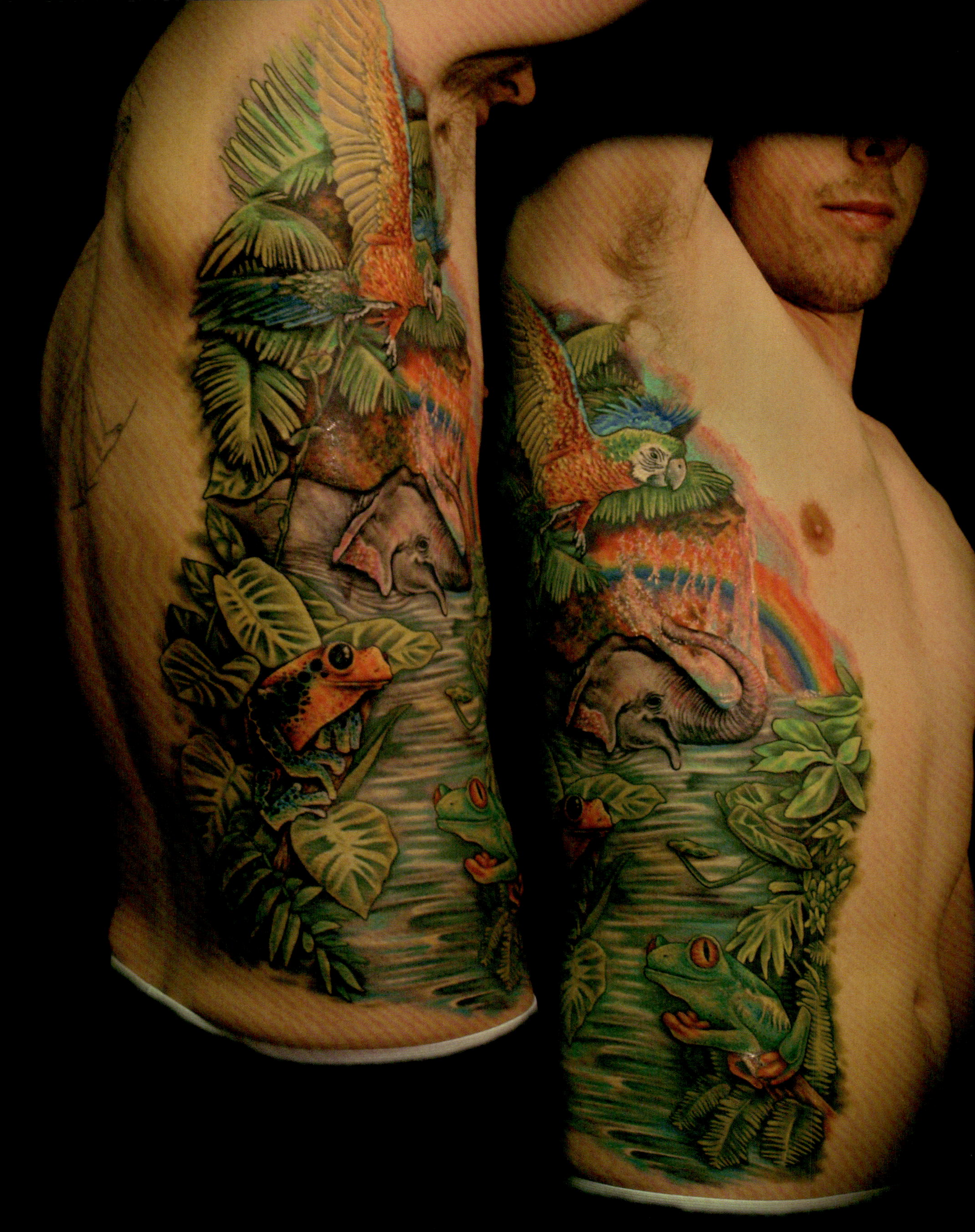

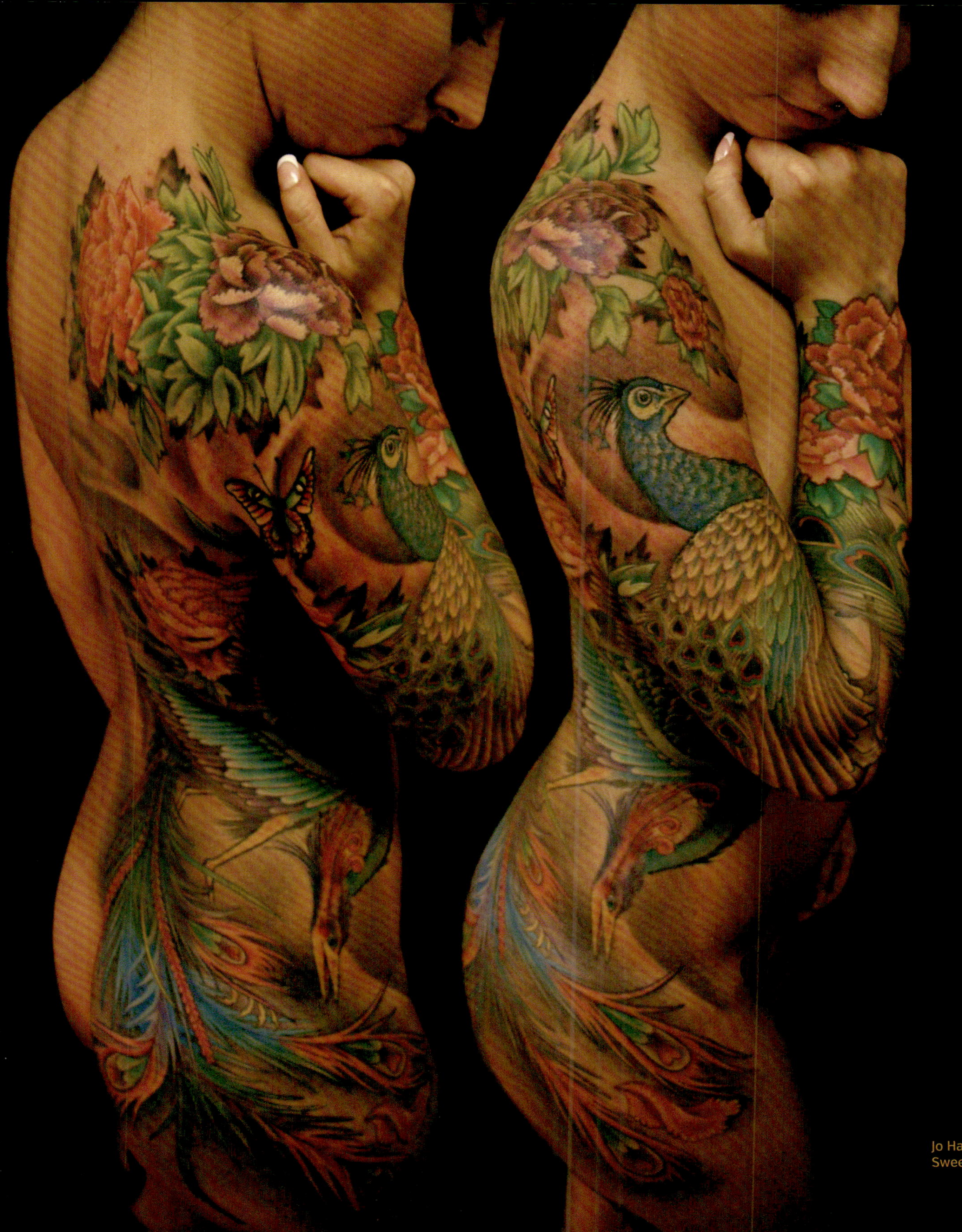
Jo Harrison
SweetStingTo

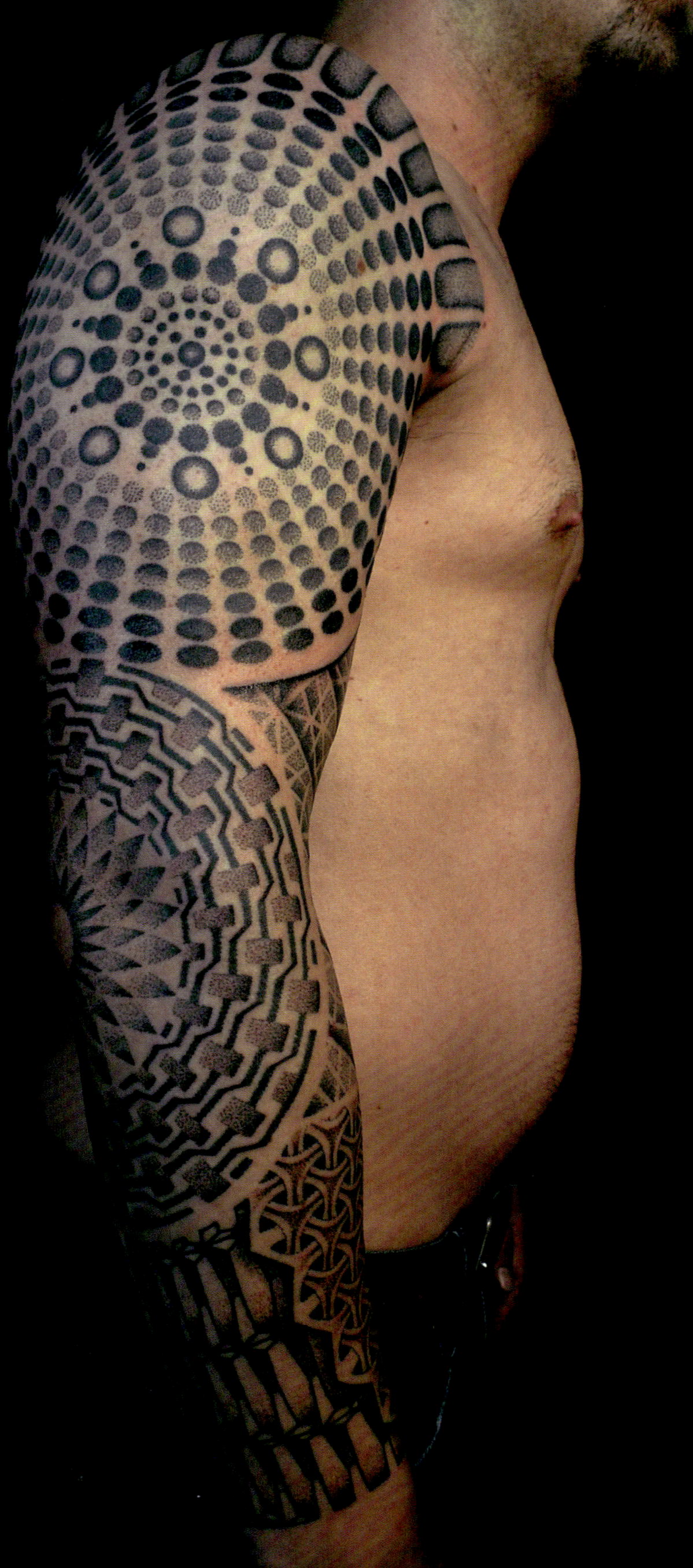

JONDIX

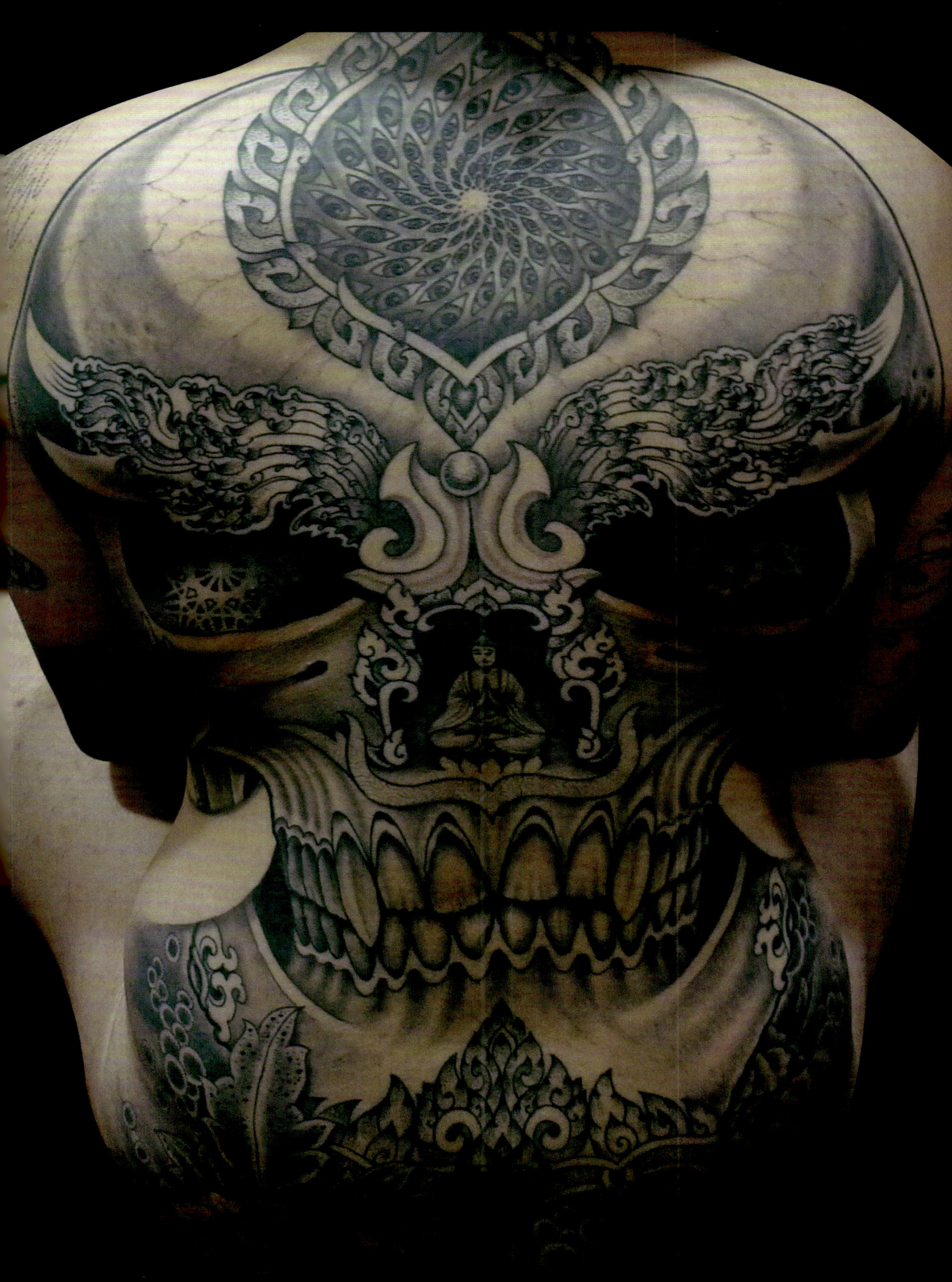

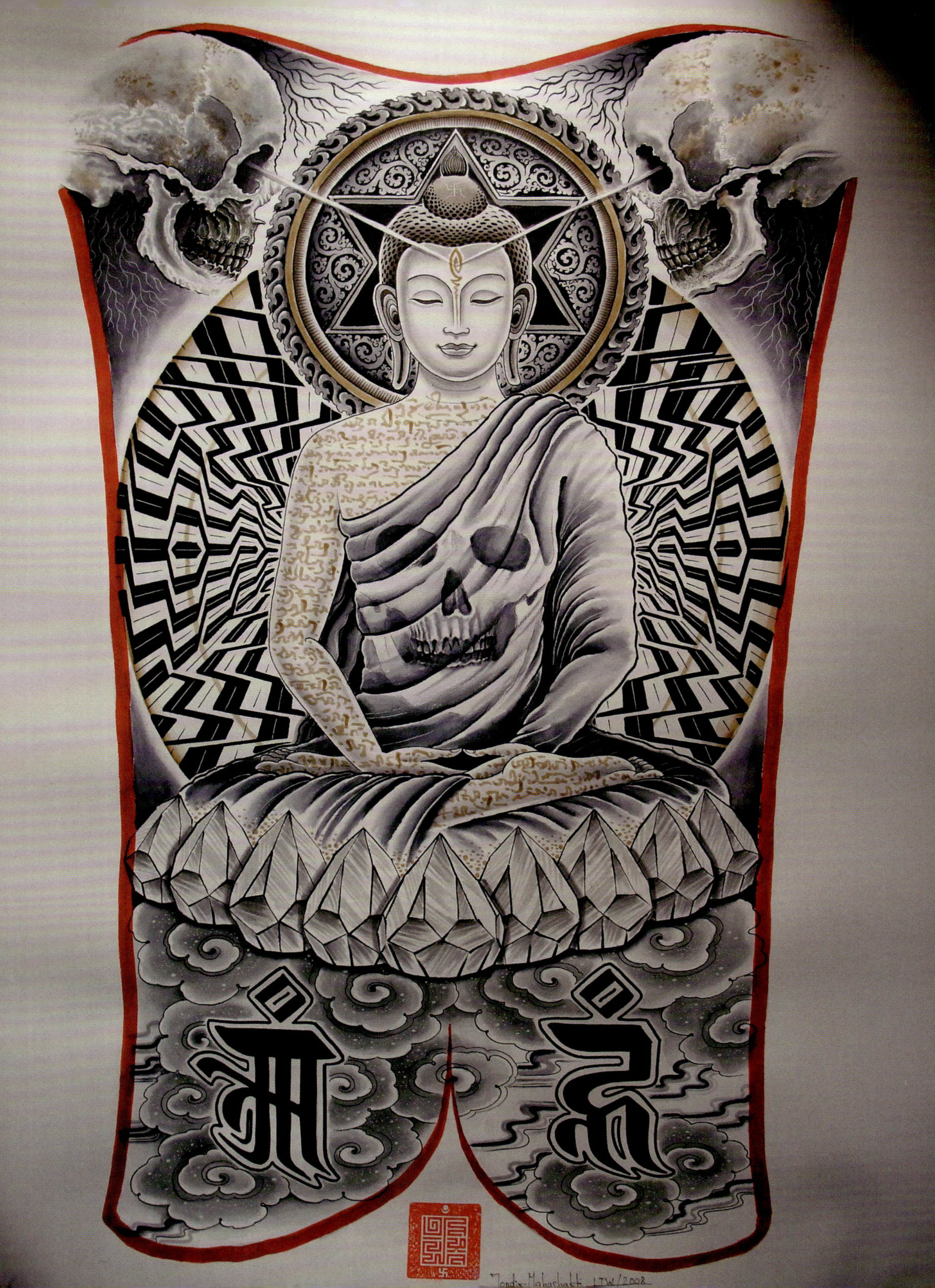

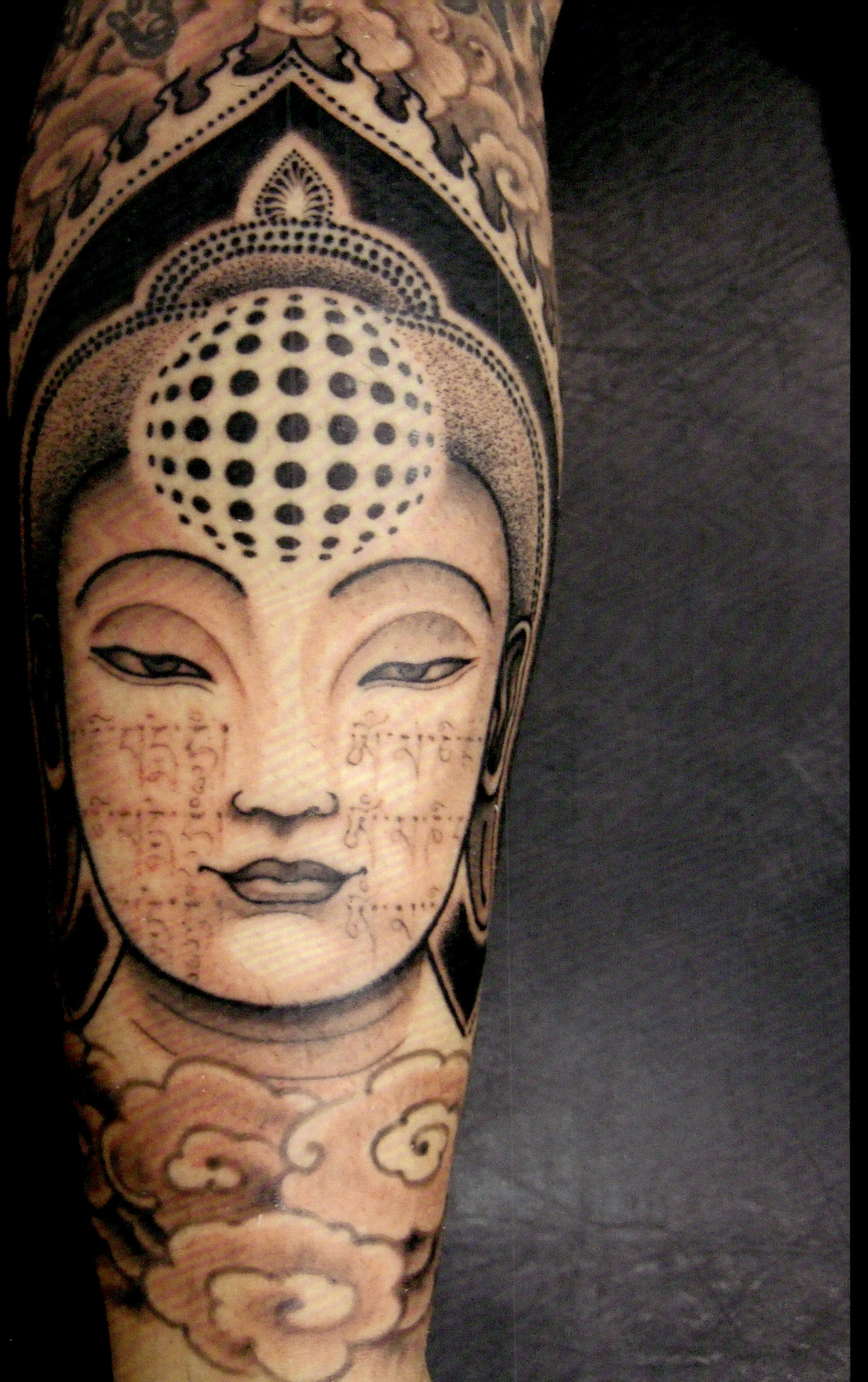

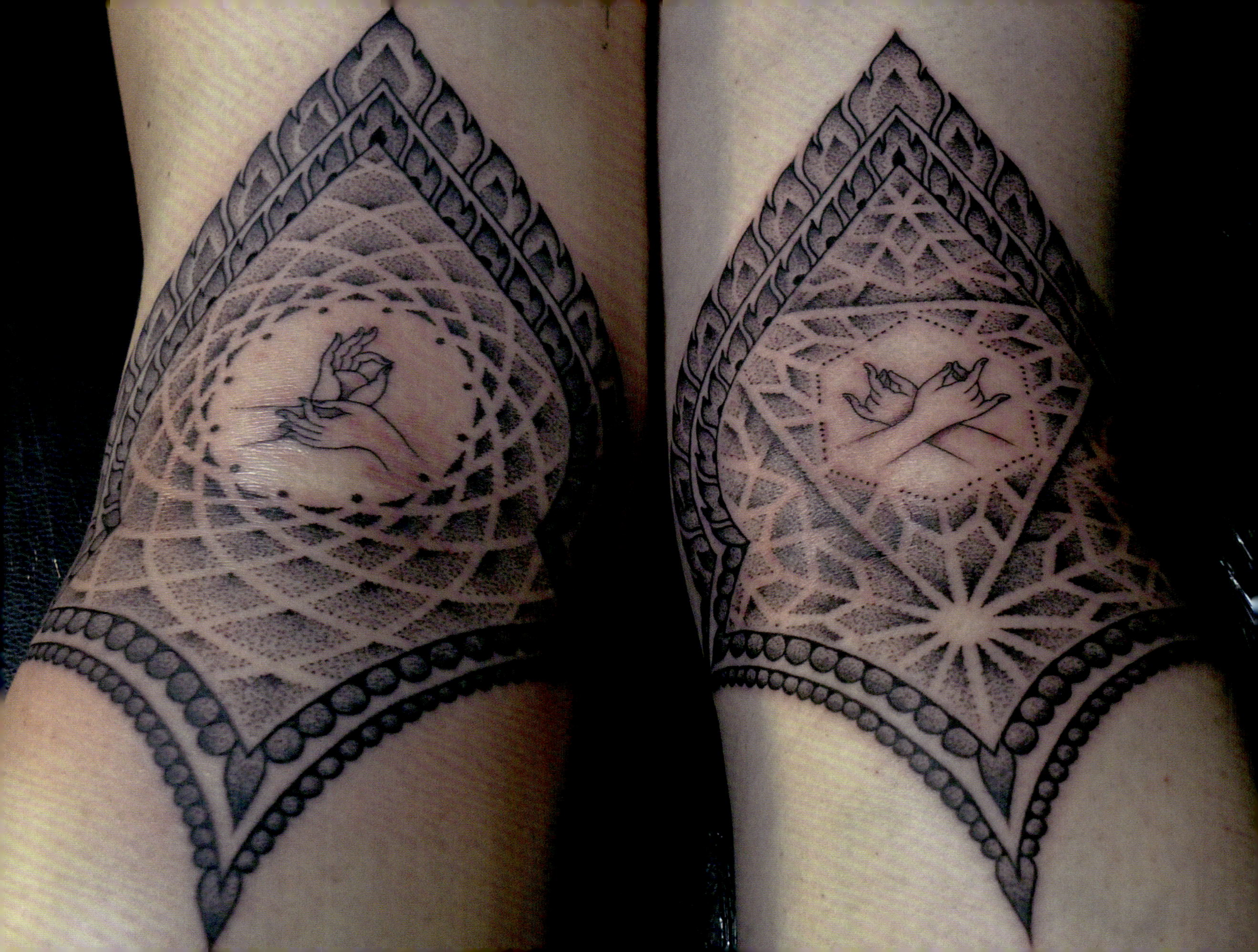

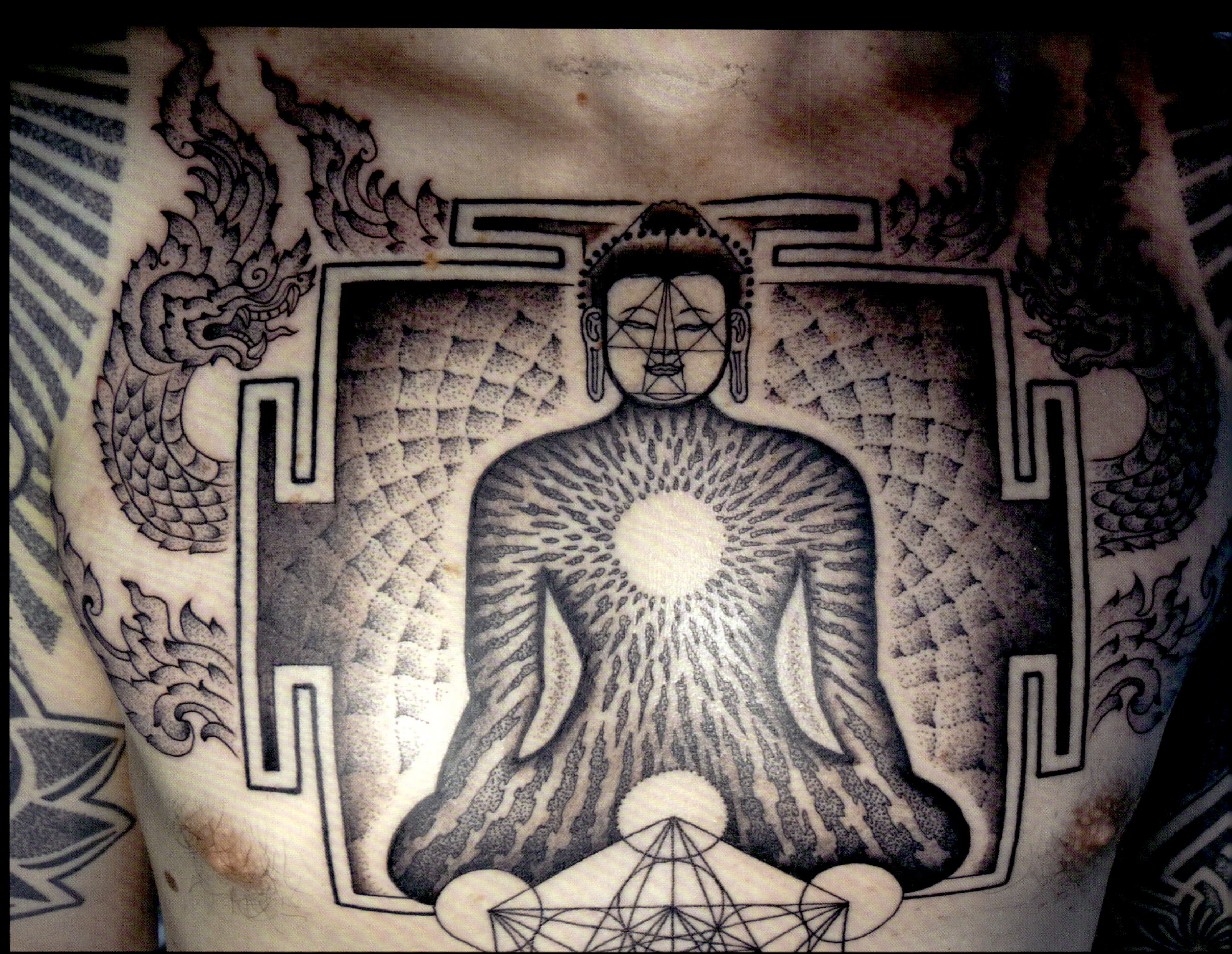
Jondix
www.holytrauma.com

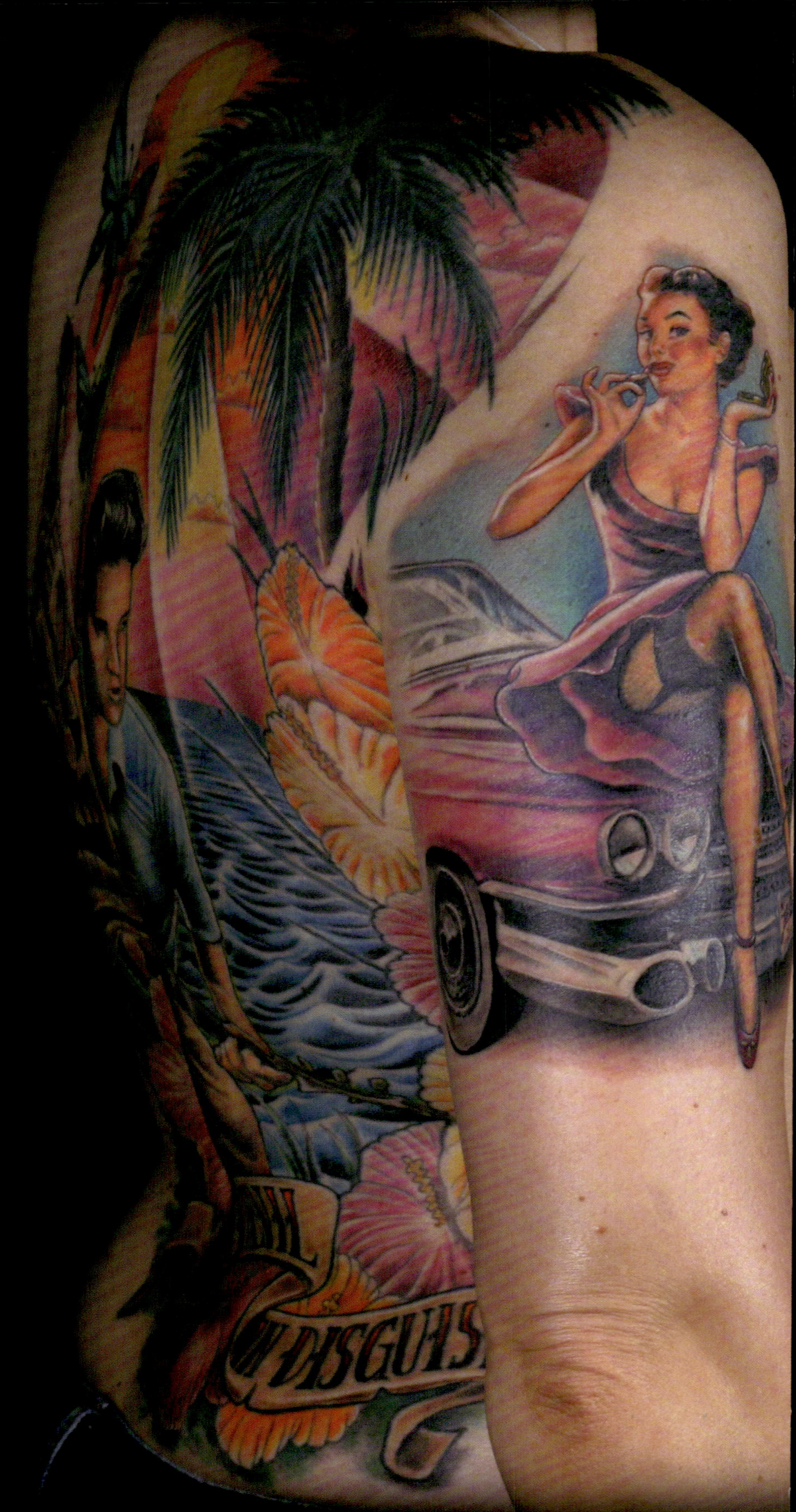

JULIAN SIEBERT
CORPSEPAINTER
TATTOO

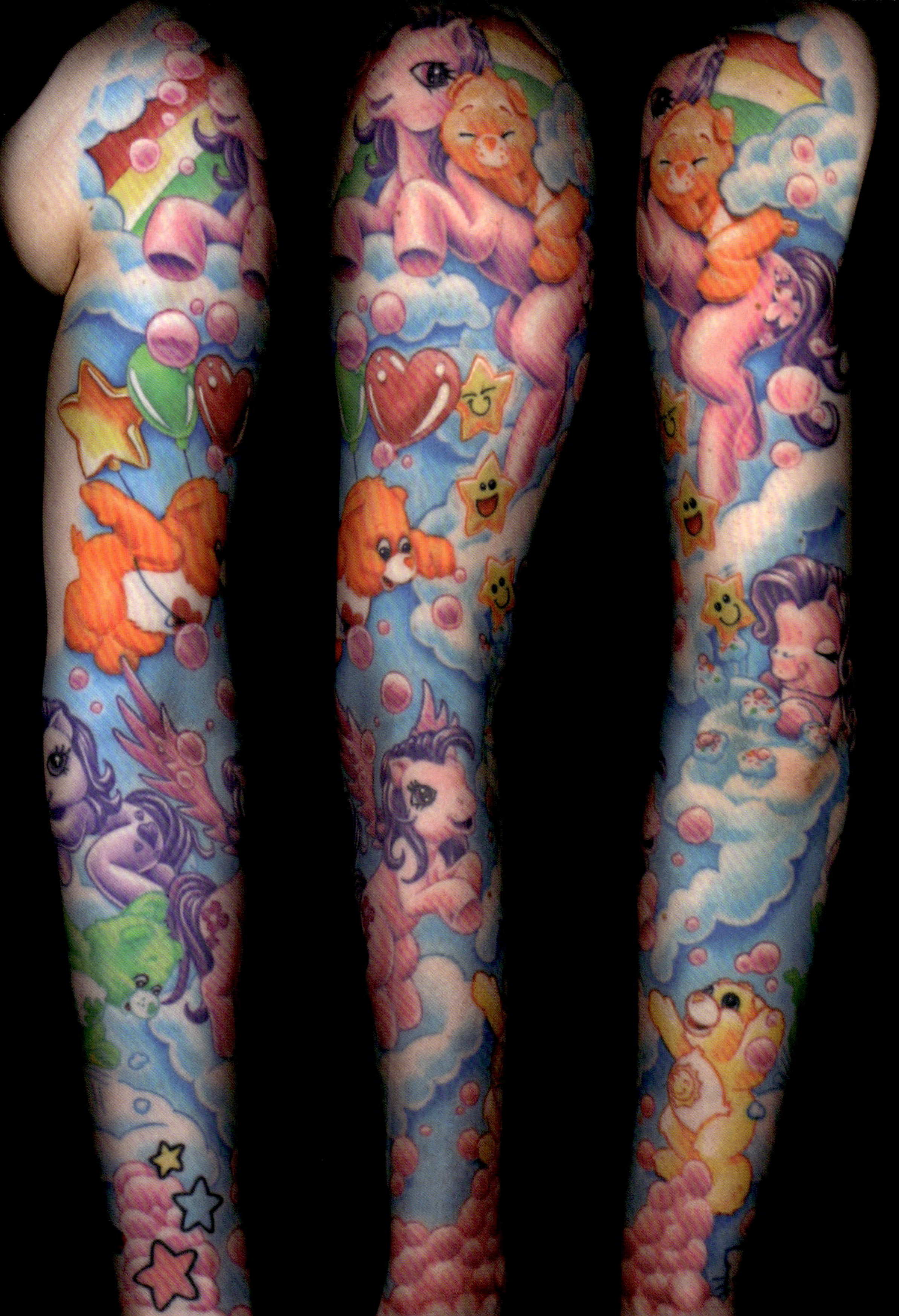

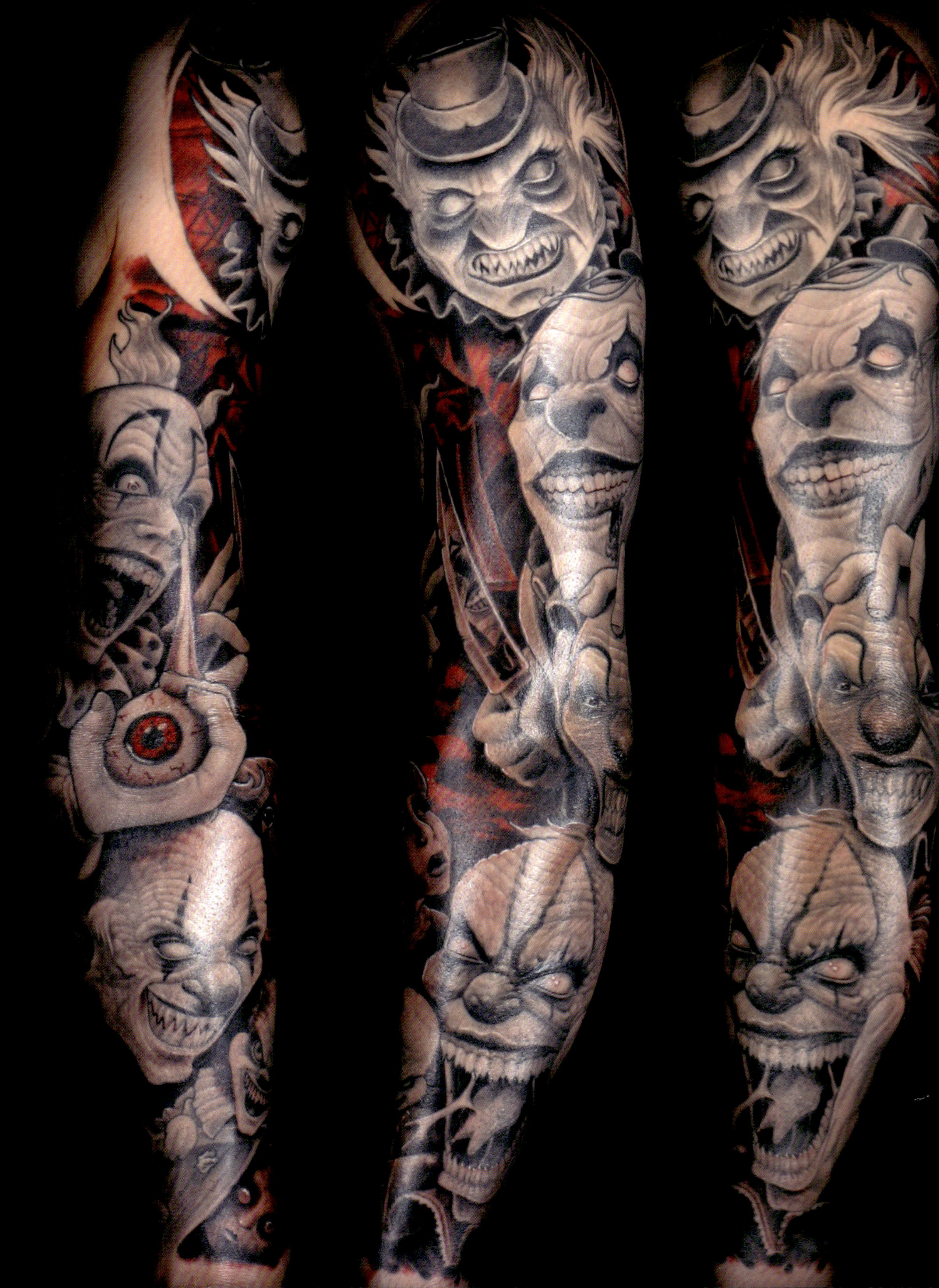

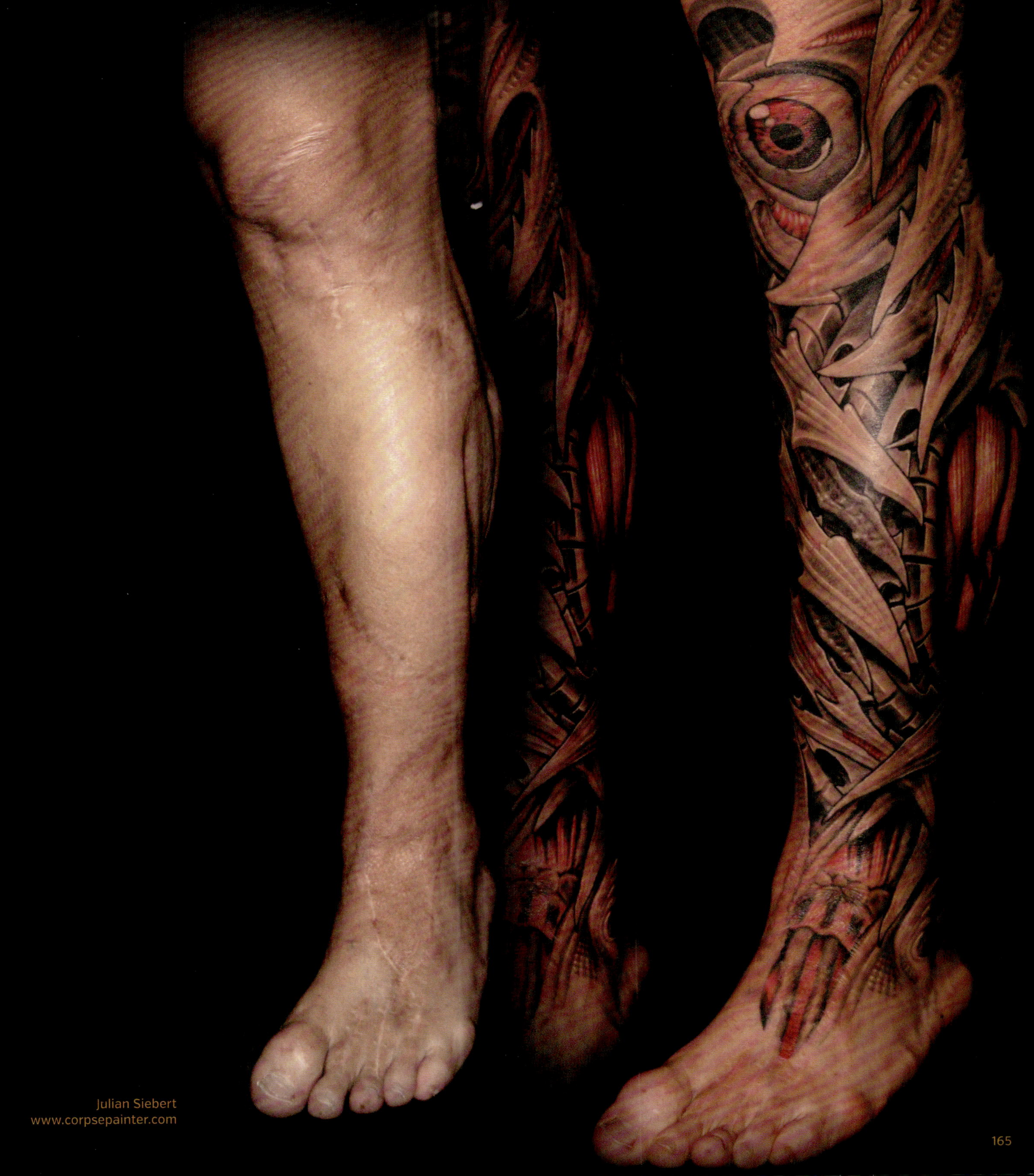

Julian Siebert
www.corpsepainter.com

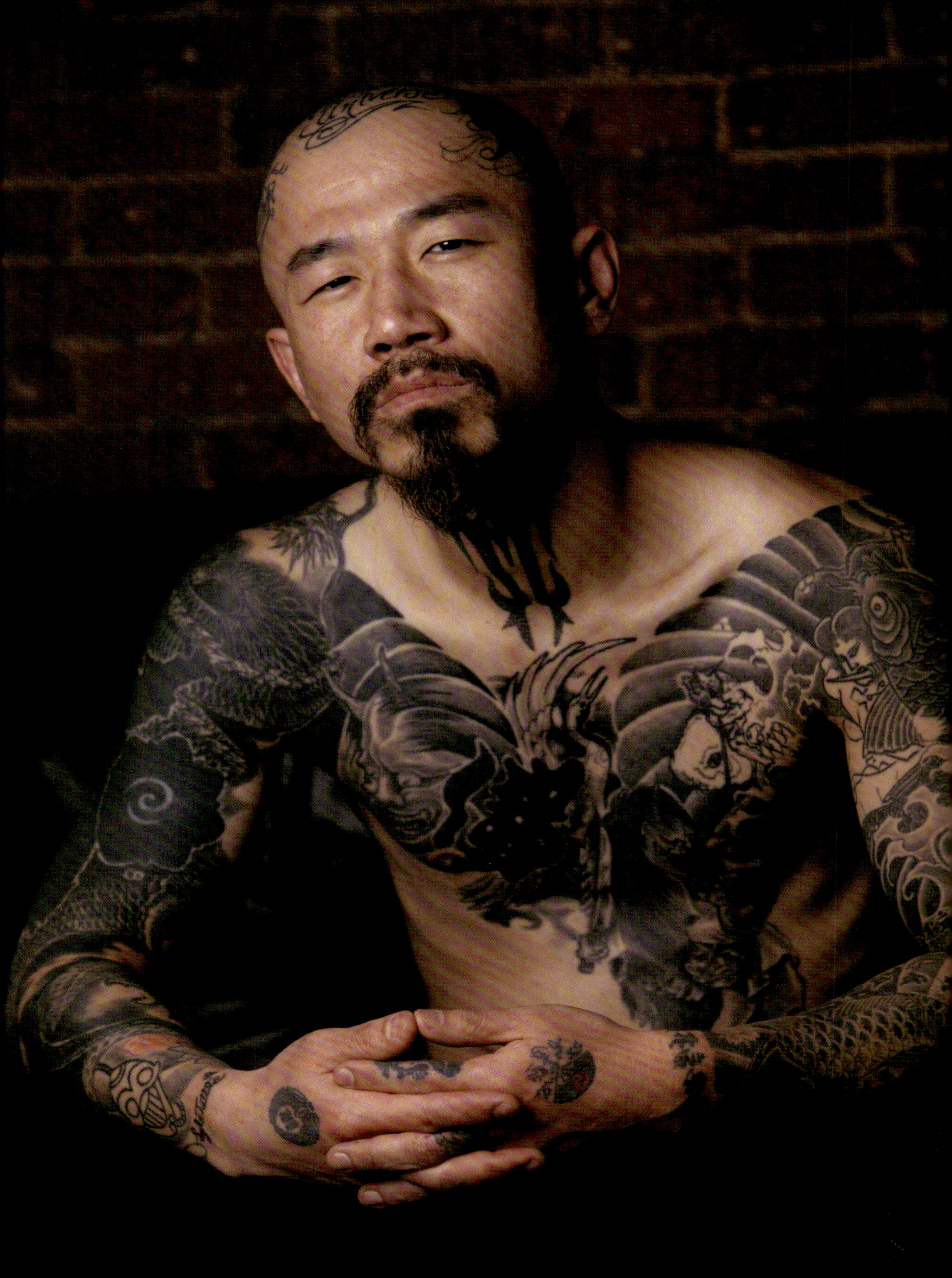

KHAN

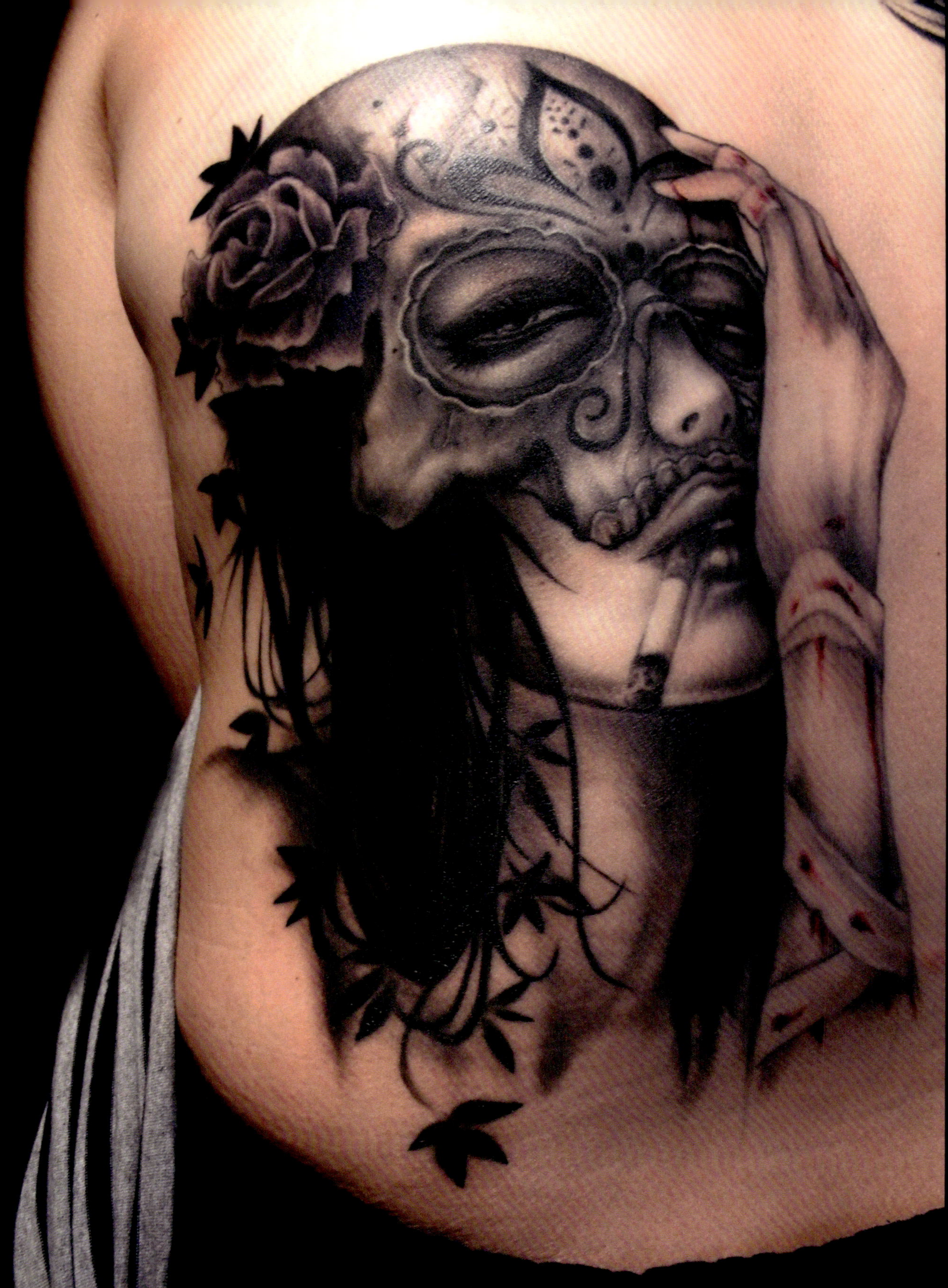

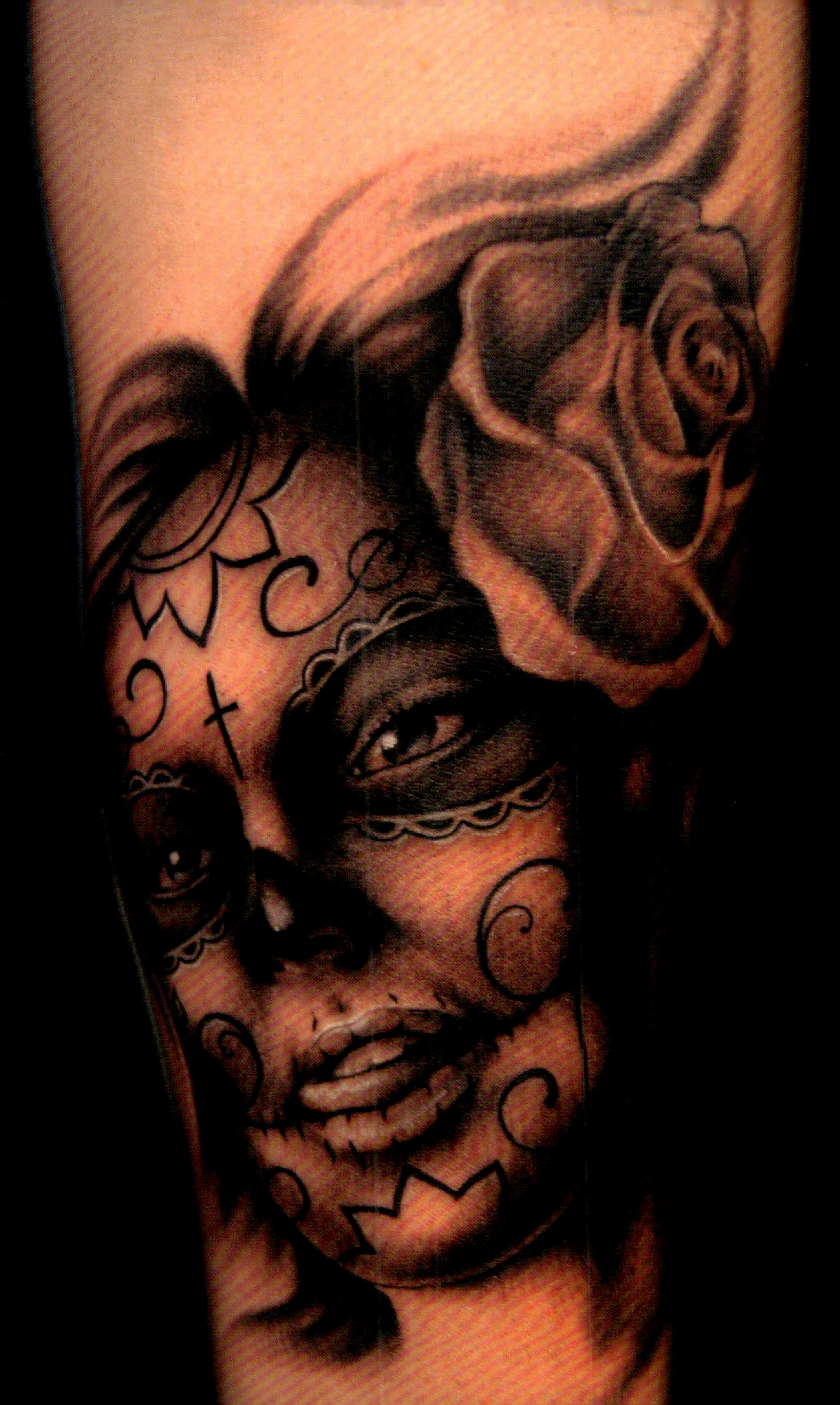

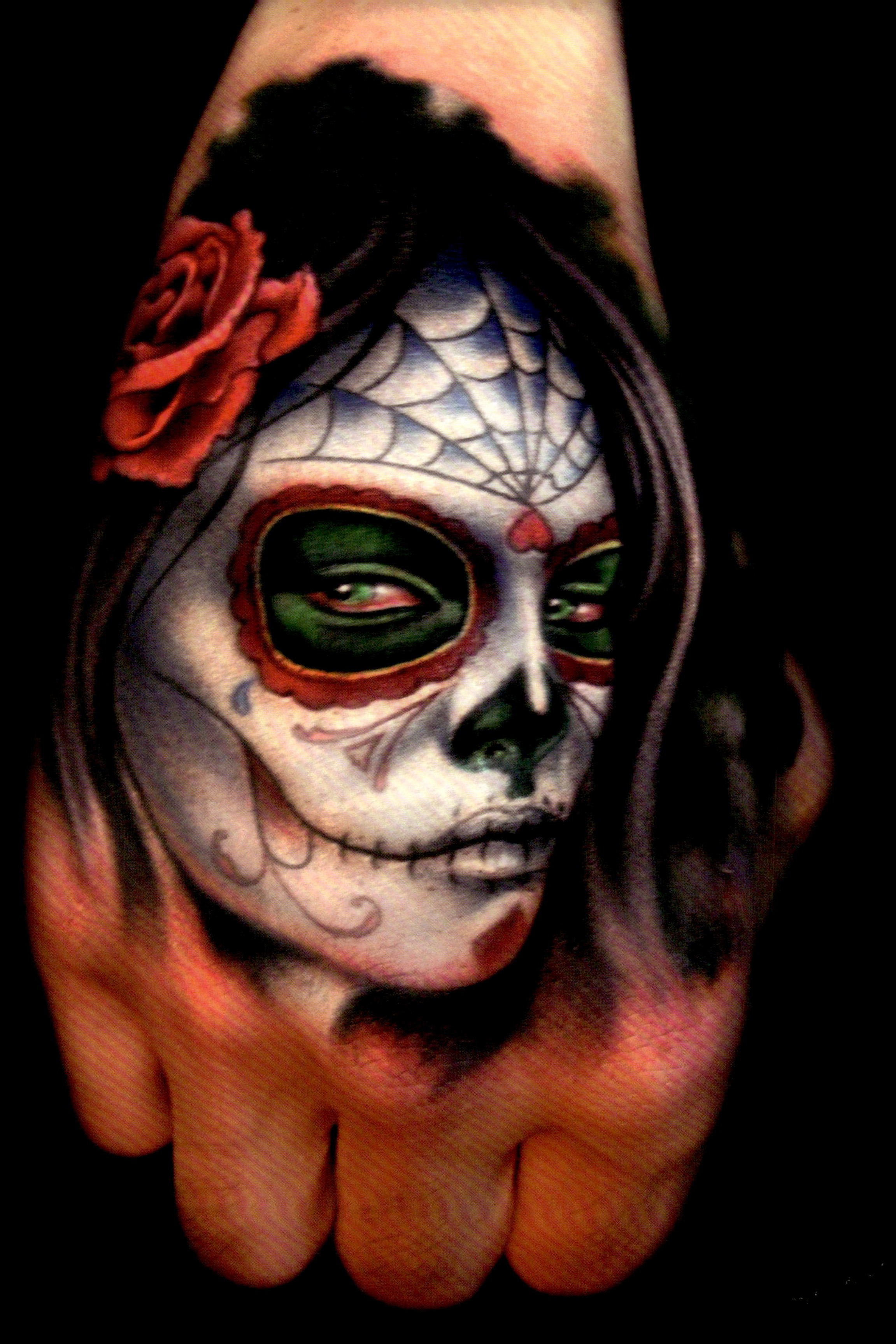

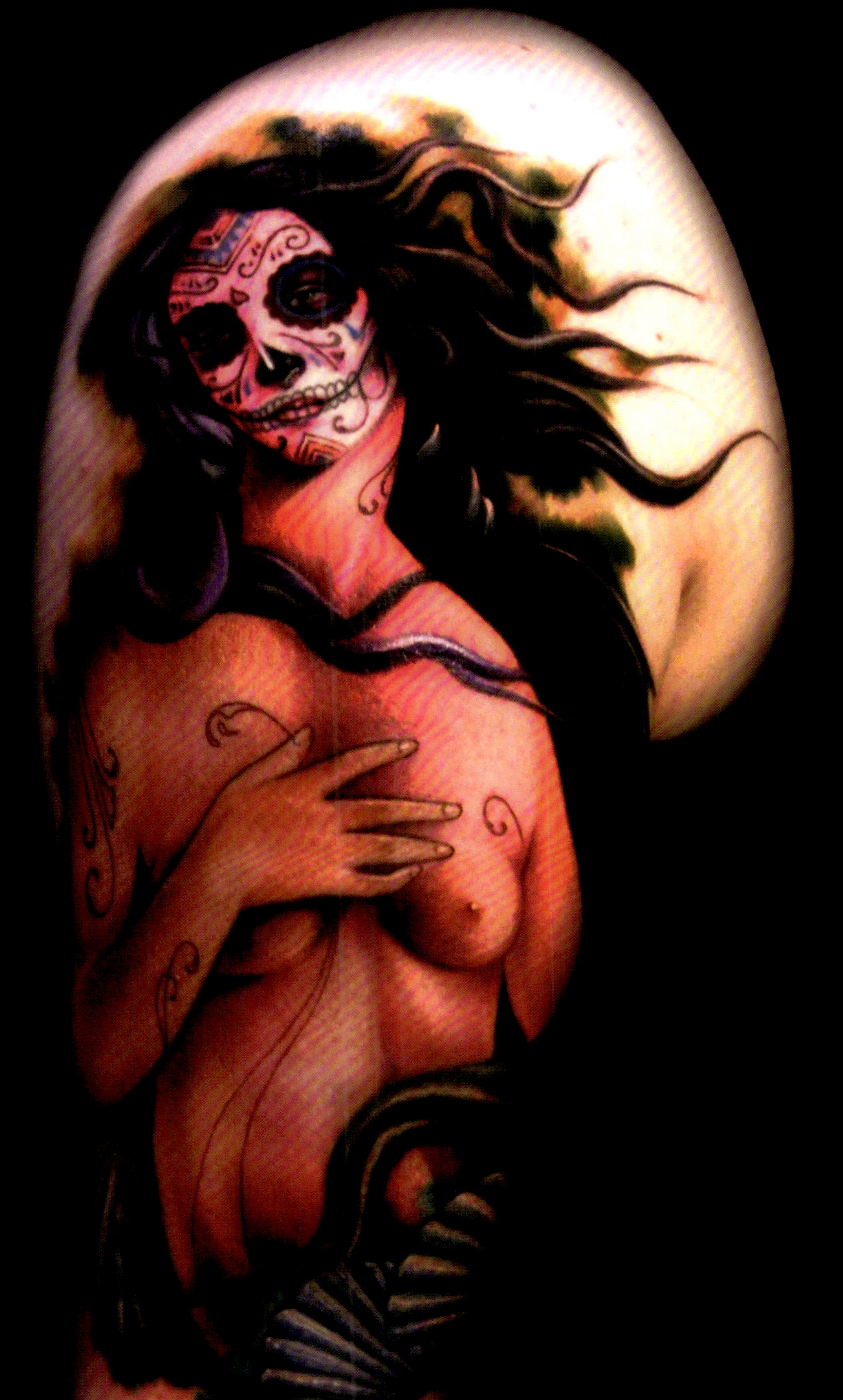

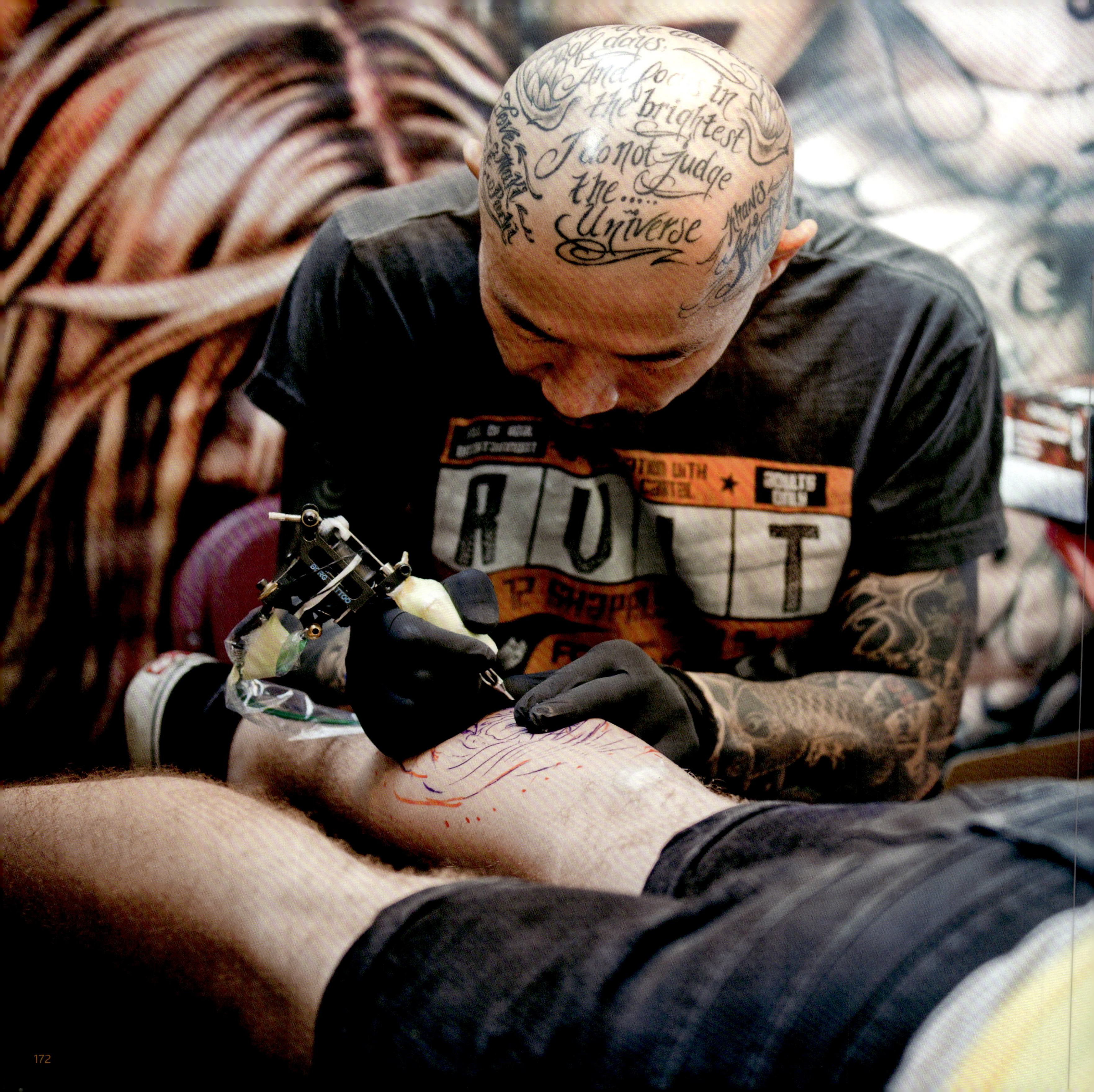
of days
And focus in
the brightest
I do not judge
the.....
Universe

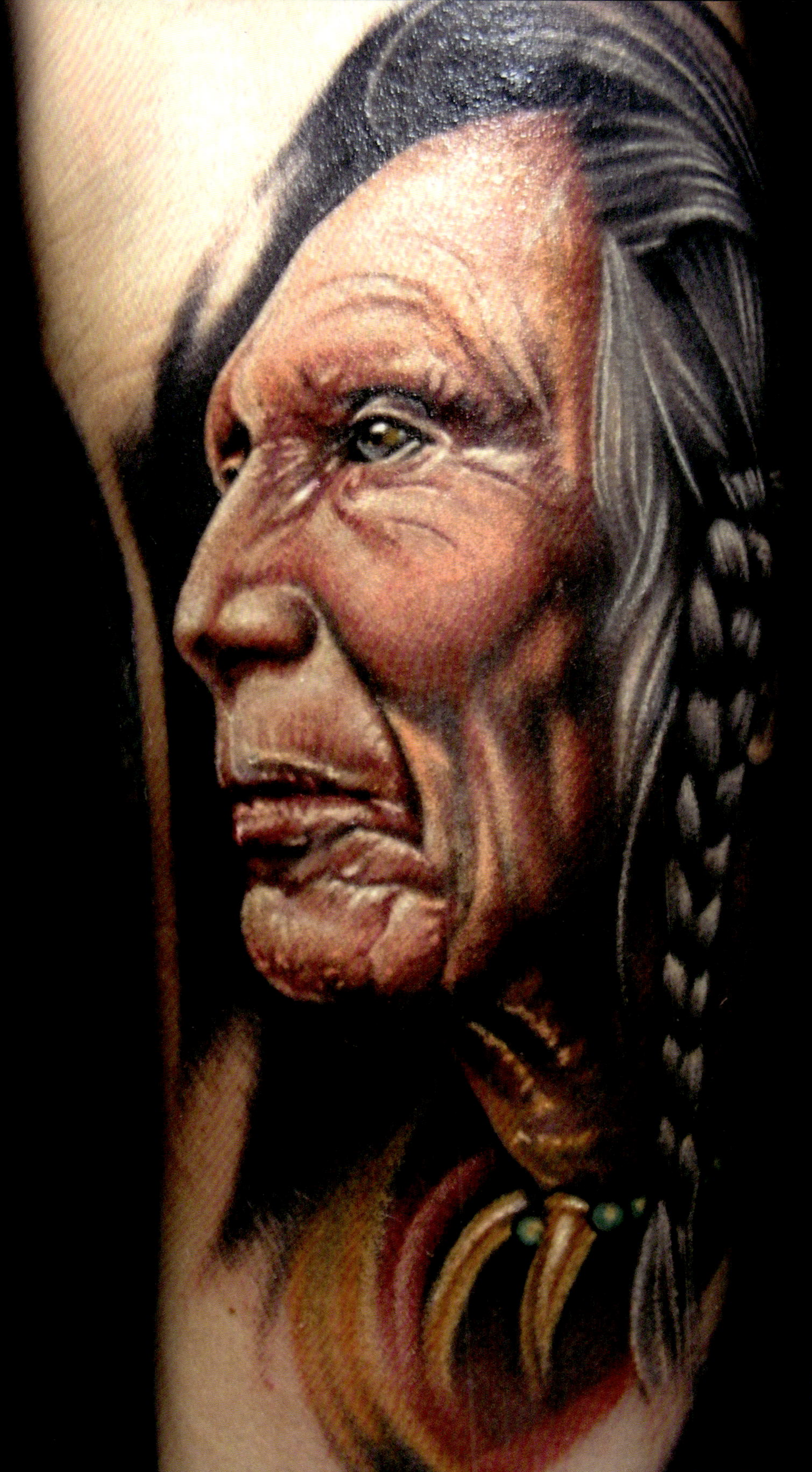
Khan
www.khantattoo

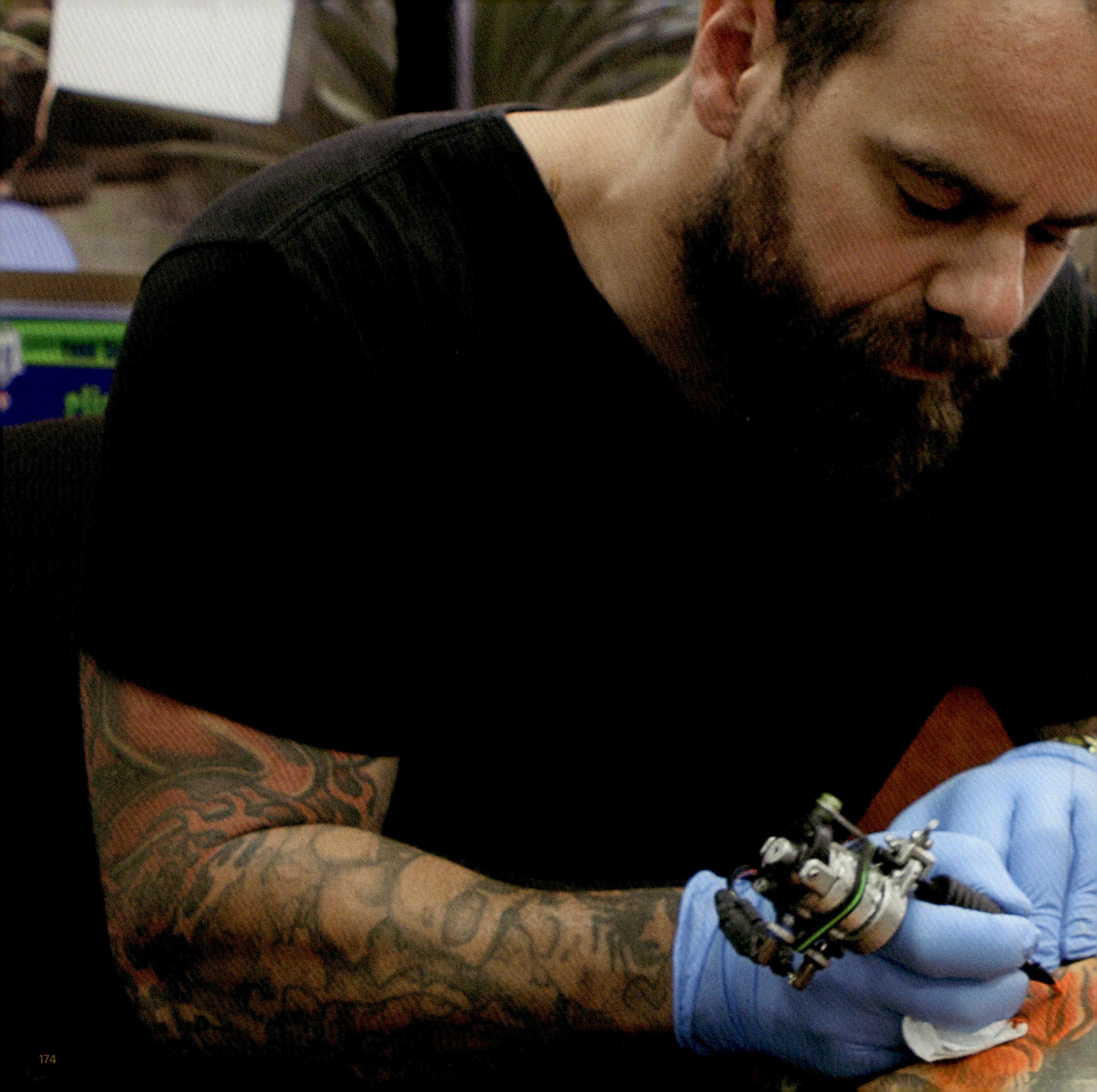

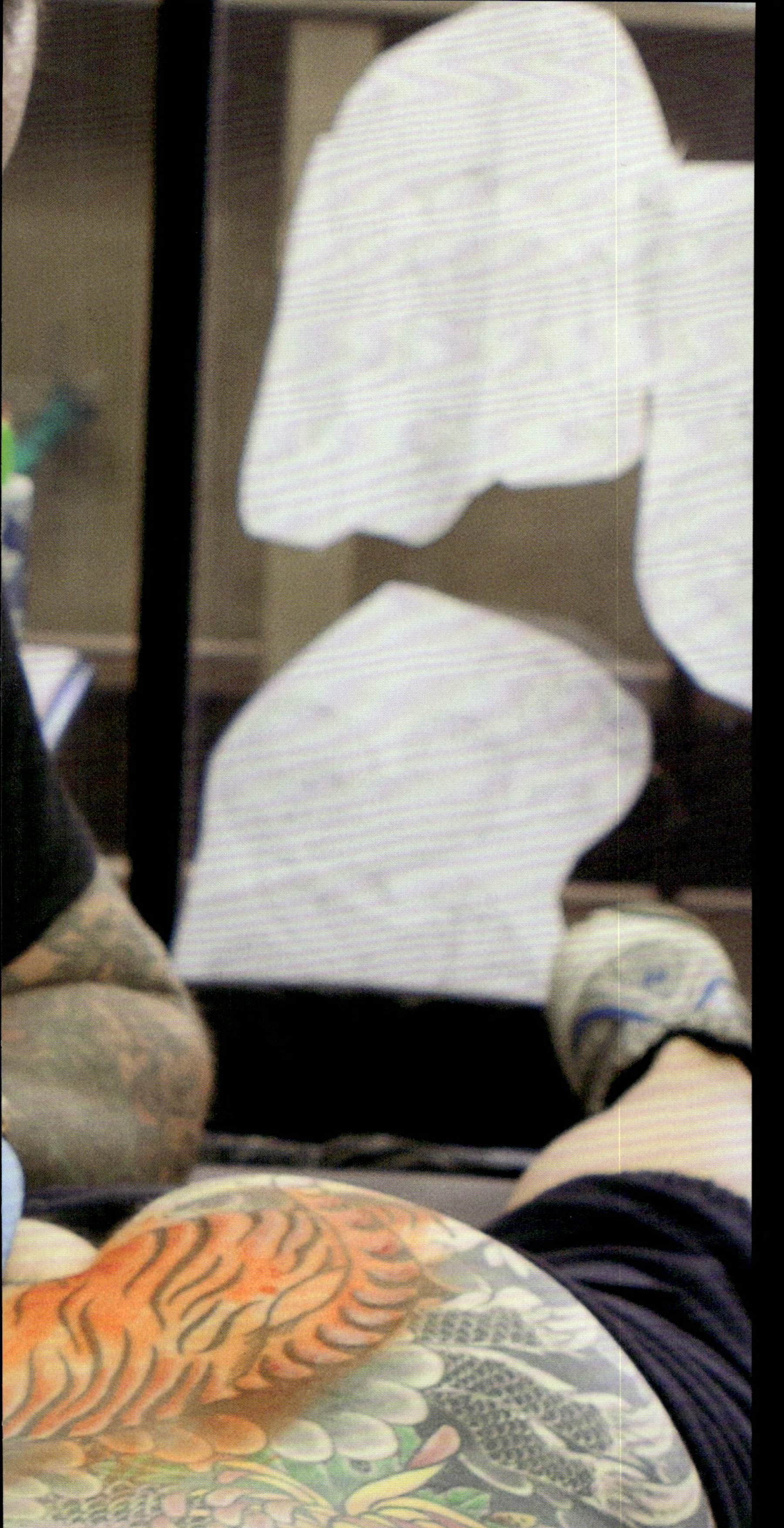

KIAN FORREAL
AUTHENT/INK

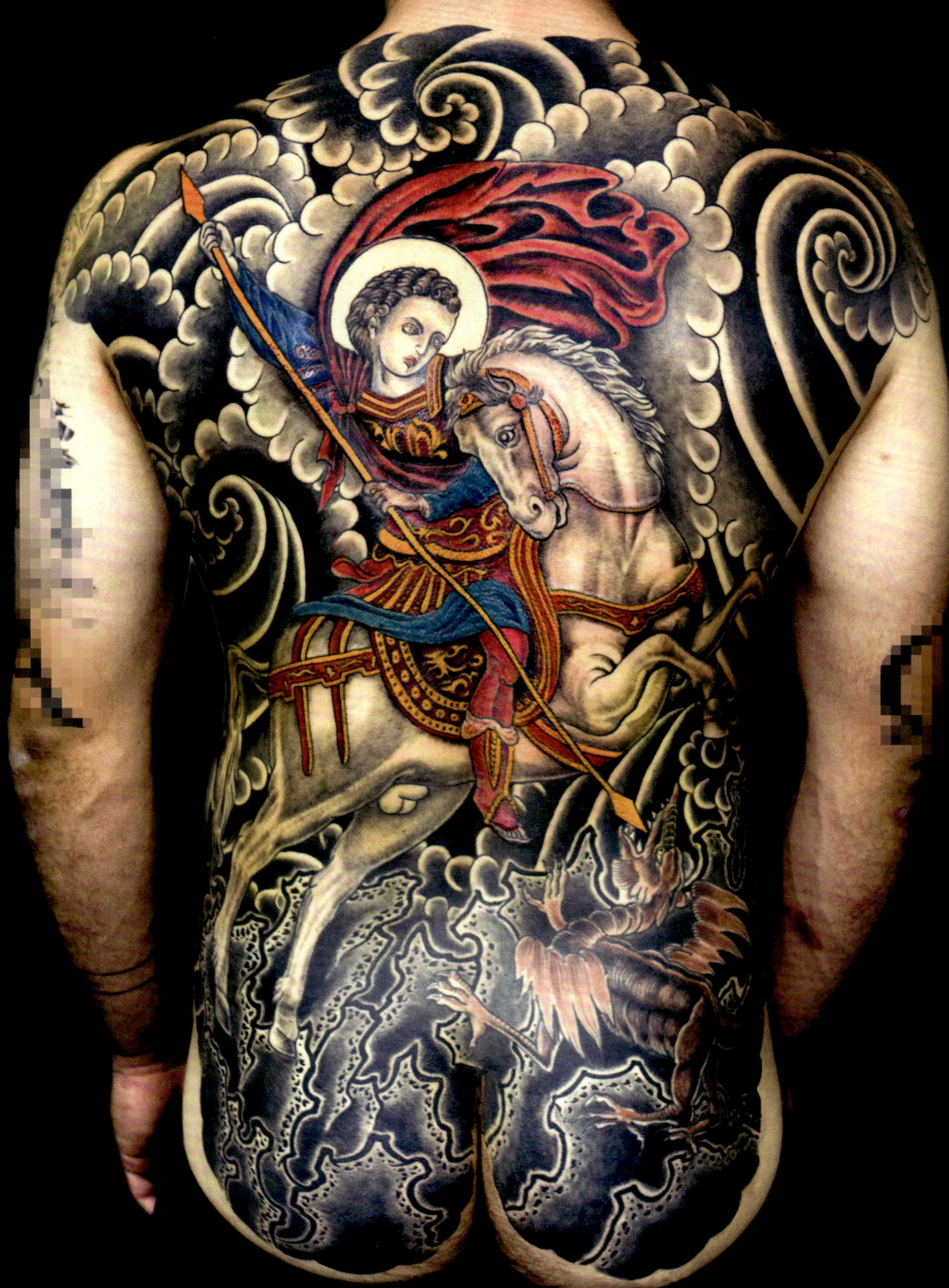

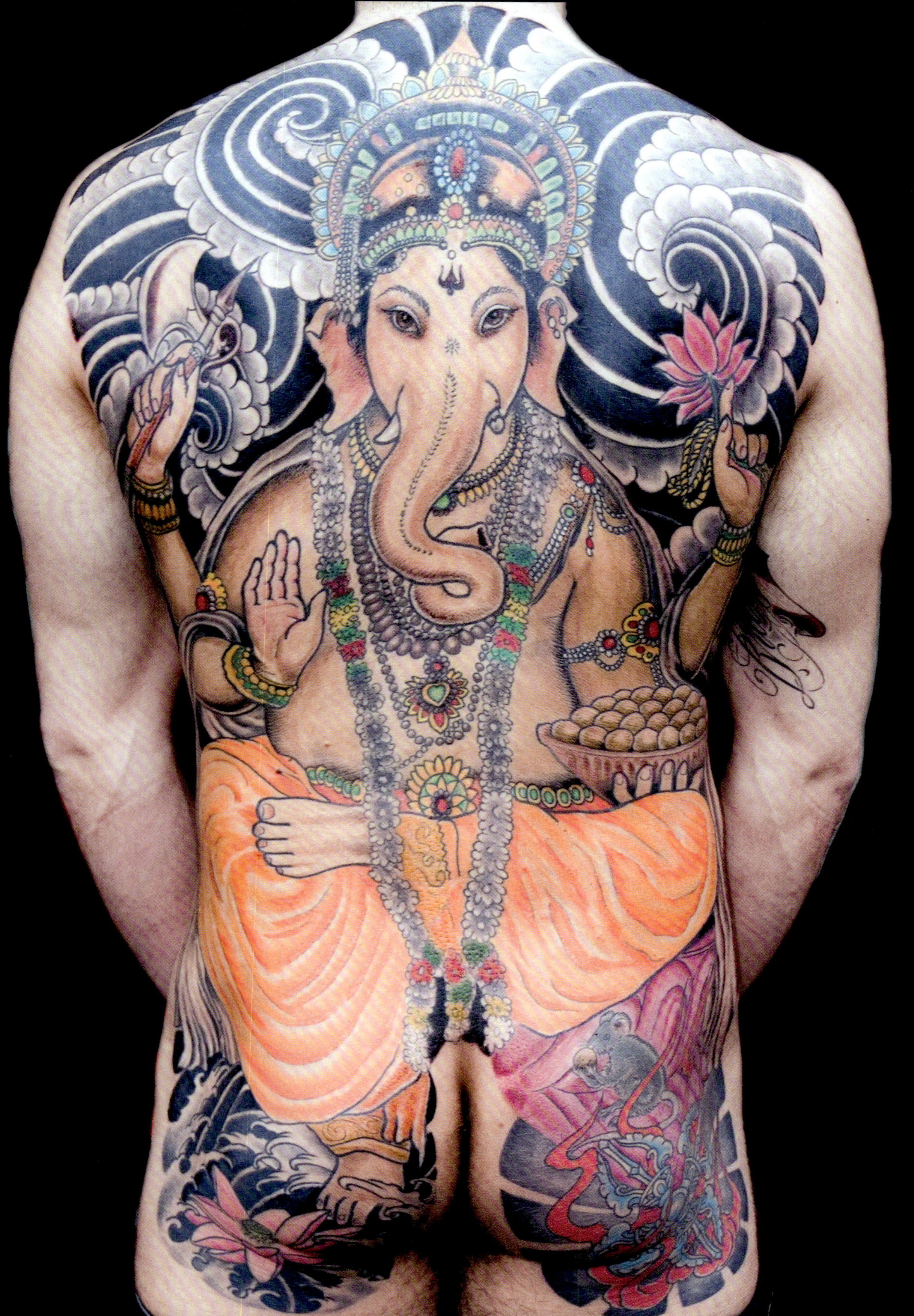

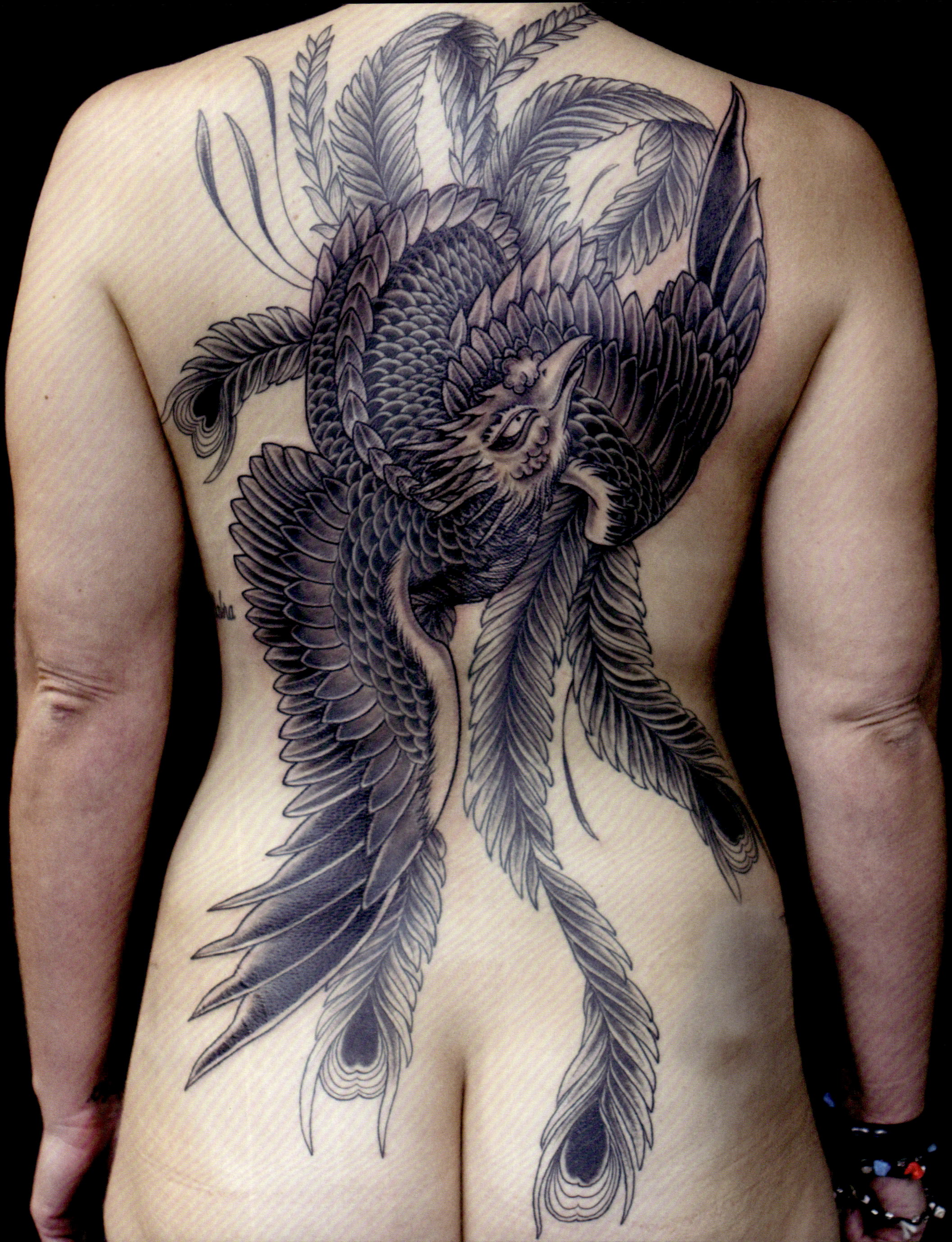

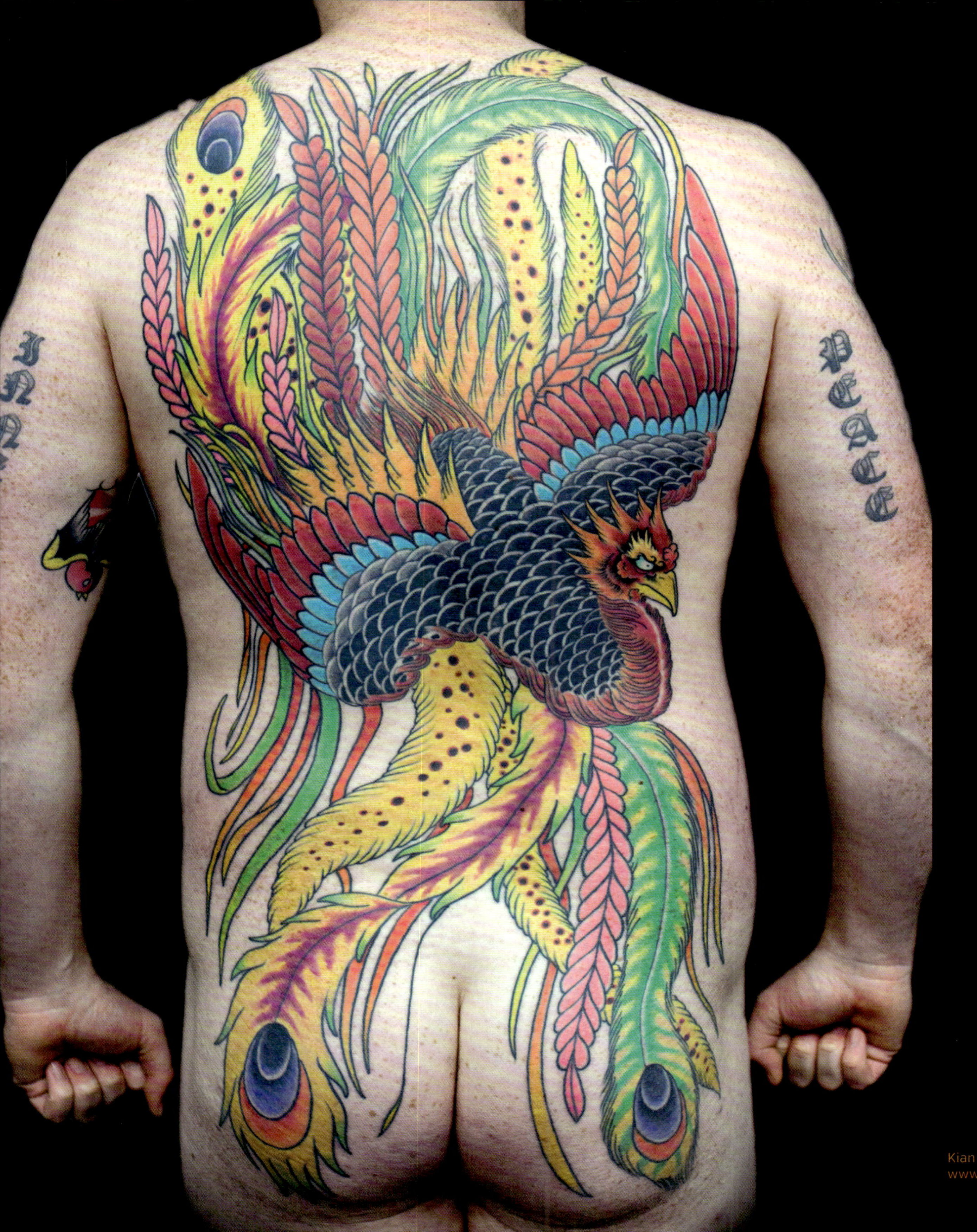
Kian Forr
www.kia

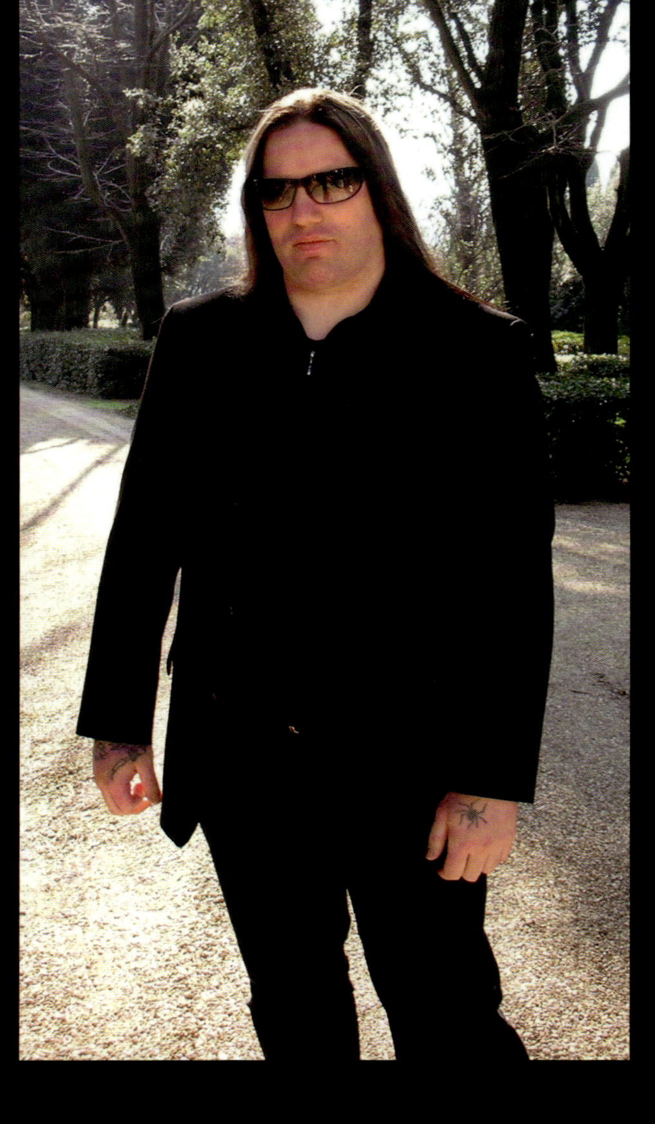

KURT WISCOMBE

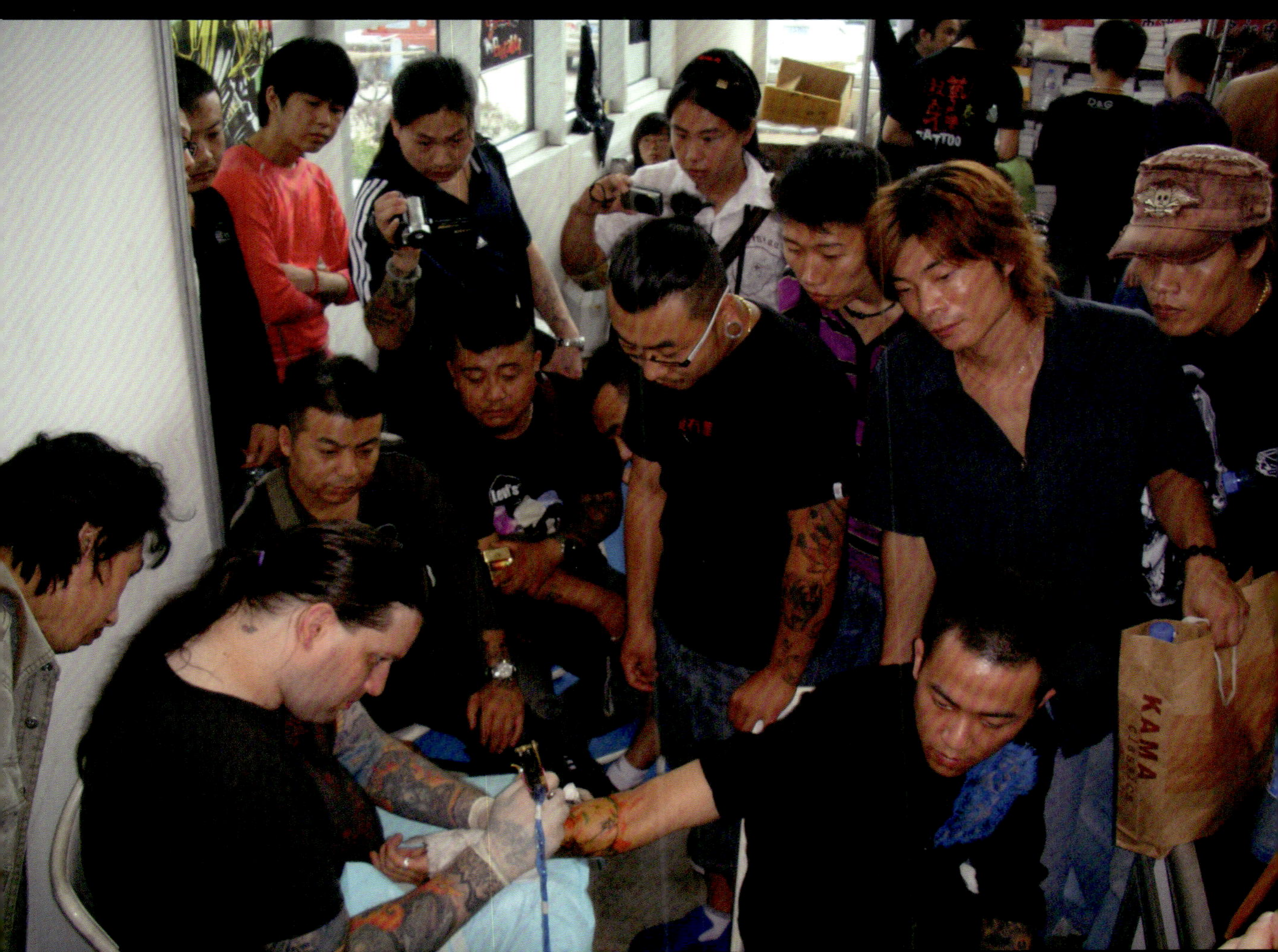

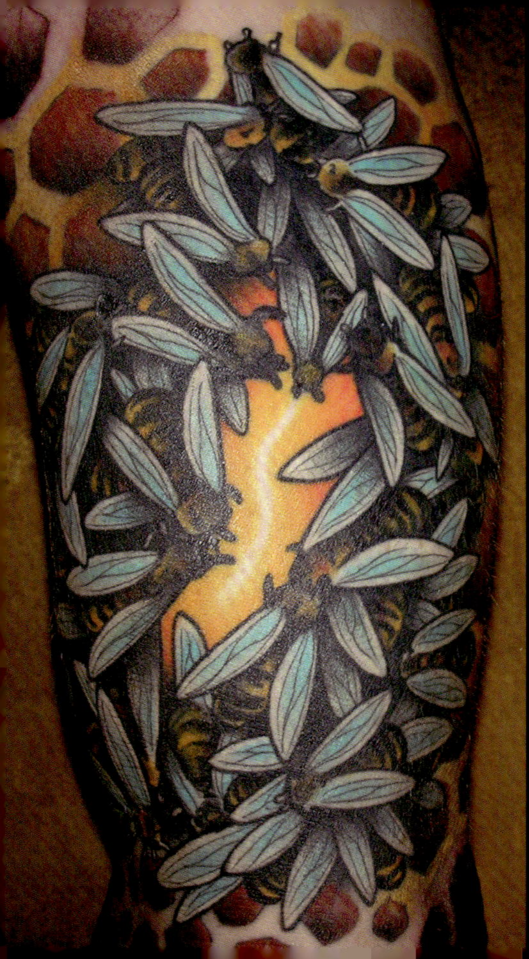

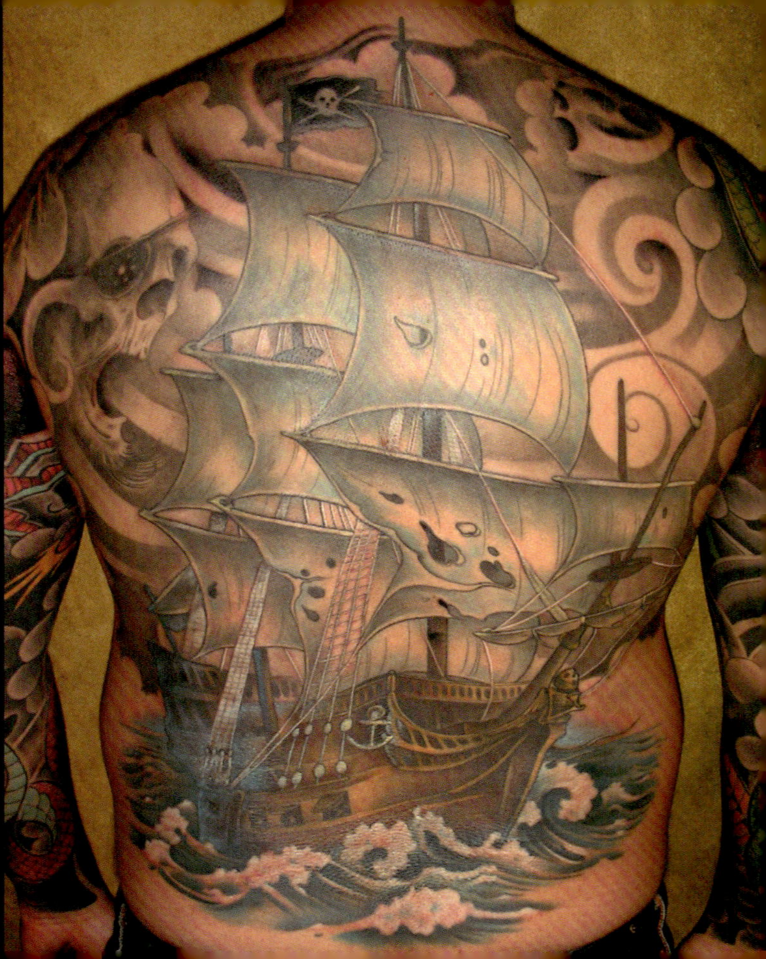

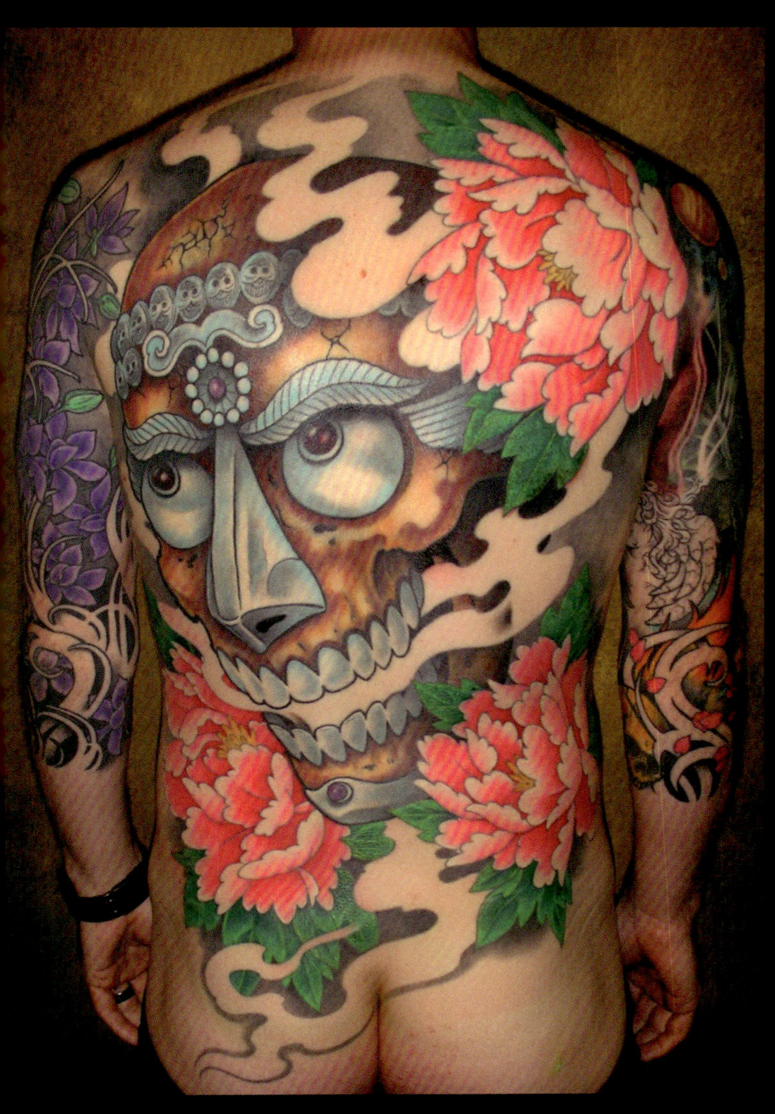
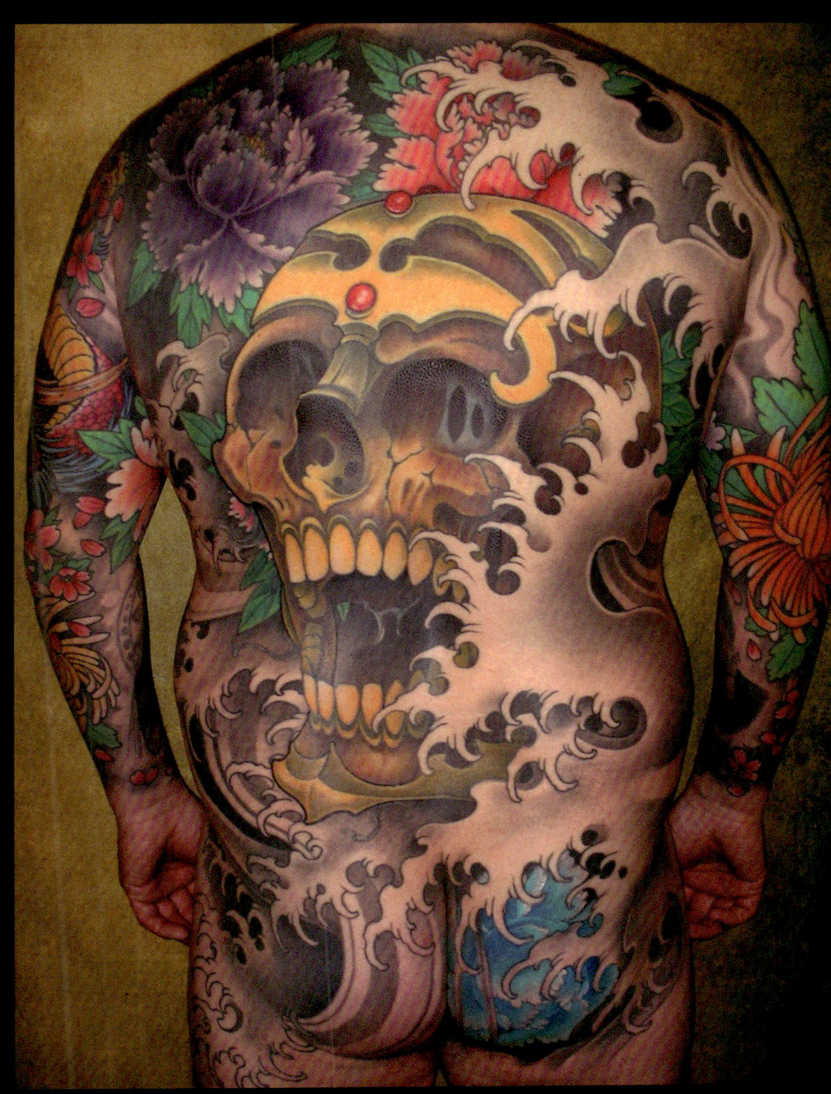

Kurt Wiscombe
www.tattooartwinnipeg.com

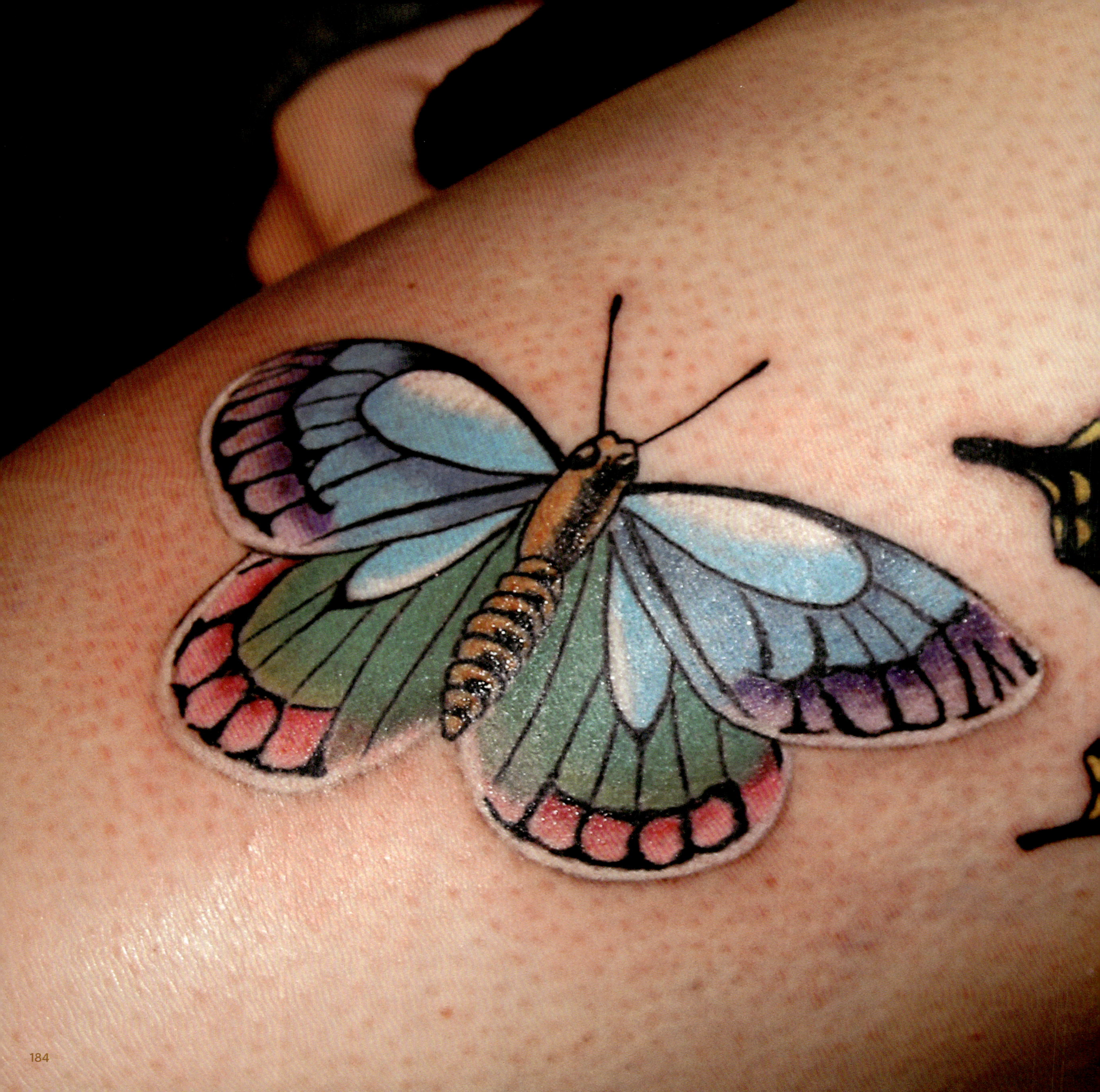

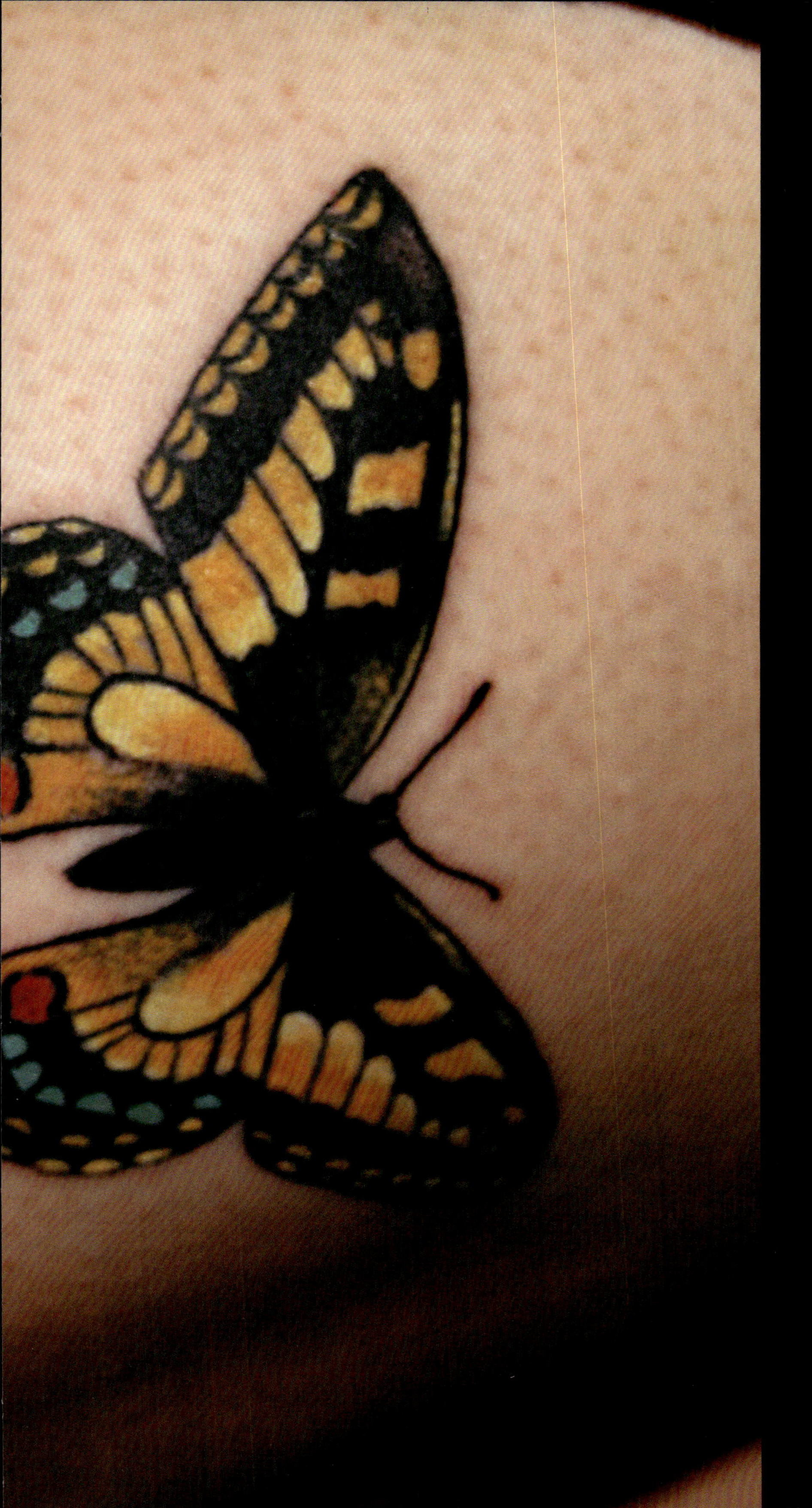
LA ASTRID

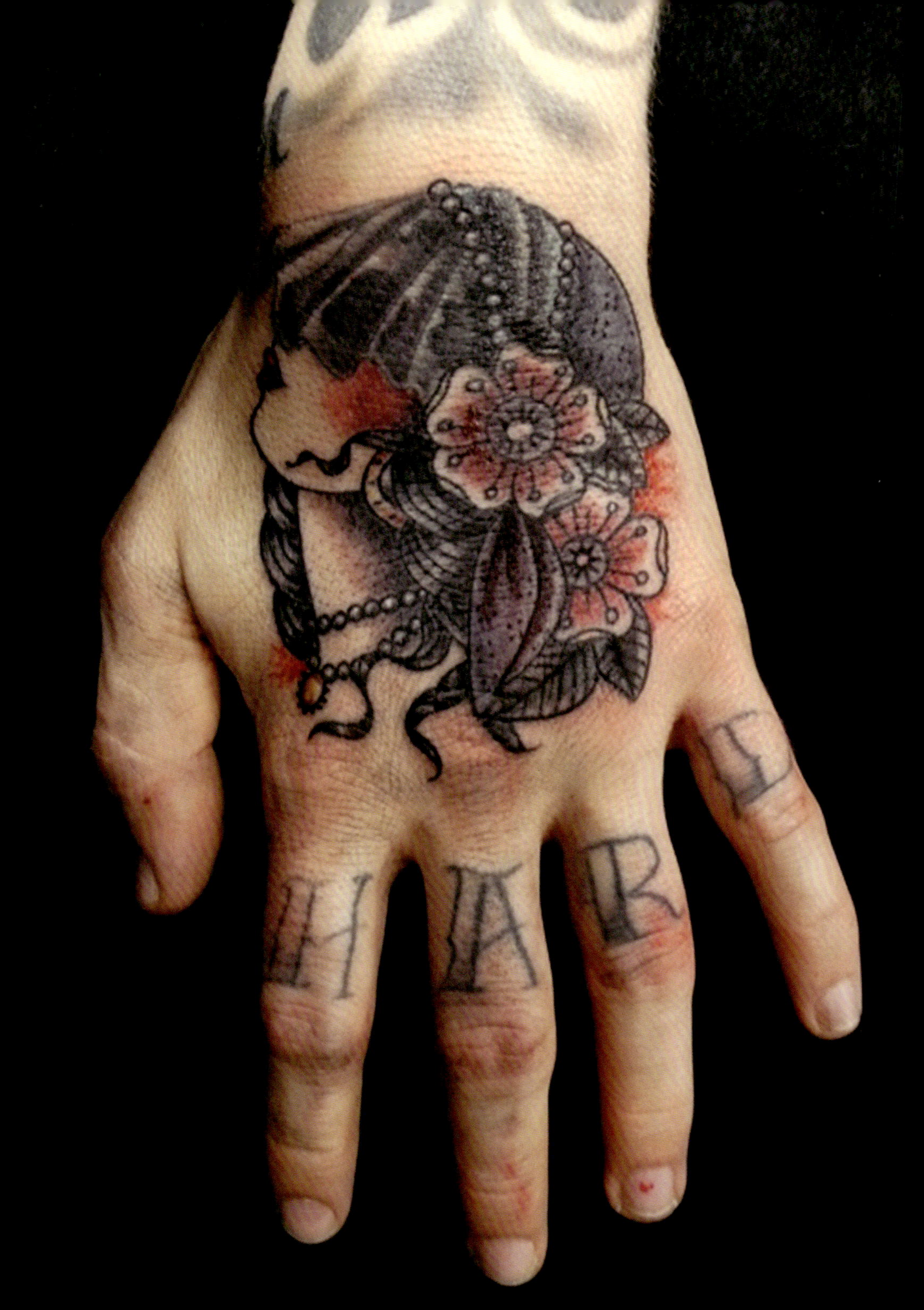

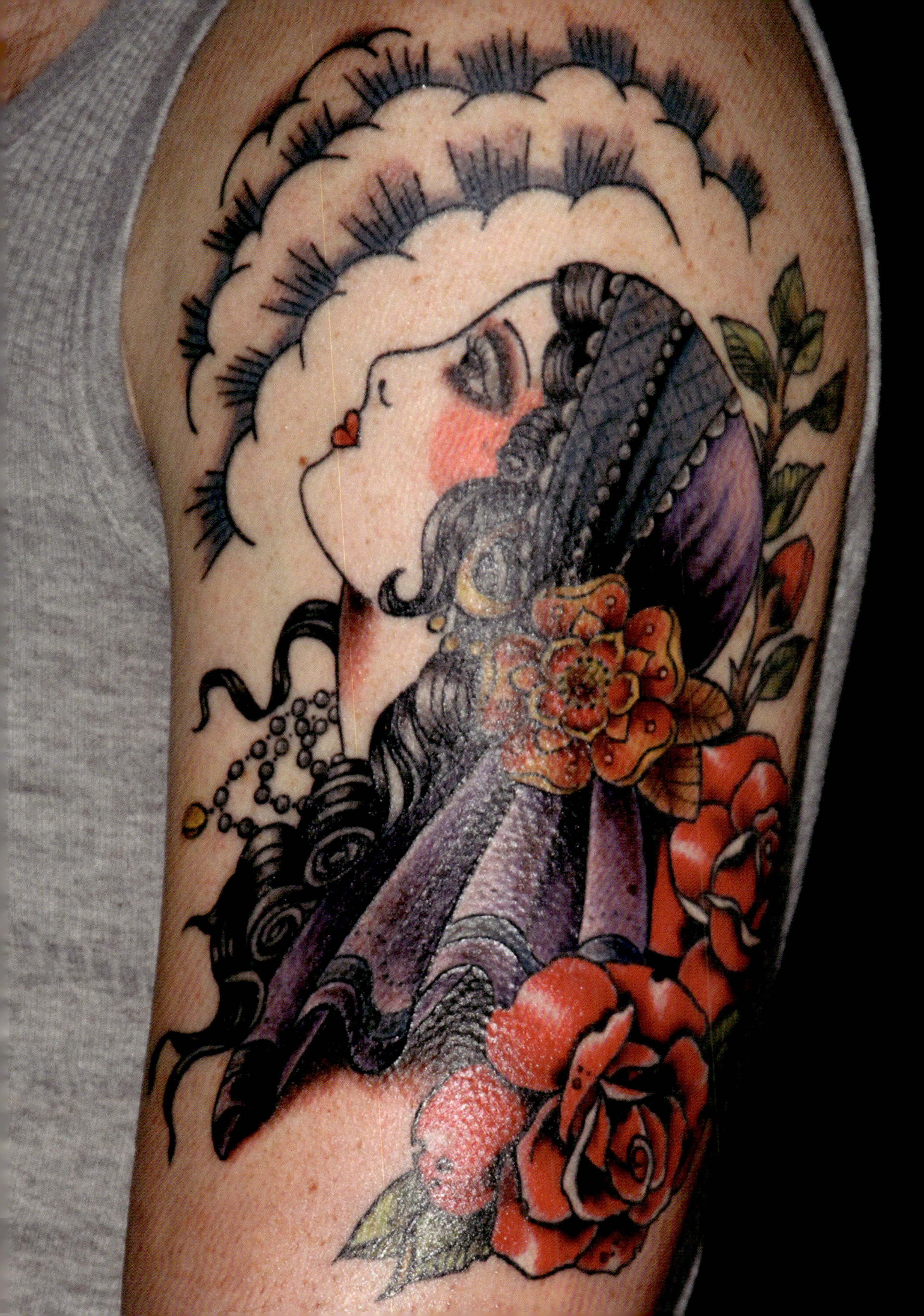

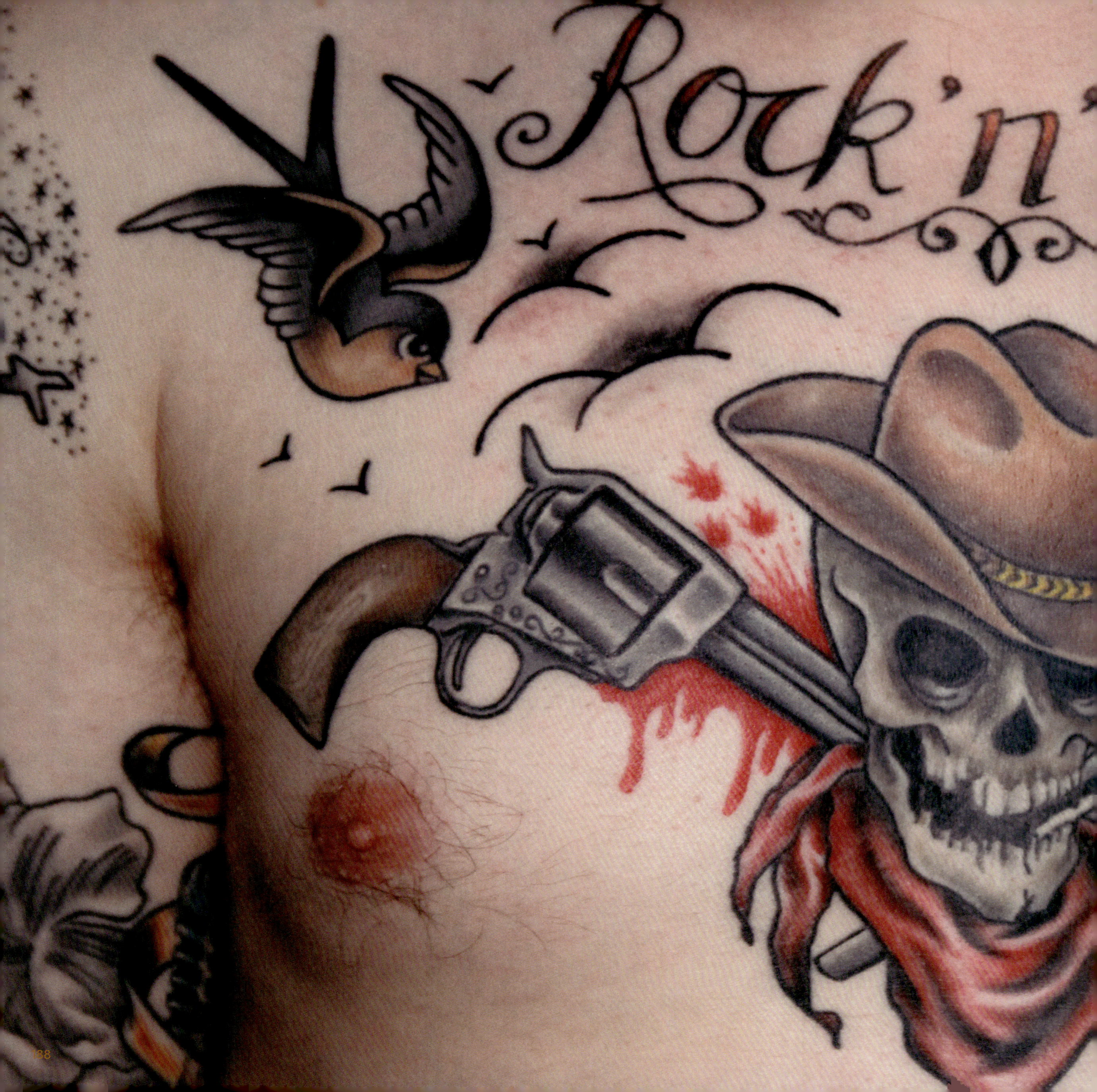
Rock'n'

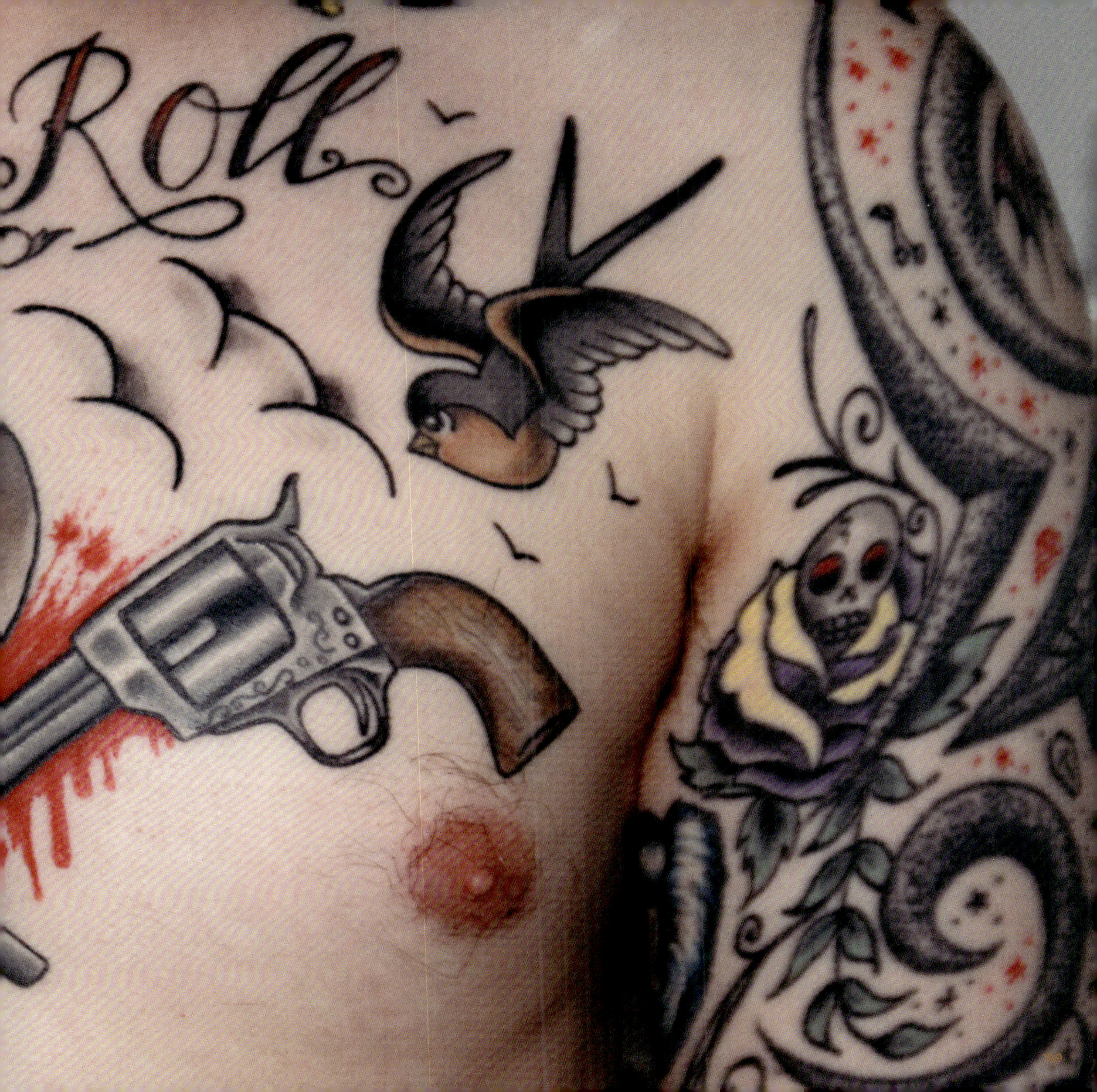

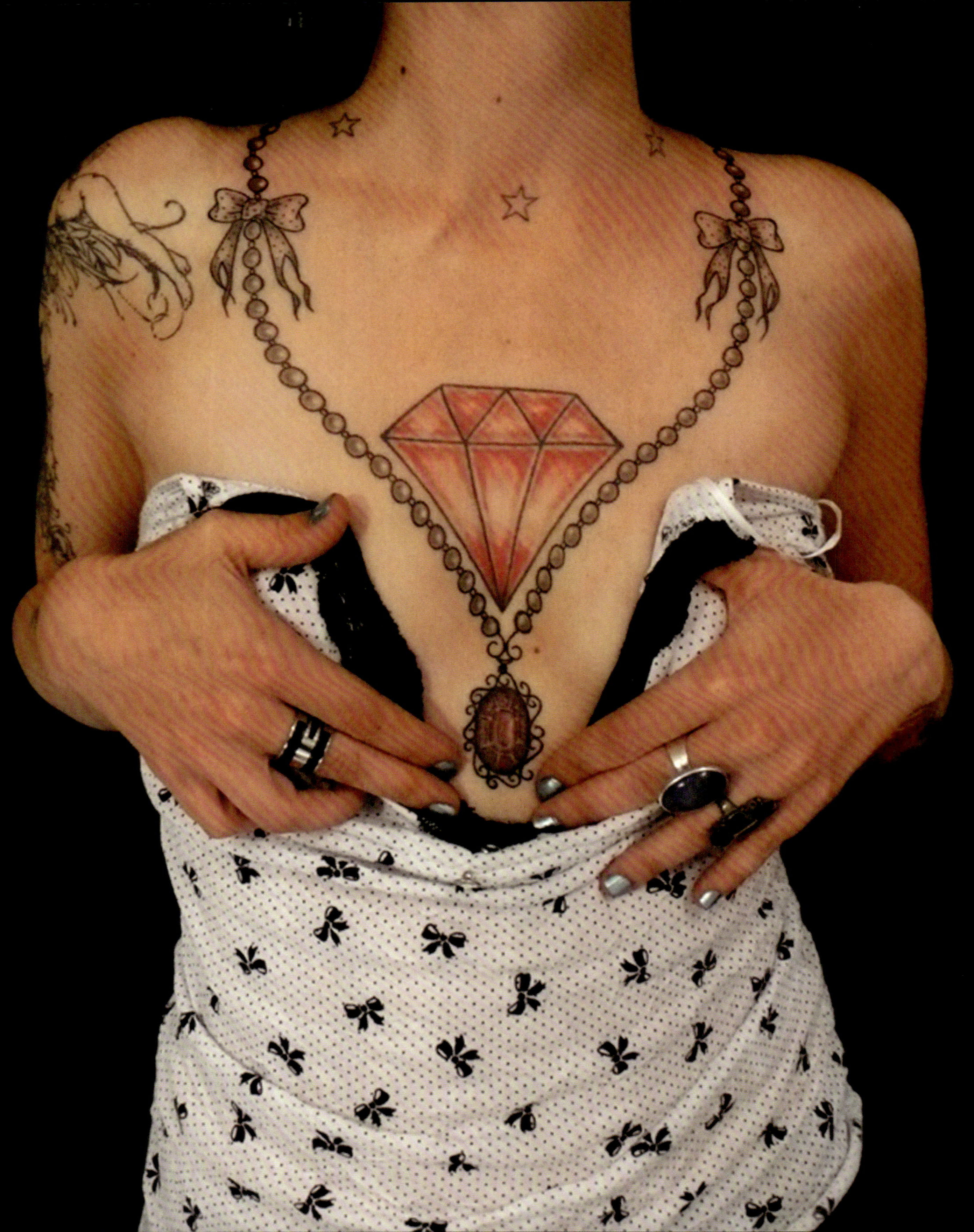

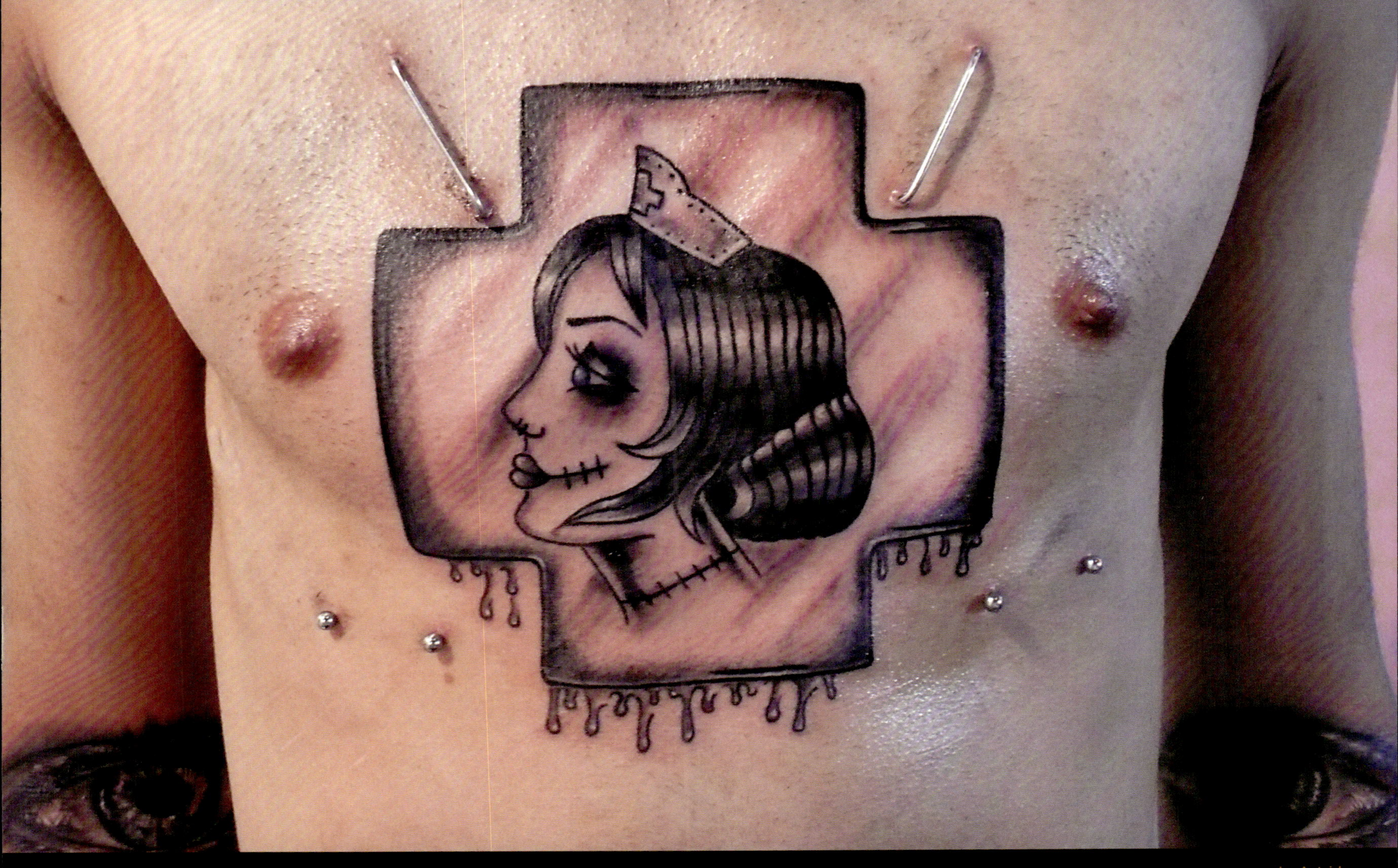
La Astrid
www.1969tattoo.no

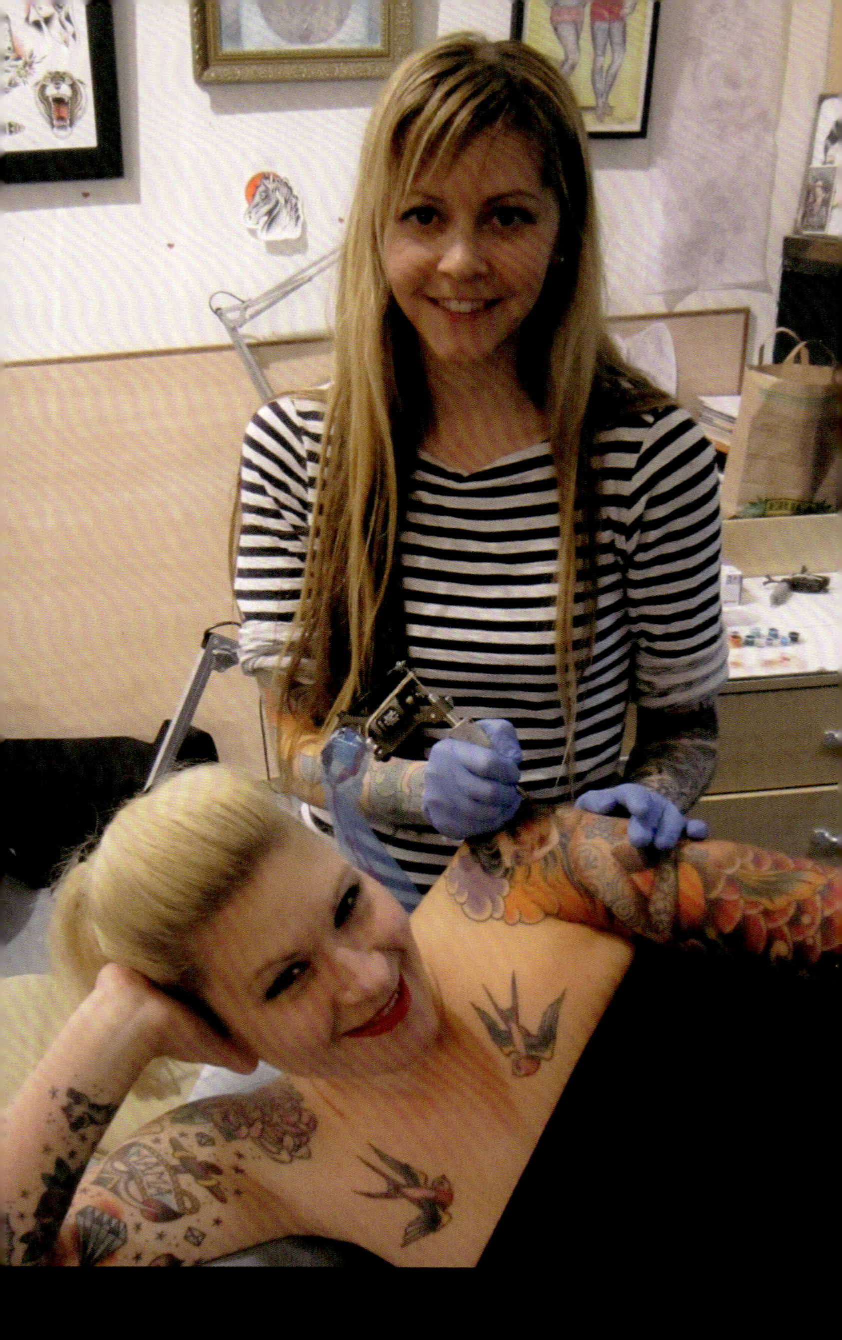

LINA STIGSSON

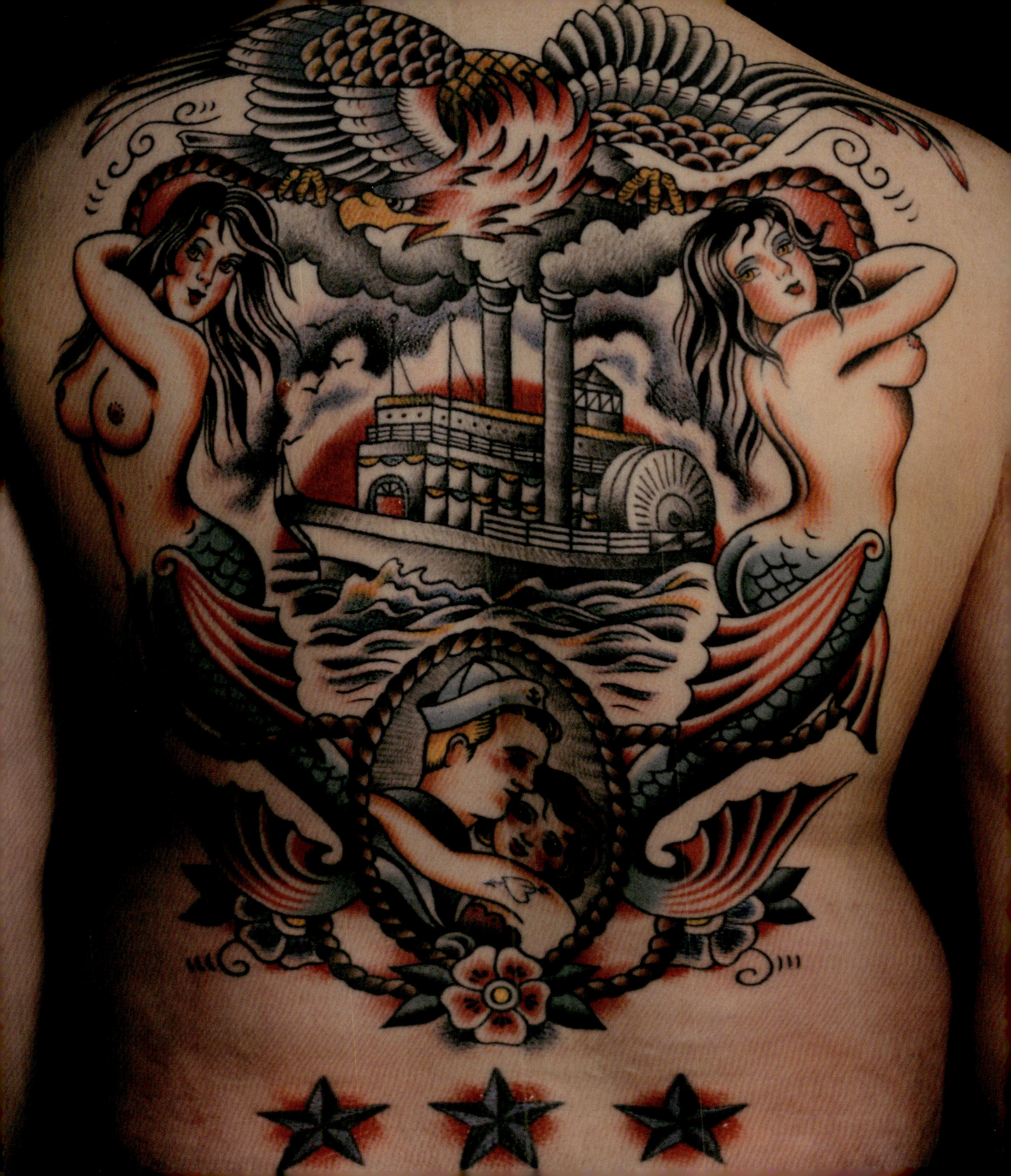

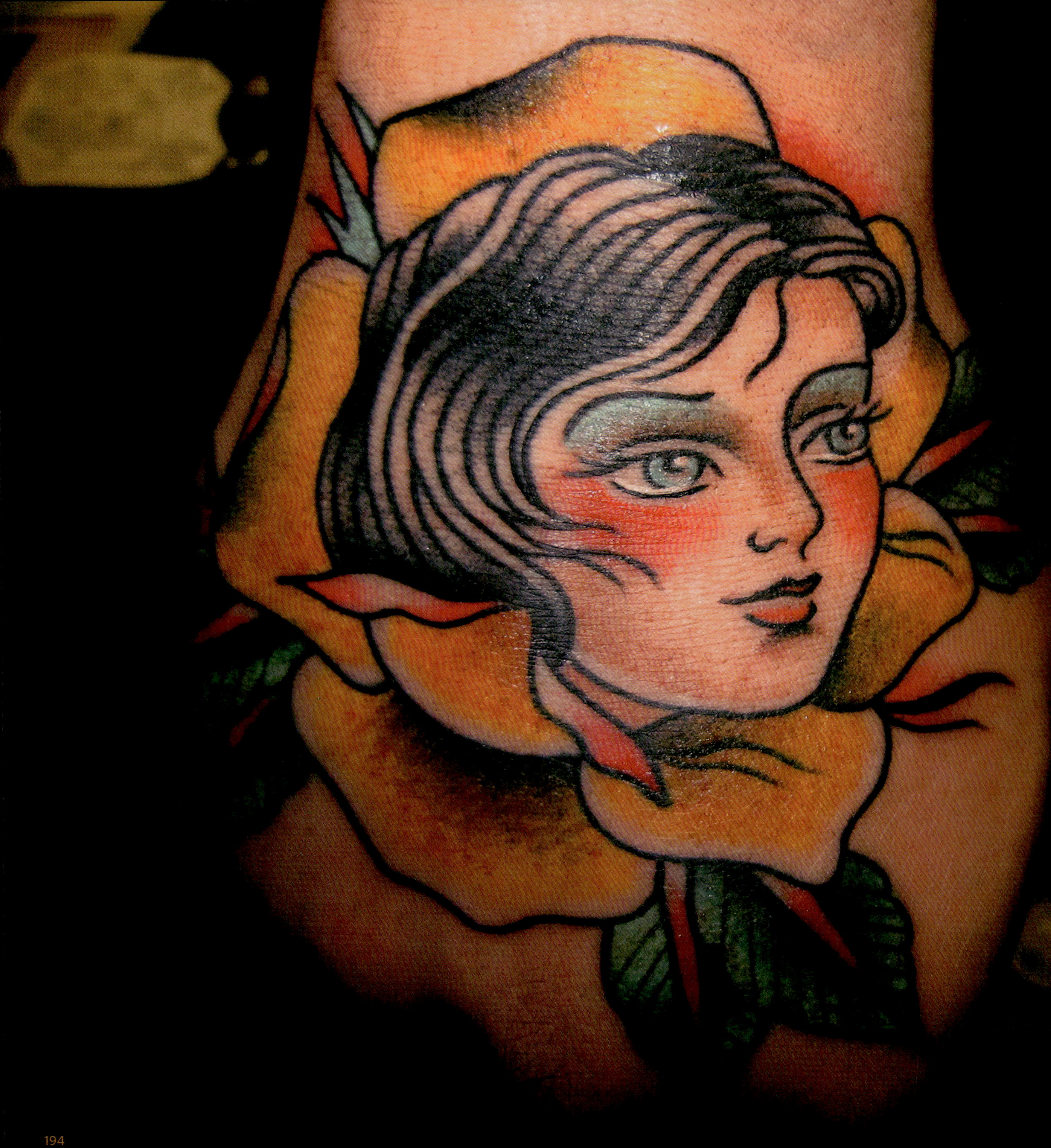

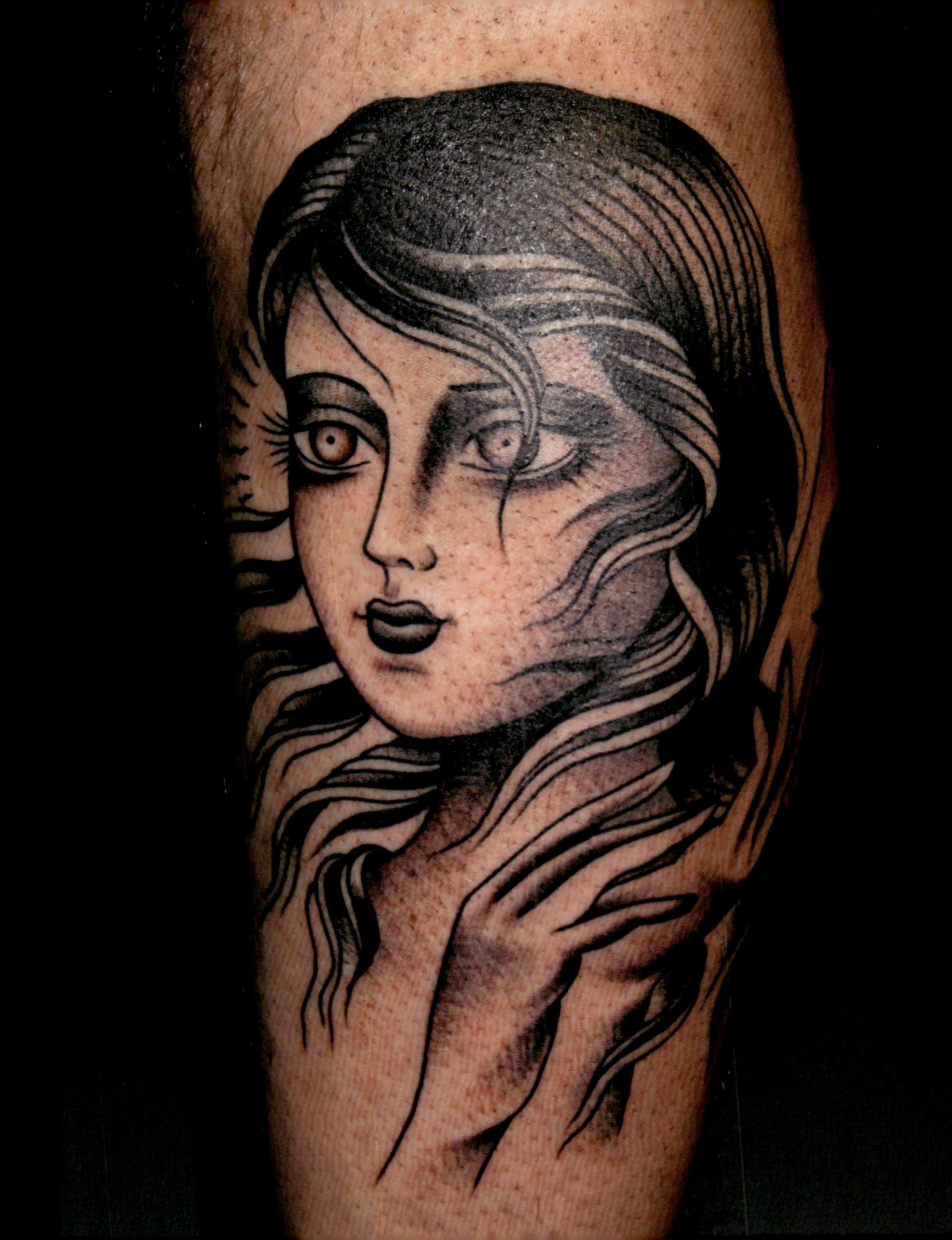

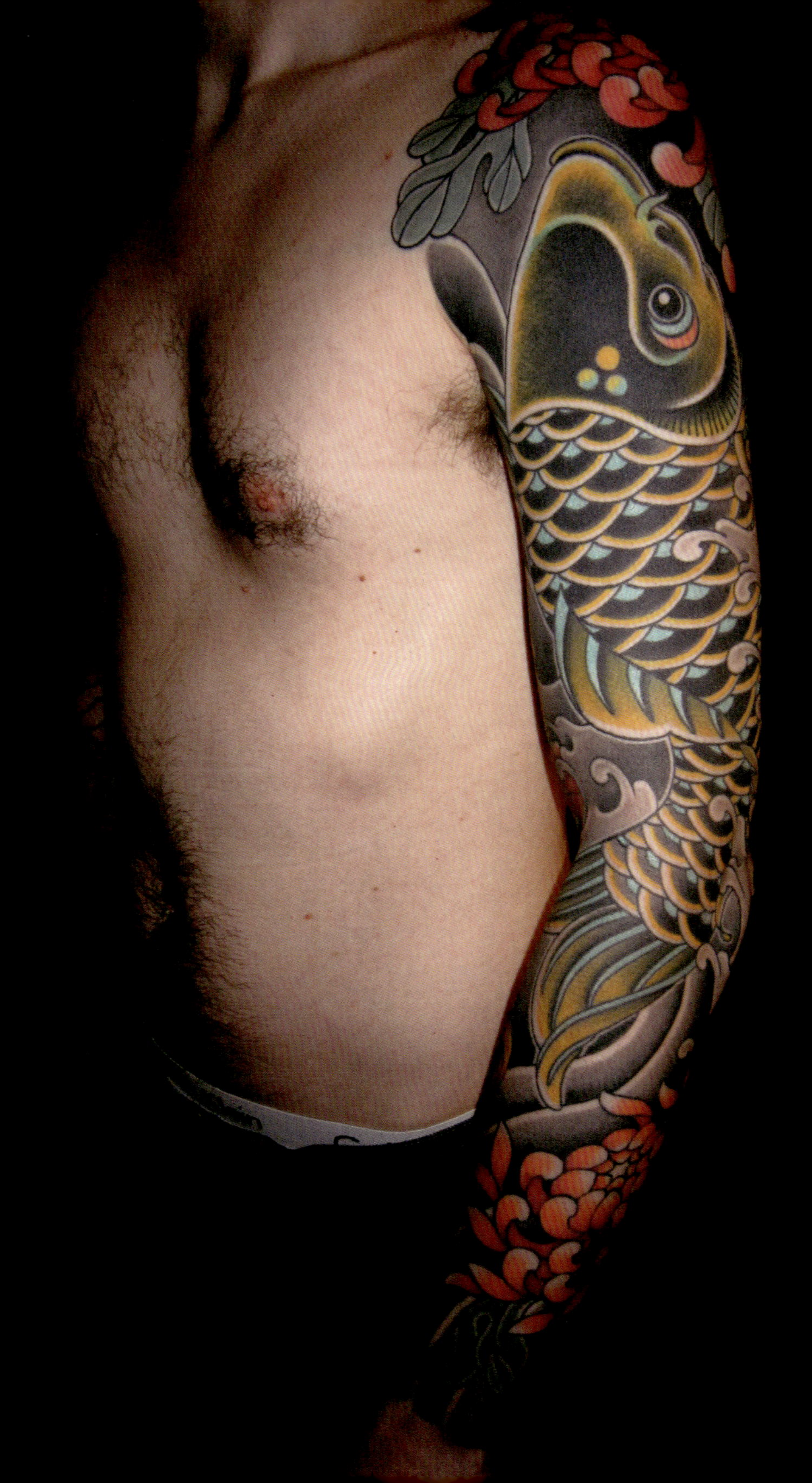

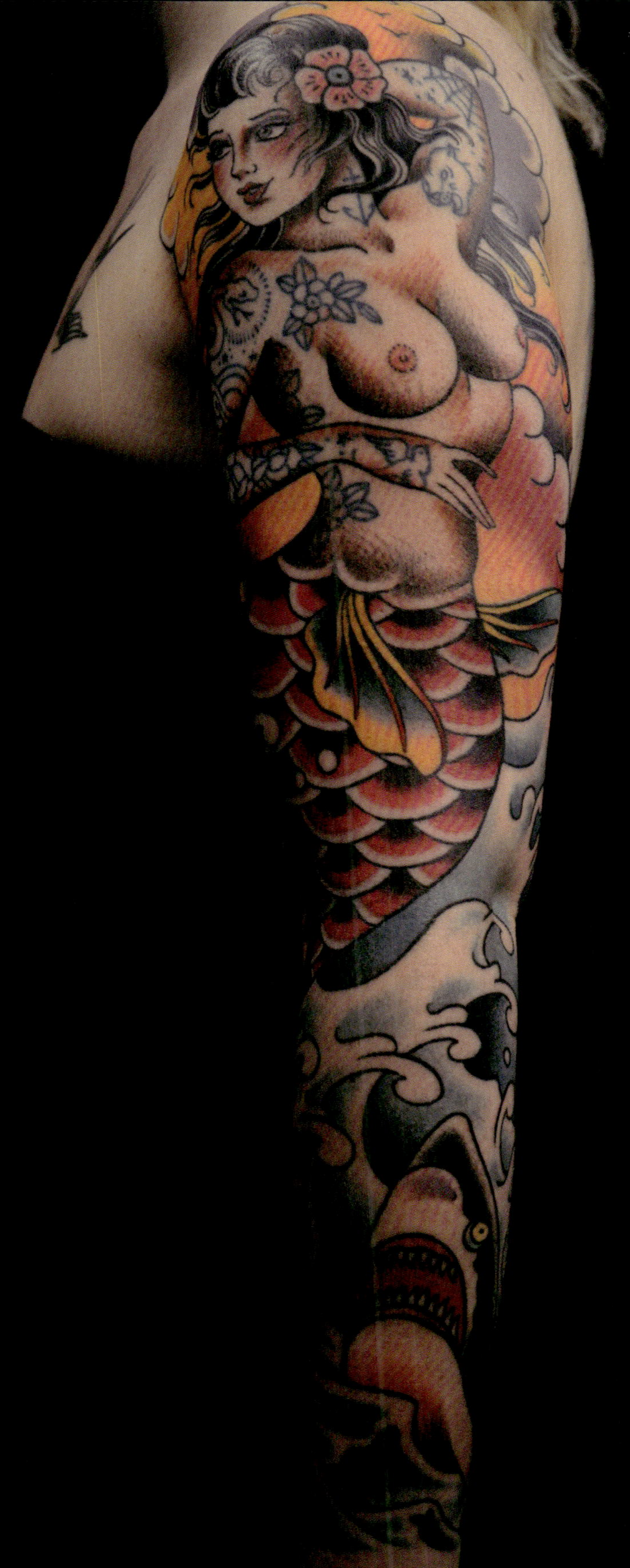

Lina Stigsson
www.linastigsson.com
www.admiraaltattoo.com

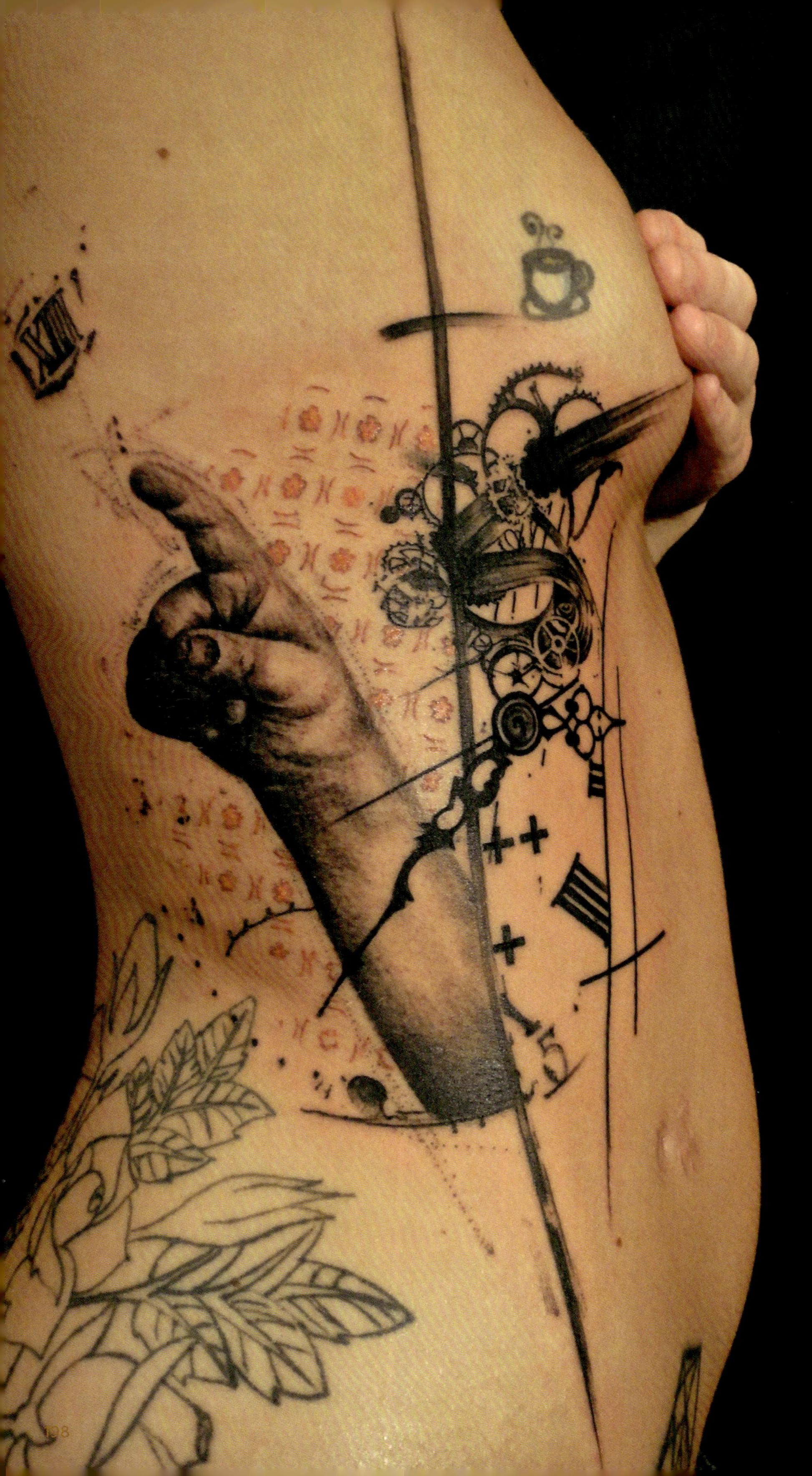

LOÏC LAVENU
A.K.A. XOÏL

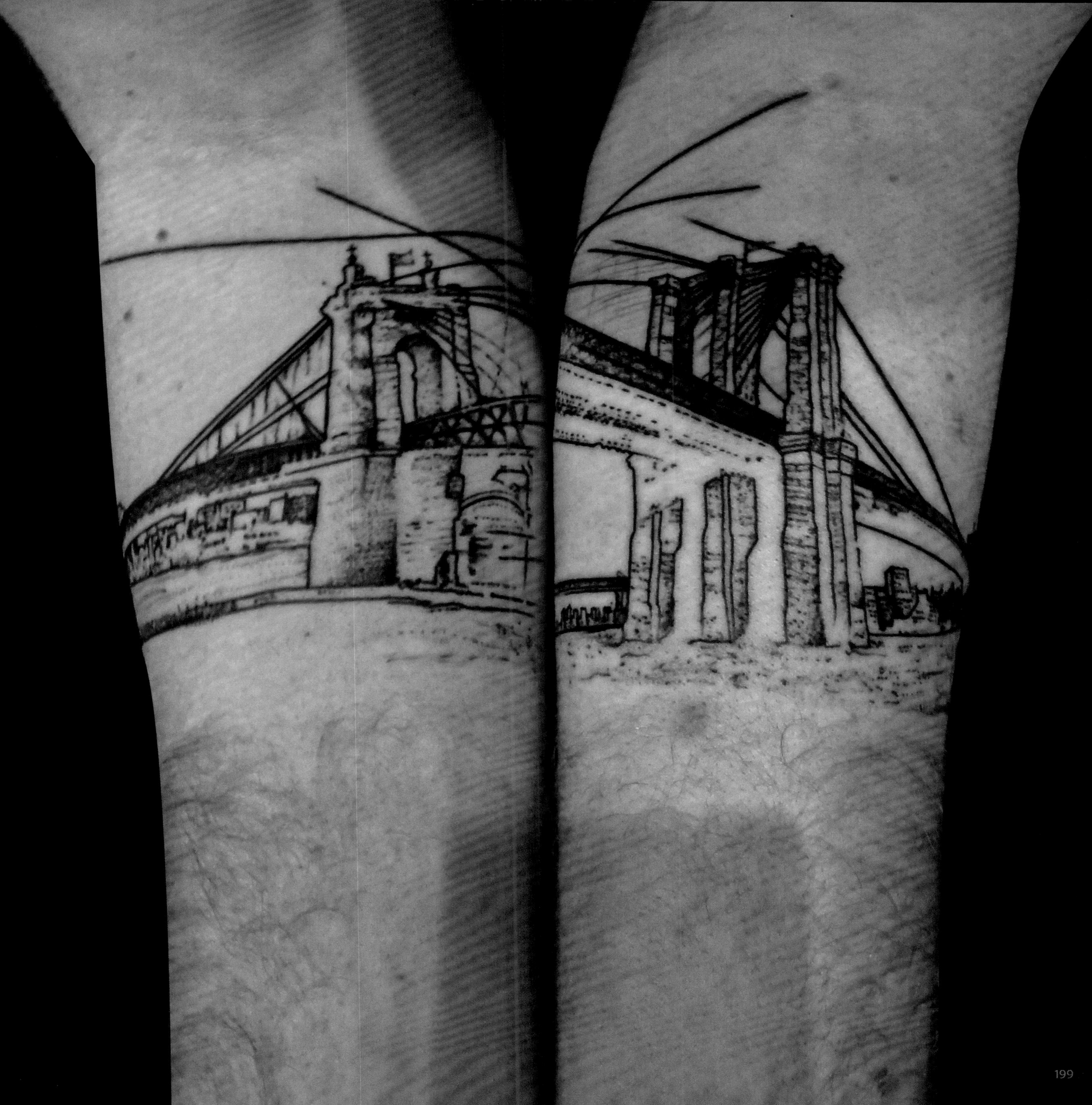

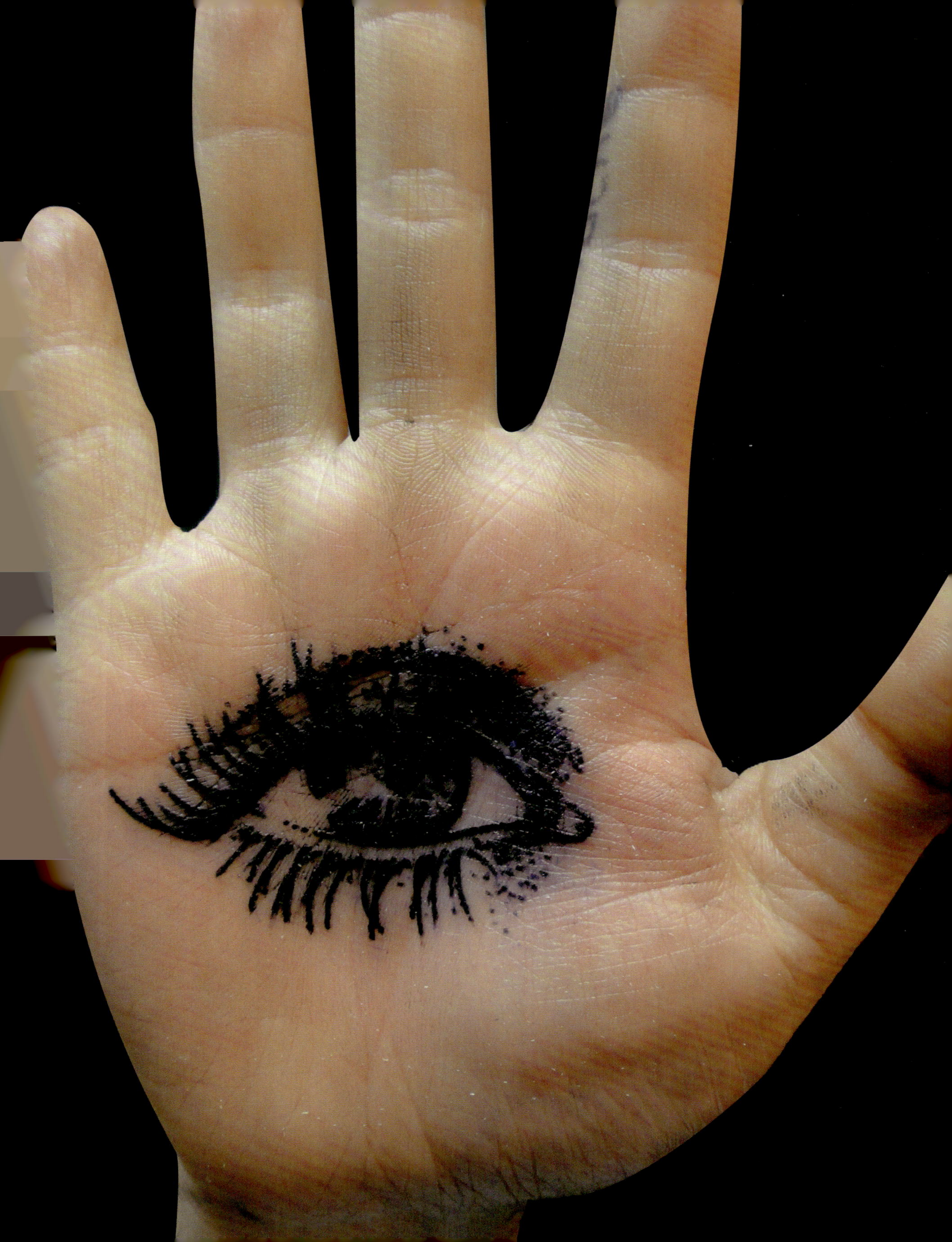

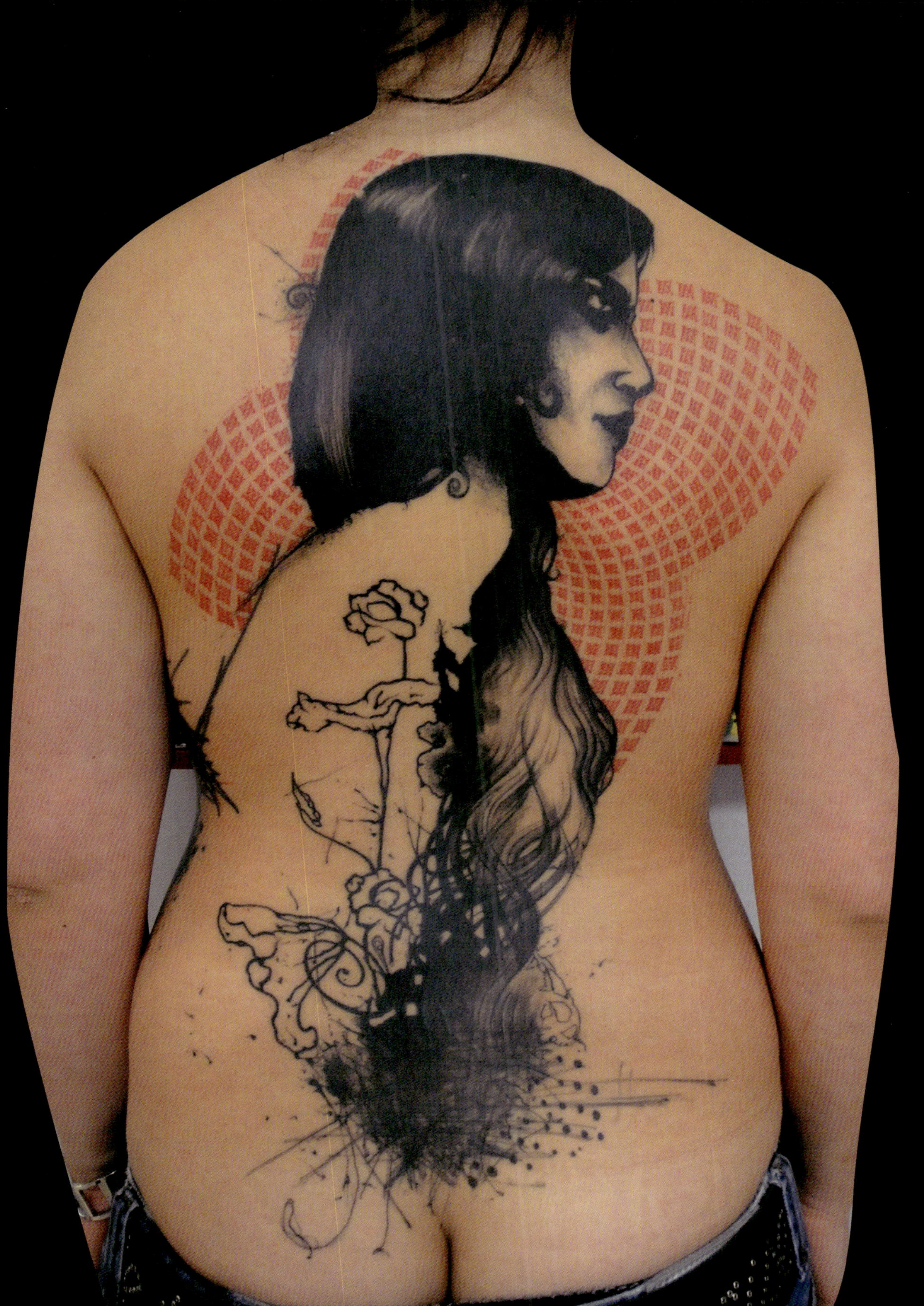

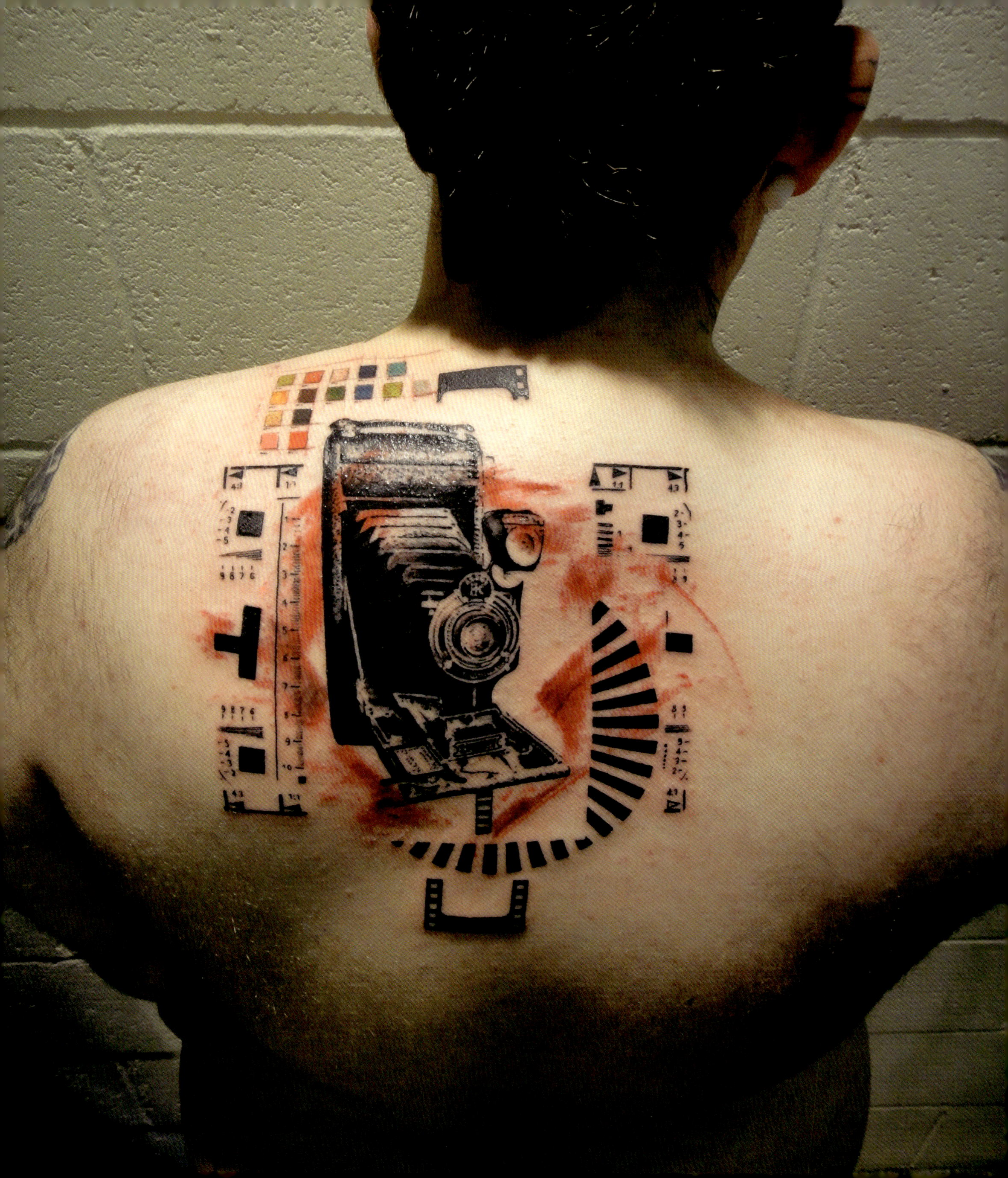

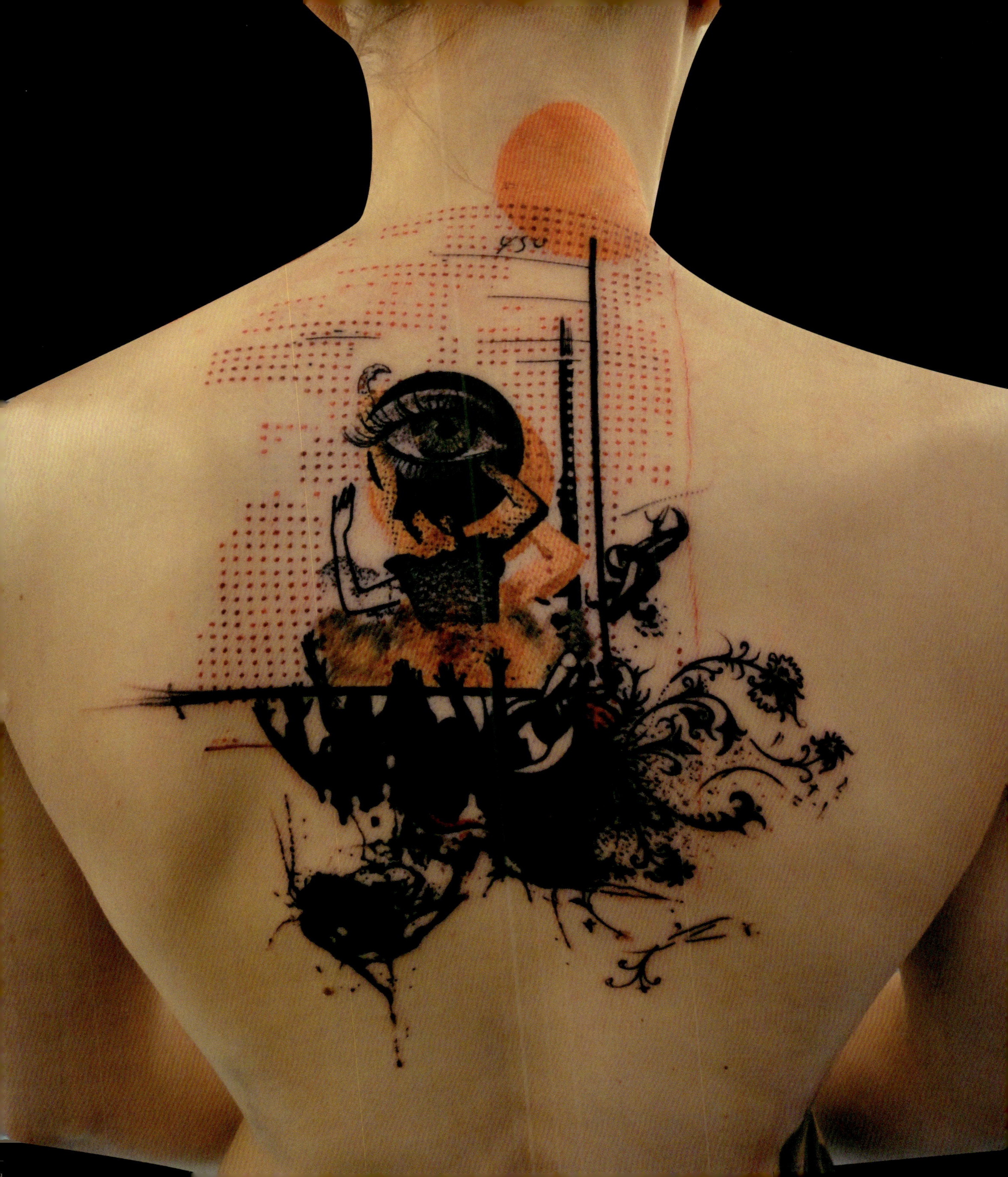

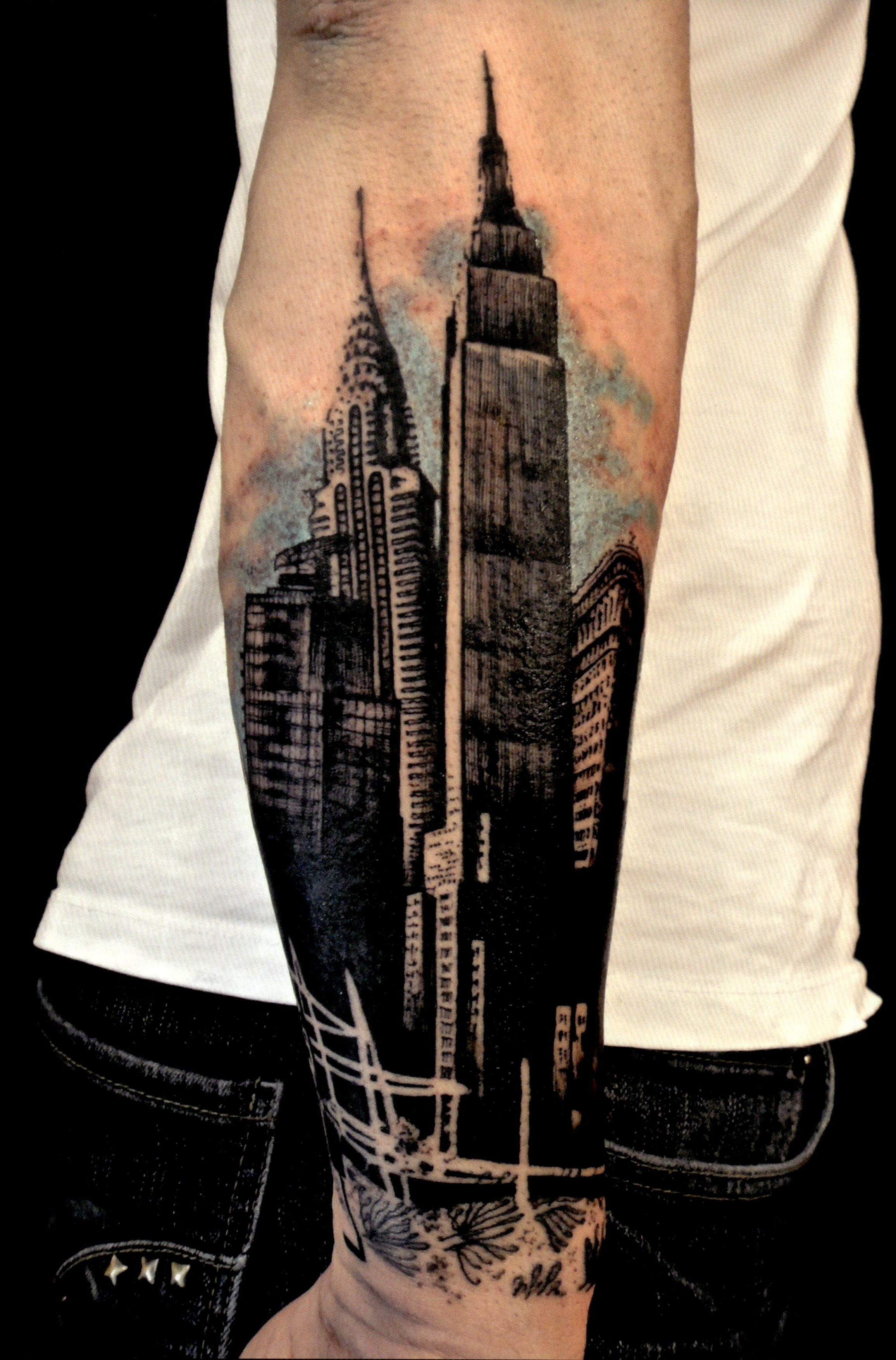

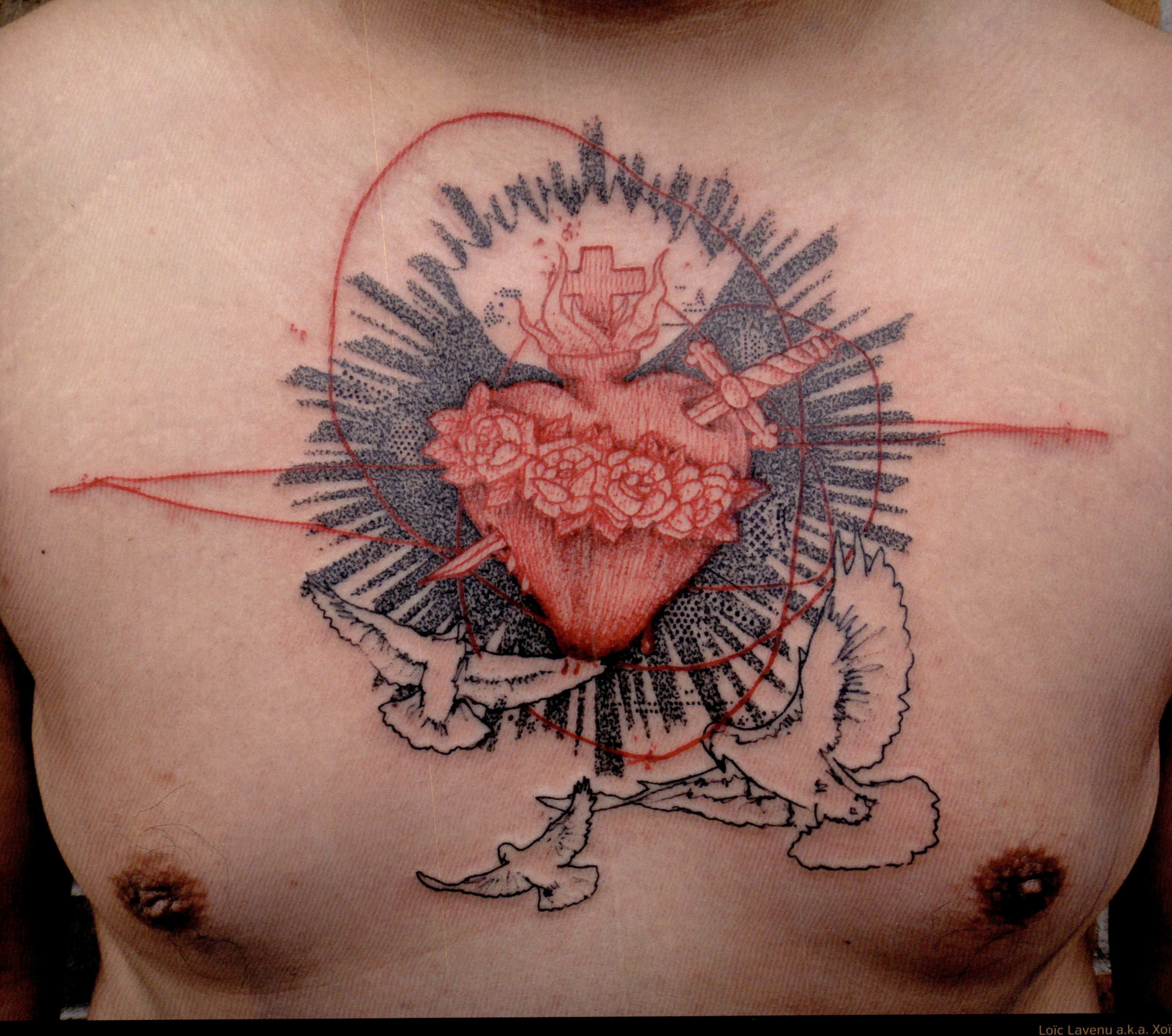
Loïc Lavenu a.k.a. Xoïl
xoilloic.faitdestatouages@gmail.com

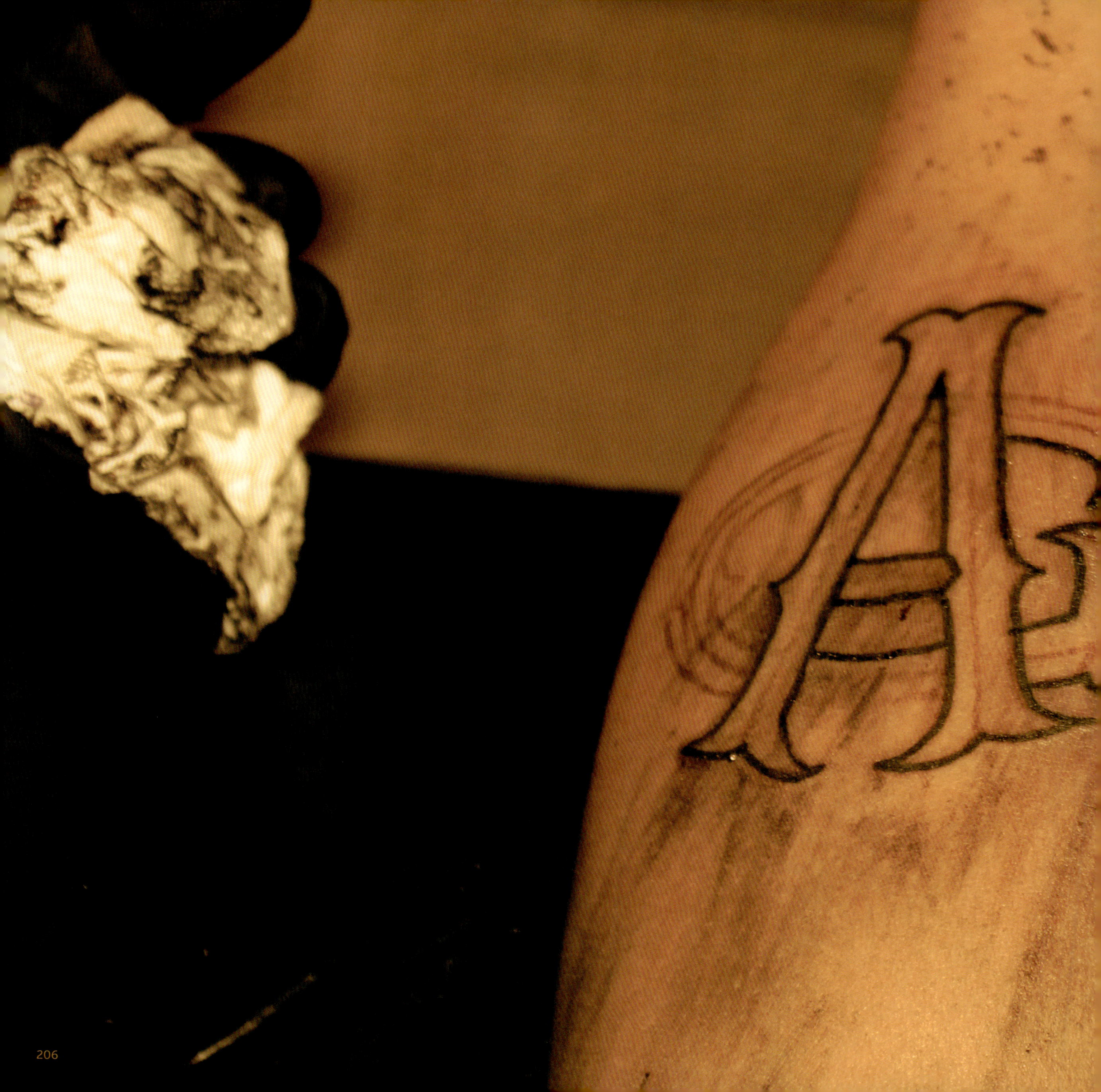

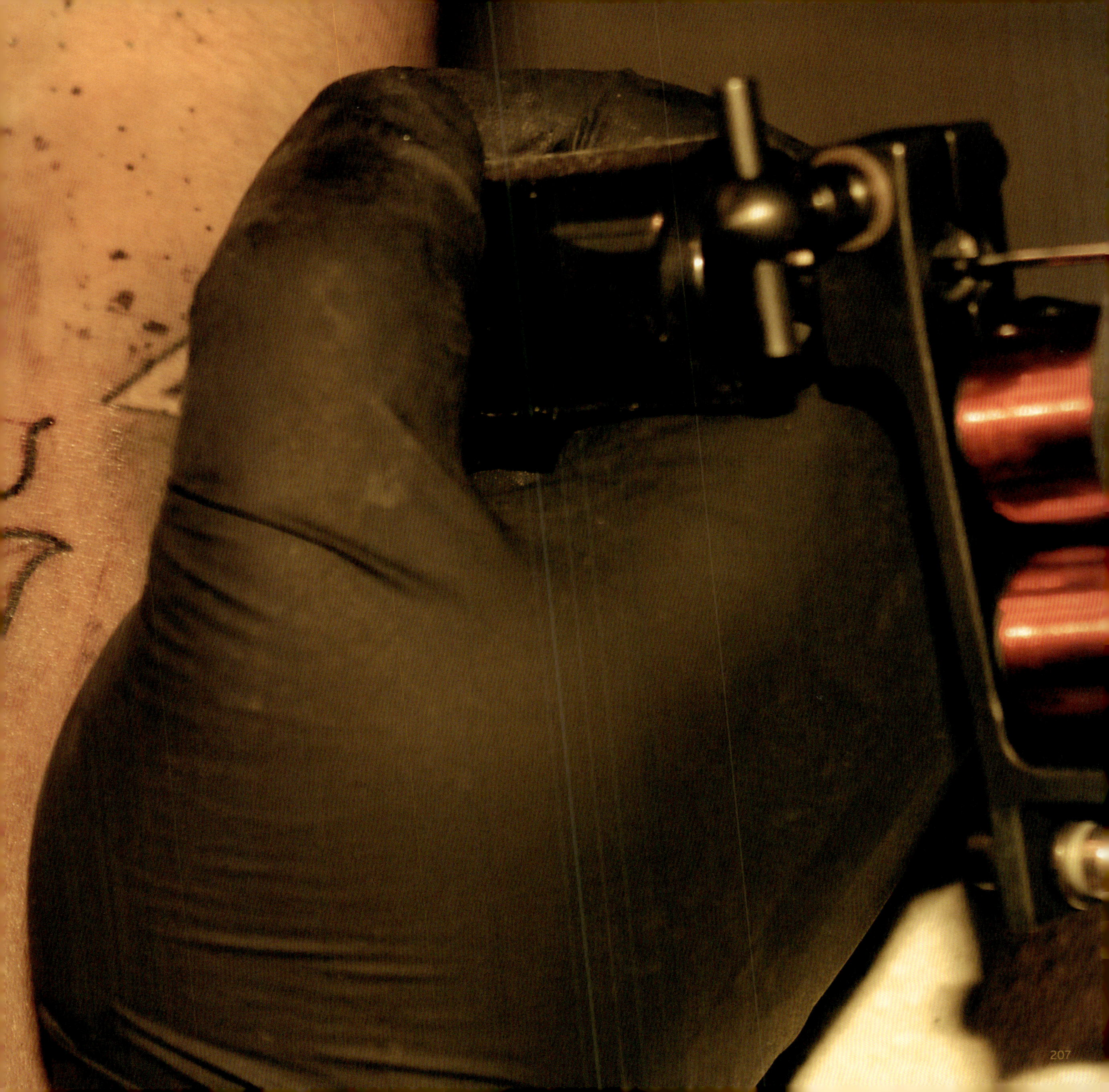

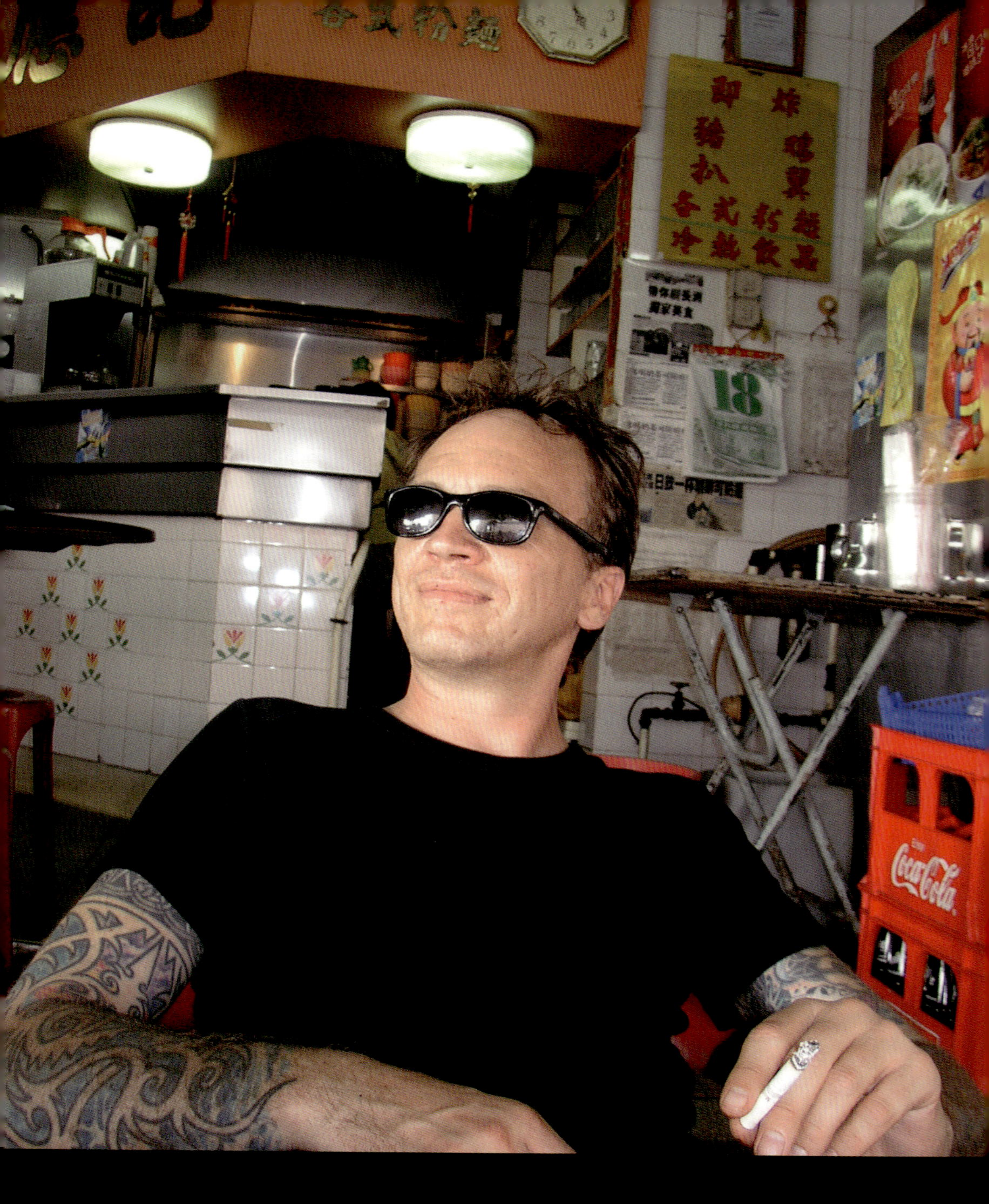

MARCUSE
SMILIN' DEMONS TATTOO

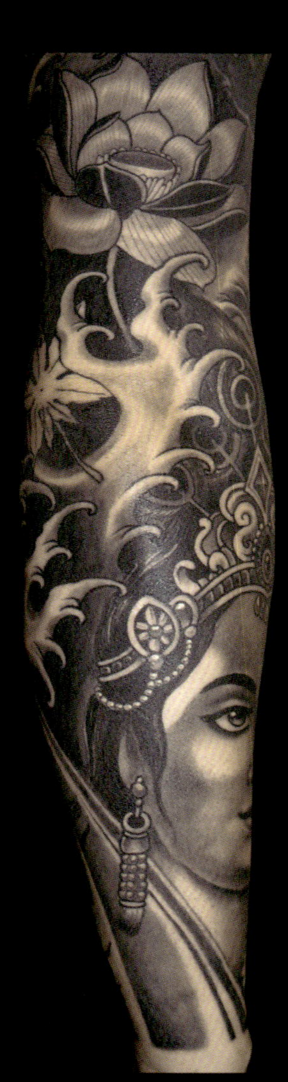
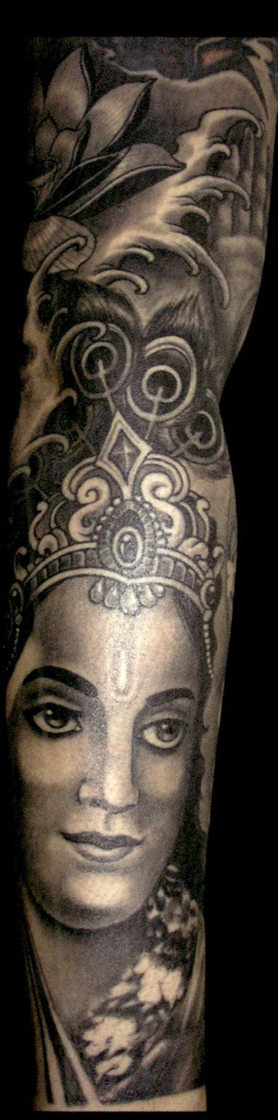
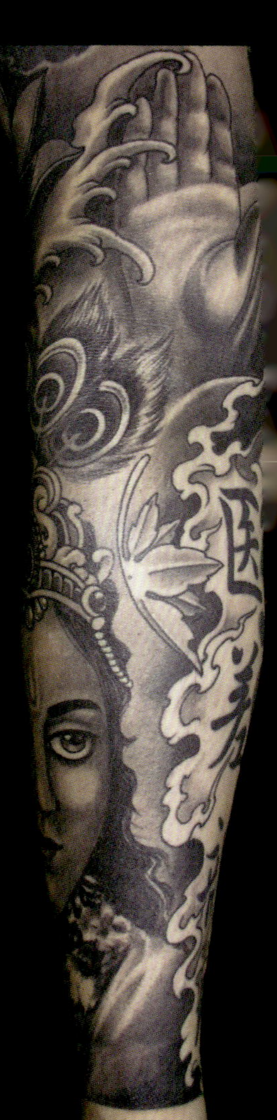

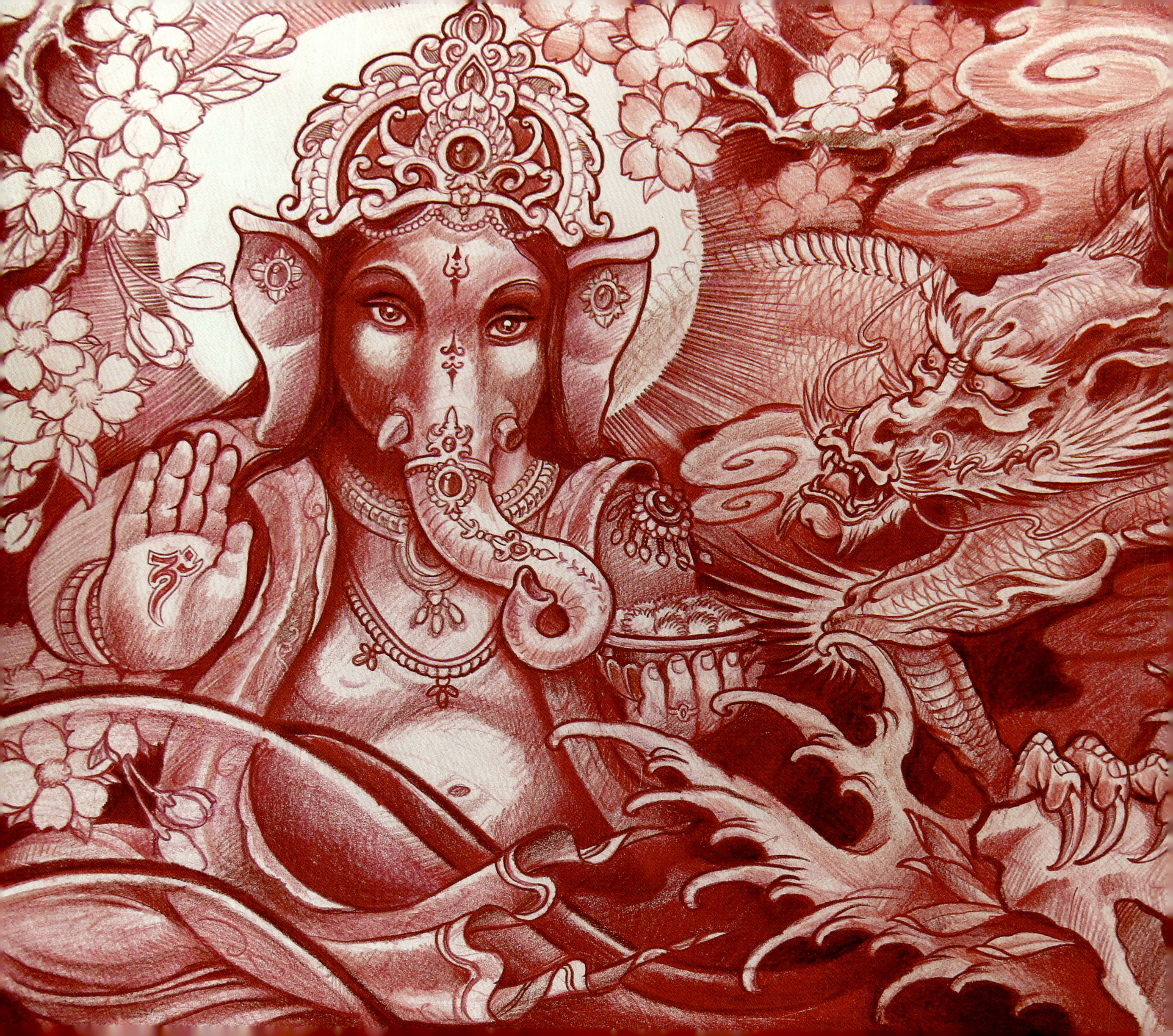

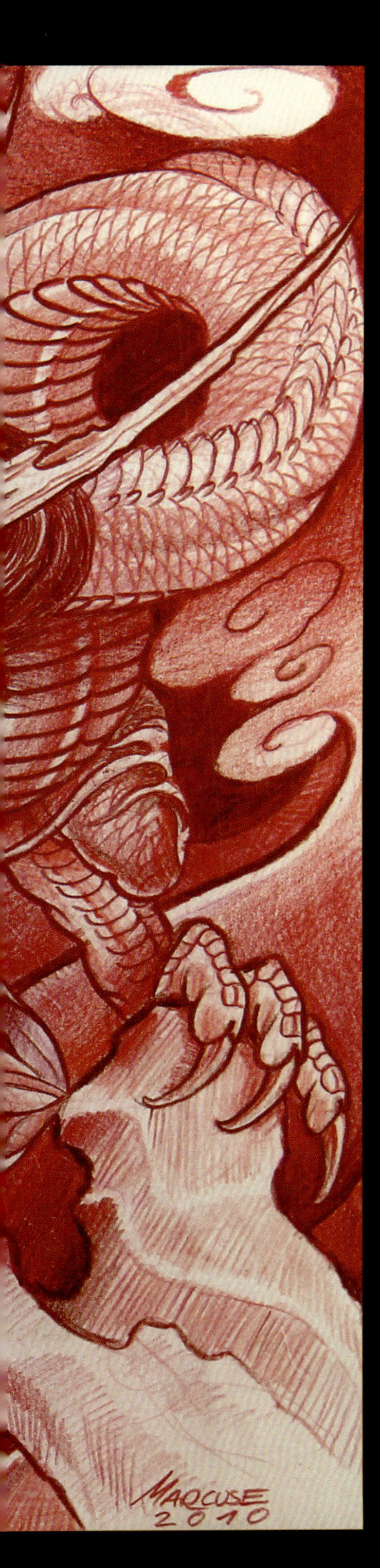

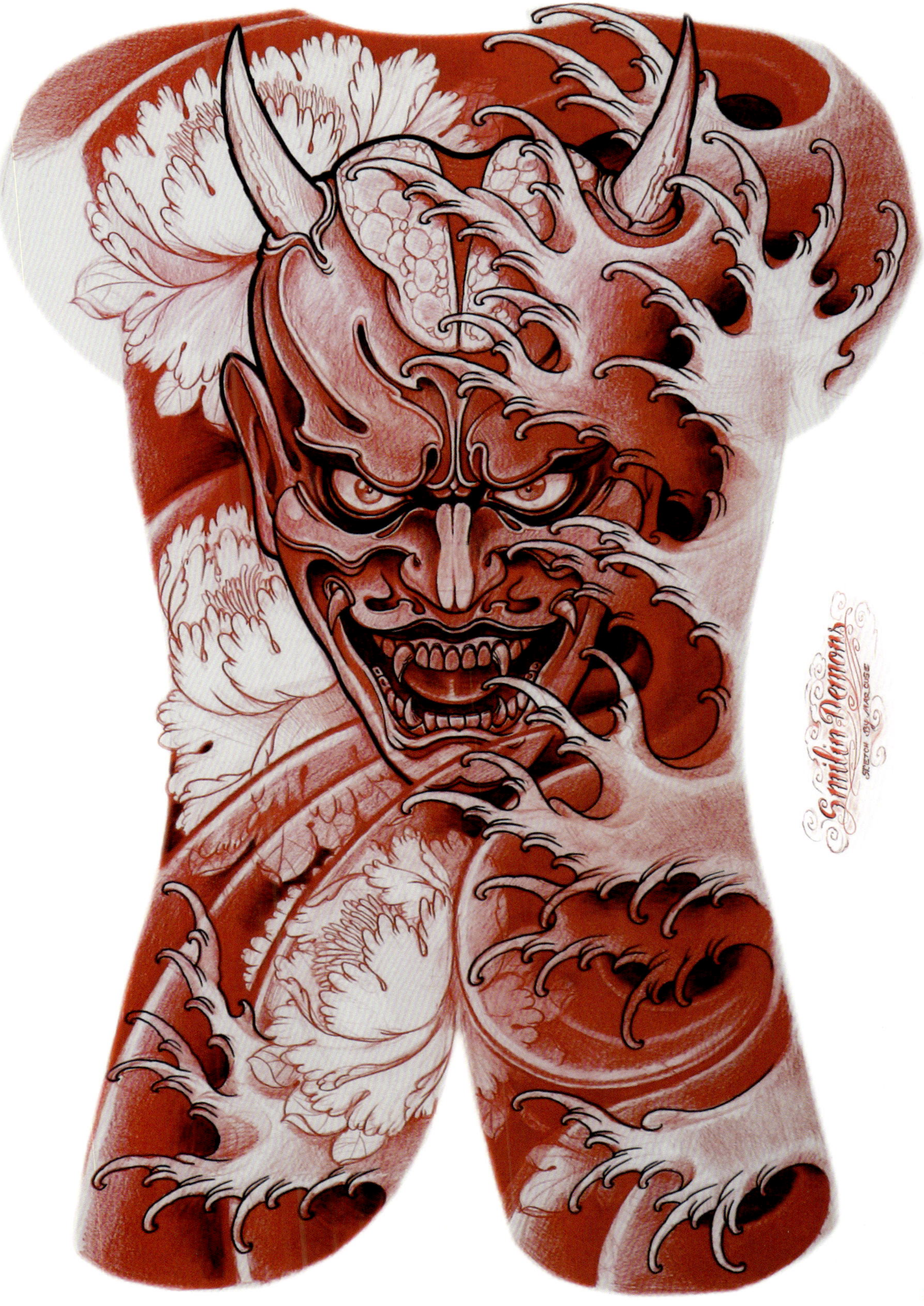

Smilin Demons
SKETCH BY MARCUSE
MARCUSE
2010

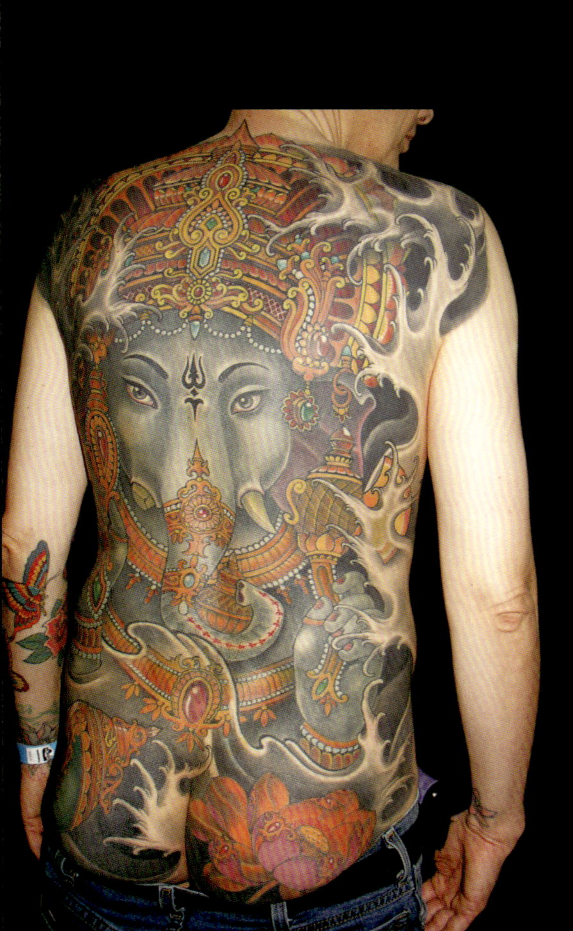
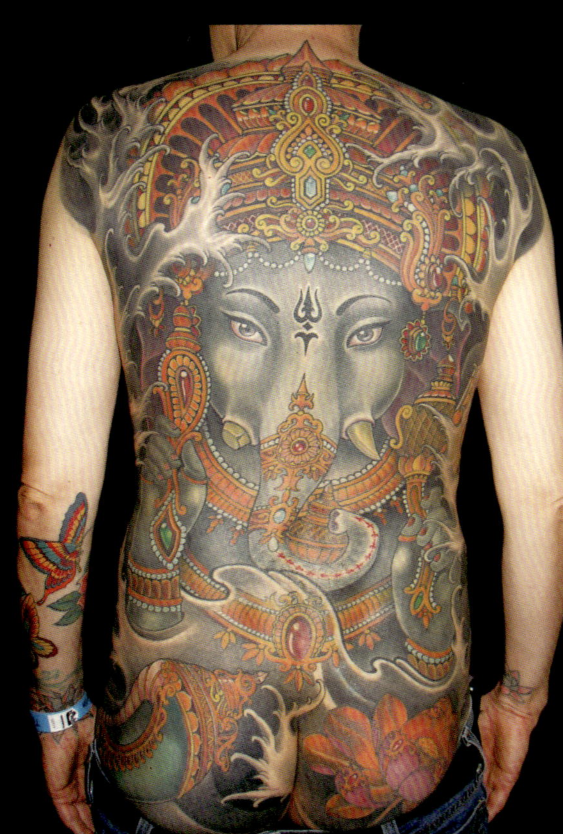
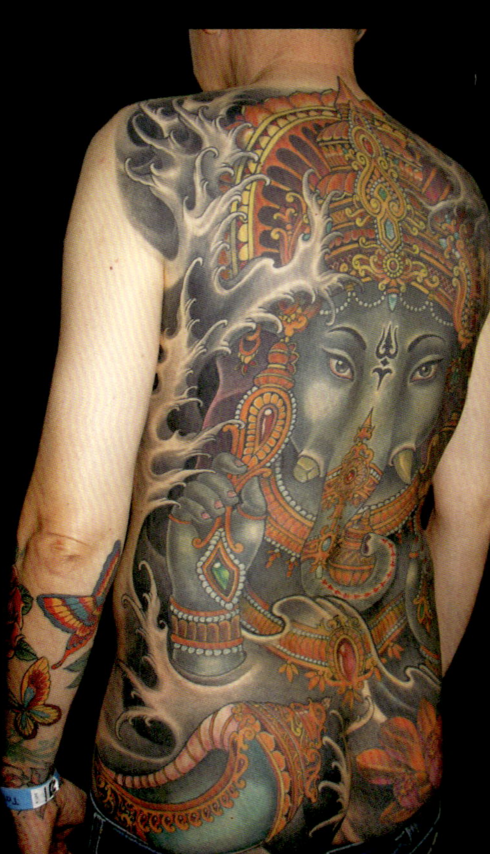

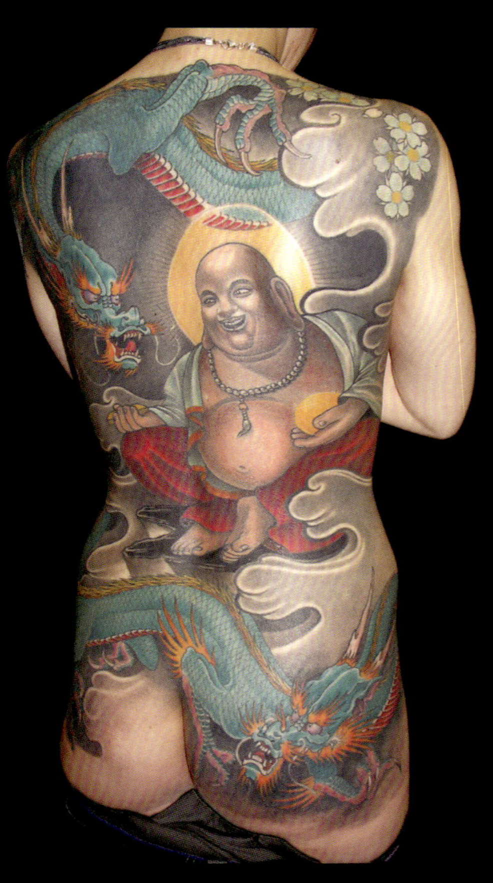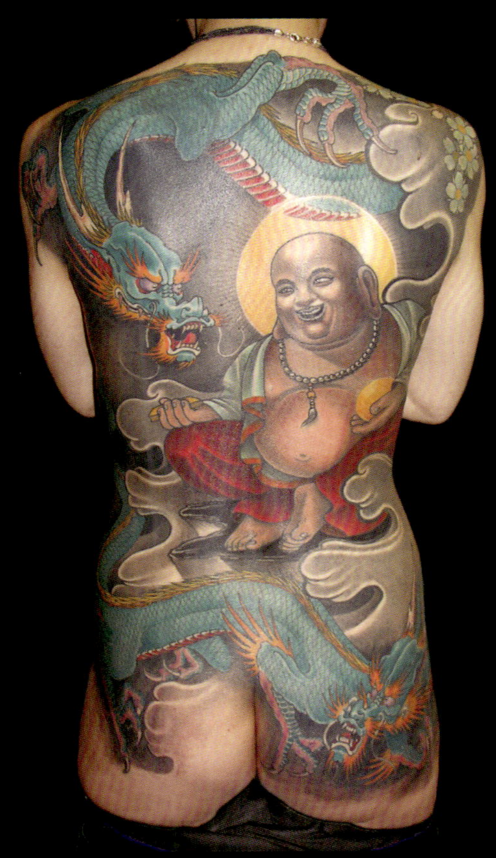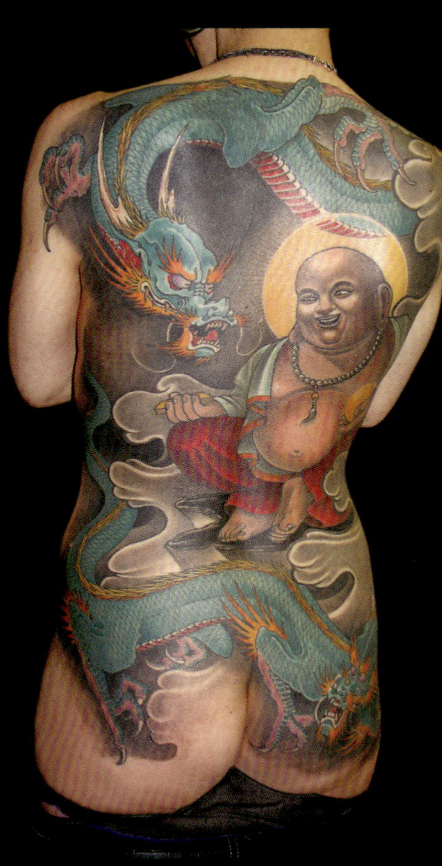

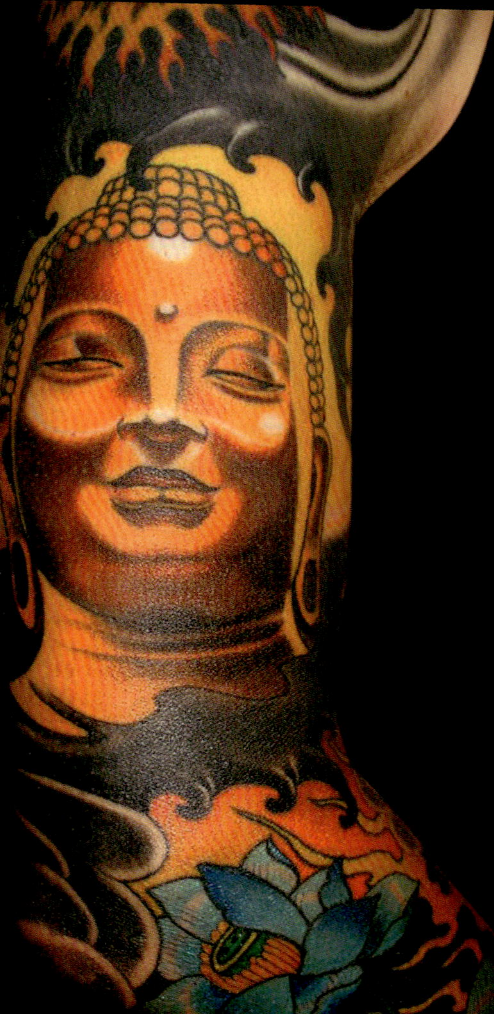

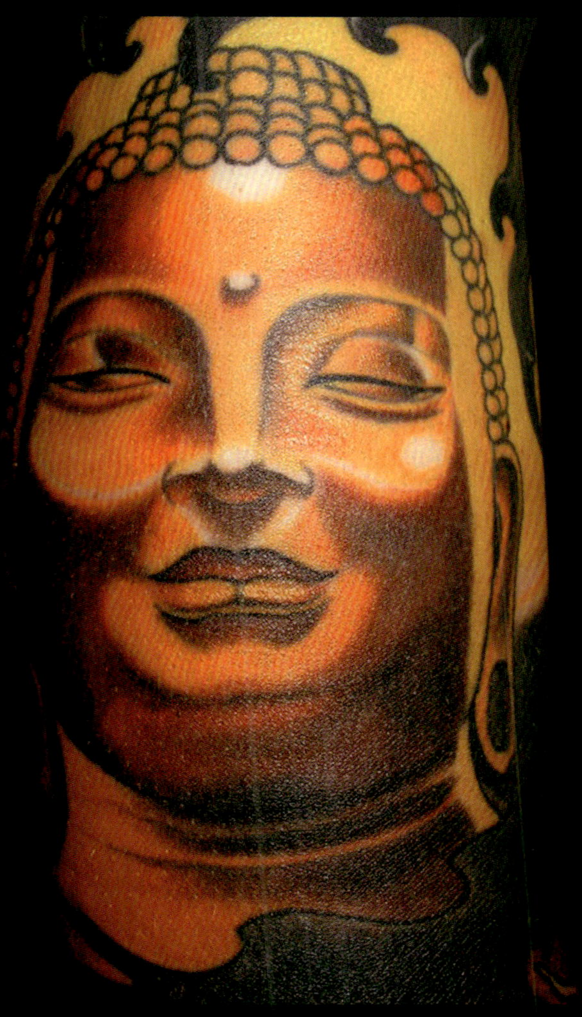

Marcuse
www.smilindemons.de

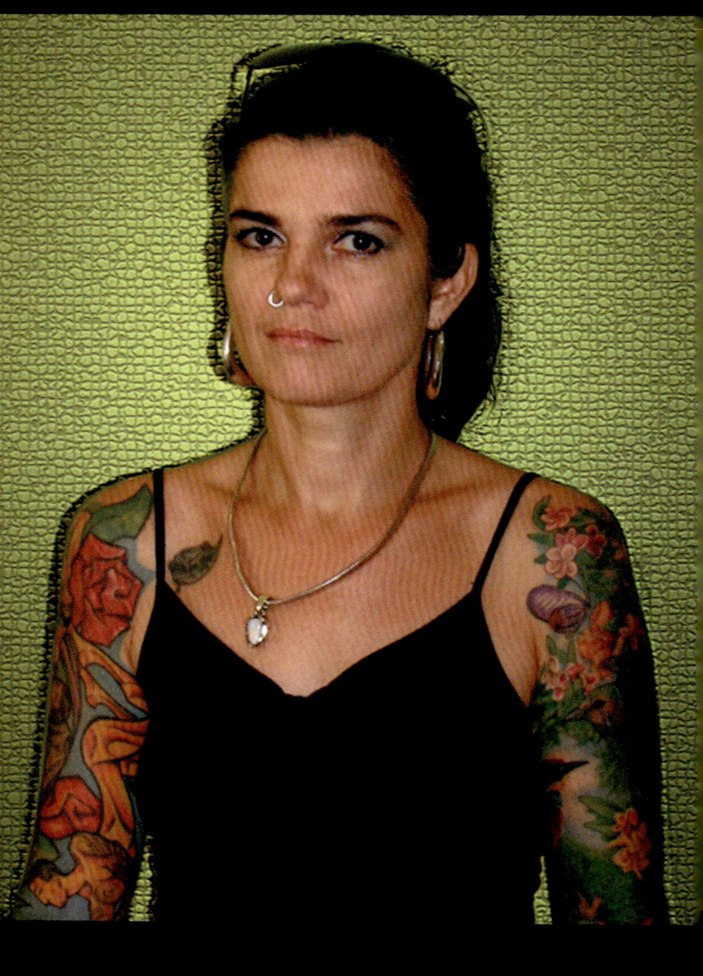

MISS NICO

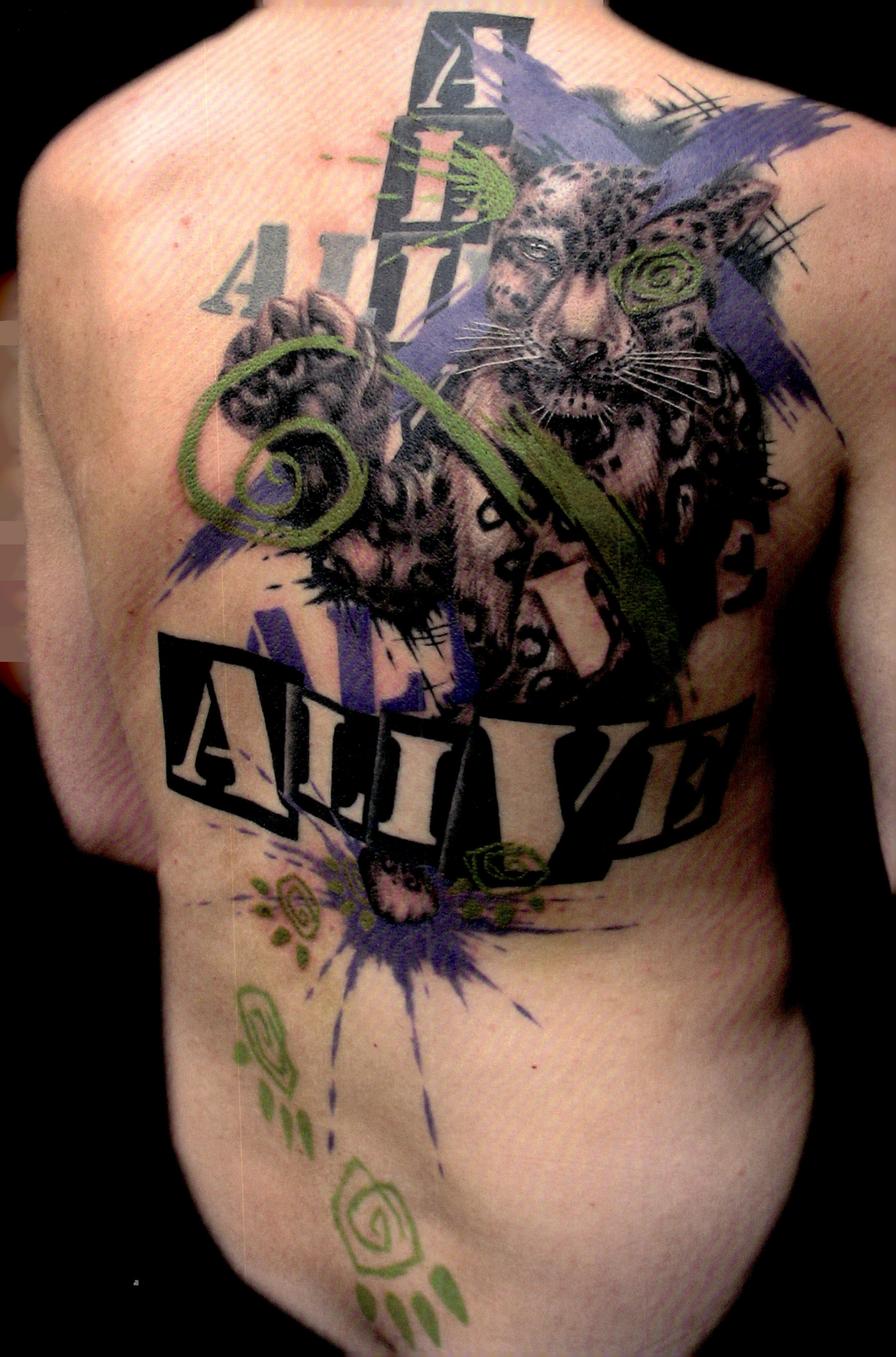

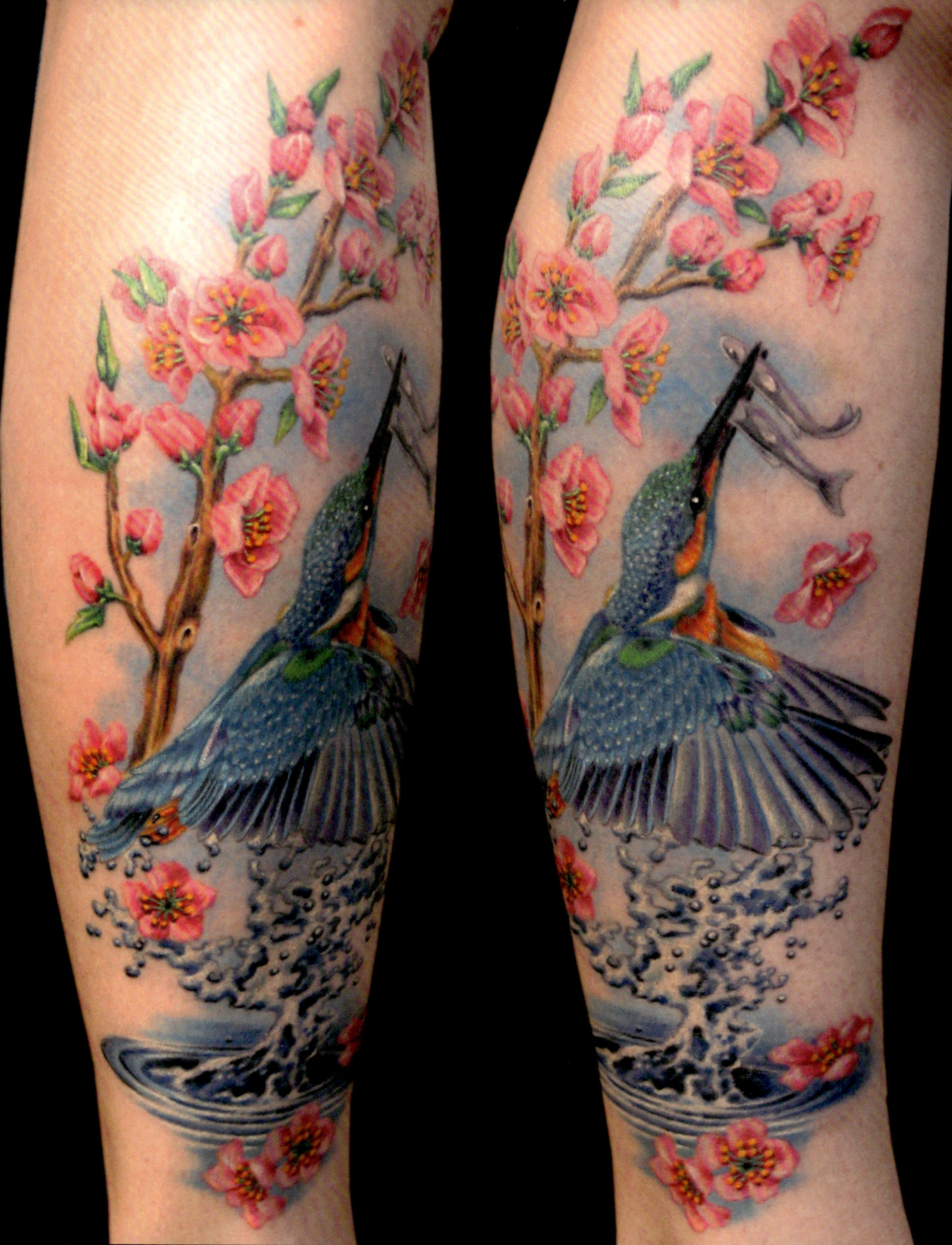

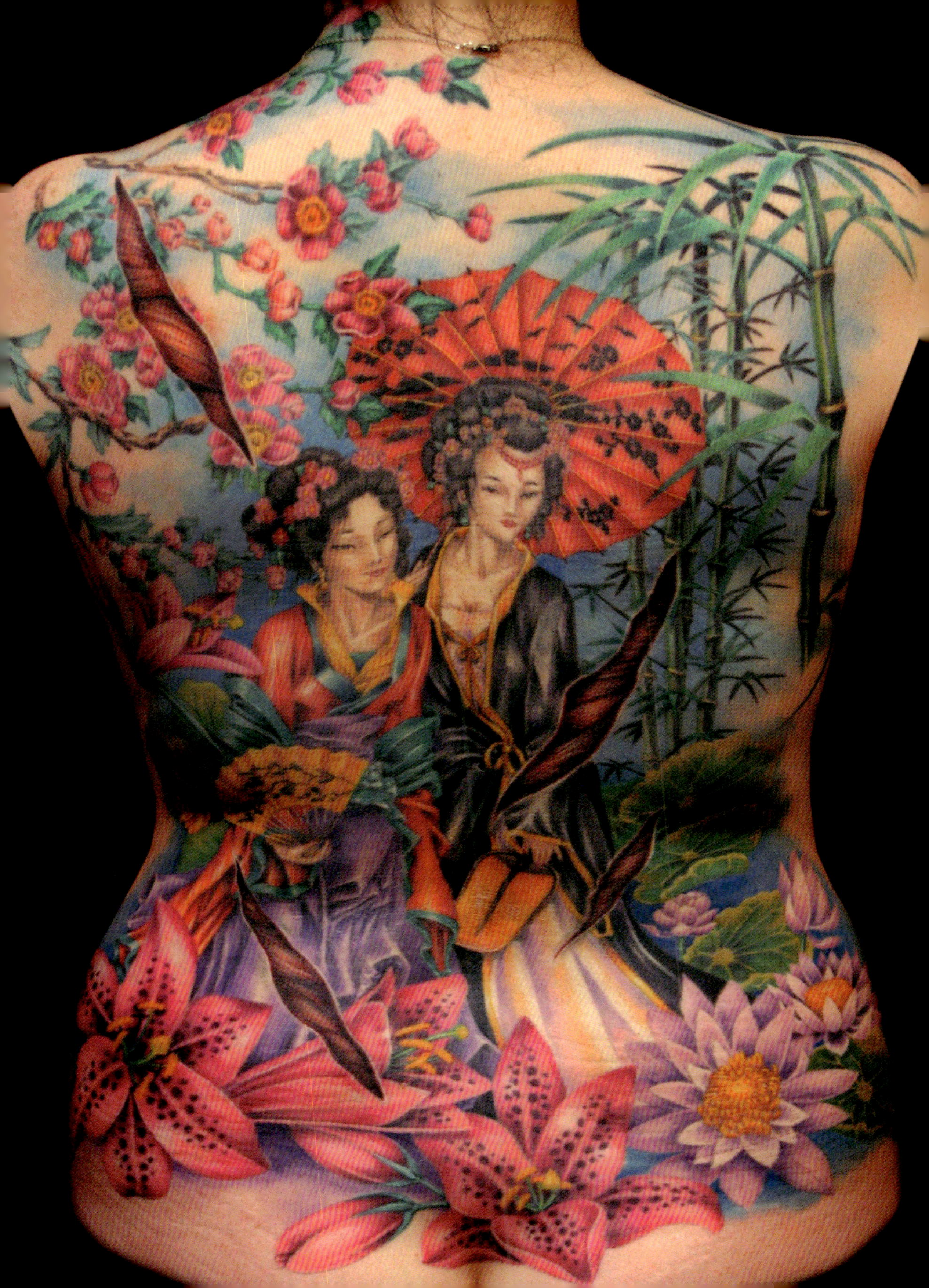

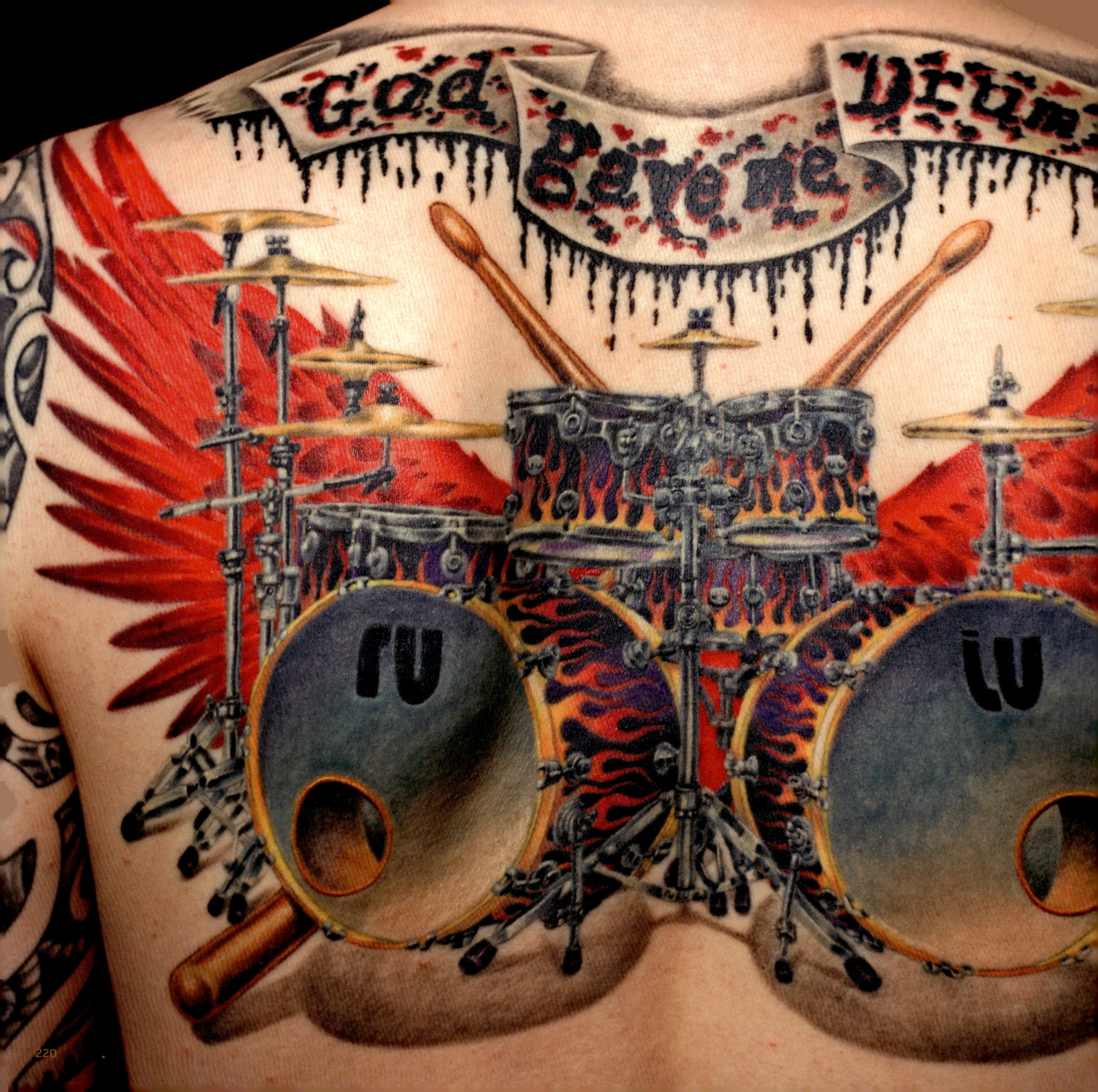
God
bayene
Drum
ru
ru

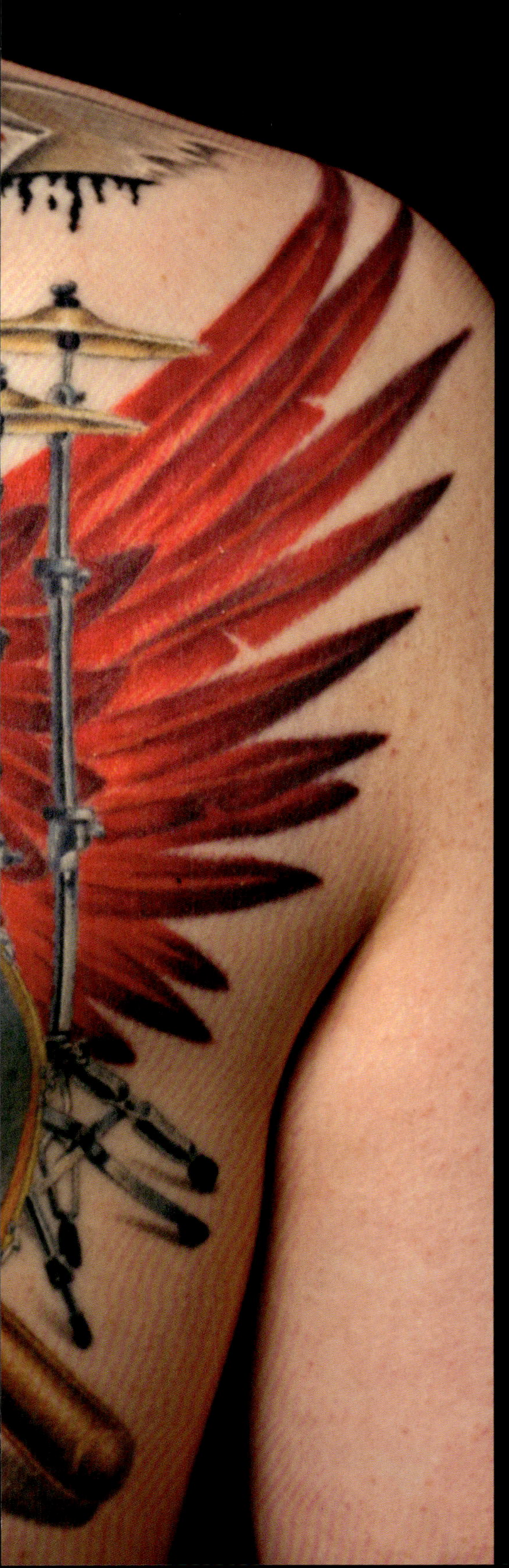

CHAMBERS

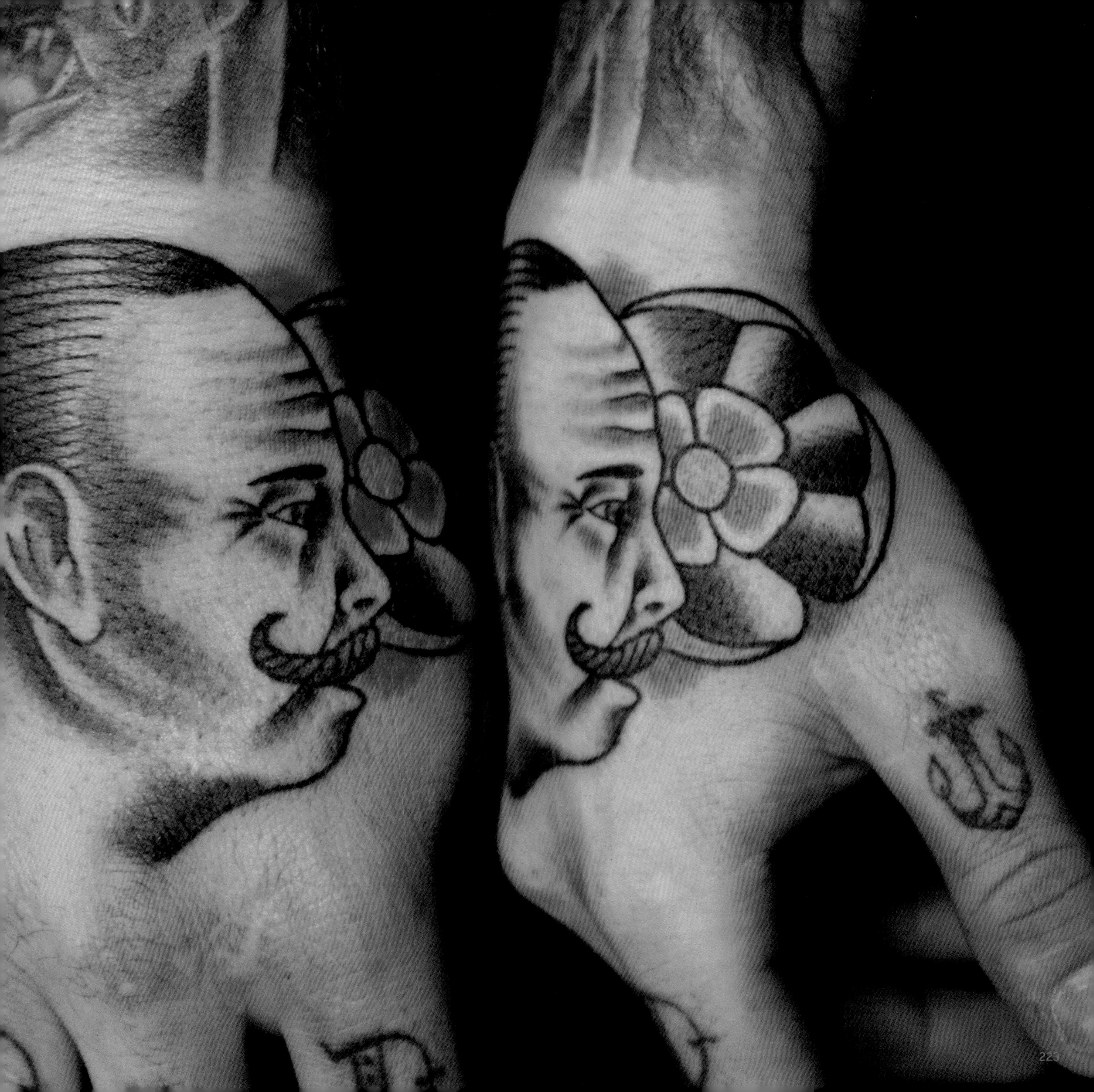

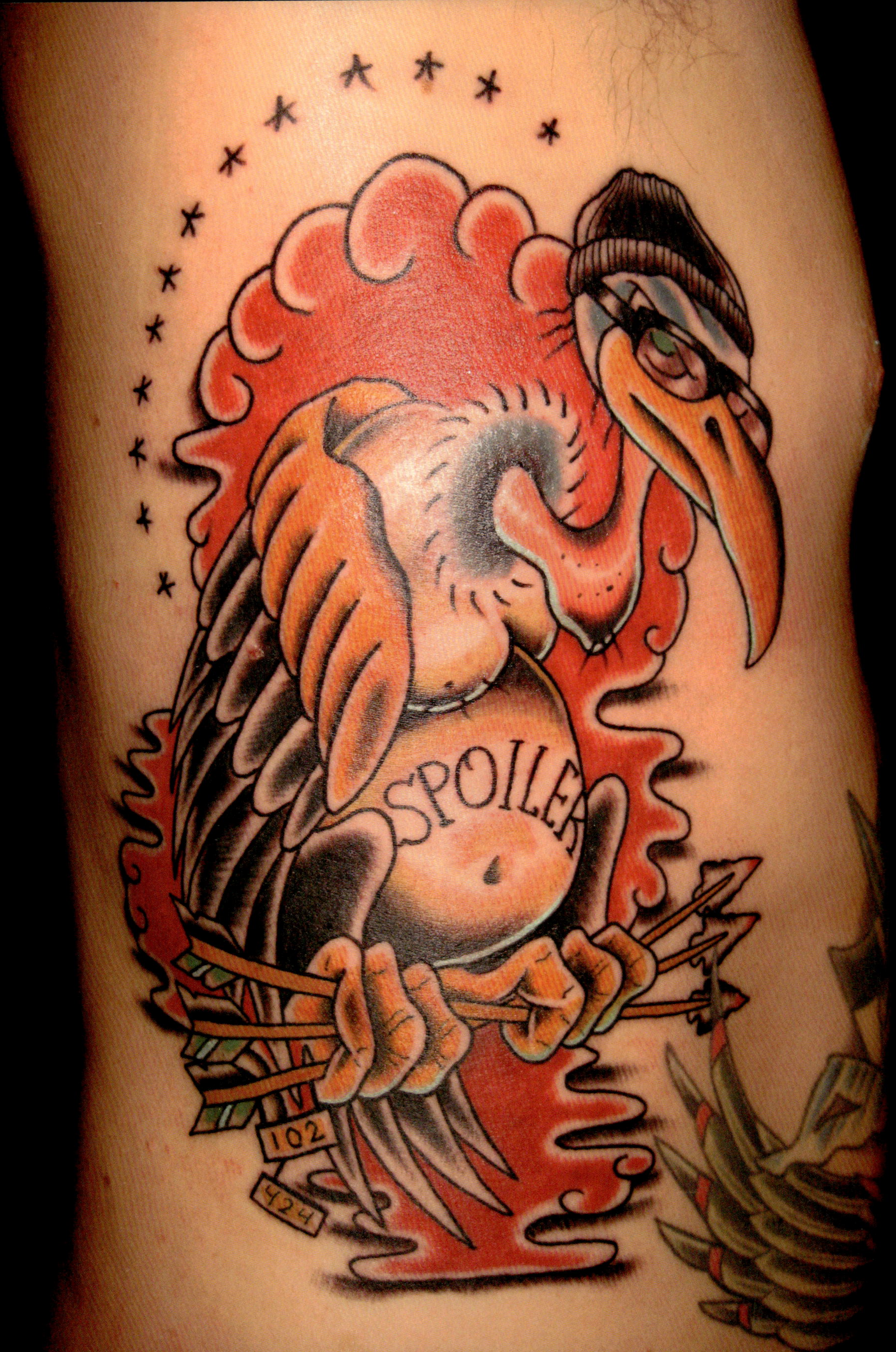
SPOILER
102
424

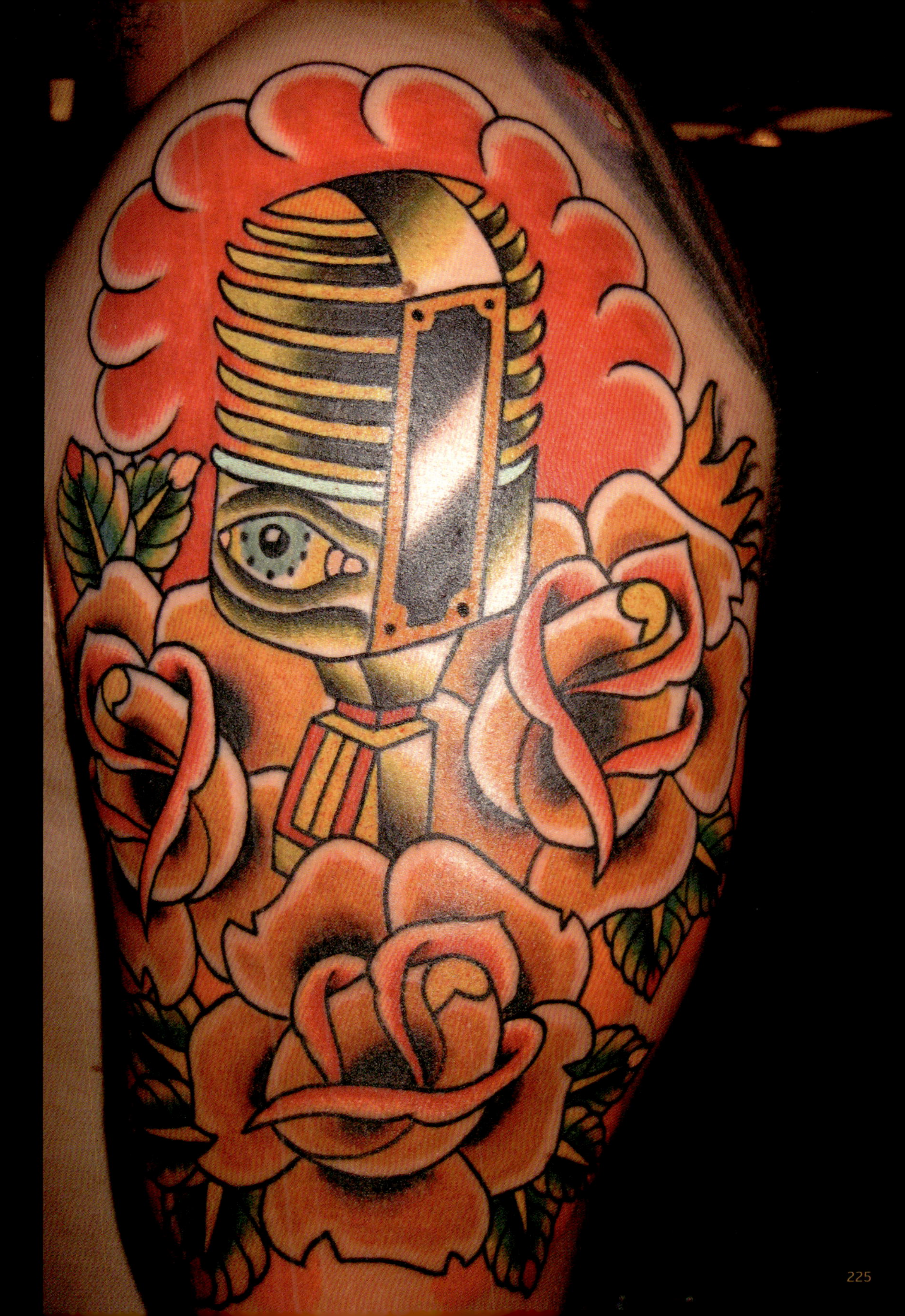

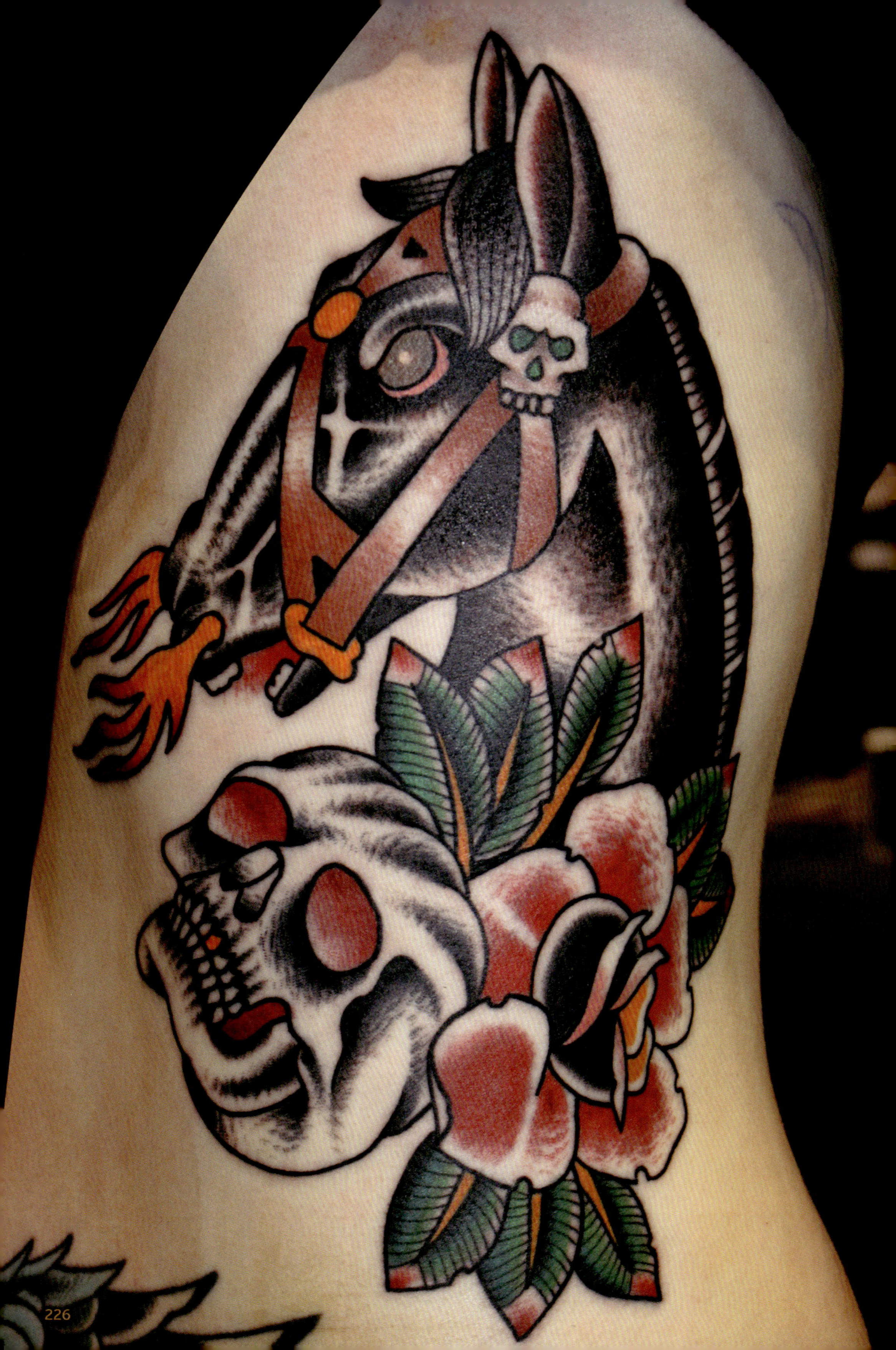

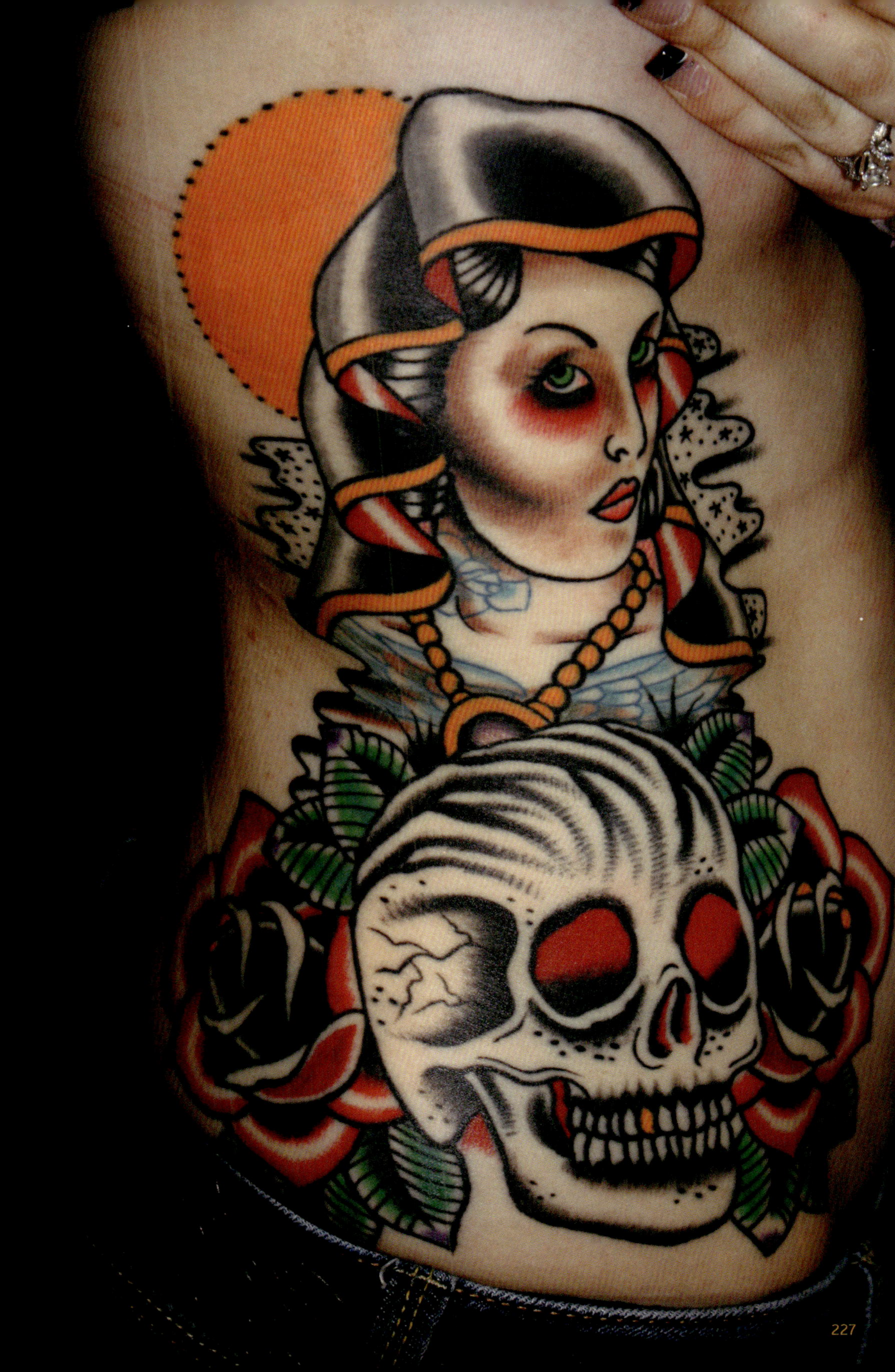

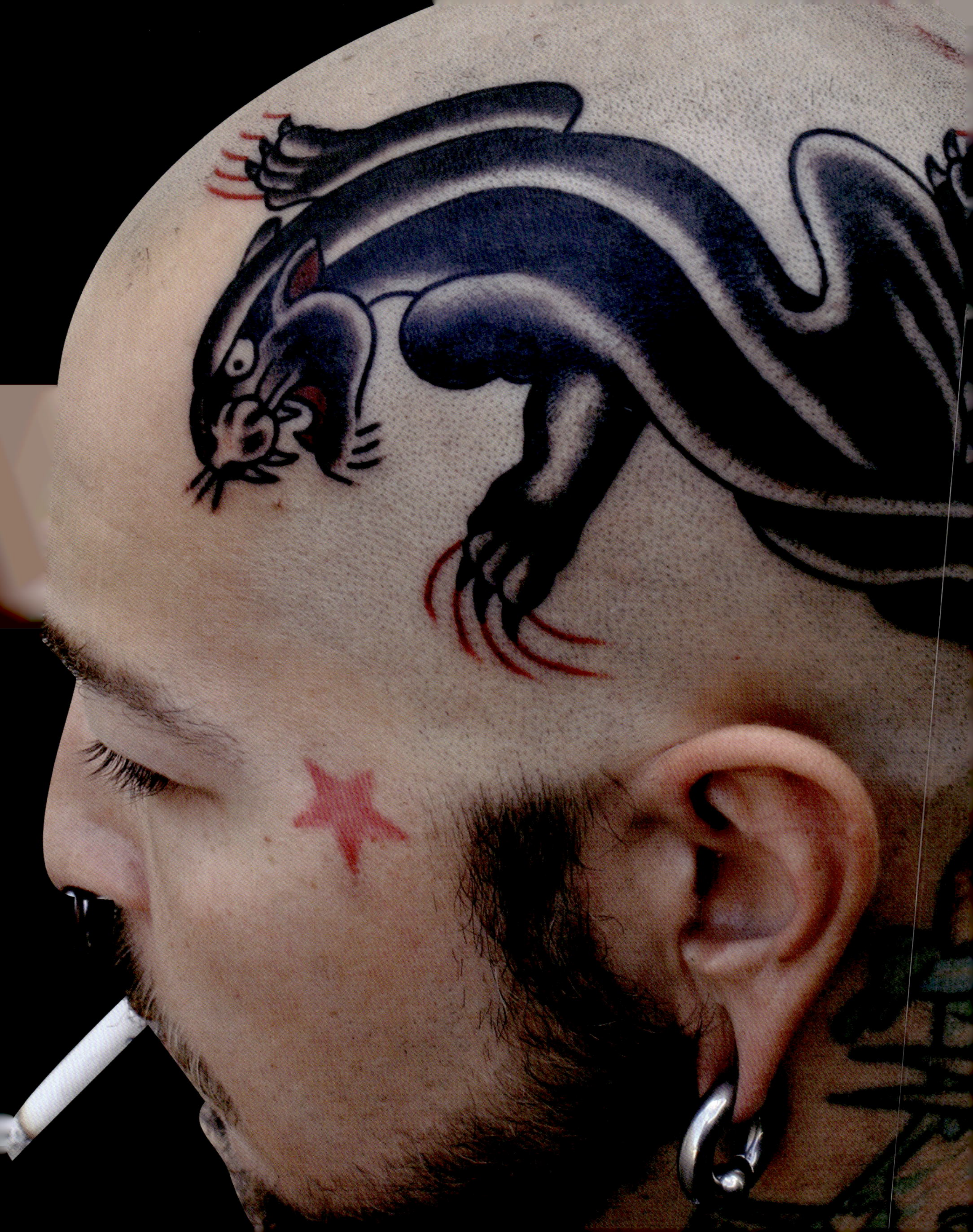

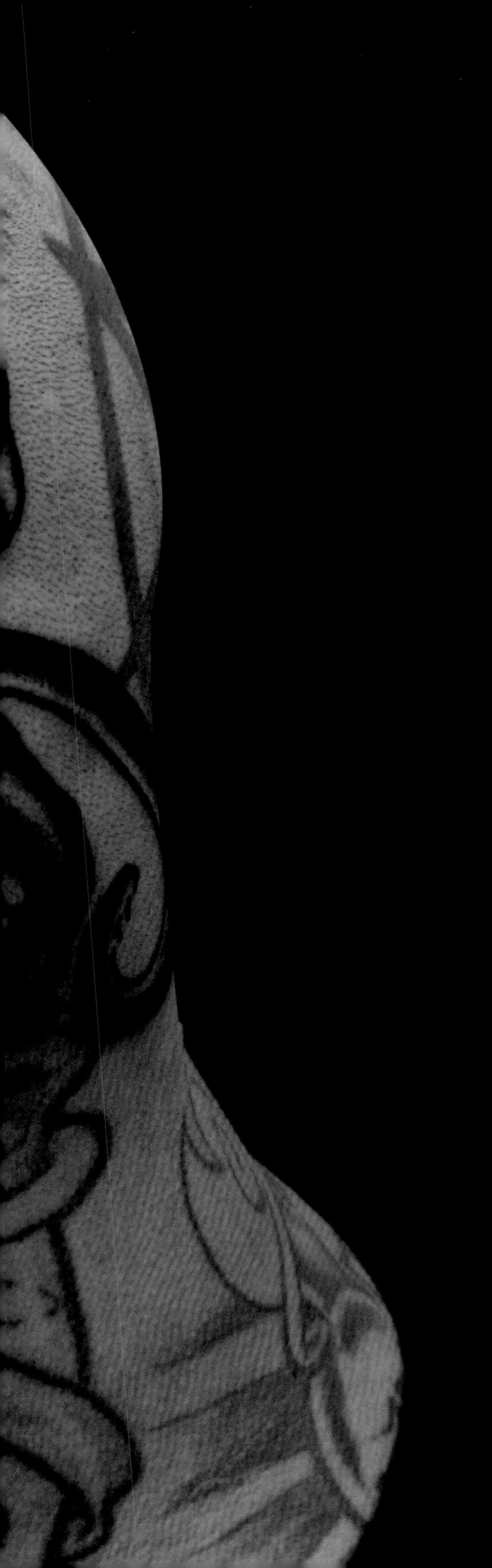

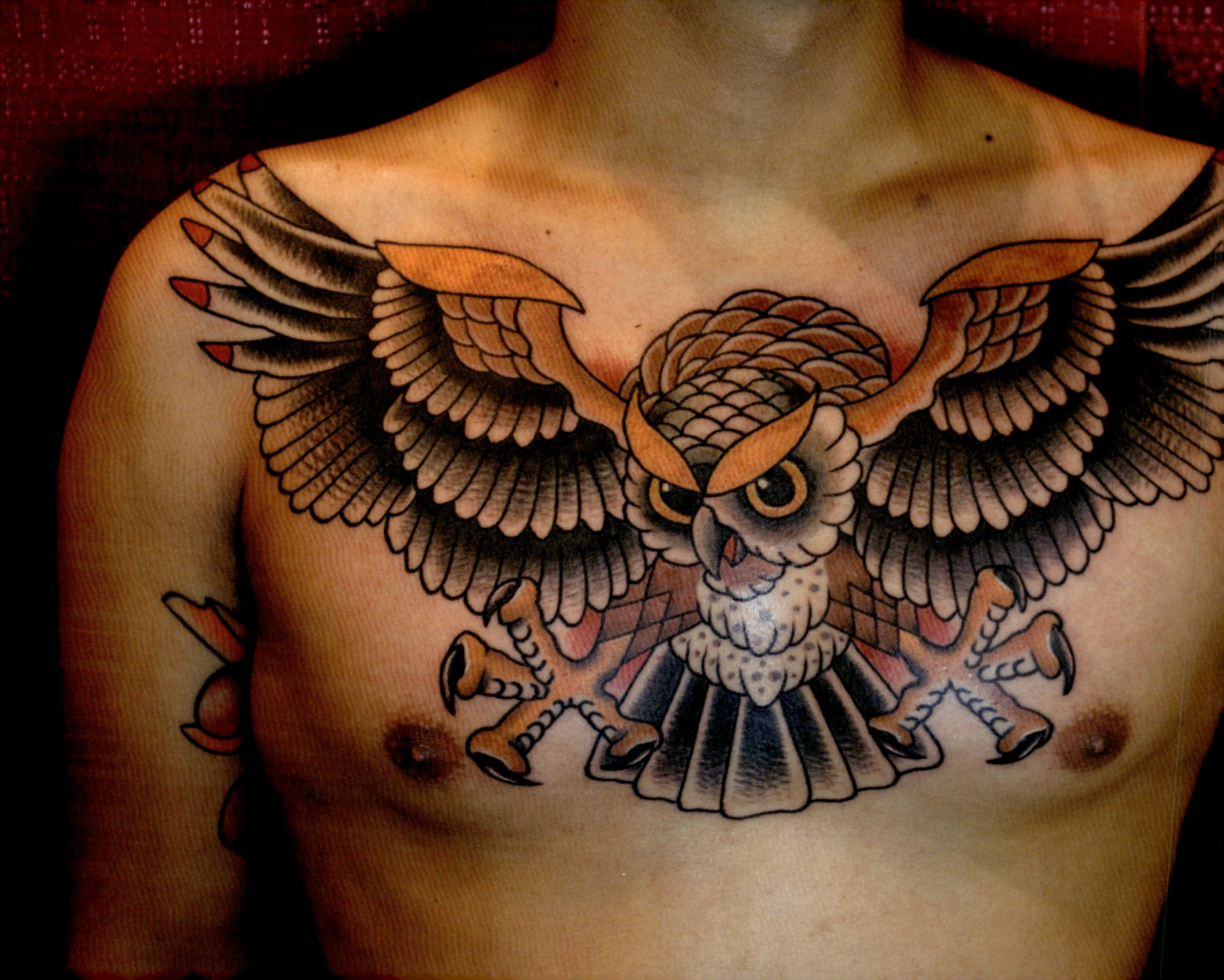

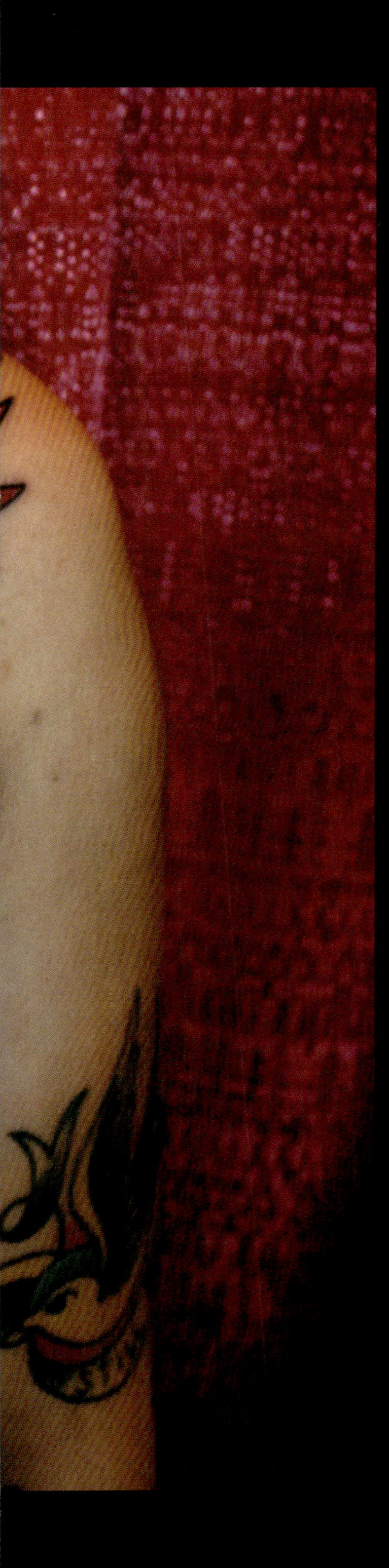

NOI SIAMESE 3

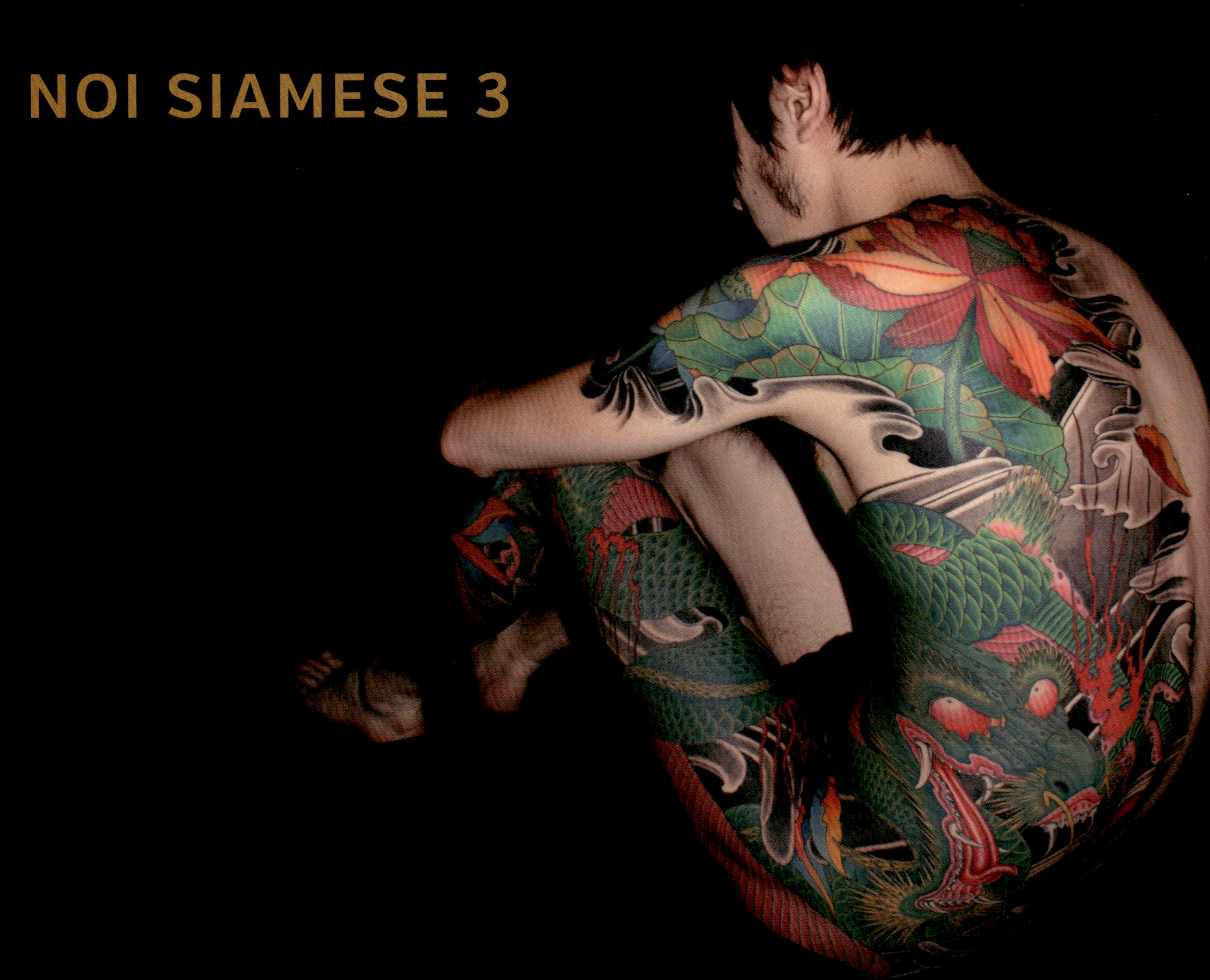

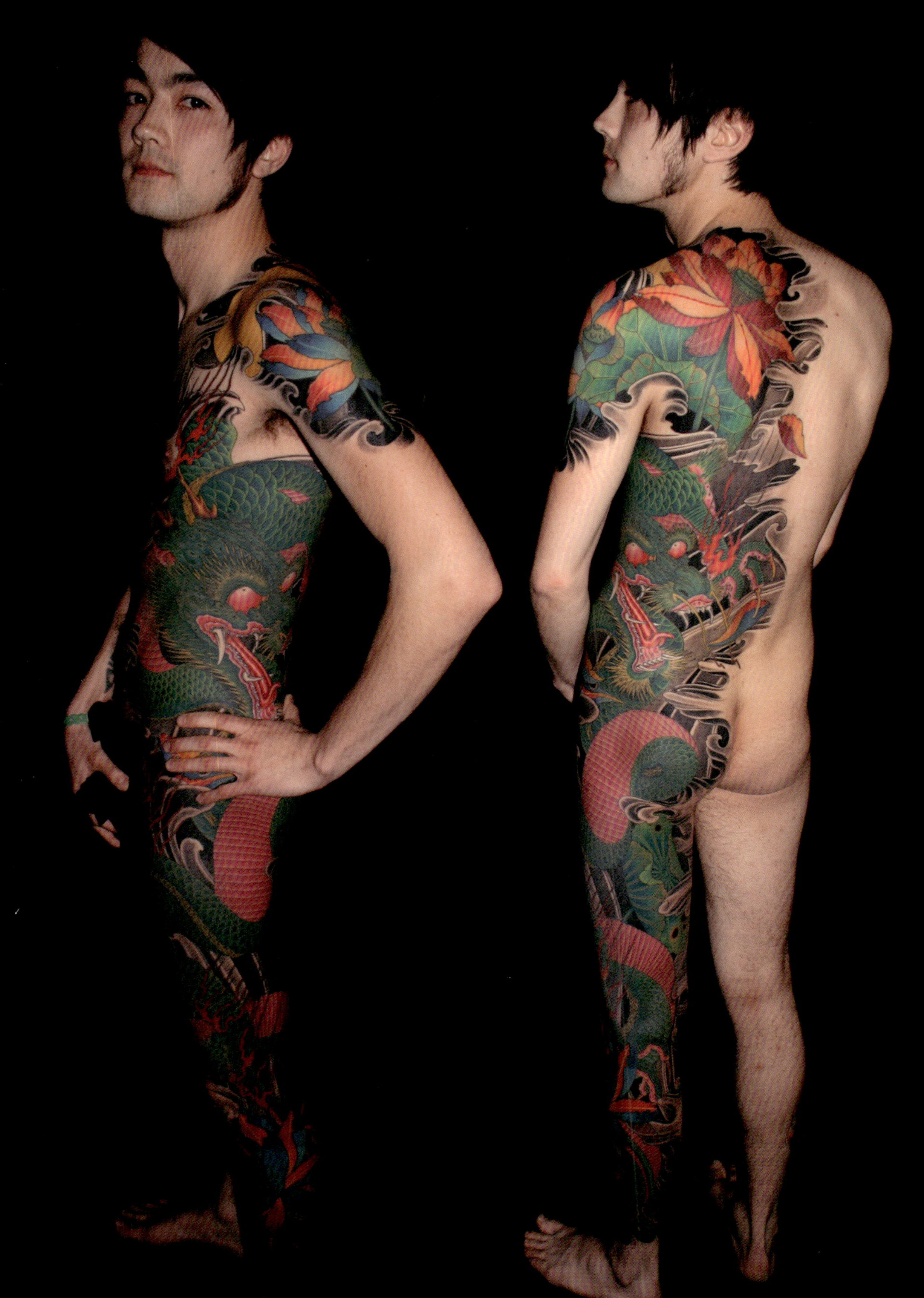

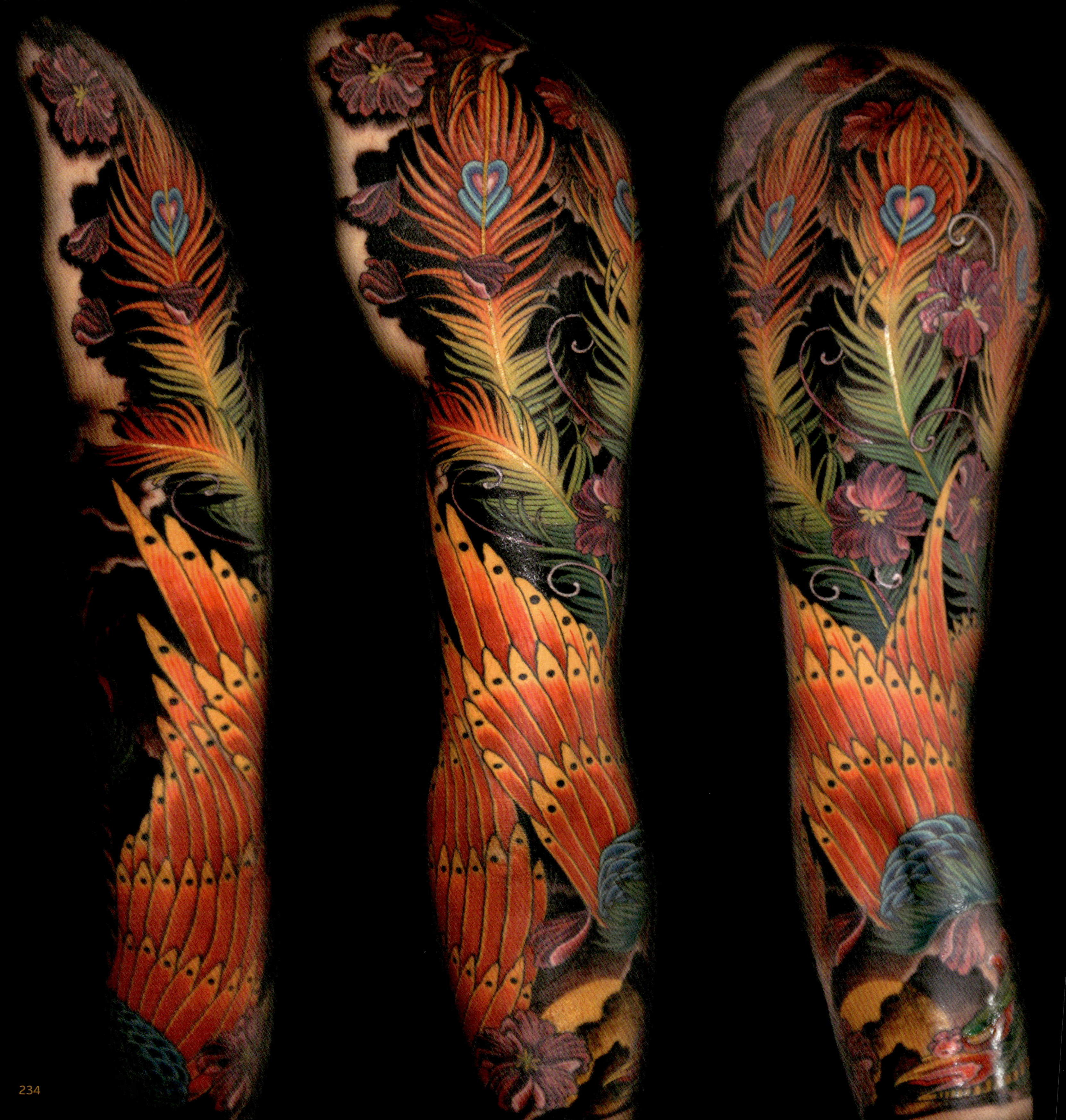

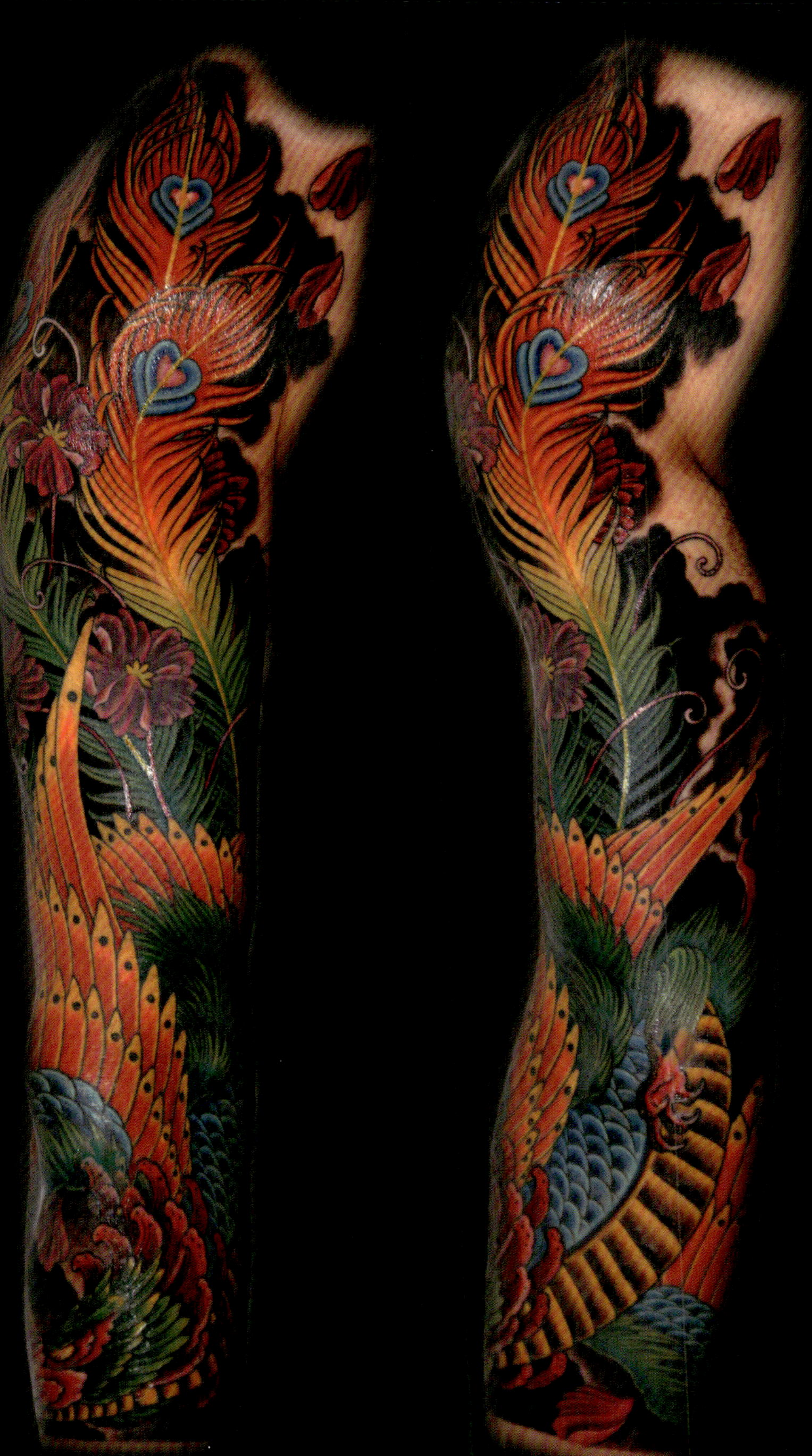

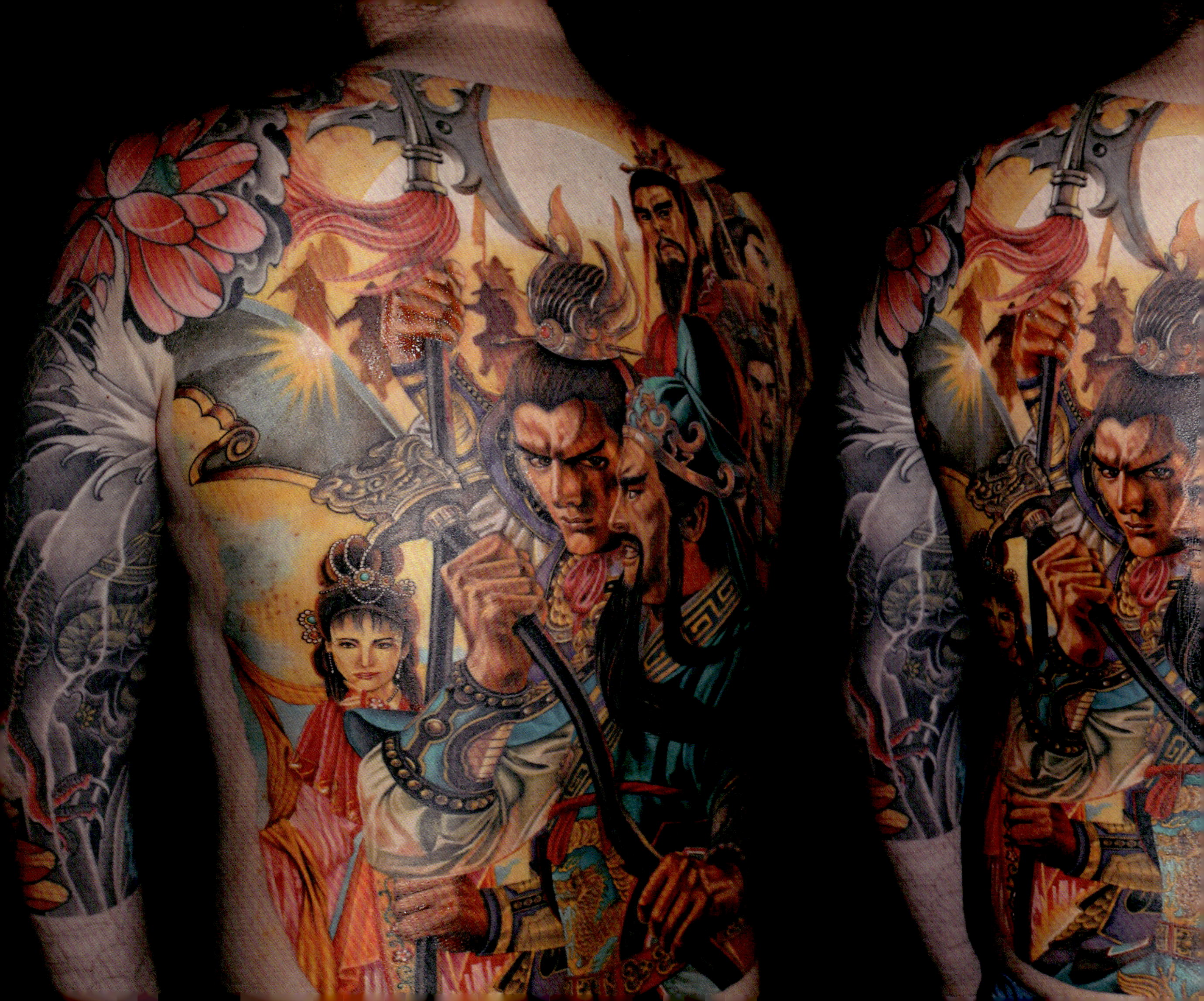

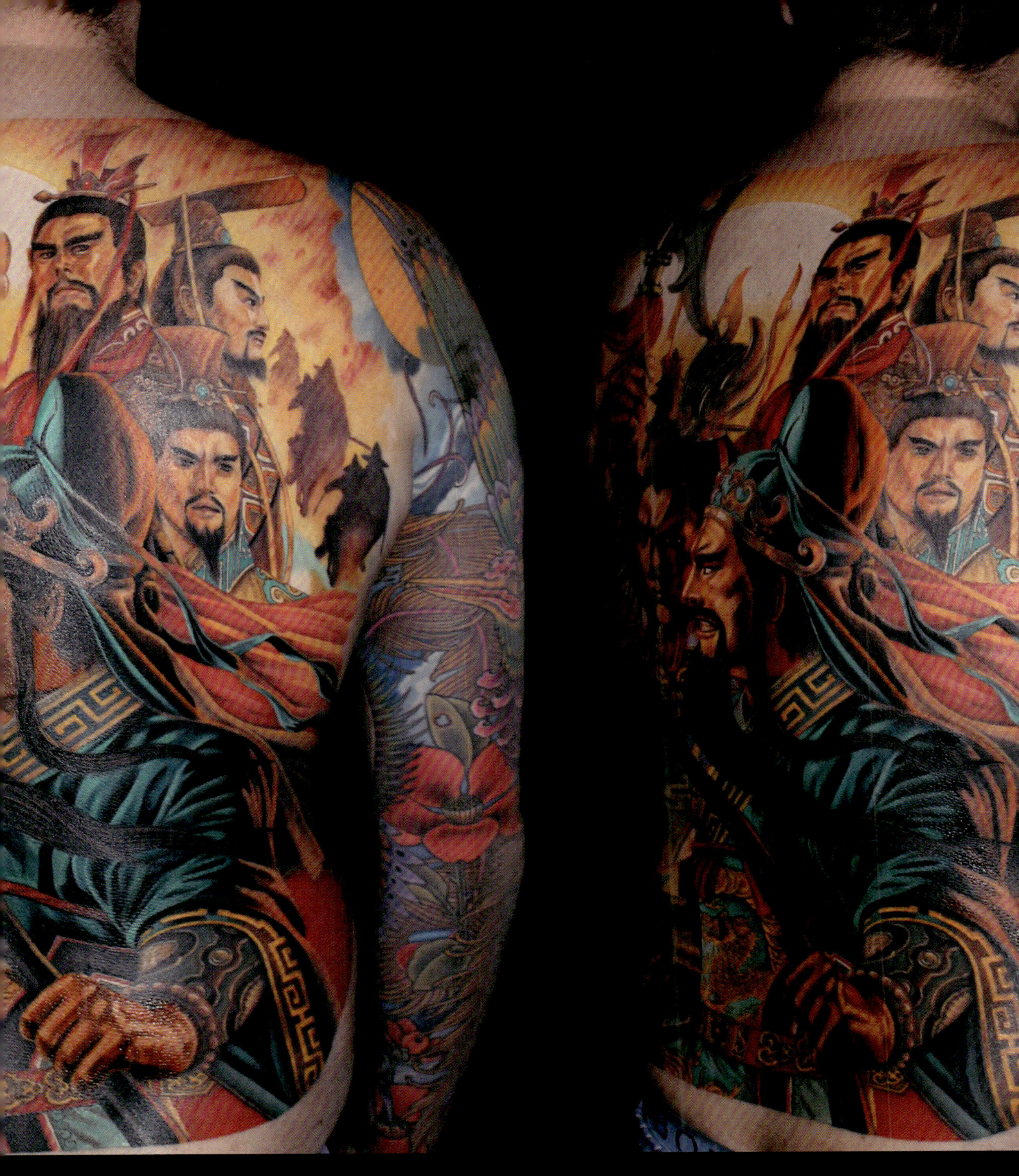

NOON

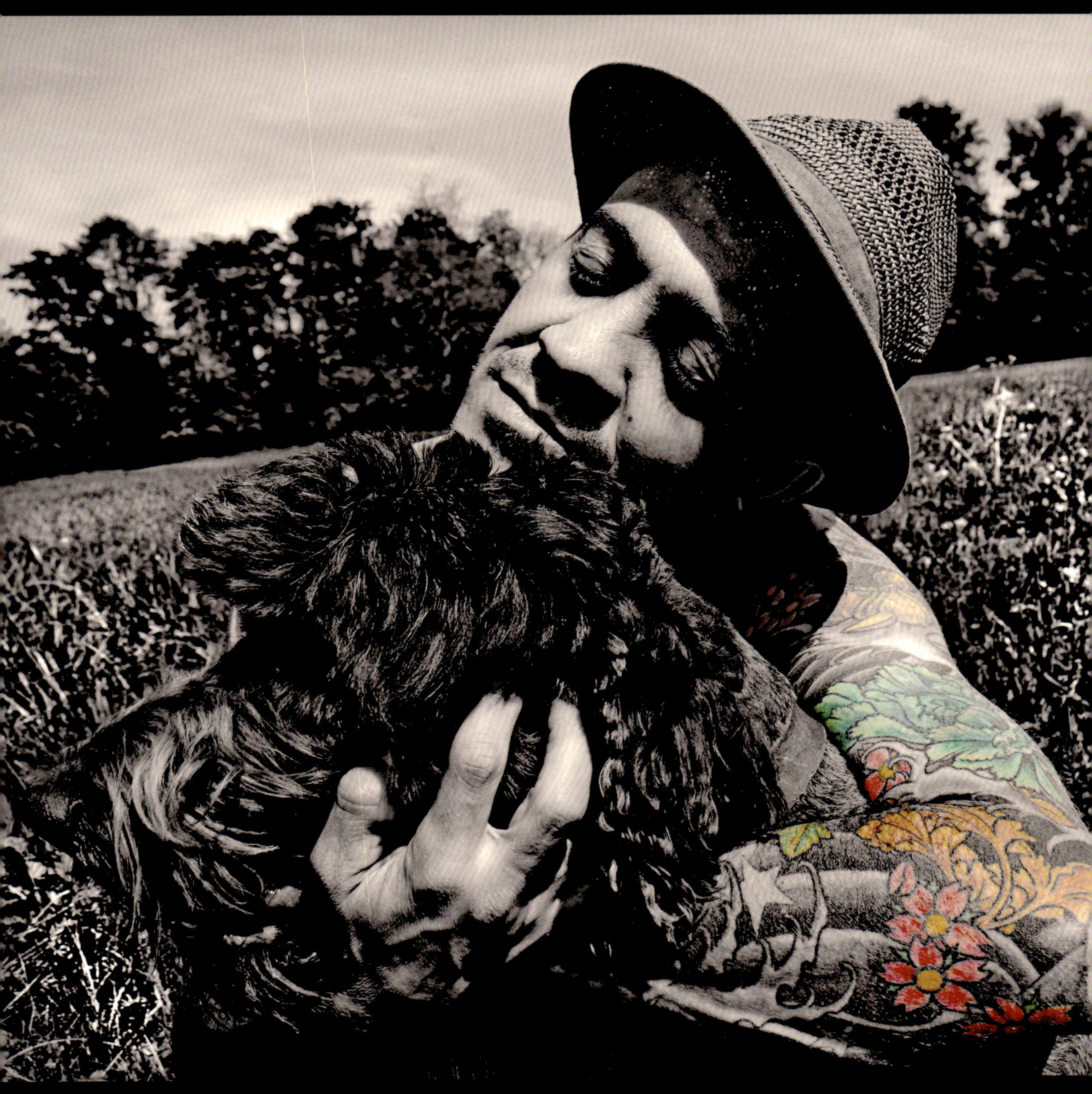

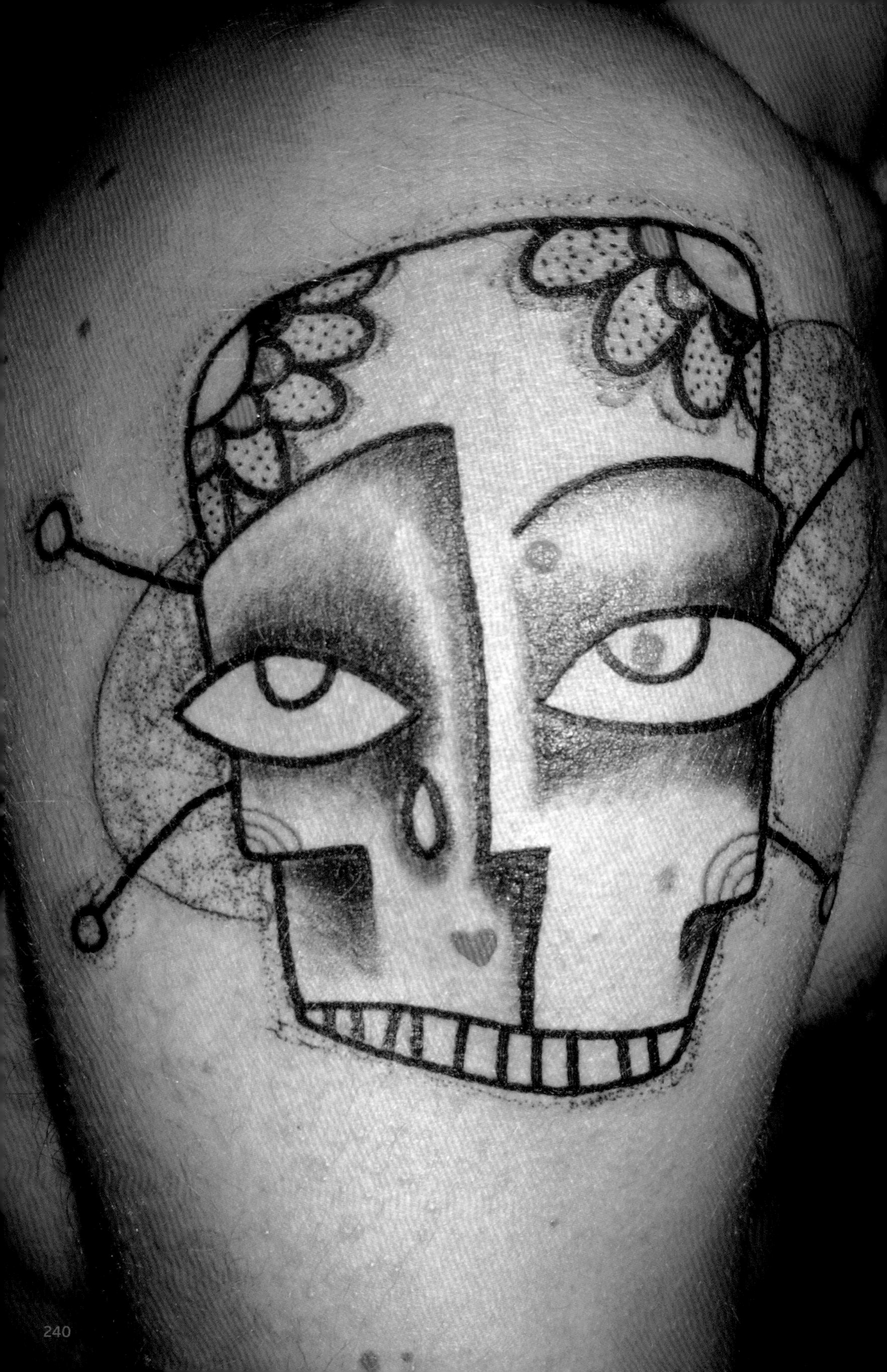

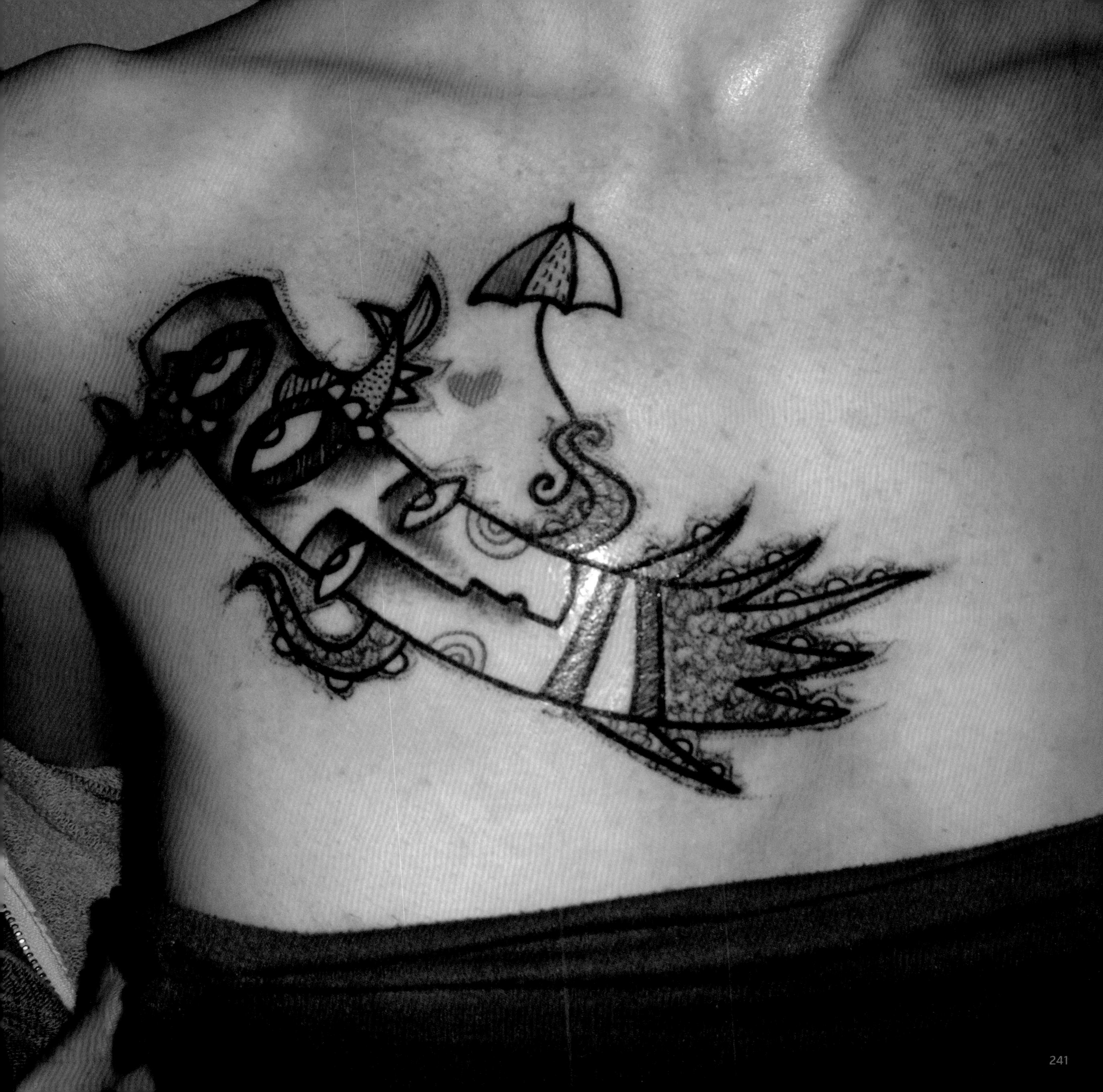

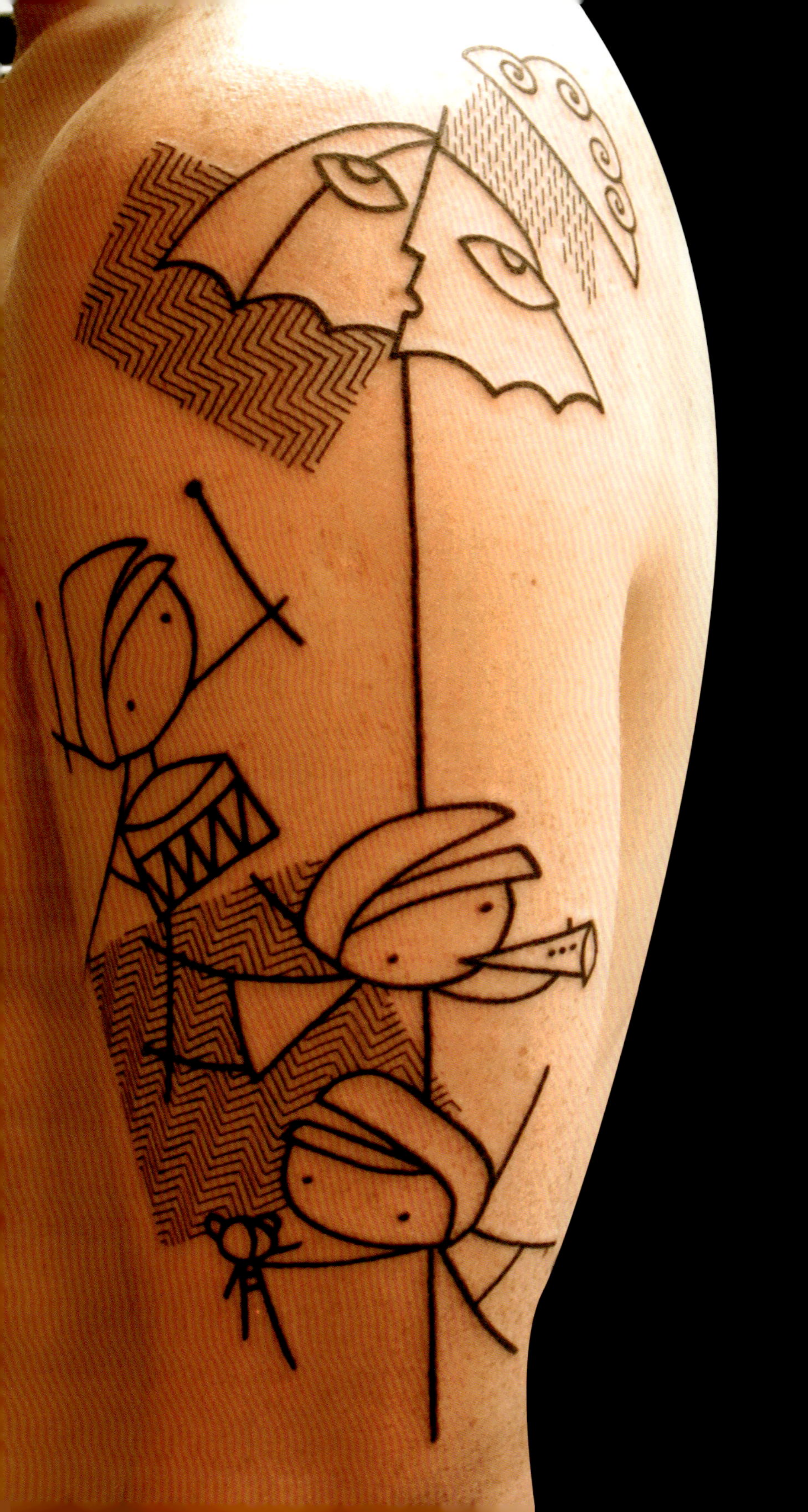

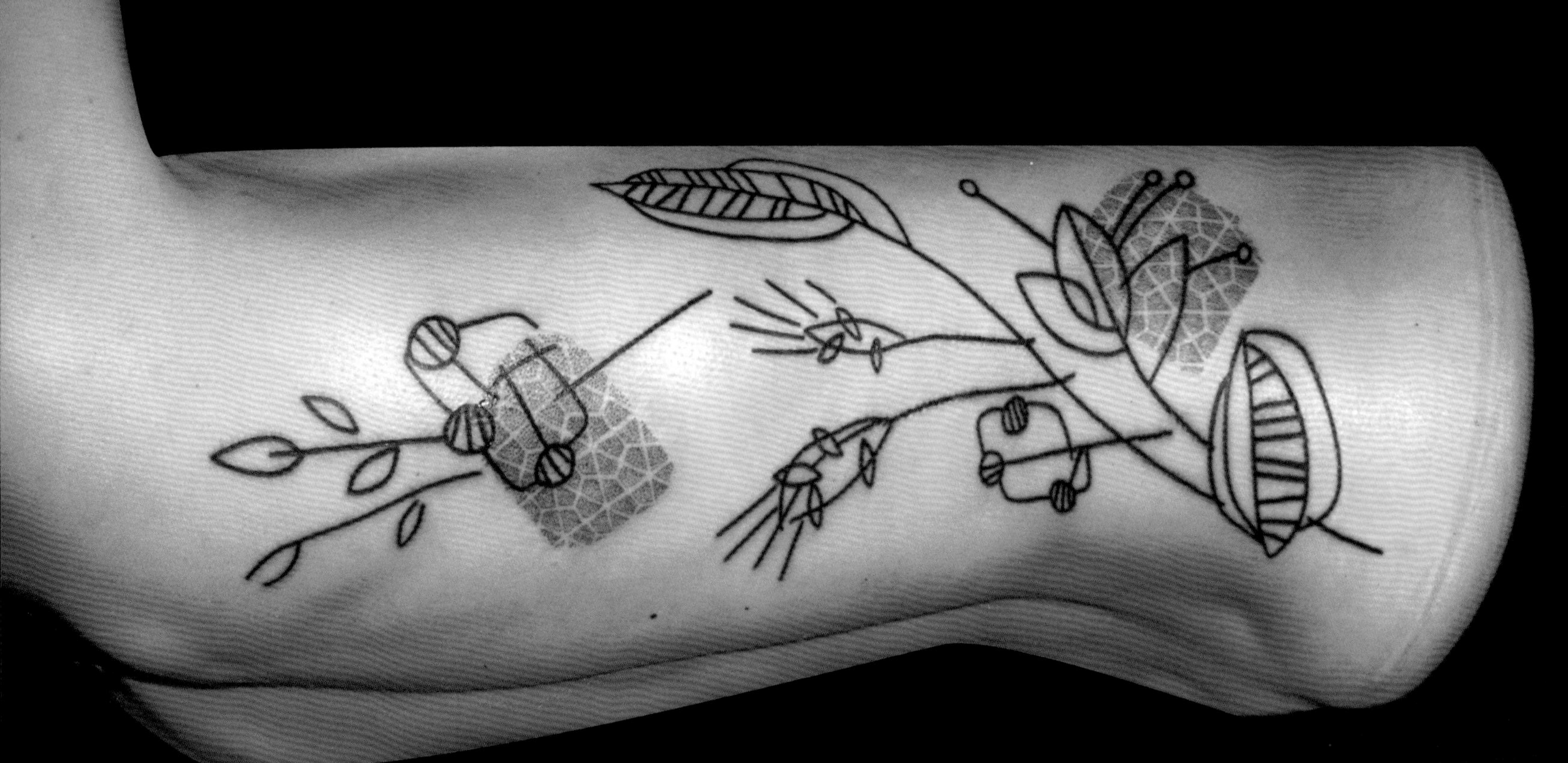

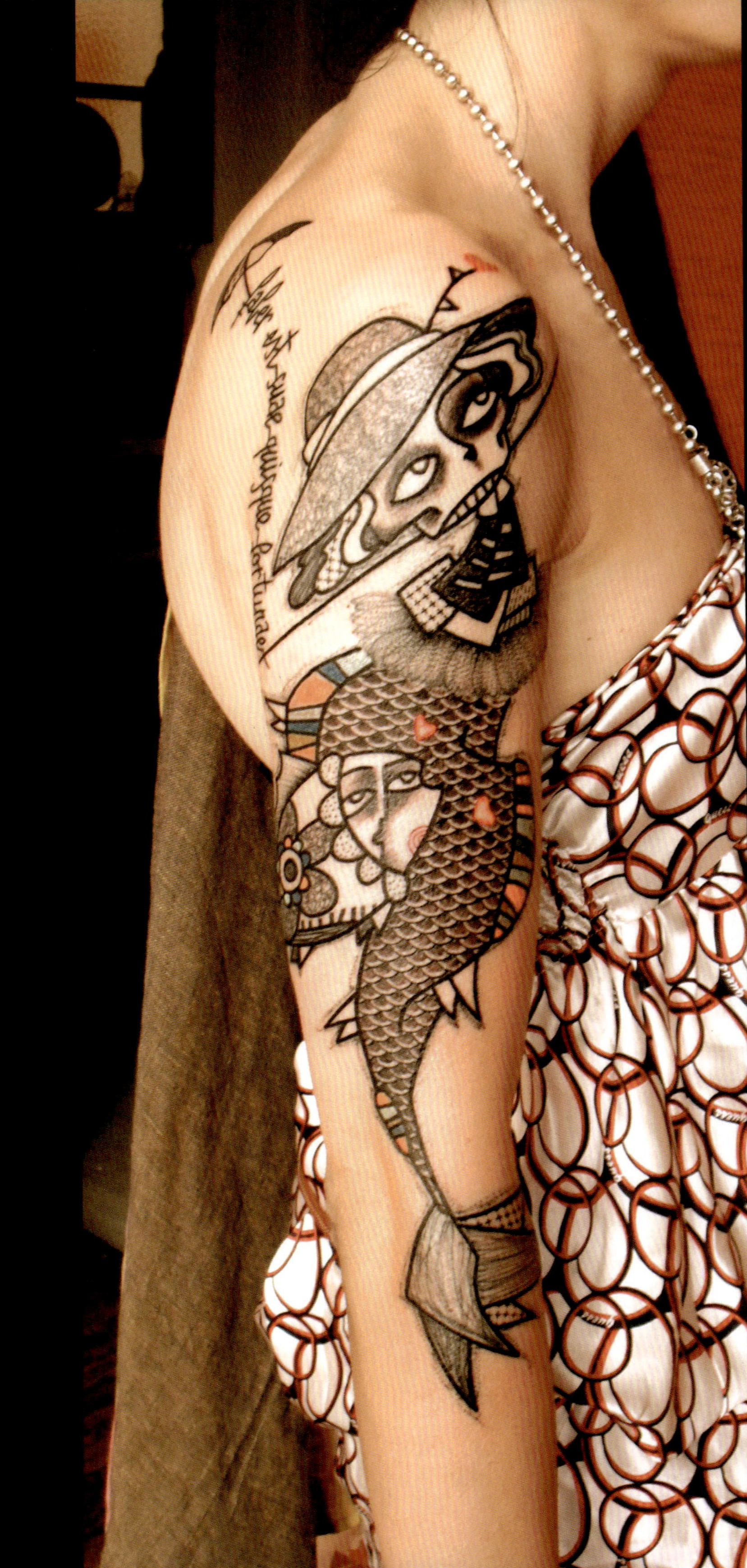

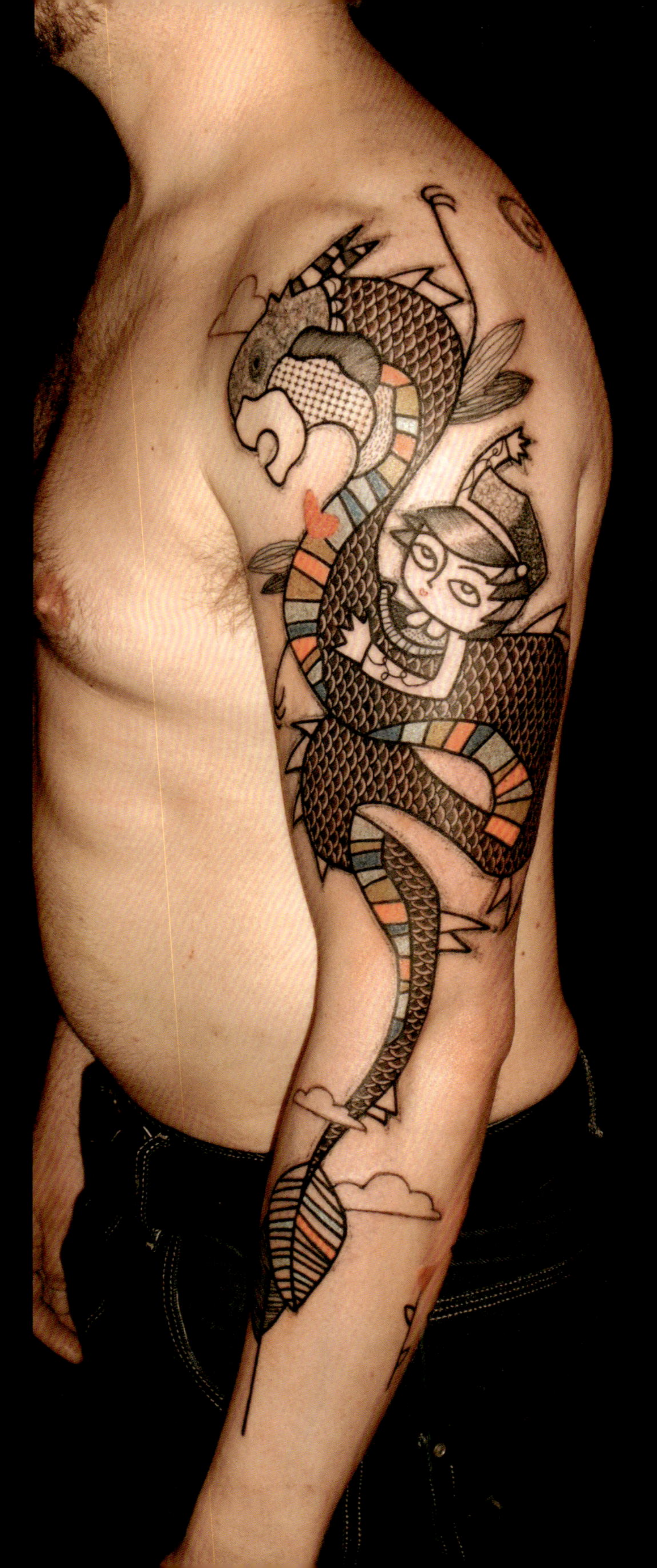

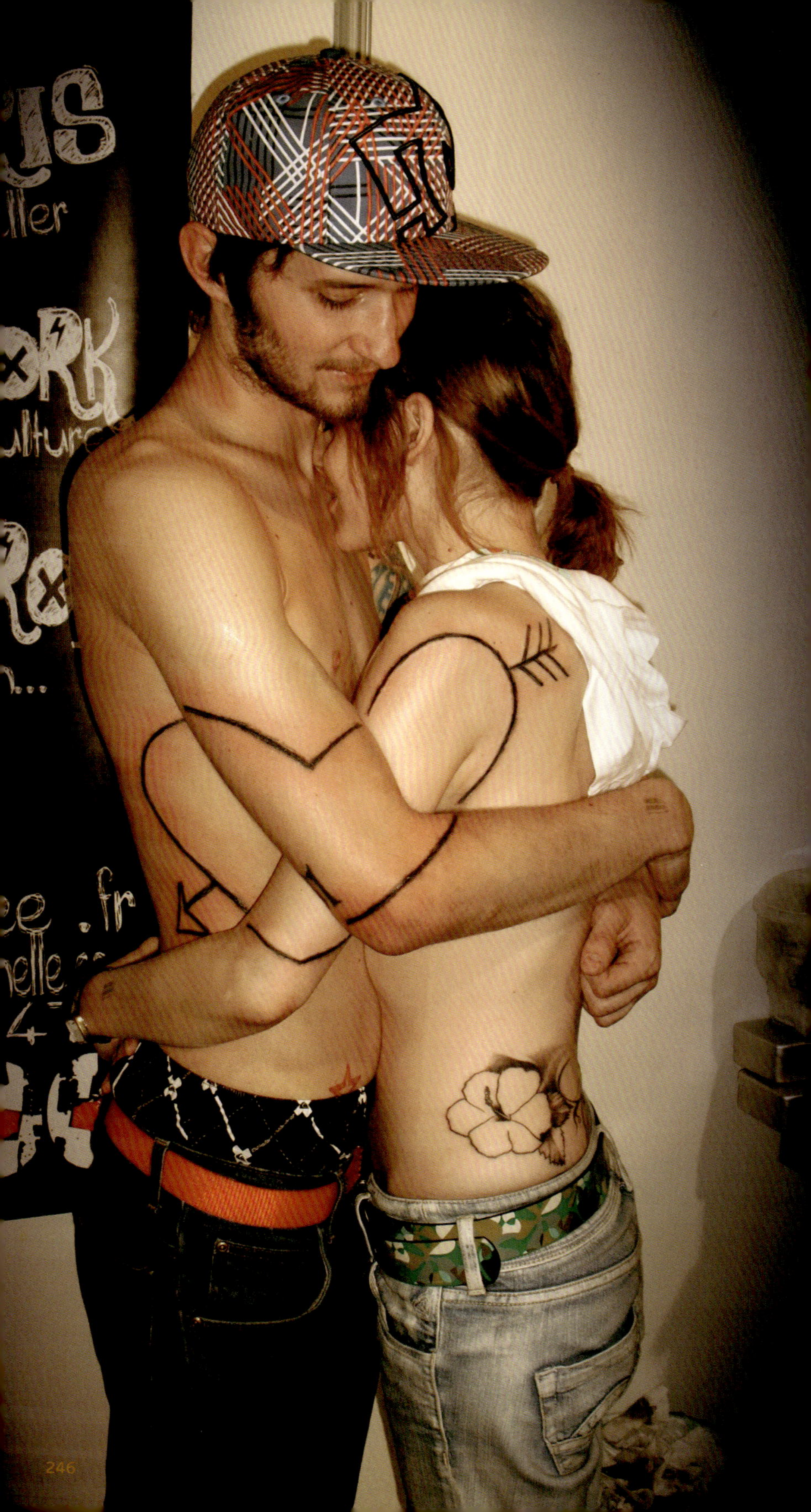
246

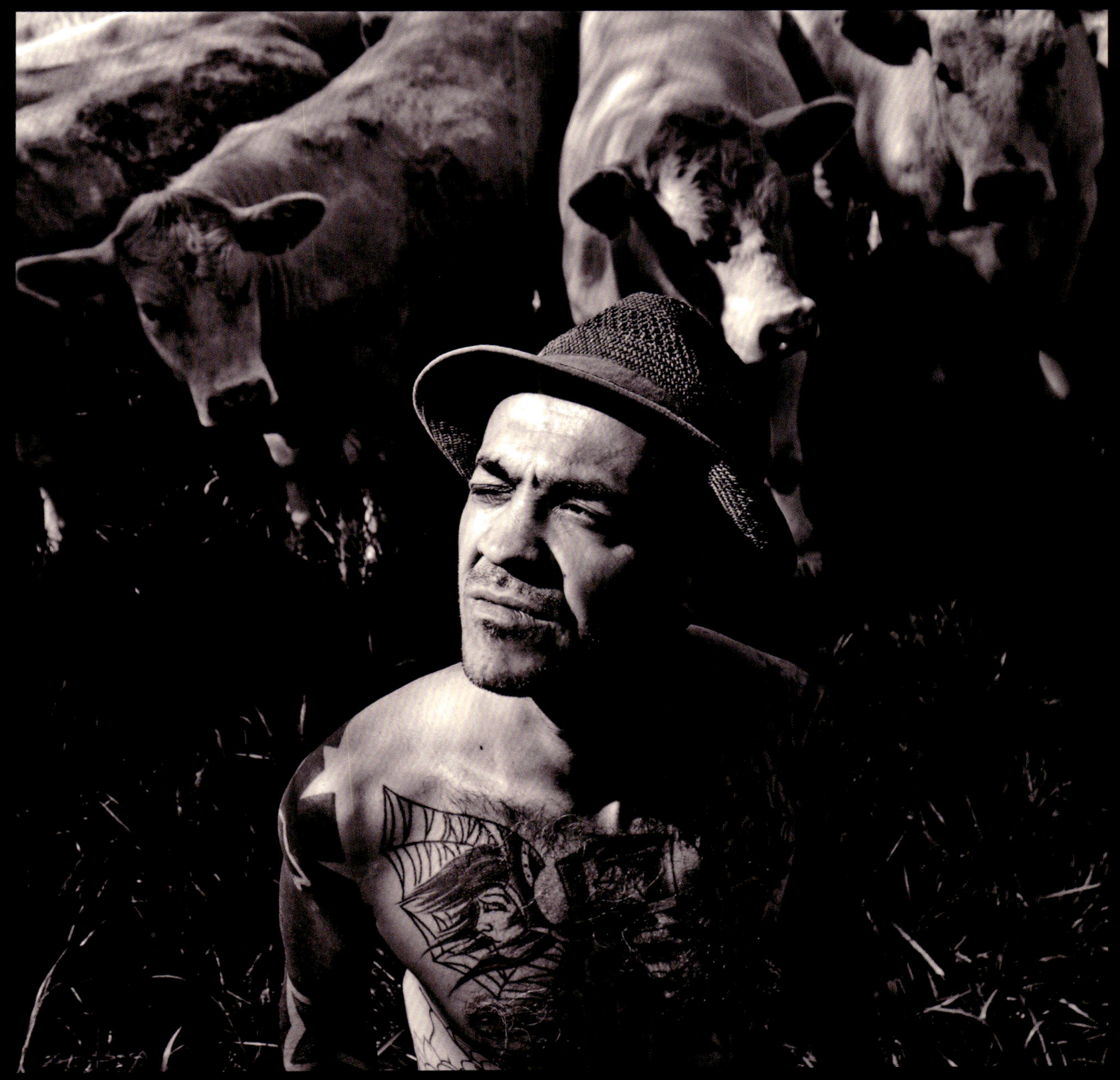

Noon
www.boucherie-traditionnelle.com

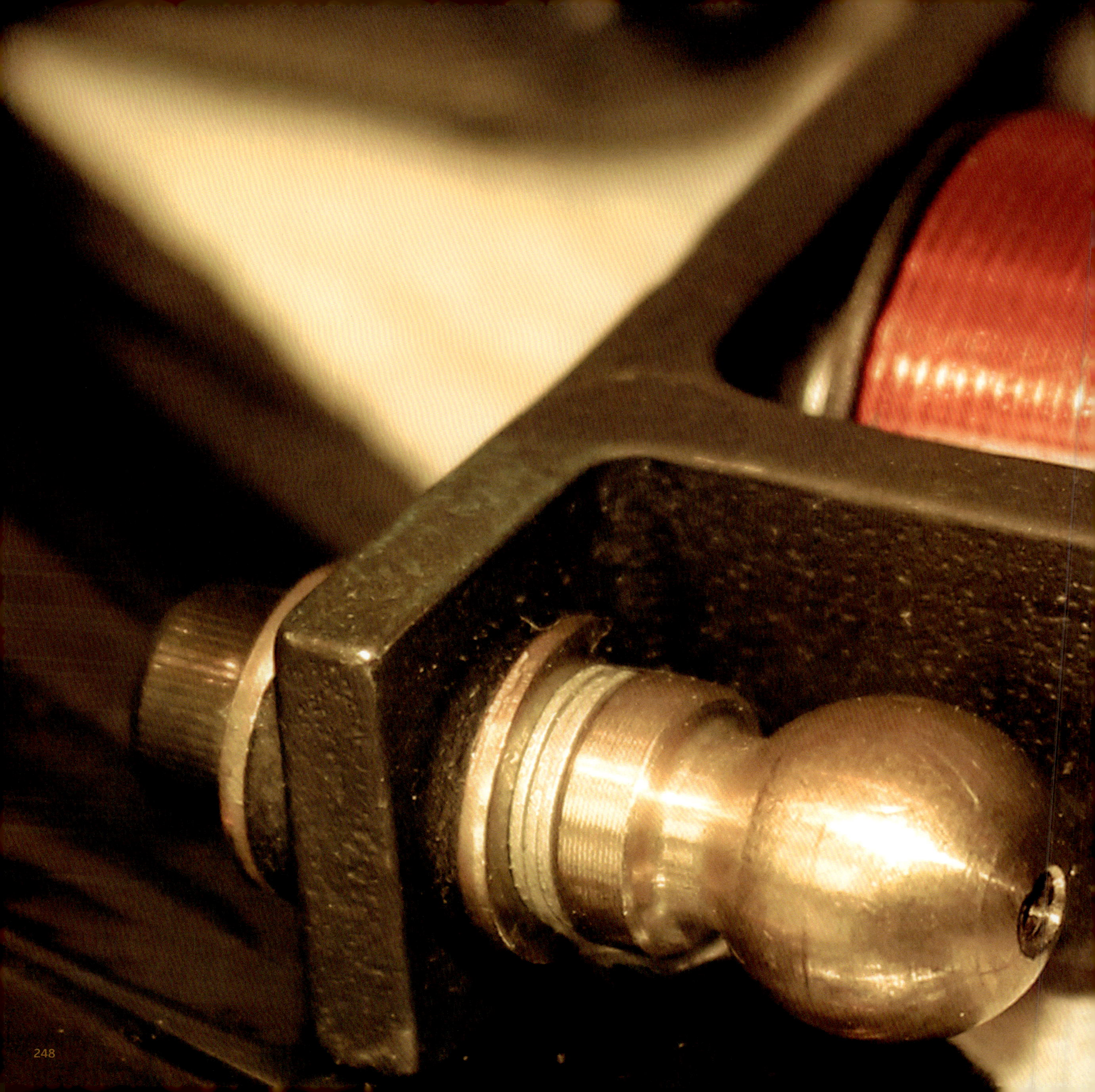

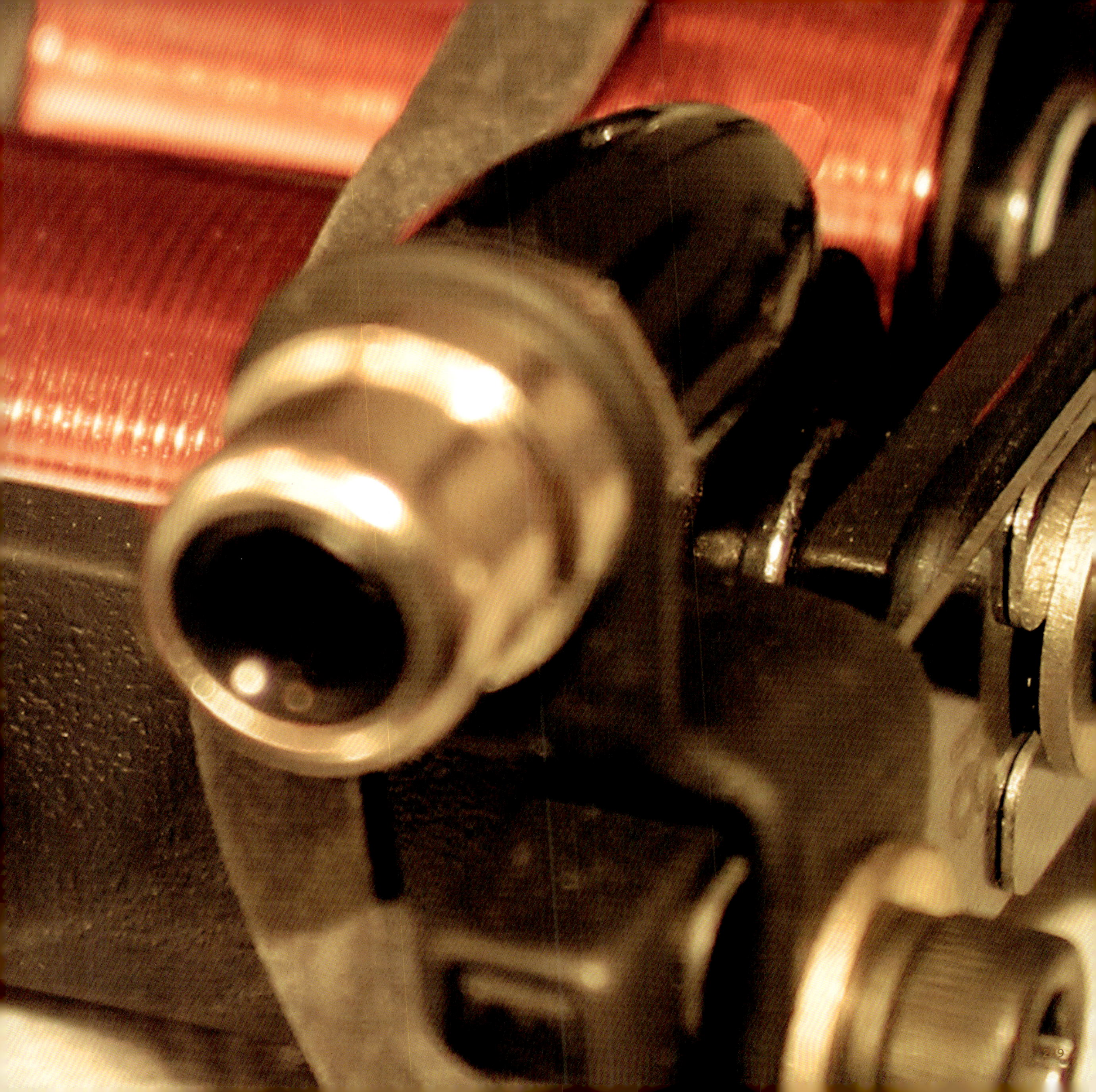

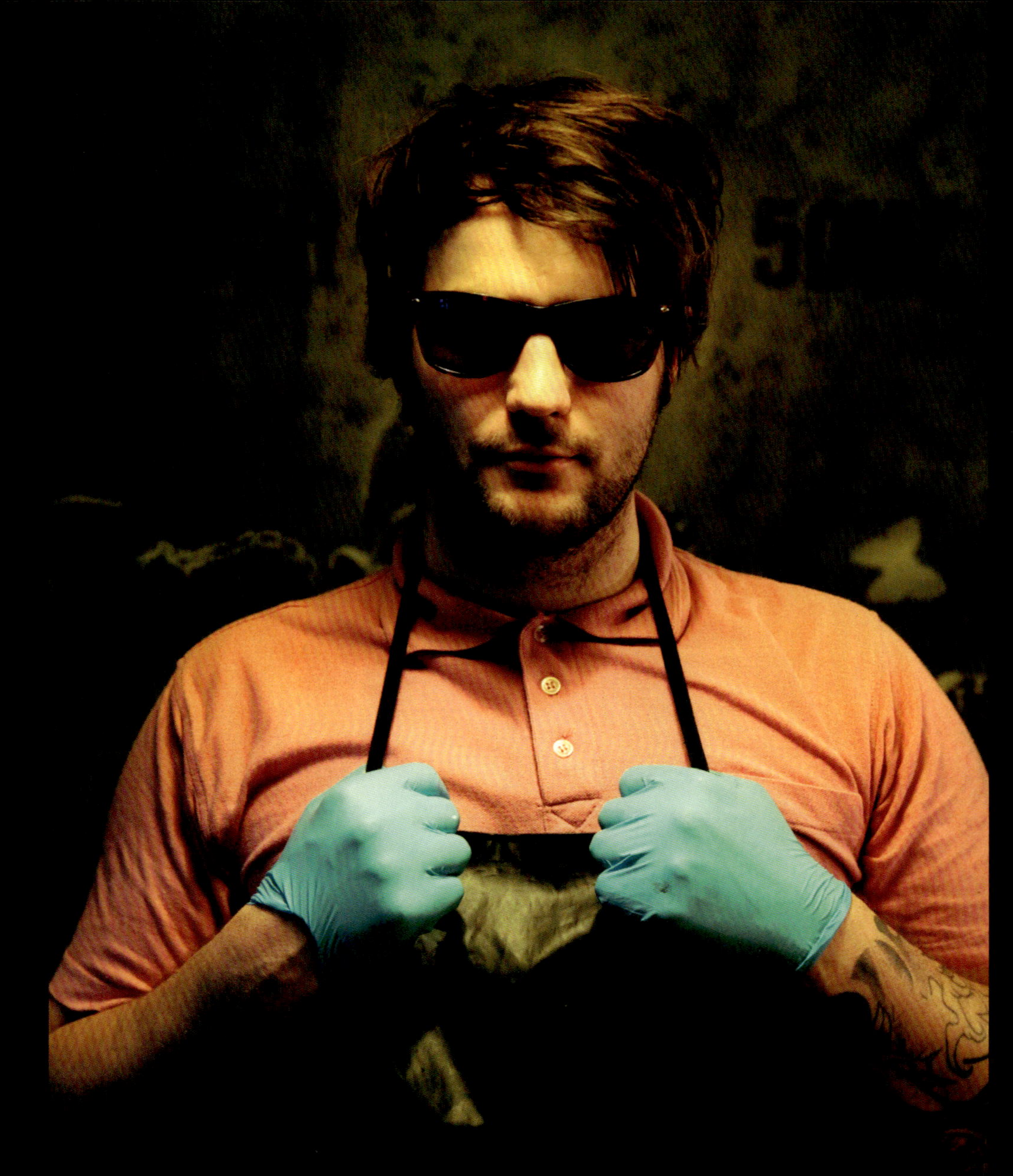

ONDRASH

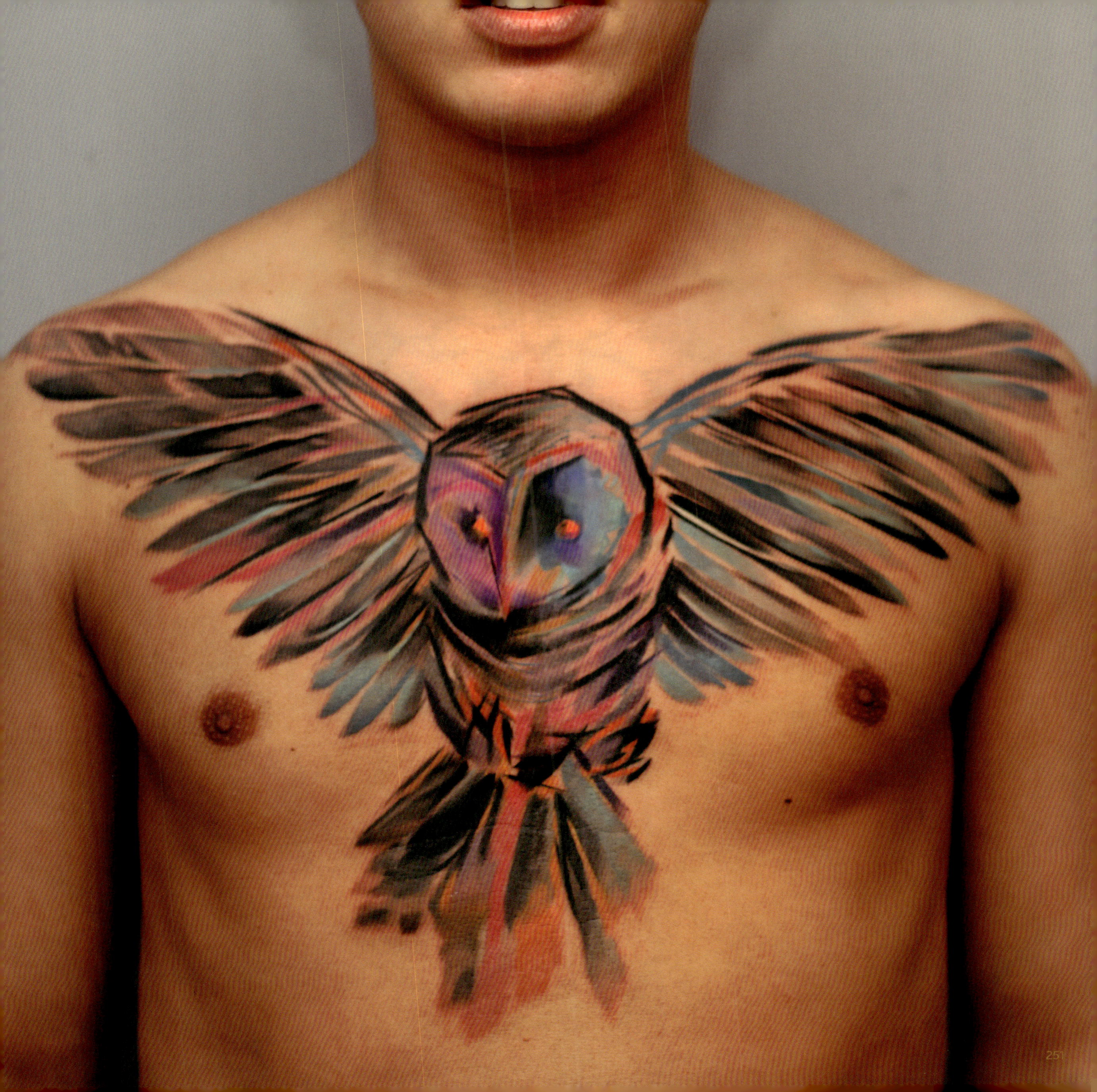

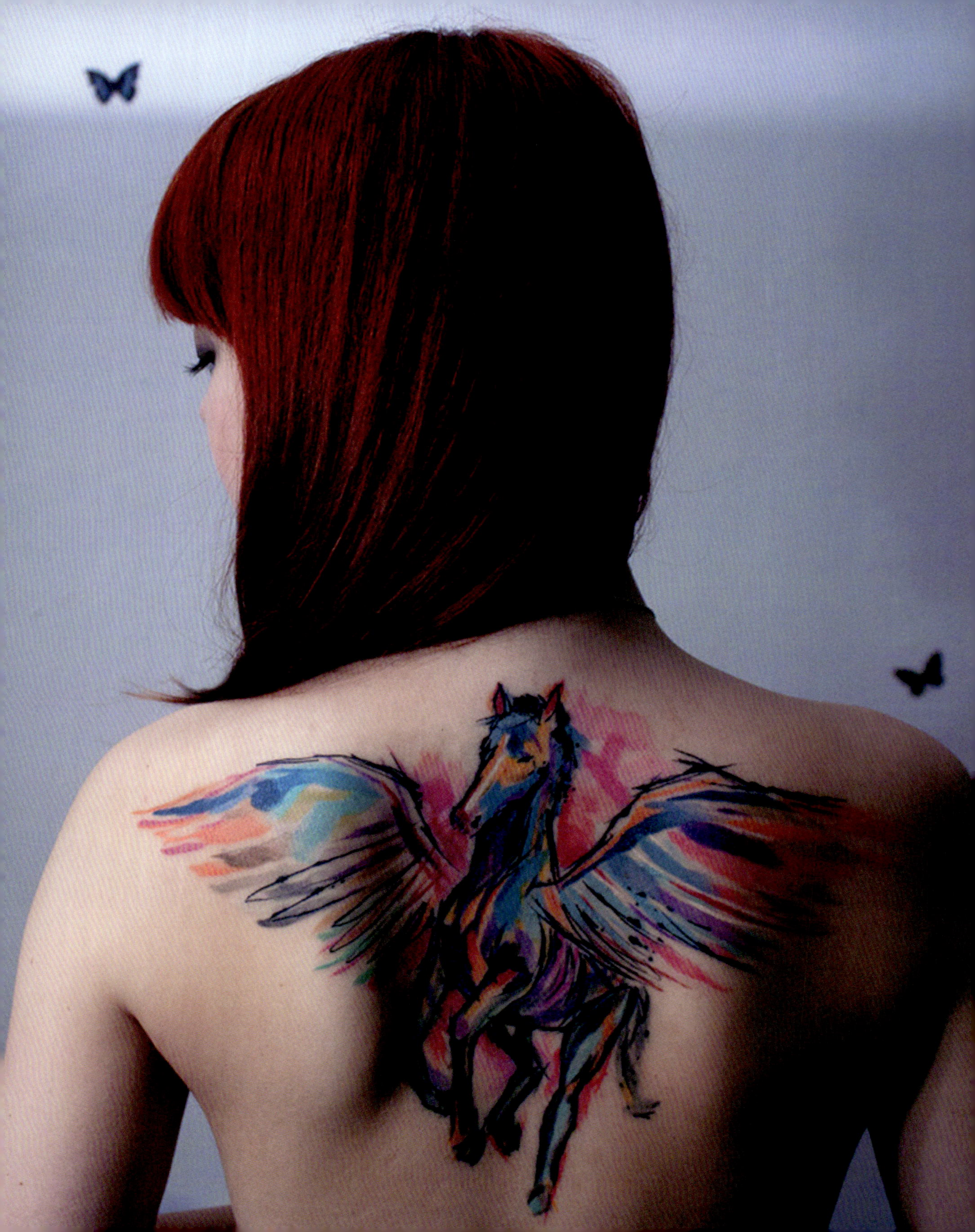

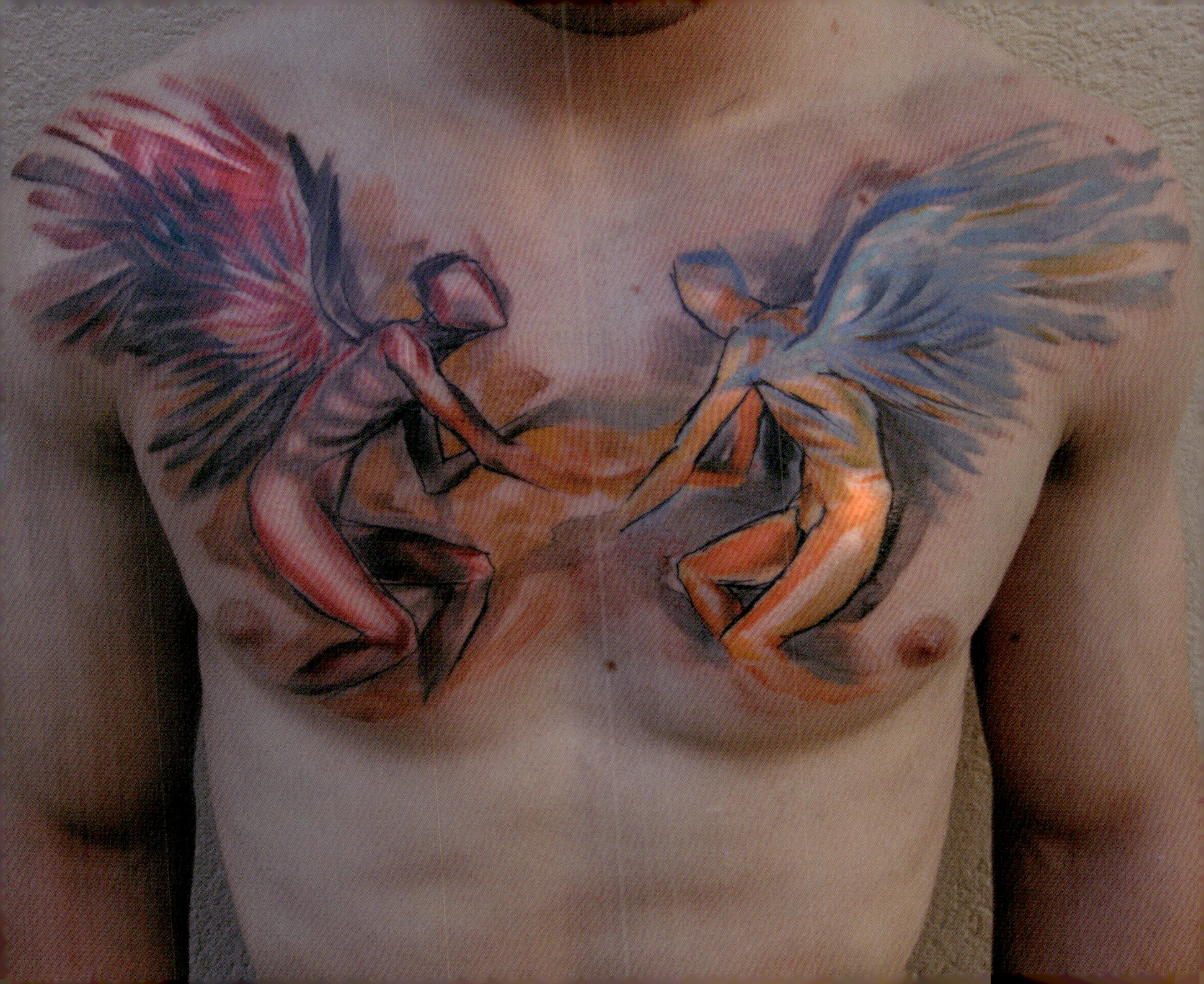

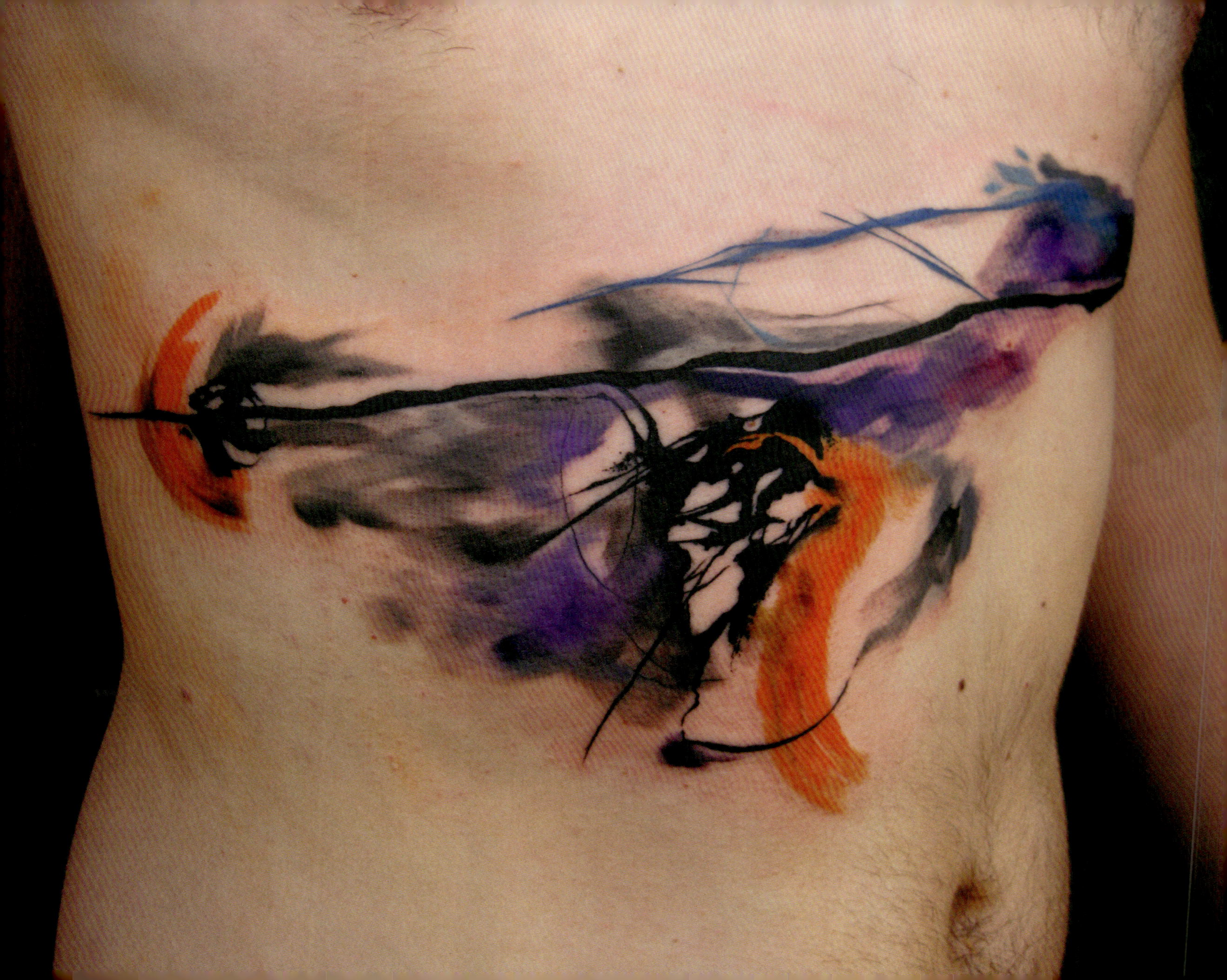

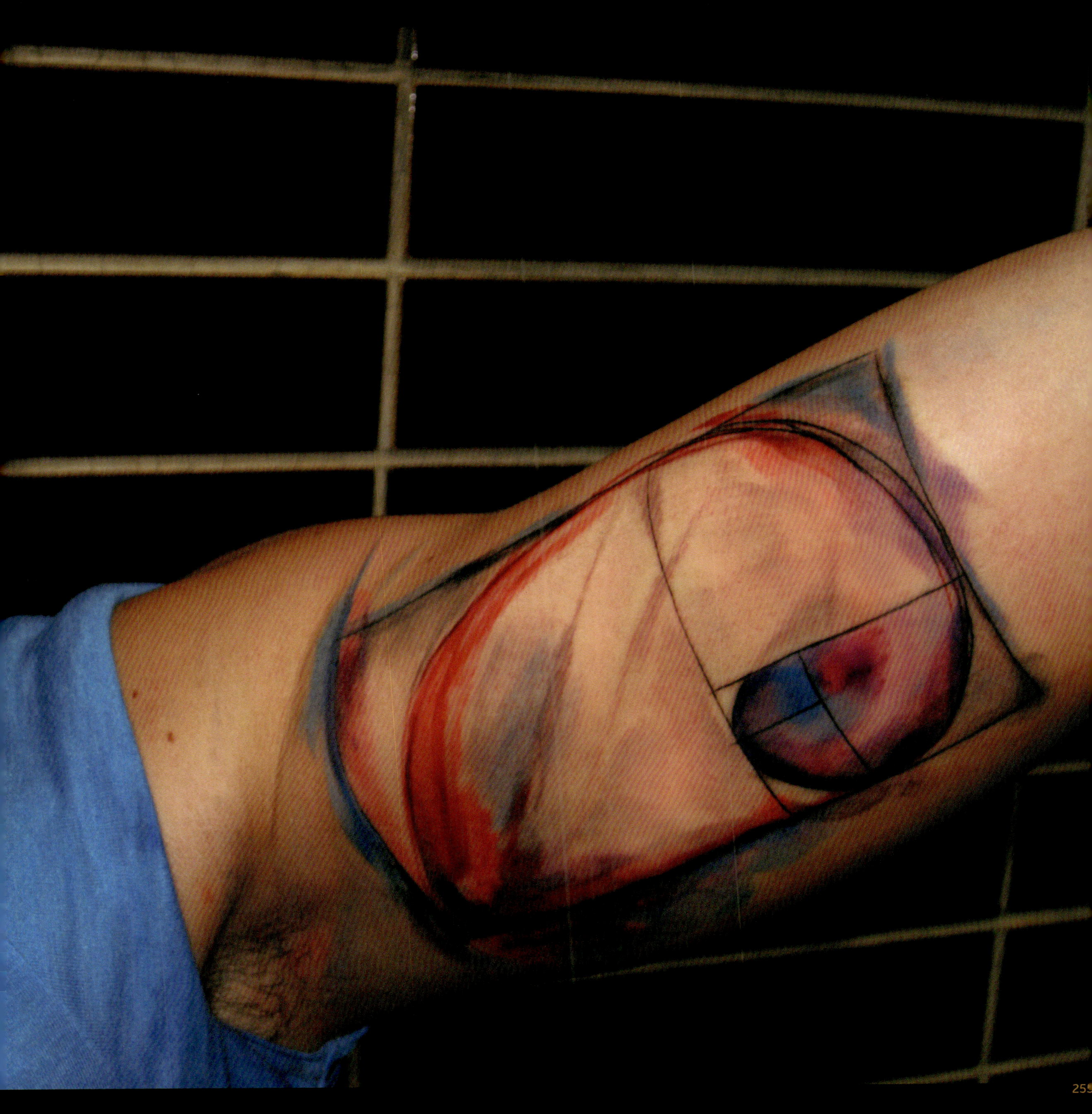

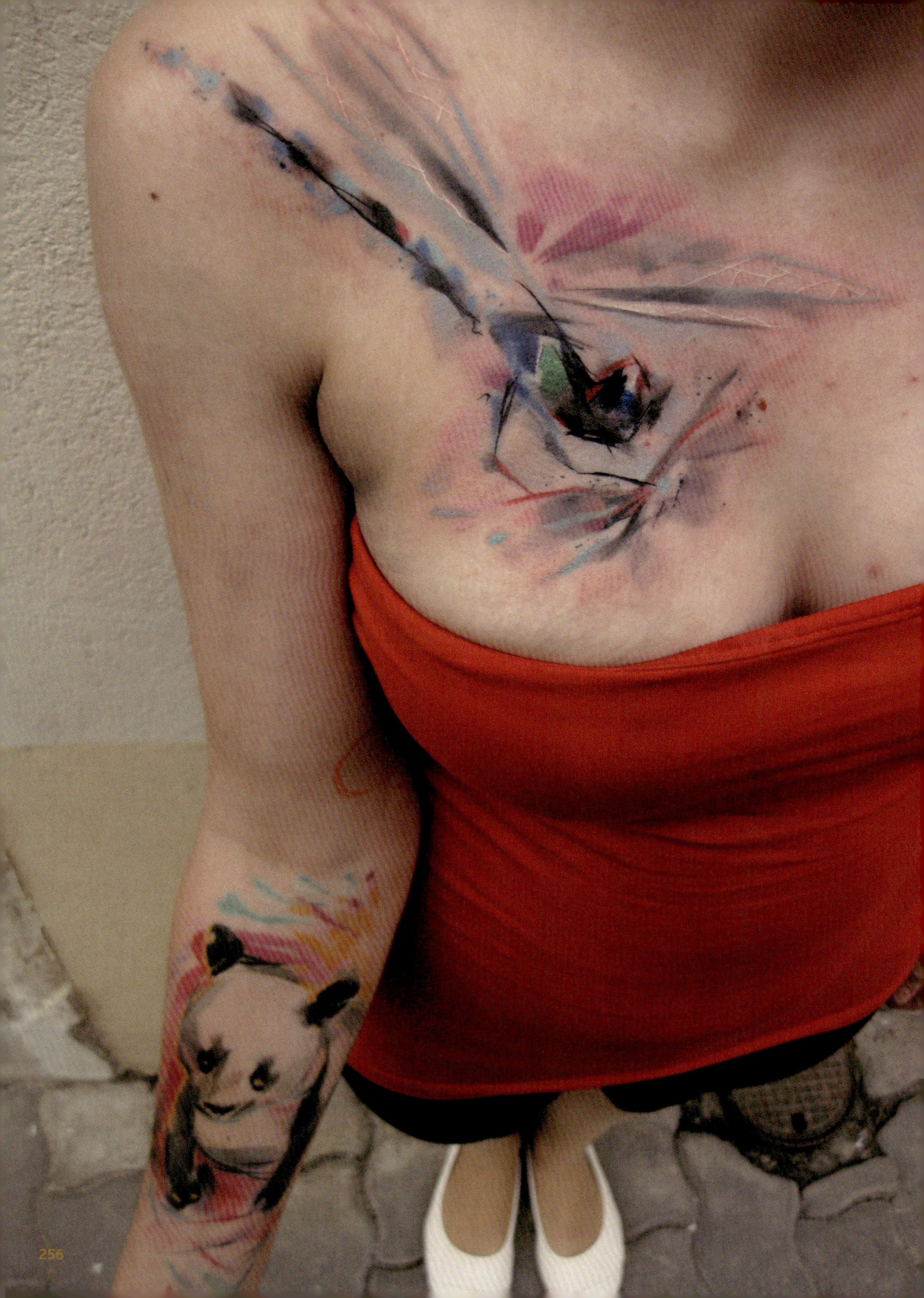

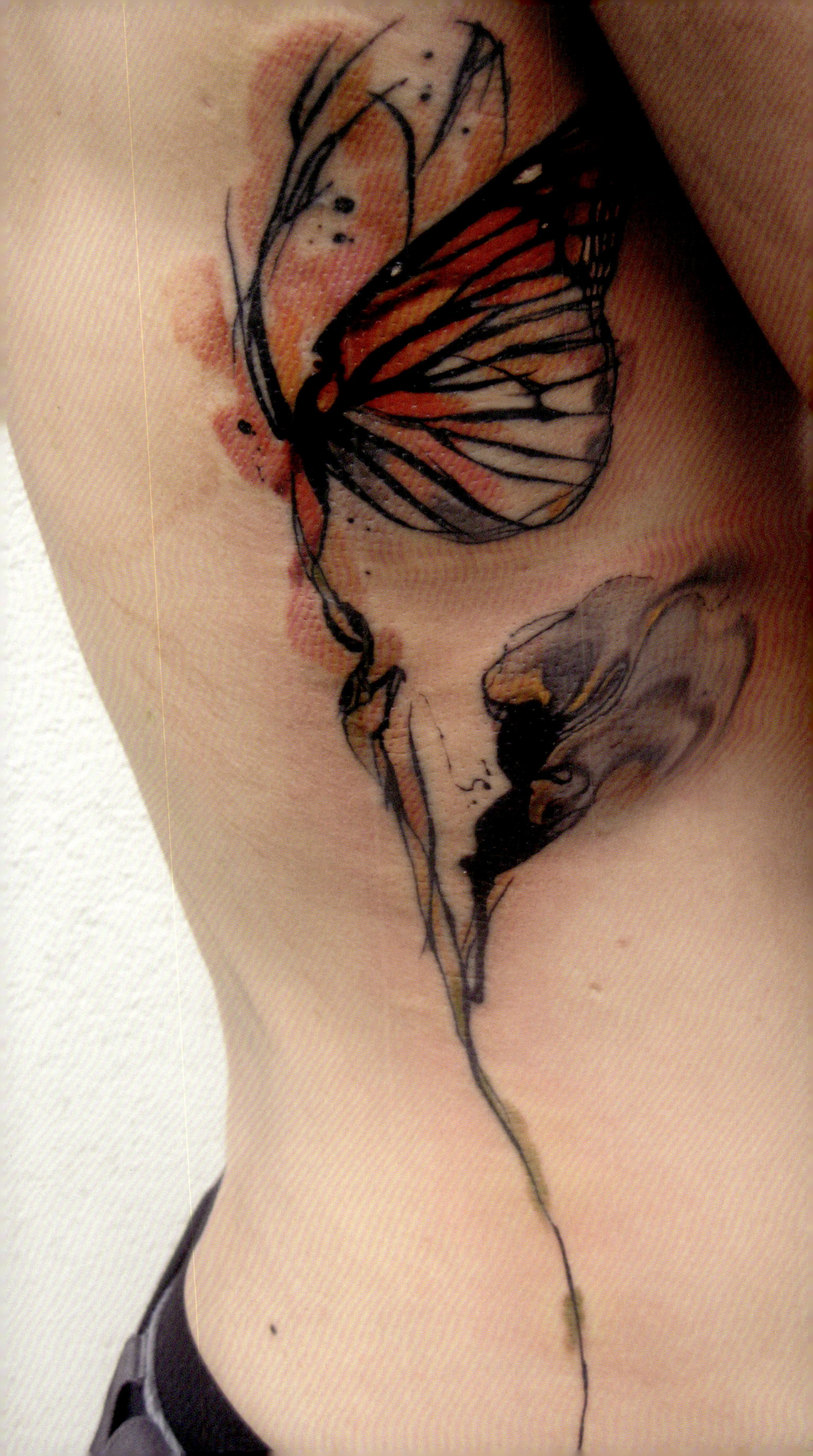

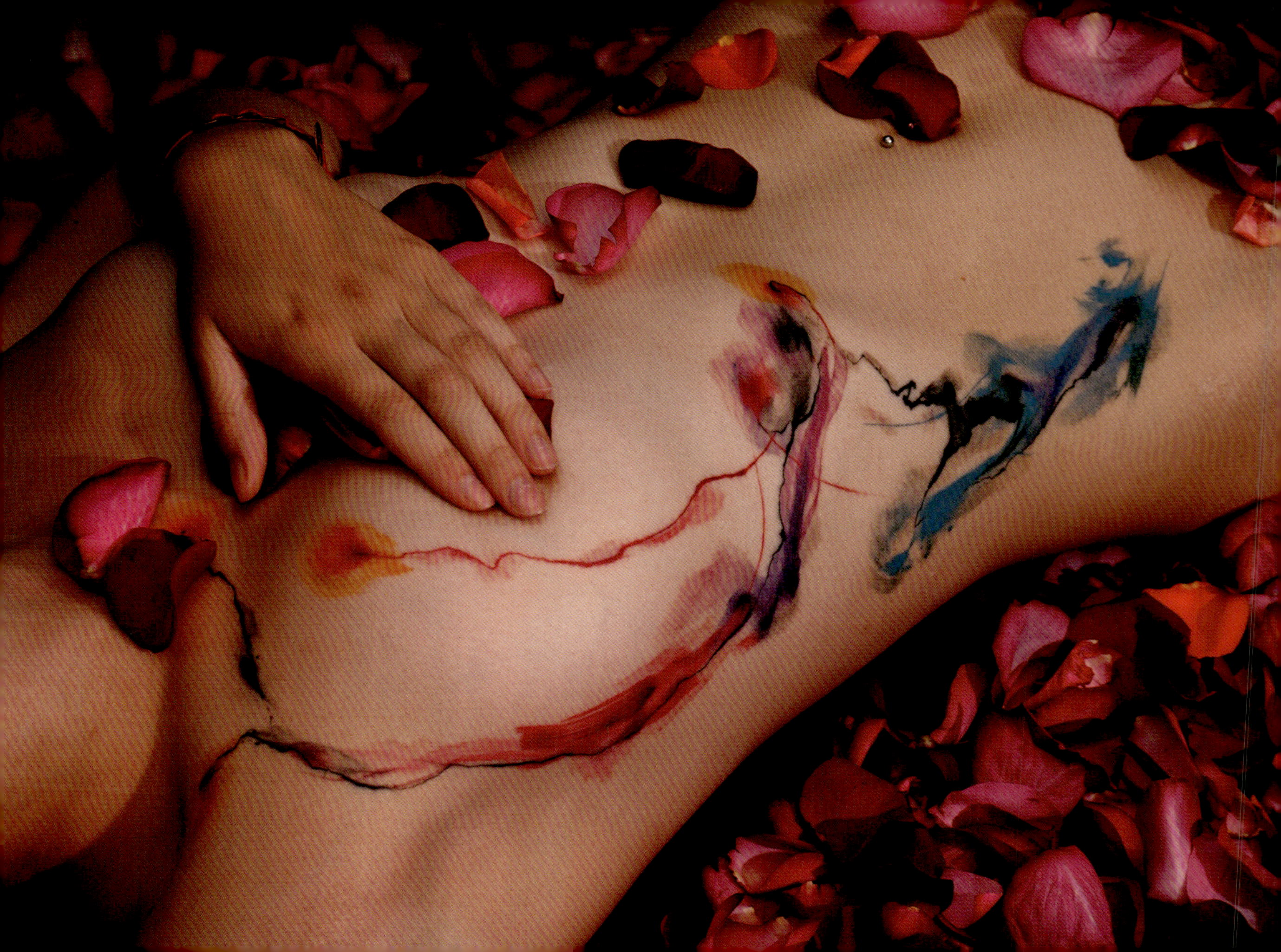

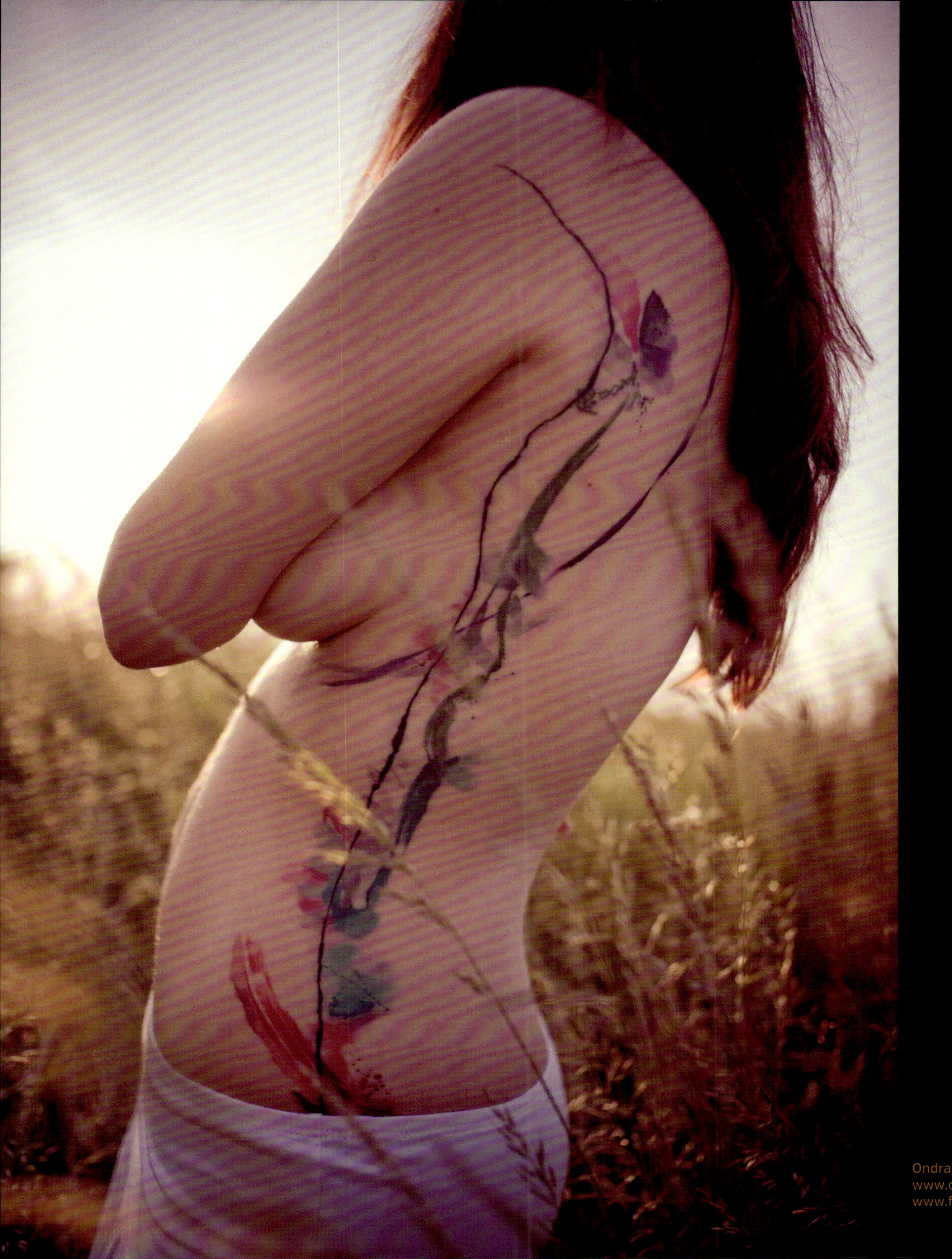

Ondrash
www.ondrash.com
www.facebook.com/ondrashtat

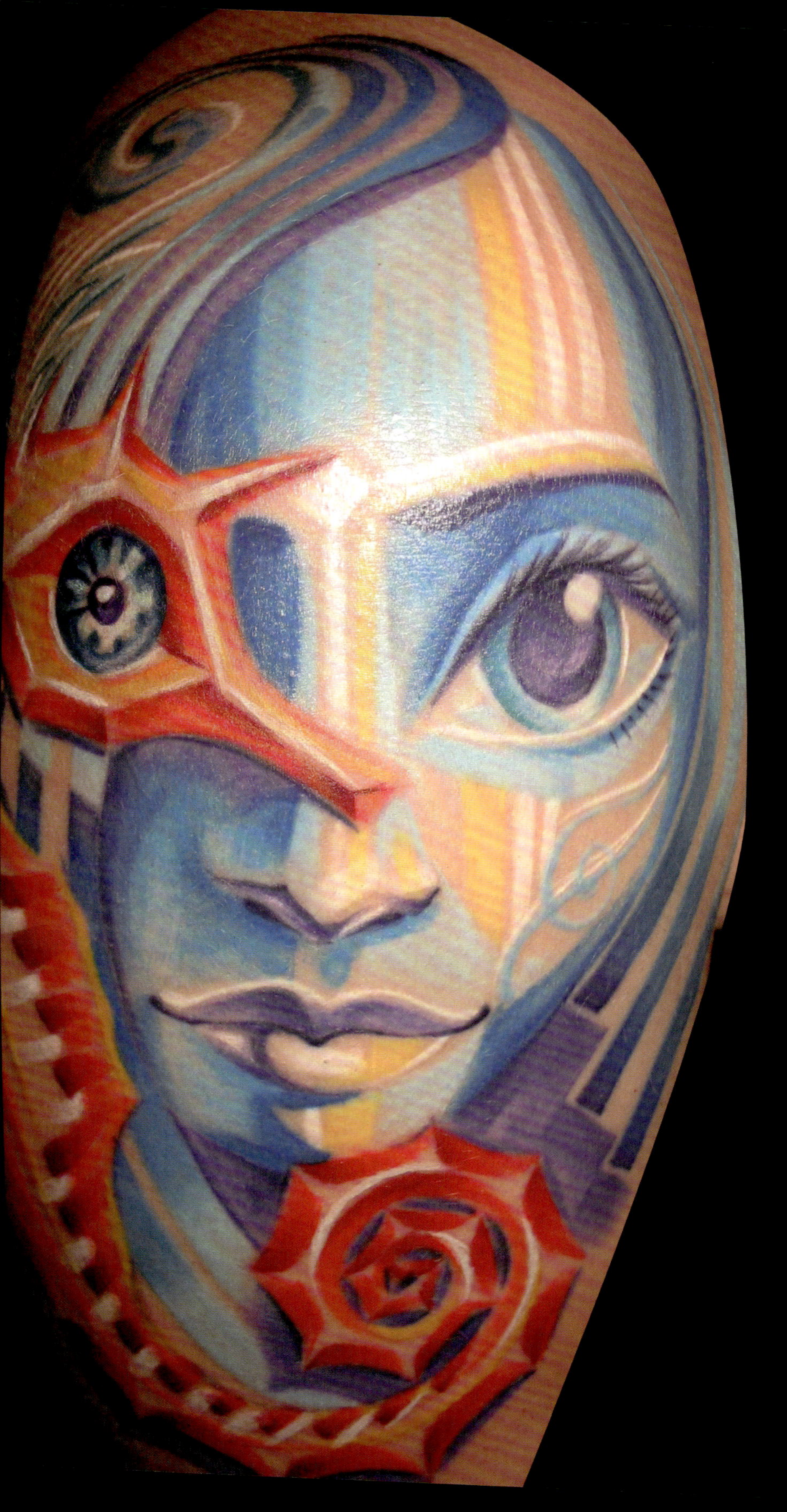

OSA WAHN
SHOCKIN' CIT
TATTOO

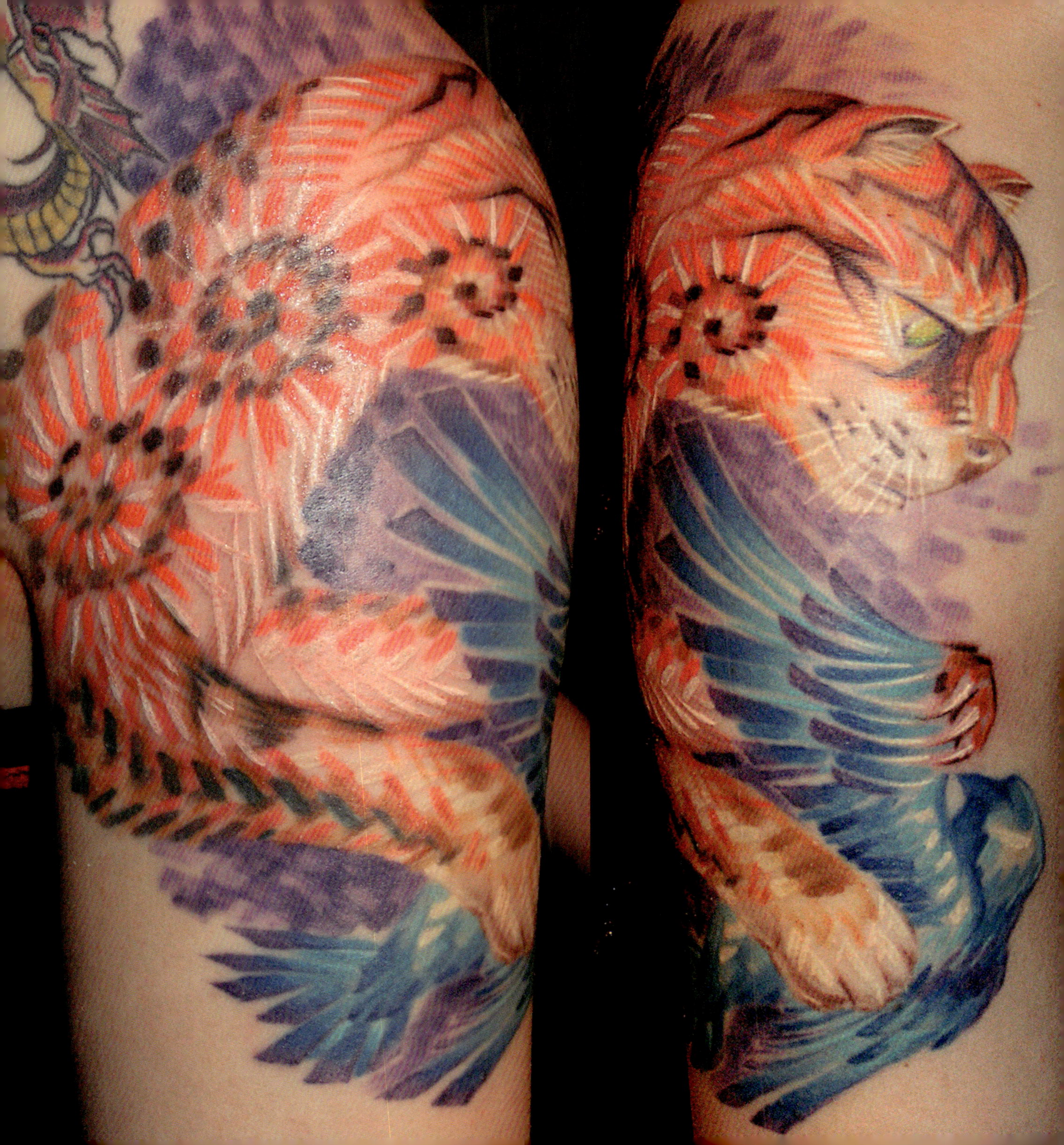

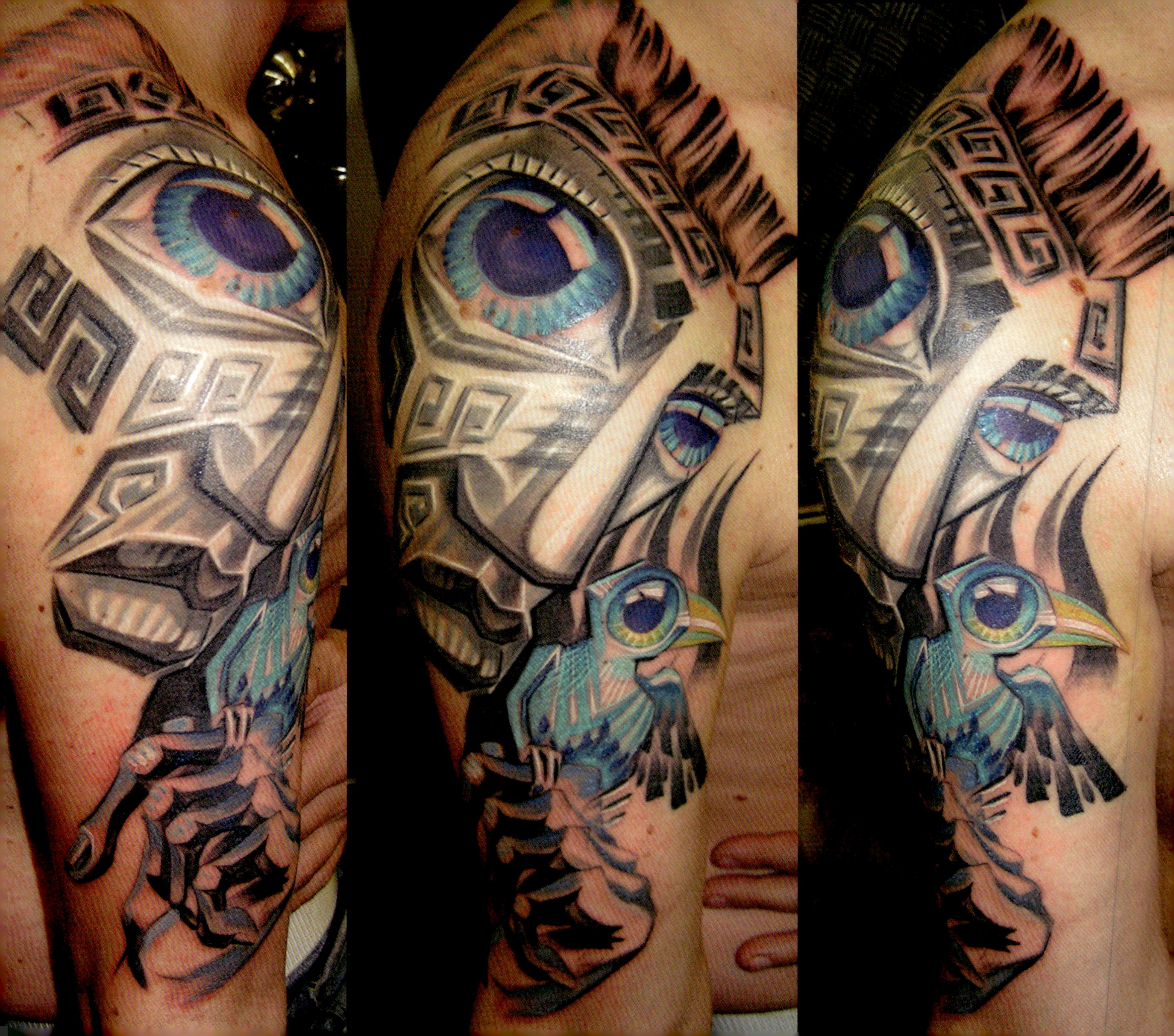

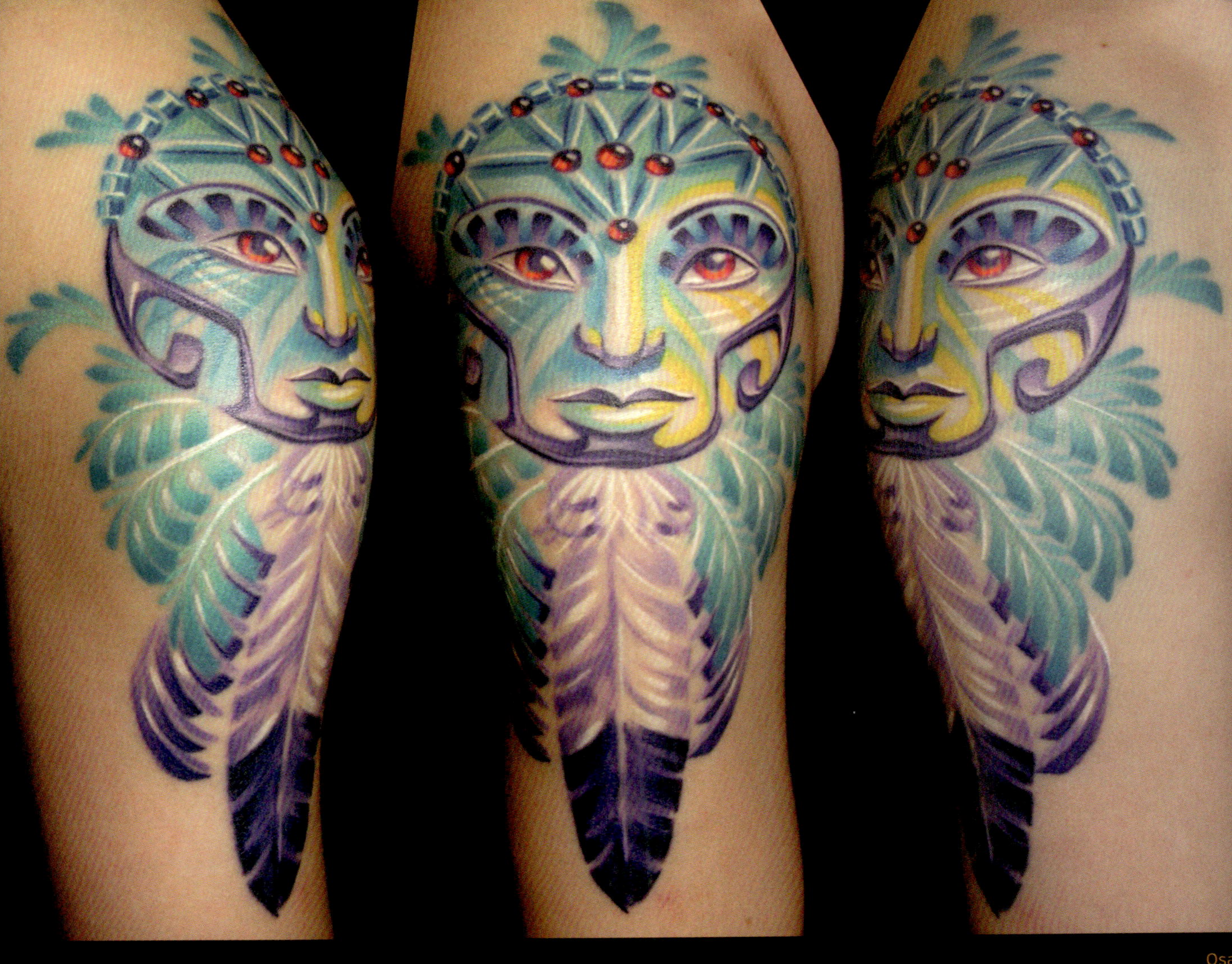
Osa
www.osatattoo.a

PHIL KYLE
MAGNUM OPUS TATTOO

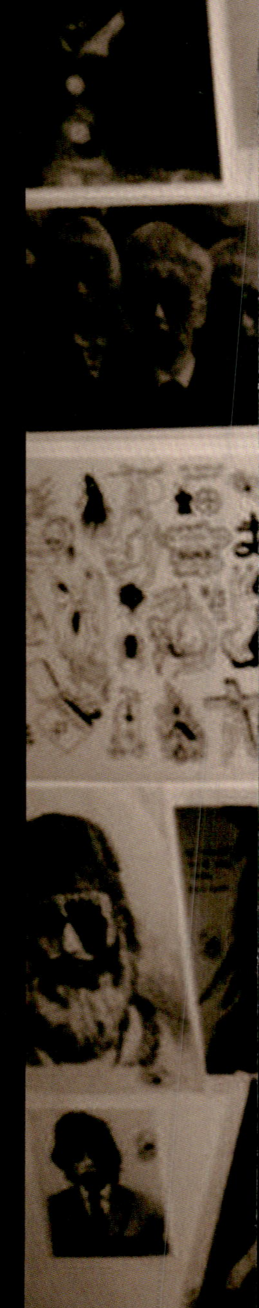

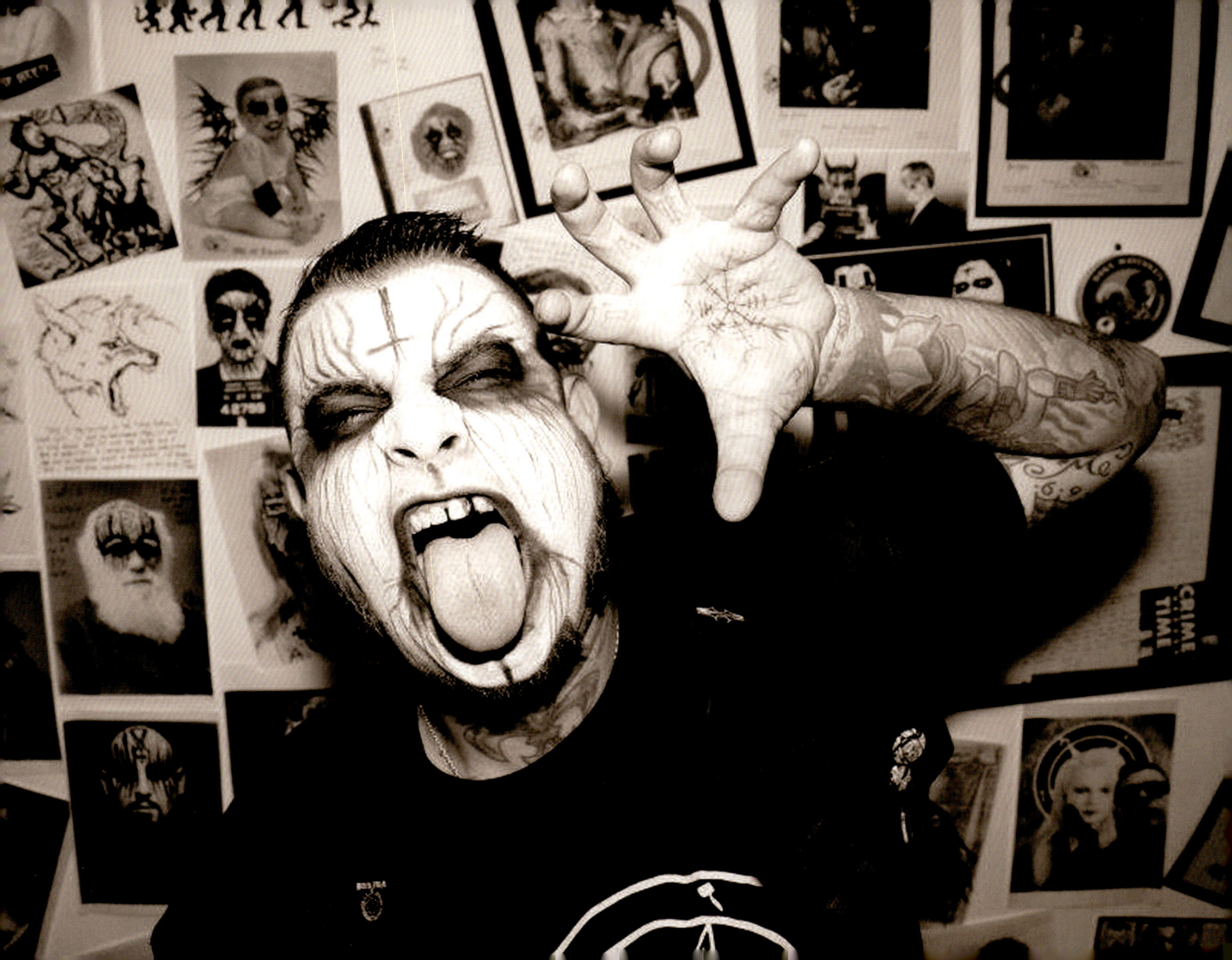

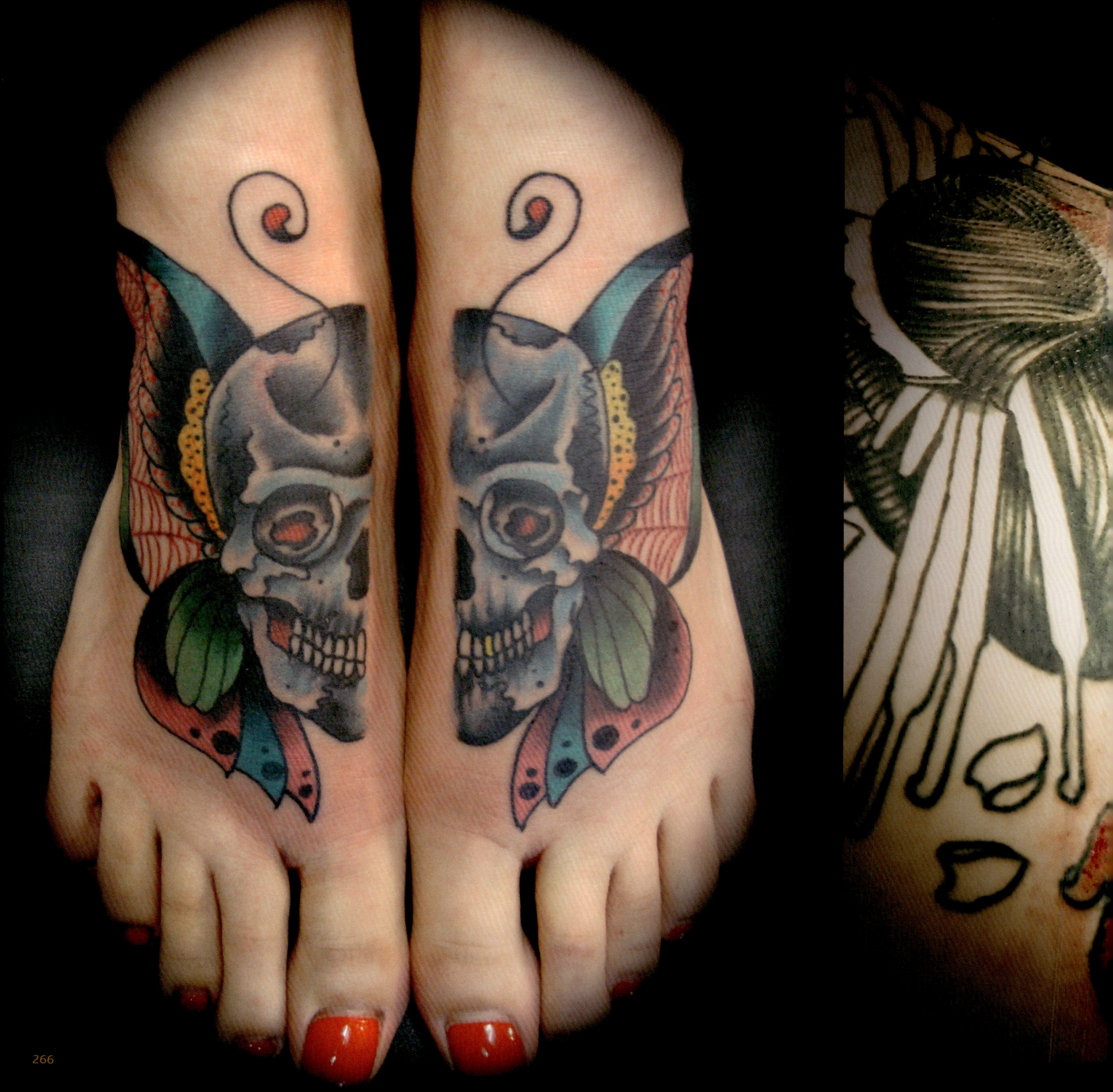

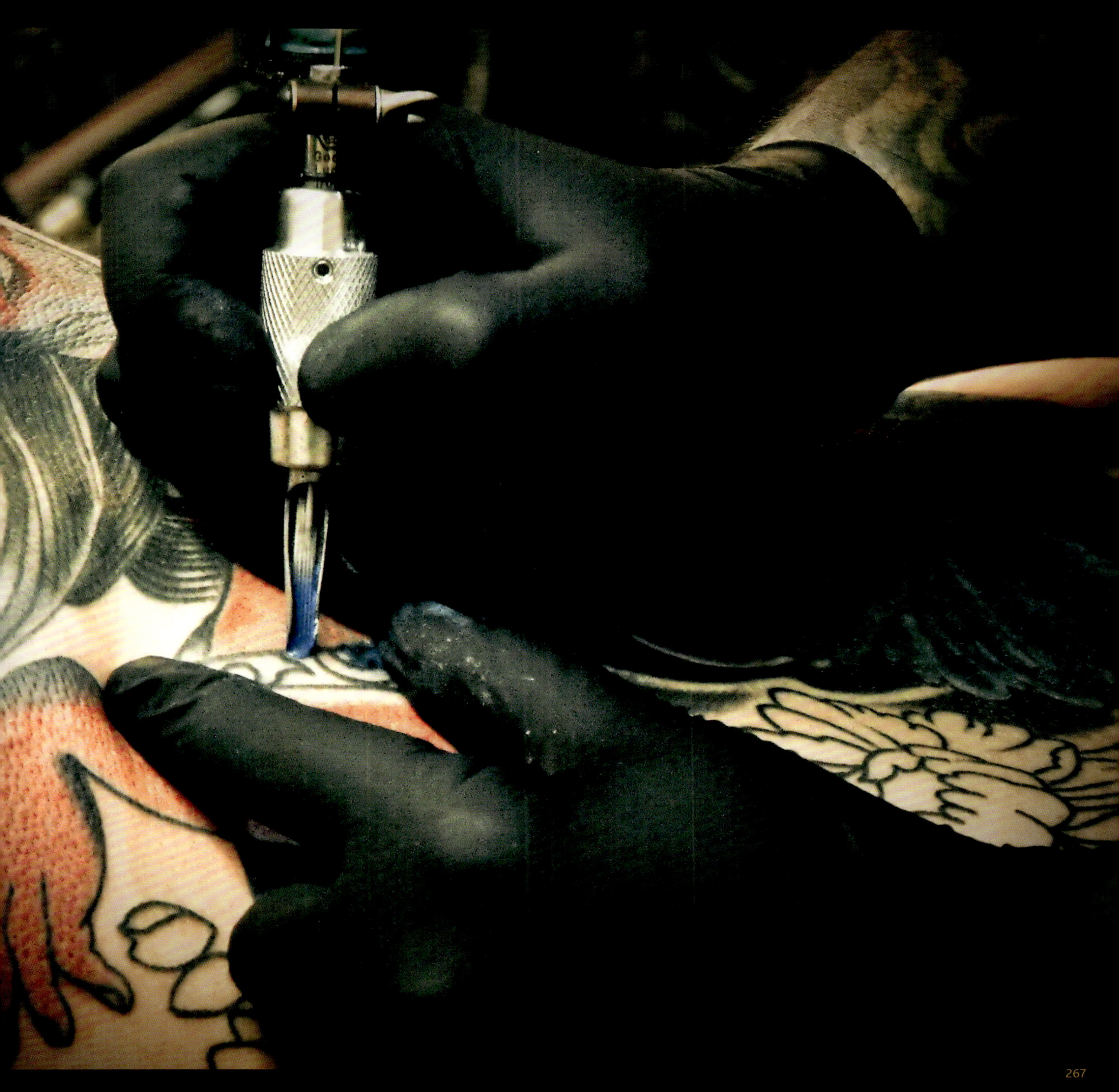

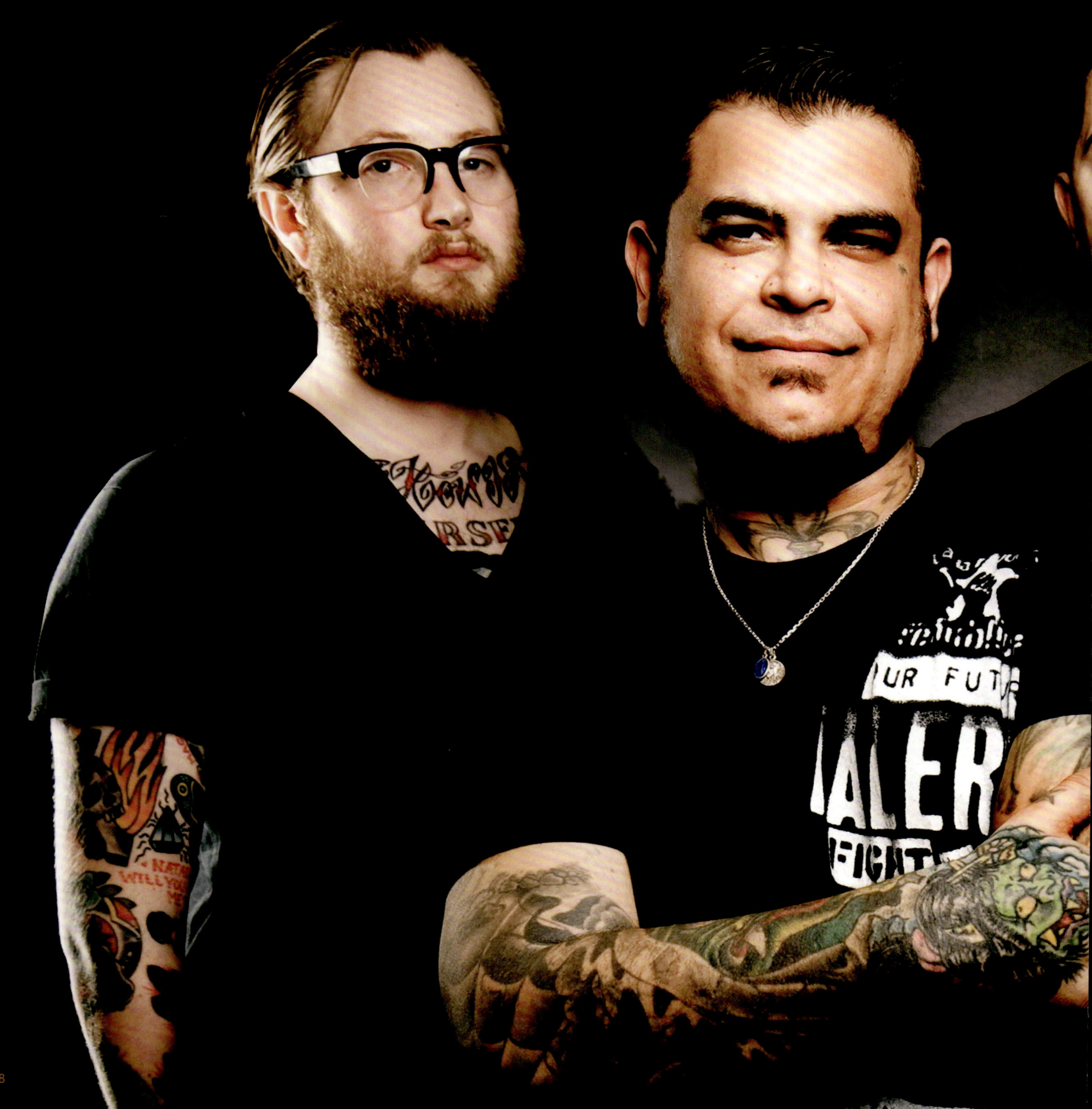

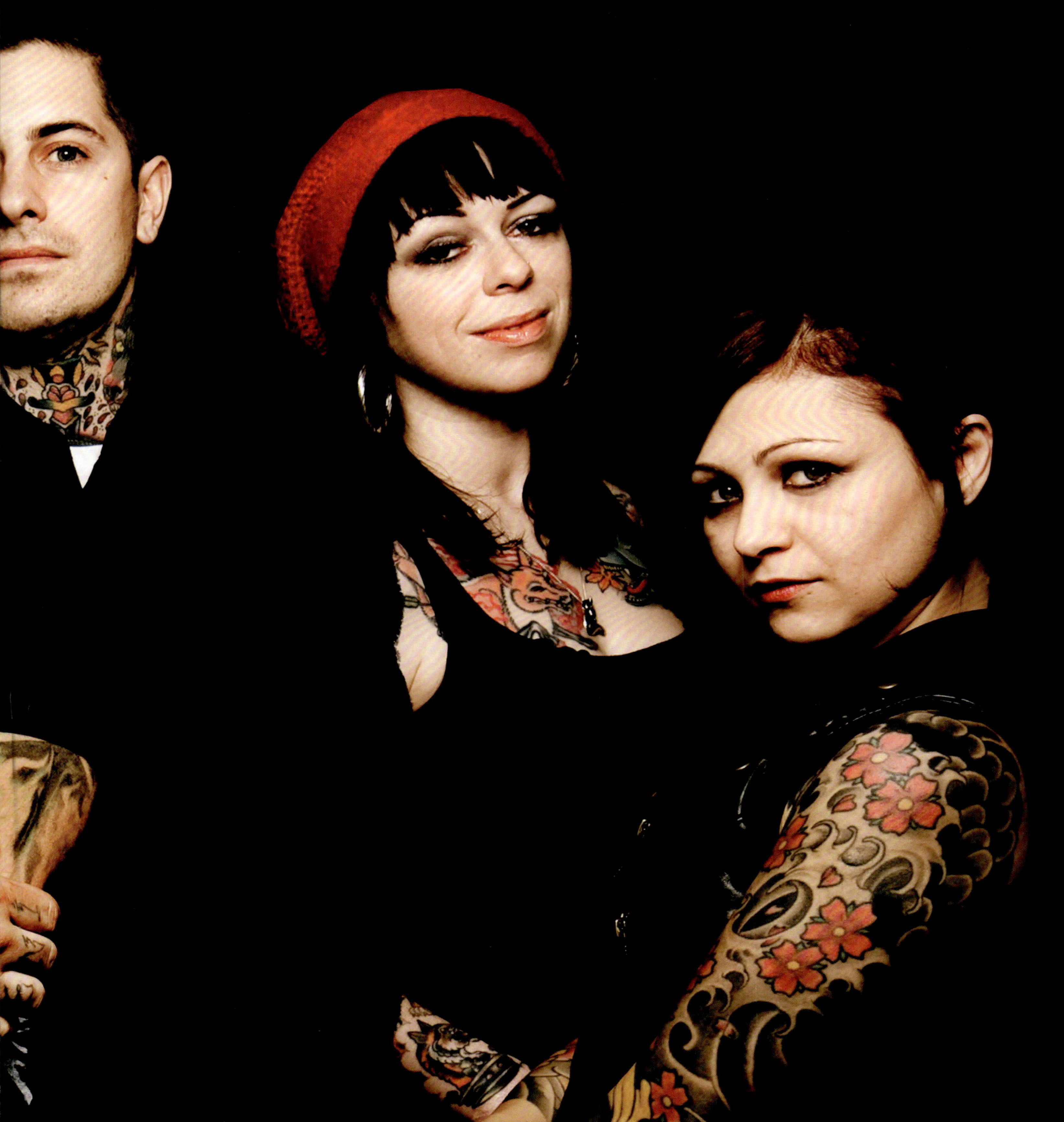

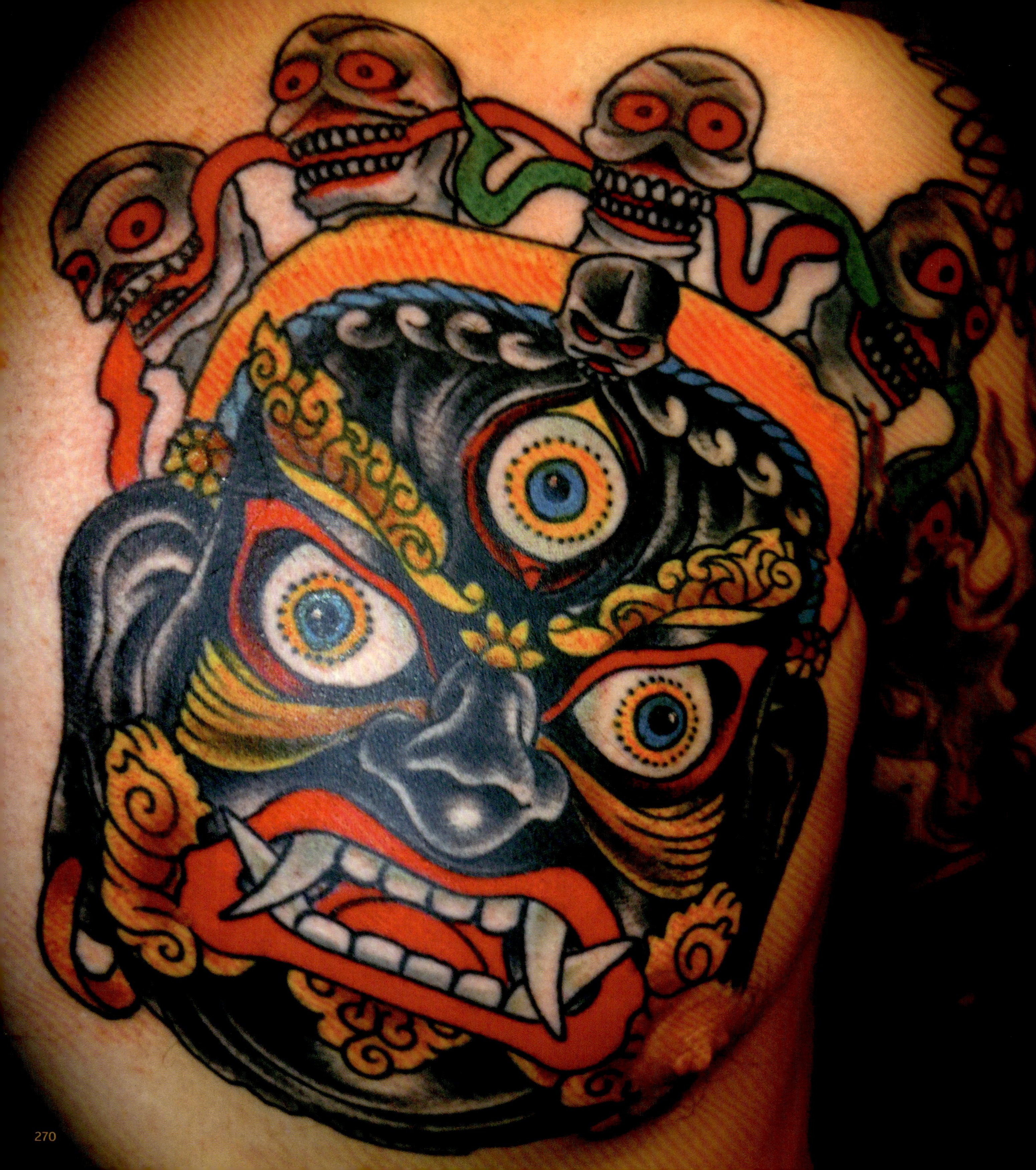

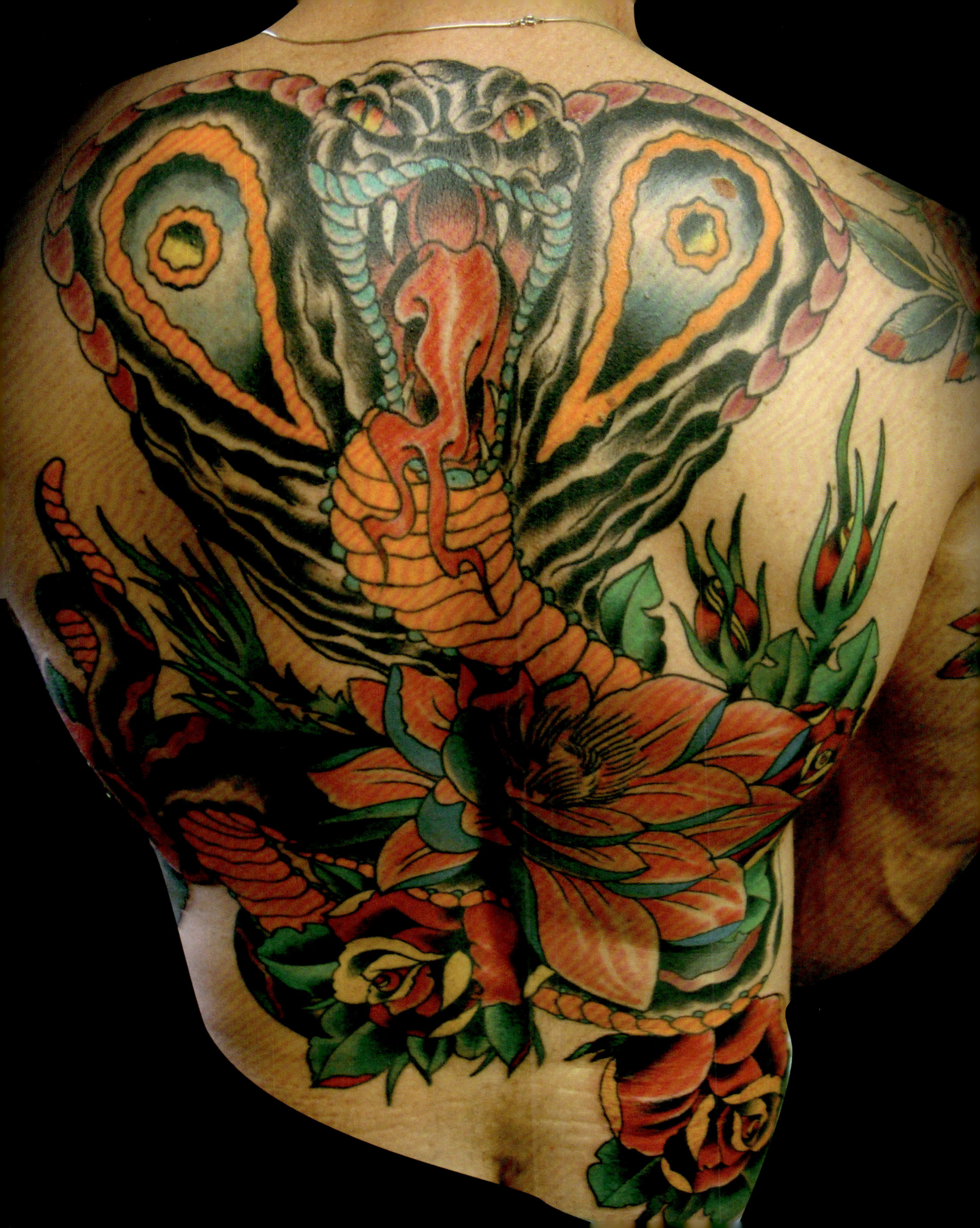

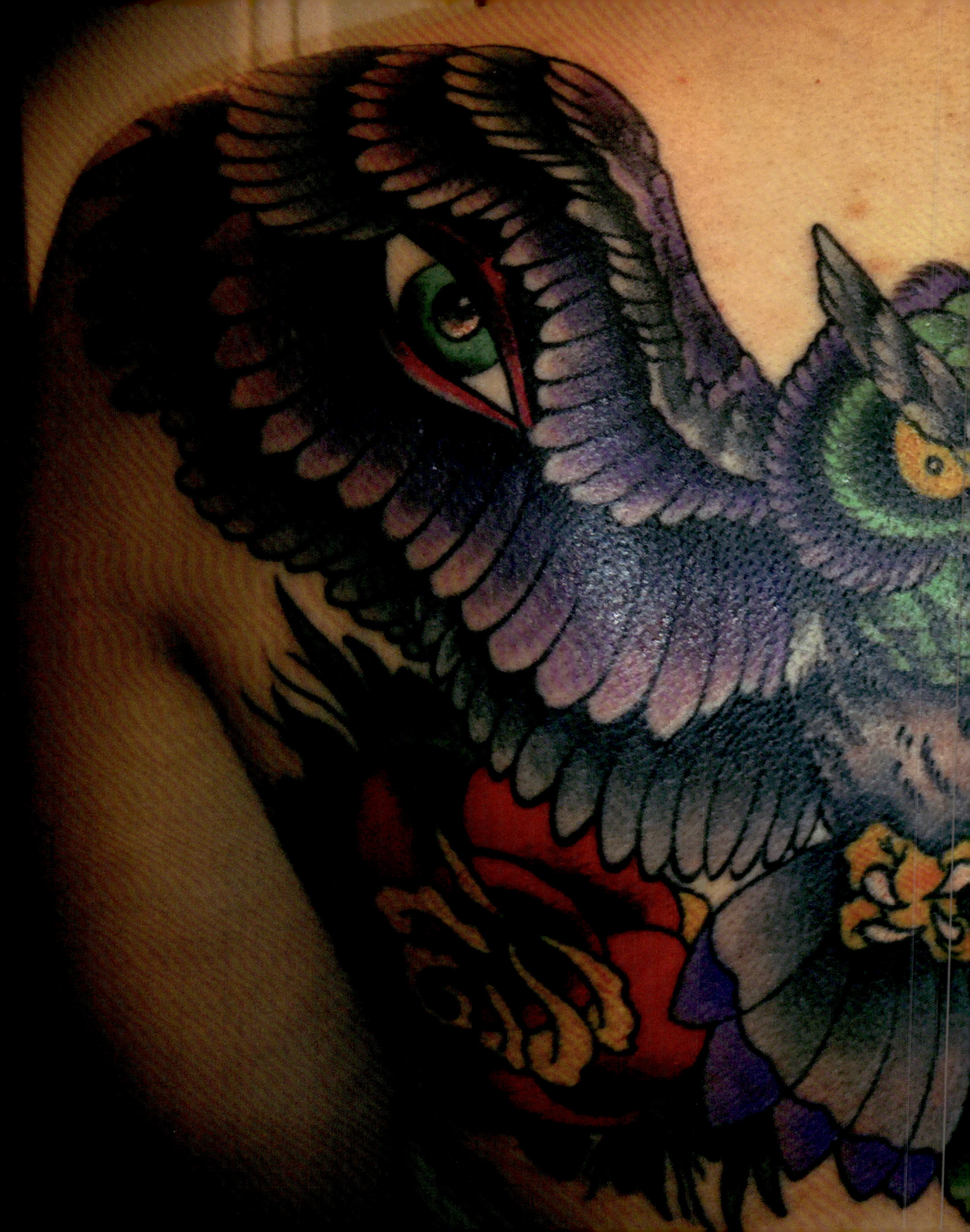

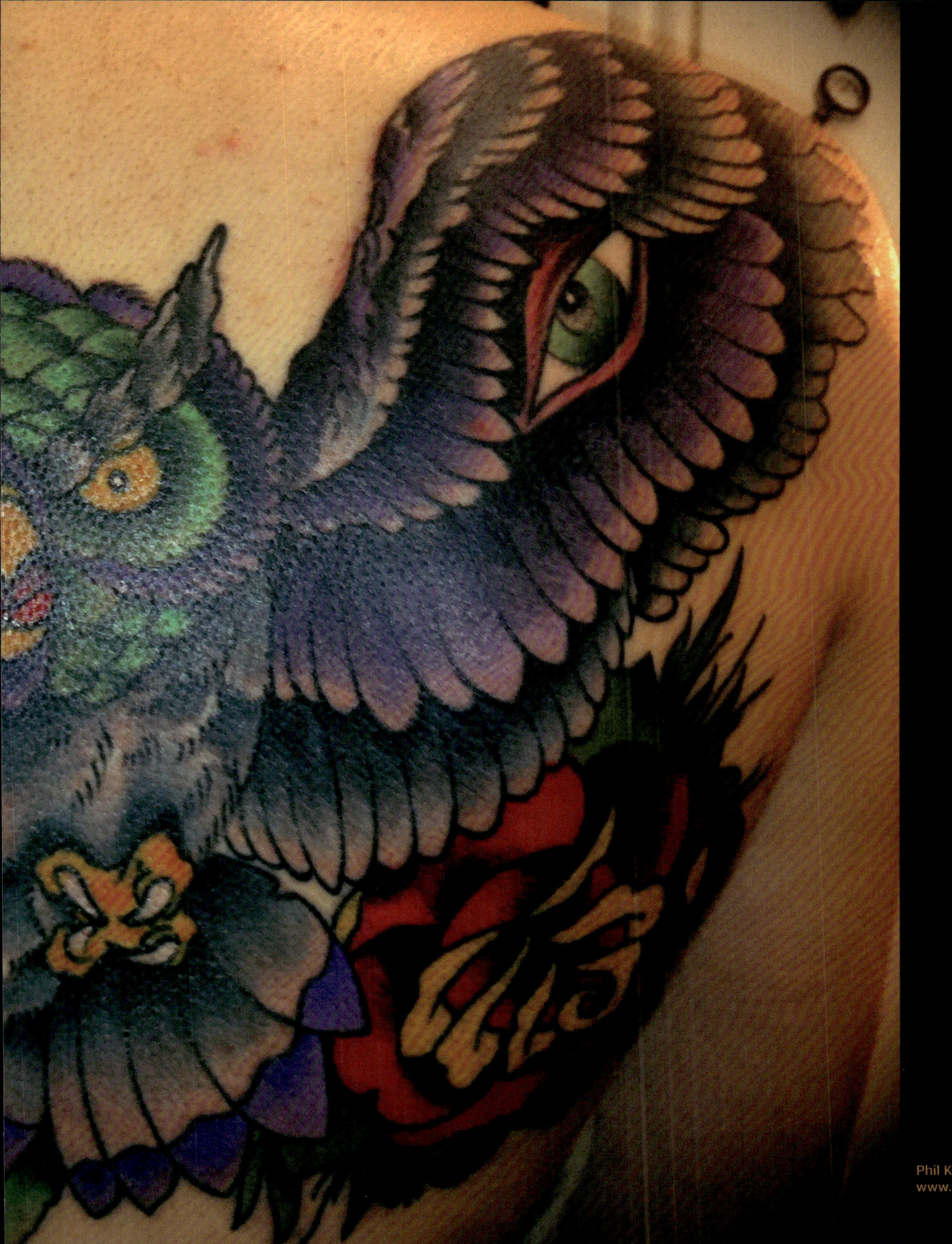

Phil Kyle
www.magnumopustattoo.co

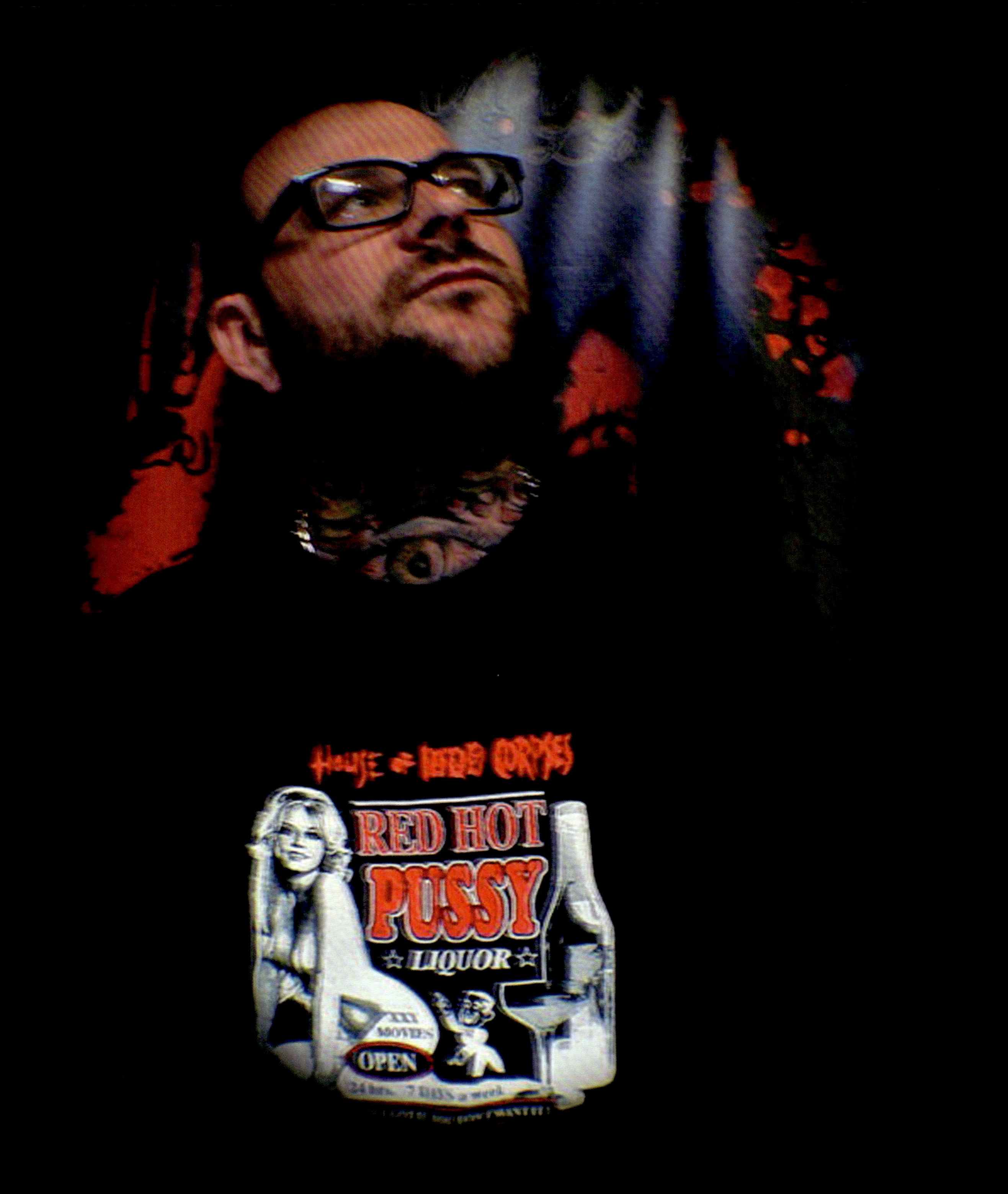

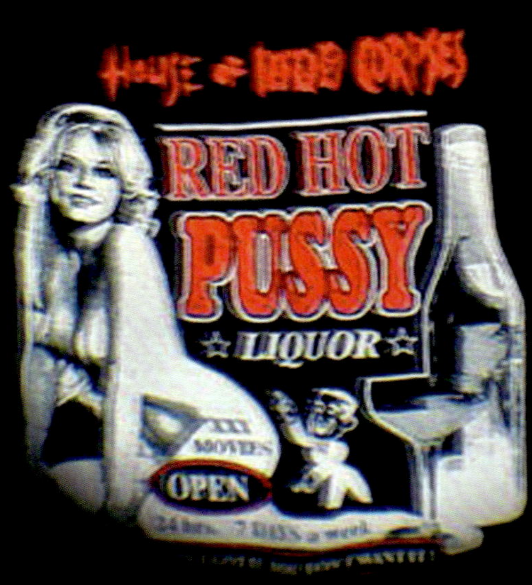

RAN MACLURKIN

ABSTRACT NOIR TATTOO STUDIO

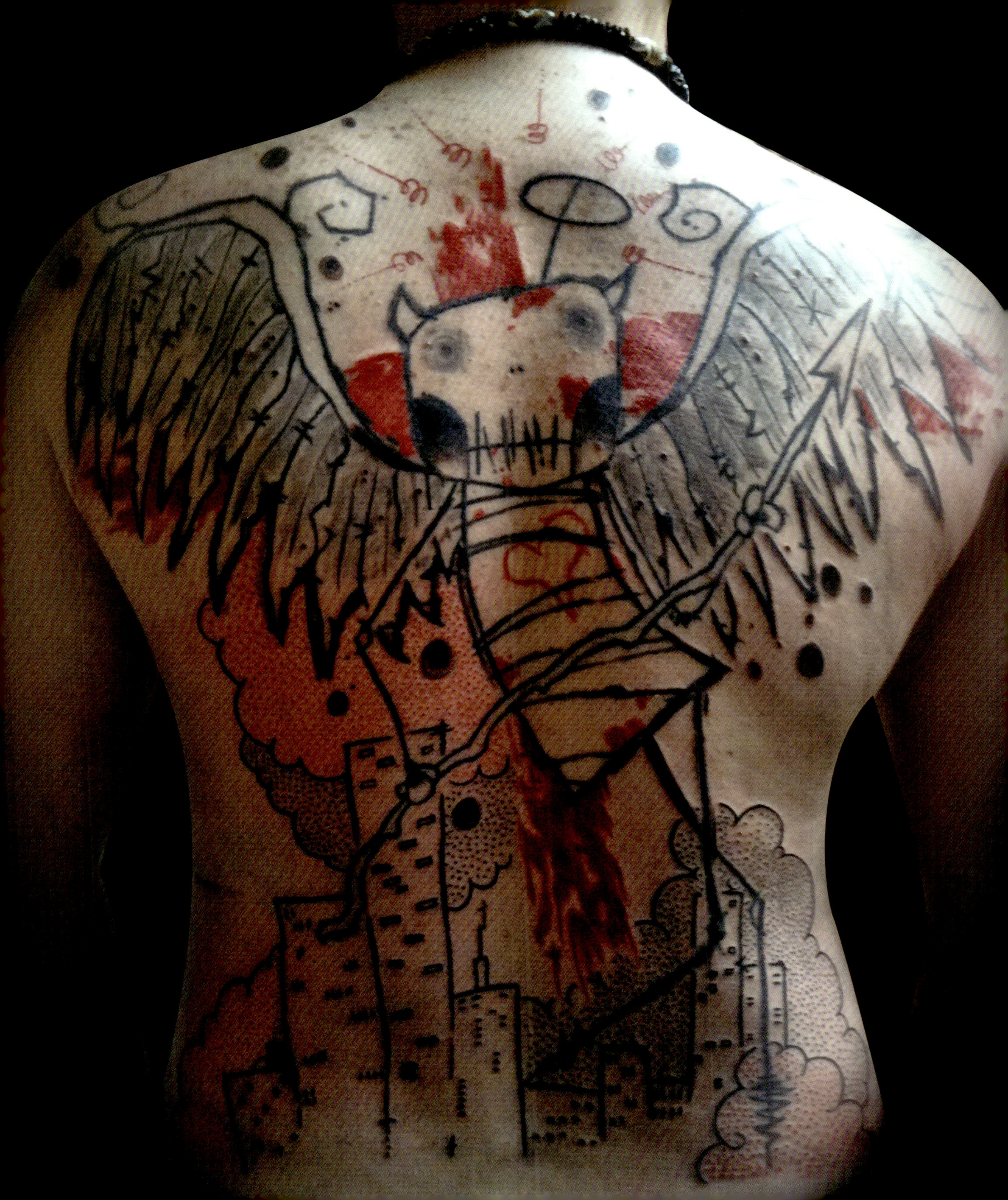

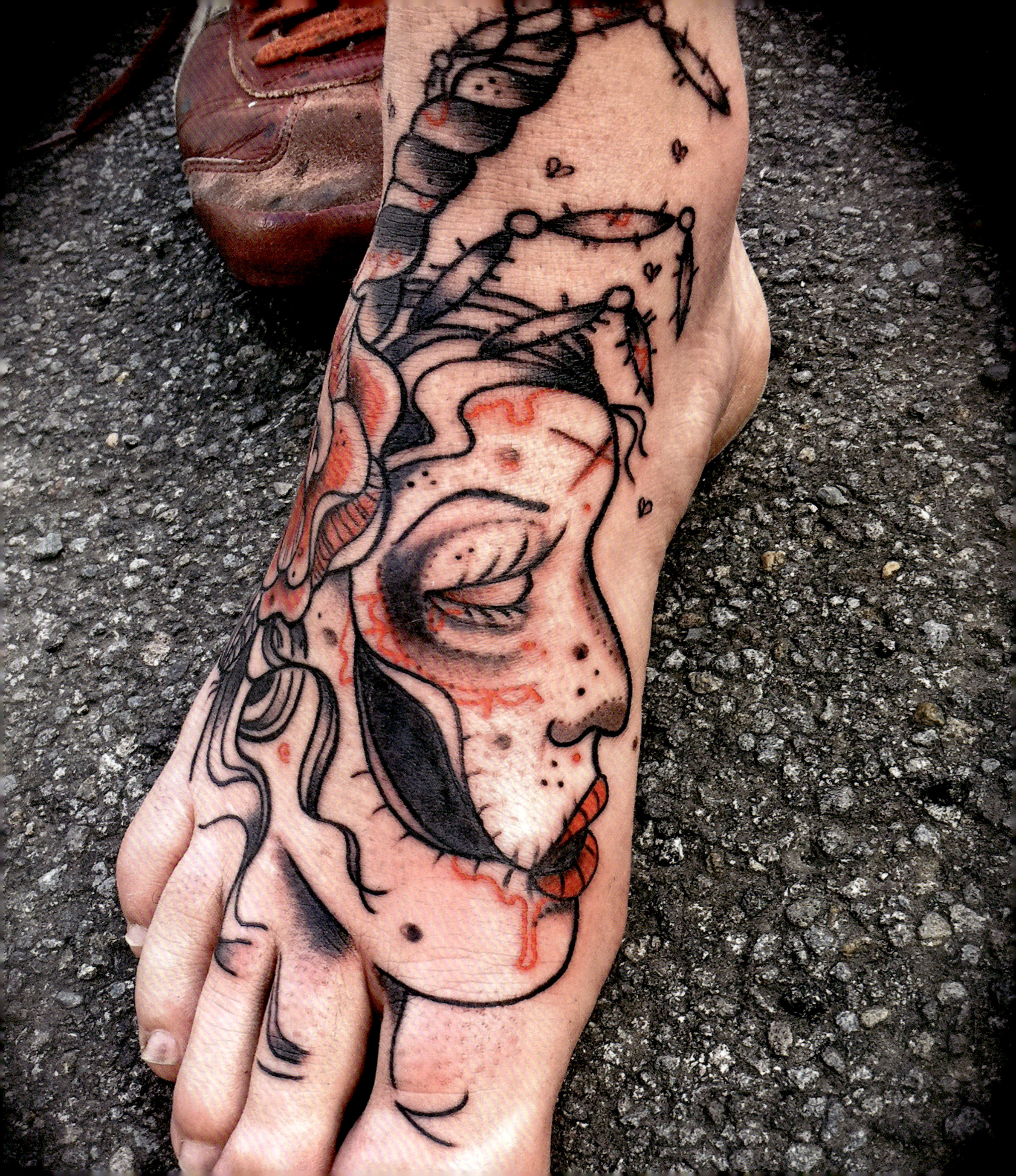

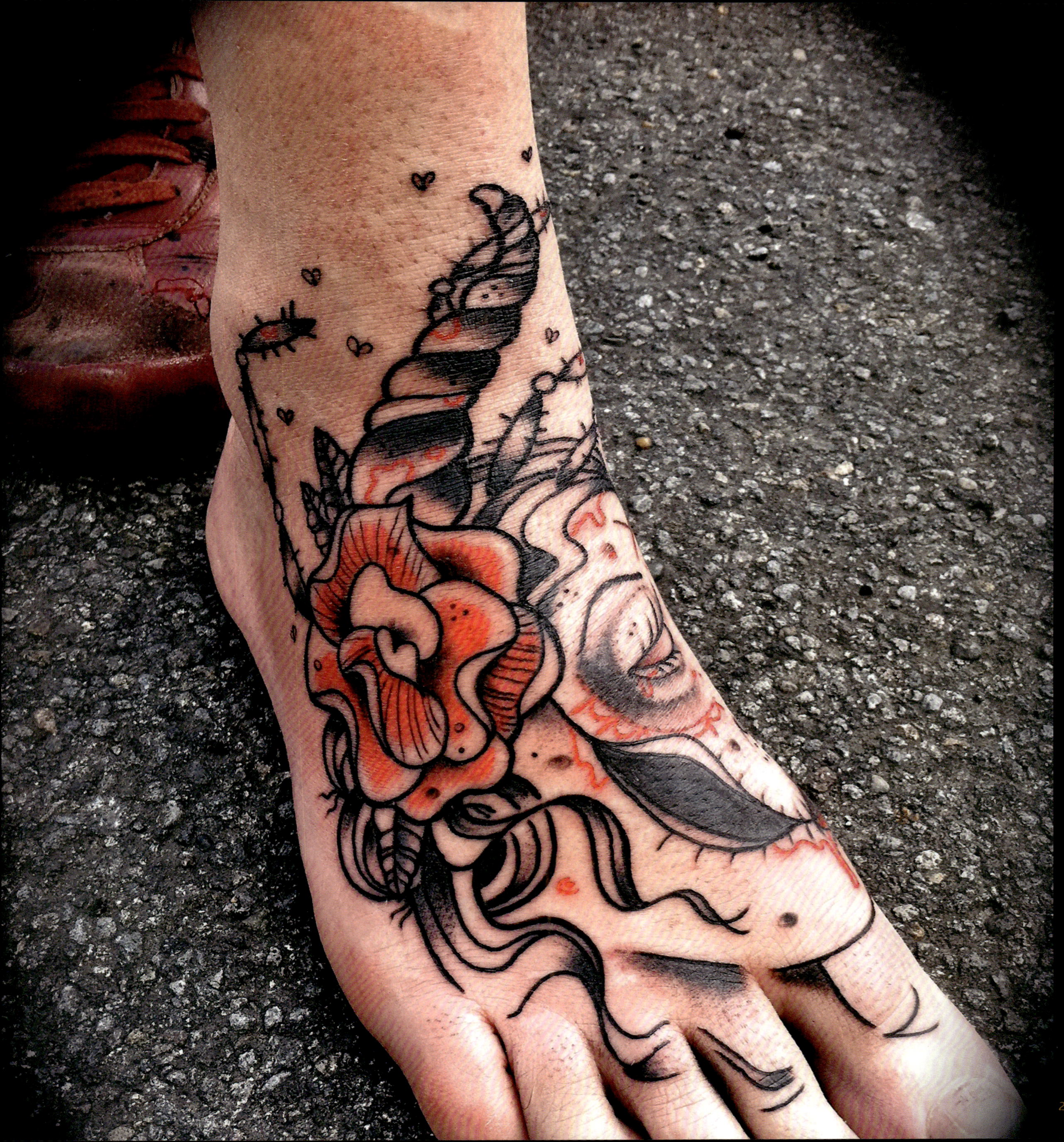

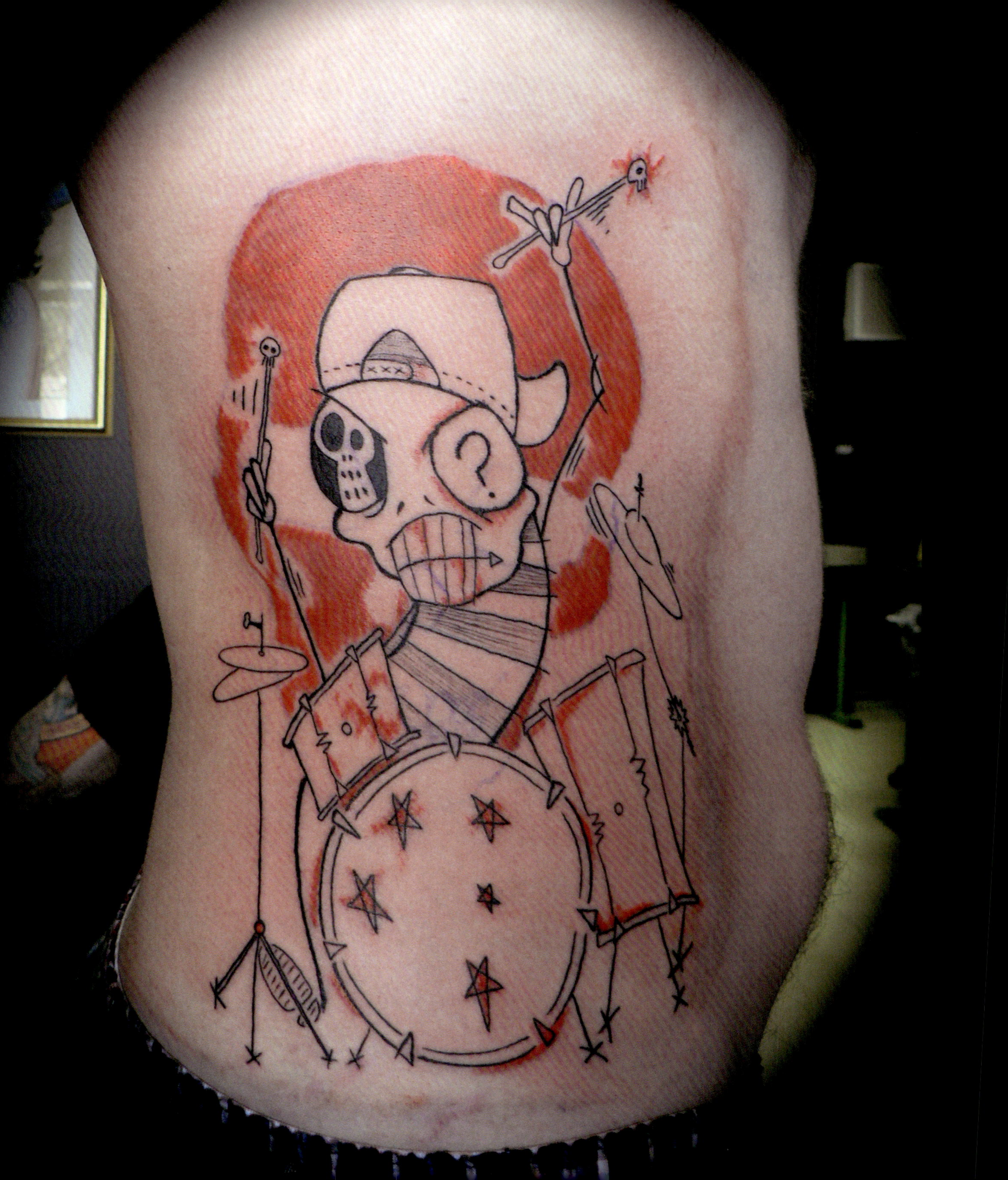

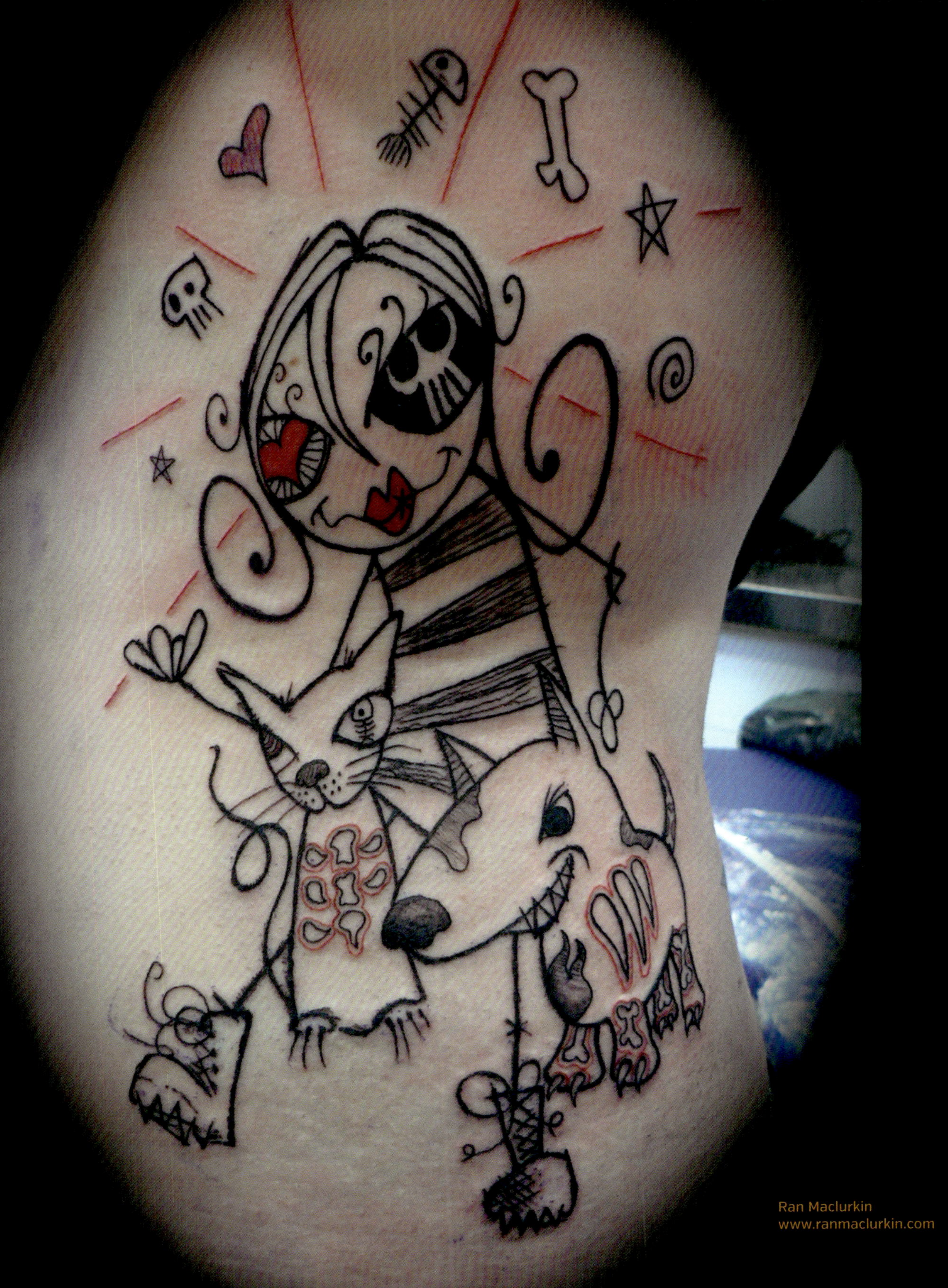
Ran Maclurkin
www.ranmaclurkin.com

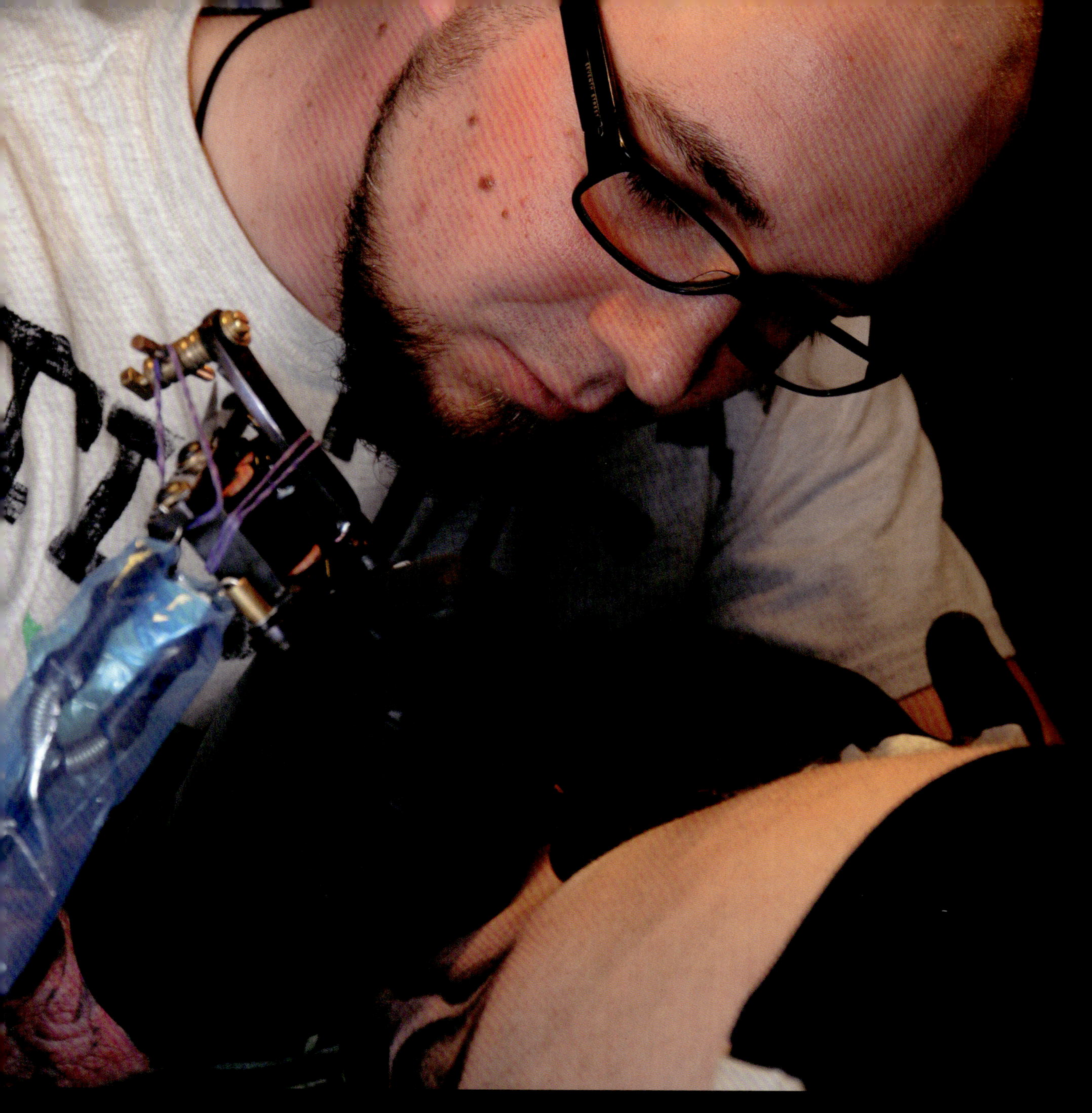

ROBERT FRANKE
VICIOUS CIRCLE TATTOO

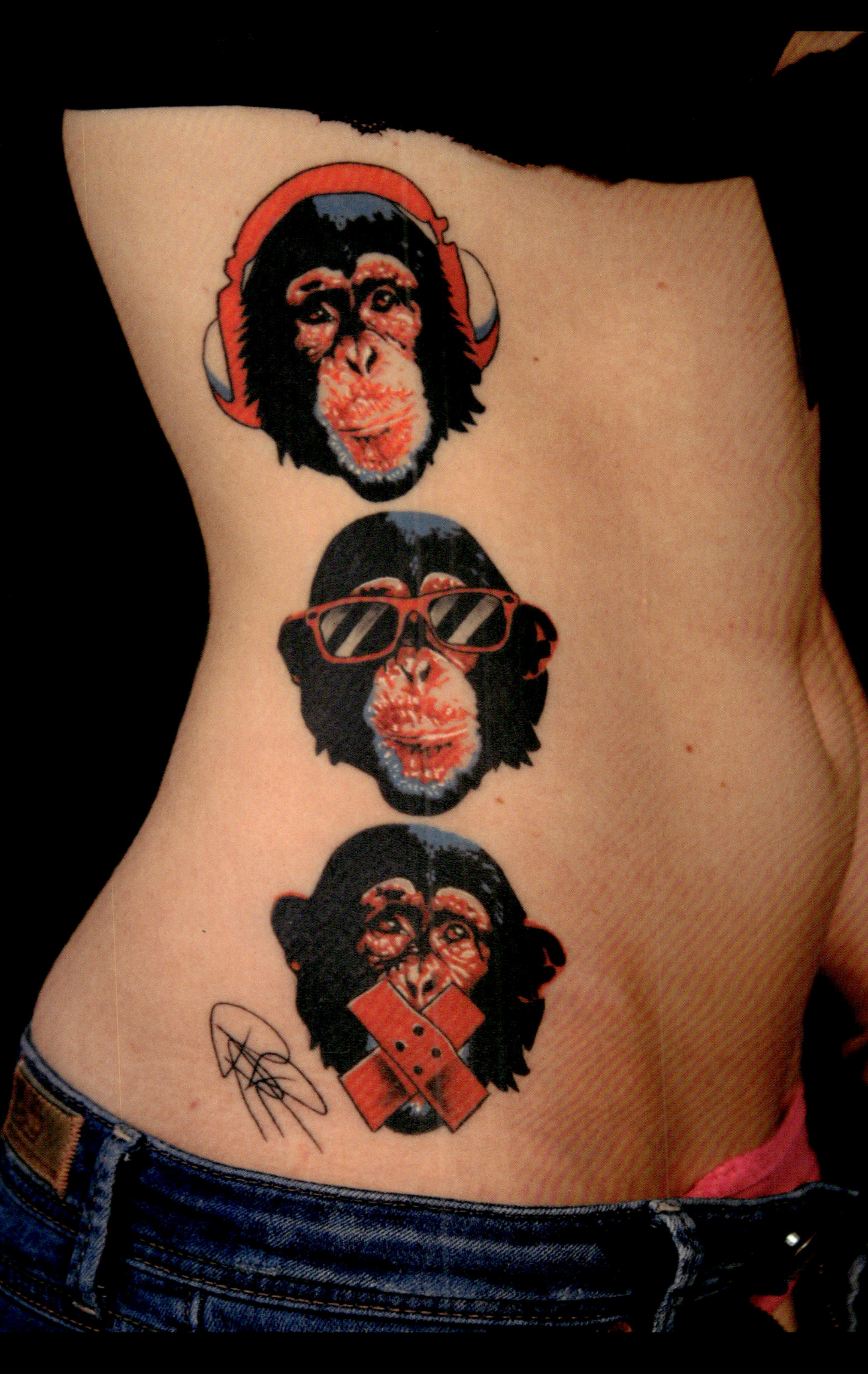

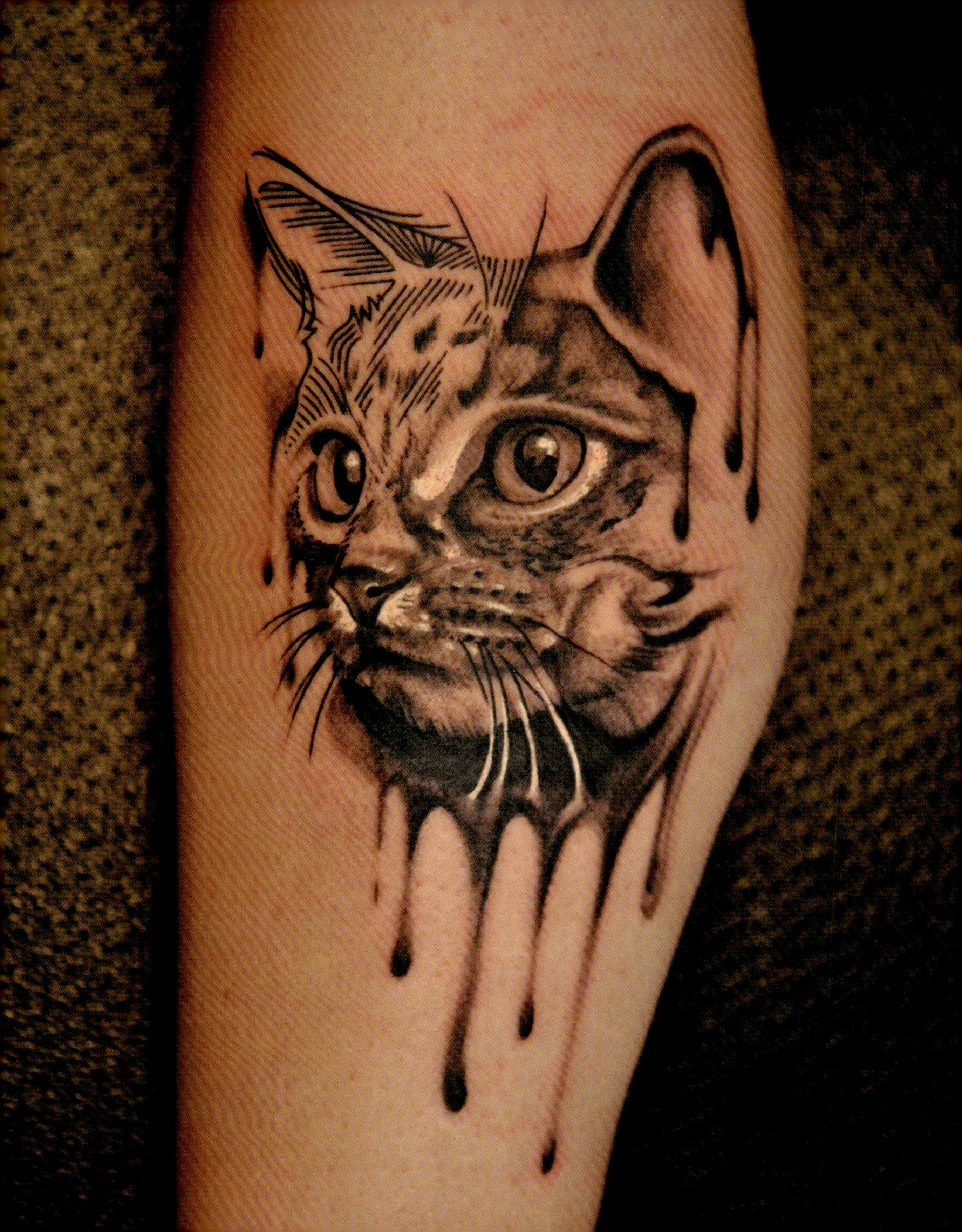

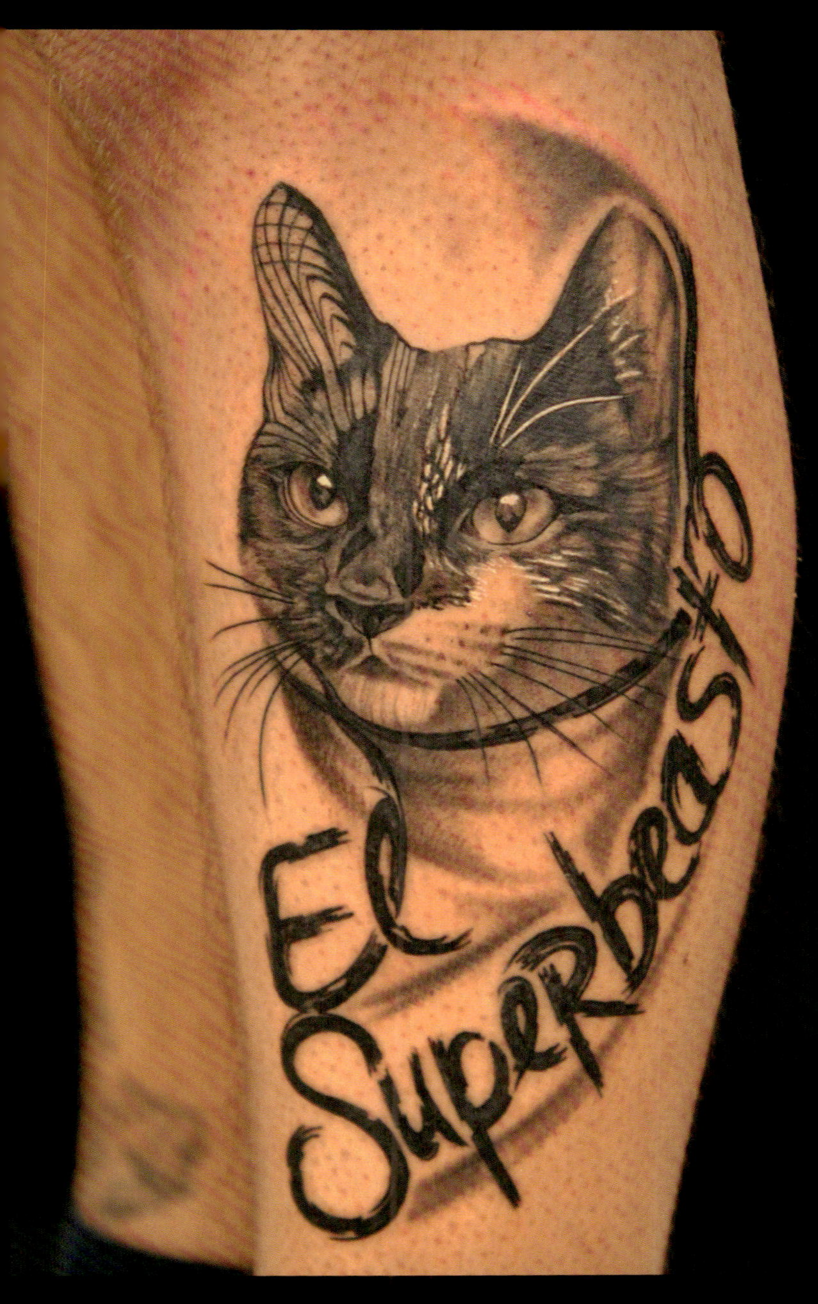
EL SuperBeasto

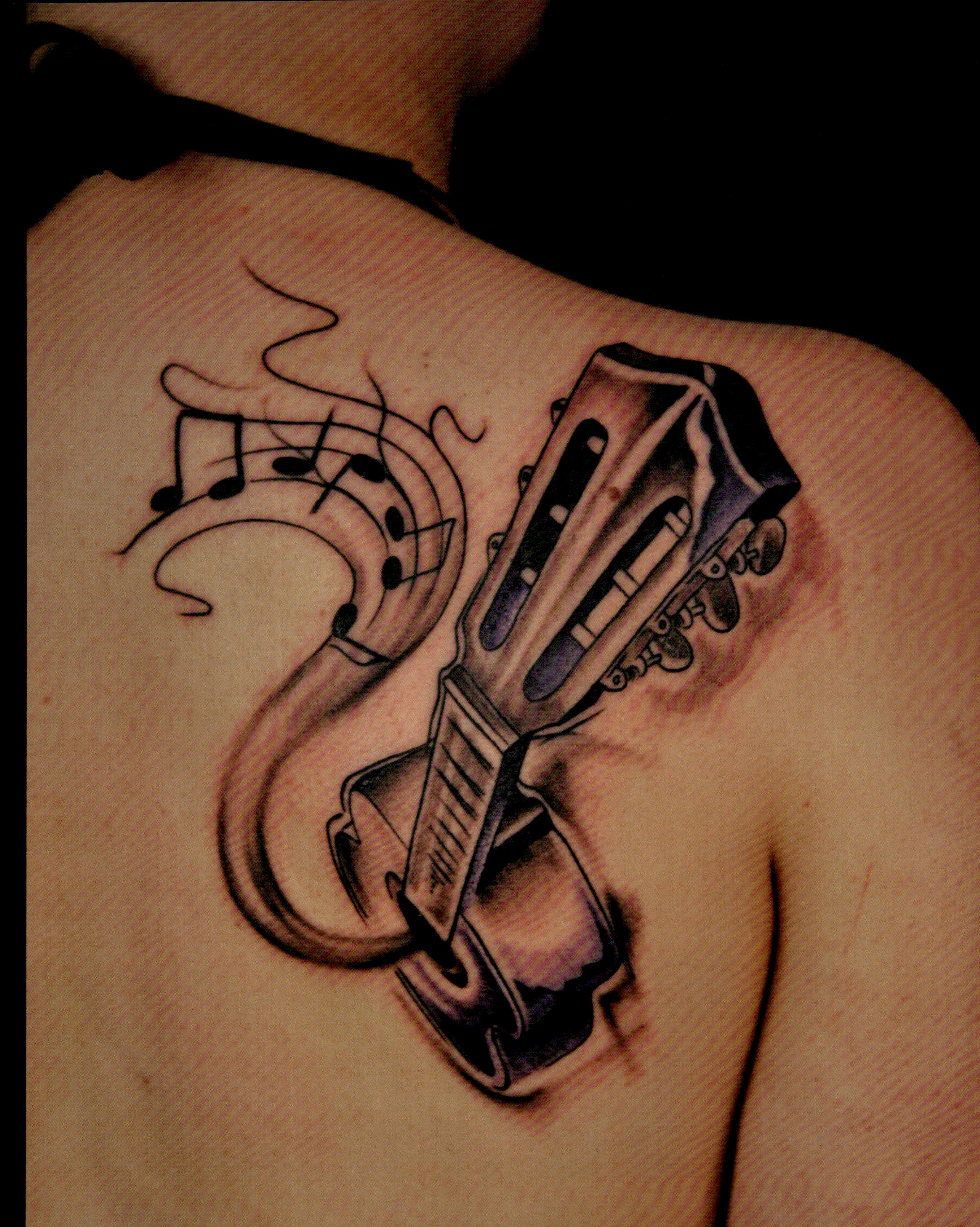

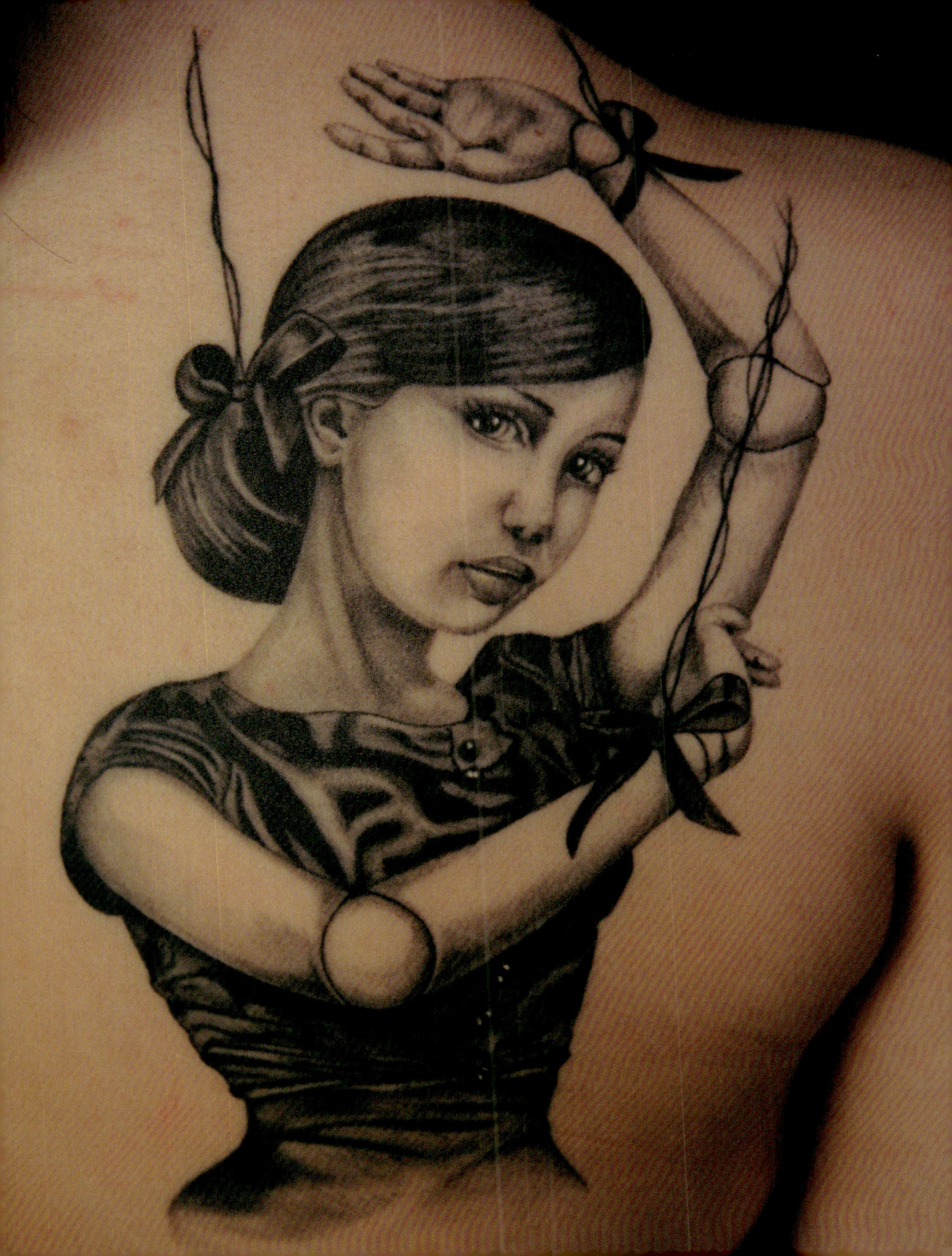

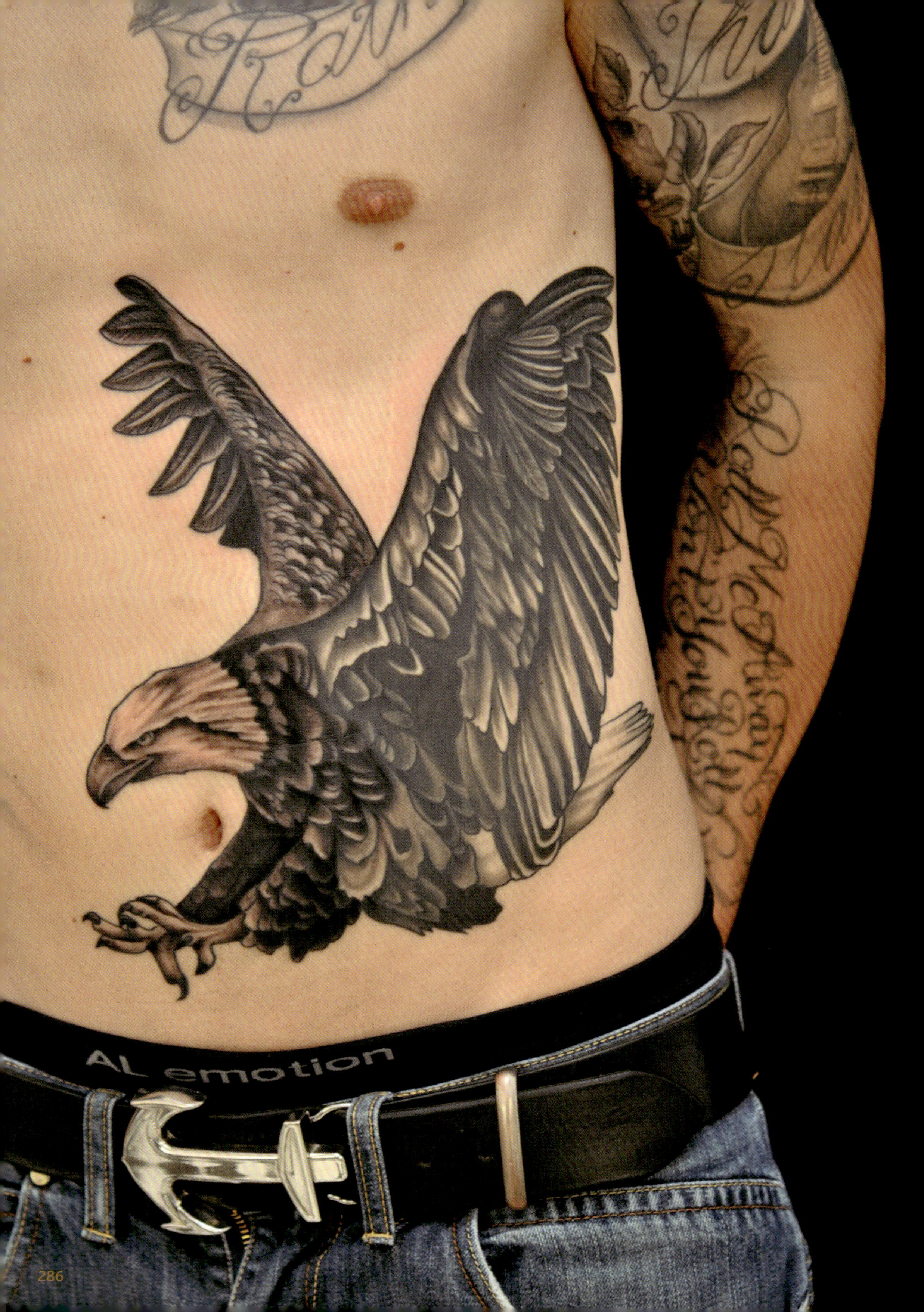

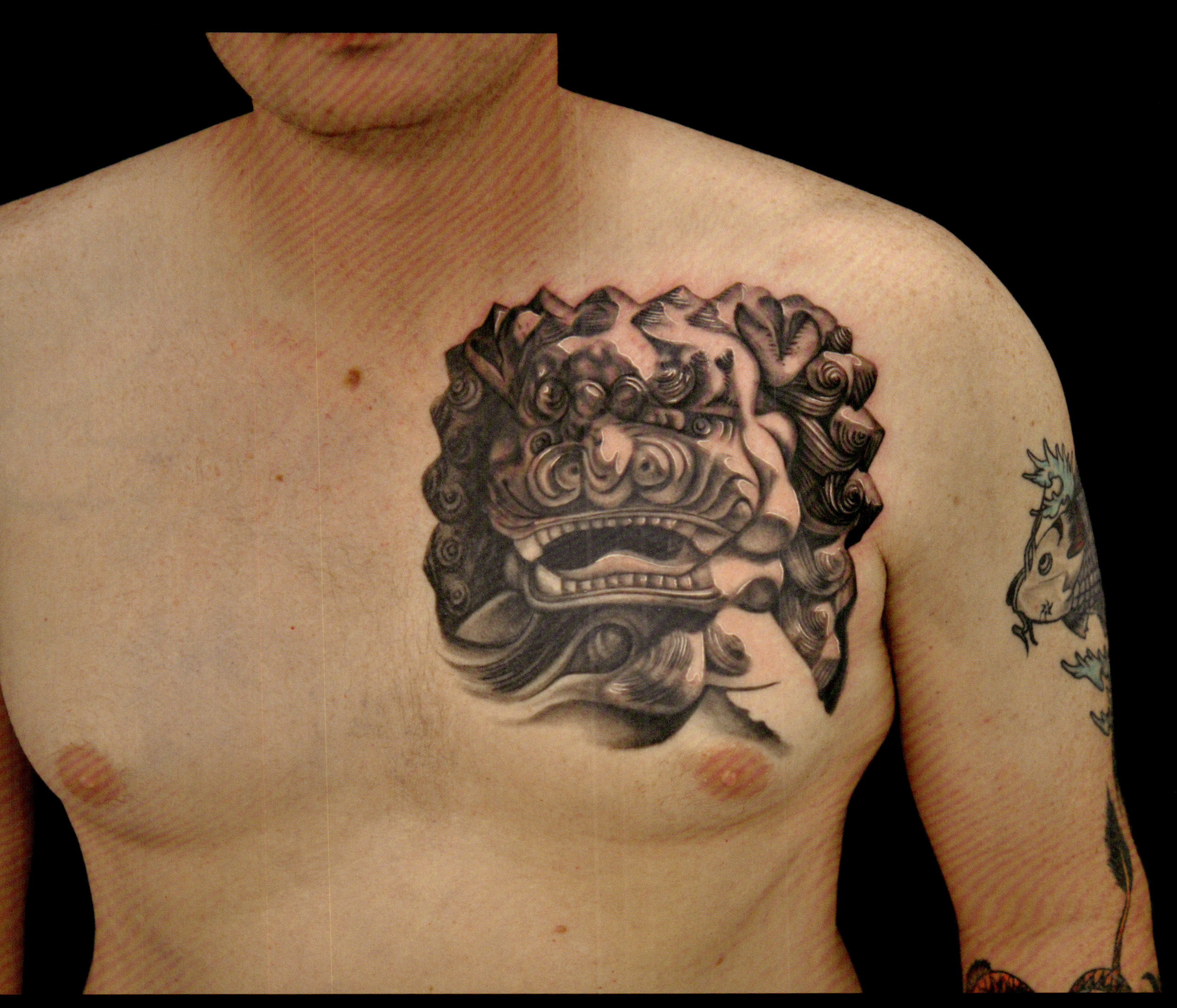

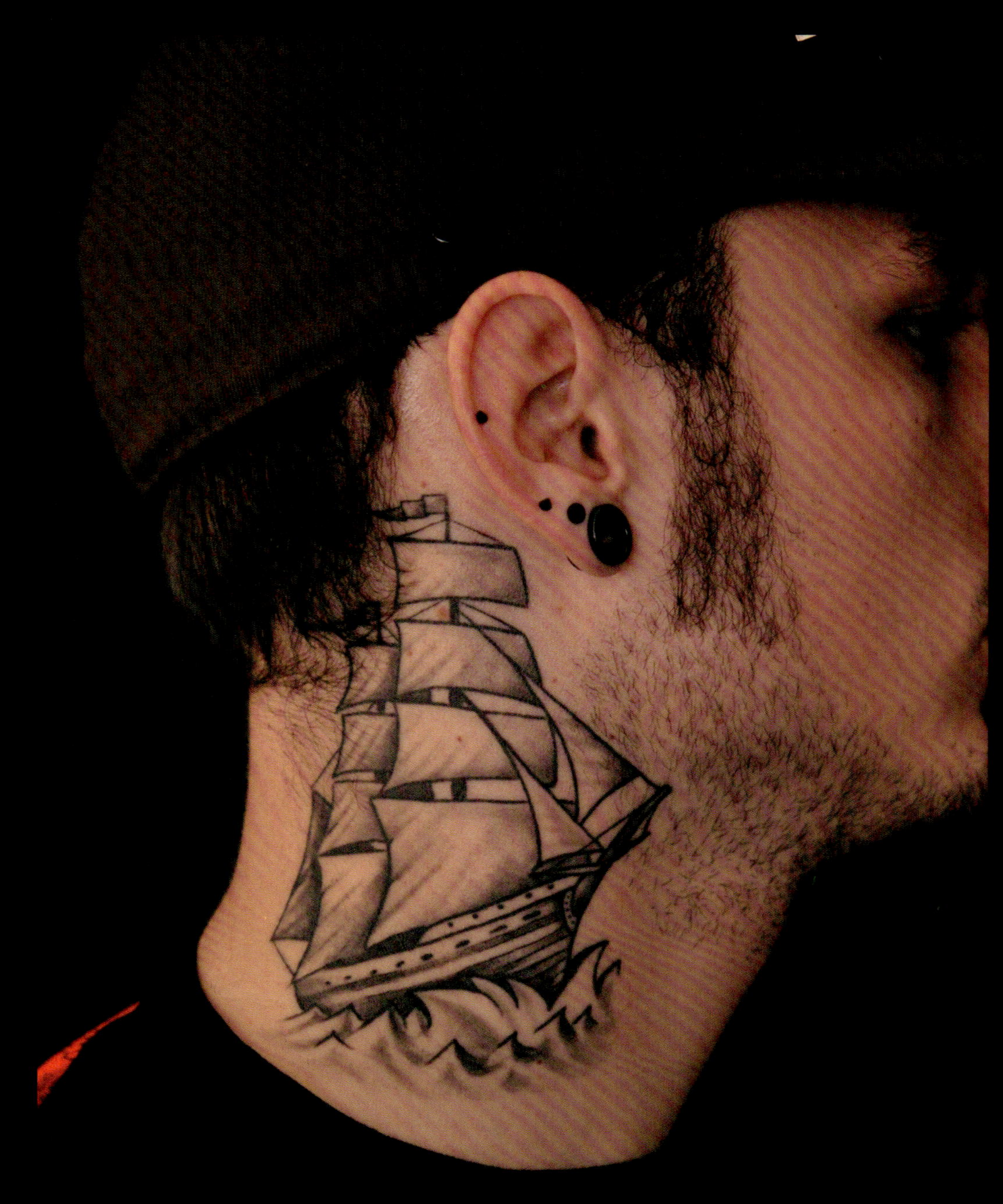

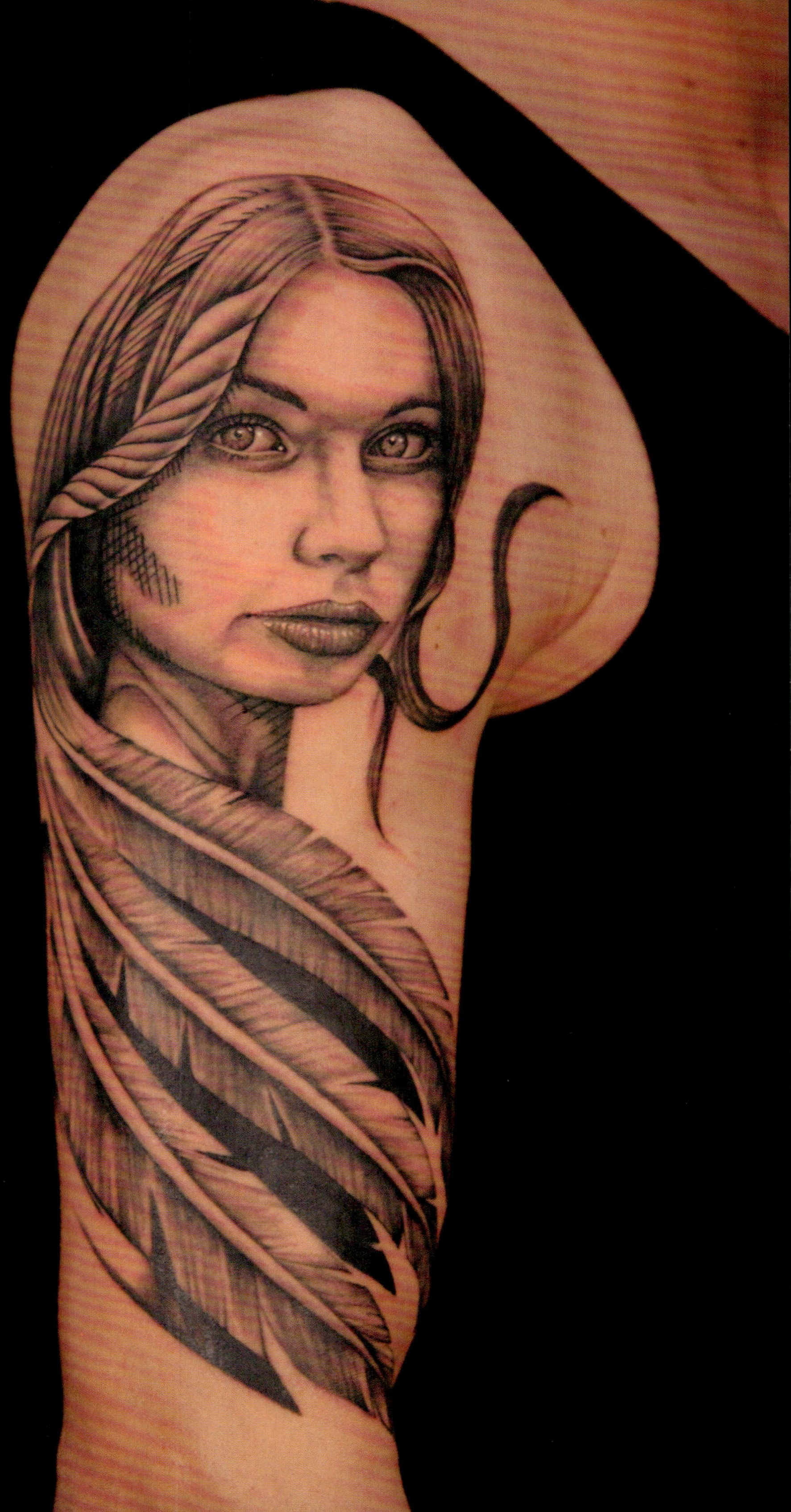

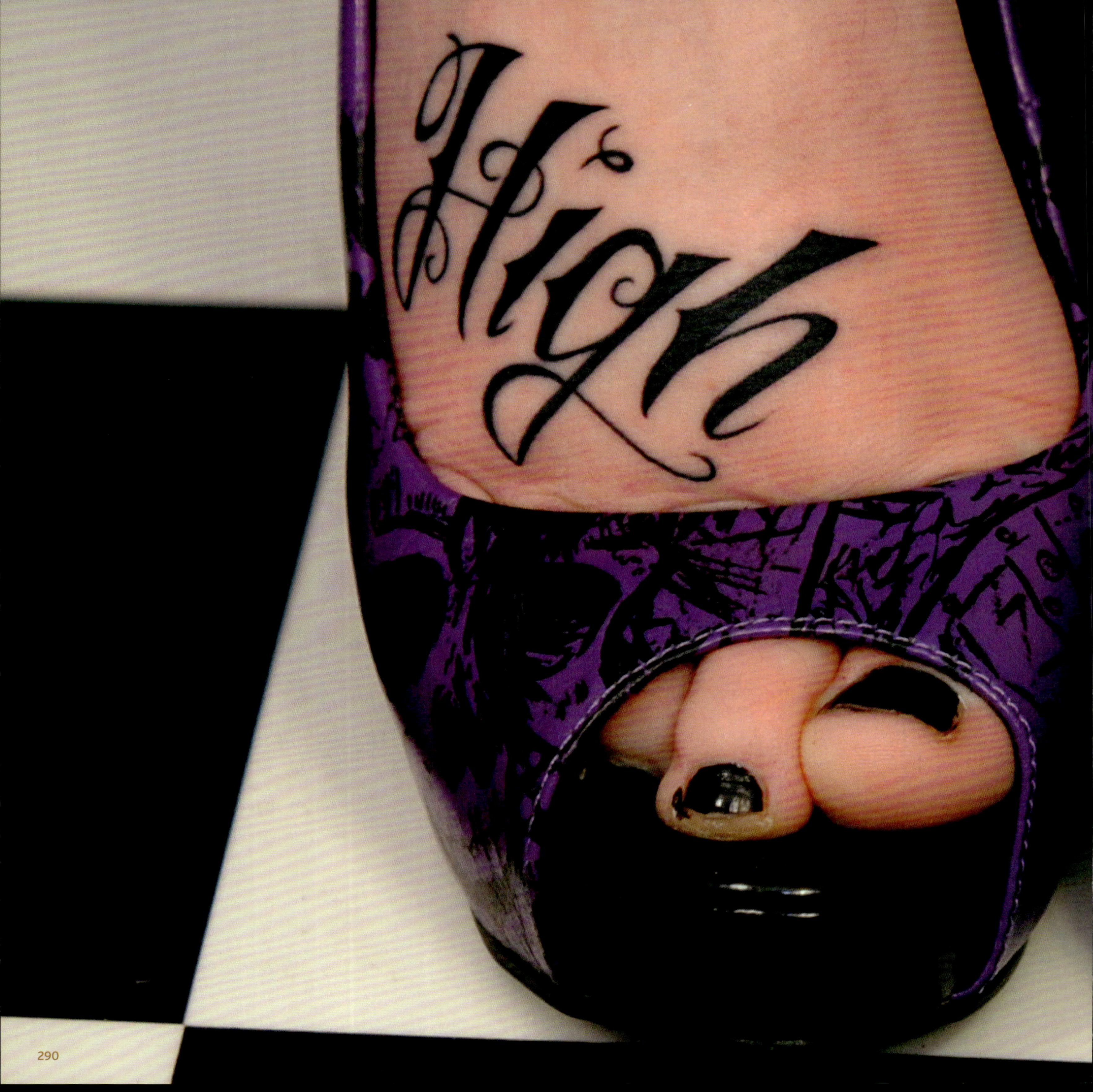
High

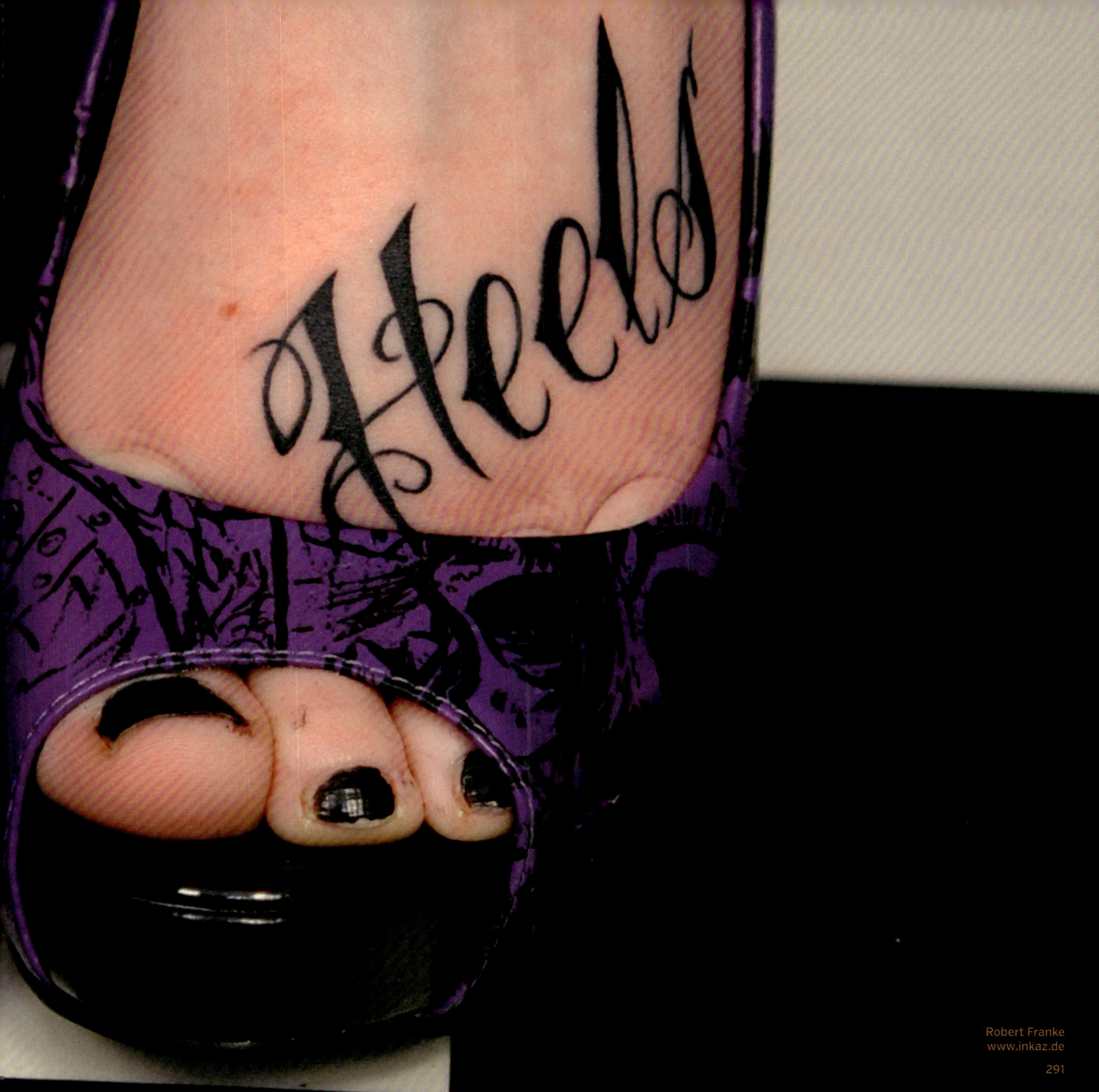

Heels

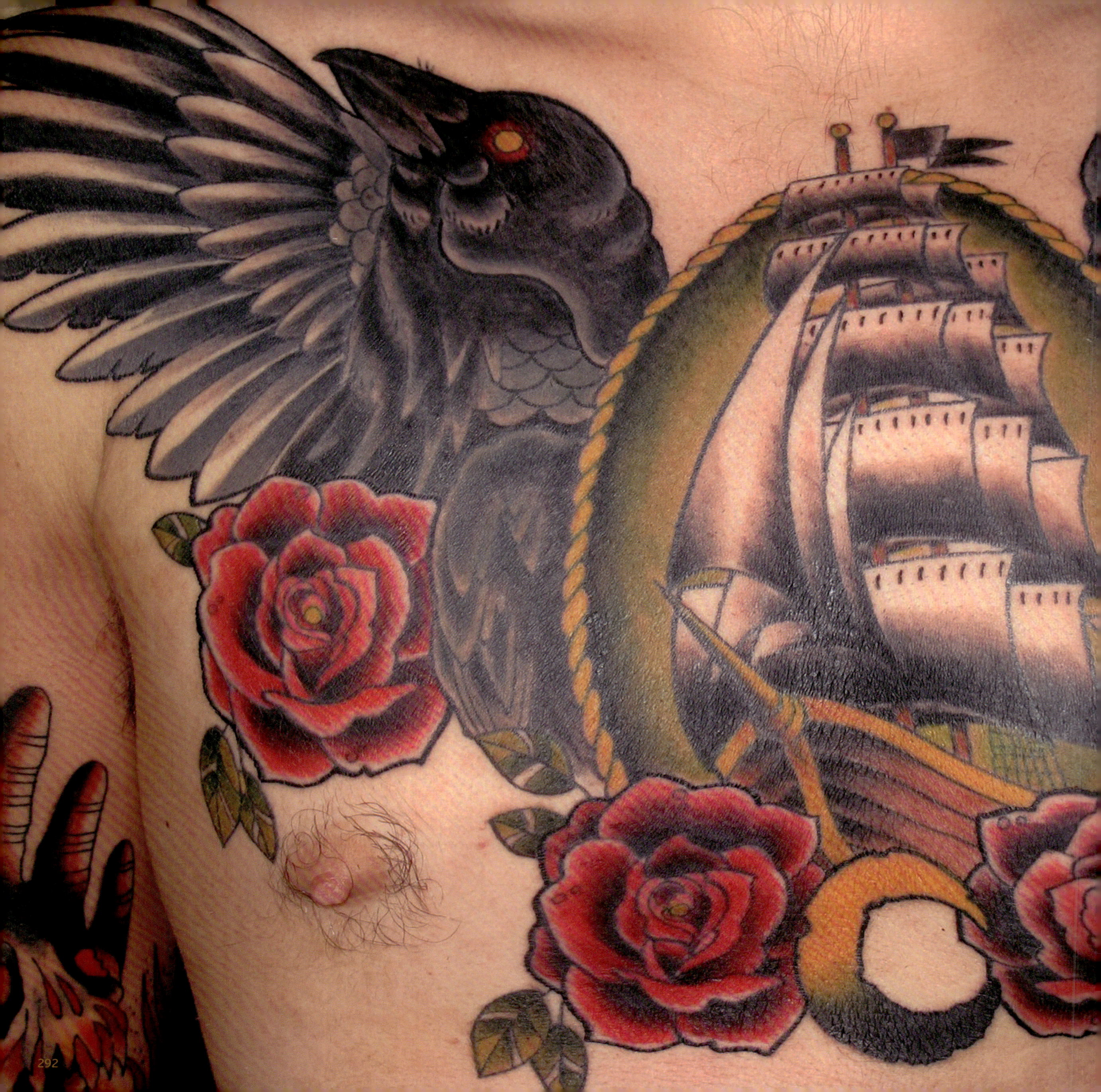

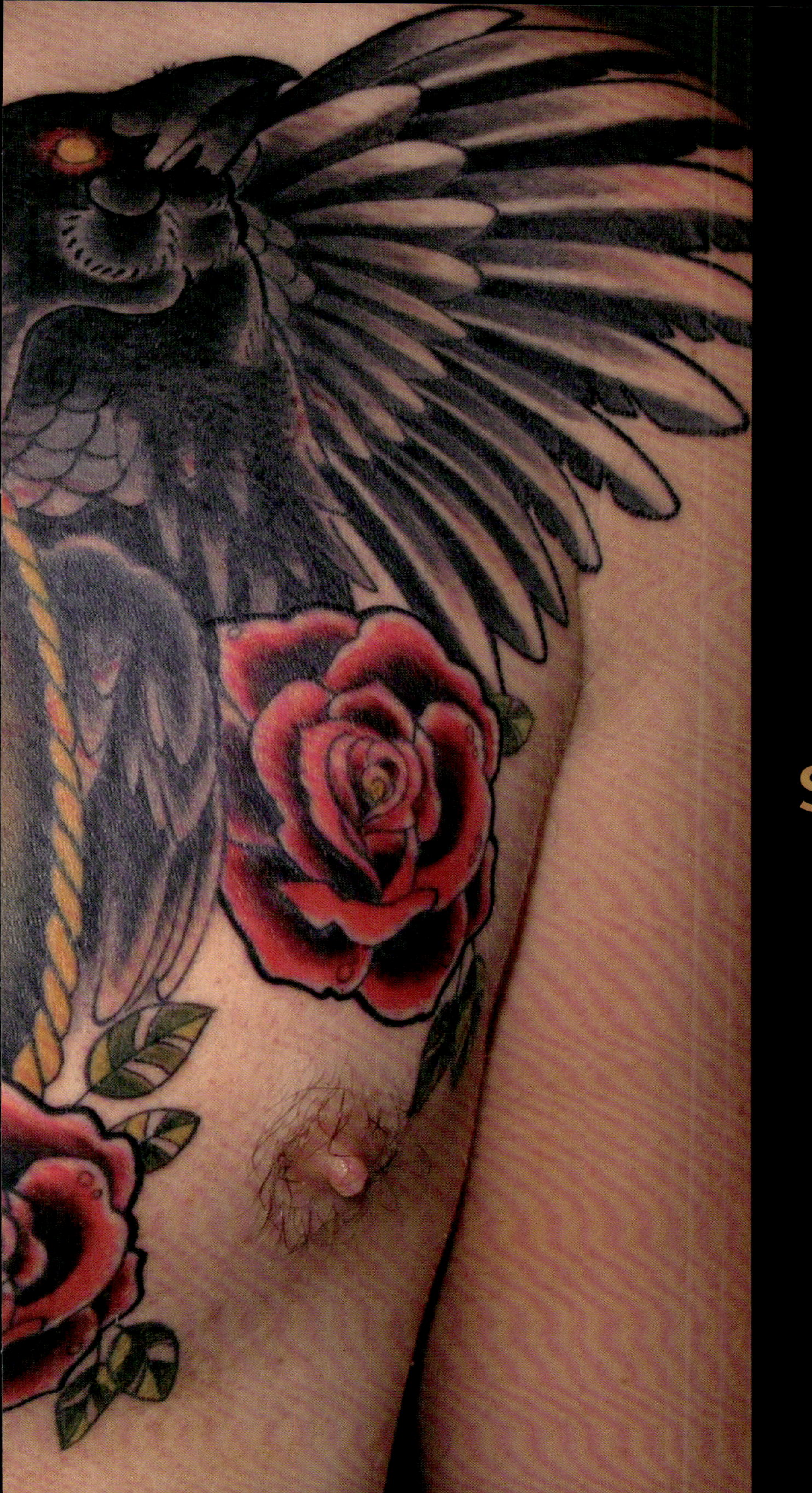

SAM

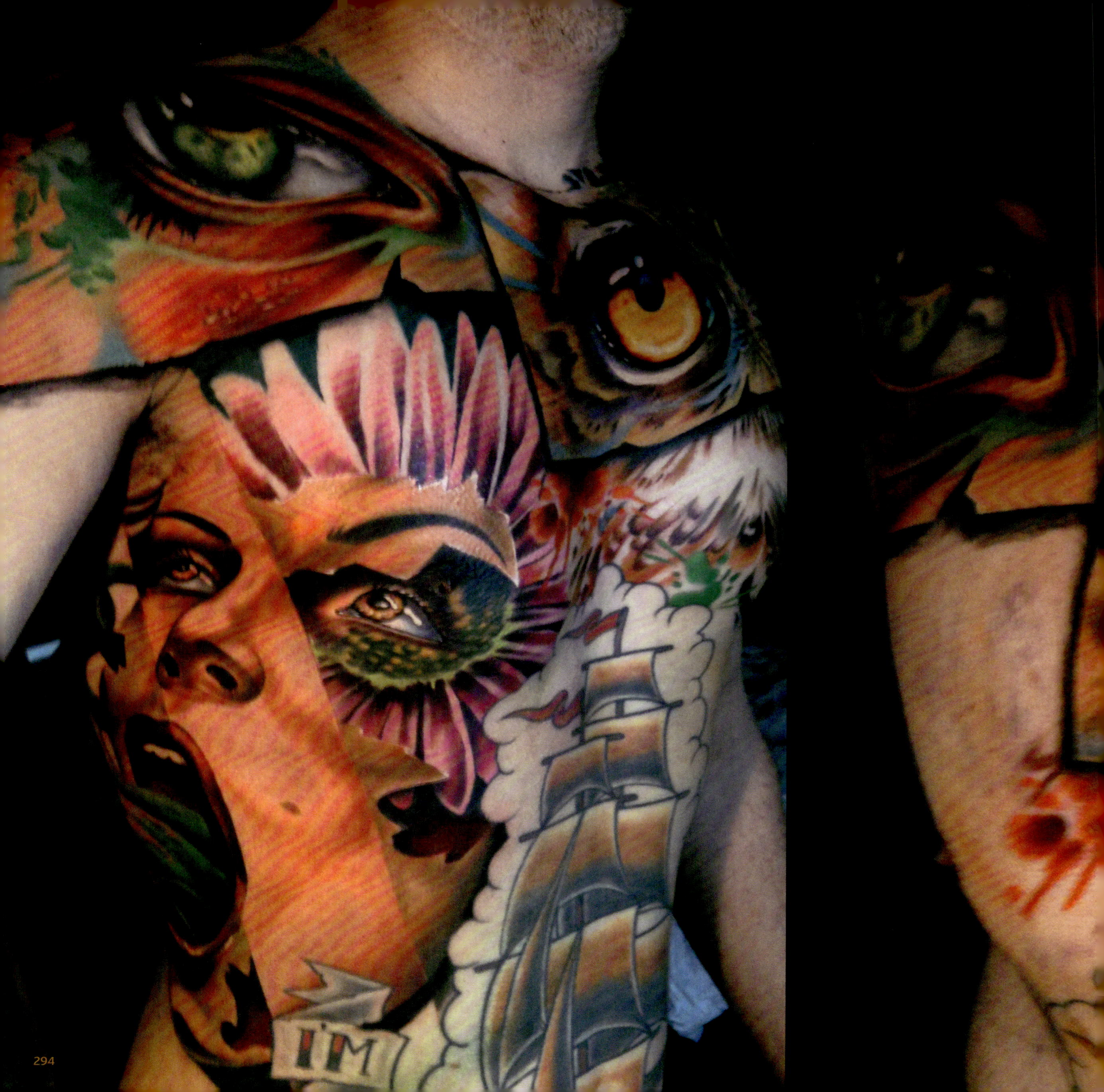
I'M

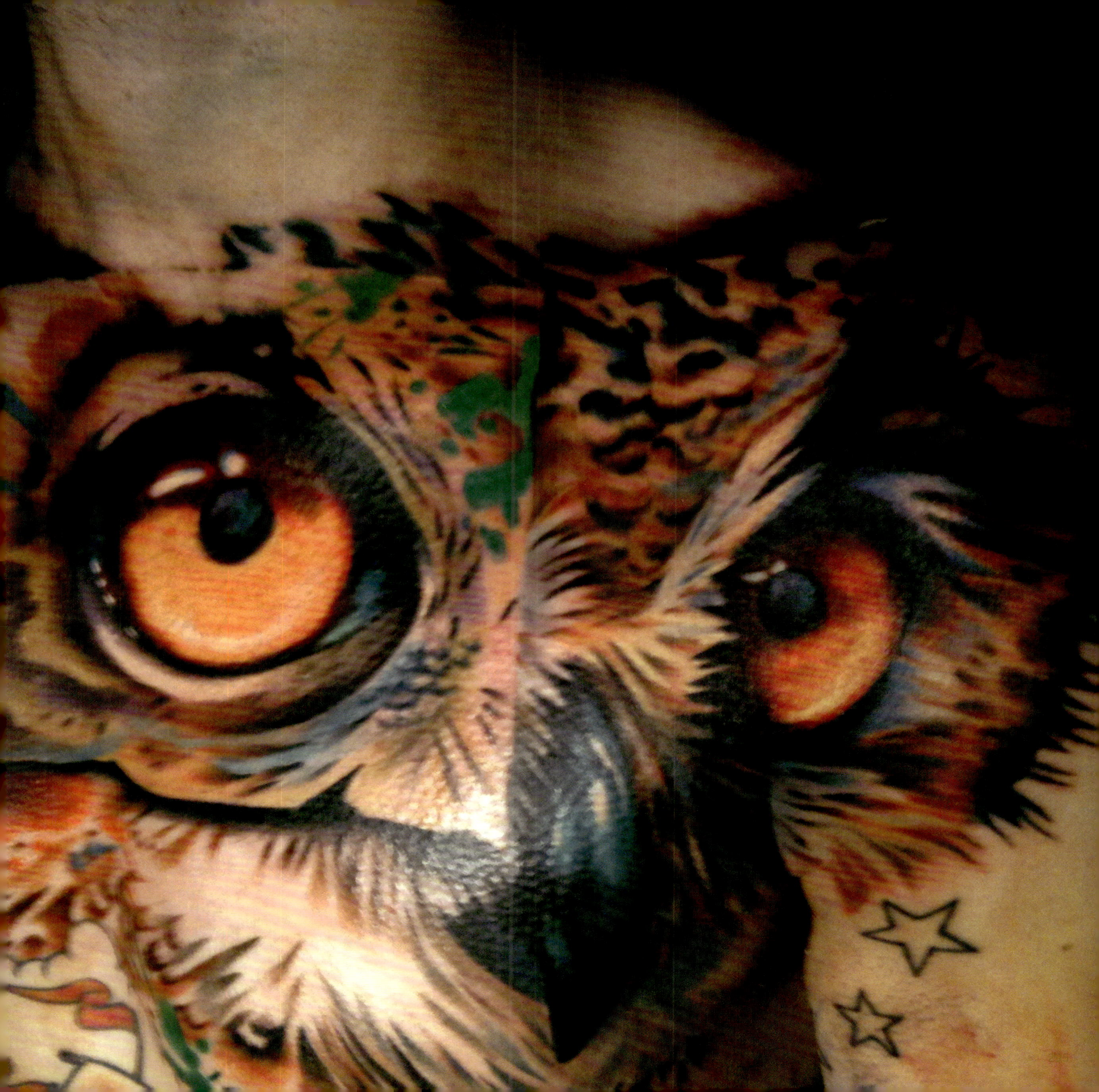

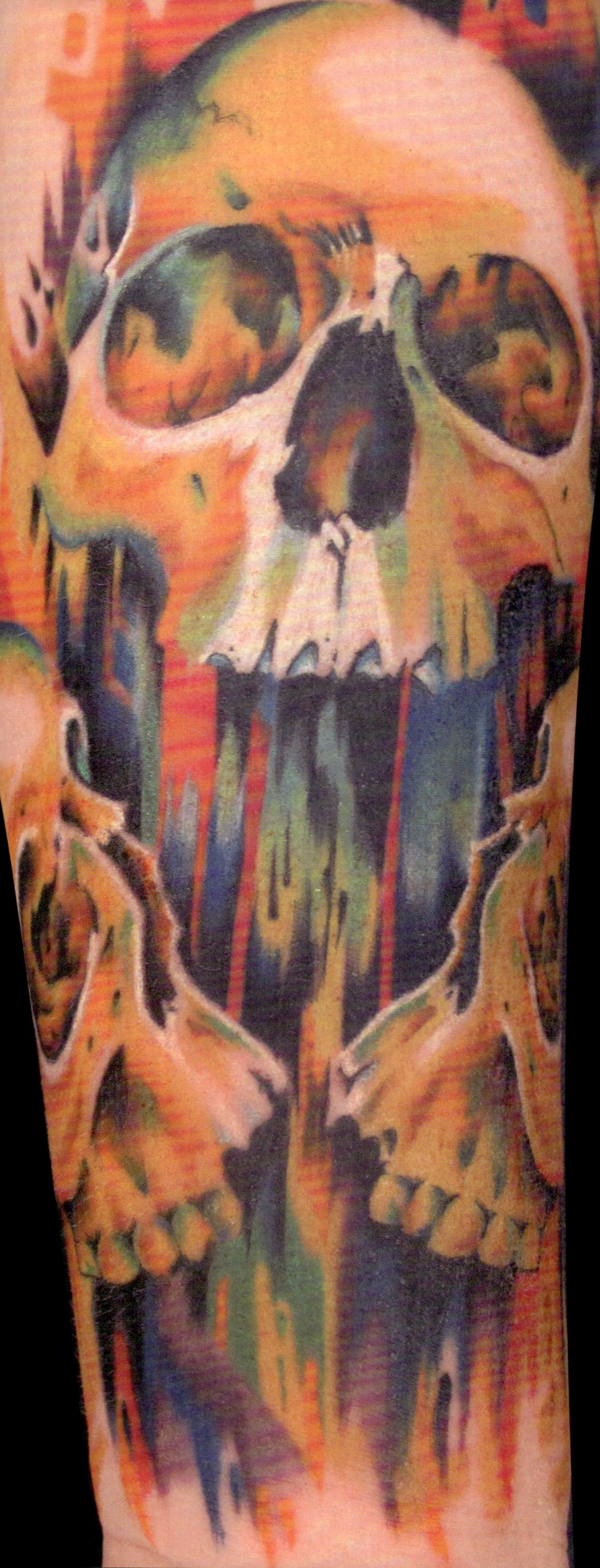

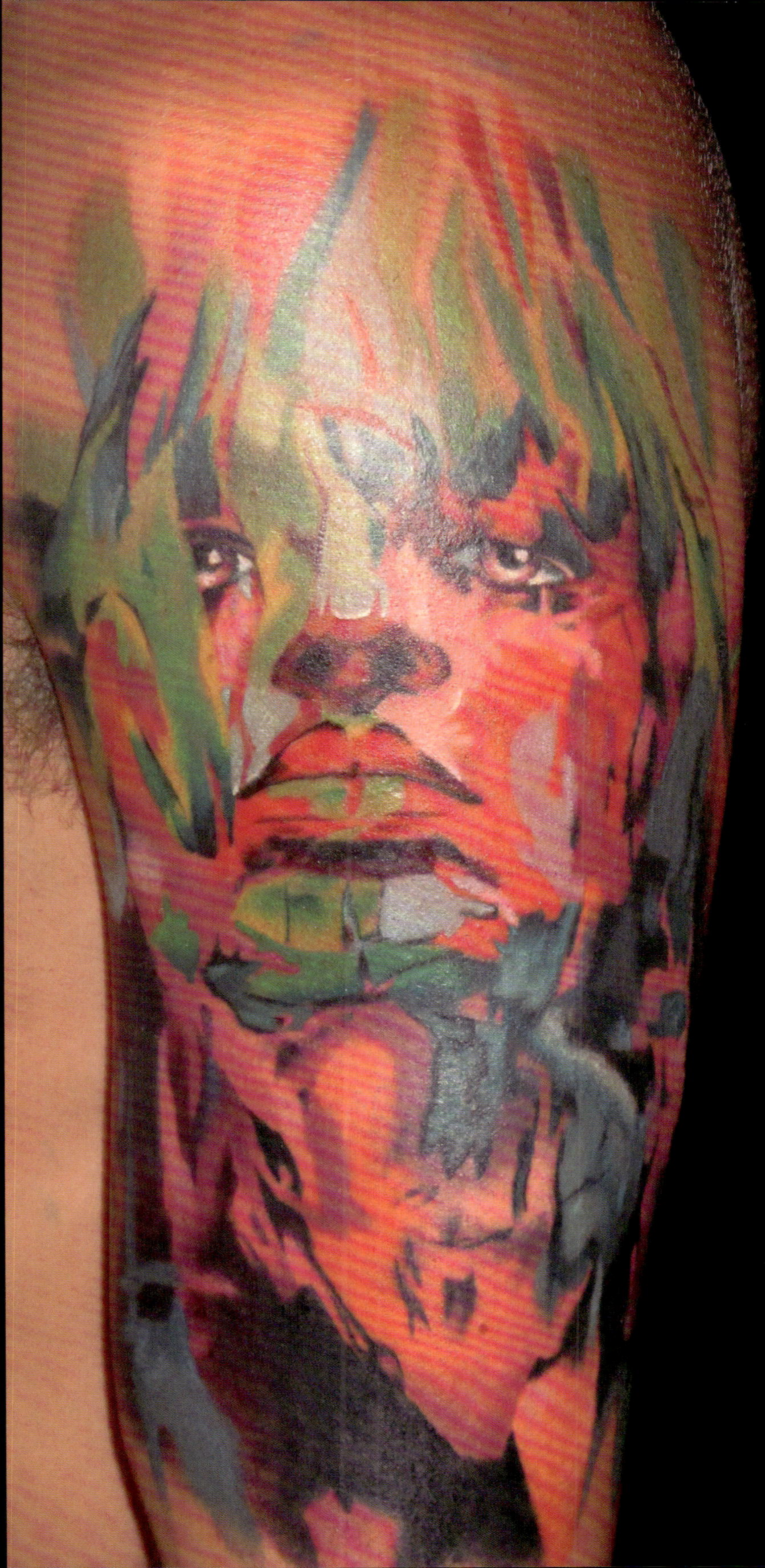

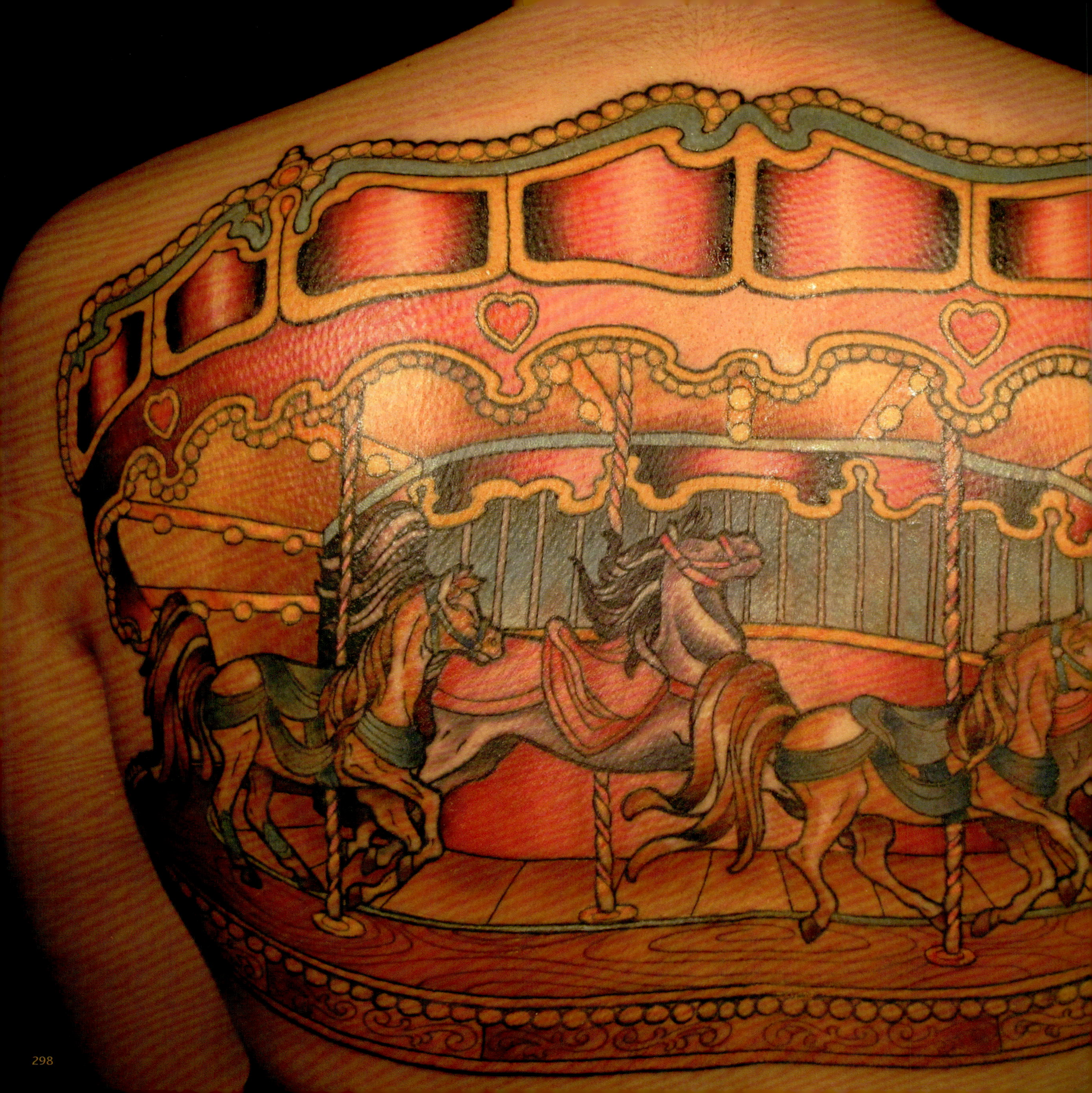

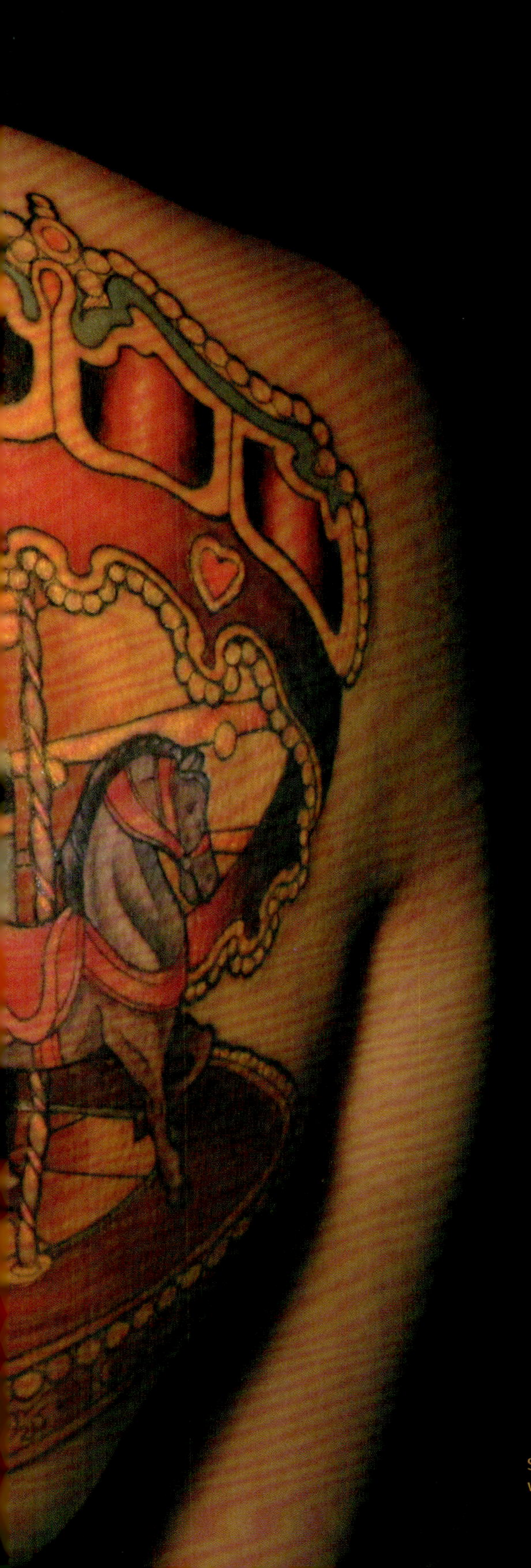

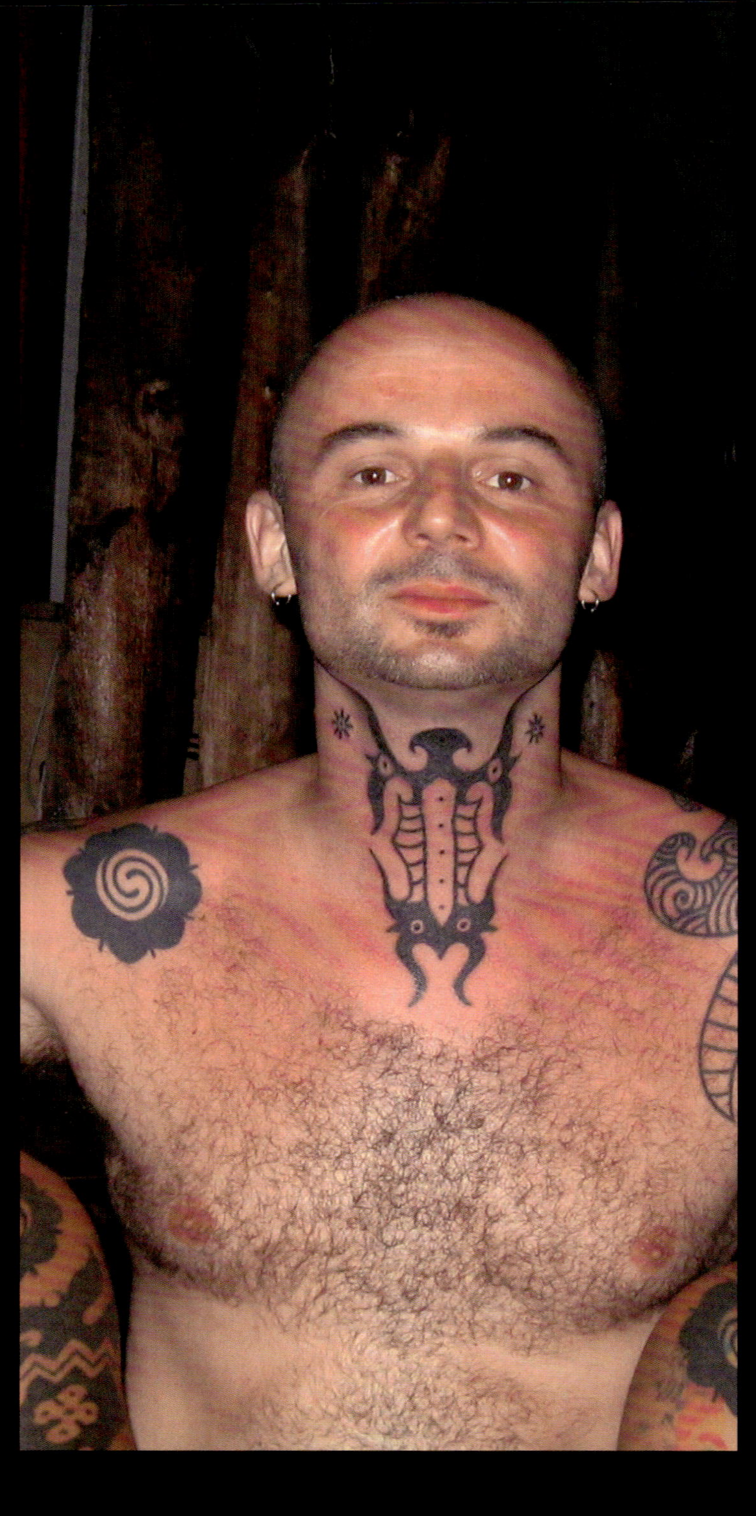

SASHA ALEKSANDAR
ORCA SUN TATTOO

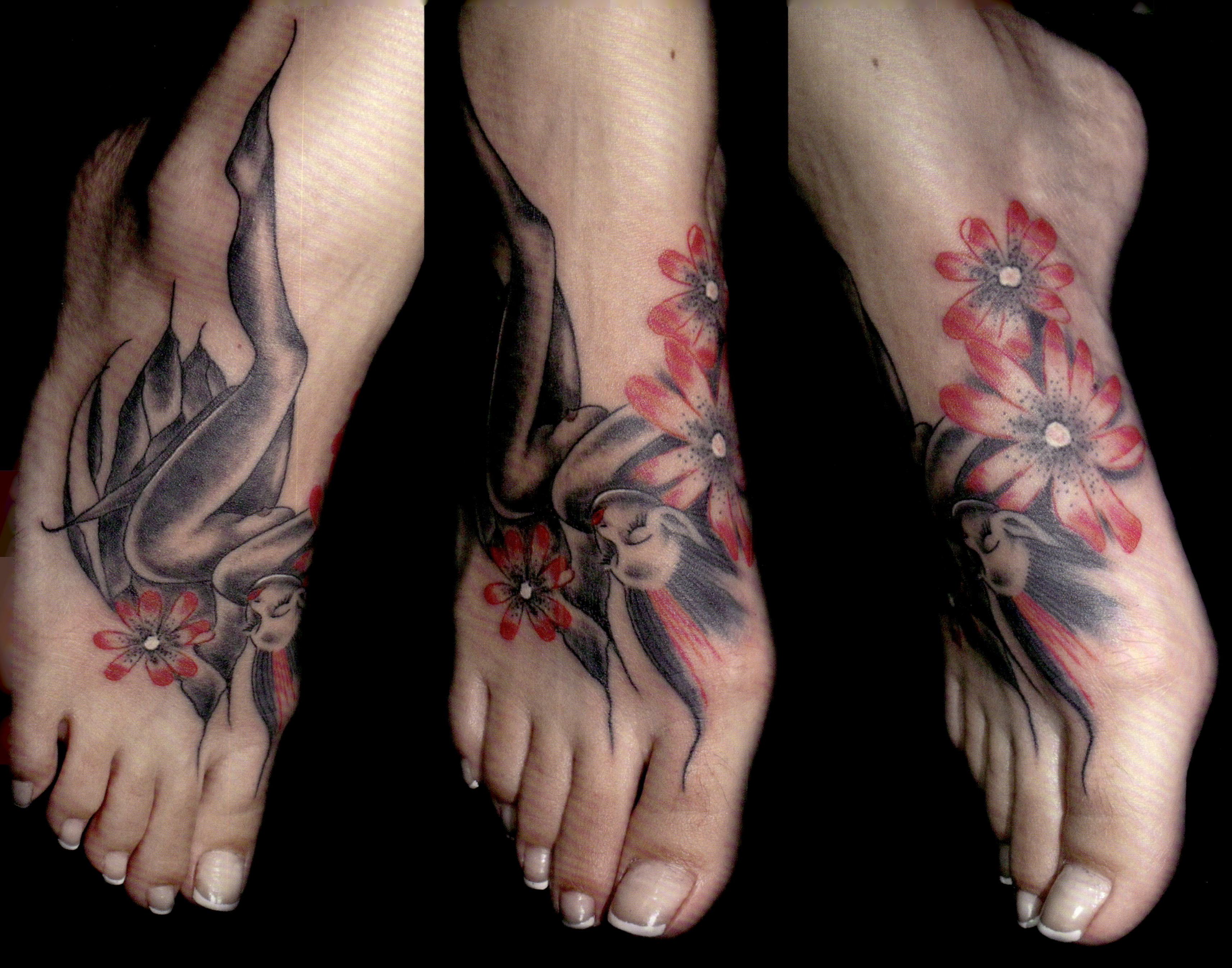

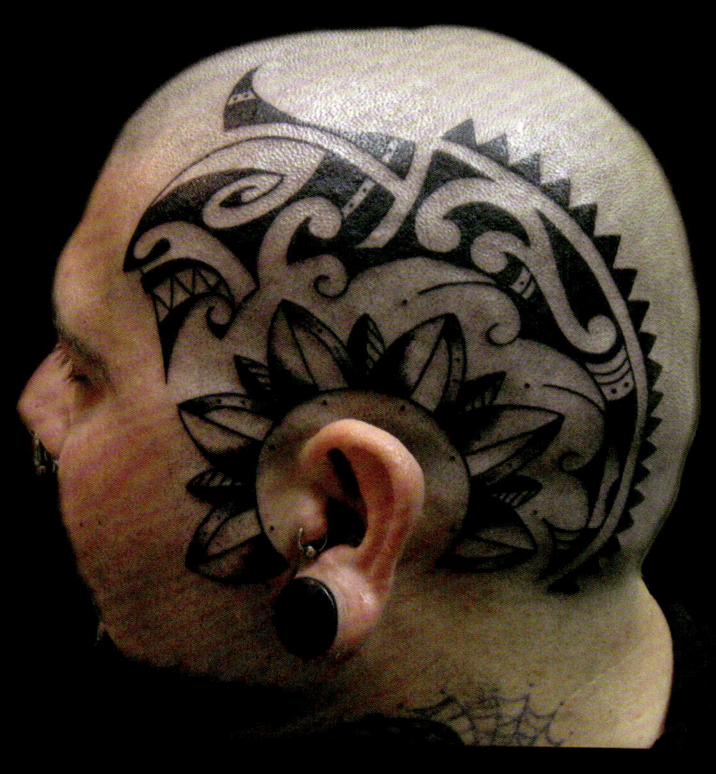

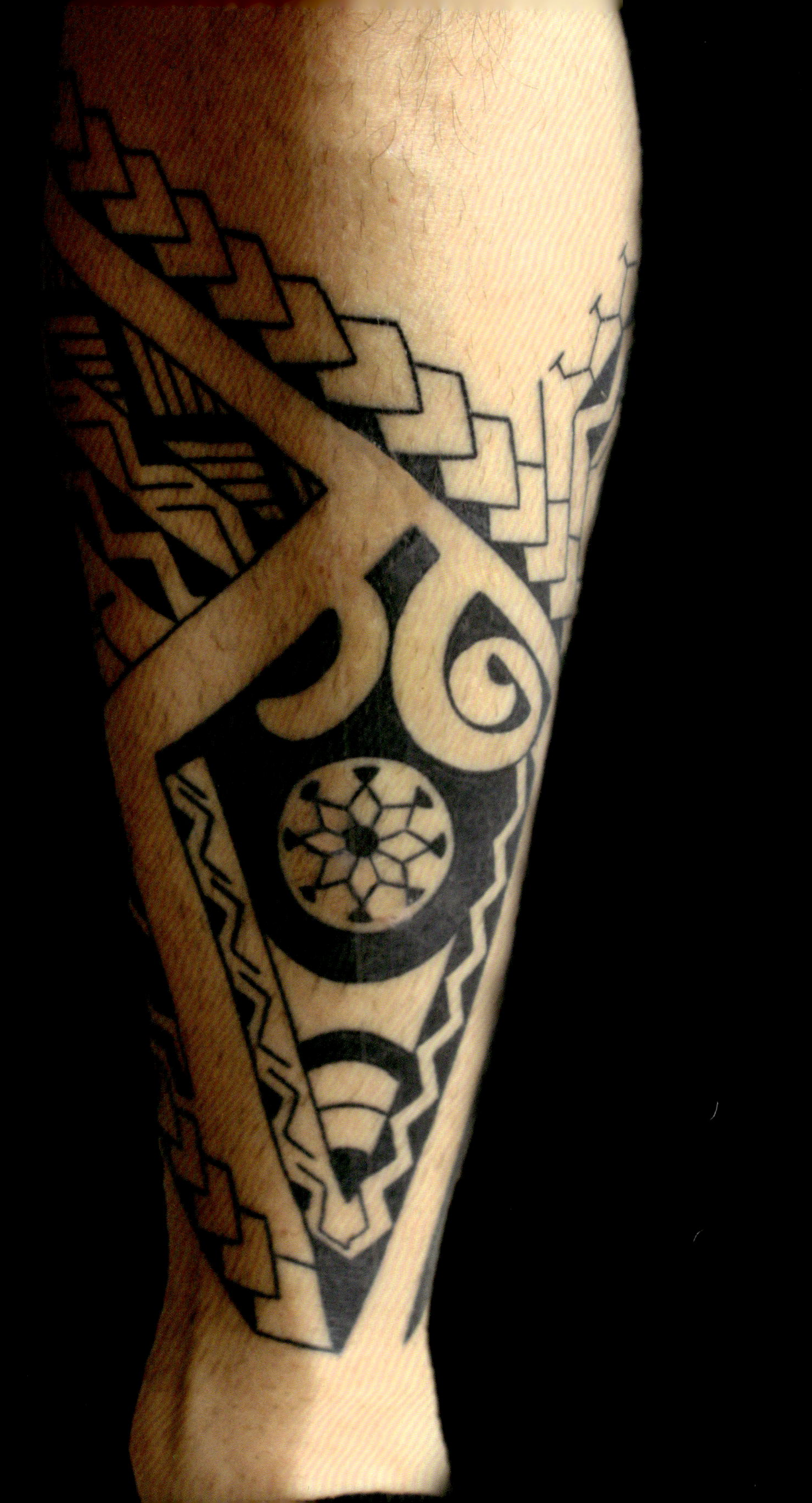

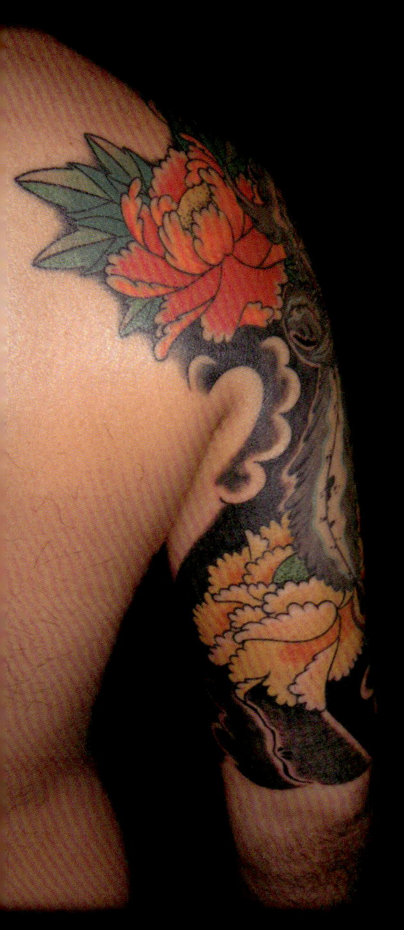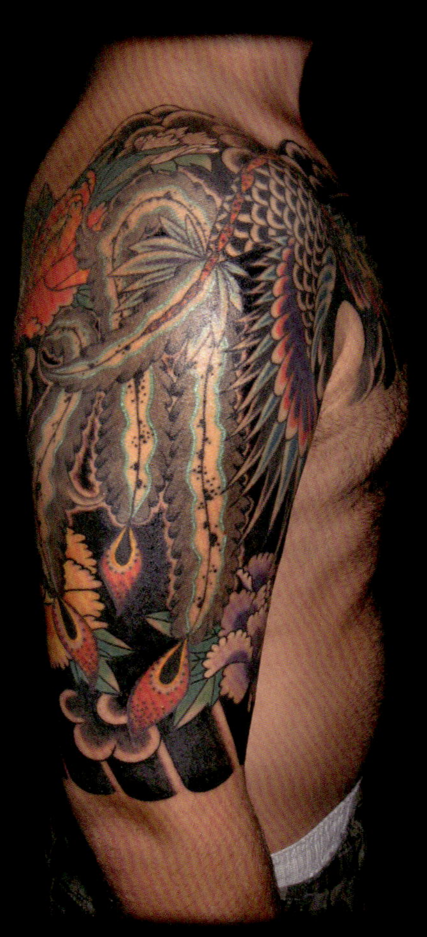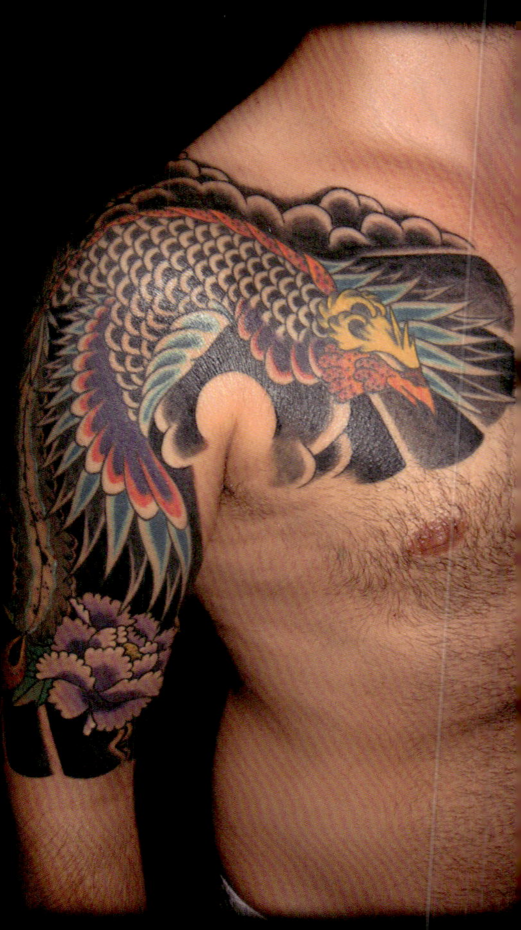

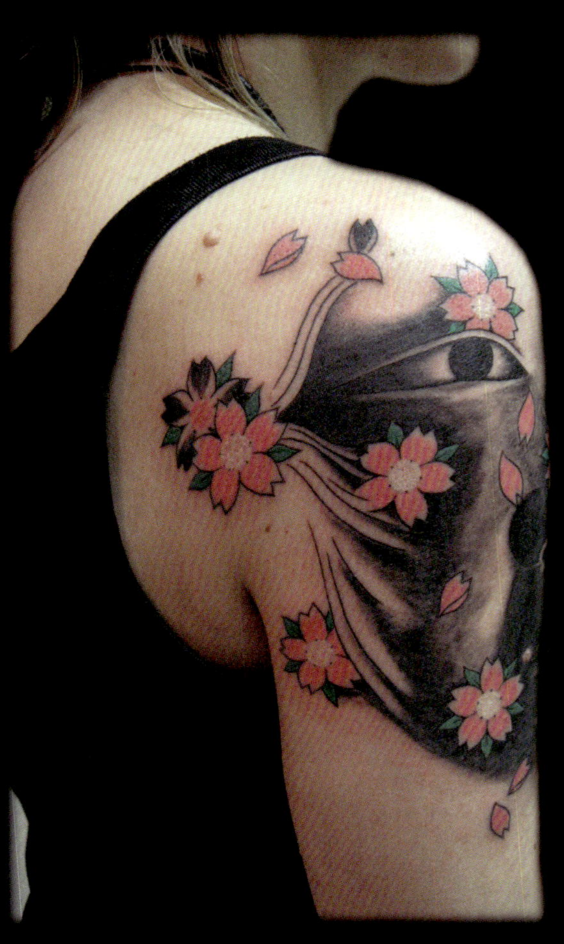
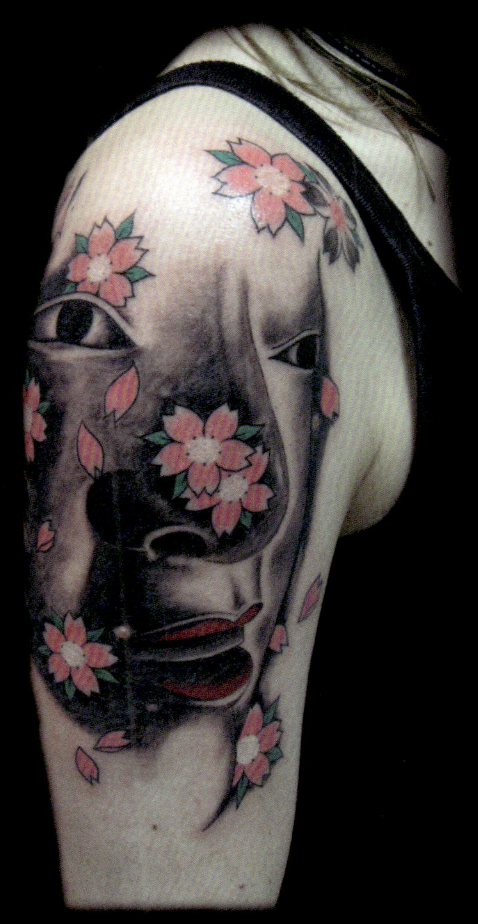
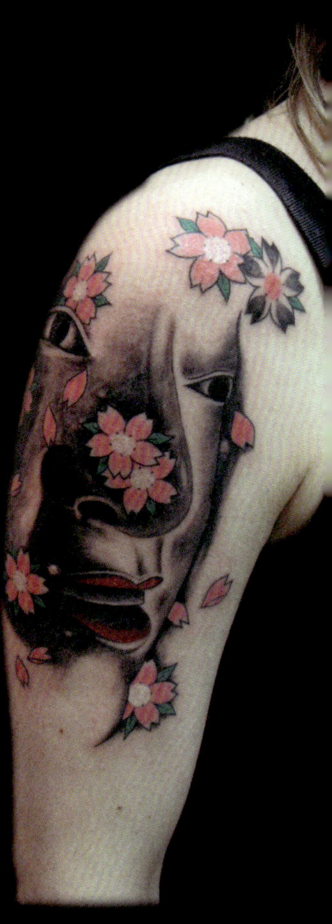

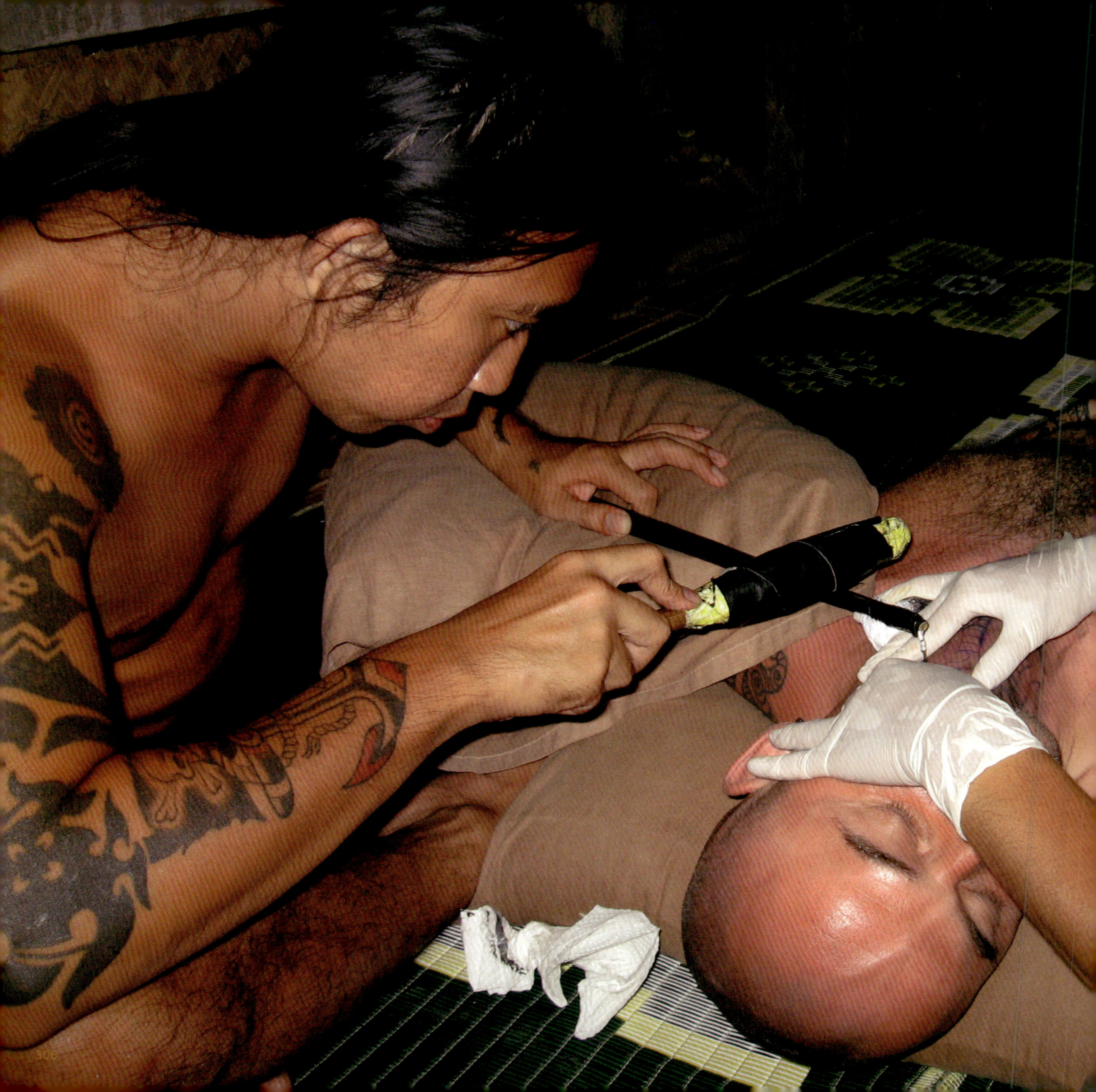

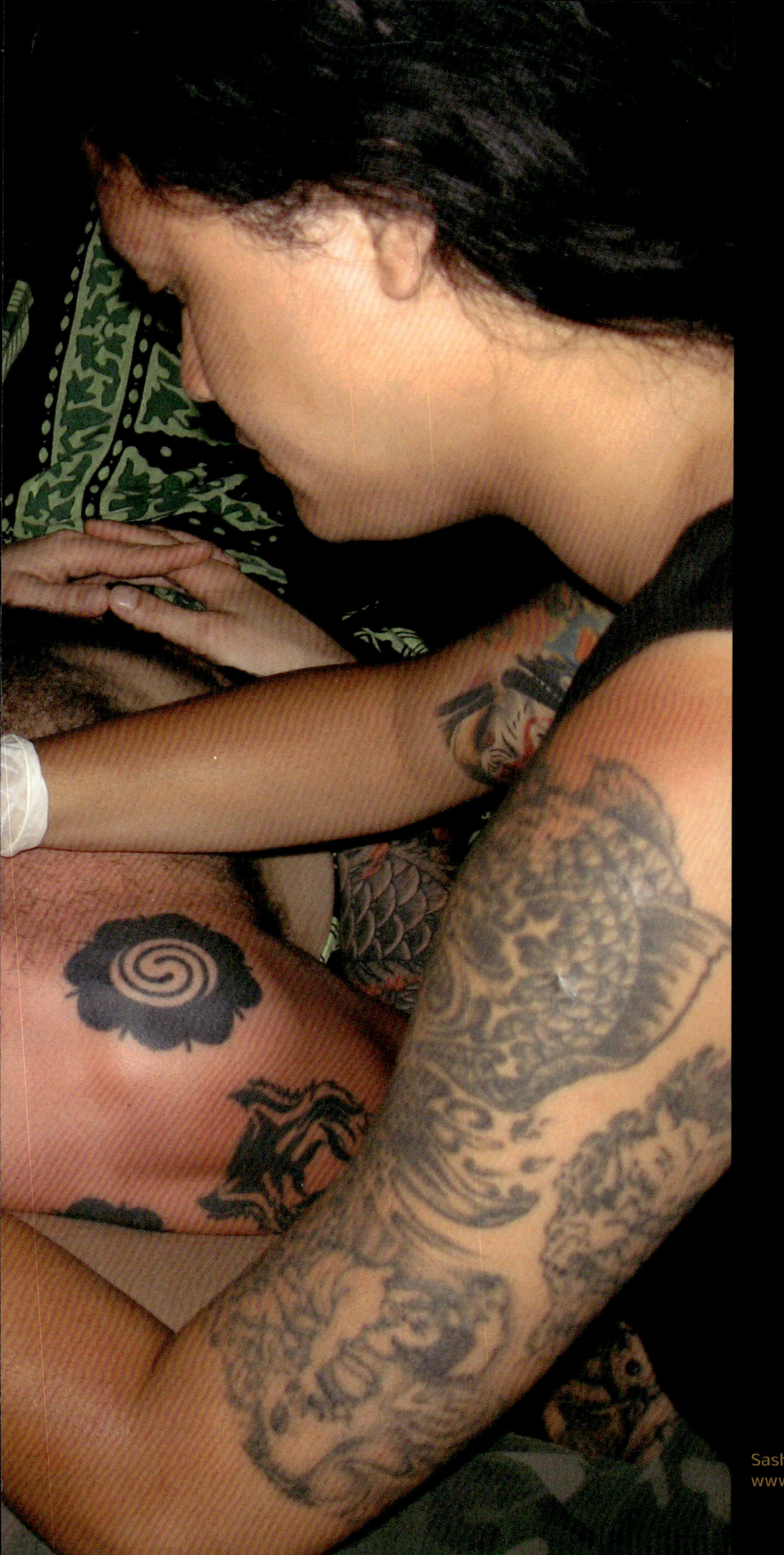

Sasha Alexsandar
www.orcasuntattoo

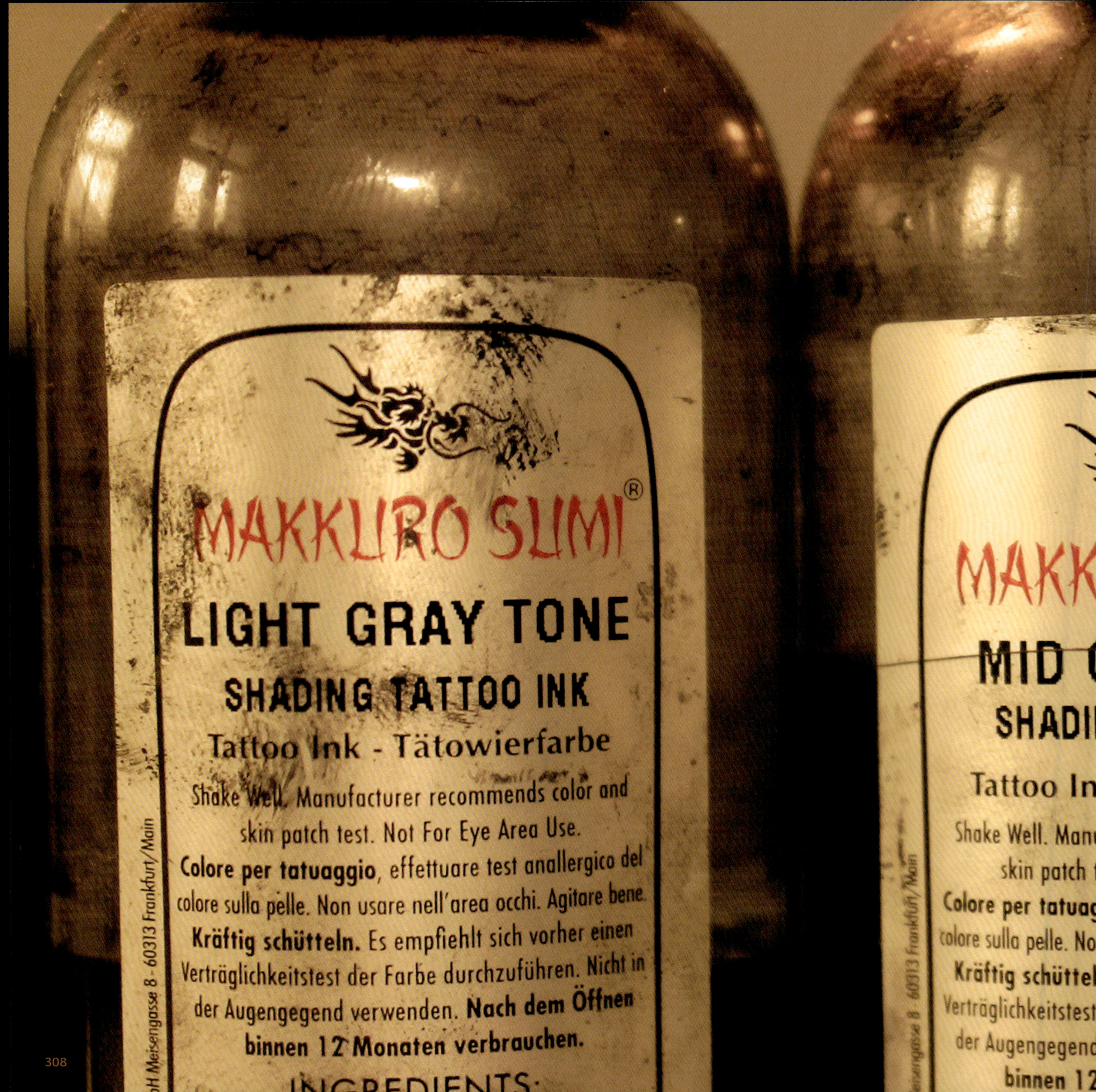
MAKKURO SUMI
LIGHT GRAY TONE
SHADING TATTOO INK
Tattoo Ink - Tätowierfarbe
Shake Well. Manufacturer recommends color and skin patch test. Not For Eye Area Use.
Colore per tatuaggio, effettuare test anallergico del colore sulla pelle. Non usare nell'area occhi. Agitare bene.
Kräftig schütteln. Es empfiehlt sich vorher einen Verträglichkeitstest der Farbe durchzuführen. Nicht in der Augengegend verwenden. Nach dem Öffnen binnen 12 Monaten verbrauchen.
INGREDIENTS:
mbH Meisengasse 8 - 60313 Frankfurt/Main
MAKKU
MID G
SHADIN
Tattoo Ink
Shake Well. Manuf
skin patch te
Colore per tatuagg
colore sulla pelle. Non
Kräftig schütteln
Verträglichkeitstest
der Augengegend
binnen 12
Meisengasse 8 - 60313 Frankfurt/Main

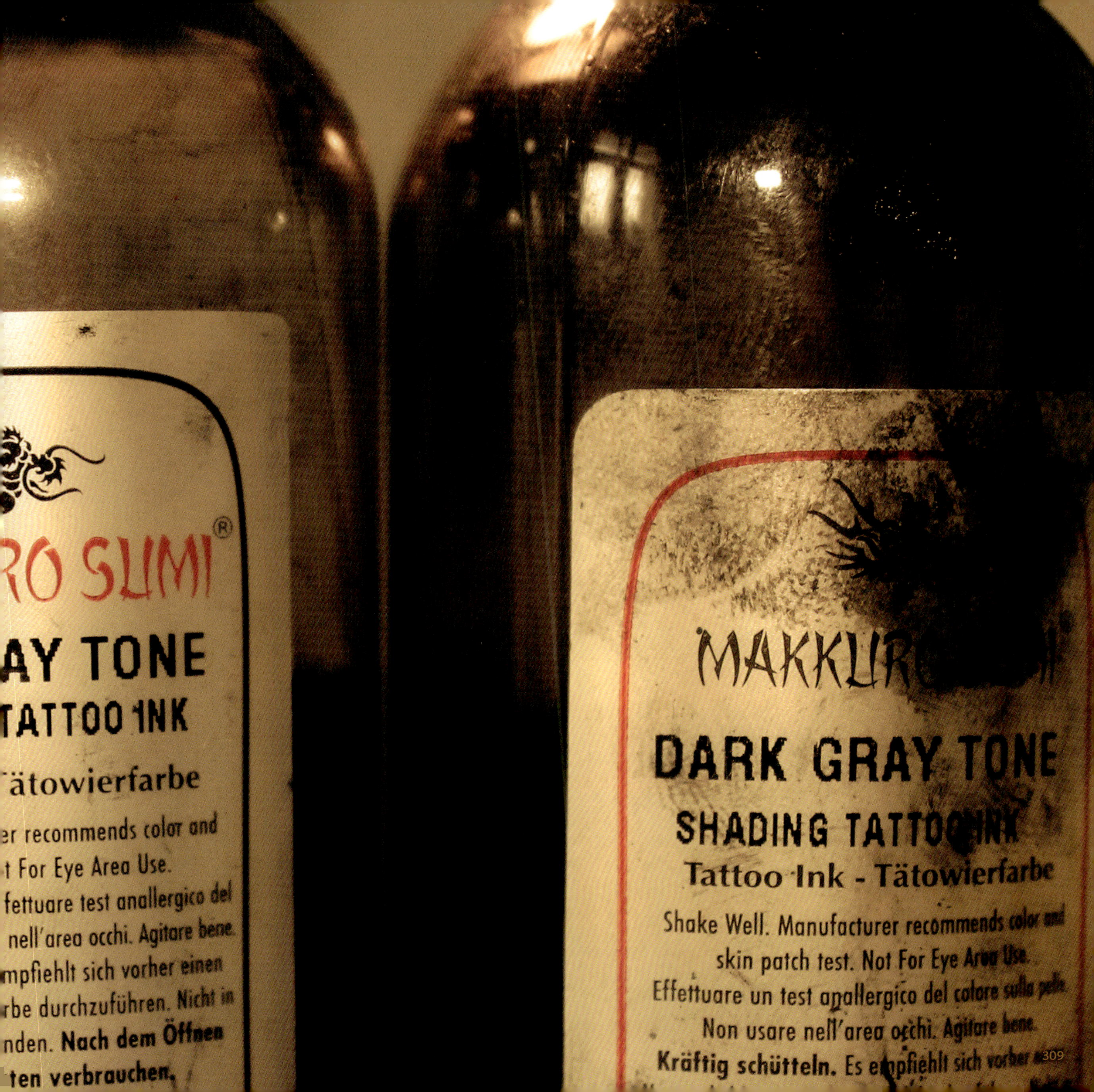
RO SUMI ®
AY TONE
TATTOO INK
ätowierfarbe
r recommends color and
t For Eye Area Use.
fettuare test anallergico del
nell'area occhi. Agitare bene.
mpfiehlt sich vorher einen
rbe durchzuführen. Nicht in
nden. Nach dem Öffnen
ten verbrauchen.
MAKKURO
DARK GRAY TONE
SHADING TATTOOINK
Tattoo Ink - Tätowierfarbe
Shake Well. Manufacturer recommends color and
skin patch test. Not For Eye Area Use.
Effettuare un test anallergico del colore sulla pelle.
Non usare nell'area occhi. Agitare bene.
Kräftig schütteln. Es empfiehlt sich vorher

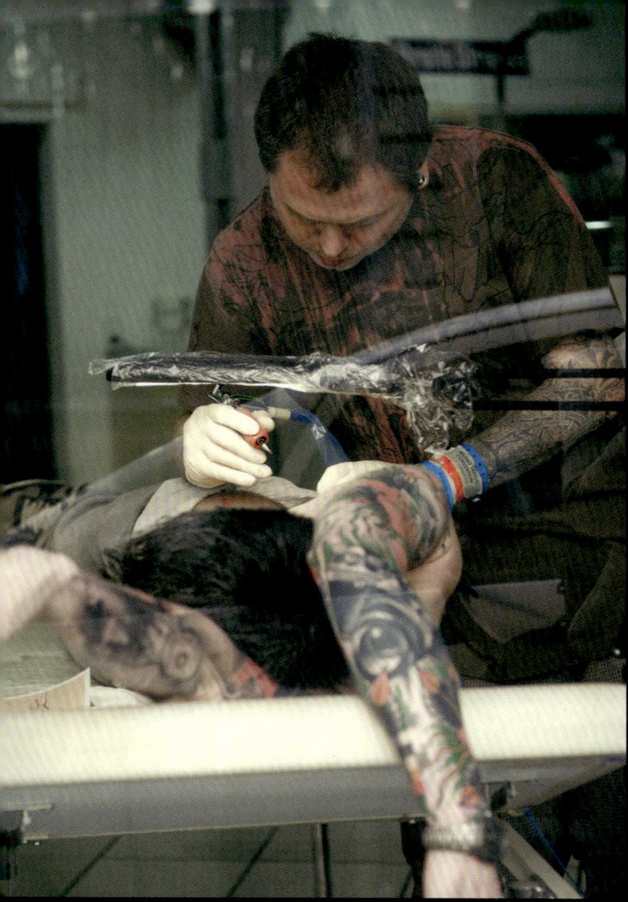

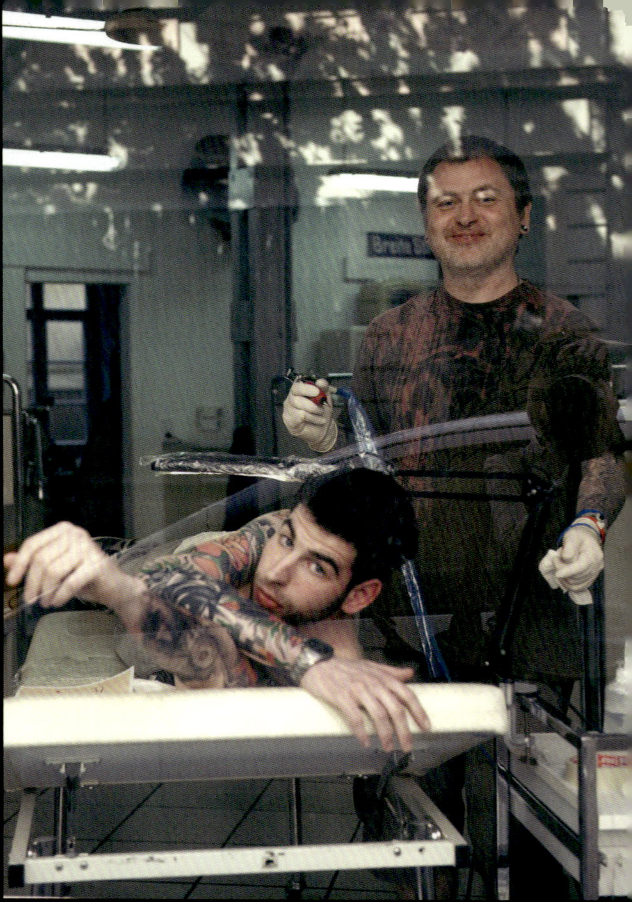

SERGEY BARDADIM
BARDADIM TATTOO ART

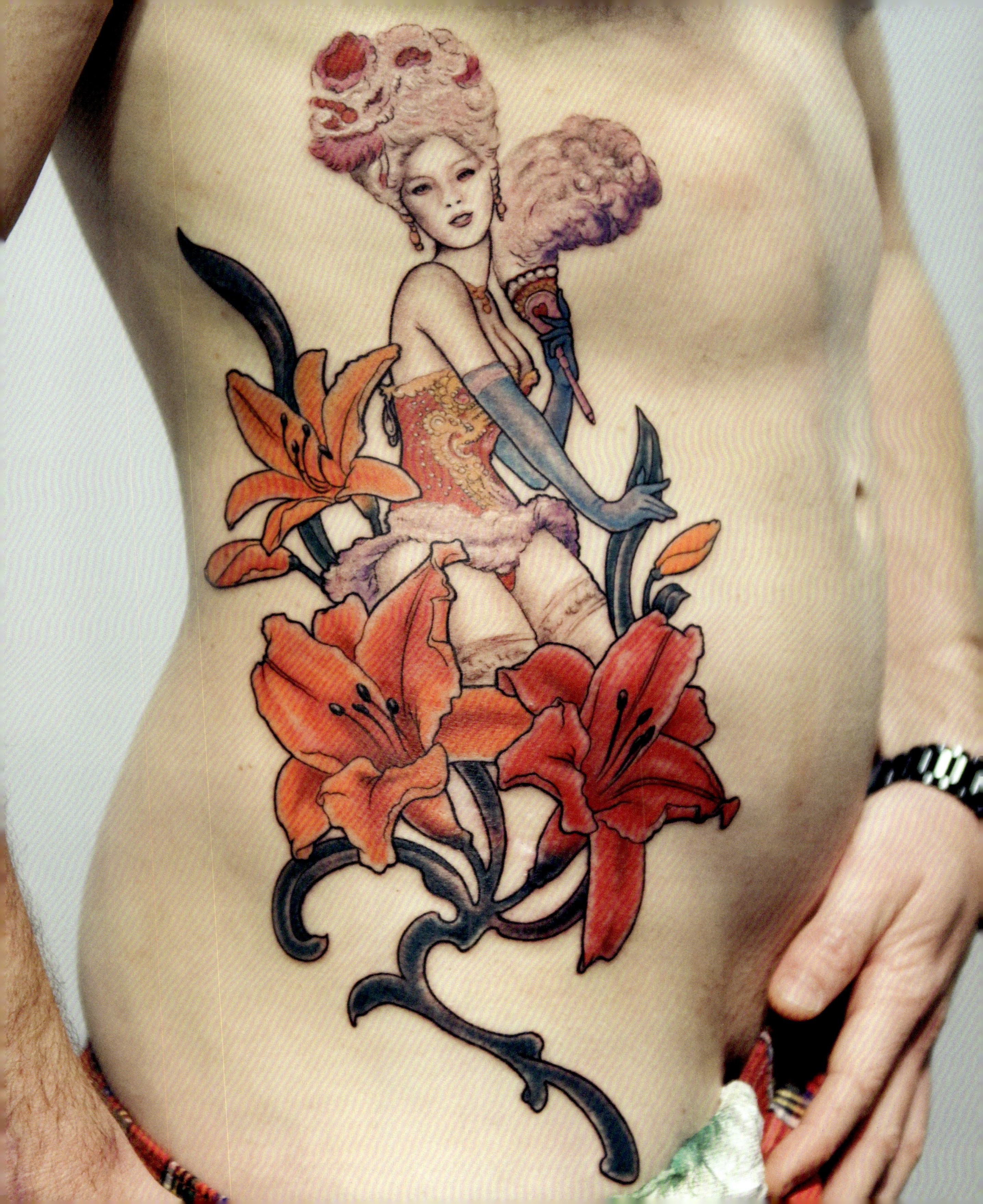

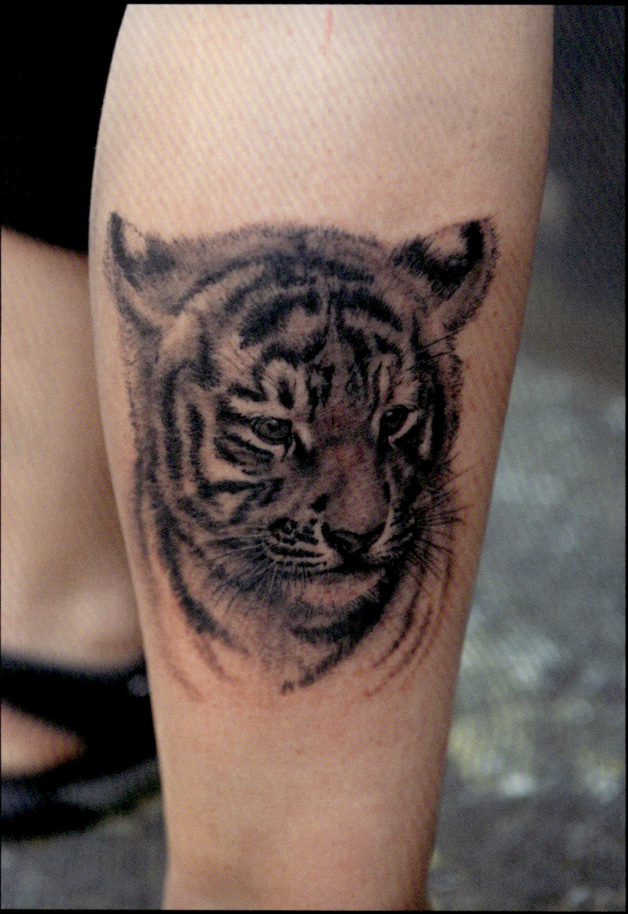

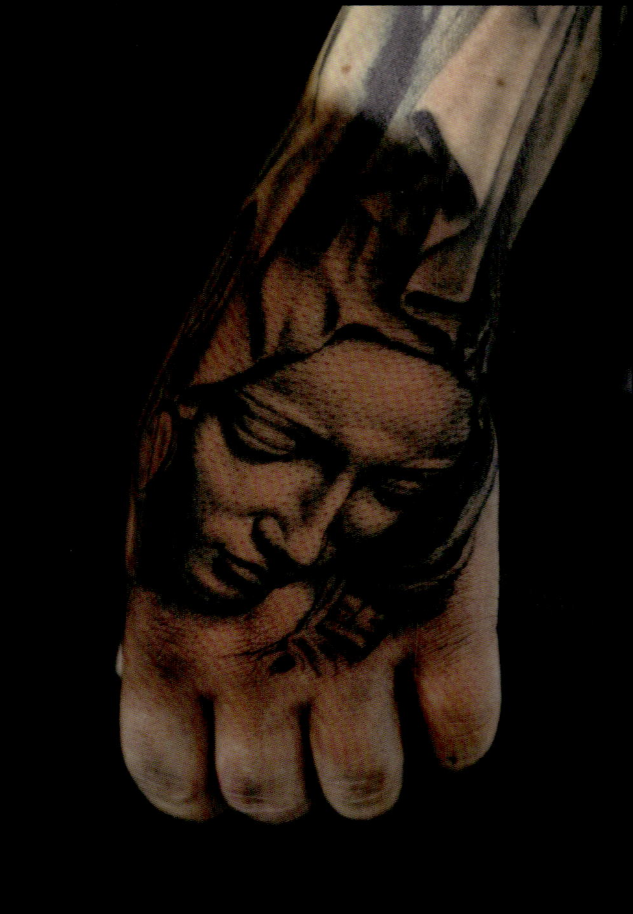

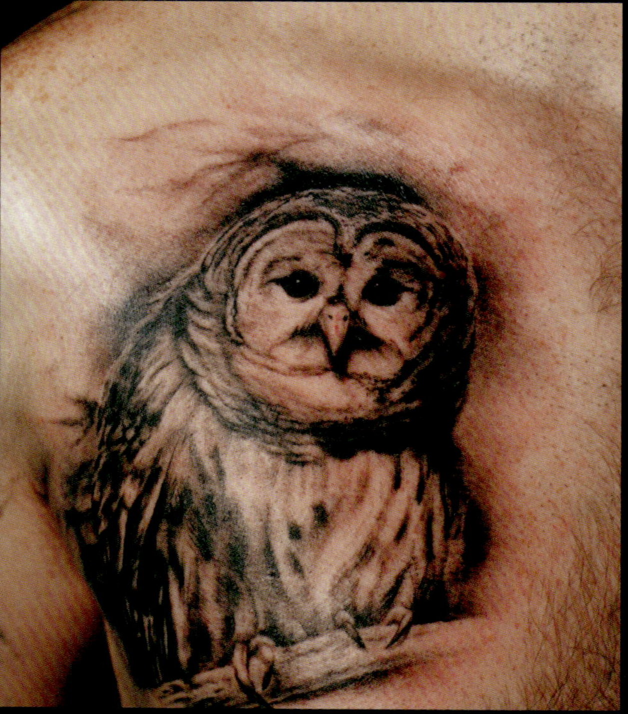

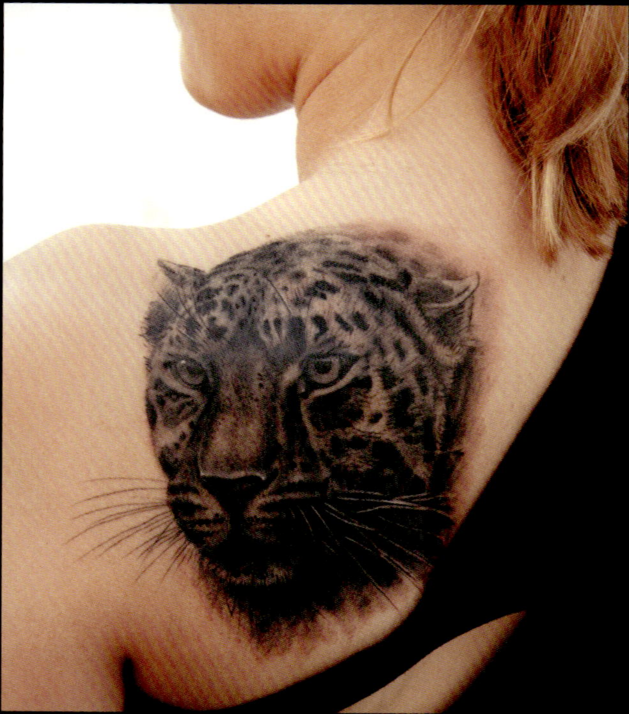

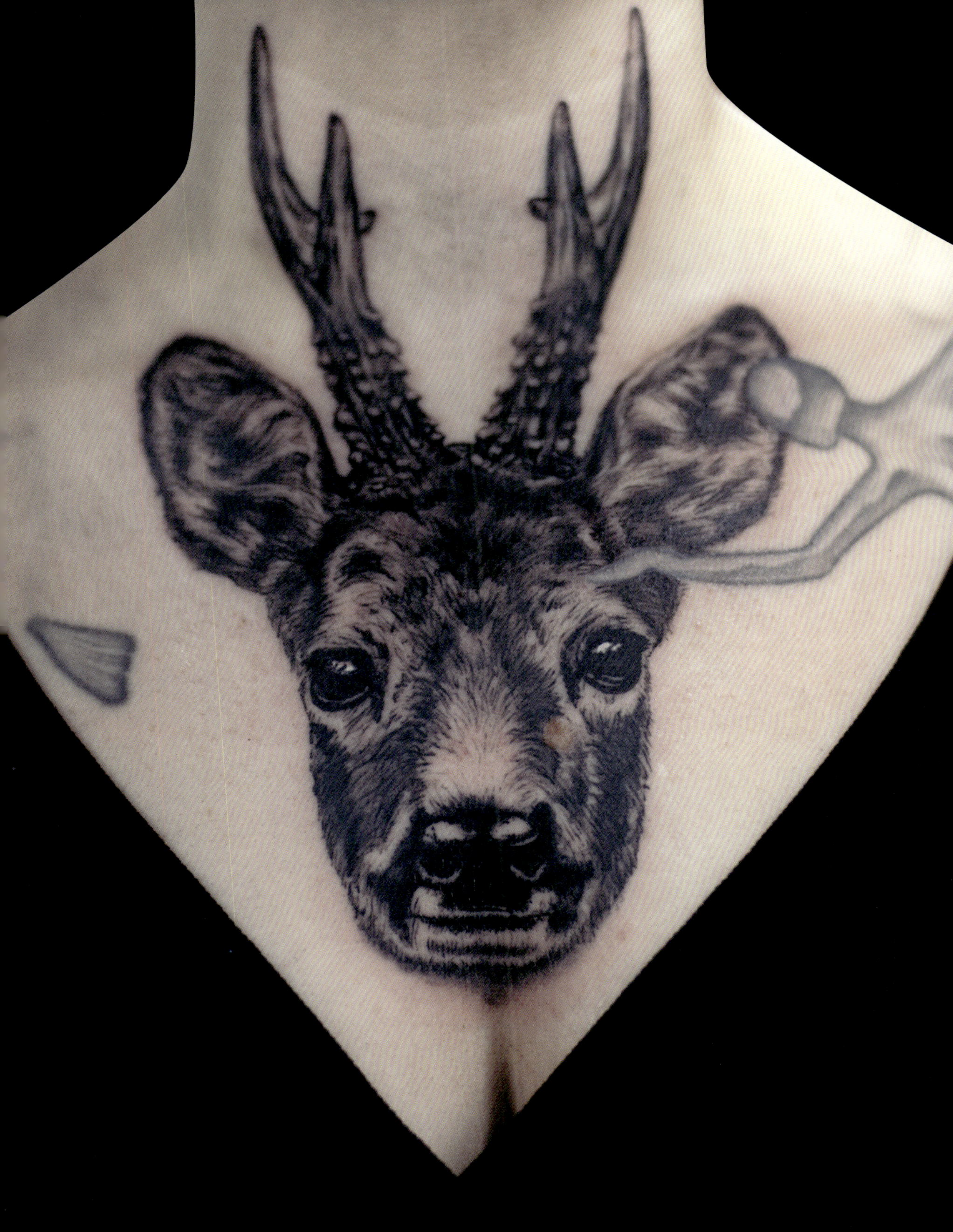

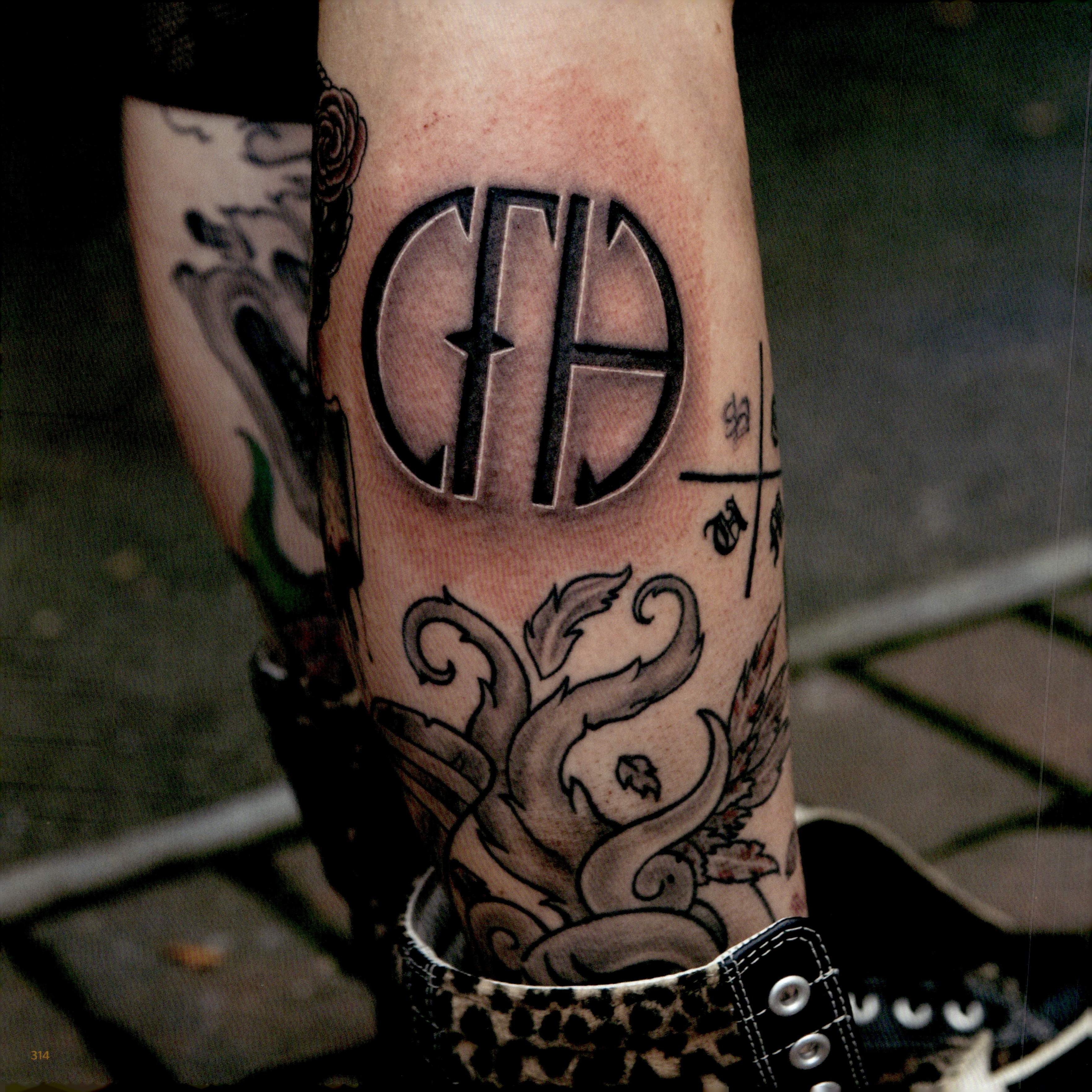

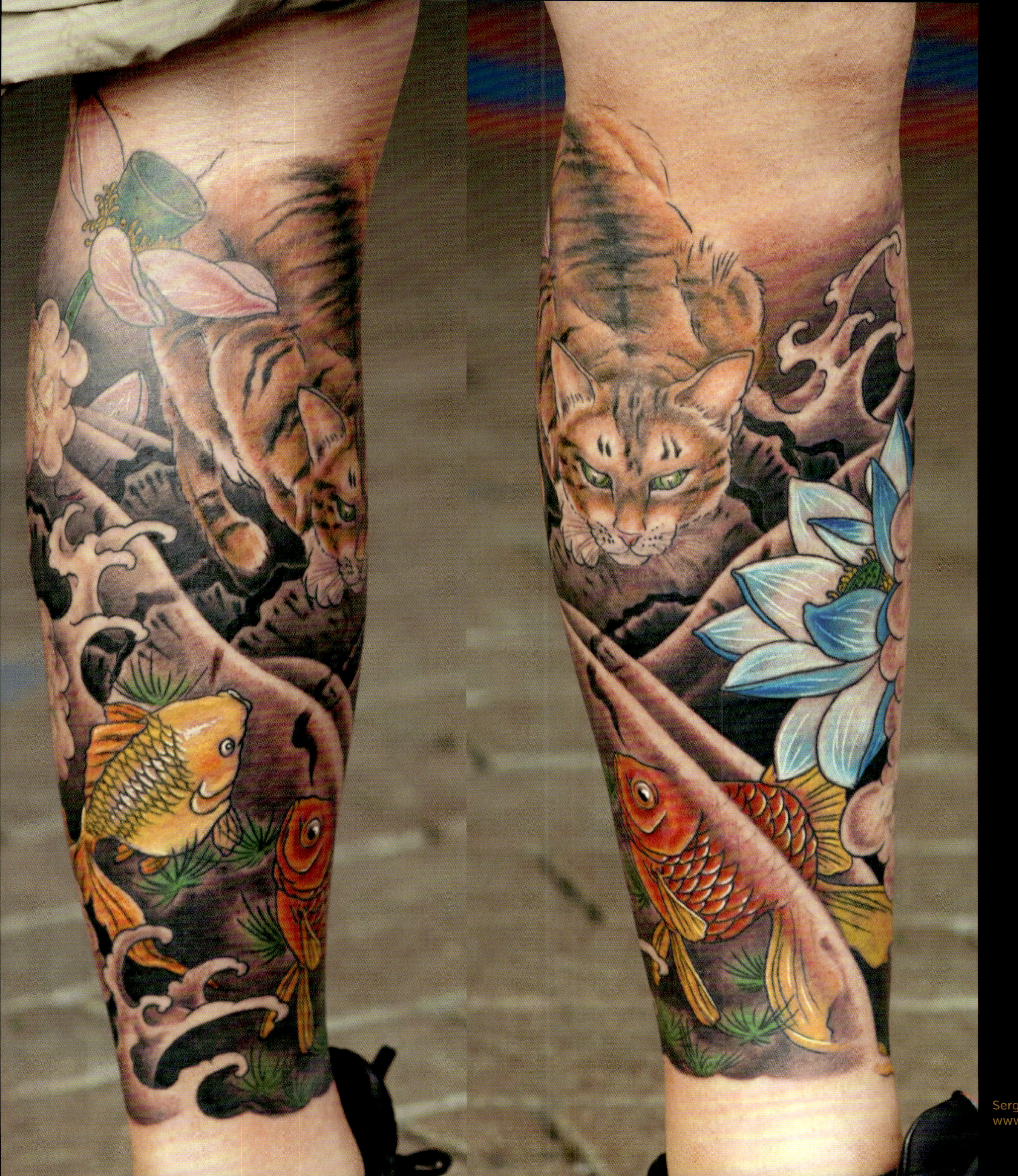

SHIGE
YELLOW BLAZE
TATTOO

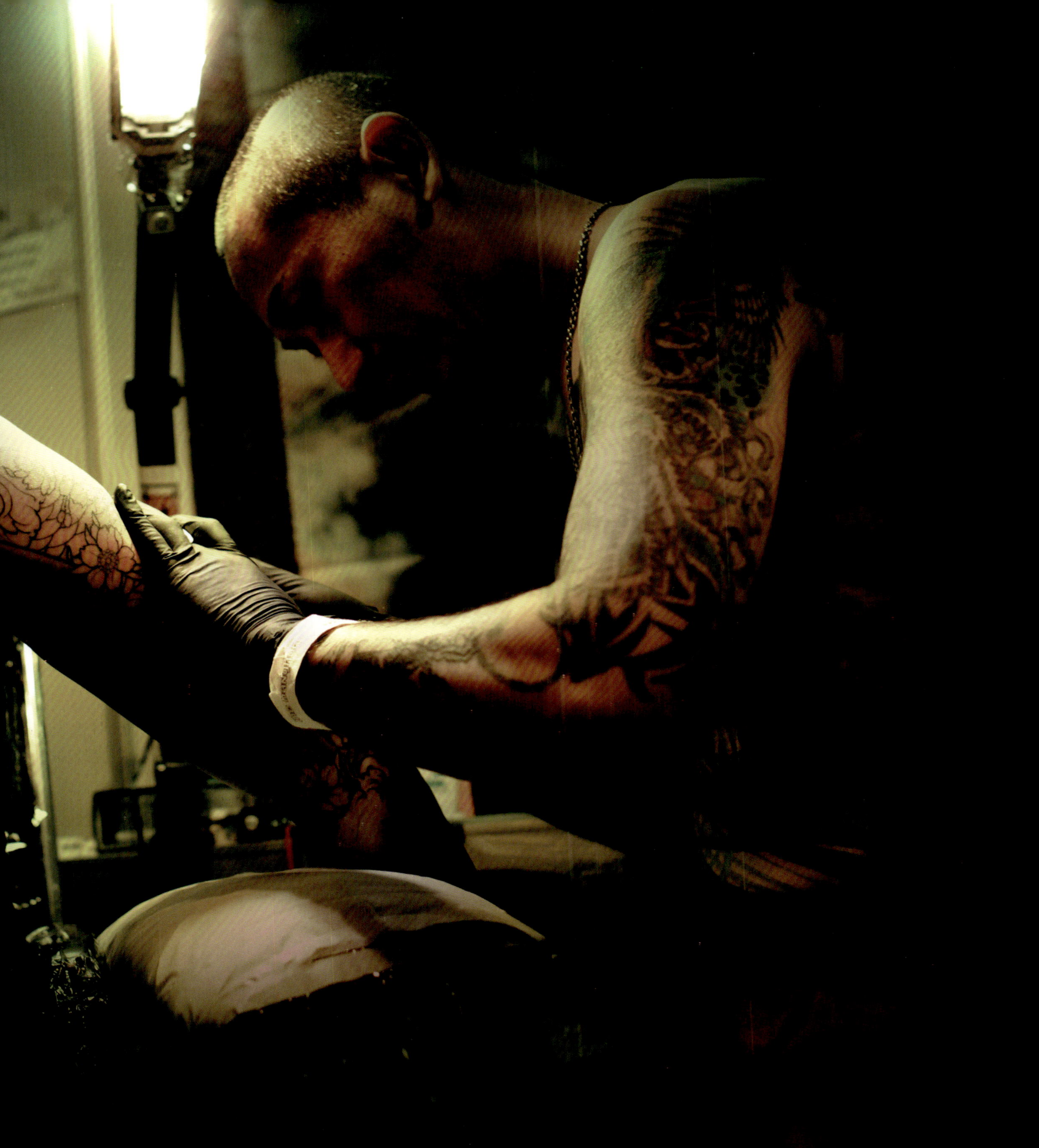

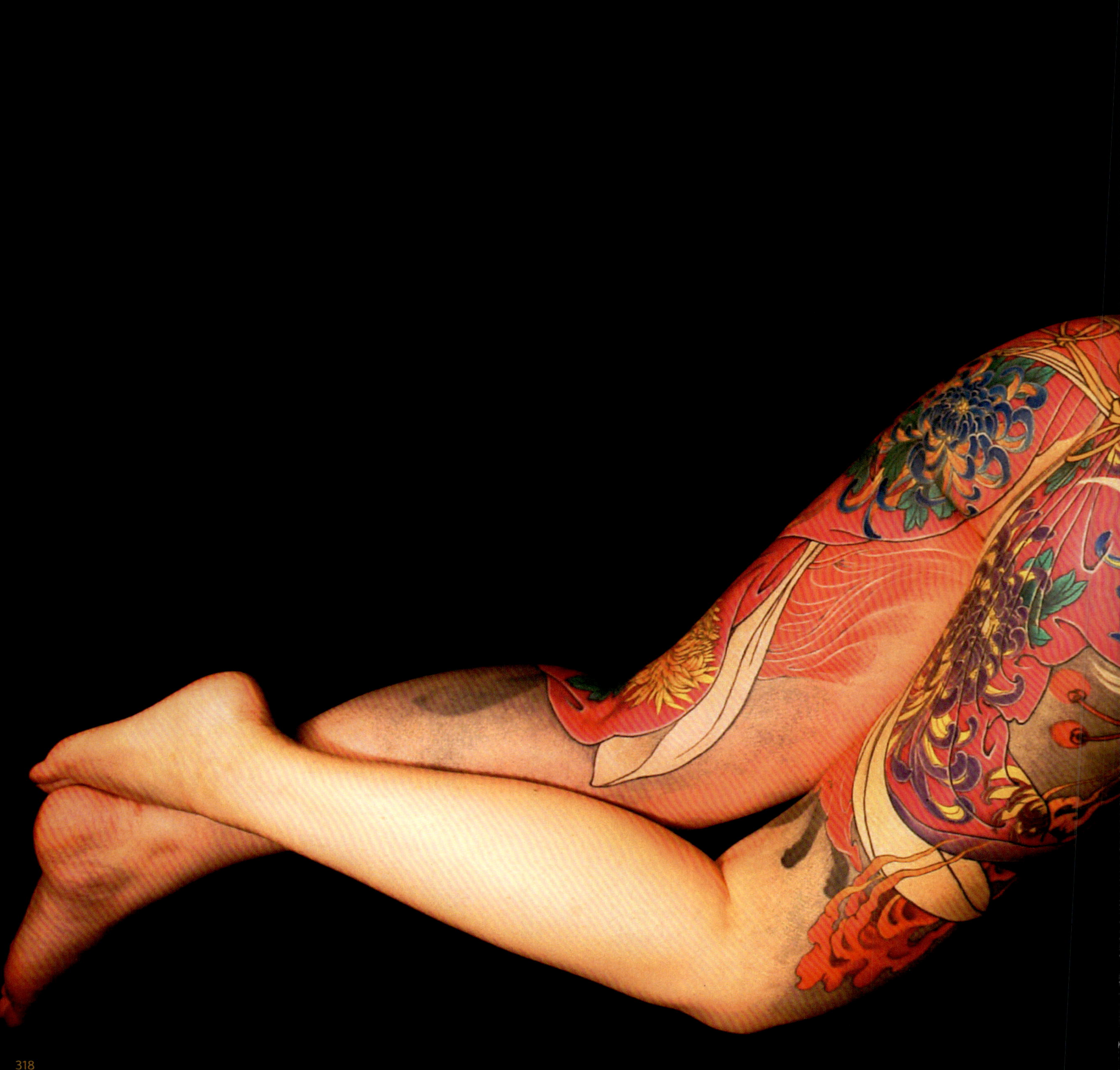

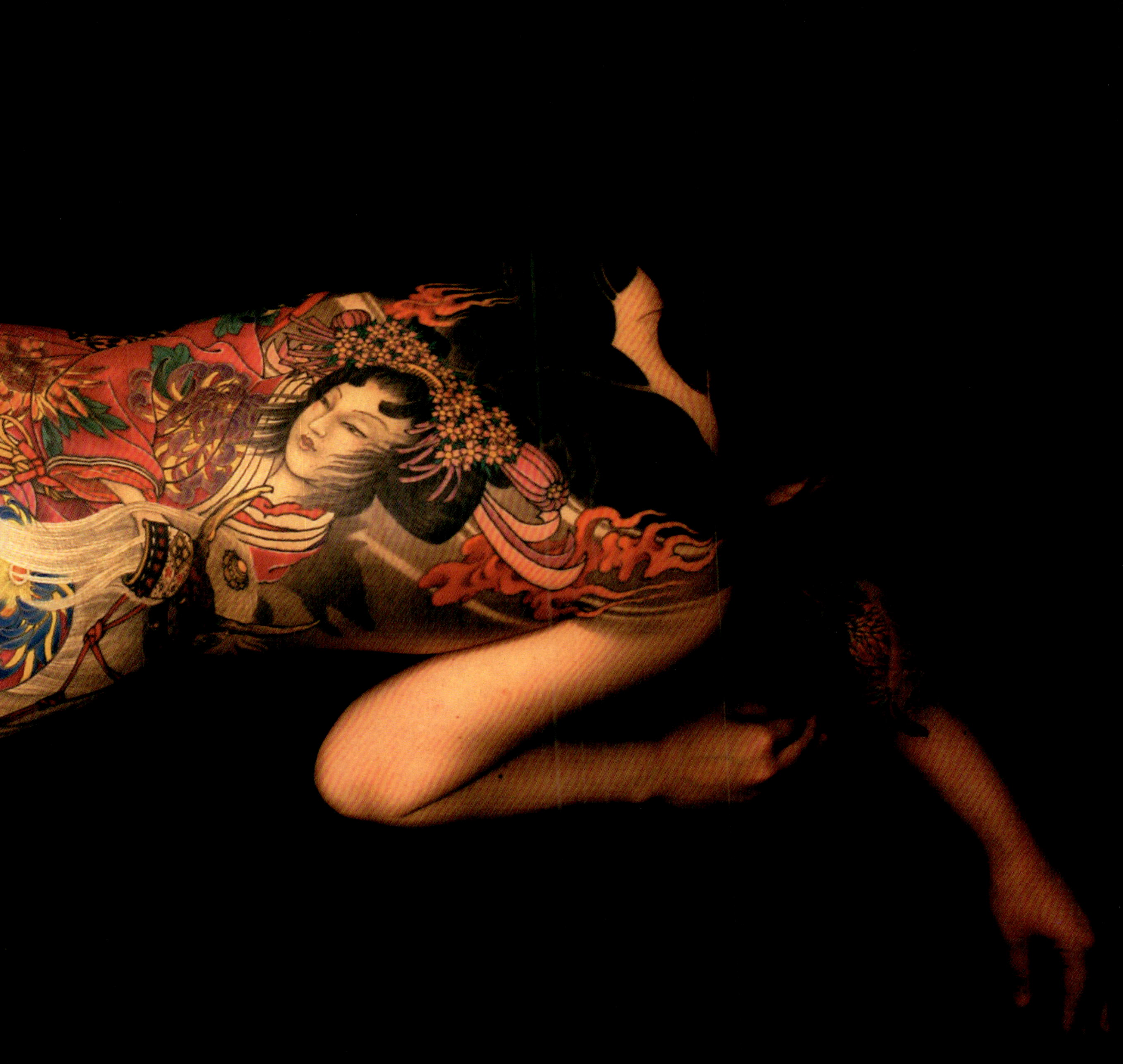

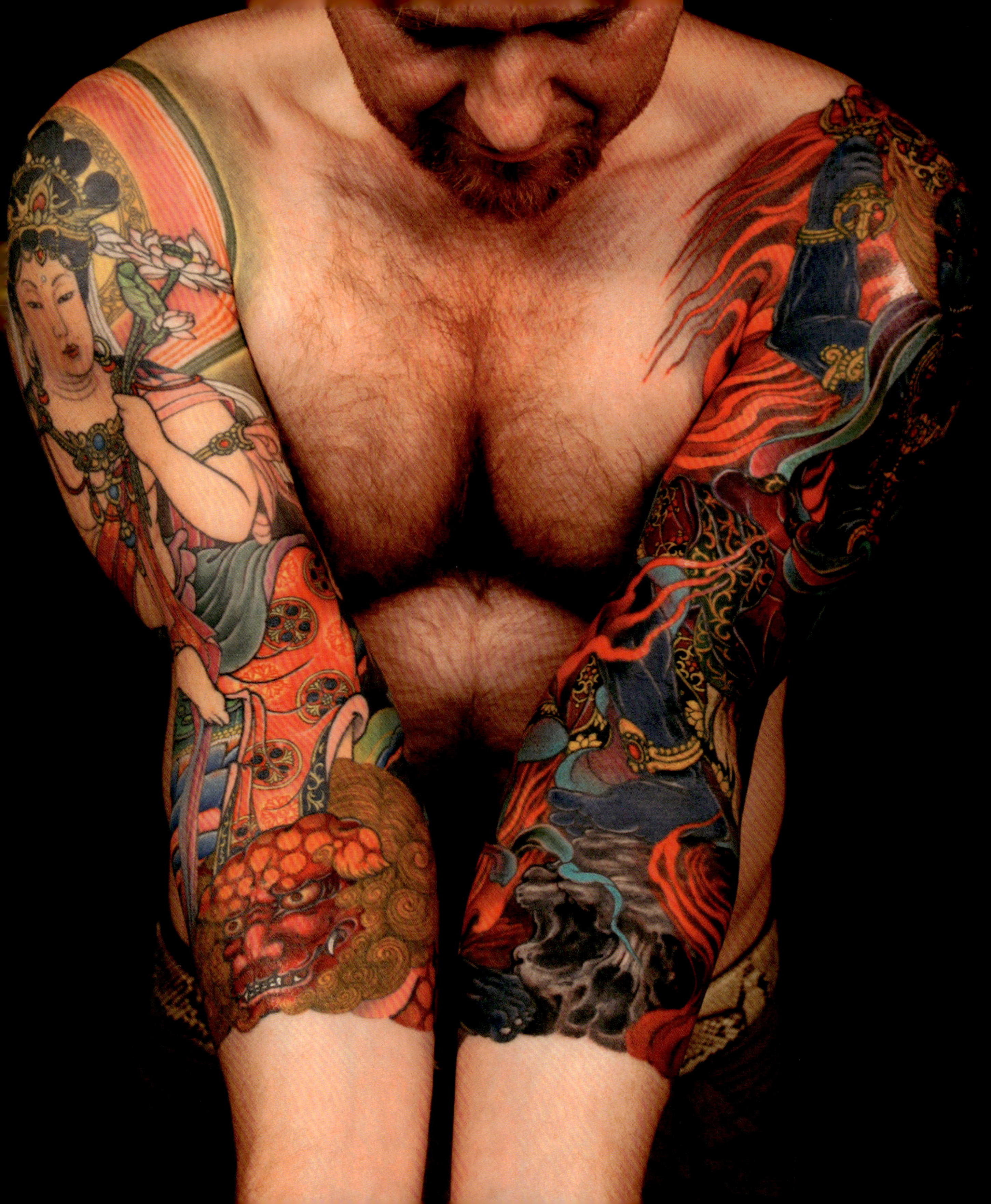

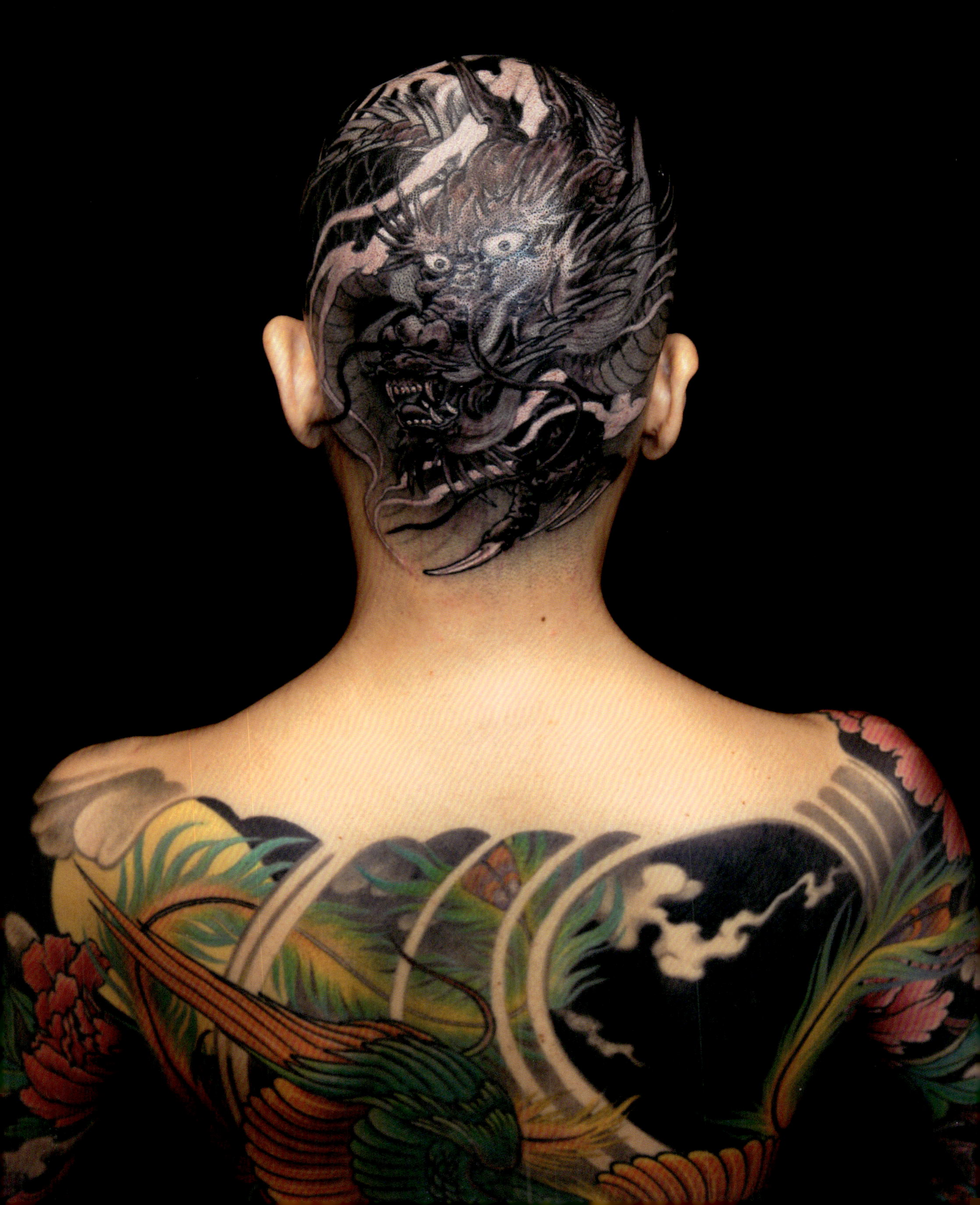

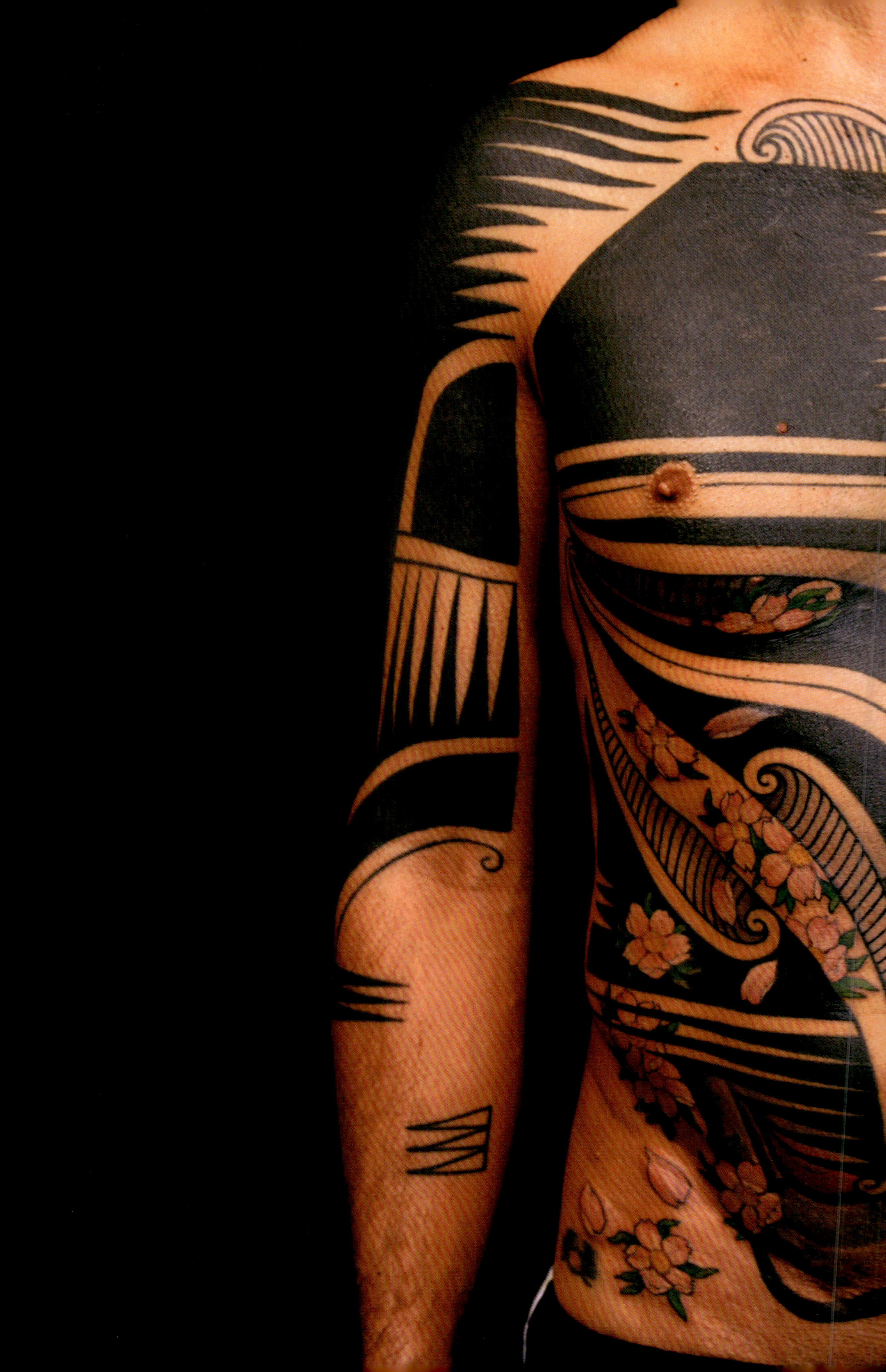

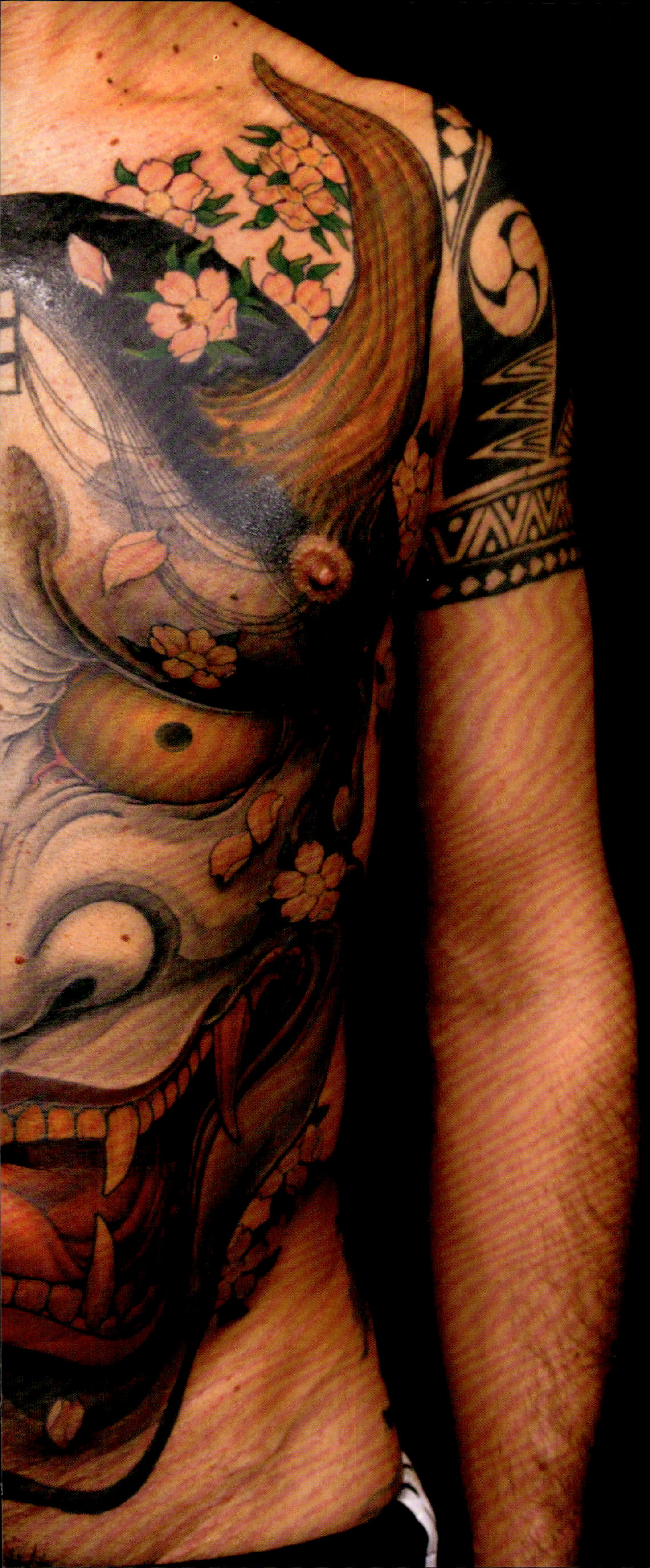

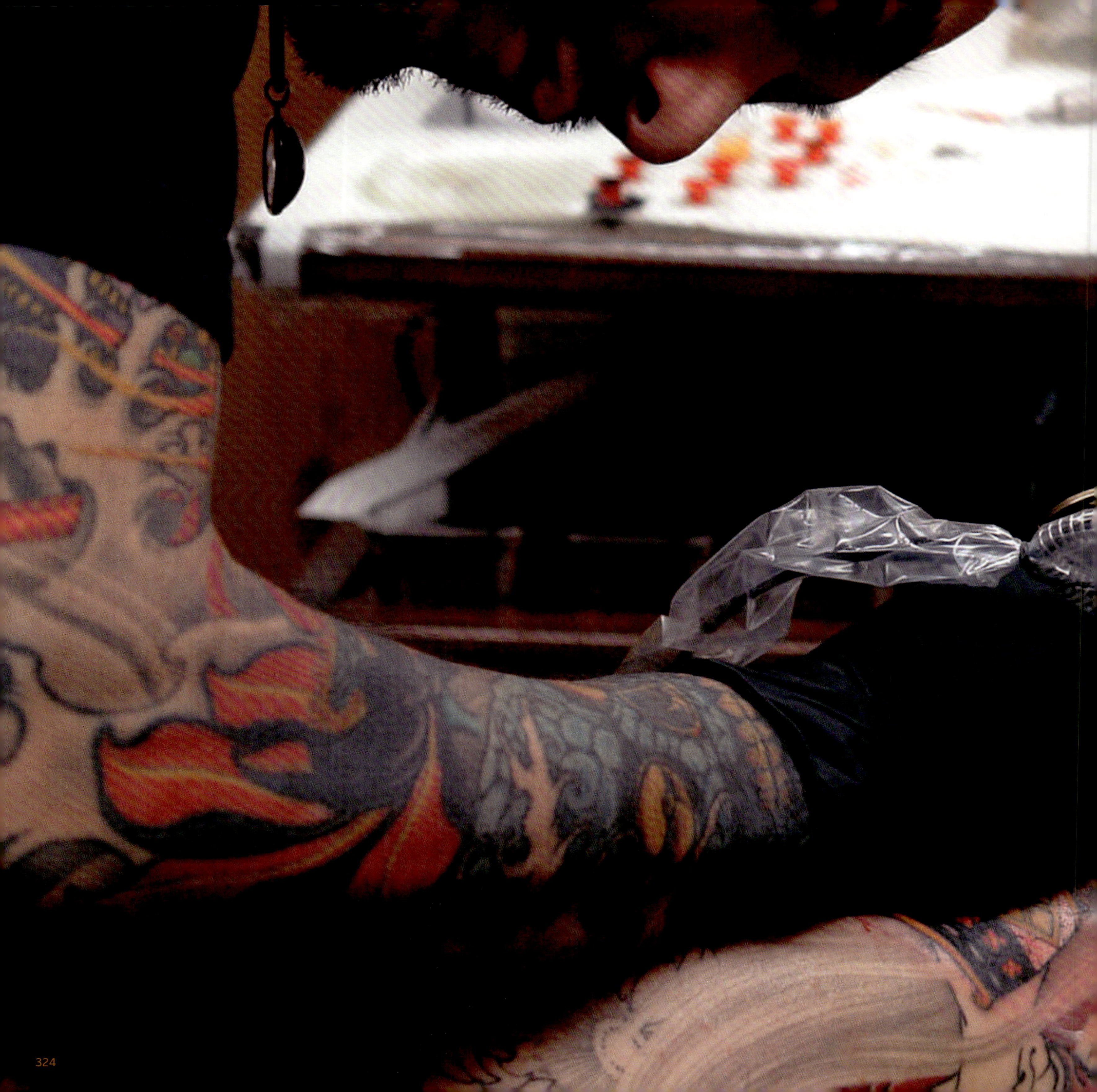

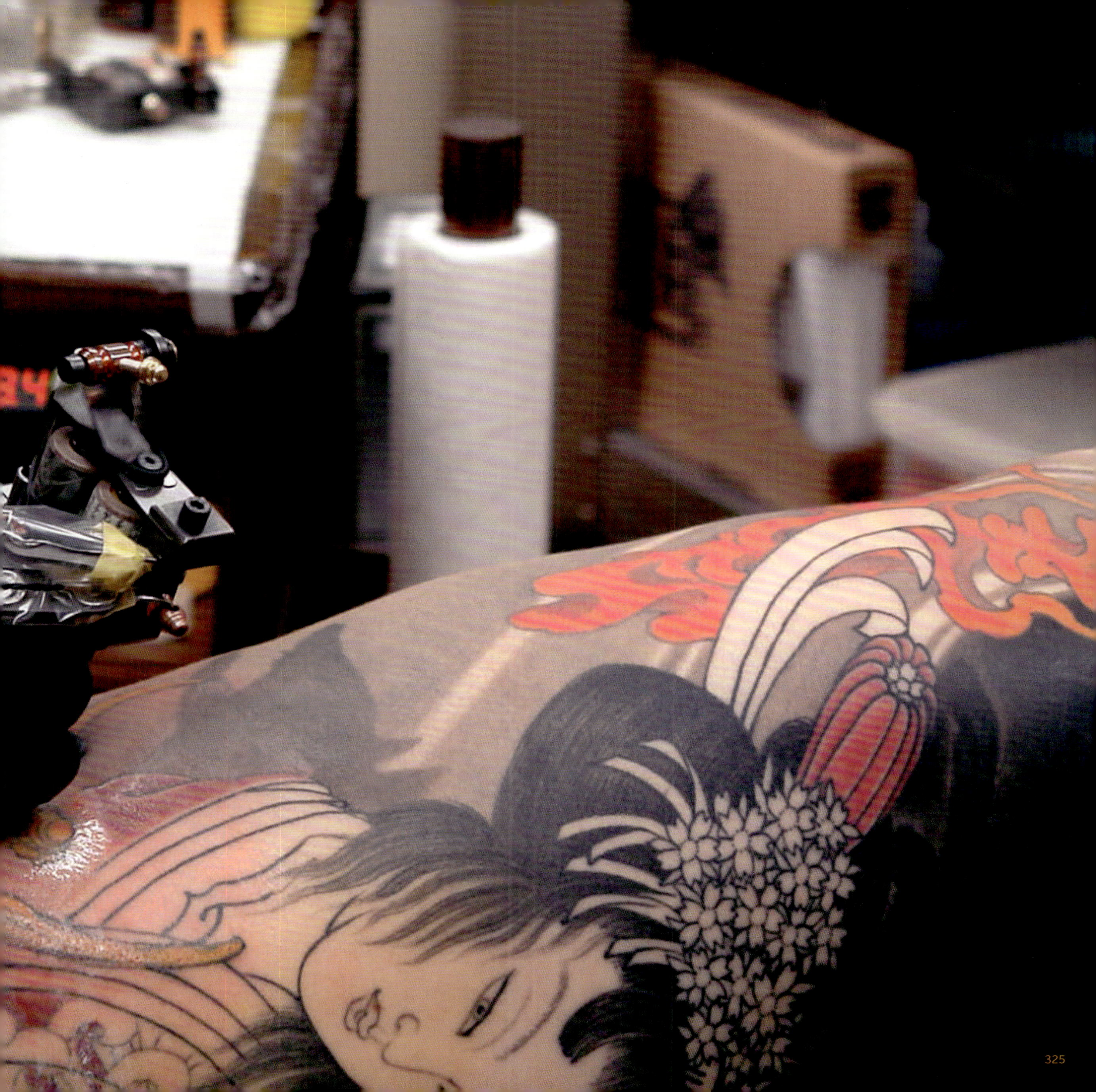

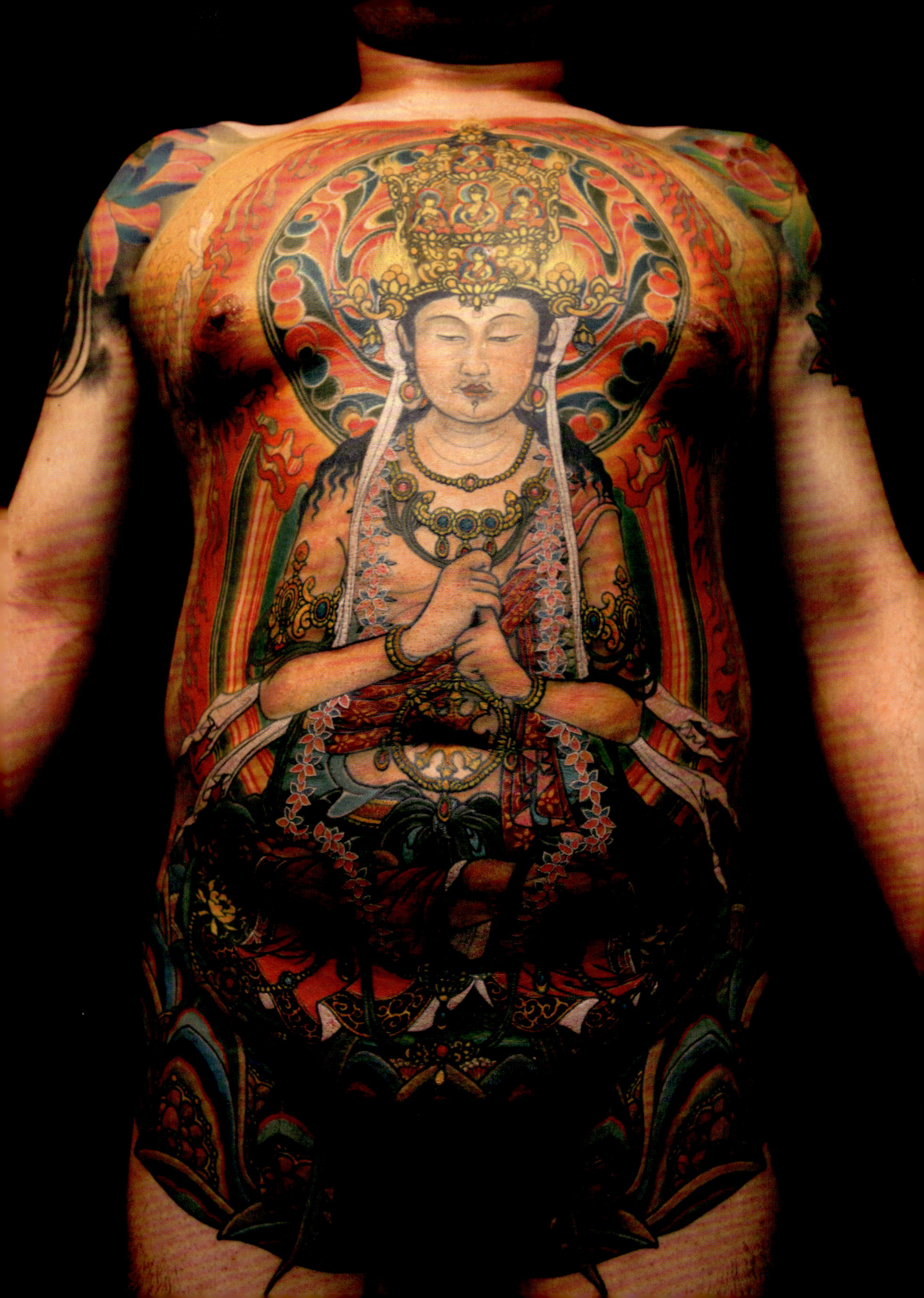

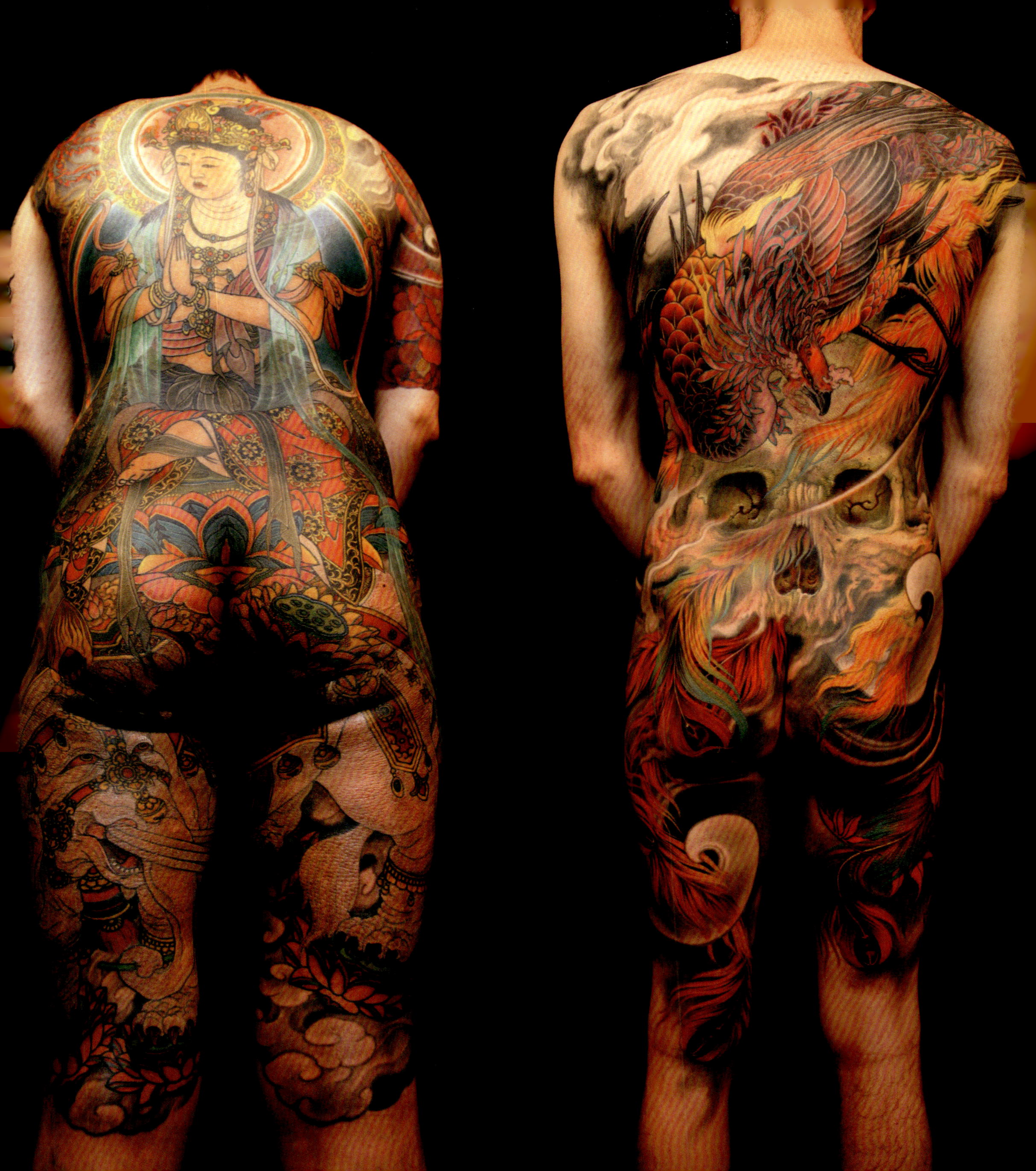

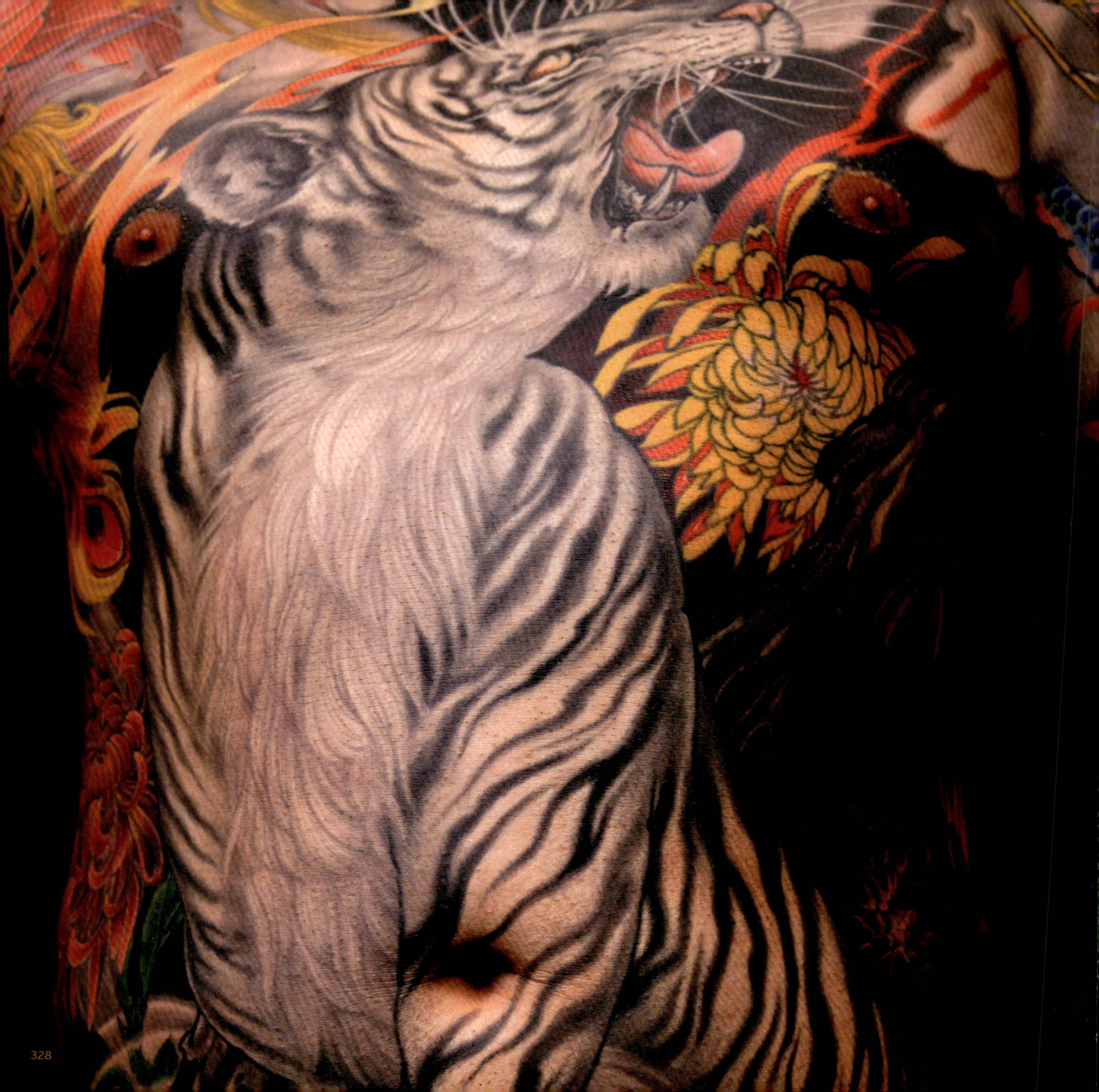

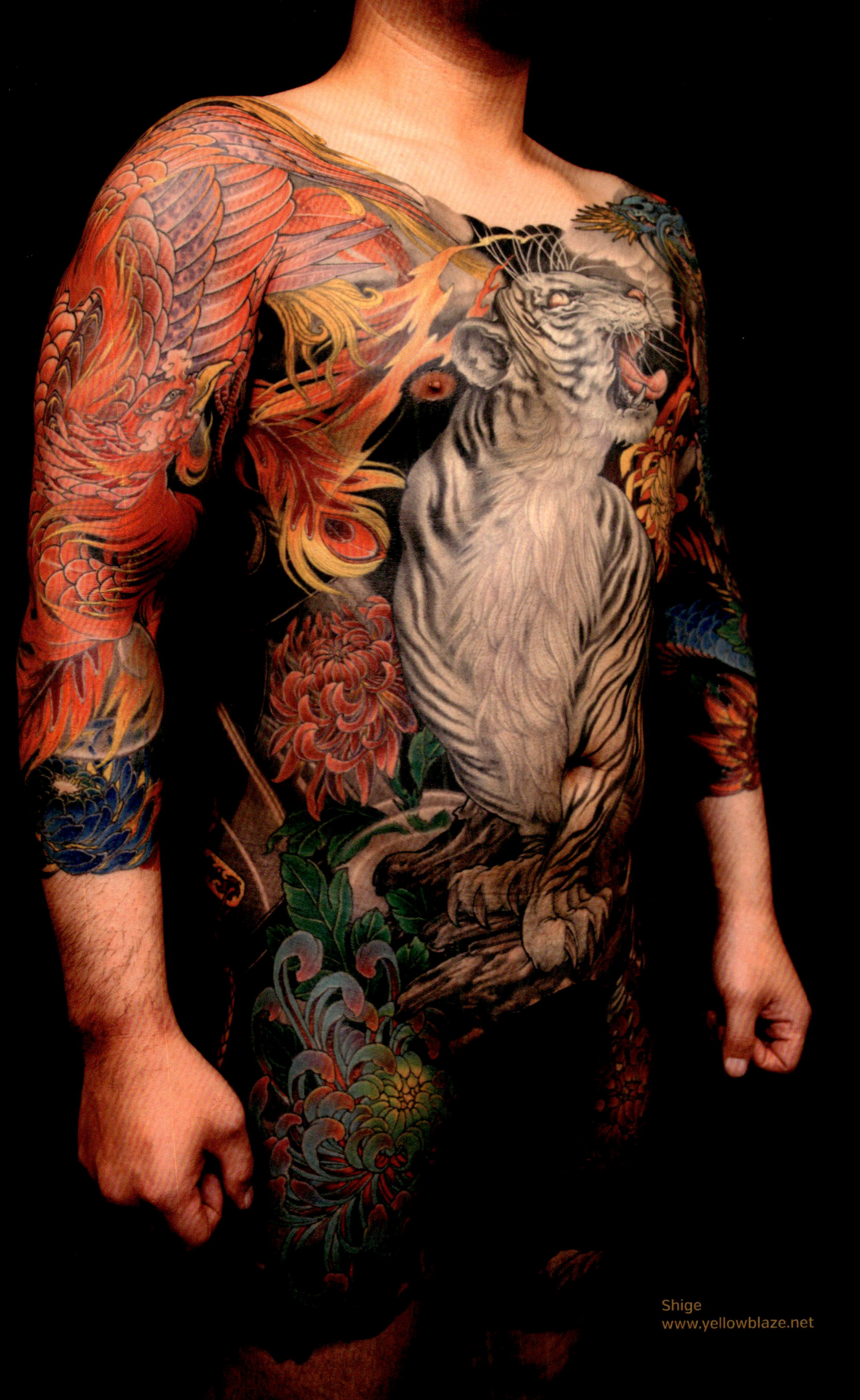

Shige
www.yellowblaze.net

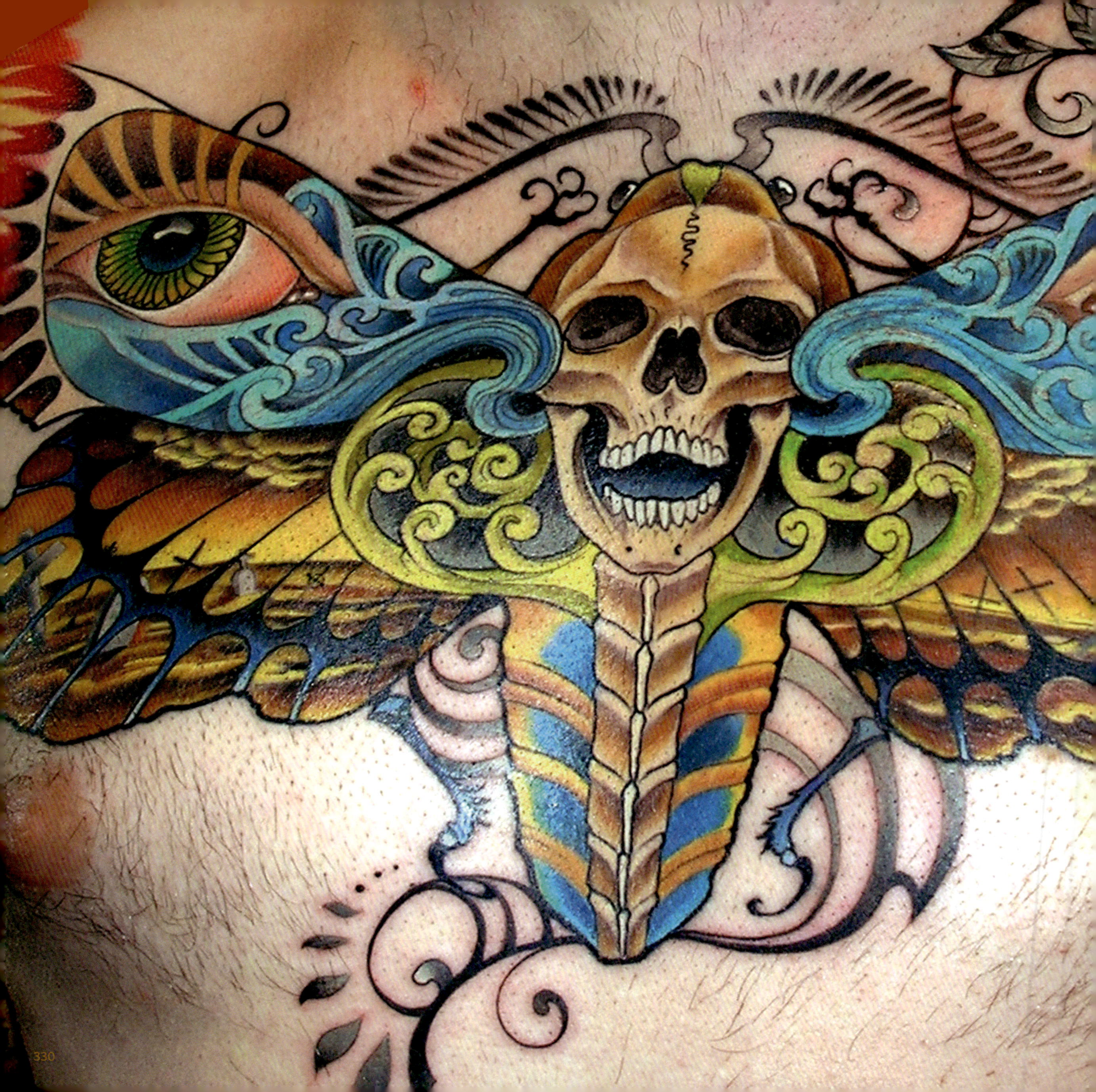

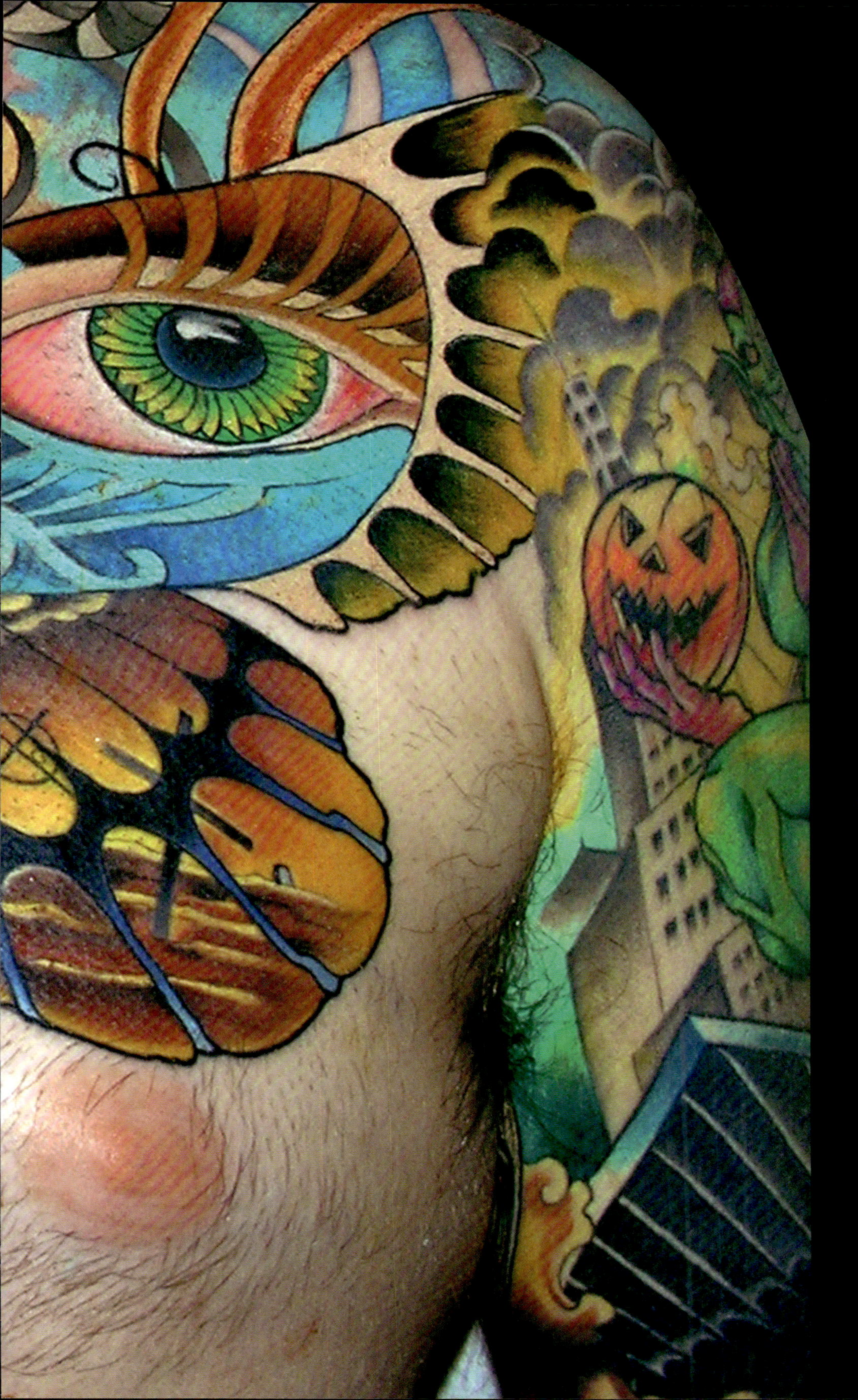

STINA NYMAN
EYESCREAM
TATTOO

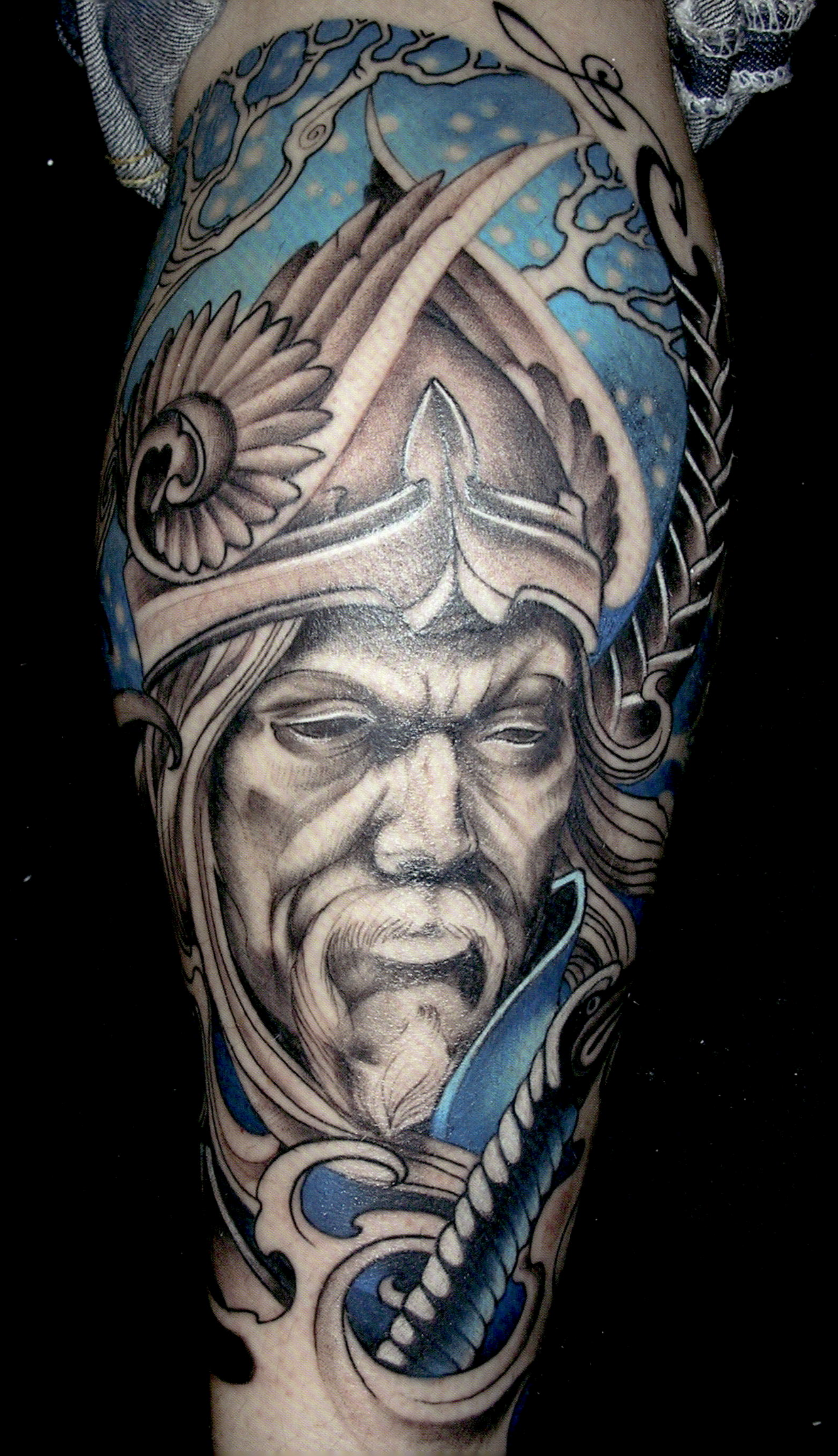

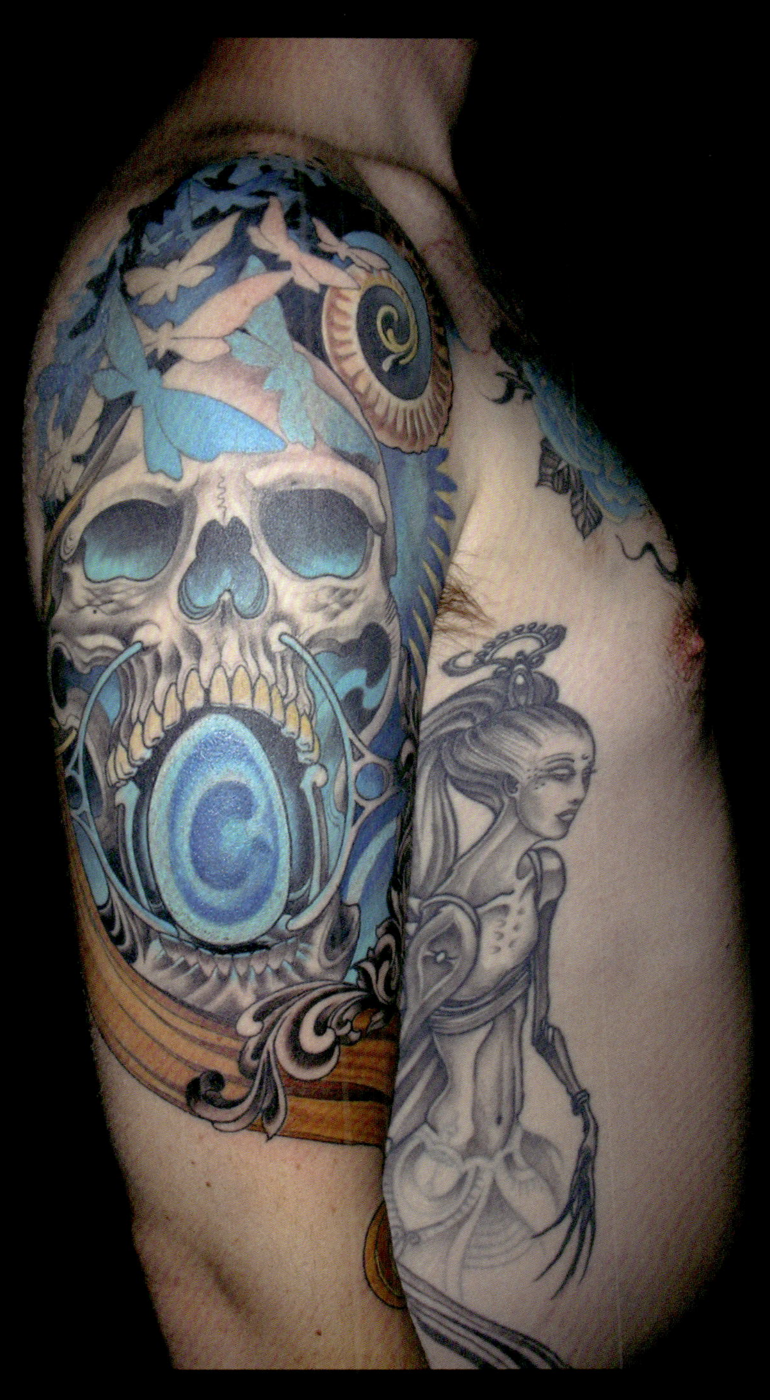

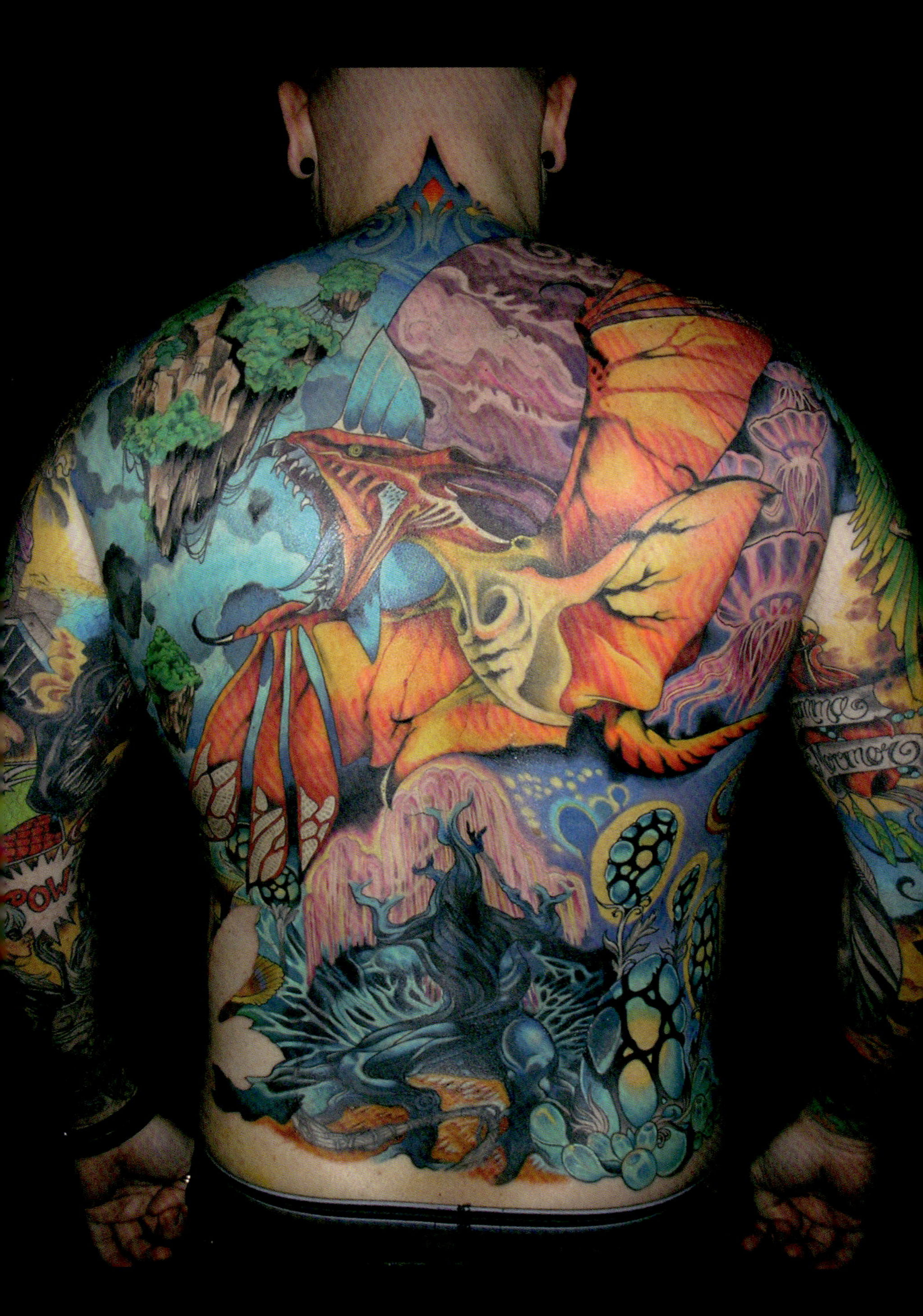

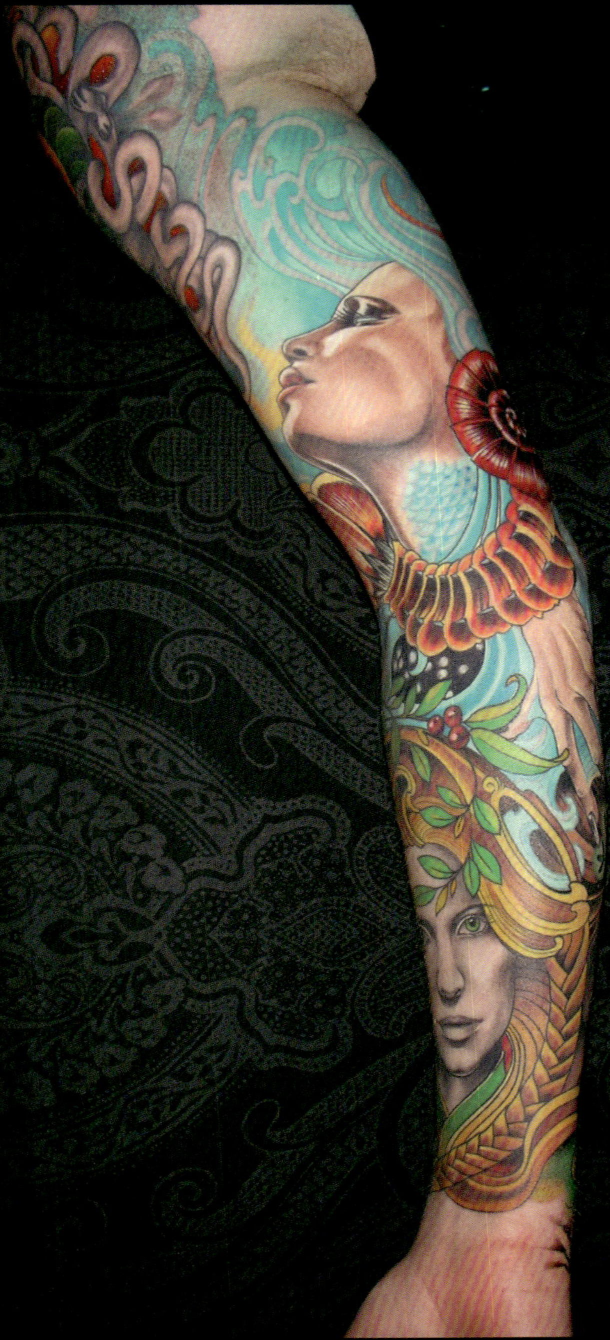

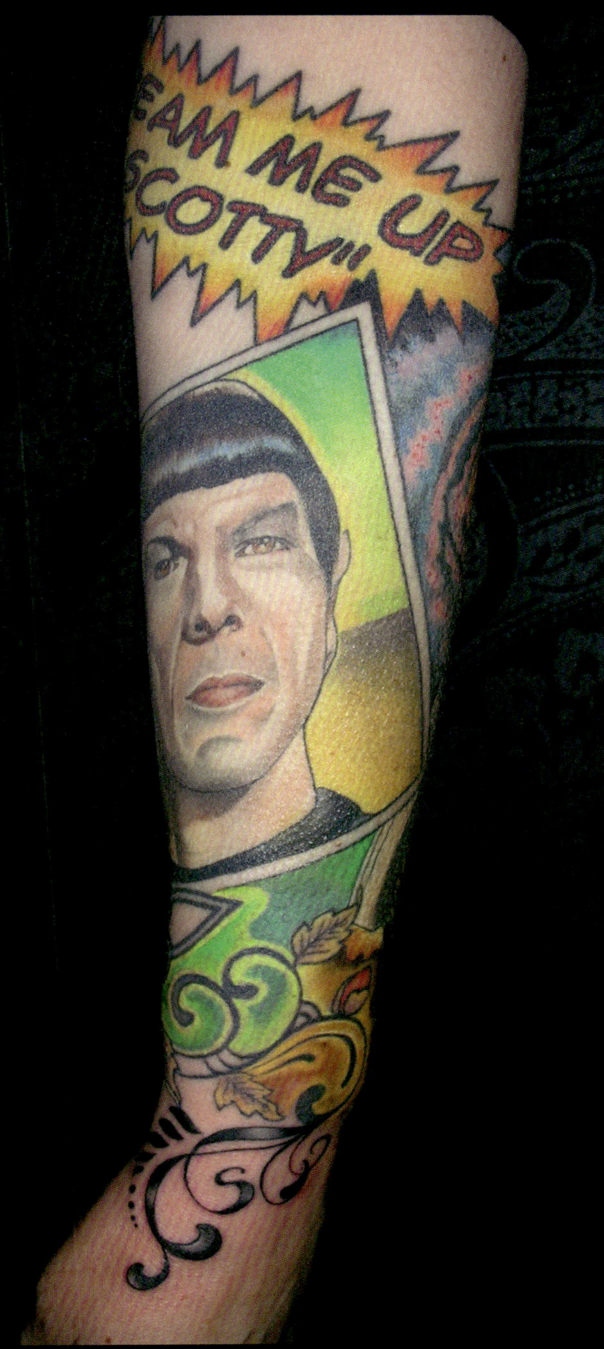

Stina Nyman
www.eyescreamtattoo.com

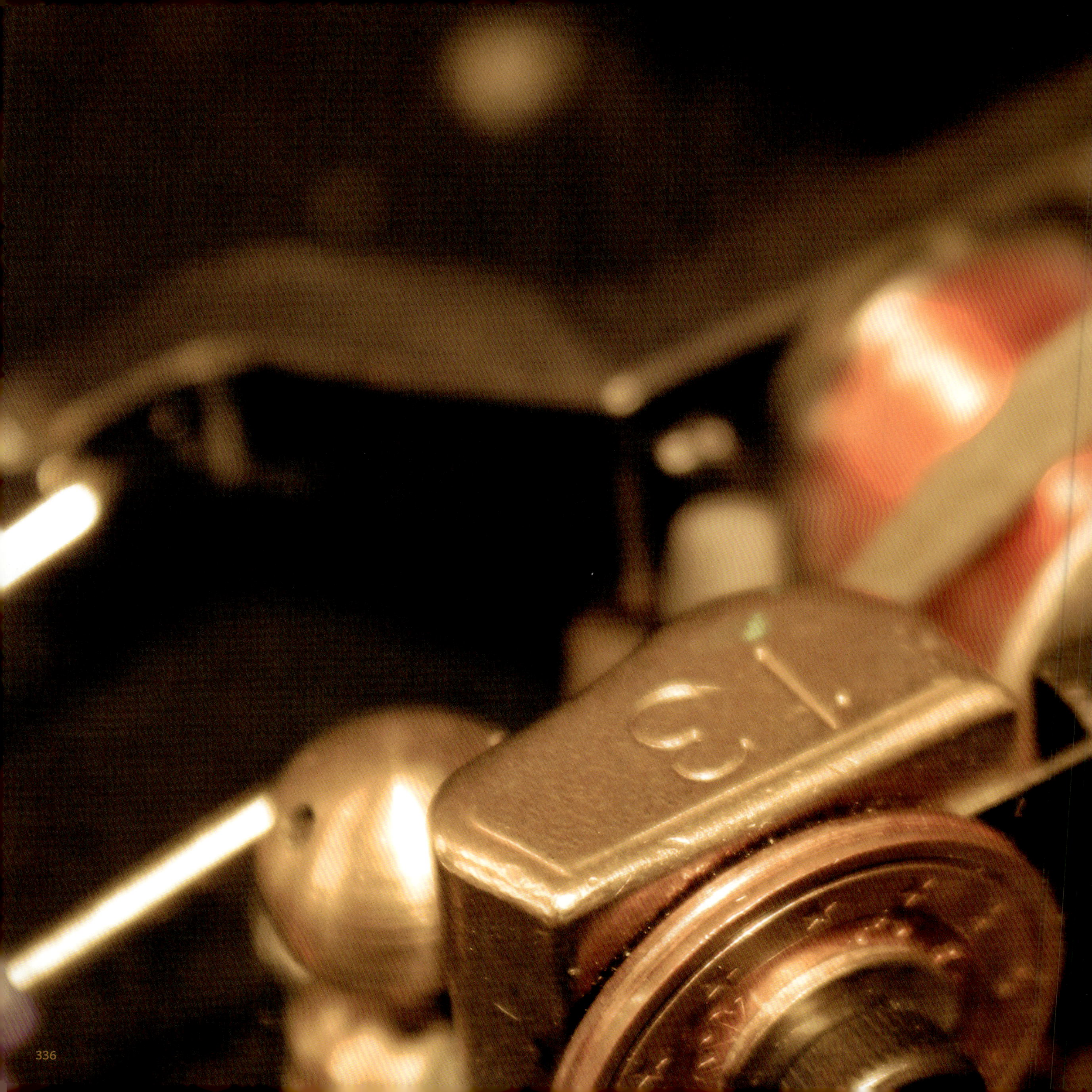

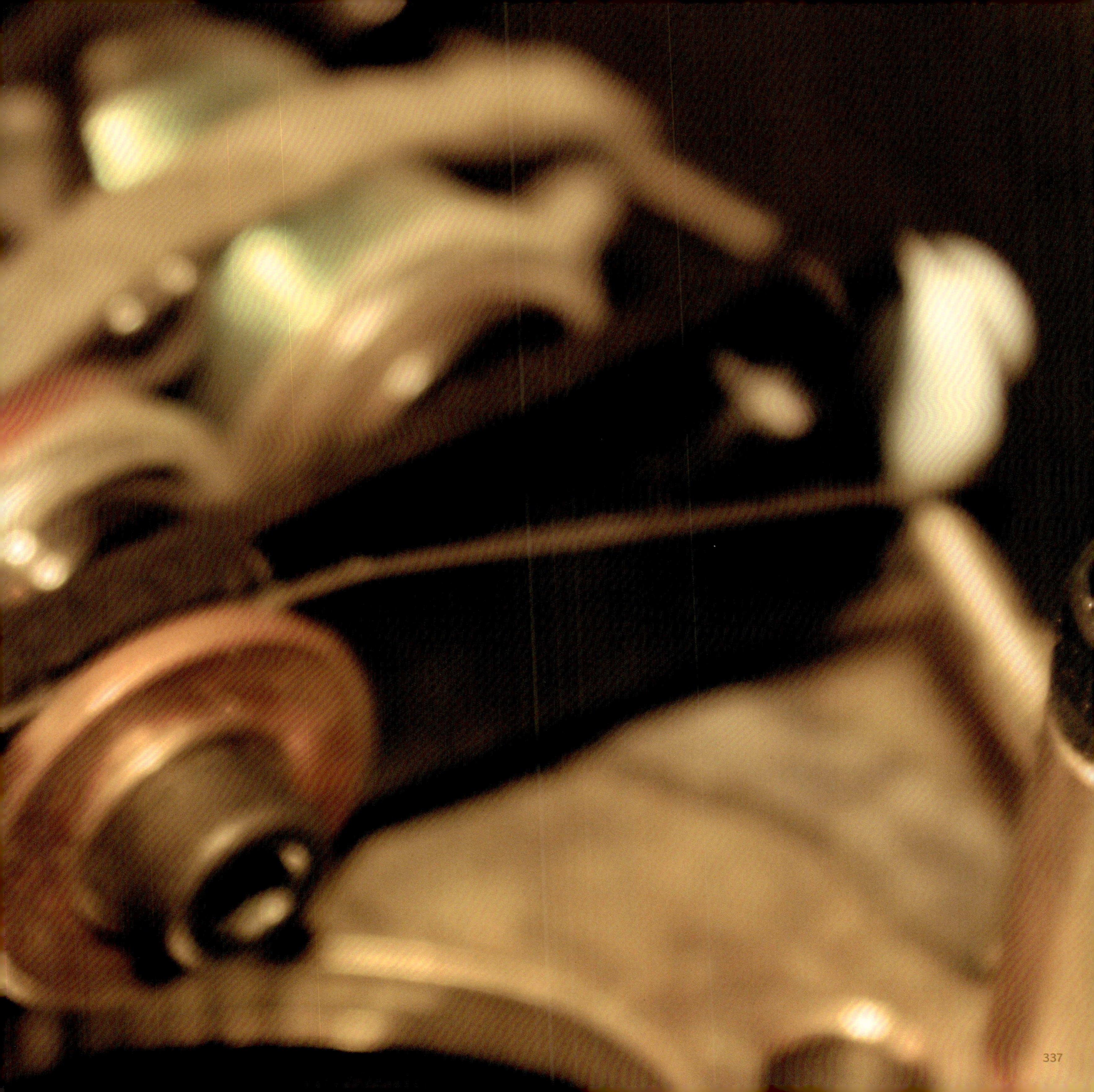

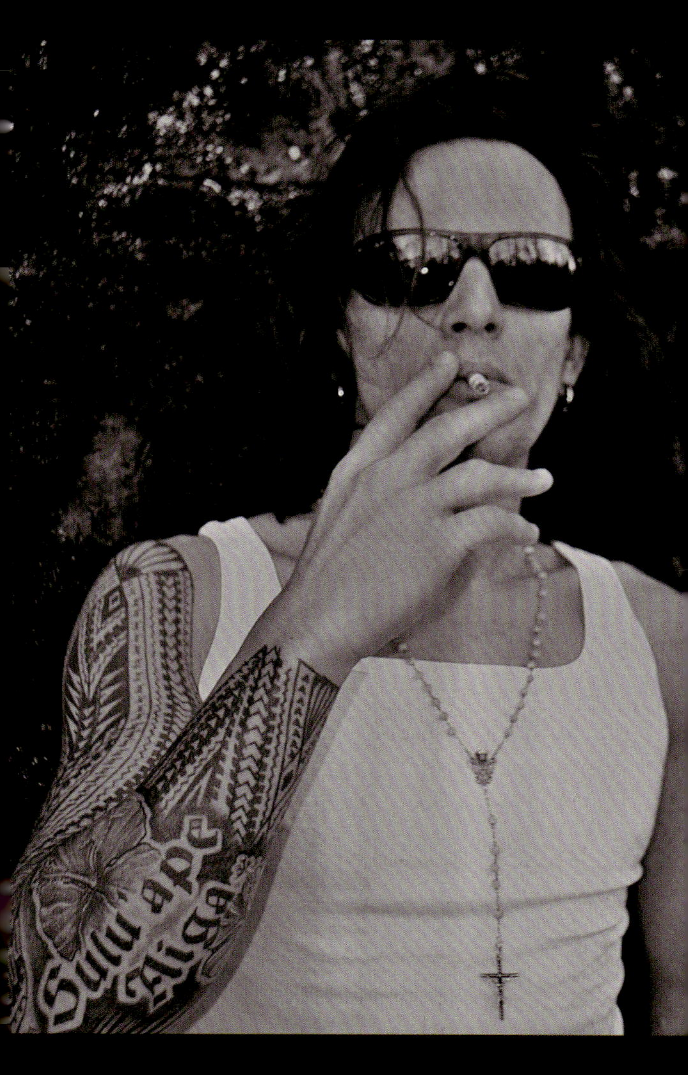

TOMASI SULU'APE
SULU'APE INK

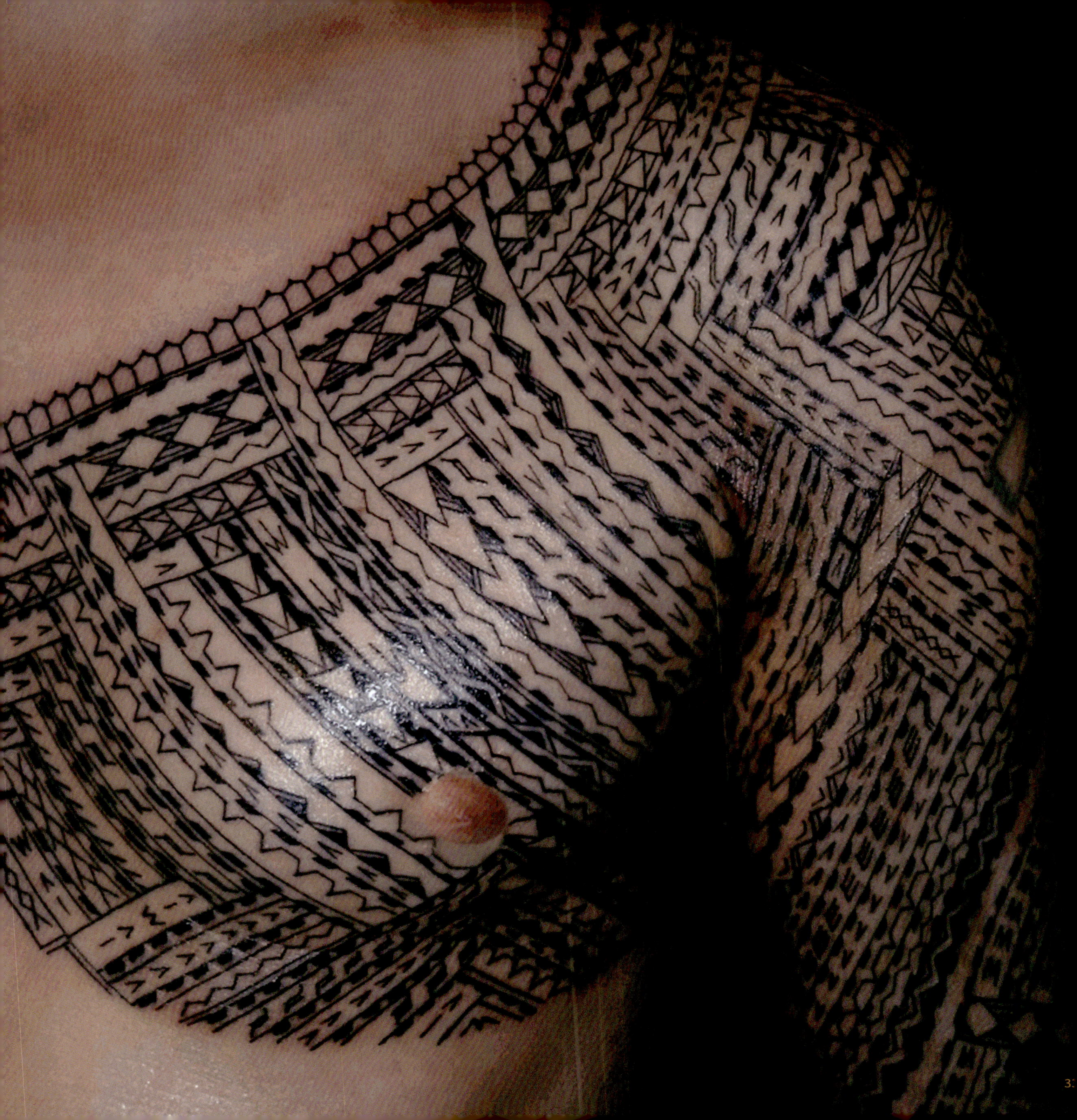

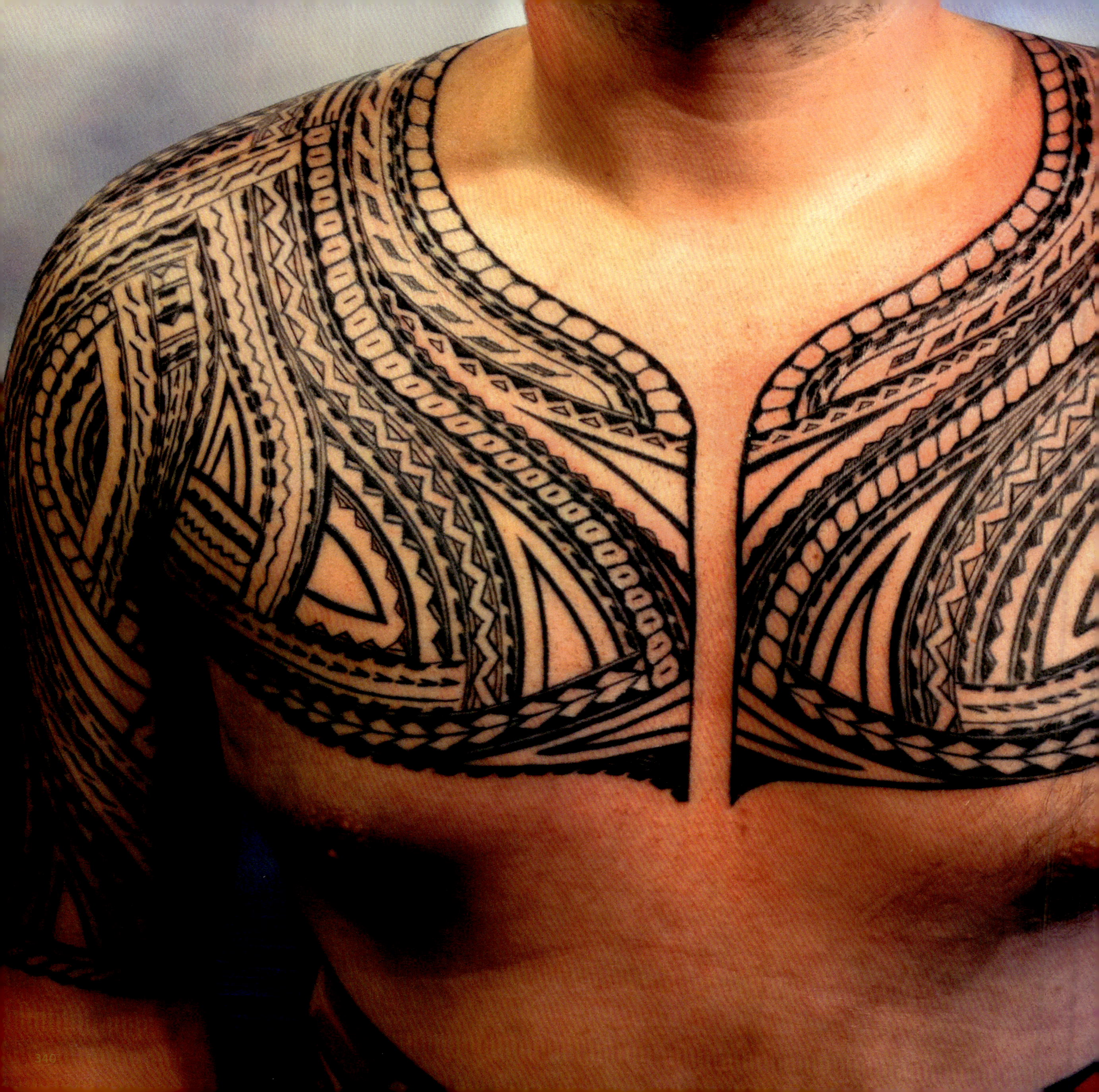

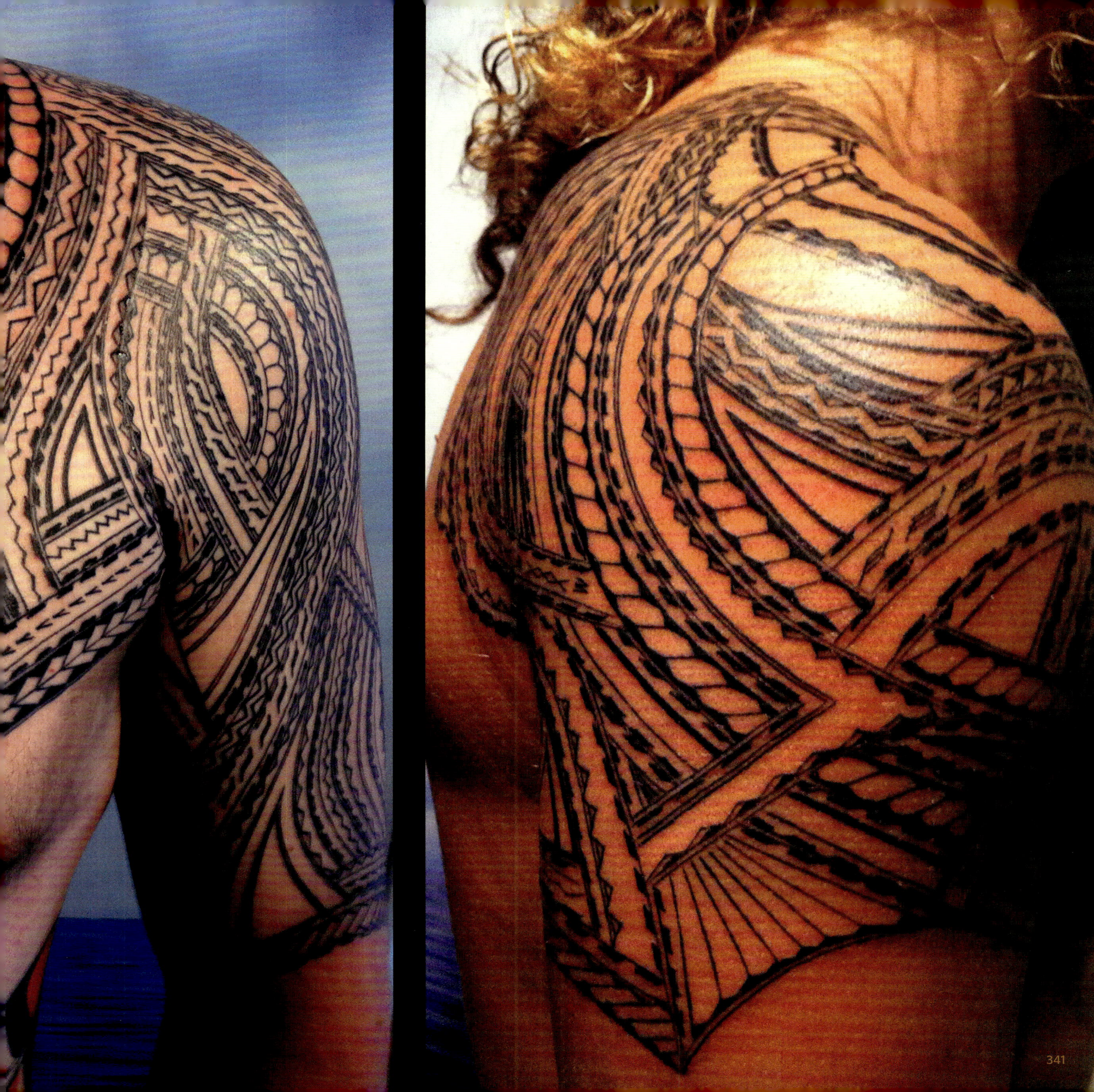

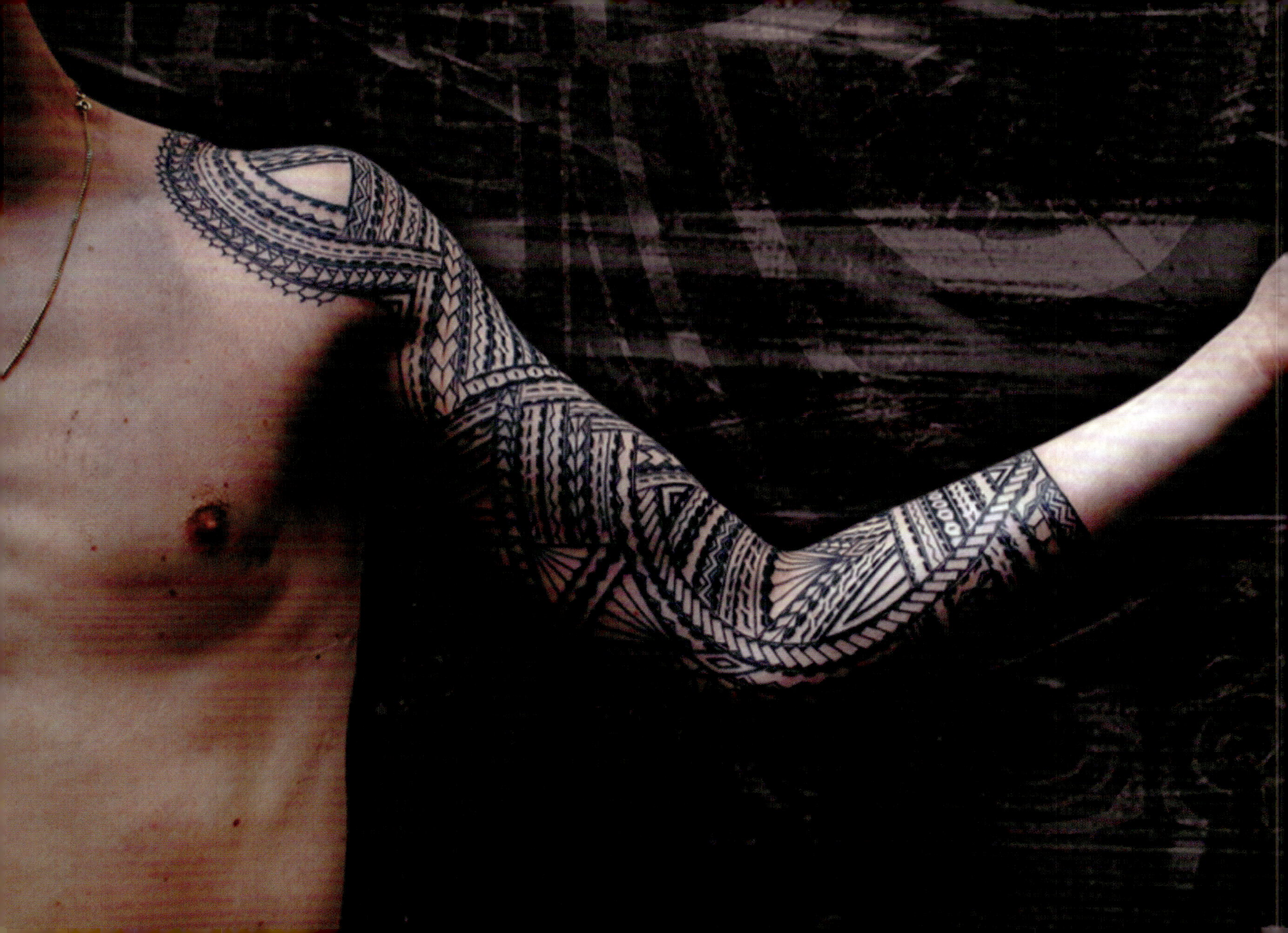

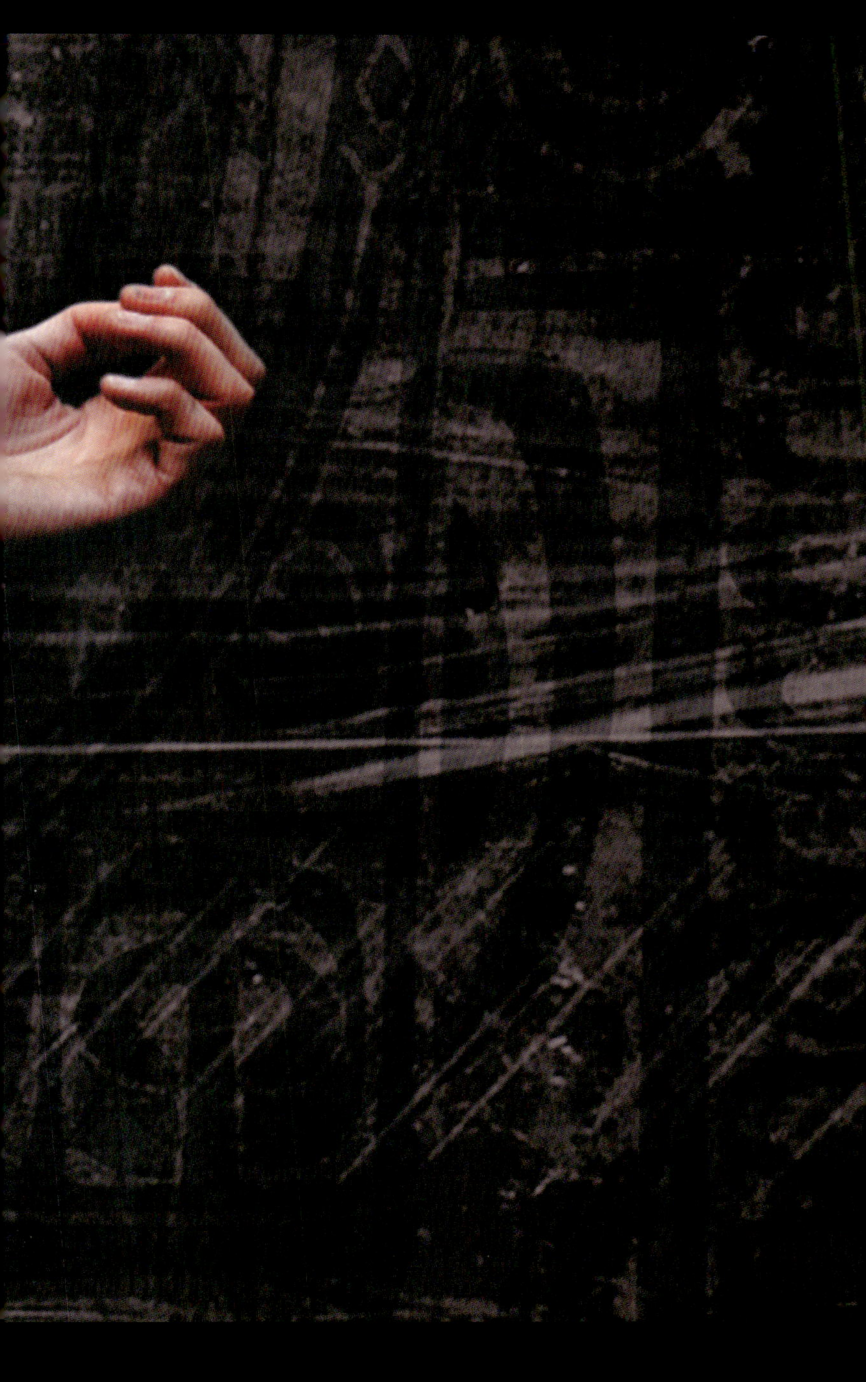

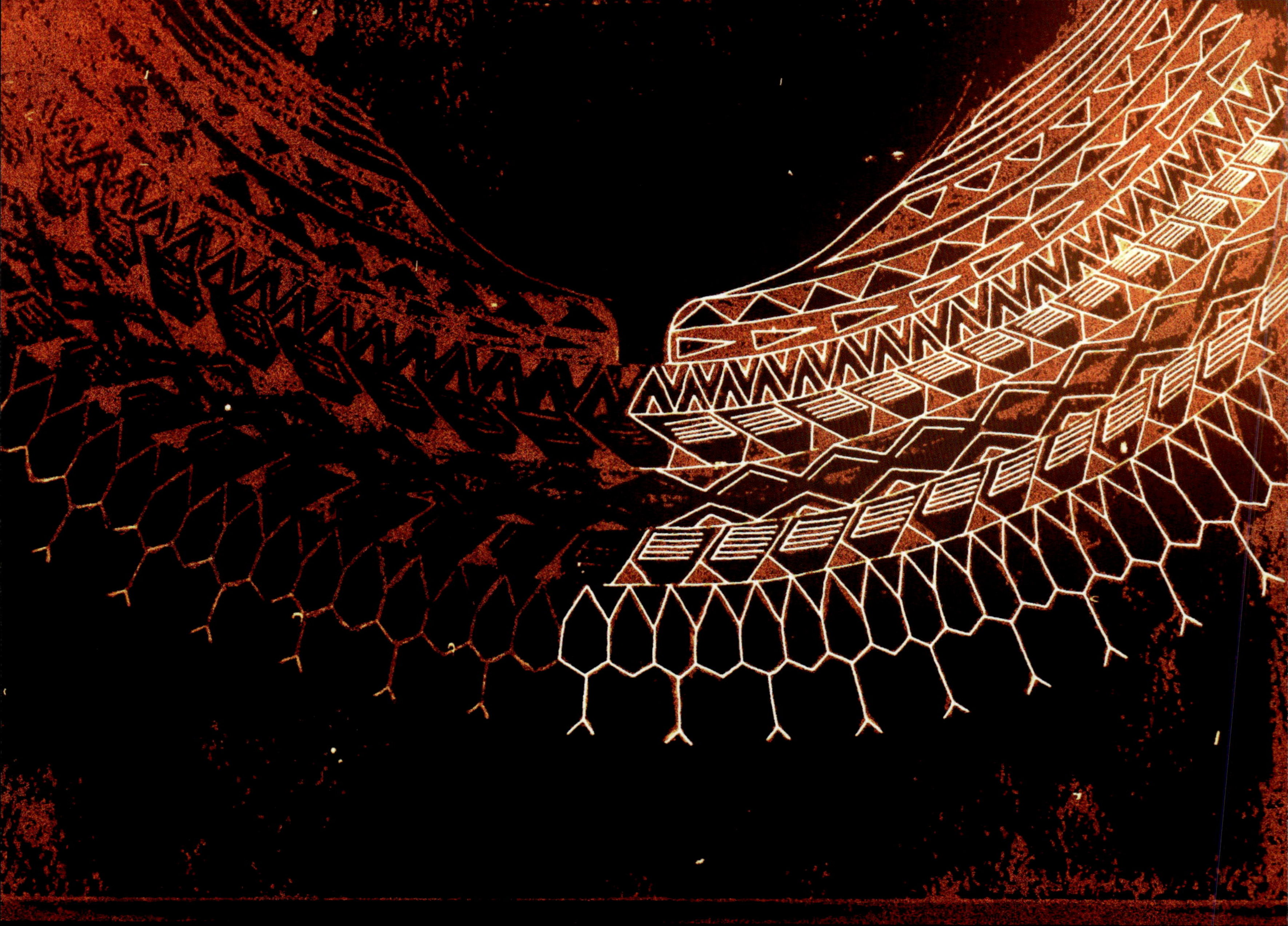

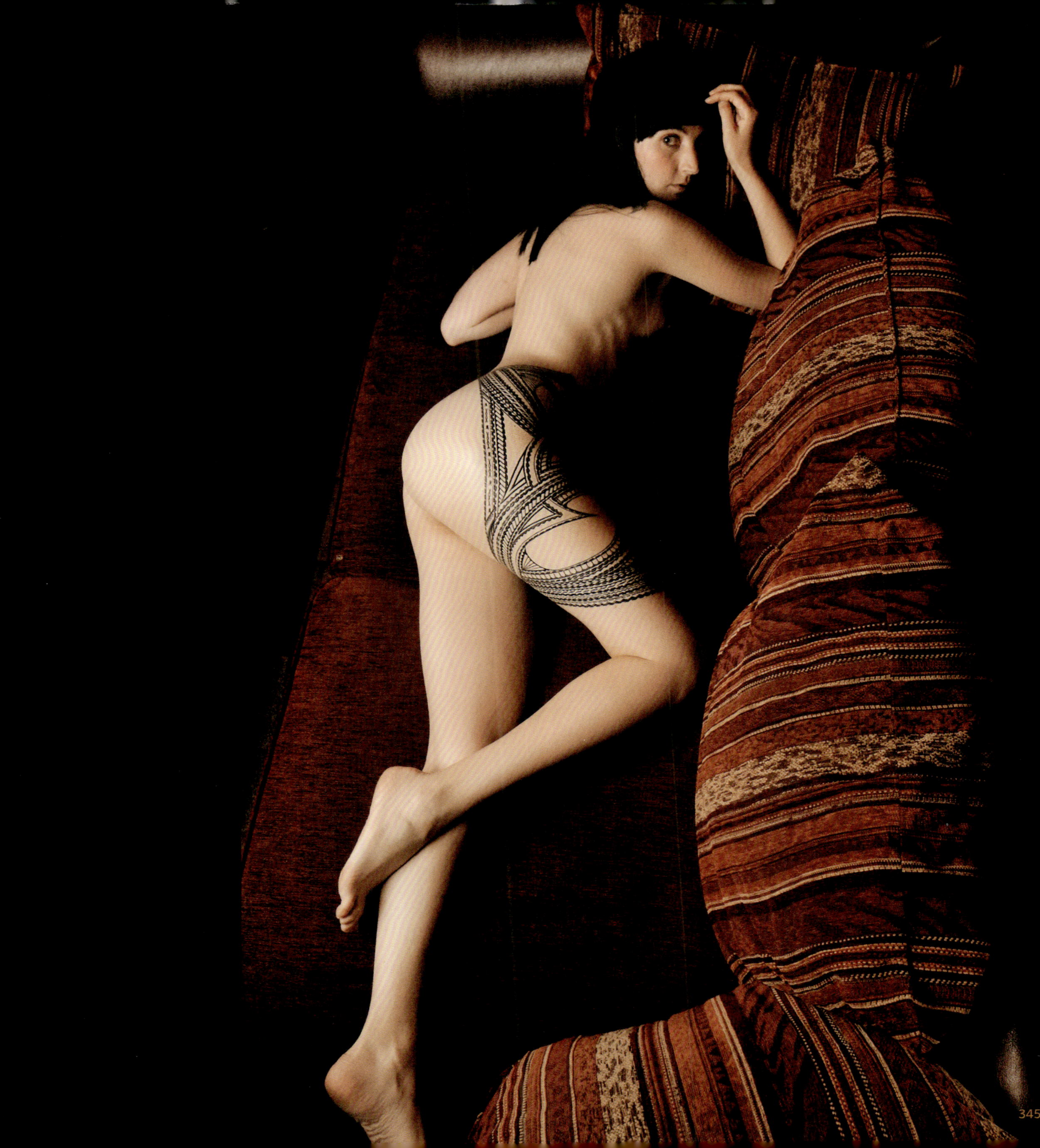

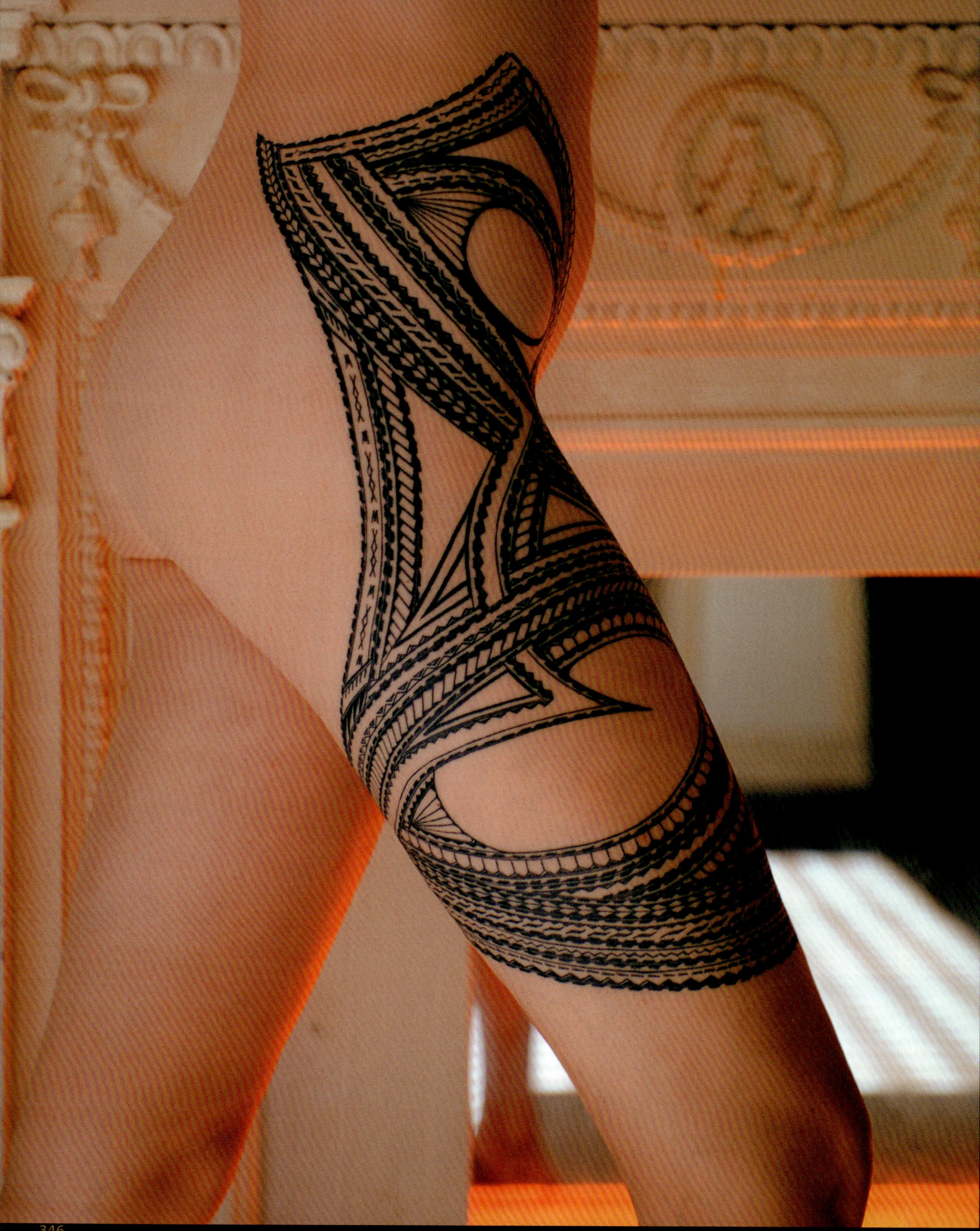

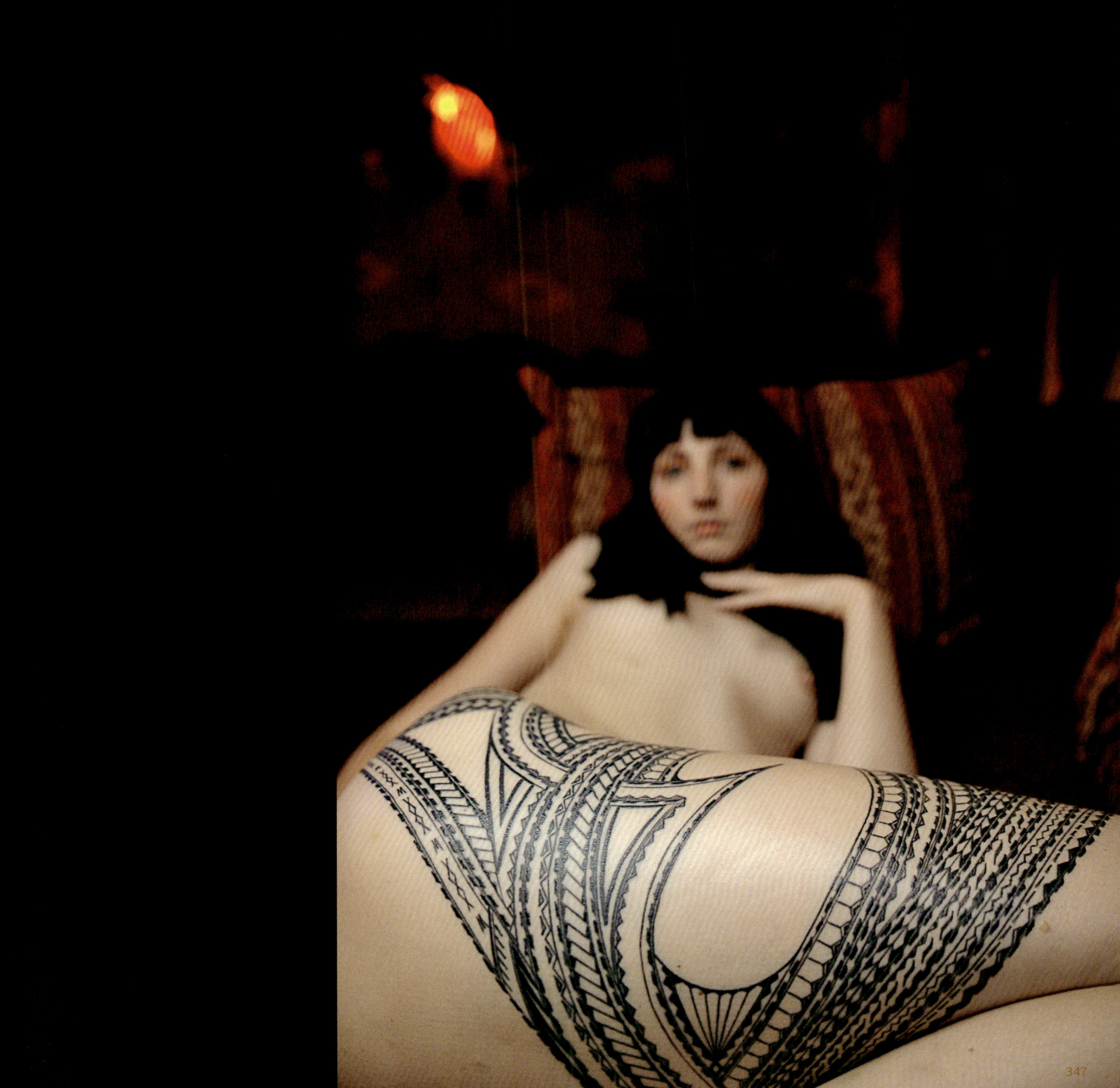

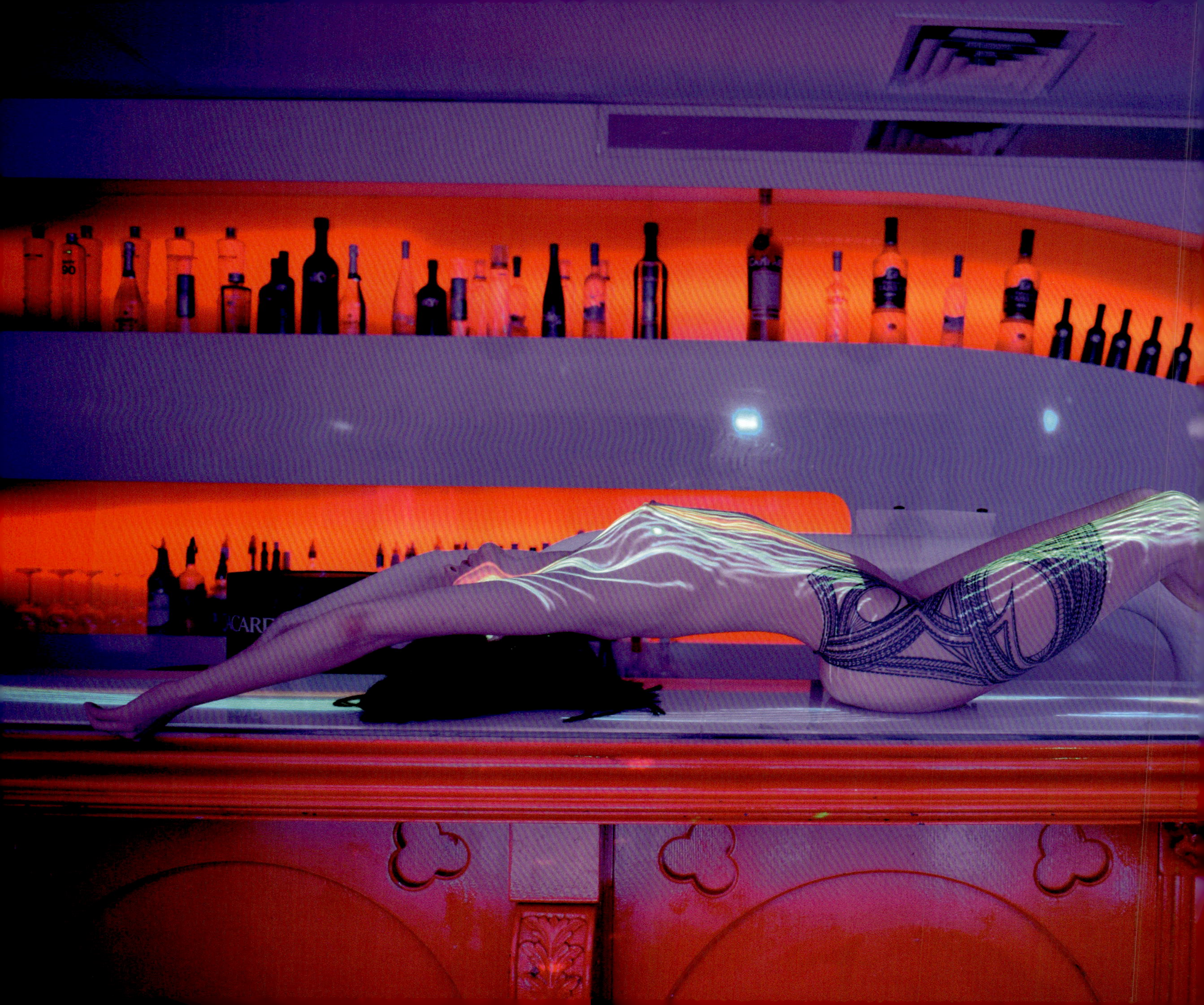

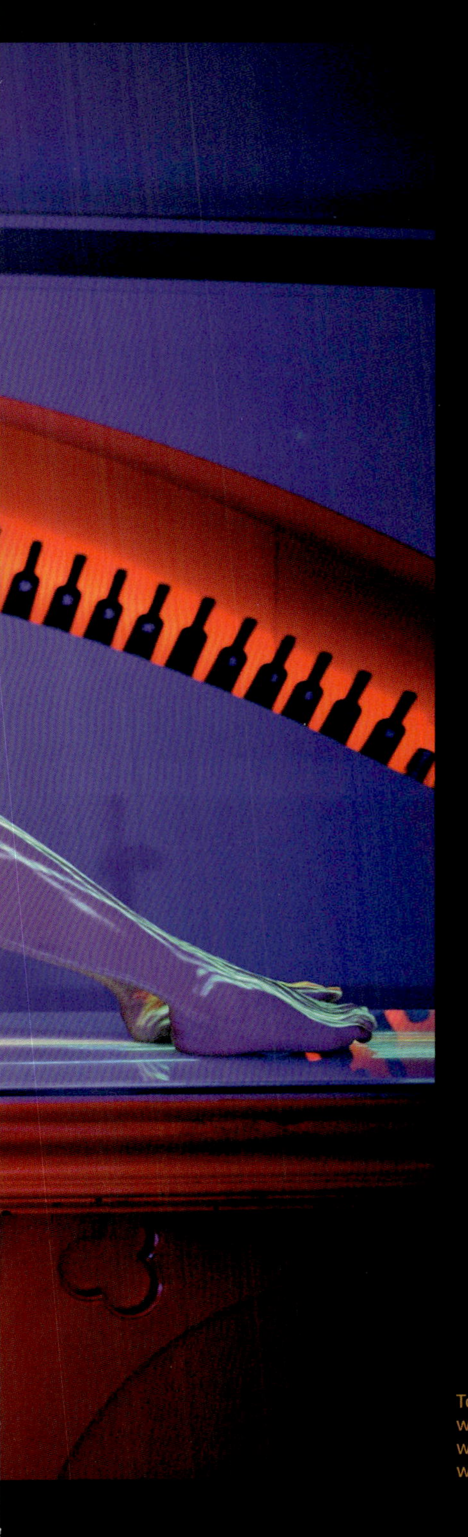

Tomasi Sulu'ape
www.tatau-samo
www.malofie.org
www.paulo-sulua

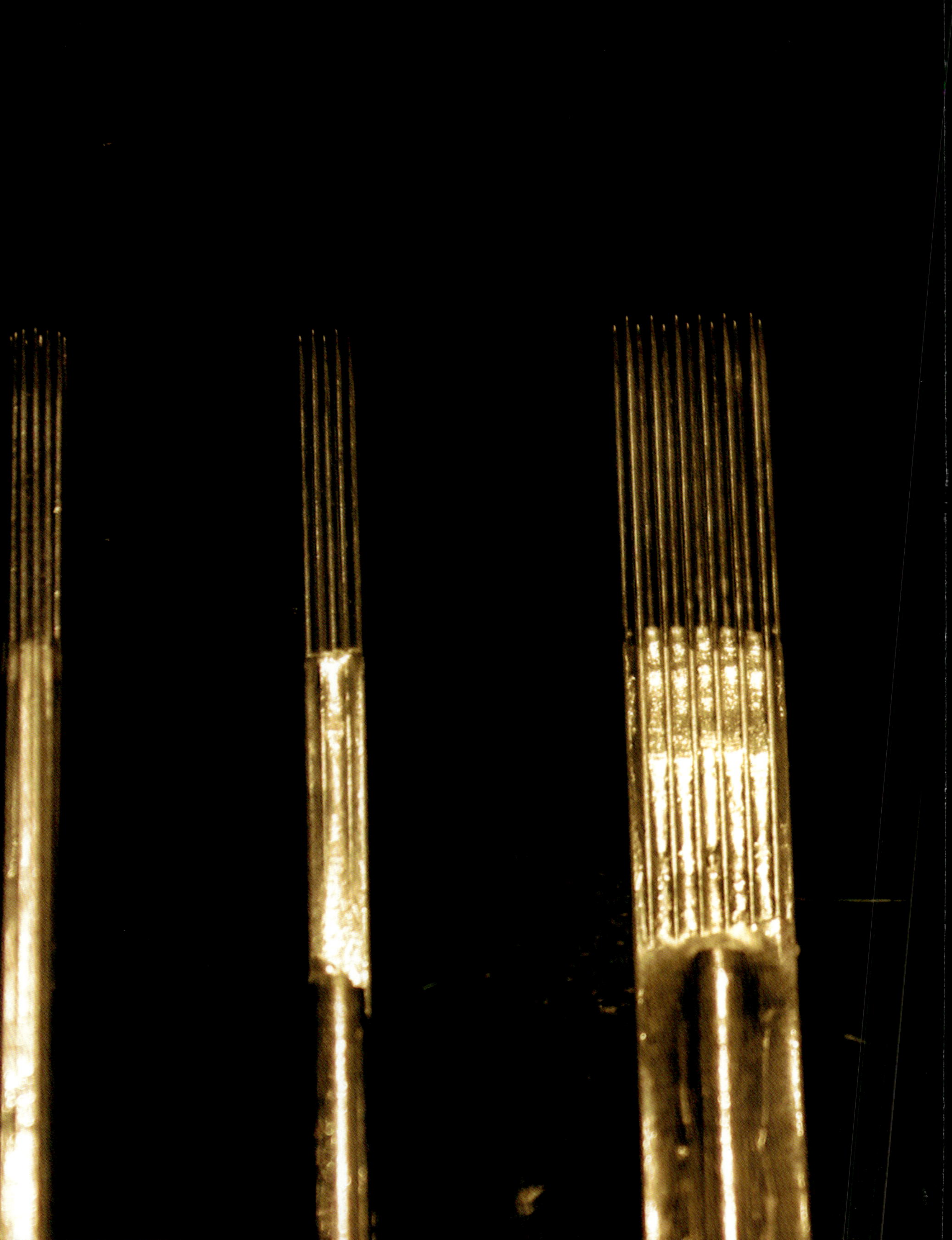

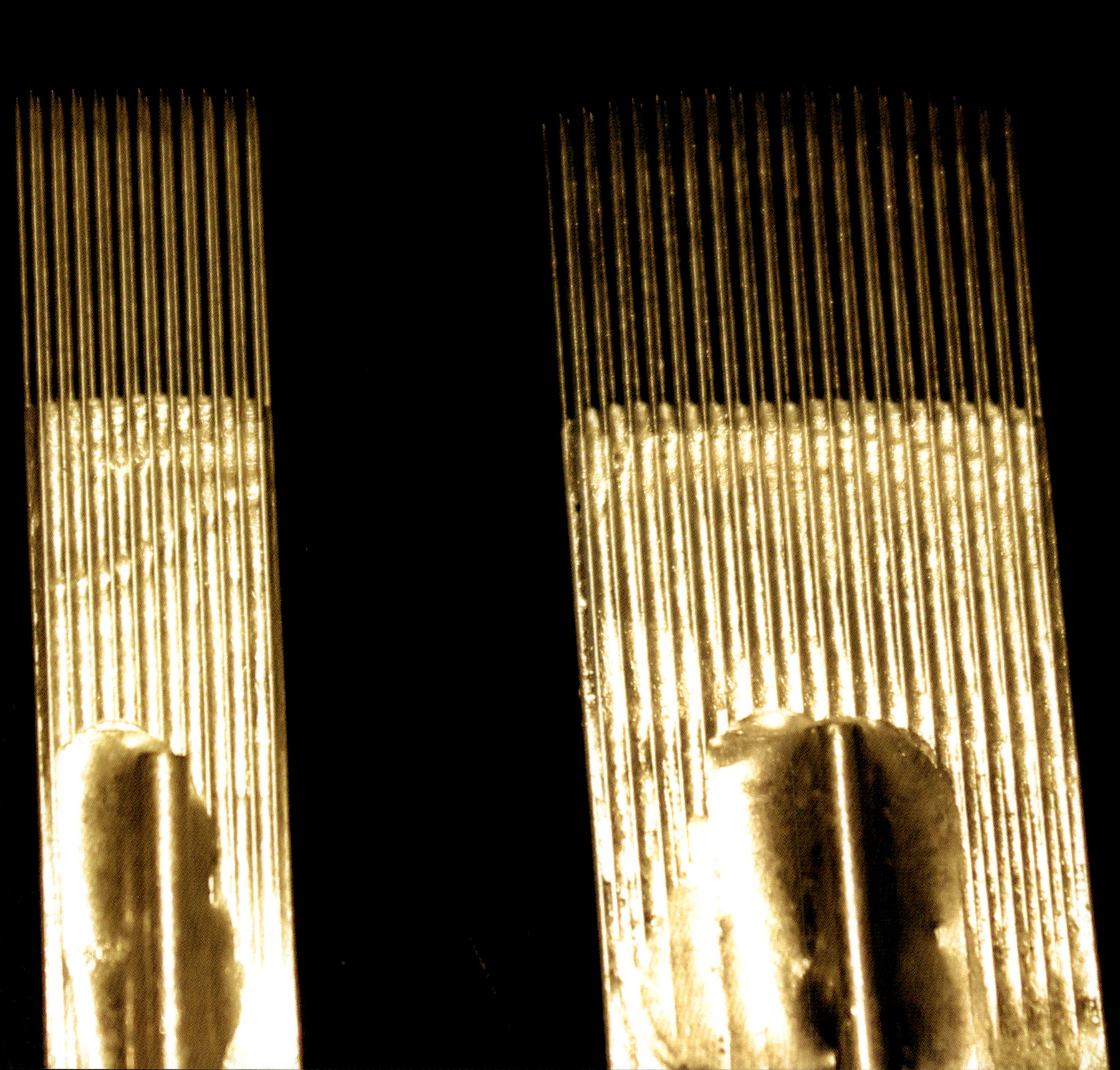

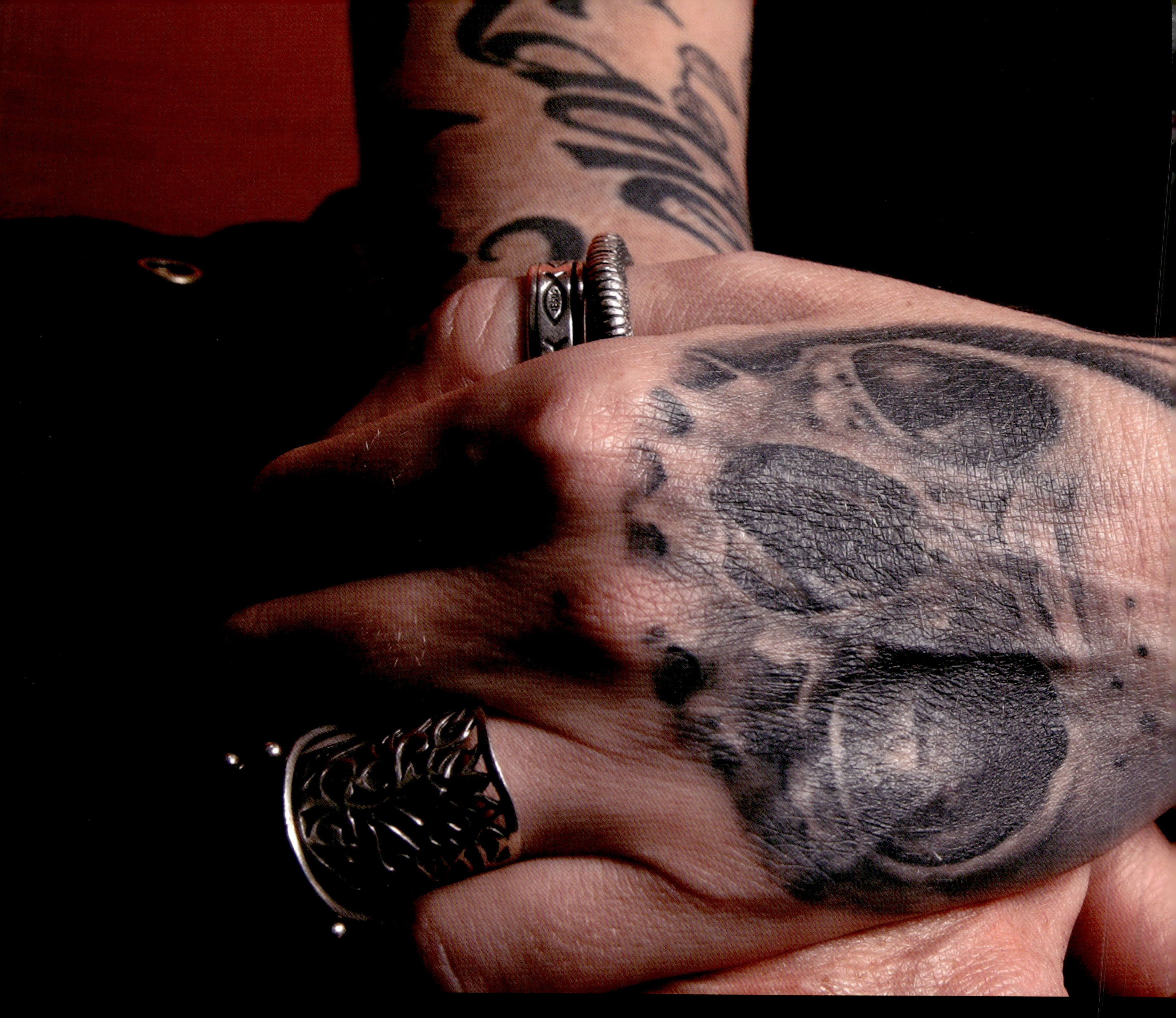

TONY WEINTRAUD
TATTOO TONY CREATIONS

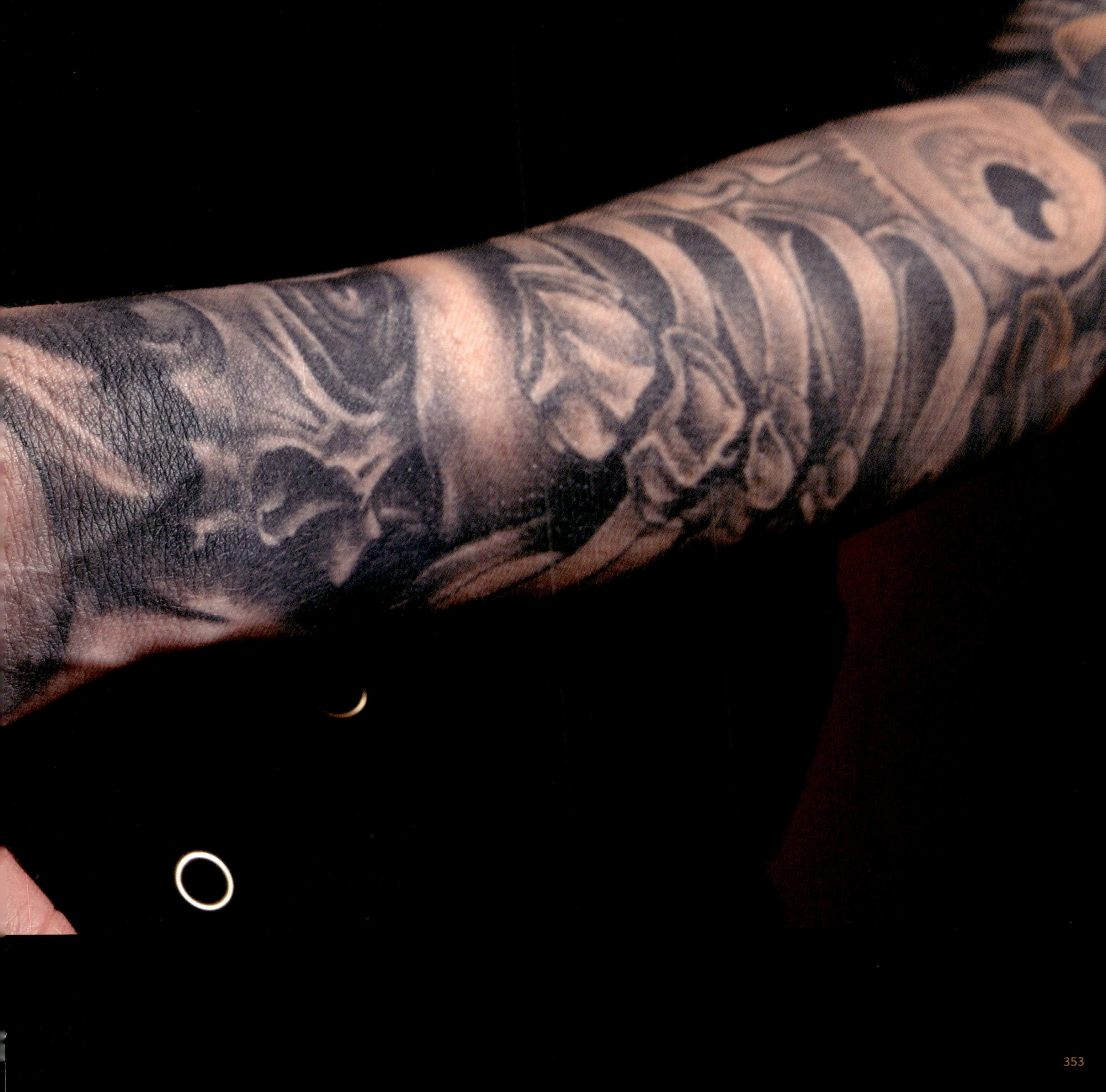

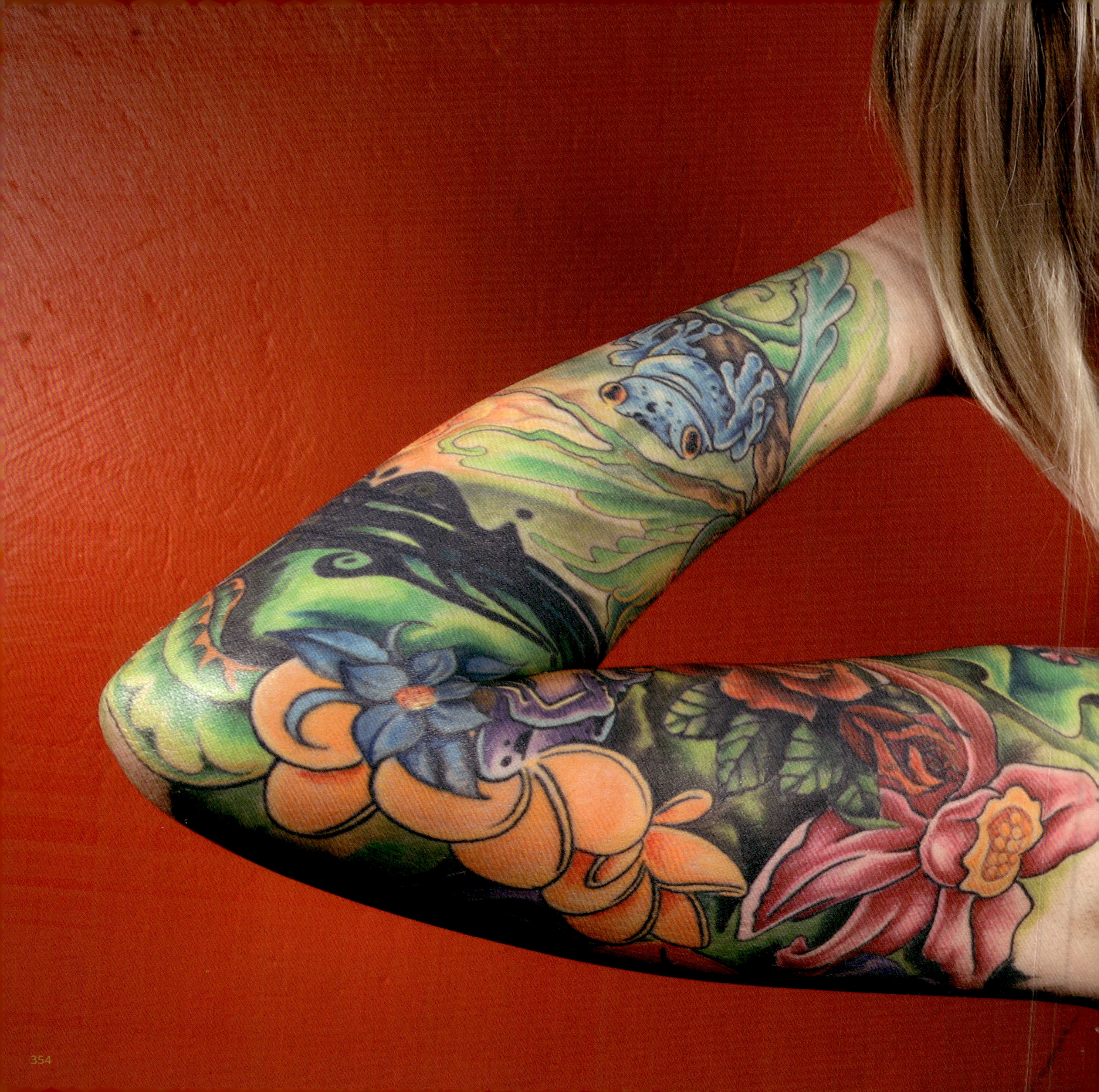

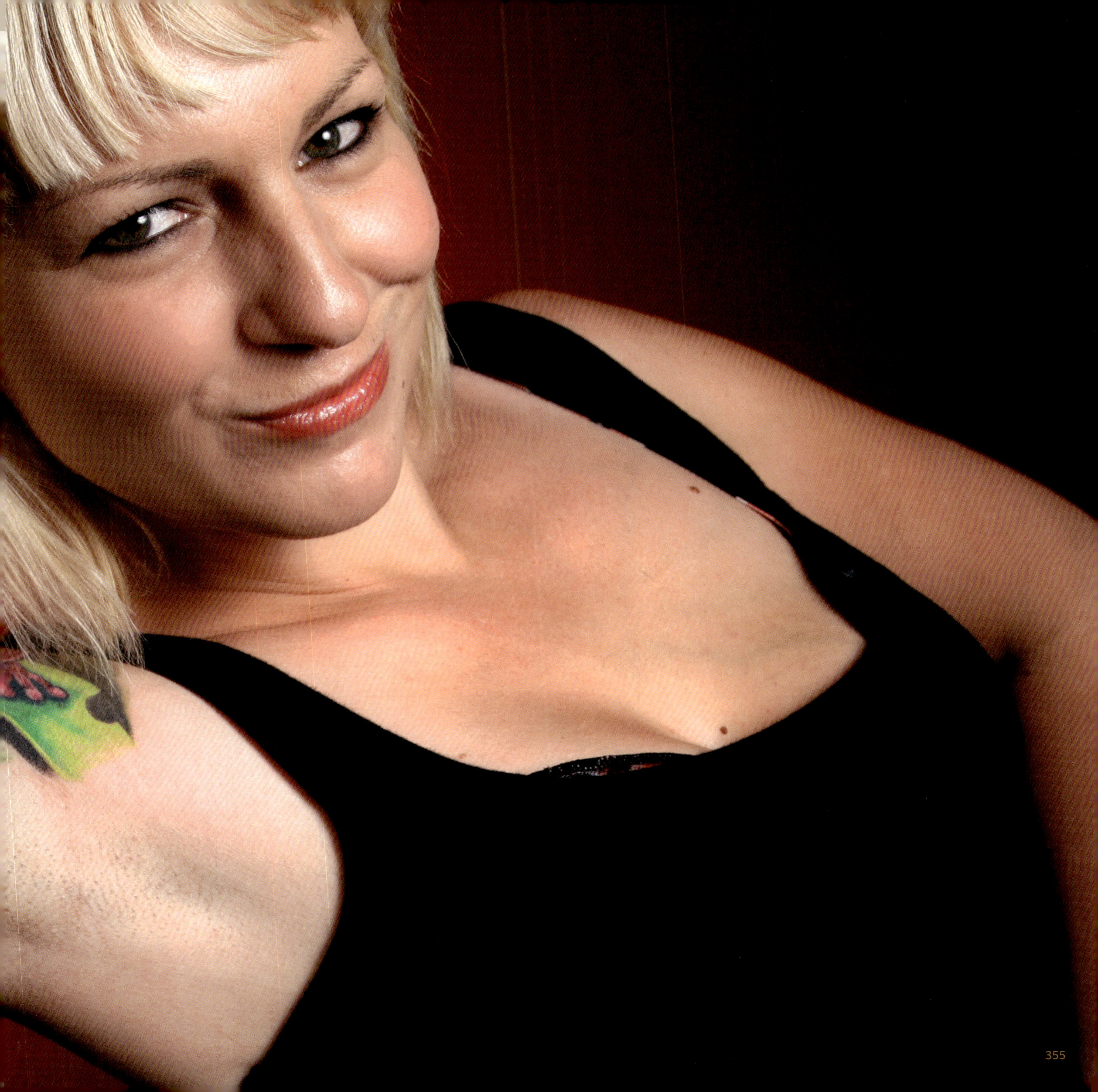

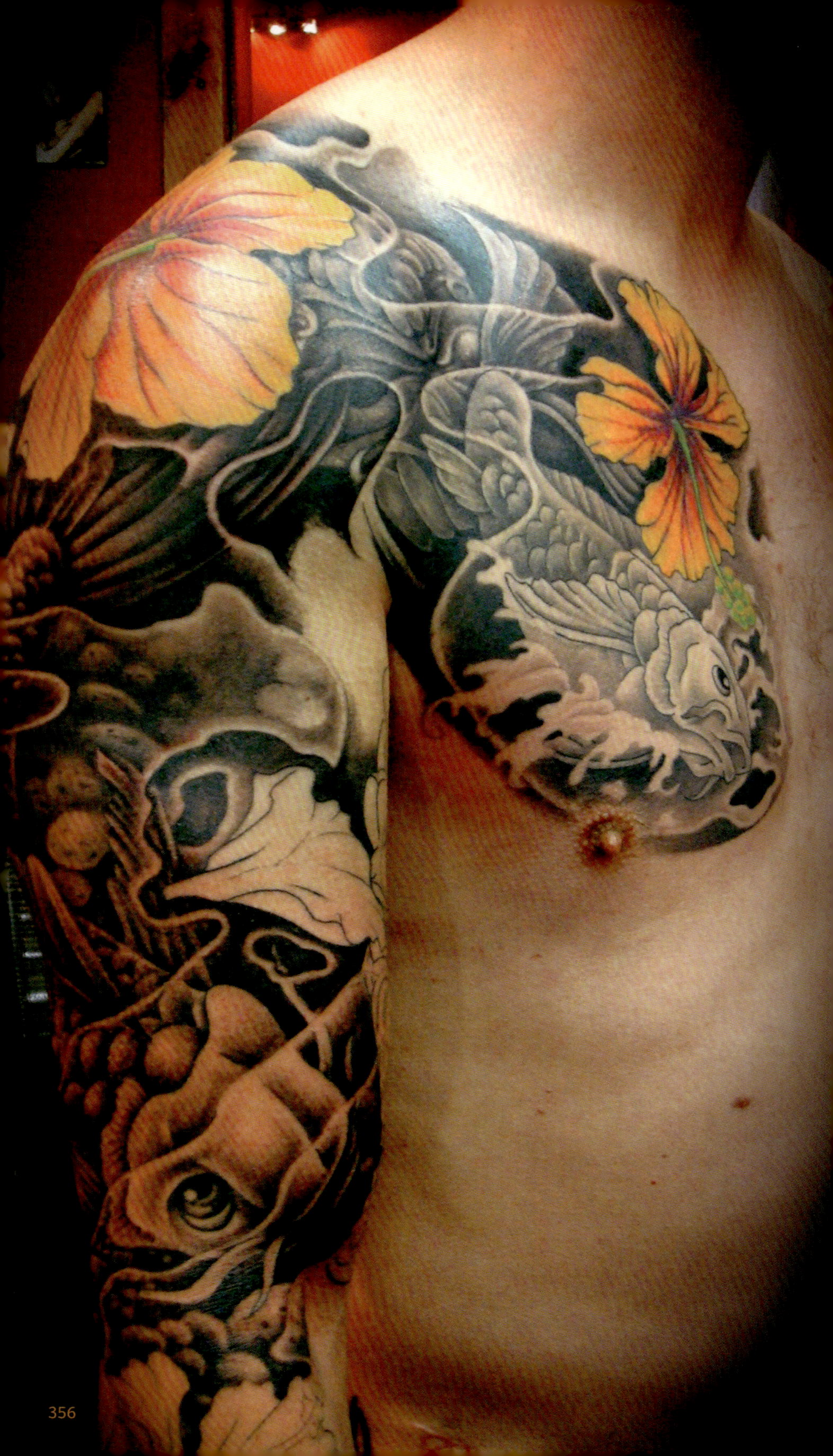

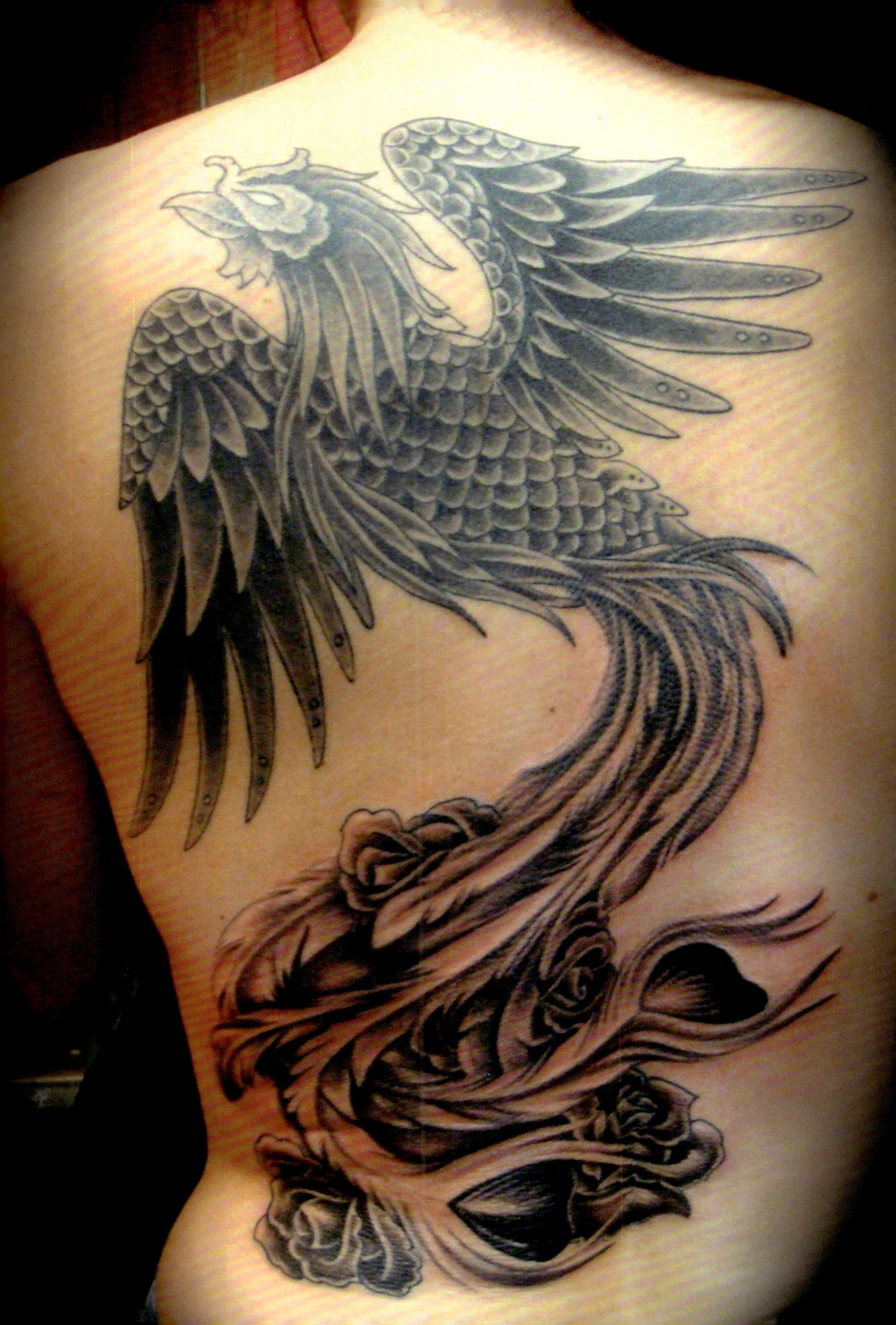

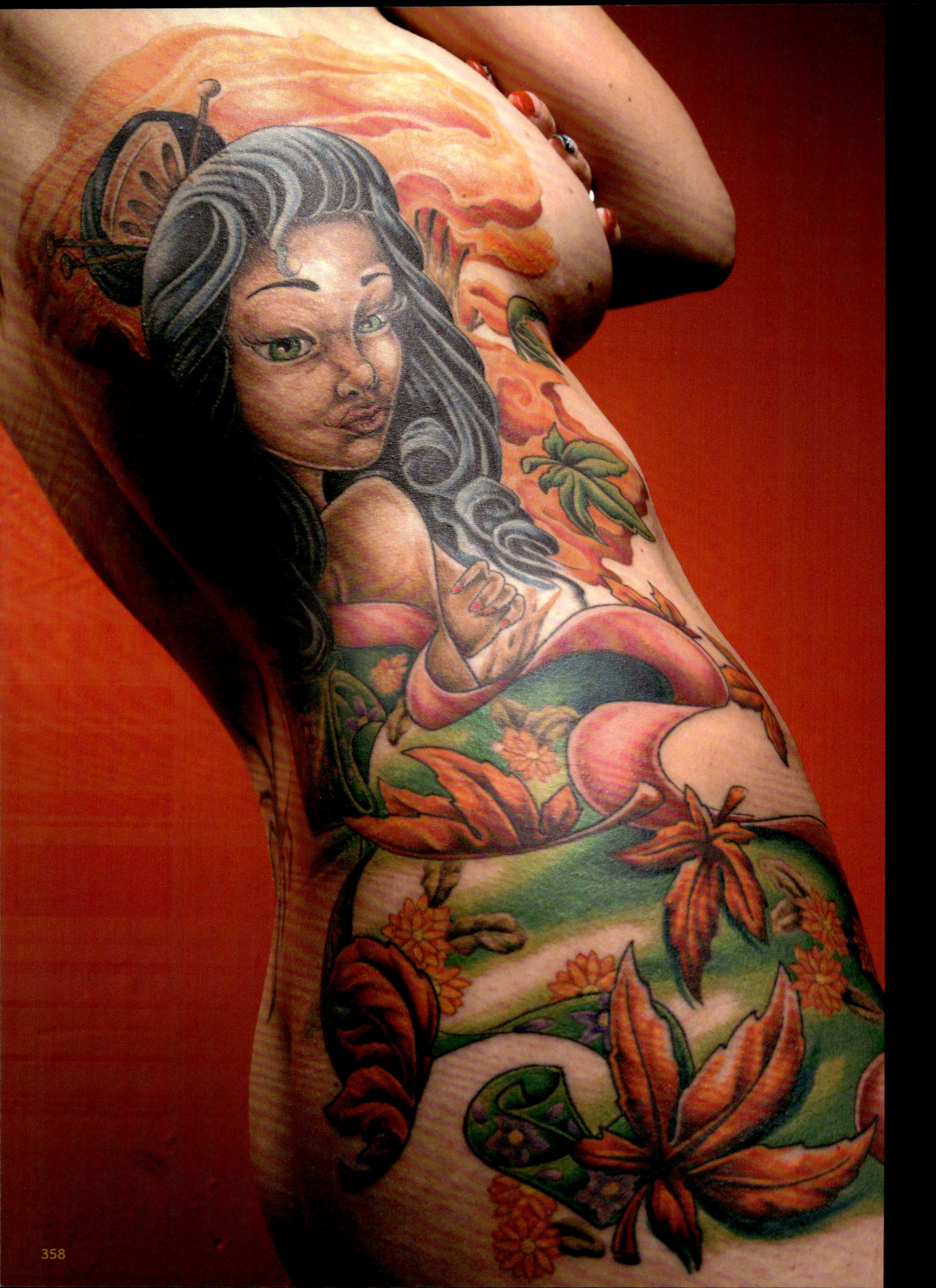

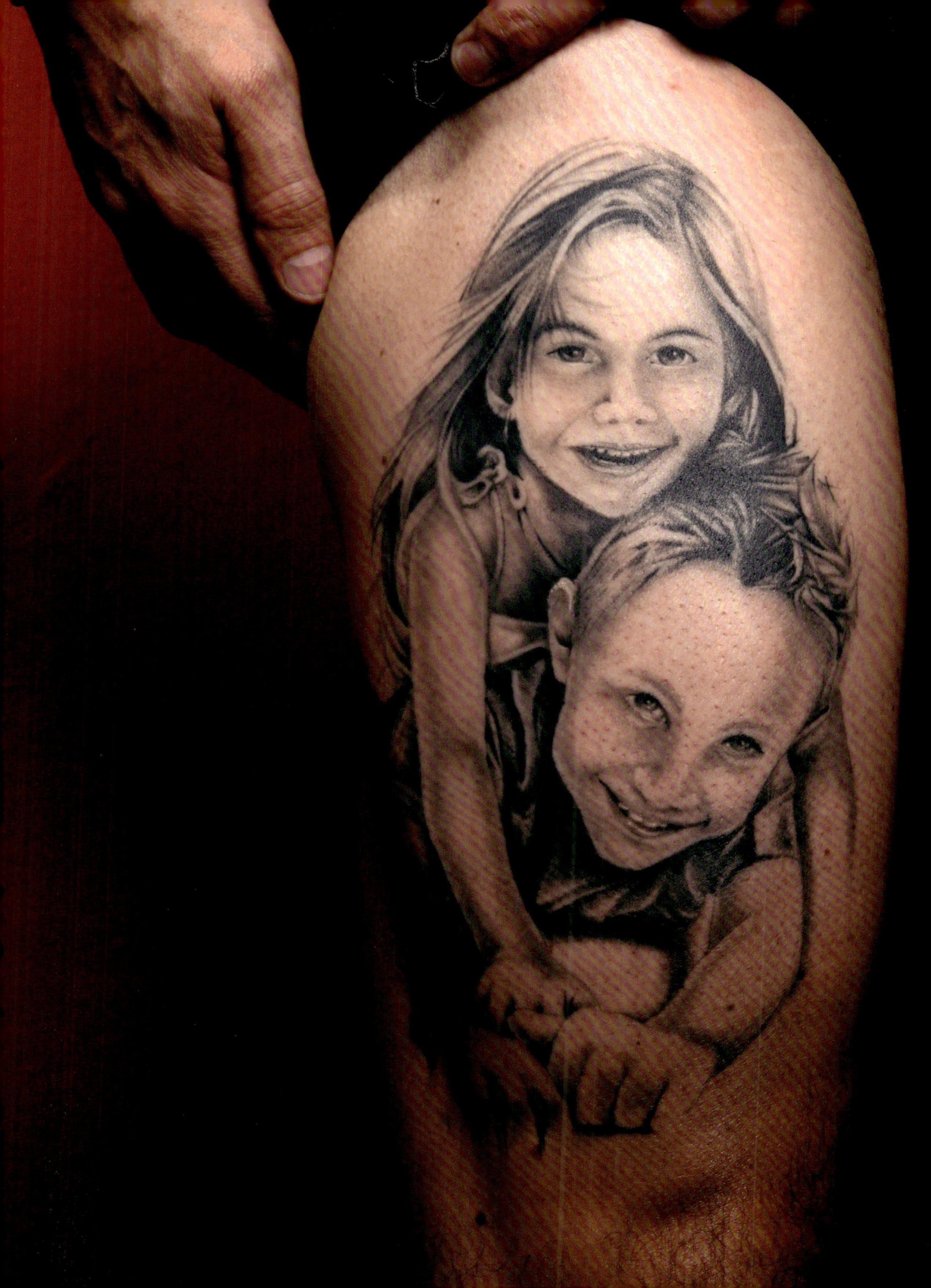

Tony Weintraud
www.tattootony.co.za